The BeatTips Manual

THE ART OF BEATMAKING,
THE HIP HOP/RAP MUSIC TRADITION,
AND THE COMMON COMPOSER

6th EDITION

Amir Said

Superchamp Books **SB**

Brooklyn, NY

The BeatTips Manual: The Art of Beatmaking, the Hip Hop/Rap Music Tradition,
and the Common Composer
By Amir Said

Copyright © 2013 by Amir Said.

A Superchamp Books Sixth Paperback Edition

All rights reserved.
No part of this book may be reproduced in any form by any electronic or mechanical means, including information storage and retrieval systems, without the expressed written permission of the publisher, except by a reviewer, who may quote brief passages in a review. Published by Superchamp Books, a Division of Superchamp, Inc. P.O. Box 20274, Brooklyn, New York 11202-0274; (347) 263-7865. www.beattips.com; Twitter: @BeatTipsManual; Facebook: BeatTips

BeatTips™ is a product and trademark of Superchamp, Inc.
BeatTip™ is a trademark of Superchamp, Inc.

Assistant Editor: Amir Ali Said

Photographs:
Front Cover photo by Amir Said Copyright © 2009, 2013 Amir Said
Interviewees photos by Amir Said Copyright © 2006-2009 Amir Said
Back Cover photo of author by Amir Ali Said © 2009, 2013 Amir Ali Said
Cover, Design, and Layout by Amir Said Copyright © 2013 Amir Said

Print History:
June 2013: First printing.
July 2013: Second printing.
December 2013: Third Printing.
February 2015: Fourth Printing.

The BeatTips Manual: Beatmaking, the Hip Hop/Rap Music Tradition,
and the Common Composer / by Amir Said – Sixth Edition
1. Beatmaking 2. Hip Hop/Rap—Production 3. Hip Hop—Histroy 4. Rap Music—Performance Practice 5. Rap Music—History 6. Hip Hop—Producers 7. Music—Technology 8. Music—Popular 9. Music—Social Aspects 10. African Americans—Music—History and Criticism 11. Popular Culture—United States 12. Music History I. Title

Library of Congress Control Number: 2013943132
ISBN 978-0-9893986-0-2

For my son, Amir Ali Said.
Amir, nobody can be a better you than you.
("When the door opens for opportunity, walk through.")
Insha'Allah…Al-Humdullilah.

DISCLAIMER: This book is designed to provide information on understanding, creating, producing, marketing, promoting, distributing, and selling hip hop/rap beats and music. It is understood that the publisher and the author are not engaged in rendering legal, accounting, or other professional services of the like. If legal or other expert assistance is required, the services of a competent and qualified professional should be sought. The author and Superchamp Books shall have neither liability nor responsibility to any person or entity with respect to any loss or damage caused, or alleged to have been caused, directly or indirectly, by the information contained in this book.

Table of Contents

FOREWORD — xvii

PREFACE — xix

INTRODUCTION — 1

PART 1: HISTORY — 13

1 BACKDROP TO HIP HOP — 15
The Story of the South Bronx Disaster

2 MOVE, ROCK, DANCE, SUCKA' — 30
The Coalescence of Hip Hop Culture
and the Birth of Hip Hop/Rap Music

3 LOOKING FOR THE PERFECT BEAT — 60
The Birth and Rise of the Hip Hop/Rap Beatmaking Tradition:
Seven Periods of Distinct Development

PART 2: TECHNICAL BEATDOWN—INSTRUCTION — 87

4 GEAR AND SOUND FUNDAMENTALS — 89
Understanding Production Setups, EMPIs, "Sounds,"
and Other Prerequisite Factors

5 DRUM SOUNDS AND DRUM PROGRAMMING — 115
The Nature of Drum Sounds and Drum Programming in Hip Hop/Rap
Music

**6 HOOK A BEAT UP
AND CONVERT IT INTO HIP HOP FORM** — 144
Composition, Programming, and Arrangement—
Coming up with the Ingredients and Putting them
All Together

7 THE ART OF SAMPLING — 193

| 8 | PRACTICE MAKES BETTER | 234 |

PART 3: MUSIC TRADITION, CULTURE, AND THEORY — 261

| 9 | FLASH BATTLED MOZART AT THE FEVER, AND MOZART GOT BURNED | 264 |

The Hip Hop/Rap Music and Beatmaking Traditions, Its Theory, and How It Does and Doesn't Jive with the Western Classical Music Tradition and Its Theory

PART 4: THE BUSINESS OF BEATS — 311

| 10 | KNOW WHERE YOU STAND | 313 |

| 11 | IT'S YOUR'S; NOTHIN' TO IT BUT TO DO IT | 335 |

Know the Angles, Because You Have the Control

| 12 | THE "BUSINESS" OF BUSINESS | 359 |

PART 5 : THE INTERVIEWS — 385

Marley Marl	387
Buckwild	401
D.R. Period	417
DJ Toomp	423
DJ Premier	439
9th Wonder	447

AFTERWORD	457
EPILOGUE	467
APPENDIX	477
GLOSSARY	492
INDEX	496

Foreword

Twelve years ago, I published the first edition of *The BeatTips Manual*. At the time, I was going through some turbulent situations. During those uncertain moments in 2001, I found solace in spending time with my son, Amir, and in making beats. Soon after the turbulence subsided, it became important to me to document everything that I knew about beats. Moreover, I wanted to share my knowledge about the art of beatmaking, hip hop/rap music, and the broader hip hop culture with my son, who at the time was turning 5 years old.

From the onset of this highly personal endeavor, I promised myself that I would meticulously record everything that I did relating to beatmaking, or saw, heard, and generally learned about beatmaking. After more than 30 yellow legal size note pads, I felt that I had created the ultimate beatmaking guide for my son. Shortly thereafter, I poured over revisions, drafting all of my notes into one cohesive reference journal. A reference journal that I hoped would one day nurture my son's understanding of beatmaking and its impact on modern music and popular culture. After reviewing the first several sections of this reference with my son, he and I both thought that it would be a good idea to share what I had created for him with the rest of the world. Thus, I decided to develop and transform my reference journal into a book for anyone interested in learning about the beatmaking tradition. Hence, *The BeatTips Manual* was born!

When I began writing *The BeatTips Manual*, I gave myself one goal: write and publish a comprehensive, relevant, and accurate book on the beatmaking tradition. In order to achieve this goal, I set out a few guidelines to follow. First, I pledged to learn as much as I could (whenever and wherever I could, from whomever I could) about beatmaking and all the aesthetics that surround it. Second, I followed what I called the "rule of inclusion." That is to say, I made a commitment to conduct extensive research on *everything* associated with beats, i.e. the art, craft, and business. To that end, I immersed myself in the study of as many relevant production methods, styles, sounds, and/or techniques that I possibly could.

The third guideline that I followed dealt with my aim to break everything down to a level where everyone could understand and appreciate. Unlike overly technical music instructional guides, self-help, how-to books and the like, I set out to write a book that was engaging, clear, and accessible, while at the same time challenging and rewarding to many different mind sets, skill sets, musical orientations, and socio-economic backgrounds.

Looking back on that first edition of *The BeatTips Manual*, I can honestly say that I've followed the same three core guidelines for this edition. And just as in my previous efforts, in this present edition, it is my sincere hope that I educate, motivate, and otherwise inform as many new, mid-level and/or advanced beatmakers as I possibly can. Indeed, if I do so, I will have done what I originally set out to do — nothing more, nothing less…

—Amir Said (Said), 2013, Brooklyn, NY

Preface

The fundamental purpose of this book is to preserve the beatmaking tradition. Moreover, I want to draw more attention to the fact that beatmaking, as a music compositional method, has increasingly become significant around the globe. Thus, in every way possible, this study seeks to take the rich heritage and traditions of beatmaking from out of the throws of obscurity, and to bring them front and center into the world of acclaimed musical processes.

In addition to the fundamental purpose of this study, there are five other auxiliary goals that I hope to achieve with this book. First, I want to provide the most crucial, most comprehensive, and most widely useful information on the beatmaking tradition. Furthermore, I want to stem and/or neutralize the increasing tide of misleading and false information about beatmaking and the most critical factors that surround it. Here, the purpose is to also reconcile the history of beatmaking with the current state of hip hop/rap music in general. Moreover, the purpose of this book is to provide a more enhanced, more nuanced understanding of hip hop/rap music and the broader hip hop culture.

Second, I want this book to establish some level of uniformity and consensus regarding the core aesthetics, concepts, and terminology of the beatmaking tradition. To that end, I hope to shed some clarity on both the well- and little-known terms, methods, practices, and themes of beatmaking that are regularly passed around with little consistency. Though there is no such thing as a "bad" or "wrong" way of making beats, there are indeed a number of standards that have been recognized over the 36 year history of beatmaking. In this study I identify and examine such standards.

Third, I hope to help unify and expand the community of beatmakers. Beatmakers are steadfastly committed to their art and craft, yet most do not recognize that beatmaking (hip hop production) is also a powerful trade. Here, my purpose is to raise attention to the artisanship of beatmaking, and to offer this book as perhaps a catalyst towards the creation of a hip hop/rap beatmakers union.

Fourth, I want to provide a path of musical guidance for those (particularly the youth) interested in making hip hop/rap music. I want *The BeatTips Manual* to serve as an investment in the youth and the future of the hip hop/rap music and beatmaking traditions. Furthermore, my aim is to fill the tremendous void, as best as I can, that has been left by the dramatic decline in the tradition of orally passing on and handing down beatmaking and general music education. Moreover, since it is my belief that we all naturally want to create music (or other art), I want to provide a source for the youth who would otherwise not be able to find a means to nurture their natural inclination for creating music. Thus, I want *The BeatTips Manual* to act as a gateway book, a conduit that further leads to learning more about the art and processes of music.

Why a book and Who Is It For?

Despite the tens of thousands of info videos and online tutorials, books are *still* the best mechanism for learning extensive processes, concepts, and ideas. Books offer the greatest opportunity for a more serious, objective individual dissemination. Also, it's worth noting that beatmaking is like crackin' a *not*-so secret code. Although there are many beatmakers who will have you believe that "you just gotta have *it*" to be a quality beatmaker, the reality is that once you acquire and apply accurate information about the key areas of beatmaking, things become much more natural, and you *and* your ideas become more intuitive. From there, you practice and develop a greater enjoyment for what you do.

This book is for anyone interested in the hip hop/rap and beatmaking traditions and the encompassing hip hop culture. Though obviously this study is geared towards beatmakers (beginners, intermediate, and advanced), it's important to note, however, that I am targeting this information also for students, professors, and other scholars as well as music writers, hip hop/rap aficionados, and casual hip hop supporters alike.

About The Slant of This Book

This book is meant to be used and enjoyed by beatmakers, hip hop/rap music fans, regular readers, and academicians alike. Moreover, I should note that this book is not a typical academic jaunt. Although I hope that *The BeatTips Manual* will be embraced by the academic community, this book is not written to be understood *only* by professional academicians and the like. Academic texts are usually written for and by professional academicians; and as such, they carry the language, feel, motives, priorities, and predilections of the members of that community. Thus, I've taken great effort to construct this study with a language and feel that is equally appealing and accessible to beatmakers, academicians, and everybody in between, while still keeping my focus first on the needs and interests of beatmakers of course. This book is not the work of someone who spent time doing "fieldwork" (admirable as that may be), but instead, it is the product of someone who's *lived in the field all of his life*.

Also, I should add that *The BeatTips Manual* is not meant to be a standard ethnographical look at beatmaking and/or hip hop culture. That being said, however, I must concede that many elements of this study will certainly appeal to both ethnomusicologists and musicologists alike. This book is also not an anthropological study of a culture for which I only have a fleeting interest in and or enthusiastic — but shaky — understanding of. I have not simply "watched" beatmaking from the sidelines. In fact, my studies in beatmaking began — I didn't know it at the time — when I was 11 years old, the exact same time I first participated in the deeply intricate hip hop/rap tradition (more than twenty years ago). I should also add that I did not just recently become aware of sampling and other beatmaking processes as legitimate music compositional methods. I knew they were legitimate back in 1986 (when I first heard Eric B. & Rakim's seminal classic, "Paid In Full"). I'm also compelled to point out that I do not consider the interviewees (whom all of which I personally interviewed face to face for this book), as "clients" or "informants." Instead, I feel privileged to see them as my colleagues and fellow members of one of the most amazing musical sub-cultures in the world.

Of equal importance is the fact that I have not merely *attempted* to make beats simply to publish my findings on the processes of beatmaking, nor have I attempted to makes beats due to some residual provocation from writing this book. I didn't decide to acquire an Akai MPC drum machine/sampler at the end of my research for this present study. I've made beats for more than fifteen years now, and I've owned various MPC models and other electronic music production instruments (EMPIs) since 1992. I was making beats well before I even considered beatmaking a possible literary topic. Moreover, any and all participation that I've had within the hip hop/rap tradition — throughout the past 20 years — has not been done so expressly for the purpose of gathering data for this study. That being said, I make no apologies for my penchant for keeping a journal of notes, incredibly memorable photos, historical party flyers, vinyl records, and cassette tapes. There are a number of my personal experiences within hip hop that have contributed substantially to the production of this manuscript. Therefore, I think that there are several key facts about my background that I should mention.

Since I was 9 years old, I have consistently collected vinyl records of all sorts. Both of my parents were *pseudo* record collectors. I took my cue from them (along with my uncle and grandmother), and I went to another orbit with it. I have listened *attentively* (at times obsessively) to more than 1,500 hip hop/rap songs, ranging in release year from 1979 to 2009. I have personally conducted, taped, and transcribed more than 75 interviews with beatmakers (critically acclaimed, well-known, and underground), engineers, label execs, accountants, lawyers, and other music insiders. In the past 15 years, I have attended more than 50 live performances and showcases at local clubs, as well as large-scale concert/tour series in New York City, and as many as 10 other states in the U.S. I have made/produced and recorded music in more than 70 separate recording studios of all varieties, sizes, and scopes — from high-end commercial labs to mid-level professional outfits, to the most bootleg, grungy bedroom setups one could imagine. Finally, since 1994, I have made/produced, recorded, engineered, and mixed more than 1,700 beats (well, at least 1700 that I care to admit to).

I also should point out that my aim has not been to be politically correct, but to be fundamentally accurate. I deal with what *was*, what *is*, what *may*, and what will most *likely be*. I do not, however, deal in what *should have been*, what it *should be now*, or what it *should be* in the future.

Finally, so that there is no confusion, I must give readers more context. This book is not concerned with the fringe musical developments of hip hop/rap music, such as the hip hop-R&B hybrid or the alternative "rocker rap." This study is unequivocally concerned with and centered around hip hop/rap music in its truest, most fundamental meaning: *beats and rhymes*. Thus, it should be clear that the beatmaking compositional methods and concepts that are explored in this book are those that are utilized by beatmakers for the purpose of creating music (instrumentals), first and foremost, for *rappers to rap over*. However, this does not mean that these methods can not be used for the purpose of creating music for other performers (that is, non-rappers).

What's In Here?

I have designed *The BeatTips Manual* to serve as both an examination of and instructional guide to the beatmaking tradition of hip hop/rap music. Thus, this book contains a wealth of information on the hip hop/rap and beatmaking traditions. Further, along those lines, I have intended for this book to be a portal or a gateway into the vast world of beatmaking. In this book, you will encounter methodical, technical, and stylistic examinations of beatmaking as well as stories of my own experiences and those of people like you. In fact, in this edition, I have again included interviews with beatmakers who are well-known and firmly established in the hip hop/rap beatmaking community.

This book is a practical tool that can be easily navigated. It is not a rigidly fashioned, cold-numbers, point-by-point-style, tech-heavy text book. Although, I should note that most of the compositional and recording "turorial style tips" — so to speak — are to be found in the **Instruction Part** of this study. Still, this book is not designed to overload you with fancy technological jargon or tricky algorithms, or the like. Furthermore, the material in this book is arranged in such a way that even if you know nothing about beatmaking, you can start on page 1 and progress through the book, moving from basics to more advanced concepts. (If you're familiar with beatmaking, you can skip around, but I recommend reading all of the material in this book at least once.) This book is easy to follow, comprehensive, straight-forward and very intuitive.

How This Book Is Laid Out

The BeatTips Manual ambitiously approaches three broad areas: history, instruction, and tradition. These areas are further organized into five parts: Part **1: History; Part 2: Technical Beatdown (Instruction); Part 3: Music Tradition, Culture, and Theory; Part 4: The Business of Beats; Part 5: The Interviews.**

This book opens with an introduction to what hip hop/rap beatmaking is, followed by Part 1: History. The history part of this book takes an extensive, rather glaring look at the historic origins of hip hop culture, rap music, and beatmaking. A thorough examination of the origins of the beatmaking tradition has never been done before, let alone even mentioned by prior publications that explore contemporary musical processes. Thus, for this current edition, I wanted to further bolster the legitimacy of beatmaking as a music compositional process, by focusing on the lesser known and often misrepresented roots of beatmaking and the hip hop/rap tradition.

The history part of this book is followed by the instruction part. Here, I dive right into all of the key aesthetics, nuances, methods, and performance practices of the beatmaking tradition. Within the chapters of this part, you will find actual instruction on such topics as: drum programming, sequencing, sampling, arranging, music theory, and more. Following the instruction part is the music tradition, culture, and theory part. This part cross examines the core aesthetic priorities and esthetic standards of beatmaking with that of those found in the Western classical music tradition. In the business part, there's an exploration of the unique business circumstances that surround beatmaking. Finally, the interviews part includes six uncut interviews with critically acclaimed beatmakers.

Helpful Icons

In this book, there are two important icons to be aware of: first, the **BeatTip** icon. I have inserted this icon as an aide to help alert readers of an especially important point and/or tip. Second, the √**Check This Out** icon. I have inserted this icon to alert readers to either a personal story of mine or an extensive discussion that further personifies the particular theme and/or idea that is currently being examined.

Note on Nomenclature and the Use of Slang
The Use of Manual, Black, African American, Afro, Western, "Hip Hop/Rap," Hip Hop — no hyphen, Beatmaking, and EMPI

The "Manual" in the title of this study is a homage to a time when all a beatmaker had was his beat machine and the equipment manufacturer's manual that came along with it. What I remember most about that time was how badly I just wanted some tips to help me thru the maze.

Next, so that readers have an understanding as to why I use certain terminology in specific areas within this study, I thought I should offer some brief explanations. First, let's look at the term "black." During the 1960s, "black" displaced the word "negro" and emerged in America as the chief designative word of ethnic identity for African Americans. "Black" represented a changing point for African Americans, as it gave many African Americans more pride and confidence in their cultural and ethnic identity. It should be further noted that "black" became even more powerful in the late 1960s, due in great part to two events in American culture: (1) James Brown's song "Say It Loud, I'm Black and I'm Proud;" and (2) the black power movement. From the latter half of the twentieth century, "black," (depending on the context), has served to represent a *collective* culture and world view associated with African Americans and people of African descent. It is because of my deference to these developments and events (in particular, James Brown's "Say It Loud, I'm Black and I'm Proud"), that I chose to use "black" — *along with* the term "African American — throughout this book.

In this study I use "Afro" to refer to the common cultural rubric that all blacks (descendents of Africa) around the globe fall under. That is to say, I use "Afro" and "black" somewhat interchangeably to represent the common cultural connection (musically and otherwise) among all peoples of African descent throughout West Africa and the African diaspora — all New World cultures that owe their history to the peculiar institution of slavery and the Transatlantic Slave Trade. Finally, I should add that in this study I also sometimes use the term "Western" to describe European-derived esthetics (and creative aesthetics) and sensibilities.

Throughout the past 10 years, the terms "hip hop" and "rap" have been so misused and misrepresented that without context, its very hard to determine what the average person actually means when they use them. For instance, there are some who attempt to distinguish "rap" as something purely commercial and not indicative of so-called *real* hip hop – this despite the fact that by 1983, all of the pivotal pioneers regularly referred to the music as "rap" (as well as hip hop). In fact, between 1984 and 1995 "rap" was the most commonly used term to describe the music of hip hop culture. However, after 1997 (around the time when beats first began to be used more prominently by other music genres that did not include rappers, i.e. the merger of hip hop and "R&B"), the term "hip hop" became the primary name used to describe the music of hip hop culture. This created a disconnect between the paramount role that the art of rapping has played and continues to play in the music of hip hop *culture*. Moreover, the misuse of "hip hop" not only minimizes the culture of hip hop down to just its musical expression, it takes focus away from the fact that hip hop culture is actually comprised of four distinct artistic expressions: graffiti, b-boying, DJ'ing, and rapping.

Also, it should be pointed out that the word "rap" has always had several distinct usages in the black community. In the 1960s and 1970s, "rap" was used to describe "talk," in particular, a heavy, intellectual (enlightening) form of speech. "Rap" could also be used to describe the slang of the urban black community. Finally, "rap" was (is) also commonly used as a word to describe the courtship language used by many black American men in their social pursuit of a woman.

In this study, I use the term "hip hop/rap" as a means to reconcile the misunderstanding of these terms and their subsequent use. "Rap" is embedded and interlocked *within* hip hop — rap explicitly means *hip hop music.* So identifiable is rap to hip hop that it's impossible to seriously discuss hip hop without recognizing the interweaving connection of rap to the music of hip hop culture. Thus, I prefer to defer to the original use and intent of these two phrases. "Hip hop," in it's original intent and understanding, encompasses and covers the *entire* cultural expression. However, I recognize, for better or worst, how contemporary lexicon employs both "hip hop" and "rap." That is to say, today, "hip hop" is often used synonymously with "rap." Thus, in an attempt to reconcile these two phrases, and to literally show their deferential link, I use the term "hip hop/rap" when referring to the music of hip hop culture. Also, in some areas of this study I *only* use the term "rap," as it is sometimes necessary to be distinguished from the hybrid of R&B and hip hop, which does not often include rapping. Finally, I use "hip hop" — no hyphen — because that is the way the original architects and pioneers of hip hop wrote it. Moreover, the first print appearance of the term "hip hop" was in Michael Holman's interview of Afrika Bambaataa in the January, 1982 edition of *East Village Eye* magazine. And in Steven Hager's seminal work, *Hip Hop: The Illustrated History of Break Dancing, Rap Music, and Graffiti,* published in 1984 uses the same spelling. My deference is to the original architects and pioneers of hip hop and the first writers to formally document the culture.

The terms "beatmaking" and "production" are often used interchangeably to describe the same thing, but depending on the context, they're actually not. It's important to note that "producing" does not always involve actual beatmaking. Still, that being said, most of those who make beats refer to themselves as "producers," perhaps because the term presumably holds more prestige. But the fact is, in the annals of hip hop/rap music lore the "beatmaker" is more prestigious, even noble in my opinion. Beatmakers literally *make beats*! Moreover, the term "beatmaker" itself is a unique term for a different kind of music composer. Because of this, and the fact that I defer to the essence and scope of the originators of beatmaking, I prefer to describe those who actually make beats as "beatmakers," first and foremost. This is also why in this book I primarily use the term "beatmaking" rather than "producing." However, throughout this book I may indeed link these terms and their variations, e.g. "beatmakers (producers)." In those cases, I'm confident that given the topic and context of discussion, readers will know which term applies more appropriately. Also, it should be understood that wherever the terms "beatmaking," "production," and the like appear, I am only referring to (unless otherwise noted) the compositional methods of hip hop/rap music.

I should also note that within this study there is a significant amount of slang. Deliberate effort was made to preserve the authenticity of these expressions and their actual or intended meanings. Finally, in this book, I use **EMPI**. It's an acronym that I created (pronounced: em-pee) that stands for Electronic Music Production Instrument. Throughout this study, all beatmaking or electronic music production gear is routinely referred to as EMPI and/or EMPIs (plural).

Case Study Production Setup
Akai MPC 4000/Akai S950/Akai MPC 60 II/Roland Fantom S 88/Propellerhead Reason Setup with Digidesign Pro Tools DAW

With a book such as this, there must be a primary beatmaking (music production) setup through which the various technical and theoretical components and principles of hip hop/rap beatmaking can be examined. For this purpose, I have chosen to use my own production setup. Because my setup is a hybrid composed of hardware (both classic/vintage and contemporary pro audio gear and equipment) and software, it is particularly well suited for the task at hand. The individual EMPIs within my setup include:

- Akai S950 Digital Sampler (maximum memory).
- Akai MPC 4000, Akai MPC 60 II
- Roland Fantom S Keyboard Workstation (88-note, standard memory)
- Mackie 32/8 Analog Mixing Console (32 inputs, 32 direct outputs, 8 bus)
- Apple Power Mac G4 Dual 933 MHz/1.25GBSDRam/80G
- Digidesign 002 Rack (not Control Surface)
- Pro Tools LE version 7.1
- Properllerhead Reason
- Numark DM 1200 DJ/Stereo Mixer
- Technics SL-1200 MK2 Direct Drive Turntable
- Mackie HR 824 self-powered Studio Monitors
- Tascam 302 Dual Cassetter Deck (with pitch controle)

Note: The setup that I use offers a variety of particular nuances that permit me to apply many different methods and techniques. However, as you will learn, the compositional and procedural aesthetics of beatmaking are nearly all universal. That is to say, for the most part, they can be applied to any setup. For instance, sampling can not be restricted to any particular hardware and/or software. But the method and technique by which a beatmaker is able to sample can vary, depending upon the setup. Furthermore, it's important to note that the setup that I use offers a number of sound and technical effects that are unique to this particular gear and software combination. It should further be pointed out that no two digital samplers, drum machines, sequencers, keyboard workstations, or even software applications are identical. There may be many similarities at their core, but each piece in any setup performs consistent to its design and design potential. Different EMPIs combine to produce various effects. What one beatmaker may be able to do on a particular setup, other beatmakers may not be able to accomplish on yet another. Likewise, where one beatmaker is limited by a particular setup, another beatmaker may discover unlimited possibilities within that very same setup. The compositional possibilities within the hip hop/rap beatmaking and production process seriously depends on how beatmakers use their gear, equipment, and other production tools. Finally, I should point out that in no way is this book about or an endorsement of a particular setup or EMPI. The center of this book is grounded upon the study of the beatmaking tradition, not a discussion of production setups.

How To Navigate Through This Book

This book is a practical tool that can be easily navigated. As I've stated before, it's not a rigidly fashioned, *cold-numbers*, point-by-point-style, tech-heavy text book. It's not designed to overload you with fancy technological jargon or tricky algorithms, or the like. I've organized and broken down the parts, chapters, and sections of this book into an order that is both logical and consistent with the time line of a typical beatmaker's progression and development. Thus, if you know nothing at all or fairly little about beatmaking and/or hip hop/rap music, you can start with the first chapter and progress confidently through this book, at your own pace. However, the more advanced beatmakers and readers should know that as this study progresses, the concepts and themes naturally become much more in-depth.

Introduction

Rap, first and foremost, is, and will always be, about the beat. –Marley Marl

Mis-teaching…fouls up the roots of the neophytes' resources and imprisons their imagination. –Wole Soyinka

Roughly 30 years after the advent of hip hop/rap music, the pop culture commodification and corporate co-option of hip hop/rap music is complete: Hip hop/rap is no longer a small, but powerful, sub-culture; it is a major part of popular American culture. On one hand, this development has clearly threatened the creative and artistic values of hip hop/rap music. On the other hand, this development has helped give hip hop/rap music a level of influence OVER the American musical psyche and, subsequently, American culture, that has not been seen since the advent of the blues and rock 'n' roll.

Hip hop, once a little known Bronx sub-culture comprised of four elements — graffiti writing, b-boying, DJ'ing, and rapping — stands today as a mighty world culture. And while the significance of b-boying and graffiti have somewhat waned through the years, rap music still remains the most powerful, and certainly the most visible, of the four original elements (artistic expressions) of hip hop culture. Thus, one might wonder, What has given hip hop/rap music its staying power? Further, What gives hip hop/rap music its richness and unique energy? Is it the no holds barred street history of hip hop culture that continues to underscore hip hop/rap music even to this day? Is it the assortment of charismatic rappers and exceptional lyricists? Sure, you can attribute it to both of those factors as well as countless others (far too many and nuanced to adequately cover in this present study). But I believe that beatmaking is one factor that stands out among the others. Moreover, just as with the blues — and all of twentieth-century popular American music — it's the beat that drives hip hop/rap music. Accordingly, this book examines beatmaking, the chief compositional process for making hip hop/rap music, in all of its glory.

Beatmaking is an art-craft that requires serious study and long hours of practice. And despite recent attempts to make it merely just another marketable idiom of hip hop culture, it's not a consumable good. Though there has been a plethora of beatmaking tools to come to market in recent years (making it easier than ever before for anyone to get into the hip hop producer phenomenon), beatmaking is not some kind of pop item that can be bought. Sure, today a production setup can be purchased for almost nothing, but a beatmaking skill-set can not be bought. Knowledge must be learned and then developed, no matter what set of music production tools one might have. In fact, I maintain that throughout the history of beatmaking, the most successful beatmakers have reached their station by engaging in the very meticulous and time consuming educational process that quality beatmaking demands.

Though some of the basics of the beatmaking art form may be learned in a relatively quick manner by the truest autodidactics, beatmaking is notoriously difficult to learn and even more arduous to master. It is a tremendously deep (and rather dense) art-craft that is marked by a rich history and a meticulously detailed methodology. And even though there are no written "rules" in beatmaking, there are, however, numerous universal norms and preferences and, more importantly, fundamental aesthetic concepts, principles, and priorities. Thus, if learning how to become a beatmaker is notoriously difficult, then you can be assured that writing about it is equally (if not more) challenging.

The first major challenge in writing about beatmaking deals with the question of how to distinguish beatmaking as its own distinct art form and musical discipline, without completely separating it from the broader cultural context of hip hop itself. There is a commonly held (but ill-informed) belief that hip hop/rap music and hip hop culture are one in the same. Semantics aside, the truth is, hip hop/rap music, which is just one component (albeit the most powerful) of hip hop culture, has its own distinct identity — an identity, I should add, that doesn't always adhere to the sentiment of a so-called purist view of hip hop culture. And even though hip hop is indeed a music-based culture, the music did not necessarily beget the culture, the music was begotten by the culture. Then after the music was born, the other elements within the culture coalesced around it. And thus hip hop culture as a whole can never be deferential to hip hop/rap music. However, hip hop/rap music is always deferential to the broader hip hop culture. Anyone can make/produce or manufacture hip hop/rap music without even attempting to subscribe to any of the original tenets of hip hop culture on the whole. Actually, there are some who believe that knowledge of hip hop culture is not necessary for making beats. I strongly disagree with that position. Not only do I believe that some understanding of hip hop culture helps beatmakers, I think it's critical to the overall creative hip hop experience.

The other major challenge in writing about beatmaking is figuring out how to accurately describe its unique compositional methods and its canon of aesthetic priorities, while at the same time present its similarities to, and in some cases its reliance upon, various concepts and aspects of traditional Western music composition and theory. Let's remember that beatmaking is first and foremost an art-craft. And at its roots and its most fundamental and most popular forms, the aesthetics of the beatmaking art form represent an unwavering preference for (really a devotion to): (1) rhythm rather than tonal harmony or melody; and (2) repetition rather than linear progression. Moreover, beatmaking can be fundamentally characterized by its use of syncopated rhythms and strong drum beats (i.e. back beats). Yet even with its most obvious differences, the art of beatmaking still conforms to some of the general practices of traditional Western music compositional practices and theory.

Beatmaking Is a Teachable Music Process

The pursuit of knowledge ("know-how") has always been an important theme in hip hop culture. Likewise, the concept of teaching has always been critical to the advancement of all hip hop art forms. In hip hop culture's infant stages, the earliest hip hop architects sought and secured knowledge when and wherever they could. DJ Kool Herc, Grandmaster Flash, and Afrika Bambaataa (the three earliest pioneers of hip hop/rap music) learned directly and indirectly from each other as well as other influential artists and figures of the time. Moreover, they willfully took advantage of whatever educational resources were available to them at the time. (For instance, Grandmaster Flash, an electronics major in high school, read books on electronics and audio systems, this helped him go beyond the boundaries of the DJ equipment of the time.)

Thus, to seek out knowledge — to read a book on beatmaking; to watch beatmaking video tutorials; to read websites that offer beatmaking information; to ask for help from other beatmakers — is not to go against the hip hop/rap tradition. Seeking knowledge is not an anti-hip hop measure. On the contrary, to seek sound knowledge — wherever it may be — rests at the very foundation of hip hop culture. That said, beatmaking, an infant music process as far as previous major music processes are concerned, is still establishing its main metrics of uniformity. Which is to say that beatmaking knowledge, something that was once acquired entirely through informal means, is formalizing just like how other music processes have.

The Democratization of Music Production Tools and Its Effect on Ideas About Music Education

Once the tools of creative production are democratized, that is to say, made more accessible, an interesting phenomenon takes place: More people create. This phenomenon, although seemingly simple on the surface of it, is actually more complex than one may gather. For instance, in the case of contemporary popular music, the more people who create music, the more blurry the line gets between what music consumers deem "good" or "bad" music. Likewise, the more people who create music, the thinner the line gets between professional and amateur musician. Further complicating this matter, especially when it comes to beatmaking, are the various notions about music education, training, and expertise. Specifically, as more and more beatmakers enter into the beatmaking community, what constitutes appropriate training and learning activities?

In the case of the beatmaking tradition, accessibility to a wide array of electronic music production instruments (EMPIs) has taken the beatmaking tradition from the obscure shadows of an otherwise underground art-world to somewhere near the front of the global pop cultural psyche. Beatmaking is no longer a secret; it's no longer a tradition inherently reserved only for a select group of individuals (like some of those beatmakers who happened to be around right when the major recording labels first began to recognize hip hop's mainstream appeal and subsequent commercial viability). Instead, beatmaking is an open pathway to anyone who dares to embark on the journey. And as with all open creative markets, this journey allows (naturally) for the inclusion of various personal commitments. In other words, some will travel farther and deeper on this journey than others; and some will commit more to the beatmaking tradition than the processes of other music traditions. That is the great reward — and risk — of a swollen number of beatmakers.

But an exponentially large increase of beatmakers aside, a bigger concern of mine is where does beatmaking stand in terms of teaching and learning? What are the educational possibilities that exist for the beatmaking tradition? And more simply stated, can beatmaking be taught? In terms of teaching and learning, beatmaking is ideal for teaching, as the educational possibilities for beatmaking are immense. As to the question whether or not beatmaking can be taught, of course it can. Beatmaking is a teachable music process; everything from its DJ sensibility, to its history, to its most complex processes and methods can be taught. Therefore, in the fundamental matter of education, teaching, and learning, beatmaking's no different than any other music process. who disagree.

Why Some Claim that Beatmaking Can't Be Taught: Self-Taught Beatmaker Ideology and the Cloak of Secrecy as Competitive Coverage

Self-Taught Ideology

Many self-taught beatmakers tend to romanticize the factors that go into developing a skill at beatmaking. Those who carry the self-taught beatmaker ideology often tend to argue (sometimes with paranoia) that beatmaking is not something that can be taught or that one can learn through books, video tutorials, and the like. These beatmakers seem to support the narrow notion that beatmaking is only learnable through a self-imposed, "trial and error" journey in one's room. Of course, the implied idea also being that they are learning through indirect means, such as the study of records and gear manuals, and other books. Then there are also some self-taught beatmakers (especially well-known vets) who openly admit that they learned directly from other beatmakers, yet ironically, they also often claim that beatmaking can't be taught.

What is often lost on many self-taught beatmakers is the fact that for many beatmakers prior to the early 1990s, beatmaking education resources where scarce. There simply weren't any books that specifically addressed beatmaking, hip hop/rap's chief compositional process; nor were there any beatmaking classes or online tutorials available. But at the same time, there were such resources available for other music forms, including the blues, jazz, rock, and, of course, Western classical. Therefore, beatmakers throughout the 1980s and early 1990s learned through a combination of indirect means, direct teachers, and a great deal of trial and error. But such learning paths, especially self-taught trial and error, shouldn't be inflated with a sense of superiority. And as honorable as being a self-taught beatmaker may be (I taught myself a number of things and I'm proud of that fact, but I'm humbled by it as well), the self-taught ideology itself should not hang over the heads of new beatmakers as the best or only legitimate model for learning the beatmaking tradition.

Furthermore, the self-taught beatmaker ideology overshadows the fundamental fact that as beatmakers, we are all students of the beatmaking tradition, no matter how developed (or underdeveloped) our beatmaking skills are. Thus, as students of the beatmaking tradition — and the broader hip hop culture — shouldn't we remain committed to studying, learning, and educating ourselves whenever and however possible? And shouldn't this commitment be applauded rather than ridiculed or dismissed? Also, shouldn't beatmakers be encouraged to follow any learning paths that recognize and authentically represent the beatmaking tradition and hip hop culture?

Look at other music forms and processes, particularly the most highly regarded tradition in Western culture: the Western classical tradition. As musicians of the Western classical tradition advance, they study and train in the areas of theory, advanced theory, form, structure, harmony, melody, counterpoint, etc. And they do so utilizing teachers (directly and indirectly), books, tutorials, and the like. It doesn't matter if beatmaking lacks the global prestige of the Western classical tradition, the fundamental point that I'm making here is that a commitment to serious beatmaking studies is valid and no less legitimate to similar commitments made in other music traditions.

The Cloak of Secrecy and Paranoia in Beatmaking

The issue of secrecy in beatmaking is complex. On one hand, secrecy in beatmaking is valid. There are some areas in beatmaking where I find secrecy to be useful, if not necessary. Along the lines of digging for records and sampling and sample source material, there's a deep rooted history in not disclosing the source material that one samples. In this regard, I'm a very strong advocate for secrecy. In this area, secrecy is appropriate not only because it helps shield samplers from unnecessary copyright infringement suits, but also because it represents a link to early DJ culture, wherein DJs notoriously hid the names of the records they used to gain an advantage over rival DJs. But useful secrecy, i.e. a cloak of secrecy about sample source material and the like, is one thing. A hard line position of secrecy about the fundamental mechanics (method, process, aesthetics, etc.) as well as styles and sounds and the history of beatmaking is quite another.

Notwithstanding the areas of beatmaking that I believe do require (and benefit from) secrecy, for the most part, I find that the cloak of secrecy that many in the beatmaking community (including notable vets) evoke is absurd and not useful. Although there is a rite-of-passage dimension in beatmaking, particularly associated with an understanding of the fundamentals of beatmaking and the embracing of canonical works, the beatmaking tradition is not a secret music society. But the simple truth is this: There has always been a cloak a secrecy surrounding beatmaking, mostly because of the lack of formal uniformity within the beatmaking tradition — due in large part to the actual "newness" of the beatmaking music process. But in no way has secrecy surrounding the mechanics, nuance, and history of beatmaking been useful. I believe that such useless secrecy has contributed to a great deal of beatmaking knowledge not being passed on, which has, in turn, also contributed to an increase of lower quality hip hop/rap music in the past decade. Imagine if musicians from other music traditions held similar positions of secrecy. Imagine if musicians from other music traditions ridiculed and dismissed the validity and usefulness of teaching their tradition.

Competitive Coverage

Looking past the conditions that merit useful secrecy in beatmaking, I believe that a new stream of secrecy emerged as a means for competitive coverage for certain beatmakers. Keeping personal methods and practices a secret are certainly understandable. If a beatmaker develops a style and sound through the ingenuity of his own device, then it's reasonable for him to protect his formulas by keeping them secret. (Some see nothing wrong with a beatmaker practicing creative protectionism with other beatmakers, but I don't practice it.) However, cloaking the mechanics of beatmaking in the same veil of secrecy smacks of something else. I think when beatmakers do this they are enacting a form of coverage against new beatmakers, or rather new competition.

Nothing demystifies the secrets (or in some cases, the talents) of beatmakers like know-how and a solid understanding of beatmaking. Therefore, given access to the know-how and understanding of beatmaking, a new beatmaker can, in time, potentially emerge as competition to existing beatmakers. But cut off the knowledge base of beatmaking, or undermine access to it by discouraging others from pursuing it, then one beatmaker — particularly one already in the beat market exchange — can dull competition by another. Now, make no mistake, I'm all for competition; it's one of the hallmarks of hip hop. But I support competition based on the merits of a beatmaker's beats, no matter how many competing beatmakers that may exist. I don't, however, support competition that's based on a rigged talent pool that's created in part by some experienced beatmakers discouraging others from learning paths that may be different than their own. Such activity is competitive coverage, plain and simple.

The Need for Beatmaking Education and Committed Training

Beatmaking is now recognized around the world. In other words, it has made it to the global stage of music processes. As such, it deserves the same treatment as any other music process. Namely, it can and should be taught to anyone committed to learning the tradition. Fact is, the number of people interested in beatmaking has gone up (and it will continue). So the need for beatmaking education and capable teachers has intensified, not just to account for those newly interested in beatmaking, but to also preserve the beatmaking tradition and culture.

Also, as the pioneers and lead architects of a tradition fade away, either by means of new career pursuits, volatile market forces, or, unfortunately, death, this task of preserving the knowledge and history of the tradition becomes ever more daunting. Just think of the alternative to no beatmaking education. Sure, one might be able to learn the functions and features of an EMPI, but without a solid knowledge of the beatmaking tradition, one might simply become well accustomed with an EMPI, not necessarily well-grounded in hip hop/rap music, or more specifically, beatmaking, its chief compositional process. If EMPI based teaching is allowed to masquerade as beatmaking (hip hop production) education, like it already is at some schools and institutions, then the beatmaking tradition, in all of its essence and glory, runs the risk of being lost to future generations. This is another vital reason why beatmaking education and training is needed.

Plus, with more beatmakers, comes more competition; with a better quality of competition, comes a better overall grade of beats. And since know-how and understanding of the beatmaking tradition directly correlates to the ability and talent of a beatmaker, then beatmakers should be encouraged to study the tradition. This is yet another important reason why beatmaking education and training is needed.

The Reality Exists

The argument that beatmaking can't be taught, that it is a non-teachable art form is not only misguided and unfounded, it's counterproductive to the advancement of the beatmaking tradition. For one thing, this argument undermines beatmaking's rich history and nuanced complexity. Further, this argument ignores the fact that beatmaking, one of the newest musical processes in Western civilization, is quickly becoming one of the most influential contemporary musical processes in the world.

Even more troubling than the non-teachable argument itself are those who maintain it. Those who argue that beatmaking is a non-teachable music process do so to the detriment of beatmaking's status among other music processes. The prosperity and/or survival of a music tradition is determined by the caliber of its primary practitioners (and, of course, the general popularity of the music a specific process produces). Therefore, if beatmakers, the primary practitioners of the beatmaking tradition of hip hop/rap music, push the argument that beatmaking is a non-teachable music process, they essentially reduce beatmaking to nothing more than a hodgepodge, trial-and-error system of tinkering that has little conscious music direction. Thus, such an argument goes against what beatmaking truly is: A serious music process that contains clear and well-defined compositional and aesthetic methods, preferences, and priorities. Furthermore, by arguing that beatmaking is not teachable, then what those beatmakers (those who presumably already have the knowledge, mind you) are essentially saying is that beatmaking is something of a rightful (natural) privilege reserved for an elite few, not something ultimately accessible for all interested in learning.

Beatmaking is in fact a teachable music process, but this does not discount one's natural affinity for or connection to beatmaking. Instead, it's a firm acknowledgement that anyone, not just a select few, in a select city, region, state, or country, can develop a skill for beatmaking through committed study and training, be it formal or informal, direct or indirect. People can be taught the mechanics and integral nuances of beatmaking; people can be taught a certain level of proficiency in beatmaking; and people can learn how to become better beatmakers through beatmaking education and committed training.

Three Spheres of Beatmaking

One of the things that makes beatmaking such a unique musical tradition is the fact that its compositional method can incorporate, integrate, and convert any other music form into its own. In fact, hip hop/rap music, in its most historical form, contains elements and direct influences of an eclectic mix of various genres and styles of music, including, most notably, funk, soul, early disco, jazz, and the blues. This is why beatmaking can also be described as the chief procedural means by which an eclectic mix of musical influences and styles are converted into hip hop/rap music.

Like all music traditions, beatmaking contains its own distinct procedure and process. Simply put, beatmaking is the fundamental process by which hip hop/rap (instrumental) music is made. As a musical process, beatmaking can be broken down into three separate but equally important spheres. The **"three spheres of beatmaking"** include: the technical, the logical, and the creative spheres. The **technical sphere** of the beatmaking process describes the mechanical procedures of making hip hop/rap music instrumentals. It involves all of the steps associated with operating various Electronic Music Production Instruments (EMPIs). The **technical sphere** is encompassed by procedures and methods like sampling, chopping, looping, sequencing, recording, mixing, mastering, and the like. The **logical sphere** of the beatmaking describes the structuring and arranging processes of making hip hop/rap instrumentals. It involves the application of one's own unique knowledge and understanding of fundamental music structures, typical hip hop/rap music arrangement practices, and traditional and non-traditional music theory. The **creative sphere** of the beatmaking describes the creative processes of making hip hop/rap instrumentals. It involves the application of one's own imagination, musical knowledge, music intuition, unique style and approach.

Taken together, the three spheres of beatmaking determine the quality of a beatmaker's instrumentals. The way in which each beatmaker can excel within the three different spheres varies because each beatmaker is different. Likewise, *how* each beatmaker handles their deficiencies within these spheres also goes a long way in determining the quality (and effectiveness) of their instrumentals.

The Accessibility of Beatmaking and the Skill Factor

During the inception of beatmaking in the late 1970s and early 1980s, the very first beatmakers were usually persons with strong DJ'ing and/or audio engineering backgrounds. Their typical setup was comprised primarily of two turntables, keyboards, and the early drum boxes and effects modules. But as hip hop/rap music's popularity grew throughout the late 1980s and exploded in the 1990s, interest in beatmaking ballooned. Taking their cue from this spotlight on beatmaking, EMPI manufacturers accelerated their development of electronic music production tools that were almost exclusively targeted to the beatmaking market. Collectively, these developments presented setup options perhaps only imagined by the earliest beatmaking pioneers. Today, would-be beatmakers are overloaded with setup choices, making the beatmaking art-craft more accessible than ever. But although beatmaking is quite accessible, it's an art-craft in which a high level of proficiency often proves allusive. Anyone can acquire EMPIs, but this acquisition (by itself) does not guarantee that anyone will develop a unique skill or great proficiency in beatmaking. And one of the biggest reasons that many people who enter into beatmaking rarely receive the opportunity to earn a living from their music production services is because they fail to master the art-craft of beatmaking.

In cases where beatmakers stop short of developing a solid proficiency of the art-craft, many simply resign themselves to being "for-the-love-of-it" hobbyists. I've known quite a few beatmakers who were quick to point out that they didn't measure success by money and paychecks; that it's all about the love and passion for hip hop/rap music. In part, I hope to always agree with this sentiment. On one hand, I do believe that a beatmaker should enjoy creating beats. But on the other hand, I believe that a beatmaker should have the opportunity to earn some form of compensation for their talent, hard work, diligence, and creativity. Still, I must acknowledge that success is something that is unmistakably relative to each individual beatmaker. For me, success is determined by the development of a beatmaker's own unique, recognizable style and sound, as well as critical acclaim and the appropriate financial compensation for that beatmaker's music-making services. Creating music for the purpose of sharing it with other beatmakers, family, friends and co-workers is any beatmaker's prerogative. But one of the main goals of this book is to help beatmakers develop their talent and skill, with the ultimate goal being that of self employment and self reliance.

Beatmakers, like other skilled artisans, have the unique opportunity to earn a living by simply doing something that they're good at, and perhaps more importantly, something that they enjoy and love. With this in mind, I designed this book to help beatmakers develop and increase or hone their beatmaking skills, while at the same time offer insight on how they can best manifest their beatmaking (production) expertise into a successful career.

The Matter of Success or Failure

There are a number of reasons that contribute to the commercial and/or critical success (or failure) of beatmakers. Only a small number of beatmakers ultimately reach a high level of commercial success; more have a chance at critical acclaim than vast riches. In either case, a beatmaker's development of their own unique style and sound is paramount. For this to effectively take place, there are many factors each beatmaker must honestly consider. For instance, what kind of person are you? Are you organized, disciplined and forthright? Or are you disorganized, undisciplined and prone to procrastination? Do you have a decent knowledge base of music, one that spans multiple music genres and moments in music history? Do you use a hardware or software setup? Do you use a classic (vintage) setup or contemporary electronic instruments and pro audio gear? Do you prefer sampling records or utilizing synthetic sounds found in keyboards and soft synths? All of these questions are critical aspects of creating beats. Hence, one of the aims of this book is to help beatmakers identify, then manipulate, the various aesthetics that are critical to creating and developing their own unique sounds and styles.

Finally, the insight offered in this book covers the fundamental, intermediate, and advanced principles of beatmaking. With regards to actually making beats, I'm much more focused on simply revealing how and what is and what works, effectively. This applies not only to the compositional and procedural characteristics of beatmaking itself, but to everything in and around the hip hop/rap music production process. Moreover, I should note that this study explores the cultural factors that have shaped and continue to underscore the hip hop/rap music and beatmaking traditions. It is my firm belief that an understanding of the unique circumstances of hip hop/rap music and beatmaking is fundamental to any beatmaker's success.

Part 1
HISTORY

Many of those new to beatmaking either haven't made enough effort to learn the art form comprehensively, or they lack the resources to do so. Therefore, they are unfamiliar with the root structure and nuance of beatmaking and hip hop culture in general. This is why a study of the history of beatmaking and hip hop culture is critical. For it is through the unraveling of this history that we are all taken towards a truer understanding of hip hop's and beatmaking's essence and significance, both then and now. Also, this part covering the history of hip hop culture, hip hop/rap music, and beatmaking is especially crucial because the best way to preserve the culture and art form is by learning about its origins and its earliest developments; which makes learning from the earliest available resources and/or devoted practitioners of the art form essential. The key to the history and initial intentions of the art form can be found in the actions of its principle architects. Regardless of other opinions, theories, or assumptions, the principle architects remain the highest authorities.

I should further add that despite what some contemporaries may have you believe, the newest thing, trend, or development is always, essentially, a throwback or a homage to an earlier time within a given tradition. Hence, with the knowledge of the historical context in which hip hop/rap music was created, as well as with a historical account of the developments that occurred in the beatmaking tradition, you will be more comfortable in your moves towards innovation. Finally, as with any art form, it is necessary for beatmakers, being the auteurs that we are, to have a solid foundation (i.e. a healthy knowledge base and accurate historical understanding) in order to more effectively make beats.

Here, I should point out what *kind* of history exists in this part of the book. First, while this book is fundamentally about the beatmaking tradition as it exists within the hip hop/rap music tradition, no musical tradition can be properly understood outside of the context from which it was born. Therefore, the history part of this book is primarily concerned with the formative years of hip hop culture, hip hop/rap music, and, of course, the beatmaking tradition. Second, my aim is to present an accurate, objective audit of hip hop, one that is based on the historical evidence as it truly was, regardless of how favorable that historical evidence may have been or is to one group or the other. Point is, frank discussions based on the factual conditions that led to the formation (or formulation) of hip hop are critical to any real understanding of hip hop culture, hip hop/rap music, or beatmaking. Finally, it is not my purpose to romanticize the early history of hip hop. I'm certainly not concerned with sanitizing hip hop's story, or presenting a neat and clean "version" of hip hop's earliest beginnings in an effort to make some readers more comfortable. If the details of the historical backdrop of hip hop and its formation cause a level of discomfort for some readers, particularly with regards to the South Bronx Disaster, then I consider the history part of this study a success.

Chapter 1

Backdrop to Hip Hop: The Story of the South Bronx Disaster

The South Bronx...was the death trap. The most ugliest place on the face of the earth was the South Bronx. –Benjy Melendez, founder of the Ghetto Brothers

The Bronx, where I grew up, has even become an international code word for our epoch's accumulated urban nightmares: drugs, gangs, arson, murder, terror, thousands of buildings abandoned, neighborhoods transformed into garbage- and brick-strewn wilderness. –Marshall Berman, ca. 1978

Patterns of Paragraphs Based on Ruin –Rakim

Like any culture, hip hop persuades its participants to adopt its style and attitude in every aspect from language to fashion to dance to even how one walks. Upon entering hip hop culture (or dare I say the hip hop way of life), those not born into the culture and traditions of hip hop learn early on that they must draft any number of unwritten rules. From street dress codes, to physical posturings, to the adaptation of a uniquely enunciated vocabulary, and, of course, an aggressive and competitive world view, hip hop culture is, in some ways, a way of life. It has often (correctly) been said that hip hop started in the South Bronx. Although this statement is true on the face of it, it's incomplete. A more accurate statement is that hip hop started in *the streets* of the South Bronx. It is that very detail — "the streets" — that gives us the most appropriate insight into the origins of hip hop and, subsequently, the longevity of it. However, for most, the story of how the ubiquitous South Bronx "streets" were created is unknown. In fact, the narrative of poverty, crime, and violence in the South Bronx is often either taken for granted or worse, over simplified. Still, the cause and reality of the backdrop to hip hop is far more sinister than one might imagine.

The principles, ideas, approaches, and traditions of hip hop culture are not manufactured components of a conglomerate enterprise or the trickle down characteristics of an elite society. The hip hop ethos has its own backdrop, a backdrop that is the result of a combination of many fascinating, inhumane, and tragic factors. The backdrop of hip hop has been described before in different texts by various scolars and historians. However, I should point out that much of what this backdrop is comprised of has yet to really reach the consciousness of those who are squarely outside of the upper echelon of academia. Therefore, in this chapter, I illuminate the backdrop, and the little-known backstory, of hip hop, not only for those who might not otherwise be privy to it, but also for those who may not be aware of the fundamental mitigating circumstances behind hip hop's origins. Also, I believe that in order for one to more accurately understand the "soul" and fundamental life force of hip hop culture and rap (its chief musical expression), it's important to first grasp some understanding of the backdrop of hip hop.

Spectacular Ruin

At the end of the 1973 blaxploitation movie classic *Black Caesar*, Tommy Gibbs, the film's protagonist, limps out of the subway into the post-industrial South Bronx. The Harlem gangster, who having just escaped an assassination attempt, sees the place of his youth as perhaps a temporary hideaway and safe haven. But when he returns to the Bronx he finds that it has been burnt out and abandoned. As he struggles to draw meaning from the hill of rubble and stones that lie where the entrance to his boyhood home used to be, he is met by a small gang of teens, who swarm on him like a pack of vultures. They beat him and take his belongings, then leave him for dead. At this point, the camera pulls back to reveal a neighborhood of ruins…and the movie ends.

If you lived in the South Bronx in the 1970s, this scene from *Black Caesar* would not have shocked you, you would have recognized it all too well. The abandoned, post-war-like world that was so accurately depicted in the movie would have been eerily familiar to you. But to the average resident of the South Bronx (then and now) and the average hip hop/rap fan, the causes of the dreadful South Bronx Disaster are little known. To truly understand the conditions of the South Bronx in the 1970s, and to really have a complete grasp of the origins of hip hop culture and rap music, you must first look at how the South Bronx of "ill repute" was actually created.

Robert Moses's People Removal

In the late 1930s and 1940s, cities across the United States enacted "urban renewal policies" and began to create redevelopment programs. These early projects, which were said to be for the "greater good" of the community, were generally focused on slum clearance and were implemented by local public housing authorities, which were responsible for both clearing slums and building new affordable housing. In some ways, urban renewal programs can be seen as an outgrowth of President Franklin D. Roosevelt's New Deal, the massive legislative agenda which sought to help the United States recover from the Great Depression that had began with the stock market crash of 1929. The most notable and prominent example of urban renewal (that was ostensibly for the greater good) took place in New York City between the 1930s and 1970s, under the direction of one man, Robert Moses.

Robert Moses, who was not an elected official but an unelected bureaucrat with immense political power and connections, gained his power through his reputation for getting large construction projects done. In fact, he had gained so much power over the years that the many elected officials whom he was supposedly accountable to instead became dependent on him. But if his power made him one of the largest political figures in New York City, then his take on modernism and urban renewal certainly made him one of the most controversial figures as well.

Robert Moses harbored an astonishingly insensitive modernist view of public structures and the public itself. Many of his most impressive and notable public projects strongly suggest that he consistently favored automobile traffic over human and community needs. Moreover, Moses was obsessed with building new projects, "I'm just going to keep on building. You do the best you can to stop it," he quipped when pressed in the 1950s about his brand and pace of building in and around New York City. Throughout the latter part of his career, Moses's public works were so immense and rampant that they displaced hundreds of thousands of New York City residents, and destroyed thousands of traditional neighborhoods along the way.

Robert Moses's controversial career in public life stretched from the early 1920s to the late 1960s. But if it could be said that Moses's earlier public works (prior to 1950) were distinguished by design and beauty, then it must be said that his projects of the 1950s and 60s were distinguished by brutality and insensitivity. To be fair, in the late 1930s and 1940s, other cities across the United States enacted urban renewal policies and began to create redevelopment programs.

However, the concept, objective, and directive of Moses's Urban Renewal was not entirely in line with that of the rest of the country at that time. Through the programs of his "special agency," the Committee on Slum Clearance, Moses masterminded innumerable construction projects that consistently displaced families, disorganized communities, and, ultimately, devastated the lives of many New Yorkers. For this chapter's purpose, it's Moses's New York City projects of the 1950s and 1960s that are of major importance. It was some of these projects — specifically, the Cross Bronx Expressway — that collectively shattered the South Bronx, and set in motion the disastrous conditions from which hip hop emerged.

For more than 30 years, beginning in the 1930s and ending in the late 1960s, Robert Moses oversaw a magnitude of immensely complex building projects that were seemingly designed to make Manhattan Island an easy commute for rich and upper middle-class whites, who had begun moving to New York suburbs and upstate during the late 1940s. There was the West Side Highway, an ambitious project (as were all of Moses's projects) that saw expressway miles stretch from the lower West Side of Manhattan all the way upstate into Westchester. There was the Belt Parkway in Brooklyn, which ran from the edge of Long Island and connected to Manhattan via the Battery Tunnel, another one of Moses's creations. There was the Tri Boro Bridge project, a true triumph of modernism that connected the Bronx, Queens, and Manhattan through a complex web of highways, parkways, and bridges. There were innumerable parks and housing developments, and then there was the Cross Bronx Expressway, a colossal expressway which carved a hole right through the center of the Bronx. Each one of the aforementioned projects did their part in displacing millions of New York City residents, and disrupting neighborhoods and communities throughout Manhattan and the outerboroughs. But of all Moses's famed construction projects, none played a bigger role in the devastation and destruction of the South Bronx than the Cross Bronx Expressway.

Construction on the Cross Bronx Expressway began in 1953. To make room for the immense and unprecedented expressway, more than a dozen solid, settled, and densely populated neighborhoods were literally blasted and bulldozed, forcing an estimated 60,000 working- and lower middle-class people — mostly Jews, but many Italians, blacks, and Irish as well — out of their homes, effectively destroying solid and settled neighborhoods that had stood for 30 years. Construction for the Cross Bronx Expressway ended in the early 1960s. But this ending was only the very beginning of the ruin and devastation that the Bronx would be forced to endure.

As more than one hundred thousand whites abruptly fled the Bronx during the late 1950s and early 1960s, in what is commonly known as the "white flight from the Bronx," the apartments they left behind (some literally overnight) were crammed with impoverished blacks and Latinos, who had been relocated under the auspices of urban renewal and the Welfare Department. This wholesale move-in spread panic among many whites who had stayed in the Bronx, and it accelerated their flight to the suburbs of Long Island and upstate New York. It's further worth noting that tens of thousands of blacks and Latinos had already been displaced before by Robert Moses's "slum clearance" programs — programs that were really nothing more than public cover for some of Moses's immense and overawing construction projects. In fact, nearly all of Moses's construction projects hurt poor non-whites the most. I note this not to imply that Moses was a racist or that he did not like black or Latino people; on the contrary, evidence suggests that Moses's wasn't particularly fond of *people* in general, particularly those he deemed as being "in the way" of his building. Instead, I want to draw attention to the fact that nearly all of Moses's immense (often over reaching) construction projects inevitably hurt and devastated poor non-whites disproportionately more than any other group in New York.

Robert Moses's slum clearance programs ended in 1965, but again, by then, the South Bronx had literally been gutted and blasted by the Cross Bronx Expressway. And as the apartments that previously housed those whites (who took flight) were emptied out, they were reloaded with poor blacks and Latinos (most of which who were evicted and displaced from long settled neighborhoods in Greenwich Village and the West Side of Manhattan, again due to a number of Moses's vast projects), this white flight accelerated. And the landlords wasted no time in raising the rents on their new "problem" tenants.

Housing Disruption

By the time Robert Moses's slum clearance programs had ended, and after his power and influence had waned completely in 1970, housing overcrowding and social disruption had just begun its path to epidemic proportions. Between 1970 and 1980, more than 1.3 million white people had left New York.[1] But there were a total of two million people who were uprooted, with more than 600,000 poor blacks and Latinos being shuttled into the South Bronx, which by then was an area large enough to perhaps house little less than half that number.

---

[1] Deborah and Rodrick Wallace, *A Plague On Your Houses: How New York Was Burned Down and National Public Health Crumbled* (London and New York: Version, 1998), pxvi.

Before Moses's reign was all over, he had effectively utilized TITLE I and TITLE III of the HOUSING ACT OF 1949 to finance the construction of non-residential public works as well as every Public Housing project in New York City. Essentially, Title I enabled the worst of the so-called urban renewal. It required a local public authority to choose the development sites in conformity to a "master plan," get approval from the local government for site plans and site preparation plans (including relocation), condemn the property, and provide the one-third local contribution. The local authority, which was controlled by Robert Moses, would then clear the site, relocate the tenants, and auction the site to private developers. Finally, all Title I and Title III projects could be coordinated under one city master plan, which of course, was developed by Moses. In actuality, however, Title I of the Housing Act of 1949 didn't merely provide Moses with two-thirds of the funding, it provided federal financing of more than 90% for his slum clearance programs — Moses's reputation for getting the federal government to pay for his projects (and ruin) was well-renown. So, in effect, Robert Moses was also successful in getting the federal government to pay for his modern vision of New York.

But if Robert Moses's vision of New York was purchased for almost nothing, the price paid by its poor non-white residents was tragically expensive. Many of Moses's slum clearance programs really worked as a "poor removal" program for middle- and upper-class housing. In the book *A Plague On Your Houses*, the seminal study on New York City's fire epidemic, Deborah and Rodrick Wallace report that one regular feature of Moses's slum clearance programs inevitably "resulted in a vastly disproportionate targeting of communities of color for relocation." Many minority-heavy slums were destroyed and replaced with more expensive housing or non-residential public works that were not accommodating to the original inhabitants.

Another alarming feature of Moses's slum clearance programs was its reliance on re-housing residents in public-housing projects that concentrated distraught families and individuals into smaller spaces — where they would soon be deemed "problems."[2] Hundreds of thousands poor and working-class blacks and Latinos were uprooted and shuffled into public housing and ugly tenements all over New York City, with the vast majority of the residents being relocated to the South Bronx, where housing shortages were already severe. By 1970, there would be a new epidemic that would further accelerate the housing shortage in the South Bronx in a much more devastating way. It was an epidemic that would eventually establish the South Bronx as America's number one urban disaster area.

---

[2] Wallace, 13-14.

Fire Epidemic: The Bronx Is Burning

> The South Bronx lay in ruins, and the fires there were becoming larger, eroding away what was left after the epidemic crest had blitzed a high proportion of the housing. The New York City burnout disaster greatly exceeds this Indian disaster by any measure: time frame, involved population, involved area, number of deaths, number of disease cases, and number of lives derailed. —Deborah and Rodrick Wallace

As a result of Robert Moses's slum clearance programs, large numbers of people were crammed into woefully inadequate housing supplies throughout New York City. But it was in the South Bronx were this theme took an even more sinister and tragic turn. Between 1969 and 1978, the population density in the South Bronx reached disastrous proportions. In its Master Plan for New York City in 1969, the New York City Department of Planning described the South Bronx as an area where most of the housing was grim, crowded tenements, where the majority of residents were black and Puerto Rican.[3] But Robert Moses had been only one contributing factor to the housing disruption and destruction in the South Bronx, the other culprit was fire.

The South Bronx fire epidemic was one of the worst urban disasters in American history. Certainly, Moses's slum clearance program was so good at disrupting housing and displacing communities that it created an even bigger housing problem for poor non-whites (blacks and Latinos) as well as other destitute and torn communities throughout New York City. And hundreds of thousands of housing units were lost in those areas where poor non-whites had been relocated to because of Moses's modernism and slum clearance program. But this paled in comparison to what the fires did to housing in the South Bronx. Many families were burnt out of there homes sometimes three and four times. In fact, the fires of the South Bronx literally created an entirely new refugee class that trumped the movements of its predecessors, who themselves were the refugees of Moses's slum clearance programs. These conditions led to a dangerously high level of housing density, which in turn made non-burnt-out housing structures susceptible to the surrounding fire wave. Indeed, throughout the South Bronx in the 1970s, seemingly whatever could burn did burn, leaving blocks upon blocks of charred and abandoned building shells. Sometimes an individual block would be destroyed in only a few months; a neighborhood would be destroyed in 6-12 months, leaving communities torn within an urban landscape that resembled the aftermath of a city bombed and blasted by war.

---

[3] *Ibid*, 26.

"The South Bronx was a real disaster," recalls Benjy "Yellow Benjy" Melendez, social activist and founder and former member of the 1970s street gang, Ghetto Brothers. "The burning buildings was widespread. Fires were happening everywhere, and you had to be on alert all the time. It was a big problem! I mean, the South Bronx looked like World War II, like Germany after World War II. When you walked down the street — especially around Freeman, Tiffany, and Fox — and you looked up, the only thing you saw was a beautiful moon on a summer night. Nothing but empty shells of empty buildings. If you didn't know, you'd think the Bronx was a war-torn area. That's what it looked like, like a bunch of tanks just blasted buildings up."[4]

What Caused the Fires in the Bronx? The Arson Stigma of Poor Non-Whites

The fires in the South Bronx leading up to 1969 could be described as the inevitable result of dangerously high levels of population density. "Large numbers of people per square mile mean that large numbers of people are crammed into housing, with more cooking, more smoking, more trash generation, more use of electricity are going on per unit area. When high population density also results in a high proportion of the housing units being extremely overcrowded, the maintenance and services of the buildings require greater effort and resources to keep fire hazards to a minimum."[5] This is not to say that overcrowded poor non-whites are naturally prone to make fire hazards (though in the following section, you will see that this was suggested by the Rand Corporation and Roger Starr), but rather to show that given the set of the previously described mitigating housing conditions and circumstances, the greater potential for fire hazards in the South Bronx was a reality. But if the fires in the South Bronx between 1965 and 1969 were perhaps the inevitable result of the mitigating housing conditions and circumstances that were created by Robert Moses's slum clearance programs, then the burnout that charred the South Bronx throughout the 1970s was the result of something far more lethal.

In 1969, the New York City/Rand Institute Fire Project conducted a study of and compiled data on fire alarms and fires in New York City. At best, the findings of the Rand Corporation Fire Project (which were heavily biased and clearly racially motivated), were negligent, incomplete, one-sided, and woefully inaccurate. At worst, the Rand findings were racist, intellectually narrow, and

---
[4] Interview with Benjy Melendez.
[5] *Ibid*, 53.

intentionally misguided and misleading. For one thing, the Rand Fire Project centered most of its attention on the contrast of racial composition of high-incidence and low-incidence areas. Next, Rand attributed nearly every fire in the South Bronx to arson. (Subsequent analysis of the data did not back this up. Of the fires in buildings, only a very small portion were arson and that portion was not higher than the rate of proven arson found in wealthier neighborhoods.)

While the Rand Institute paid major attention to the neighborhoods that were "heavily Negro and Puerto Rican and mostly poor," it curiously avoided addressing several key factors that helped to create the fire epidemic in the South Bronx. For instance, it did not address the concentrated reductions in fire service (fire house closings and defunct fire alarm boxes) that were disproportionately carried out by the city in non-white and impoverished areas, most notably in the South Bronx and the Brownsville section of Brooklyn. Also, it did not account for, or even acknowledge, landlord (slumlord) and business-owner arson. And it did not account for the fact that many of the fires in the Bronx weren't even arson at all, but rather the expected result of devastatingly poor housing conditions, community disruption, and an overall reduction in public safety resources in the South Bronx. Furthermore, the Rand Fire Project not only labeled nearly all fires in the South Bronx as arson, it also, in effect, laid the blame of this arson on poor non-whites — i.e. blacks and Puerto Ricans.

The unfortunate truth about the Rand data is that most major political figures in New York City knew that the fire service reductions between 1969 and 1976 further devastated poor neighborhoods (which had already been vastly disrupted by Robert Moses's slum clearance programs), and helped destroy huge numbers of housing units much more rapidly than Moses ever could. Yet rebuilding and/or repairing these disastrously torn communities was not the response of New York City policy makers. Instead, the response was something even more sinister and inhumane: benign neglect and planned shrinkage.

Benign Neglect & Planned Shrinkage
The 1-2 Punch that Knocked Out the South Bronx

> Not an arsonist at first glance, Daniel Patrick Moynihan burned down poor neighborhoods in cities across the country as surely as if he had doused them in kerosene and put a match to them. —Deborah and Rodrick Wallace

If Robert Moses's slum clearance programs set the stage for a collapse of the South Bronx, then the benign neglect policy — inspired by Daniel Patrick Moynihan's now-infamous memorandum to President Richard Nixon — opened the show with a number that inevitably assured the destruction of the South Bronx. In January, 1970, Daniel Patrick Moynihan, then an Urban Affairs Advisor within the Nixon Administration, wrote and sent a memo on race relations to President Nixon. Drawing on national census and employment data, as well as data on fire alarms and fires in New York City forwarded to him from the 1969 New York City/Rand Fire Project, Moynihan's memo advised that the nation might "benefit from a period of 'benign neglect.'"

The now-infamous "benign neglect" memo, which was printed in its entirety in the New York Times in March, 1970, was itself highly controversial and absurd. The memo portrayed poor blacks (specifically black males) in urban America as "socially pathological," "antisocial," and racist — even going as far as to blame these blacks, in part, for shaping white radical attitudes. What's more revealing about this portrayal of poor non-whites (blacks in particular) is Moynihan's underlying thesis that they were unredeemable and a "threat" to the "socially stable elements of the black population."

But there were two other features of the memo that were even more alarming, and, subsequently, damaging to the people of the South Bronx. First, there's Moynihan's thesis on fires in New York City. Using the flawed Rand data, Moynihan asserted that the great majority of the fires in New York City were arson, and that poor black slum dwellers were the blame:

> In New York, for example, between 1956 and 1969 the over-all fire alarm rate more than tripled, from 69,000 to 240,000. These alarms are concentrated in slum neighborhoods, primarily black…Many of these fires are the result of population density. But a great many are more or less deliberately set…Fires are in fact a "leading indicator" of social pathology for a neighborhood. They come first. Crime, and the rest, follows. The psychiatric interpretation of fire-settings is complex, but it relates to the types of personalities which slums produce.[6]

The second damaging feature of the memo can be found in Moynihan's one-sentence suggestion to Nixon on how to solve his administration's "ineptness" for appropriately handling relations with the black population:

> The time may have come when the issue [sic] of race could benefit from a period of "benign neglect."[7]

Hardly a direct national call for the abandonment of urban (black/Puerto Rican) neighborhoods; nevertheless, New York City officials took the "benign neglect" tagline, combined it with all of Moynihan's damaging assessments of

---

[6] "Text of the Moynihan Memorandum on the Status Negroes," *New York Times*, p.69, March 1, 1970.
[7] *Ibid.*

poor non-whites, and used it to formulate and justify a new, more dastardly urban policy: "planned shrinkage."

When Roger Starr first articulated his theory of planned shrinkage in his book *Urban Choices: the City and Its Critics* (1966), one might have known, given the political and racial climate of the time, that he and his book would eventually influence New York City policy makers. As the Executive Director of the Citizens' Housing and Planning Council of New York (1959), Starr's directive should have been to facilitate the mandate of the Council, which was to "educate New Yorkers about the housing problems, and to lead city and state governments to programs for the alleviation of some of the accumulated housing miseries"[8] of New York City. However, planned shrinkage, the program that Starr *lead* city officials to, was not only ill-conceived, it was better equipped for extending rather than alleviating some of the accumulated housing miseries. Moreover, it could not have been designed with any other intention, except to kill off New York City's poor non-white neighborhoods, in particular, its poorest and biggest eyesore: the South Bronx.

Planned shrinkage (the de facto name for the New York City's war on the poor), was what ecologists Deborah and Roderick Wallace called "the New York City expression of Moynihan's benign neglect." More sinister and inhumane than Moynihan's benign neglect might have ever intended to be, planned shrinkage was truly an all out frontal assault on the poor. The policy (program) dictated the direct withdrawal of essential services from so-called "sick" neighborhoods, which were all poor and non-white, and seen as unable to survive or *undeserving of survival* and, therefore, unworthy of the level and quality of services afforded to white middle- and upper middle-class neighborhoods. The range of services that planned shrinkage snatched from the South Bronx and other poor non-white New York City neighborhoods left no doubt about the real intention and scope of the policy. To Starr and other elites, the notion of community did not exist in these poor neighborhoods, therefore, there were drastic reductions in everything from libraries and public transportation service to social and health services and, most alarmingly — but fitting to the task at hand — fire service. It was the withdrawal of fire service that "left burned out communities defenseless and insecure and churned out wounded spirits as surely as the Viet-Nam War did."[9] It should be noted that as all of these services were "freed up" from the "sick" neighborhoods, they were routinely shuttled into the ones deemed to be "healthy," which were all middle- to upper-class and mostly white.

---

[8] Roger Starr, *Urban Chronicles: The City and Its Critics,* (New York: Coward–McCann, 1967), front matter.
[9] Wallace, 113.

Equally destructive of poor neighborhoods like the South Bronx was Roger Starr's use of the notion of *non-community* in poor neighborhoods as the intellectual basis for the massive demolition of housing for the poor. And rather than repair or rebuild the damaged housing within these neighborhoods, Starr urged instead to let the land "lie vacant" until a new use, such as industry, could arise.[10] Thus, in the final analysis, if benign neglect was the call for the intentional abandonment of urban poor non-white (particularly black) neighborhoods, then planned shrinkage was the devastating blow used to outright kill them off.

The Aftermath and Foreseen Fallout

Community Destruction

Prior to the fire epidemic, which was the direct result of New York's war on the poor, which itself was made up of Robert Moses's slum clearance program and the benign neglect and planned shrinkage policies of Daniel Patrick Moynihan and Roger Starr, respectively, poor and lower middle-class non-white neighborhoods were stable. Communities in very poor and lower middle-class areas rely on social and mutual-aid networks in ways different from the American majority. Families and individuals depend on their communities for necessary resources, emotional support, and news and information in direct proportion to their poverty, lack of education, cultural sensibility, and ethnic difference from the American majority. Moreover, within the communities of the poor, social networks form through intergenerational links, and may or may not be familial. In fact, in poor communities, the extension of kin relations to non-kin is expected, because it helps allow for the creation of mutual-aid networks — networks that fundamentally reserve strategies of survival. Yet anyway you look at it, New York's war on the poor destroyed these communities and their vital networks, and made survival within them harder than ever for its residents. Nowhere was this more apparent than in the South Bronx.

By 1975, the South Bronx was the most devastated urban landscape in the United States. According to Demographia, the three community districts that comprise the core of the South Bronx had fallen 57 percent in population from 383,000 in 1970 to 166,000 in 1980, which has to rival the greatest short term population loss in any urban setting with the possible exception of war's devastation. Furthermore, until around 1990, almost no housing replaced the

---

[10] *Ibid*, 25.

1970s destruction that was created by planned shrinkage. But by then, hundreds of thousands of units had already been burnt out or abandoned. The war on the poor had consequences which the previously planned and mitigated slum clearance did not: Deterioration in public health, deterioration in public safety, and serious decline in the life expectancy of both elderly and young blacks citywide. The slum clearance programs that proceeded the benign neglect and planned shrinkage policies and the fire epidemic of the 1970s were of such a magnitude that they constituted a disaster, a truly calamitous event, that caused widespread destruction and great loss of life, damage, hardship, and "a situation of massive collective stress."[11]

During the 1970s, the South Bronx was transformed into an isolated war zone. Out of any other area in New York City, its neighborhoods had suffered the most intense social destabilization and destruction of community. As the burnout, and the city policies that gave rise to it, rapidly continued to scuttle their neighborhoods, the black and Latino populations were increasingly fragmented and left for dead. And as the firewave reached an epidemic level, and housing shortages rose to dangerously high proportions, and as unemployment rose, residents were repeatedly burned out and/or evicted and relocated into city-owned tenements that were worse slums than the ones from which they came. Because families could not move far enough from the fangs of decay and ruin, they were sometimes burned out (and/or evicted) two or three times in a few years.[12] At at the same time that people in the community were being assaulted by this, the community institutions — churches, political clubs, social clubs, stores, and small factories, which normally would have buffered the outfall of displacement — weakened dramatically.

Though the burnout ebbed around 1977, after 1978, housing overcrowding rose again. All of the families who were able to move out did so, soaking up what little housing availability that existed in and around New York City, which forced the majority of South Bronx residents to double and triple up inside already cramped housing. And when there was a call for federal funding for housing construction efforts for the poor in 1978, Daniel Patrick Moynihan (who at that time was a U.S. Senator), opposed it, stating that: "People in the South Bronx don't want housing or they wouldn't burn it down. It's fairly clear that housing is not the problem in the South Bronx."[13]

---

[11] *Ibid*, 18, 60.
[12] Interview with Benjy Melendez.
[13] H. Raine, 'US Housing Program in South Bronx Called a Waste by Moynihan.' *New York Daily News*, 20 Dec. 1978, p. 3

The combined factors that led to the disaster in the South Bronx destroyed the community immeasurably, but perhaps the areas in which the aftermath of the devastation manifested itself the most was along the lines of unemployment, crime, and the social health of the youth. It has been well-known that stable communities do a better job of maintaining law and order within their community than the police. Such was the case in the South Bronx, that is, until the disaster hit.

One can only imagine the various emotional and mental effects caused by the wild swings of widespread housing disruption. Unfortunately, the unemployment side-effect takes little imagination. Even before the citywide slum clearance programs uprooted hundreds of thousands of Black and Latino residents from solid and stable communities (communities wherein a majority of these residents worked) and relocated them to decaying slum areas in the South Bronx, the unemployment level in the South Bronx certainly wasn't admirable. But after the disaster, the unemployment level skyrocketed. Throw in the dual deathknolls for the poor that the policies of benign neglect and planned shrinkage were, and the result was ever-expanding incomless periods for many of the South Bronx residents during the disaster period.

For certain, these long stretches of incomeless periods added to the strain of an already distressed family nucleus. Many families in the South Bronx were split up and permanently scarred. Fathers vanished, sometimes voluntarily because of the anguish and humiliation the disaster placed upon them; other times they were removed "involuntarily" due to prison stints, drug usage, and/or violence — all significant by-products of the South Bronx disaster. The departure of many fathers was particularly hard because it left single mothers to struggle alone as the single bread-winner. It also meant that grandmothers, aunts, and other family members (including extended family) had to help pick up the weight and take in those too young to provide for themselves, straining an already distressed housing situation even further.

The Social Health of a Disconnected Youth: Fragmentation, the Code of the Streets, Survival, and the Rise of South Bronx Street Gangs

> In the South Bronx today, death is an ironic but frequent event among the youth of this community. And the fist of irony is clinched within the knowledge that death — violent death — is often most heavy here among the poor, who seem to have so little to lose. Here, perhaps because of its frequency, sorrow is never born of any sense of form. To live in this community today may be to share in an inhuman existence. One must learn, from implausible models, the speciality of survival. One must be…relentless in the pursuit of this survival…with hands to steal and legs

to run, eyes that view life and death, which unless one is stronger than the strong, crush whatever human sensibilities left remaining. One might ask how does one learn the specialities which separate man from what we consider the lower animals. On these streets, the youth of the South Bronx is molded and educated in the rules of the survival game… In this neighborhood one is lucky, only if one learns the wisdom of the street, early. Here, to be lucky is to stay alive!
–Tony Batten, *Ain't Gonna Eat My Mind*, 1971

Before the South Bronx Disaster, parents in stable communities were able to rely on the extended networks and relationships within the community to reinforce the socialization of their young. But now, with parents struggling to survive and these networks and relationships weakened — if not outright destroyed — a great number of children emptied out of broken homes into the streets, where there was little to no adult supervision or responsible mentorship. For the overwhelming majority of young blacks and Latinos in the South Bronx, the peer groups that they found and created in the streets, not the traditional familial nucleus, became their chief support system.

Because of the South Bronx Disaster, these fragmented groups were exiled far outside of the mainstream, and as such, they where forced to establish new modes and structures for living that were predicated upon daily survival. And with little to no economic opportunity and weakened community social networks, the youth of the South Bronx (and other similarly hard-hit areas) were left without a structure to responsibly nourish them and their time. Thus, the youth — who like all South Bronx residents at the time — became the target of destruction; and they were highly susceptible to the kind of contagious, destructive/self-destructive behavior that runs through the streets. Over time, the "behavioral codes" transmitted between groups and coalesced into a more aggressive street code (i.e. "code of the streets"), which inevitably informed the youth on how to act and survive in the streets.

In order for each group to distinguish themselves (and in order to simply survive), each group had to out-do the other. Aggressive competition became one of the norms of the street, and each group found that not only did their representation of the street code have to be solid, they had to be even more daring and anti-social than the next group. In this context, all anti-social behavior was amped up, because in the competition for distinction, groups became bolder, more riskier, more brazen, and, subsequently, more violent. Eventually, for the majority of the youth in the South Bronx, it was street gangs (and then later crews) that would become their new family. And for many, it was street gangs that would also serve to formulate their primary social and information structures, and, in many cases, their chief means of survival.

The slum clearance programs, the city's ill-fated benign neglect and planned shrinkage policies, and the burnout collectively helped to usher in a new and rather severe New York City street gang culture. As it probably should have been expected, the street gang culture of 1970s New York City was much more extensive and alarming than that of the 1950s. For starters, during the 1970s, the sheer number of gangs and gang members and affiliates throughout all of New York City dwarfed that of the 1950s. In 1971, there were more than 50 gangs, with total membership in the South Bronx exceeding 60,000 members, by far the most street gang activity in New York City.[14] Next, the gangs, which in many cases grew from childhood friendships on neighborhood blocks and disbanded social clubs, were much more aggressive and brazen. And while the street gangs of the 1970s permeated throughout the five boroughs of New York City, it was quite extensive and more deafening in the South Bronx and Brooklyn. It is further worth noting that all of the top three pioneers of hip hop — DJ Kool Herc, Grandmaster Flash, and Afrika Bamabaata — at one point during this era either belonged to or had an affiliation with one of the major street gangs of the South Bronx. In fact, Afrika Bamabaata was at one time a well-known member of the Black Spades, one of the biggest, most infamous and influential street gangs in the South Bronx and Harlem.[15]

Segregation

The aftermath of the slum clearance programs, the benign neglect and planned shrinkage policies, the burnout (which had been set in motion by the aforementioned programs and policies), the community destruction of the South Bronx, and the high level of street-gang activity in the South Bronx, tells many stories.

There's the tragic story of housing disruption and destruction, wherein the impoverished or lower middle-class neighborhoods in New York City are made up almost entirely of black and/or Latino families, with the bulk of the city's public housing projects mirroring this tragic ratio even more disproportionately. By 1990, the number of extremely overcrowded housing units had reached about double the epidemic 1970 number.[16]

There's the story of crime and especially crime disproportion as it relates to incarceration. Since 1980, over 75% of the prisoners within New York's upstate

---

[14] Estimate provided by Benjy Melendez.
[15] The story of the 1970s South Bronx street gang culture is itself an explosively extensive topic which I cover in my forthcoming book with Benjy Melendez *Ghetto Brother: How I Found Peace in the South Bronx Street Gang Wars*.
[16] Wallace, xvi.

facilities have come from only seven New York City neighborhoods — three of sections are located in the heart of the South Bronx; and 85% of the prisoners are Black or Latino.[17] As the number of employment opportunities rapidly declined, and as the housing crisis intensified, and the family nucleus broke down and the gang era erupted, the level of crime ballooned. As should have been expected, there was a dramatic increase in every type of crime associated with poverty. The number of burglaries and armed robberies went up; the drug trade (specifically heroin) spiked out of control, as the disaster worsened and drug usage/abuse became a means of escape for the poor minority, both young and old. Ecologists Deborah and Roderick Wallace insist that planned shrinkage "seems to have enabled drugs to be flooded all over the South Bronx, Upper Manhattan, the Lower East Side and East Village, the poverty corridor and transitional neighborhoods of Brooklyn, and the immigrant neighborhoods of Queens. Even Staten Island did not escape; it grew a drug problem on its north shore which received the spillover of refugees from Brooklyn and Lower Manhattan."[18] Finally, the murder rate skyrocketed, no doubt due to the result of violent robberies, street gang wars and other street gang activity, drug usage and distribution, and heightened, war-like induced stress.

But of all of the stories that the aftermath of the South Bronx disaster tells, it's the story of segregation that, here, for the purposes of this discussion, the hip hop/rap and beatmaking traditions, warrants special attention. The increased level of community segregation played a pivotal role in the origins of hip hop culture. Prior to the disaster, the South Bronx was fairly integrated with a healthy mix of Jewish, Irish, Italian, Black, and Latino residents. But after the disaster, the South Bronx was mashed up and torn into such an isolated area that it rivaled the level of segregation found in rural Jim Crow South.

For all of its diversity, New York City has in fact been made up of deeply segregated populations, particularly in the outer boroughs like the Bronx and Brooklyn. And as we have seen, the particular brand of segregation in New York City wasn't brought on by some obscure, radical sense of racism or white supremacist ideology. No. The class and racial segregation of New York City was caused, first and foremost, by a war on the poor that was waged by New York City's elite class. The slum clearance programs and public policies of benign neglect and planned shrinkage, which were orchestrated and enacted at the behest of city officials Robert Moses, Daniel Patrick Moynihan, and Roger Starr, created a New York City disaster that was most devastating in the South Bronx.

---

[17] *Ibid*, 212. See also, "Ex-Inmates Urge Return To Areas of Crime to Help," Francis X. Clines, (*New York Times*, December 23, 1992).
[18] *Ibid*, 114.

In the minor, these policies legally intensified already separate and unequal social and economic spheres throughout New York City. In the major, these policies created a fire epidemic and a disaster in the South Bronx that resembled a post-war bombing. And as this disaster and its effects became more apparent throughout the 1970s and 1990s, there was no real effort to rescue those who had essentially been left for dead in a segregated oasis of vast ruin.

The Black and Latino people of the South Bronx (and other similarly hit areas throughout New York City, especially the Brownsville and East New York sections of Brooklyn), were forced into segregation and further discriminated against. The youth of the South Bronx understood very well that the "greater" society had caused the South Bronx disaster; they that the South Bronx was under siege. Perhaps they didn't know the intellectual directive, that the twin polices of benign neglect and planned shrinkage were an attempt to kill off and quarantine New York City's poor non-whites, especially those in the South Bronx. And maybe they didn't know that the reductions in fire houses, health care and transportation services in the South and West Bronx were a prescribed death sentence for the Americans living there. But they knew something much more practical: They knew that the South Bronx was attacked and left for dead. They knew that the dominant culture had rejected them; so they further disconnected themselves from *it*, rejecting and turning mainstream (elite-class dominated) society, philosophy, and culture into a rival mode of living.

Things They Took from the Disaster

The South Bronx Disaster created a cemetery of hope that was bordered by despair, destruction, fire, drugs, violence, and tragic death. But even in a land where the damned were intentionally oppressed and abandoned (in the form of "benign neglect"), then outright attacked and left for dead (in the form of "planned shrinkage)," the resilient pulse of humanity never completely extinguished. It was this left-over pulse, this "beat," that a large band of young Black and Puerto Rican adults from the South Bronx rallied around. And in this process of coming together around that beat, they formulated a new outlook on life. It was an outlook on life that was dynamically infamous. It incorporated the pain of neglect, the spirit of vengeance, the essence of street-knowledge, and the pure focus of survival. It moved to a new rhythm, rhyme, and reason. And it turned style, attitude, and the quest for respect into a powerful force. In time, this new cultural movement became known as hip hop.

Chapter 2

Move, Rock, Dance, Sucka
The Coalescence of Hip Hop Culture and the Birth of Hip Hop/Rap Music

> Gospel, blues, jazz, no one person invented it. It was the social result of a painful existence. –Quincy Jones

Unprecedented Cultural Autonomy and the Seeds of an Invisible Culture

In Chapter 1, I discussed how the South Bronx Disaster destroyed a community and in the process created a pool of disconnected youth. In this chapter, I examine how the young of the damned — the so-called disconnected youth — re-connected with one another, came together, and used an unprecedented level of autonomy to not only forge a new community, but to formulate one of the most powerful subcultures in modern history.

Of all of the preexisting conditions necessary for a new subculture to emerge and thrive, autonomy is the most important. For a community to have true control over the innovations, developments, and advancements of its culture, its people must have the independence, the freedom, and the will to choose and orchestrate its own actions. The more autonomy that a community has, the more freedom its people will have to develop its culture. No doubt in the case of the hip hop subculture, the autonomy factor played an pivotal role. And what's most important to note about the role that autonomy played in hip hop's origins is how and where exactly this autonomy was created: Nowhere was this autonomy more visible than in the streets of the South Bronx.

"The streets" have long been one of the most durable institutions of urban America, but inside of the 1970s South Bronx, this institution was further emboldened by one of the worst cases of municipal malpractice in United States history. The South Bronx Disaster destroyed a community, tore up neighborhoods, and threw the lives of hundreds of thousands of people into a post-war-like chaos. Because of their shared socio-economic backgrounds and environmental circumstances, the youth of the South Bronx made the streets their home and a world within a world. It's where they spent most of their time, it's were they learned how to navigate the disastrous conditions of their community (conditions, we must remember, they themselves did not create), and more importantly, it's where they found their greatest level of communal autonomy.

History has shown us many examples of the resilience and creativity of mankind in the face of grave tragedy and disaster, but perhaps it's those cases in which malfeasance serves as the catalyst for disaster and abject poverty that reveals the most about a given dominant culture and the victims of its assault. From impoverished areas sprout practical, unique, and often ingenious subcultures that grow in the face of on-going malfeasance. These newly formulated subcultures emerge with a number of unifying characteristics; most telling of these are the practical ways in which the victims blend and use themes and elements of their indigenous culture, along with fragments of the dominant culture (society at large), to stake out a new life full of meaning and dignity. Such is the case with the people of the South Bronx Disaster.

The people of the South Bronx knew they were under siege. Yet remarkably, even though they were the victims of an urban renewal catastrophe and municipal malfeasance, they never looked at themselves as such. In the face of hopelessness, despair, and a dilapidated physical environment, most surviving victims of the South Bronx Disaster still tried to carve out a life as best as they could. And as the decade of the '70s stretched on, the forgotten and purposely neglected poor black and Latino youth developed a new mind state and a new attitude, one that allowed them to not only deal head-on with the low quality of life inside the South Bronx disaster zone, but one that allowed them the wherewithal to improve upon that quality of life.

Hip hop culture and, subsequently, rap music may not have been inevitable, but because the disastrous 1970s South Bronx backdrop helped create an unprecedented autonomous zone for the South Bronx youth, *some* sort of subculture was inevitable. Afterall, when the pressure drops and the squeeze is put on a group of people, it should be expected that a new culture will emerge. And the squeeze, in this case, came in the form of an epidemic burnout, which itself was spawned by ill-advised slum clearance programs and insensitive, ill-fated public policies. Thus, in the process of being pressured into reconstructing a new community, the youth of the South Bronx (and later other poor non-white areas throughout New York City) amalgamated one of the most formidable, durable, and resilient music-based cultures of the twentieth century.

The "Culture of Sampling"

> How do you master yourself after catastrophic circumstances — poverty, dilapidated housing, dysfunctional educational system? –Cornell West

Before I move forward with an examination of the direct origins of hip hop culture, it's necessary to first describe the culture of sampling that underscores communities that are forced to undergo catastrophic circumstances. One prominent result of an oppressed people and their isolated, fragmented community is that its residents learn to incorporate (salvage) any element within and outside of their environment that they see fit to forge and fortify their culture. The fragmentation caused by the South Bronx Disaster, in effect, led to a "culture of sampling," one in which residents of the South Bronx (and other similarly hard-hit cities across the U.S.) learned to take pieces from the mainstream American society then convert them in accordance to their own needs and values. In a culture of sampling, everything is fair game — language, fashion, automobiles, and the like. If it can be converted and flipped (according to the predilections and priorities of a particular community), it will be. The "culture of sampling" sensibility permeates throughout the entire hip hop culture. For example, there's the b-boy fashion, which featured sportswear and casual attire for comfort and flexibility; there's hip hop terminology, which often converts all sorts of words (even tragic ones) into terms of triumph — words like "dope" and "sick" become impressive expressions of magnificent creativity and authenticity. In fact, all of hip hop culture involves sampling and "flipping" something.

Where They Jamming At? Street and Party Cultures Collide

Partying is one of the most vital cultural events that take place within ghettos.[19] In ghettos, parties serve two very important functions. On one hand, parties allow for a temporary relief or escape from the harsh realities of an impoverished environment. On the other hand, parties form a celebration of the resilience of the human spirit in the face of hopelessness and despair. Thus, aside from the conditions of the South Bronx Disaster itself, the other two primary sources of consistent familiarity for its residents were parties and

---

[19] Hip hop culture did not grow out of the street gang era of 1970s New York City as some writers and historians have insisted. The street gangs, in particular, the organization of the street gangs, served as one conduit (there were others) for which hip hop was able to travel and mobilize into one formidable force. They represented a street level organization of would-be party goers. Street gangs may have committed crimes and acts of violence, but their favorite past time was partying.

music. Throughout the most dire times of the South Bronx Disaster (1969 to 1979), impromptu parties or "jams" and music provided much needed healing and entertainment.

What's particularly important and distinct about the 1970s South Bronx party scene is how it was further bolstered and unified through the arts and talents of its partygoers. To be sure, there were parties before that fateful day in 1973, where the first unofficial hip hop party (or coming together) took place. There were parties held at other community and recreational centers, ballrooms, churches, school gymnasiums, and street blocks. Even by Kool Herc's own admission, he played nothing new — i.e. any music that wasn't heard before at parties ot he time — at that initial hip hop gathering. Kool Herc tells us that he "gave the people what they liked," and all of the partygoers took to the floor, knowing exactly how to *move* to it. But it was this one party, and many others like it (particularly the ones given by Grandmaster Flash and Afrika Bambaataa) that soon followed, that served as the initial breeding ground or force that would merge the individual art forms together into one mighty subculture: hip hop.

The Unification of the Four (Original) Elements of Hip Hop Culture

The culture that would eventually be dubbed hip hop was actually brewing before the famed Sedgewick Rec Party in 1973. But historians prefer clear benchmarks. Moreover, historians favor the prospect of assigning definitive historical developments to key figureheads. And so it would seem, the fewer the number of key events and figureheads, the easier it is for historians to draw a clean narrative. This is why the story of hip hop, for better or worse, always conveniently begins with the Kool Herc/Sedgewick Rec Party storyline. The story of Kool Herc DJ'ing at the Sedgwick Rec Room on August 11, 1973 has been offered up by hip hop historians, prime hip hop architects, and common fans with such reverence that it has risen to the level of romantic legend. But even if one does just a surface read of the 1973 Sedgewick Rec party storyline, it's clear that the event didn't emerge as if Kool Herc had said, "Hey, I'm going to throw a 'hip hop' party."[20] Thus, one of the biggest misconceptions about hip hop culture is that it was the initial product of one lone force: hip hop music, and one lone person: Kool Herc.

---

[20] *Why* the famous Sedgwick party took place at all is based on two stories: (1) Cindy Campbell's birthday party; or (2) Cindy Campbell's idea for money under the guise of a back-to-school party. Accounts given in 1984 and then in 2005 by DJ Kool Herc and his sister, Cindy, differ. In 1984, Herc refers to it as a "birthday party." In a 2005 interview with Jeff Chang, Cindy describes it differently — as a back to school party to raise money for new school clothes. I suspect the truth is somewhere in the middle.

Though the music of hip hop did indeed drive the entire culture as it further developed, hip hop/rap music did not spawn each element of hip hop culture. There were many simmering creative impulses leading up to the first hip hop party. The hip hop movement formulated with a wide range of expressions that were moving parallel to one another in the South Bronx and other areas throughout New York City (most notably Brooklyn) at the same time. So it should be understood that hip hop culture is not the story of a single event or invention of a single person, but rather it's the story of the coalescence (unification) and formalization of seed elements that were already present within a community devastated by the South Bronx Disaster. B-boying (later to be known as "break dancing" or "breakin'"), DJ'ing, rapping (MC'ing or emceeing), and graffiti writing, all sprang up from the same cultural and social conditions described in Chapter 1 of this study. What follows in this section is a brief historical breakdown of each of the four original elements of hip hop culture, along with an examination of the aesthetics, tenets, priorities, values, and principles that underscore all of the elements of hip hop collectively.

Though each of the original elements — art forms — of hip hop culture represented its own distinct tradition and subculture within the broader hip hop tradition and culture, it must be noted that the development of each of these elements overlapped and cross-fertilized throughout the 1970s and early 1980s. All of the early hip hop pioneers participated in at least two (if not all) of the four elements of hip hop. (For example, Kool Herc was first a graffiti writer before he became a DJ.) Thus, it's necessary to spend some time exploring the origins and development of each element and their role in the development of hip hop overall. Also, the notion of cross fertilization is particularly important in this scope. Since all of the earliest pioneers participated in more than one of hip hop's art forms, all of the pioneers had a keen awareness of each of the art forms that came together to comprise the collective hip hop culture.

Graffiti

In New York City between the 1950s and late 1960s, graffiti was mostly used by street gangs to mark turf and some political activists to make statements. But the underground art form that would take hold in NYC actually had its roots in Philadelphia, PA in the late 1960s. The two writers from Philly who are credited with the first "conscious bombing efforts" are CORNBREAD and COOL EARL. It's unclear exactly how the Philly concept of graffiti made its way to New York City, but by 1971, it was apparent that the form was rising.[21]   That year, the *New York Times* published an article on TAKI 183, a teenage graffiti writer from Washington Heights. The article was very influential in that it not only made TAKI 183 (real name Demitrius) the first graffiti writer in New York City recognized outside of the newly formed subculture, it also helped push forward an already growing underground NYC graffiti movement. As the article noted, TAKI 183 worked as a foot messenger who, being on the subway frequently, wrote motion "tags" in subway stations and on subway cars as well as buildings all across NYC.[22]   But TAKI 183 certainly was not the first graff writer in NYC, nor was he even considered to be one of the graffiti "kings." During this time, JULIO 204 was most widely credited as being one of the first writers of significance. After noticing JULIO 204's, TAKI 183 took up writing his name and street number (with a wide marker) wherever he went. Other significant writers who appeared in 1971 were LEE 163, SLY II, and PHASE 2, LEE 163's cousin.[23]

Between 1971 and 1974, the first pioneering period of graffiti, hundreds of new graffiti writers emerged, and the art form continued to grow in both volume and, more importantly, in style throughout the five boroughs of NYC. Tags were the norm for most writers, and competition was a major driving force. Writers competed with each other all over the city, seeing who could get the most tags up as possible. At first, buses, handball courts, schoolyards, and other locations were hit, but soon, as graffiti grew more competitive and writers grew more daring, subway cars became a favorite target. Not long afterward, the concept and method of "bombing" (painting subway cars as they sat parked in train yards) was born.

During this period, writers experimented with script and calligraphic styles. Flourishes, stars, crowns, and other similar designs also marked the earlier part of this pioneering period. It was also during this period when writers began to experiment with the size (scale) of tags. Using the creative commons of their craft, writers began to create tags that were larger, with letters that were thicker and outlines with additional colors. After writers began to use caps from other aerosol products, they learned that the width of the spray could be increased. This discovery, credited first to SUPER KOOL 223, who used the cap from an oven cleaner can, led directly to giant signatures known as "masterpieces" (or

---

[21] For an extended history of graffiti see: @149st (http://www.at149st.com/history.html). Also, see: *Subway Graffiti: An Aesthetic Study of Graffiti on the Subway System of New York City, 1970-1978*, by Jack Stewart; and the classic for the newer school, *Subway Art* by Henry Chalfant and Martha Cooper; and "History of Graf," daveyd.com.
[22] *New York Times*, "'Taki 183' Spawns Pen Pals," July 21, 1971.
[23] History of Graffiti, Part I," @149th Street (http://www.at149st.com/history.html). It must also be noted that there was a burgeoning graffiti movement growing on the streets of Brooklyn at this very same time, with FRIENDLY FREDDIE being one of the most recognizable Brooklyn writers at the time. Also see: Stephen Hager, *Hip Hop: The Illustrated History of Break Dancing, Rap Music, and Graffiti* (New York: St. Martin's Press, 1984), 13.

"pieces," for short). These were large-scale visual themes or statements, with bigger letters and bolder styles and ideas. Credit for the development of the first masterpieces is commonly given to SUPER KOOL 223 (of the Bronx) and WAP (of Brooklyn). Soon pieces began to appear on the entire height of subway cars. These pieces were known as "top-to-bottoms;" RIFF 170 is credited for having revolutionized top-to-bottoms. During this period, style became the most important aspect of graffiti, as it was more prestigious for writers to create original lettering styles. Lesser writers who merely imitated others became known as "toys," and writers whose tags were *just* local and not "all city" (scene in all five boroughs) were described as DGAs: "Doesn't Get Around."[24]

With competition steadily driving the movement, forcing less talented writers out of the limelight, styles began to move away from the typical tag pieces. The Broadway style, introduced by TOPCAT 126 (who had moved from Philly to New York City), emerged. The Broadway style led to block letters and leaning letters. Then came the Bubble letters, a style first developed and credited to PHASE 2. It was the combination of PHASE 2's work and competition from other style masters that began what became known as the style wars. "Style wars" was the term used to describe the period in which there was an explosion of writers who took ideas from each other, improved upon them, and brought them to another level. During this period, pieces became more complex in style, especially in size, depth, and meaning. Finally, by 1974, works with scenery, illustrations, and cartoon characters (popularized by TRACY 168, CLIFF 159, BLADE ONE) started to appear.

It was also during this period when writers began gathering in loose-knit groups that mirrored small artistic professional associations. "Meetings were held at various 'writers' corners' around the city, the two most prominent of which were located at a subway station at 149th Street and the Grand Concourse in the Bronx, and on the corner of 188th and Audubon Avenue in Manhattan." Wherever writers gathered, they shared sketch ideas from their personal art books, compared notes on various lettering styles, and generally talked shop about their craft. Through their various writers meetings and gatherings and artistic protocols, graffiti writers, like b-boys, soon developed their own slang and fashion styles.

It's widely considered by all graffiti historians that by 1974, all of the graffiti standards (foundation) had been established. That being said, the period between 1975-77 marks the time when the heaviest bombing in NYC took place (no doubt due in some part to NYC's mid-1970s fiscal crises). During this time,

---

[24] *Ibid*, 19-24.

"whole car" pieces became standard fair, and the "throw up" became the definitive form of bombing. The throw up, a style based on Bubble lettering, is a piece (hastily rendered, usually just two letters) that consists of just a simple outline and a fill-in. Just like competition had driven writers in 1971 to put up as many tags as they could, competition for the most throw ups exploded throughout the city between 1975 and 77. Incidentally, during this time the number of graffiti crews increased dramatically.[25]

Between 1978 and 1981, there was a graffiti revival of sorts, brought on by the new style wars between major writing crews like UA, CIA (founded by style master DONDI), TDS, TCF, RTW, TMT, and more. But this period also marked the final wave of bombing before the New York City Transit Authority ratcheted up their efforts to end graffiti on trains. Though graffiti writing would continue on through the mid-1980s, by 1985 the NYC street graffiti culture would deteriorate dramatically.[26] However, due in large part to the efforts of graffiti writer (and sharp self-promoter) Fab 5 Freedy, graffiti would find a new audience in the downtown NYC art scene.[27] It should also be noted that the NYC subway system played a tremendous role in the development of NYC's graffiti culture. Both in terms of being a de facto art canvas and, more importantly, as a line of communication and a unifying element for all of the different graffiti writers and separate graffiti developments (movements) throughout the five boroughs. Finally, it's worth mentioning that graffiti culture is parallel to beatmaking culture, in that it became quite racially and ethnically inclusive. Although during the first pioneering graffiti period (1971-1974) many writers were Puerto Rican, it's a little-known fact that most of the first writers in the South Bronx were black.

B-Boying ("Break Dancing") and DJ'ing

Dance has always played an integral part in the development of the African American (Black) music tradition. But the explosive new dance style that was taking hold in New York City in the early 1970s was quite different. "Going

---

[25] *Ibid.*
[26] The Transit Authority tried two main solutions. First, they tried the "buff," a giant subway car wash. This didn't work, as the buff rendered subway cars a "dirty" and "desolate" color. After the buff, came the yard fence with barbwire, coupled with guard dogs. This second solution, along with more serious penalties for graffiti writers, became the chief deterrent for bombing. There are many reasons for the decline of graffiti culture in the mid-1980s, notably the stepped-up anti-graffiti efforts of the Transit Authority, stiffer penalties for graffiti, drug usage, and the allure of hip hop/rap music as a "safer" and more profitable career path.
[27] Fab 5 Freddy's efforts in the downtown New York City art scene of the mid-1980s not only helped popularize graffiti, it also helped break rap music and hip hop to a wider (white) audience.

off," "burning," or the "good foot" (named after the James Brown song of the same name) were the names used to describe what would become "b-boying," and later on, widely known as "break dancing." "Going off" was a dance style that featured an erratic assortment of floor drops and spins and other James Brown-inspired leg movements. Dancers who "got wild" would wait for the "break" (the part in the record where the song is stripped down to just the high energy of the rhythm section — the drums, guitar or bass licks, maybe some additional syncopated percussive elements, no melody), then they would get out on the dance floor and go wild.

At the same time dancers were getting wild, Kool Herc was building a name as a DJ. After seeing these dancers go wild whenever he played the breaks, Herc began calling them "break boys," which he shortened to "b-boys." And in the dialogue between Kool Herc and the b-boys (and b-girls), it was the b-boys who perhaps had the most influence. B-boys pushed Herc just as much as he pushed them. But in addition to helping the b-boys further develop their art form, Herc also found that by using two turn tables, a DJ mixer, and two copies of the same record, he could not only keep the b-boys engaged, he could also keep the party going for everybody, *without* interruption.

Herc wasn't the first American DJ to use two turntables; club DJs, especially New York disco (early disco) DJs, were already using two turntables before Herc. But the club/disco DJs played one record at a time; that is, they let one record play all the way through before playing the next one. It was Herc who first came up with the style of only playing the breaks (continuously) with two turntables. And Herc was directly influenced by a DJ named John Brown. While still in high school, Herc (not yet Kool Herc) used to hang out at a small nightclub called the Plaza Tunnel. By his own admission, he spent time at the Plaza Tunnel soaking up the records (mostly early funk) that John Brown played and his style of DJ'ing as well. It was this experience and interaction at the Plaza Tunnel that led directly to the style of DJ'ing that Herc showcased at the infamous Sedgwick party in 1973 and other subsequent parties.

As Herc, and other DJ's like Grandmaster Flash and Afrika Bambaataa, continued to pioneer the hip hop DJ style (Herc's style), specifically the elongation of the break of early funk records (the "merry-go-round" technique), the b-boy culture continued to solidify and become more definitive. B-boys would create "ciphers," dance rings (circles) in which b-boys would enter one at a time and compete against each other. Now that the music had been extended, the energy level had gone up, and more intense competition sparked new moves. Early b-boys like the Nigger Twins (Kevin and Keith, who were only 12 years old when they attended their first Herc party), the Zulu Kings, and "Clark Kent" continuously borrowed moves from each other and used the *extended* break to experiment and come up with new moves. During this time, spins became more prominent and footwork grew more complex. Floor drops, where b-boys dropped to the ground and popped back up again *on beat*, became basic stuff for all b-boys worth their weight. Arm- and hand-use for body support developed quickly; freezes and leg shuffles became big; knee spins and butt spins emerged. And around this same time, out in Brooklyn another early funk-based dance style known as the "Brooklyn Uprock" or "Brooklyn Rock" (soon it would come to be known as "uprocking" in the South Bronx) was serving as the foundation for another pivotal dance movement. Each of these moves, and others based upon them, eventually all became part of the definitive architecture of the b-boy dance style.

And just as graffiti was developing into its own subculture with its own slang, fashion, and crews, b-boying was quickly morphing into its own subculture, complete with its own slang, fashion (at first jeans and sneakers, then sportswear, usually warm-up suits and sneakers), and crews. Moreover, b-boying was just like graffiti, in that it "was all about battling…Breakin' on somebody was the attitude you had to have if you called yourself a b-boy. You had to be ready to battle at the drop of a hat, whether you were on the street, in a park, or at a jam, and you had to be on your shit if you dared compete."[28]

By 1977, many DJs had followed Kool Herc's lead, but none were more notable than the first two who appeared directly after him: Grandmaster Flash and Afrika Bambaataa, respectively. Although Herc was the first DJ to use turntables as instruments, it was Grandmaster Flash who took the art of hip hop DJing to the next level. While Herc had developed the style of elongating the break, he used the "needle-drop" technique. That is to say, he dropped the needle of the turntable on the groove of the record where he *thought* the part he wanted began. Flash moved past the needle-drop, and developed techniques and methods for *blending* records, mixing them, and cutting the beats together all *on beat*. Rather than simply keep records playing continuously, Flash wanted to create a continuous groove, one that was made up of all the "reorganized pieces of songs" he'd found. He wanted to "keep the beat." That is, he wanted to figure out a way to start and stop records on the left and right turntables, without listeners knowing where one record stopped and the next one started.[29]

Grandmaster Flash became the first DJ to actually *physically* put his hands on the vinyl while the turntable's platter was spinning, giving him a level of control previously unrealized by other DJs. Using his hands to wind the records back and forward, a technique he dubbed the "spin back," and

---

[28] Grandmaster Flash and David Ritz, *The Adventures of Grandmaster Flash: My Life, My Beats* (New York: Broadway Books, 2008), 39.
[29] *Ibid*, 54-84.

keying in on the *marks* (pencil lines at first) that he placed on the labels of his records, Grandmaster Flash developed what he called the "clock theory." Soon, he took the clock theory further and developed the "quik mix theory," which was a collective of his own techniques for quickly cutting back and forth between records *on beat*, making one musical passage flow seamlessly to the next. Flash's "quik mix theory" included a number of firsts, but it most notably included the "spin back," a method for quickly rewinding records, and the "punch phase," which was a method for *punching* a record forward, right on the break.

While Kool Herc was winding down his career, and while Grandmaster Flash was pioneering the use of turntables as instruments, Afrika Bambaataa was making a name for himself as a cultural unifier and DJ whose stash of records knew no bounds. The term "hip hop" is curiously credited to being first used by Lovebug Starski, but by most accounts, it was Afrika Bambaataa (ca. 1975-76) who first (consciously) used "hip hop" specifically to describe the type of jams (parties) he was throwing. And thus, it was perhaps because of Lovebug Starski and Afrika Bambaataa that "hip hop" came to (informally at first) describe the collective culture (movement) that encompassed the four separate NYC underground street elements — art forms: DJ'ing, graffiti writing, b-boying, and rapping. While a Grandmaster Flash music set was characterized by turntable wizardry and precision, an Afrika Bamabaataa set was personified by an eclectic musical mix. Bambaataa experimented with other forms of music, particularly late 1960s and early 1970s rock. Finally, even though Kool Herc, Grandmaster Flash, Afrika Bambaataa, and other pivotal DJs of the time ultimately developed distinct hip hop DJ performance styles (all based upon Herc's original innovation), it must be remembered that the parties that each threw between 1973 and 1978 were really more like events, wherein all four of the elements hip hop culture were well-represented.

The Late "Early" Years of B-Boying and the Birth of Break Dancing

After developing the b-boy style for more than five years, many blacks stopped by 1978. But it was at this time that Puerto Ricans had just started getting into b-boying. By 1979, b-boying, which had once been a movement almost exclusively practiced by blacks, had become a new movement that was now lead by Puerto Ricans. New crews like Rockwell Association, TDK, TBB, and the Rock Steady Crew (founded by Jimmy D and JoJo) emerged, taking over where the earliest b-boys (like the Zulu Kings, Profile, and The Nigger Twins) had left off. During this period, b-boying moved forward, then suddenly in

1980, it begin to enter a new decline. That's when 14-year old Richie Colon stepped up and changed everything.[30]

Having grown up in the Bronx most of his life, Richie Colon moved with his family to Manhattan in 1980. Before he moved to Manhattan, he had spent two years practicing the b-boy style in hopes of one day joining Rockwell Association. He had changed his name to Crazy Legs, and he was now ready to join the ranks of master b-boys. But Rockwell Association and Rock Steady Crew were no longer dancing as much as they had been in the previous two years. So Crazy Legs was forced to find his own crew. After getting permission from Jimmy D (co-founder of Rock Steady Crew), Crazy Legs started a Manhattan branch of Rock Steady Crew. It was Crazy Legs and this branch of Rock Steady Crew that would bring the most fame to the RSC name.

The early and mid-1980s brought the advent of "power moves," dance moves that emphasized more spinning action and gymnastics. From this period, dances like the infamous "windmill" (credited to Crazy Legs), and "1990s (one-hand-stand spins) emerged. The early and mid-1980s also brought a level of media coverage of b-boying that had previously been unimaginable. This is when the Rock Steady Crew, along with another pivotal New York City b-boy crew, New York City Breakers, and movies like *Style Wars* (1982), *Wild Style* (1982), *Beat Street* (1984), *Breakin'* (1984), and *Breakin' 2: Electric Boogaloo* (1984), combined to spark a break dance explosion all across America.

While b-boying was developing in the South Bronx and Brooklyn uprocking was happening in Brooklyn (the latter dance form unifying into the b-boy movement), there was a parallel dance movement — "locking" and "popping" — happening on the West Coast. Like b-boying in the South Bronx, locking and popping were inspired by funk music as well. However, early West Coast funk, which too focused on the groove, was slightly different than East Coast funk. Out of this separate early 1970s "funk movement" in Los Angeles, California emerged Don Campbell, aka "Don Cambellock," originator of "locking" (ca. 1970-73). Locking, a dance somewhat based on the "funky chicken," another popular dance at the time, featured a locking motion of the joints of one's arms and the bending of one's elbows. Soon after introducing locking, Cambellock formed a group called The Lockers. The Lockers were very influential in that they pioneered a number of new moves and other dances that made up the locking repertoire, including "knee drops," "butt drops," the "stop n' go," "the

---

[30] Hager, 86-89. Also, information extracted from interviews with various 1979s Bronx and Brooklyn residents, specifically my close family friendCanell Johnson.

fancies," "the lock," and "scooby doos." And as with some of the later b-boys of New York City, some of the west coast lockers incorporated dives, drop downs, and other gymnastic moves.[31]

"Popping" was introduced in 1976. Originated by Sam "Boogaloo Sam" Soloman, one of the three founders of The Electronic Boogaloo Lockers, "popping" was a dance that featured the tick-like contraction movement of hands, arms, neck, chest, and legs, which gave off a mechanical or smooth robotic effect. There are conflicting stories as to how "locking" and "popping" made their way to the Bronx and the rest of New York City, but it's widely regarded that the dance was picked up (and initially misnamed "electric boogie") by dancers in NYC, after groups like The Lockers and The Electronic Boogaloo Lockers appeared on 1970s television shows like "Soul Train," "Saturday Night Live," "The Dick Van Dyke Variety Show," and the popular sitcom "What's Happening."

By the mid-1980s, mainstream media had grouped together most of these dance forms — both from the East Coast and West Coast — and called it all "break dancing." Soon, break dancing became over-commercialized, and all of the separate art forms that comprised hip hop dance lost emphasis on their root structures and nuances. More specifically, the essence and spirit of b-boying culture faded and seemingly disappeared, until a resurgence in the late 1990s and early 2000s.

Rapping (MC'ing or Emceeing)

To truly understand the force that is rapping, one must accept the conceptual heritage and material artifacts and their authentic significations — in history, origin and social intercourse, and orature.[32] The roots of the art of rapping go back much farther than most people recognize. In fact, rapping, a clear example of the broad black vernacular tradition, is a continuance of the African American

---

[31] Information extracted from interviews with various b-boys and dancers, including King Uprock, Mariella Gross, and Canell Johnson. Also see: Jorge "Popmaster Fabel" Pabon, "Physical Graffiti: The History of Hip Hop Dance," DaveyD.com. Furthermore, see: episodes of television dance show "Soul Train" (ca. 1976), as well as other television shows of the same period, including: "Dick Van Dyke Variety Show;" and "The Carol Burnett Show."

[32] For context and reference, see Wole Soyinka, "The Critic and Society: Barthes, Leftocracy and Other Mythologies," *Black Literature & Literary Theory* (New York and London: Methuen, 1984), 44. In his essay, Soyinka illuminates the problem that arises in academia when *critics* of African literary theory attempt to *teach it*. Specifically, Soyinka points out that because these critics of the African literary tradition "refuse to accept the conceptual heritage or even material artifacts and their authentic significations...as valid dialectical quantities" for any literary theory, the "roots" of African literary are mis-taught, and students are ultimately "imprisoned" by the subsequent mis-teachings. I find the same parallel in the ways in which the various elements of hip hop — specifically rapping and beatmaking — are taught. Because many contemporary teachers willfully refuse to accept the roots of rapping and beatmaking, new rappers and beatmakers are often imprisoned by mis-teachings, and are, therefore, prone to misrepresenting these two art forms.

"toasting" tradition, an oral tradition of lively verbal art that stretches back from the Reconstruction Era to the jazz age to the social movements of the late 1960s and on through to the present. A uniquely urban phenomenon, the African American toasting tradition — *not* to be confused with the Jamaican toasting tradition of the late 1960s and early 1970s[33] — is a dynamic poetic performance art, traditionally learned directly from or by studying other "toasters" and through intense verbal training. African American forms of "toasts," which often feature boasts, "trickster" tales, adventures, and social commentary, are typically laced with slang and profanity, and center around some form of heroics or uplift made by a central black character, who *beats the odds* (a tragic event, a villain, etc.) by using his wits and common skills. Often in toasts, the central character "top talks" (out talks) a clear opponent, often a dangerous or tyrannical authority figure. Also, within this toasting tradition, versioning, improvisation, and using one's individual style is highly valued. It's also worth mentioning that while some women have participated in the African American toasting tradition, toasts were mostly performed by black males. Finally, I should point out that before rapping emerged, the three most common forms of African American toasts were: (1) "signifyin' toasts;" (2) "radio DJ toasts;" and (3) "hustler toasts."

"Signifyin' toasts," which appeared in both print and music stem from the African American vernacular practice of "signifyin'(g). Signifyin' describes a verbal process of using the direct (denotative and figurative) meanings of words to say something *else* indirectly, and it is typically used to parody or satirize a character, theme, subject, or event. Signifyin' emphasizes the connotative (secondary), context-bound significance of words or expressions in addition to their explicit or primary meanings, which is accessible only to those who share or well-understand the unique cultural values of a given speech community. Signifyin' involves the conscious use of "specific language" and slang and concepts specifically understood by a given speech community. In signifyin' toasts, performers tell "trickster tales" in which central characters use the aforementioned verbal strategy to cleverly tap the *direct* meanings of words, while summoning *indirect* meanings, often for the purpose of obtaining "hidden," but intended outcomes.[34]

---

[33] The Jamaican toasting tradition of the 1970s has been widely considered to have played a major role in the art of rapping in hip hop. This is inaccurate.

[34] Two of the most popular African American signifyin' toasts are "Shine and the Titanic," and "The Signifying Monkey." In "Shine and the Titanic," a black stoker named Shine uses his wit and common abilities to both escape the sinking of the Titanic and the threat of a hungry whale. In "The Signifying Monkey," the Signifying Monkey in the jungle cleverly dupes a Lion. See: Henry Louis Gates, Jr., *Black Literature and Literary Theory* (New York and London: Methuen, 1984), 288.

"Radio DJ toasts," which were pioneered in the 1950s by Philadelphia, PA radio disc jockey Douglas "Jocko" Henderson ("JOCKO" & The Rocket Ship Show),[35] were quite different than signifyin' toasts. Unlike signifyin' toasts, radio DJ toasts were typically not too narrative in nature, and they were most often not characterized by a central character, but rather a "hip," improvised telling of the moment. That is to say, radio DJ toasts were rapid, quick-witted radio "raps" (rhymes) or "skats," usually simple one- and two-liners filled with "hip" urban slang. Radio DJ toasts were impromptu and performed *throughout* radio shows, but particularly before and after records were played. DJs like Jocko would use toasts to help keep their shows moving or to boast about themselves, their radio shows, and/or the hit records they played. Often, Jocko would say things like, "Eee-tiddlee-dock, this is the Jock! Back on the scene with the record machine," or "Oo-papa-doo, how do you do?" "He ain't mean, he just wanna be seen;" "Mommy-Os and Daddy-Os;" "The Ace from outta space;" and similar toasts all exemplify the kinds of toasts black radio DJs performed and their limitless ability to improvise hip rhyming slang. Black radio DJs used these toasts to build up their radio shows and to communicate in a more personal way with their listeners.

By the early 1970s, there were a number of black radio DJs who performed radio toasts, but the clear leader in 1970s New York City radio was Frankie Crocker "the chief rocker." Frankie Crocker, who was also the MC (Master of Ceremonies) at the Apollo during the mid- and late 1970s, said toasts like, "More dips in your hips, more glide in your stride;" and "If Frankie Crocker isn't on your radio, your radio isn't really on." Frankie Crocker, and later some NYC disco radio DJs, would have some role in the development of rapping in hip hop.

"Hustler toasts," which reached prominence in black street corner culture and black prison culture between the mid-1960s and early 1970s, shares more similarities with signifyin' toasts than radio DJ toasts. Hustler toasts are mostly narrative and carry a message; but that's where the similarities stop. While signifyin' toasts often emphasize the connotative and are indirect, hustler toasts usually emphasize the straight-forward (often confrontational) and are mostly direct. While signifyin' toasts are often *versions* of well-known toasts, hustler toasts are often the true accounts — experienced or witnessed — of the individuals who perform them. Finally, while signifyin' toasts are generally humorous and contain profanity in a passive context, humor (when it's used) in hustler toasts is often sinister, and profanity is used much more aggressively or matter-factly.

---

[35] Other important pioneering black radio DJs of the time who performed radio DJ toasts include: Maurice "Hot Rod" Hulbert, Jr. and Rufus Thomas. It should further be noted that the radio DJ toast tradition was pioneered first on rhythm and blues radio stations.

Although all three common forms of African American toasts played a role in the development of rapping in hip hop, no form had more direct influence than the hustler toast. And the most important hustler toasts to hit the streets of the South Bronx was James Brown's version of "King Heroin" and the infamous Lightnin' Rod album *Hustler's Convention*.

Released in 1973 and performed by Jalal Nuriddin, under the pseudonym, "Lightnin' Rod," *Hustler's Convention* became the single biggest inspiration for the early formulation of rapping in hip hop. Set to the music of Kool and The Gang, Bernard Purdie, Billy Preston, and Colonel Dupree, *Hustler's Convention* masterfully demonstrates the African American toasting and rapping traditions. The album contains a series of "rap songs" (prison-style toasts) that tell the story of two hustlers, Sport and Spoon, as they hustle their way through the ghetto one summer. Each rap spares know punches, as stories of drug use, dice and pool games, sexual episodes with random women, drug sales, and shoot-outs color the balance of the album. Told through the first-hand account of Sport, the story begins with Spoon coming home from jail, and ends with Sport going back to jail, where after "twelve years of time," he realizes that he was just a "nickel and dime hustler," and that the "real hustlers are those rippin' off billions from those millions who are programmed to think they can win."[36]   There can be no doubt that James Brown and, more importantly, the album *Hustler's Convention* were the two biggest and most direct influences on the development of early rapping in hip hop. All of the earliest hip hop/rap pioneers who have spoken on record maintain this. In fact, the first hip hop/rap music architect and pioneer, Kool DJ Herc, directly said as much more than 25 years ago: "The inspiration for rap is James Brown and the album Hustler's Convention."[37]

Rapping in Hip Hop

Early on in the development of hip hop, rapping was very simple and rappers (MCs/emcees) were primarily a sideshow to the DJ. The first hip hop toasts (raps) ever performed were by Kool Herc, who, inspired by James Brown and the album *Hustler's Convention*, would say impromptu toasts while DJ'ing.

---

[36] *Hustler's Convention*, (United Artists, 1973). At the time of the release of *Hustler's Convention*, Jalal Nuriddin was the leader of The Last Poets, a group of Harlem poets and musicians who earned acclaim through their searing social commentary and oft-described black nationalist sympathies. It's perhaps worth noting that prior to becoming the leader of The Last Poets, Nuriddin was, in fact, incarcerated.
[37] Hager, 45-49. Famed early rapping pioneer Grandmaster Caz of the Cold Crush Brothers makes a similar unwavering claim: "I knew the entire *Hustler's Convention* by heart. That was rap..." See also, Toop, 53-58: "James Brown was the most direct connection between soulful testifying and Bronx poetry... His position as spokesman for black consciousness and minister of super-heavy funk might have been on the wane by the '70s, but for the b boys he was still Soul Brother Number One."

The toasts that Herc performed were not long or particularly narrative, they were nothing more than simple expressions designed to keep the energy of the party going. He would say things like, "Yes, yes, y'all, it's the serious, serio-so joint*ski*," or "YES-YES, Y'ALL! TO-THE BEAT, Y'ALL." He would also say expressions that singled out the names of some of the party-goers, combining these shout-out-like expressions with rhymes and some of the well-known slang of the day: "As I scan the place, I see the very familiar face…of my mellow;" or "Wallace Dee in the house. Wallace Dee, freak for me." Soon, Herc added Jay Cee and Clark Kent (The Herculords) to the show, and the Herculords would rap the same type of toasts first performed by Herc. [38]

Interestingly enough, it was another DJ who pushed rapping in the direction that eventually lead to modern rapping. In an effort to keep pace with Kool Herc, Grandmaster Flash wrote a rhyme (sometime between 1974 and 75) that would prove even more influential than Herc's initial toasts. The rhyme went like this: "You dip, dive and socialize. We're trying to make you realize. That we are qualified to rectify that burning…desire…to boogie." Hardly the sort of lyrical dexterity that we associate with modern rap, but what Flash's rhyme did was open up the possibilities for *how* rhymes could be written and performed.

Grandmaster Flash was not consciously trying to advance the art of rapping, he was simply acting out of necessity. According to Flash, "vocal entertainment became necessary to keep the crowd under control."[39] Flash soon put together a group of rappers to be part of his DJ show. The group, The Furious Five, composed of rappers Cowboy (Keith Wiggins), Kid Creole (Nathaniel Glover), Eddie "Mr. Ness/Scorpio" Morris, Guy "Rahiem" Williams, and last but not least, Creole's younger brother, Melle Mel (Melvin Glover), would quickly become one of the most pivotal rap groups of all time, almost immediately sparking similar groups like the Cold Crush Brothers and The Treacherous Three.[40]

Between 1975 and 1979, rap styles were an assortment of party rhymes, nursery rhymes, boasts, and comic book inspired joke rhymes. Rap routines, like the ones first performed by The Furious Five, became more elaborate and more entertaining in the late 1970s. The quintessential "rap routine" was perhaps most personified (and perfected) by The Cold Crush Brothers and The Fantastic

---

[38] Hager, 47. Also, Flash and Ritz, 102.
[39] *Ibid*, 47.
[40] There were a countless number of rappers who helped advance the art of rapping, but some of the most notable rappers of the period include: The Furious Five (Melle Mel, Cowboy, Raheim, Mr. Ness, and Kid Creole), The Cold Crush Brothers (Grandmaster Caz, Whipper Whip, Dot-A-Rock, Easy A.D., DJ Charlie Chase, Kay Gee, DJ Tony Tone, J.D.L., and Mr. Tee), Double Trouble (Lil Rodney Cee and KK Rockwell), The Treacherous Three (Kool Moe Dee, Special K, and LA Sunshine), Funky Four Plus One More (Lil Rodney Cee, KK Rockwell, Sha Rock, Keith Keith, and Jazzy Jeff with DJ Breakout), and Spoonie Gee.

Five. Just as with graffiti, b-boying, and DJ'ing, rapping became increasingly more competitive. Rap "battles" became a defining event of the time. It was also during this time that personal styles, like those from Grandmaster Caz, Kool Moe Dee (The Treacherous Three), and Spoonie Gee, were rapidly developing.

By 1980, the art of rapping had begun to shift towards the style and structure we recognize today. Most paramount to this broad directional shift in rapping was Kurtis Blow and Melle Mel. Kurtis Blow's big hit — in terms of sales, critical acclaim, and influence — was "The Breaks." Neither a party rhyme, a boast, or a joke rhyme, "The Breaks" was the first attempt at serious subject matter, albeit to a party-style backing track. Using an updated, hard-hittiing version of the studio-band sound of the time (inspired by the approach used for the Sugar Hill Gang's "Rapper's Delight), Kurtis Blow articulated a much more direct and consistent flow, one that was more rhythmically balanced than any other rap previously recorded.

In 1982, barely two years after "The Breaks," and just months after the release of "Planet Rock" (the breakaway hit by Afrika Bambaataa), Melle Mel — a former b-boy — pushed the art of rapping into another stratosphere when he and The Furious Five released "The Message."[41] Building off of Kurtis Blow's pioneering efforts of serious subject matter, Melle Mel and producer Duke Bootee (leader of Sugar Hill Record's in-house studio band), created what was, in effect, the very first "reality rap" song. "The Message," which featured a grim, down-tempo rhythm track created by Duke Bootee, was a stark departure from the club rhymes and *light* (party) subject matter of the period. Reminiscent, both in tone and performance, to Lightnin' Rods' *Hustler's Convention*, "The Message" tells the stories of many typical figures living in the ghetto, and it ends with a youth going to jail, where, after being raped, he commits suicide. Equally impressive to the straight-forward subject matter of the song, was the structure of the rhyme itself. The meter that Melle Mel used was much more rhythmic in nature, and the bars that made up each stanza were quite conversational, moreso than any rap that had previously been recorded. "The Message" marks the beginning of the rhyme style in which a rapper seemingly talks directly to individual listeners, rather than addresses an audience.

In 1983, just one year after Melle Mel laid down the foundation of modern rapping, Run-DMC released their first single, "It's Like That." Similar to "The Breaks," and "The Message," "It's Like That" was a rap retelling of "the way it is"

---

[41] Although "The Message" is attributed to Grandmaster Flash and The Furious Five, the truth of the matter is that Grandmaster Flash fought against the record and had no real involvement with it. Furthermore, Melle Mel wrote every verse of the song, except for one, which was co-written by Duke Bootee (Ed Fletcher).

in the hood. However, what set "It's Like That" apart from those other earlier efforts is the fact that the rhymes were set to a sparse, drum programmed beat, something that seemingly inspired rappers Run and DMC to merge the rhyme styles of Kurtis Blow and Melle Mel, respectively.

In 1984, T La Rock broke on the rap scene and introduced the "complex lyrical rhyme style" with the single, "It's Yours," produced by a then unknown producer named Rick Rubin. Unlike the message-driven and crowd-moving rhymes of Kurtis Blow, Melle Mel, and Run-DMC, T La Rock's "It's Yours" was a celebration of lyricism. Backed by a sparse drum track (a sound that would come to personify the period), T La Rock put forth a lyrical arsenal that clearly separated his style from the less complex rhyme structures that preceded him. Rather than use the typical "A B A B" structure, T La Rock instituted a rhyme style that completely abandoned conventional rhyme structure, offering up stanzas in "A A A B" and "A A A B B" form. Eschewing simple rhyme patterns and easy metaphors, T La Rock introduced an entirely new rhyme structure, one that was much more dense and layered than anything before. Until T La Rock, words were mostly used to set up the rhyme that came at the end of each line. T La Rock pioneered the rhyme style in which any word in the meter could be rhymed. (In addition, the use of more multisyllabic words emerge at this point.)

Finally, between 1985 and 1988, there were six new rappers who emerged and solidified (cemented) the modern style of rapping: LL Cool J, KRS-One, Rakim, Slick Rick, Kool G Rap, and Big Daddy Kane. (*Rapper Silver Fox, who unfortunately recorded very little, must be credited for his influence over the lyrical style and technique of LL Cool J and Kool G Rap*).[42] With his debut album, *Radio* (1985), LL Cool J summoned the collective lyrical energies that proceeded him and furthered the tradition of *aggressive rapping*, an approach that was perhaps first pioneered by Grandmaster Caz. Incorporating the blastmaster skills of the Cold Crush Brothers, Kurtis Blow, Melle Mel, and Run-DMC, and utilizing the dexterity of T La Rock's rhyme structure, LL Cool J (only 15 or 16 years old at the time), put together a lyrical force that married the complex rhyme style with the blastmaster approach.

With his first two singles in 1986, "Eric B. Is President" and "My Melody," Rakim (of Eric B. and Rakim fame) immediately secured his position among the most influential rappers (lyricists) of all time. Using a rhyme style perhaps inspired by T La Rock, Rakim pushed the boundaries and dimensions of the poetics of rap in a way in which new structures could be explored. Coupling

---

[42] After 1987, most "new" rhyme styles were really stylistic innovations that were based upon the canon of lyrical work produced prior to 1988.

both complex and easy riddles with a dead serious rhyme flow and an uncanny knack for using breath control and delivery to accentuate each word in a rhyme, Rakim established a dense, multilayered rhyme scheme approach that helped revolutionize the complex lyrical rhyme style.

Not to be outdone, in that very same year, Kool G Rap met Marley Marl (DJ, first modern beatmaker/producer) and made the single "It's a Demo." Although he was also most likely inspired by T La Rock, Kool G Rap shattered the previous complex lyrical rhyme style. With "It's A Demo," Kool G Rap further pushed the complex lyrical rhyme style. He aggressively attacked the basic poetic structure and exhausted simple meter; he doubled-, tripled-, and even quadrupled-up hyperactive rhyme couplets, judiciously stretching and chopping words and using slant rhymes more as a means for tempo control and stylistic intonation than for their explicit value. And like Rakim (perhaps even more so), Kool G Rap demonstrated an extensive understanding of breath control and its effect on delivery and flow. Together, Rakim and Kool G Rap helped establish the complex lyrical rhyme style architecture that later influenced many lyricists of the same cloth like Nas, O.C., AZ, and Black Thought.

In 1987, the South Bronx crew Boogie Down Productions (BDP) dropped the seminal album *Criminal Minded*. An album distinguishable for many reasons, not the least of which for containing a song that sparked one of the most infamous "beefs" in hip hop/rap history,[43] *Criminal Minded* featured KRS-One using yet another new rhyme style. Drawing on his true experiences in the streets of the South Bronx, KRS-One introduced a new style of "reality rap," one that was defiant, in your face, conversational, pulled back in pace, and educational — that is to say, educational in the same vein as Lightin Rod's *Hustler's Convention*. One year after *Criminal Minded*, KRS-One and BDP dropped *By Any Means Necessary*.[44] Although the album still featured KRS-One's own brand of reality rap, it also presented a much more educational minded KRS-One. It's woth pointing out that while KRS-One and Chuck D of Public Enemy laid down the foundation for so-called "conscious rap," both rappers were not considered as such at the time; they were merely thought of as dope rappers with unique rhyme styles that were well-grounded in hip hop's rap tradition.

---

[43] The album *Criminal Minded* (1987) included the songs "The Bridge Is Over" and "South Bronx," both diss records aimed at Marley Marl and M.C. Shan and the Queensbridge Housing Project (Long Island City, Queens, New York), where KRS-One apparently believed that Marley Marl said hip hop started. Truth is, Marley Marly never made such a claim. Instead, KRS-One lobbied the first strike over what he felt was a slight. As the story goes KRS-One tried to give his demo to Marley Marl, but Marl didn't accept). Whatever the actual causes were, the songs personify the classic BDP/Queensbridge battle.

[44] Months after the release of *Criminal Minded*, BDP member Scott La Rock was murdered. Some attribute this tragedy to KRS-One's "educational" approach.

As far back as 1975, the storyteller rhyme style was, in effect, in hip hop's rap form. But prior to 1988, the form was used rather sparingly. That changed, however, after the release of *The Great Adventures of Slick Rick* (1988), an album that was completely dominated by the storyteller rhyme style. Unlike the storyteller rhyme style of the 1970s, Slick Rick's style, which was modeled off of the South Bronx reality rap style, featured a narrative approach that was both broad and meticulously detailed. Moreover, Slick Rick's rhyme flow was easy and not overbearing, something entirely unassuming yet incredibly engaging. The modern standard for the storyteller rhyme style was established with Slick Rick and his album *The Great Adventures of Slick Rick*.

Finally, in the same year that Slick Rick made his debut, Brooklyn rapper and Juice Crew member Big Daddy Kane dropped his debut album, *Long Live the Kane*. As far as rhyme *styles* go, Big Daddy Kane falls somewhere in between Rakim and Kool G Rap. However, Big Daddy Kane introduced a consciously "smooth" element to the art of rapping. Before Kane, rappers were not particularly concerned with the "polish" of their rhyme style, but instead the rawness of it. Kane, who could just as easily rip the complex lyrical rhyme style as he could the more straight-forward rhyme styles, introduced an entirely new component to rhyme styles, something that I call the "showmanship delivery." The showmanship delivery refers to the delivery style in which a rapper delivers lines in such a way that they resonate much more clearly and come off more profoundly (perhaps even more than they really are). Using the showmanship delivery and his mastery of rhythm and tempo, Big Daddy Kane carved out a rhyme style that on the one hand, mirrored the confidence of Grandmaster Caz and the mid-1970s MCs, and on the other hand, personified the structural dexterity of the newly created modern rhyme style.

To sum it all up, rapping itself was certainly nothing new. In fact, it was a continuum of the Black American oral tradition, specifically the vernacular tradition of toasting in the United States. Rapping was a blend of the signifyin', radio DJ, and hustler toasts of the African American toasting tradition. However, that being said, the art of rapping in hip hop did distinguish itself and present a new development in the black vernacular tradition. From simple toasts, nursery rhymes, boastful and light subject matter, to complex lyrical structures and serious content (reality rap) and concepts, rapping developed into the newest and one of the most powerful vocal strategies of the twentieth century.

The Hip Hop Sensibility and the Hip Hop Attitude

Having looked at the development of the four original elements (art forms) of hip hop, we can conclude that hip hop clearly has its own esthetic standards as well as its own aesthetic priorities. More importantly, I believe that together, these standards and priorities form what I call the **"hip hop sensibility."** To understand what the hip hop sensibility is and how it drives and informs creativity in hip hop, you must look at the five fundamental properties (traits and attributes) that personify it.

First, there was the importance of style; more specifically, there was a sharp focus and emphasis on individual style. Style identity was an important factor in the development of the four original elements of hip hop. The early hip hop pioneers were completely consumed with forming and representing their *own* style. In fact, to the pioneers, originality was not based so much on arbitrary "newness," but instead on the stylistic innovations of the creative commons that one was able to make.

Next, there was the transgressive philosophical approach to creativity. As is often the case in ghettos, and their subsequent street cultures, there exists a **"culture of sampling."** That is, a culture which enabled its residents (in this case, the South Bronx and other similarly hard-hit sections in New York City) to take and make use of pieces of culture from both within *and* outside of their own settings, particularly from the mainstream American society. Immersed in this culture of sampling, hip hop pioneers learned how to convert those pieces of mainstream American culture in accordance to their own needs, principles, priorities, and values. Thus, the hip hop pioneers openly relied on their ability to convert traditional forms and elements of music, art, and fashion into a distinctly hip hop aesthetic. In this way, hip hop has always been a transformative, transgressive culture. For example, b-boys reconceptualizing karate moves and gymnastics, and converting popular black American dance moves like the "bus stop" or James Brown's "good foot" into an entirely new dance form, simultaneously turning sportswear into a new fashion — casual streetwear.[45] And consider how hip hop DJs use turntables as instruments, that is to say, in a way that transgressed their traditional use and designed bounds. Then there's the case of graffiti writers — painters — who used aerosol paint cans to create a fresh new art form, which they applied on non-traditional

---

[45] It should be recognized that b-boys (and the b-boy culture) are most responsible for why sneakers are *fashionable* (a legitimate daily fashion) today. Prior to b-boys, sneakers were something mostly worn for sporting events and children's play.

canvases. And finally, we see this culture of sampling at work when we look at how rappers (MCs) break up and extend the implicit and indirect meanings of words (even inventing some words), formalize slang, and reconstruct traditional poetic (rhyme) forms and meter.

Hip hop's transgressive nature is governed by what I like to call its "rules/freedom duality." The "rules/freedom duality" describes the sensibility that hip hop practitioners *consider* (consciously or subconsciously) before they use something — a form, expression, element, etc. — outside of hip hop. This simply means that hip hop practitioners work with a sense of freedom to use tropes and elements from other traditions or cultures, provided they can convert these tropes and elements into the hip hop form.

Communal creativity is another important attribute of the hip hop sensibility. All of the early hip hop pioneers participated in and mastered their art forms through the process of communal creativity. In other words, whenever a new style and method emerged, it entered directly into a well-known creative commons. From this creative commons, wherein canonical works, styles, methods, and techniques were developed, the architects of hip hop openly drew (as they were expected to) ideas and knowledge. And in turn, they further created new styles, methods, and techniques that also went directly into the creative commons, further codifying the hip hop tradition.

This communal creative pipeline was perhaps best personified by the practice of "versioning." **Versioning** can best be described as the stylistic reworking of established (popular) styles and/or works. Versioning was critical to the overall creative process of all of hip hop's earliest pioneers. When PHASE 2 introduced Bubble letters, every graffiti writer thereafter developed their own *version* of the new style. Incidentally, it's important to point out that although PHASE 2 is credited with having introduced the style, it was not considered *his* style; it was well-understood to be *one* established style that, once created, entered directly into the creative commons, and therefore, it belonged to all graffiti writers. Similarly, when Kool Herc began using two turntables and two copies of the same record, focusing exclusively on the break, his style, method, and technique entered directly into the creative commons, which other DJs used to develop new styles, methods, and techniques.

Within hip hop's early communal creativity, syncretism played a major role. Syncretism, as I use it here, refers to the combination or fusion of the inflectional forms (slang), practices, principles, presuppositions, or ideologies (not necessarily opposing) of each of the original four elements (art forms) of hip hop. Cross-fertilization of the four elements of hip hop culture and cross-participation by the architects of hip hop in the four elements was not only very common, but expected. (Again, most of the pioneers participated in at least two of the four elements, while many participated in *all* four of the elements.)[46] In this way, each element influenced the other in a uniquely reciprocal manner. Thus, the incredibly high level of syncretism that occurred between the four distinct (separate) elements of hip hop led to their unification and, ultimately, to the formulation of one common hip hop ideology and philosophy.

Finally, because of hip hop's early communal creativity, many of the architects of hip hop willfully entered into short and long-term apprenticeships. In hip hop's developmental years, there was an objective reverence for the "masters" of the art forms. As such, most (if not all) style masters took on apprentices — often as an obligation to the development of the art forms. And because they understood the importance of training and having the proper foundation (knowledge), many budding style masters actively (and unshamefully) sought to be apprentices.

After the transgressive attribute, the next important trait of the hip hop sensibility is competition. The *competitive consciousness* of the architects of hip hop was second only to *style consciousness*. That is to say, the earliest hip hop pioneers saw competition not only as a necessary component of creativity, but also as a critical means to individual recognition. Through their commitment to regular, intense competition, the architects of hip hop were successfully able to police the overall level of originality and quality of each art form. It is also worth mentioning that the hip hop pioneers competed based on their knowledge and mastery of established styles as well as the styles and innovations that they were able to bring to the table. In other words, although competitors were revered for their ability to introduce something new and innovative, they were also judged by their knowledge and manifestation of the core tenets of the art forms that they represented. Finally, it's important to understand that through such vehement, quality-based competition, the architects of hip hop were able to maintain a strong sense of artistic integrity and pride. Moreover, they consciously established the process of intense individual practice as a critical rite of passage.

The last, but certainly not least, attribute of the hip hop sensibility is the "hip hop attitude." The **hip hop attitude** is best be described as an anti-establishment, me-against-the-world sentiment that grew out of the harsh socio-economic backdrop of hip hop's beginnings. The architects of hip hop took to heart the

---

[46] This means that the pioneers and original architects of hip hop were embedded with a deep overall understanding of the culture, in particular, how and why it coalesced into a movement. Today, this understanding is basically mute. More and more people enter into beatmaking with little to no understanding of hip hop culture. This disadvantage threatens the preservation of hip hop culture and rap music, as a widespread lack of knowledge leads to a misrepresentation of hip hop.

notion that "This is a tough world," one in which, "Nobody gives you anything;" and therefore, "You gotta take chances, because you can't sit back and wait for things to happen — you gotta make it happen!" Within the DNA of the hip hop attitude is the ever important idea of survival, which means that there's no room for weakness. Thus, the hip hop attitude is in-your-face and often confrontational.

Here, it's worth remembering how this hip hop attitude was created. Hip hop culture represented a cultural and social change from the bottom-up. And among the many emotional and philosophical conditions that the South Bronx Disaster bred, a heightened level of urgency and uncertainty about the future were two conditions that profoundly and disproportionately affected the South Bronx youth — hip hop's most earliest architects and pioneers. This urgency and uncertainty was predicated primarily upon one thing: daily survival. Therefore, it should really come as no surprise that hip hop/rap music, and the encompassing hip hop culture, has a distinct sense of urgency and chaotic certainty (controlled chaos) that is governed by a proactive, "Get Yours!" attitude. Perhaps a fair analysis would deem this attitude pragmatic, given the socio-economic climate and urban renewal circumstances that flanked hip hop's earliest pioneers from every angle.

The Evolution from Hip Hop to Rap Music

By 1978, a noticeable change had emerged in hip hop culture. Though DJs, for the most part, were still the central figures, rappers were now almost at par with them. Between 1976 and 1978, rappers had developed their performance showmanship and lyrical content so significantly that crowds were steadily coming to parties to see *them* almost as much as they were coming to see (hear) DJs. Cassette tapes of "rap music" (then the only means through which hip hop/rap was documented and distributed) were becoming ever more popular, delivering even more notoriety to rappers. Then, in 1979, one single event instituted a seismic shift in hip hop that would never be reversed.

"Rapper's Delight," released in 1979 by Sugar Hill Records — *six years* after hip hop music had been brewing in the South Bronx, was the first bonafide hit rap record on radio airwaves.[47] The story surrounding the song itself is as much legend as the milestones that it set and the doors it opened up. Sugar Hill Records owner, Sylvia Robinson, who lived in and operated her label (with her husband, Joe Robinson) out of Englewood, New Jersey, became interested in the commercial prospects of hip hop music, purportedly after noticing her children's affection for rap music. (By 1979, rap tapes were traveling throughout New York City and in some parts of New Jersey, where people there had family in NYC, thus this story appears to be the most accurate). The Sugar Hill Gang, the *performers* of "Rapper's Delight," were actually not an original Bronx hip hop group of rappers at all; they were a manufactured, make-shift hip hop/rap concoction that assembled by Sugar Hill Records label-head Sylvia Robinson.[48]

Despite the Bronx-style unauthenticity of "Rapper's Delight," the record went on to popularize rap music nationally, setting the stage for rappers to become as iconic as soloists and lead singers from other music forms. Thus, of the four original elements that comprised early hip hop culture, rap music would become the most far reaching, most visible, most commercially viable one of them all. Rap music stepped out of the park jam and off of cassette tapes directly into the recording studio and, subsequently, the music business. It went from a mainly live performance medium to a more fine-tuned recorded medium. Once this happened, rap music garnered a widespread acceptance from both the music industry and the mainstream media. In no time at all, the term "rap music" — the music *of* hip hop — was shortened to rap.

Soon, hip hop culture in general and rap music in specific, was co-opted and commercialized by corporate America. After this, many self-described hip hop purists and traditionalists began arbitrarily rejecting the "rap" classification, ignoring the fact that it was the architects of hip hop who first described the music as rap, and instead began referring to the music synonymously with and exclusively as hip hop. Perhaps this was a means to both reclaim the music as well as distinguish and signify a more truer, supposedly more traditional form of hip hop — a brand of hip hop that was seemingly more influenced by the love for the art-craft, and less influenced by the spoils of commercialism. Whatever the real cause, this conscious move to not use the rap designation has opened up

---

[47] "Rapper's Delight" was not the first rap song ever commercially recorded and released. That distinction belongs to Brooklyn's The Fatback Band, which released the single "You're My Candy Sweet," which had on the B side a rap called "King Tim III (Personality Jock)." Neither the Fatback Band's song or the Sugar Hill Gang's song was considered to be the *authentic* hip hop of the time, primarily because each song's musical track was performed by a band rather than a DJ.

[48] David Toop, *Rap Attack: African Jive To New York Hip Hop* (New York: Pluto Press, 1984), 71-81. Information also extracted from my interviews with Marley Marl and Minnesota. Although "Rapper's Delight" is the first rap record on the radio and first rap hit, it's widely considered to be one of the most non-authentic renditions of rap music ever offered.

hip hop music to much more broader interpretations than it can fundamentally hold. Finally, it should be pointed out that inevitably, as rap music grew, the significance of the rapper increased, while the role of the DJ decreased. But it was also inevitable that the beatmaker would become paramount as well.

Refuting the Jamaican-Origins Narrative of Hip Hop

For a proper perspective of the roots of the hip hop DJ style and the sampling tradition of hip hop/rap music's true lineage, as well as the birth of rap music (rhyming in hip hop culture), the popular legend that hip hop was directly shaped by reggae and dub music deserves some attention here.

The historical accuracy of a given event or movement or moment in time is inevitably doomed to be misrepresented in the future whenever the most critical variables of that event or movement are inaccurately recorded or misinterpreted. Such is the case with the mythical Jamaican-origins narrative of hip hop's beginnings. To be certain, Kool Herc *did not* take Jamaican reggae or dub music or the Jamaican toasting tradition to the South Bronx and use it to *invent* hip hop. That narrative, either explicitly or implicitly, is wrong! Yet today, the Jamaican-origins narrative of hip hop's beginnings continues to be advanced by key historians, musicologists, and other scholar, as well as countless music critics, pop culturists, and hip hop aficionados alike. Thus, in this section, I soundly refute the Jamaican-origins narrative of hip hop's beginnings and show how (and perhaps why) this narrative was able to advance in the first place.

No matter how accurately an author examines and present facts outside of the direct nucleus of hip hop culture's origins, those findings can never supplant the actual framework from which hip hop culture emerged. And although Jamaican music culture is significant in its own right and for its own merits, in nearly all recent historical accounts of hip hop's beginnings, writers have (at some point or another) overzealously played up the Jamaican-origins narrative of hip hop's beginnings. Even in the face of evidence that directly and unequivocally contradicts such a narrative, these writers have forged ahead with the story; and in doing so, they have (some knowingly) completely advanced nothing more than a myth.

So how did the Jamaican-origins myth begin? Essentially, what happened is that at some point, probably around 1987, the story surrounding the migration of Clive Campbell (DJ Kool Herc) to the South Bronx was greatly misinterpreted. The facts — confirmed by Kool Herc himself — are that he arrived in the South Bronx in 1967 *at the age 12*. More importantly for the purposes here, it should be clear that when he came to New York he was *not* a DJ, nor did he have any experience with DJ'ing. In fact, it wasn't until six years *after* he arrived in the South Bronx that he began to DJ. But the myth, most likely first set in motion by author Dick Hebdige, is that Clive Campbell came to New York *as* "DJ Kool Herc" and brought along with him key tenets of the Jamaican music culture, which he used to formulate hip hop music. In the section rather curiously titled, *"The beginning of hip hop,"* from his 1987 book, *Cut 'N' Mix,*[49] Dick Hebdige writes:

> **In 1967 a dj called Kool Herc emigrated to the States** [United States] ***from Jamaica*** and came to live in the West Bronx. **Herc knew the Jamaican sound system scene**, and had heard the early talk overs of the new djs like U Roy. By 1973 Herc owned his own system." [emphasis mine][50]

There are several points that must be made clear about this misleading account. First, Hebdige either misread the facts concerning Clive Campbell's migration to the United States or he intentionally played loose with them. In 1984, three years before Hebdiges' *Cut 'N' Mix* was first published, two different and rather pivotal Kool Herc interviews appeared in two separate books: *Hip Hop* by Steven Hager and *The Rap Attack* by David Toop — Hebdige lists the latter book by Toop in two separate end notes of his own study. What's important about both of these 1984 interviews is that each are consistent and clear and about the details surrounding Clive Campbell's (Kool Herc) migration to the Bronx. In each interview, Herc reveals that in 1967, Clive Campbell — not yet Kool Herc — was only 12 years old and certainly not a DJ when he migrated to the Bronx. Each interview plainly makes it clear that it wasn't until high school in the Bronx that he got the nickname "Herc," which was short for "Hercules."[51] Moreover, both interviews also revealed that Herc didn't even begin DJ'ing until 1971, and that at that time, his biggest influence was John Brown, an American DJ from the Bronx who played breaks of funk records, not Jamaican music.[52] Then there's the issue of Herc "knowing" the "sound system scene." By Herc's

---

[49] Published in 1987, *Cut N' Mix* was a seminal work on the study of Caribbean music and culture. The book is ground breaking for its findings; however, the connection that author Dick Hebdige draws between the Jamaican music culture of the early 1970s and hip hop's beginnings during the same period is inaccurate.
[50] Dick Hebdige, *Cut 'N' Mix* (New York: Methuen, 1987), 137.
[51] Herc was given his nickname by an American friend in high school.
[52] For some of the clearest and earliest evidence that refutes the Jamaican-origins narrative of hip hop's beginnings, see Hager, 31-33, and especially 45: "'Jamaican toasting?' said Herc. 'Naw, naw. No connection there. I couldn't play reggae in the Bronx. People wouldn't accept it. The inspiration for rap is James Brown and the album *Hustler's Convention.*'"
It's also worth seeing: Toop, 18-19, 39, 60-63. Note, Hager's interview with Kool Herc is more extensive and detailed, and therefore, more revealing and reliable. In Toop's *Rap Attack*, it's Afrika Bambaataa, *not* Kool Herc, who suggests that Herc took "Jamaican toasting" and brought it to the Bronx. But that statement is inconsistent with what Herc himself adamantly says in Hager's *Hip Hop*.

own admission, he was "too young" to get into the legendary Jamaican sound system parties.[53] Therefore, he could not have "known" the Jamaican sound system scene in the way that Hebdige says that he did. Finally, the third point that must be made clear is the fact that Clive Campbell ("Kool Herc) was already in the Bronx when Jamaican DJs like U-Roy pioneered the Jamaican dub and toast sound. In other words, he wasn't a DJ in Jamaica listening to U-Roy or the other "Jamaican toast masters." In fact, a Brian Lehrer Show interview with Kool Herc in 2009 reveals much about this:

> **Brian Lehrer:** "So you must remember toasts like that from Kingston in the 60s, before you moved to New York. Do you think you were influenced by that for your early composing in the Bronx?"
> **Kool Herc:** "**No, it wasn't all about that! I was a kid.** All I know is the Skatalites, Don Drummond, Barry Reed, and the Dragonaire, you know, Toots and the Maytals. And U-Roy and Big Youth and I-Roy was doing things like that. **I didn't — we didn't try to come and play reggae music; American people wasn't feelin' reggae music… I used other records that had a beat to it more than a reggae beat to it. I never hide the fact that I was Jamaican,** [but] *I wasn't here reppin' Jamaica. I was just a kid.* You know, I was born in Jamaica; I knew what time it was, far as me leaving from a country coming to another country. I was there when Jamaica got its independence. I remember historic things like that. You know, I admit the fact that when I migrated to the United States, I don't remember those art forms, but **I would never try and take nothing away as far as, but it [Hip Hop] didn't have nothin' to do with Jamaica.**… And as far as Jamaican toasting and DJ'ing, it wasn't two turntables they used. They used one turntable. It wasn't two turntables, it was *one!*" [emphasis mine][54]

If Dick Hebdige is most responsible for putting in motion the Jamaican-origins narrative of hip hop's beginnings, there is no commentator more responsible for prolonging this myth and, subsequently, the misrepresentation of hip hop's earliest roots, than Jeff Chang. In his book, *Can't Stop, Won't Stop: A History of The Hip Hop Generation*, author Jeff Chang constructs a narrative that is at times so at odds with the evidence of hip hop's early origins that it includes a chapter on the rise of Jamaica's "roots generation" and the turmoil of Jamaica's two warring political parties in the 1970s. Despite the fact that neither the Jamaica Labor Party (JLP) or the People's National Party (PNP) had nothing to do with the South Bronx Disaster, its causes, or the South Bronx street culture in the 1970s, Chang still incorporates such material into his study. Although it's engaging information, the Jamaican political climate has no connection to the birth of hip hop. At best, Chang's curious choice to include this chapter misleads

---

[53] Chang, 68, Kool Herc: "I was too young to go in. All we could do is sneak out and see the preparation of the dance throughout the day."
[54] *The Brian Lehrer Show*, WNYC Radio, February 26, 2009.

readers to believe that the political climate of Jamaica had some connection to the origins of hip hop culture — it didn't. At worst, Chang's inclusion of this chapter misleads readers to believe that the political climate of Jamaica somehow had a direct impact and influence on the origins of hip hop culture — it didn't.

As I pointed out in Chapter 1, among all of the travesties that the residents of the South Bronx were forced to endure, benign neglect was front and center. In other words, the South Bronx youth did not participate in New York City politics. They did not enter into any political squabble between New York's Democratic and Republican parties. Furthermore, during the 1970s, New York City was infamously under the death grip of fiscal malfunction — the city was teetering on bankruptcy and sinking fast. There was no intense "power grab" situation in play for two opposing political parties. And even if there was one, there certainly wasn't a place for the disconnected South Bronx youth to join in the fray and aid one side or the other.

In his book, Chang also surveys the history of Jamaican dub music and the musical developments that grew out of Lee "Scratch" Perry's Black Ark recording studio. Chang maintains that "Dub's birth was accidental…" and the goes so far as to say that **"it would become a diagram for hip-hop music.** *A space had been pried open for the break, for possibility."* [55] Dub as "a diagram for hip-hop music" is more than an overreach, it's flat-out wrong. But while Chang is occupied with trying to connect dub music to hip hop/rap's origins, specifically trying to demonstrate how dub music was the precursor to break-beat music (b-boy music) and, subsequently, hip hop/rap music, he fails to include critical details, which of course completely undermine his theory.

First, let's look at the year 1967, a crucial year to many of those who push the Jamaican-origins narrative of hip hop. On the surface, the way the story goes is that Kool Herc came to New York in 1973 *as a Jamaican (dub)* DJ. From the start, the trouble with this narrative is the fact that Clive Campbell ("Kool Herc") came to New York in 1967, *at the age of 12* — and as noted earlier in this section, he certainly wasn't yet a DJ either. Also, as it so happens, 1967 is widely considered by Jamaican music historians to be the first year in which dub music emerged in Jamaica. And according to even the most basic historical reading of dub's development, dub music isn't fully realized and developed until around December, 1973 — the date associated with the start of Jamaican producer and dub pioneer Lee Perry's Black Ark studio. Chang, too, no doubt is aware of this date, as he mentions it in his study. So this raises a couple of questions. First, if by December, 1973, Kool Herc had already given the notorious Sedgwick

---

[55] Chang, 30, emphasis mine.

party, the party that is widely recognized for having kicked off the hip hop movement, how could he have been using the *underdeveloped* Jamaican dub style as "a diagram for hip-hop music?" Second, if funk — a music tradition which is widely considered by most soul music historians to have begun in 1964/1965 with the James Brown releases "Out of Sight" in 1964 and "Papa's Got a Brand New Bag" in 1965 — was indeed the music from which hip hop was spawned, why does Chang claim that Jamaican *dub* was "a diagram for hip-hop music?"[56]

Now, let's look at what Kool Herc — the most important link in the Jamaican-origins narrative — has repeatedly and quite clearly said about this issue. In 1970, while still in high school, Herc (then not yet "DJ Kool Herc") started hanging out at a disco called the Plaza Tunnel, formerly located on 161ST St. and the Grand Concourse, in the South Bronx. By Herc's own admission, the deejay at the Plaza Tunnel, John Brown, was the first to play records like "Give It Up or Turn It Loose" by James Brown, and "Get Ready" by Rare Earth, and "Soul Power" by James Brown. Herc has long conceded that it was John Brown who influenced him to spin funk records and the like, and that it was what John Brown, not Lee "Scratch" Perry, who was doing the style that led him to kick off what would become the formulation of the break-beat DJ phenomenon and subsequent hip hop DJ tradition. Herc has never said that Jamaican dub music, Jamaican toasts, or any part of the Jamaican music culture was the inspiration for what he and the other earliest hip hop DJs were doing. Again, from Kool Herc:

> Jamaican toasting? Naw, Naw. No connection there. I couldn't play reggae in the Bronx. People wouldn't accept it. The inspiration for rap is James Brown and the album Hustler's Convention.[57]

Further, it was a well-known fact of the time that "while most other deejays played disco…Herc played hard-core funk…"[58] So if Kool Herc himself has noted quite clearly — on numerous occasions since 1983 — that the inspiration for what he and, subsequently, the others that immediately followed him did was not Jamaican dub music, Jamaican "toasters," or Jamaican DJs, but rather black American funk and a 1970 funk-based DJ named John Brown, how can Chang's claim possibly be accurate? Moreover, if in two separate interviews, appearing in *Hip Hop* (1983) and *The Rap Attack* (1984), two books that Chang cites (multiple times) in the end notes of his own study, Kool Herc makes it very clear that he was influenced by a South Bronx *funk* DJ (John Brown), and

---

[56] *Ibid*, 30.
[57] Hager, 45.
[58] Hager, 45.

that the inspiration for rap (what he and others were doing) was James Brown and the album *Hustler's Convention*, how can Chang project that Jamaican dub music was the "diagram" for hip hop/rap music?

But while Chang curiously plays-up hip hop's alleged indebtedness to Jamaican music culture, author Tricia Rose does not attempt to draw out (or dwell) on the same. Instead, she seems to actually play it down. In the end notes of Chapter 3 of *Black Noise*, her seminal cultural study of hip hop and rap music, she maintains (in just one brief sentence) that "Rap music is heavily indebted to Jamaican musical practices." Aside from this, she offers no further examination of the overread connection between the Jamaican music culture of the 1970s and that of the South Bronx during the same period.

Here, it's also worth examining three other areas of contention: (1) The importance of audio/sonic quality in hip hop/rap music; (2) The history of park jams, block parties and the like; and (3) The Jamaican toasting tradition of the 1970s. To be certain, Kool Herc's understanding of sound systems was primarily influenced in America. In fact, it was in America where Kool Herc made the discovery that allowed him to make his sound system more powerful (amplified) than most. Prior to Herc's discovery in America, neither Herc or his father knew how to increase the peak level sound in their family's system.[59] The importance of Audio/sonic quality and bass tones was already a preference of black Americans before Clive Campbell ("Kool Herc") came to the Bronx. For example, in 1975, in both Chicago and New York City, at least three of my uncles had hi-fi sound systems. (My father had a hi-fi system as early as 1971.) It's probably worth mentioning that neither my uncles or my father were from Jamaica, they were all born and raised in America. Furthermore, one of my uncles played bass guitar in a band throughout the 1970s and early 1980s. In his band, as with other black American bands, the bass tone was always highly valued. Finally, in my interview with DJ Toomp, Tomp shared a story about a time in Atlanta (throughout the 1970s), wherein he checked out what kind of speakers DJs were using at house parties. This indicates that speakers and sonic quality were not only valued, they were both expected at parties and black American homes during the 1970s and early 1980s. Also, Toomp recalls how people were often remembered by the sound systems they had and how much bass each system kicked out.[60]

As for park jams, block parties and the like, my mother attended multiple

---

[59] Chang, 68-69.
[60] Information extracted in my interview with DJ Toomp.

live shows. Also, some close family friends, like Canell Johnson, as well as Ghetto Brother founder Benjy Melendez, have shared many stories about partying in parks and "on the block" as early as 1965. Hence, recorded or live music and parties at parks or on the block were certainly nothing particularly new when Clive Campbell ("Kool Herc") arrived in the Bronx. And it's worth mentioning that Herc's decision to move his "rec room jams" over to Cedar Park (right up the corner) was not inspired by, nor had anything to do with, the yard parties of Trench Town, Jamaica. On the contrary, the decision was a practical one: Herc simply needed a bigger space to accommodate the growing number of party-goers, who had typically ranged in age from as young as 8 to as old as 50 — the late night yard parties of Trenchtown, that many researchers have tried to link to Kool Herc, were for adults only. Finally, what about the Jamaican toasting tradition? Again, in Kool Herc's own words:

> Jamaican toasting? Naw, Naw. No connection there. I couldn't play reggae in the Bronx. People wouldn't accept it. The inspiration for rap is James Brown and the album *Hustler's Convention*.[61]

Final Analysis of the Jamaican-Origins Narrative

Overall, for their tireless research and work and invaluable contribution to hip hop studies, I respect Jeff Chang and similar authors; some of their other findings were and are still in-line with the realities of hip hop/rap music, then and now. But with regards to their advancement of the Jamaican-origins narrative of the creation of hip hop/rap music, they are wrong. To equate Kingston, Jamaica as the cradle of hip hop/rap music, in a similar way to how one equates Mississippi and Chicago with the blues, or the way one equates New Orleans, Chicago, or Kansas City with jazz is, at worst, a conscious attempt to overstate Jamaica's non-existent influence over the origins of hip hop/rap music. At best it's a woefully misleading exaggeration.

Hip hop was not directly shaped by Jamaican dub and reggae; moreover, Jamaican music did not provide the "diagram" for hip hop. Parallels existed, mainly in terms of (1) sonic priorities — bass and volume; (2) a focus on rhythm and groove — tropes important to all popular black musics of the period; and (3) DJs as figureheads (in the Bronx, a descendent link to disco DJs is more appropriate for understanding the early development of hip hop/rap music). But these are parallels between two burgeoning music traditions — one in the United States and the other in Jamaica — that were functioning at roughly the same time. It's not however an instance of one music tradition giving rise to or

---

[61] Hager, 45.

guiding the other. Did Clive Campbell bring some Jamaican musical customs with him when he migrated to the South Bronx as a child? Perhaps. About as much as any 12-year old kid could have when he migrated to the United States at the close of the 1960s.

Kool Herc's role in the development of hip hop/rap music and hip hop culture in general is unquestioned. His contributions are absolutely central to the birth of hip hop/rap music and the formulation of the collective hip hop cultural movement of the time. For that, he should always be remembered and revered, and his efforts should never be tarnished. However, in the interest of historical accuracy, Kool Herc's contributions should never be misrepresented or overstated, or air brushed into a flawed historical narrative of the beginnings of hip hop/rap music — a narrative that even Herc rejects. Likewise, the contributions of DJ Grandmaster Flash and Afrika Bambaataa, respectively, should not be understated or conveniently neglected to support such an inaccurate historical narrative.

Finally, In lieu of the features and developments of the Jamaican music culture — ca. 1968 to 1973 — we must look at those features and developments for what they are: The ingredients of an absolutely amazing musical culture that made a major contribution to twentieth-century popular music, but a musical culture and tradition that did not have a direct connection to or major influence on the origins of hip hop/rap music in the specific, and certainly not on hip hop culture in general.[62] Although my findings contradict earlier research on this matter, it should really come as no surprise to the authors that I've mentioned in this section. After all, in their bibliographies, they've cited some of the very same books that I do. And two books in particular that appear in the bibliographies of some other hip hop historians, Stephen Hager's *Hip Hop* (1984) and David Toop's *Rap Attack* (1984), leave little room for misinterpretation; and both books offer evidence that debunk the Jamaican-origins narrative of hip hop/rap music's beginnings.

Whatever parallels that existed between Jamaican music culture of the early 1970s and hip hop/rap music of the same period are merely examples of the type of similarities (and perhaps coincidences) that can often be found throughout all musics of the Afro-diasporic. To misread these parallels, or worse, to misinterpret them as having had a pivotal role in the creation of hip hop/rap music is not only detrimental to accurately understanding the roots of hip hip hop/rap music and the art of sampling in the hip hop/rap music tradition, it's detrimental to comprehending the unique origins and scope of hip hop culture itself. What was happening in the Bronx, ca. 1970-1973, was developing irrespective of what

---

[62] The fact that there were no b-boys and/or graffiti writers in Jamaica in 1973 can not be ignored. And as it has been noted earlier in Chapter 2, Kool Herc was influenced by the "b-boys" just as much (if not more) as they were influenced by him.

was going on in Jamaica during the very same period.

Move, Rock, Dance, Sucka: The Summary

Although hip hop is indeed a music-based culture, it should be understood that it grew from the coalescence and informal unification of four distinct art forms (graffiti writing, b-boying, DJ'ing, and rapping) that were brewed first in the streets of the South Bronx, then soon after in other areas throughout NYC. And prior to Afrika Bambaataa dubbing his parties "hip hop parties" (ca. 1975-76), each artistic expression represented its own subculture, complete with its own creative aesthetics and priorities, its own slang, and even its own fashion. And it's important to remember that most early hip hop pioneers participated in at least two of the four elements. Because of the heavy cross-participation in each of the four elements, there was much creative (especially stylistic), ideological, and philosophical overlap. And the hip hop sensibility was the common thread that underscored and linked the four original elements. Thus, by the time that the 1970s had drawn to a close, hip hop had been established as a New York City subculture, one complete with its own music, dance, graphic art, fashion, slang, and underlining philosophy. It would not be long, however, before this little known NYC (mostly Bronx-based) subculture would explode around the rest of America, and then the globe. But the catalyst of this explosion would not be hip hop DJs, who up until 1979 were the central figures in hip hop; it would be rappers.

Finally, I'm compelled to point out that there were countless graffiti writers, b-boys (and b-girls), DJs, and rappers that never quite made it to the "top." But this does not erase the critical roles that these unsung architects played in the development of hip hop. In history, it's those names that rise to or near the top that are the ones most often remembered. But it's the flooded ranks of the unknowns, who no doubt contributed immensely to the purpose, that we must never forget to also honor. Therefore, I honor the less-known contributors and shapers of hip hop. And I offer this chapter as a humble re-payment for a debt of gratitude that I've carried for them all.

"Move, rock, dance, sucka!" That says it all.

Chapter 3

Looking for the Perfect Beat
The Birth and Unique Rise of the Hip Hop/Rap Beatmaking Tradition: Eight Periods of Distinct Development

DISCLAIMER:
The purpose of detailing the developments of the eight periods of the beatmaking tradition is to document (objectively) each period as it occurred in the past 40 years. I've made no attempt to present one period as superior to another; effort has only been made to show the actual developments (or lack there of) within each period of beatmaking, and how these developments have affected hip hop/rap music overall. I encourage you to draw any additional conclusions that can be reached about each period. Likewise, it's my hope that the information presented in this chapter further informs and helps beatmakers make those compositional choices that are right for them individually.

MAP OF THE DEVELOPMENT OF
THE HIP HOP/RAP BEATMAKING TRADITION

AFRICAN AMERICAN (BLACK) MUSIC TRADITION
(blues + gospel + rhythm and blues → soul•)

Time Line

1965 — funk

1971 — Pete DJ Jones — John Brown — early disco

1973 — **BREAK-BEAT PERIOD** • 1973-1978 (1ST PERIOD, FIRST GOLDEN ERA)
HIP HOP DJ ERA BEGINS
Kool DJ Herc

1974 — DJ Grandmaster Flash — DJ Afrika Bambaataa — late funk

1975 — Grand Wizard Theodore — DJ Red Alert — late disco
DJ Charlie Chase — DJ Breakout — DJ Jazzy Jay
DJ A.J.

1979 — **STUDIO-BAND PERIOD** • 1979-1982 (2ND PERIOD, FIRST RADIO/NATIONAL EXPOSURE)
"label bands"
(in-house session musicians
Ed Fletcher, et. al) — Kurtis Blow — *EARLY SAMPLING*

1982 — electro funk → Arthur Baker

1983 — **ELECTRONIC DRUM MACHINE PERIOD** • 1983-1987 (3RD PERIOD)
Grand Mixer DXT — Larry Smith — Steinski — Rick Rubin

1984 — Dr. Dre — DJ Lonzo Williams — DJ Jam Master Jay — Amos Larkins
(earliest years) — electro-hop — (AKA Peter Rocker)
DXJ (AKA Maggotron)

1986 — Marley Marl — DJ Jazzy Jeff
Prince Paul — Hank Shocklee — Mr. Mixx — Miami bass
SAMPLING — and the Bomb Squad — *MODERN* — DJ Toomp — (bass music)
ERA BEGINS — Easy Mo Bee — *HIP HOP/RAP* — (earliest years)
— *ERA BEGINS* — Ced Gee — Mannie Fresh
(earliest years)

1988 — **PIONEERS/AVANT-GARDE PERIOD** • 1988-1994 (4TH PERIOD, SECOND GOLDEN ERA)
Paul C. — *SAMPLING-MAJOR* — DJ Pooh — Erick Sermon — Dr. Dre
Large Professor — *ERA BEGINS* — DJ Clark Kent
Showbiz

1990 — Ali Shaheed Muhammad — DJ Premier — Pete Rock — RZA — DJ Quik
& Q-Tip — Ski Beatz — Trackmasters — G-funk
The Beatnuts

1993 — Domino — No I.D. — Modern Beatmaking Blueprint — Buckwild
Havoc
(of Mobb Deep) — The Hitmen

1995 — **POST-PIONEERS PERIOD** • 1995-2000 (5TH PERIOD)
Rockwilder — Dame Grease — DJ Shadow

1996 — The Ummah — J-Dilla — DJ Toomp — Swizz Beatz — Mannie Fresh
(aka "Jay-Dee") — Timbaland — (early years) — Lil Jon — DJ Muggs

1997 — Bink — The Neptunes — Nottz — (earliest years) — Kanye West — Mel-Man
Just Blaze — The Heatmakerz — crunk — Statik Selektah — The Alchemist
Madlib

2001 — **SOUTHERN-BOUNCE PERIOD** • 2001-2004 (6TH PERIOD)
9th Wonder — DJ Toomp → trap music — Scott Storch — Jazze Pha
Kev Brown — Marco Polo — Lil Jon — *SAMPLING DECLINES DRAMATICALLY*
DJ Khalil

2005 — **RETRO-ECLECTIC PERIOD** • 2005-2009 (7TH PERIOD)
Keak Da Sneak — Danjahandz — Shawty Redd — snap music — Bangladesh — Black Milk
hyphy — (aka "Danja") — Jake One
Droop-E — *SAMPLING REVIVAL BEGINS* — Don Cannon — J.U.S.T.I.C.E. League

2009 — **TRAP BASED/PERFORMANCE-EXPERIMENTAL PERIOD** • 2009-2015 (8TH PERIOD)
Flying Lotus
Cardiak — Lex Luger — Jahlil Beats — Boi-1-da — Noah "40" Shebib
slump — Mike Will Made-It — Knxwledge — Frank Dukes — T-Minus
Dibiase — Harry Fraud — DJ Mustard — Vinylz — Young Chop — Metro Boomin

2015

Hip Hop/Rap Beatmaking Tradition Map, Copyright © 2009-2015 Amir Said

Figure 1 Map of the Development of the Beatmaking Tradition

> To Herc, a DJ set was one continuous piece of music. My man was composing something. And if he was a composer, that went for me too. –Grandmaster Flash

> Fuck the melody, forget the chorus, and leave the verses alone; we're talking about the pure rhythmic groove. –Grandmaster Flash

Beatmaking, the chief compositional process of hip hop/rap music, has been a part of the hip hop/rap music tradition right from the start. In addition to rockin' the crowd or providing music to party to, early DJs like Kool Herc, Grandmaster Flash, and Afrika Bambaataa considered what they were doing (the DJ element of hip hop) as a form of music composition, not just as a process of spinning records. The DJs of hip hop's first era used the breaks and other fragments from records (mostly funk, some disco, and other genres that fit the hip hop style) to make completely new musical statements. But in the earliest years, beatmaking, as a stand alone element of hip hop, had yet to formulate into what we commonly know it as today. Thus, what follows is an examination of the eight developmental periods of the beatmaking tradition, from 1973 to 2015.

Break-Beat Period, 1973-1978

Between 1973 and 1978, the first five years of what can be described as the "hip hop movement," the job of making beats through the use of turntables was something done only by qualified DJs. All of the pivotal developments of this period were actually discussed in detail in Chapter 2, but here's a brief recap of what must be noted. A use of a particular brand of funk records — that became the foundation for hip hop/rap music — was first performed in 1970 by a lesser known South Bronx DJ named John Brown. John Brown was the DJ at a place called the Plaza Tunnel, a local South Bronx spot. It was at the Plaza Tunnel where what would become known as the "hip hop *style*" of DJ'ing was first born in the mind of a young Kool Herc.

Herc's style of DJ'ing, which he first showcased in 1973, was influenced as much by dancers ("b-boys") as it was by John Brown, centered around the use of a mixer, two turntables, and two copies of the same record on two separate turntables. Herc would go back and forth between each record (mostly funk), only playing the "breaks" — the raw rhythm section, stripped of melody and underscored by the pulse and groove of the drums, bass guitar, and rhythm guitars. He would extend these breaks continuously, pumping up the action by b-boys on the dance floor. Herc was the first person to use turntables as *instruments*, thereby setting the tone for a new group of non-traditional musicians. As Herc's new DJ style took the South Bronx by storm, other DJs soon followed; most notably Grandmaster Flash and Afrika Bambaataa. Between 1973 and 1978, DJs emerged as the most powerful and revered figures of the hip hop movement.[63]

It was also during the Break-Beat Period that the break-beat style or hip hop style of DJ'ing began to lay the foundation for the modern beatmaking tradition. First, Herc developed the "merry-go-round" technique, a process of using two copies of the same record — one to play and one to cue up while the other was playing. Next, Grandmaster built upon the merry-go-round technique and invented new techniques, including: the spin back, a method for winding records back and forth; the clock theory, a method for quickly spotting where sections where on a record; and the quik mix theory, a collective of his own techniques for quickly cutting back and forth between records *on beat*, making one musical passage flow seamlessly to the next; and the punch phase, a method for *punching* a record forward, right on the break.[64] To create a continuous groove, Flash began *blending* records, mixing them, and cutting the beats together in exact syncopation and meticulously planning out his DJ sets. In his pursuit to develop his own unique DJ style and to outdo and surpass Kool Herc once and for all, Grandmaster Flash became the first DJ to actually *physically* put his hands on the vinyl while the turntable's platter was spinning, giving him a level of control previously unrealized by other DJs. In effect, Flash had developed a method for looping the breaks and other segments of the same record. Thus, it was the pioneering developments of Grandmaster Flash that first hinted at the looping, cutting, and chopping techniques of the modern beatmaking tradition.

Grandmaster Flash must also be recognized for other innovations that laid the groundwork for the modern beatmaking tradition. In addition to being the first DJ to "rig" his mixer, specifically for the purpose of creating his own headphone input jack (yes, he was a techie), Flash was also the first DJ to use an electronic beat box, incorporating additional percussion sounds and effects with his regular DJ setup. And finally, it should be recognized that while Herc was the originator of the "break-beat" style and Grandmaster Flash the first true *technician* and the closest link to the modern beatmaker, it was Afrika Bambaataa

---

[63] Of equal importance, it was during the Break-Beat Period wherein the first DJ/rapper (MC) crews were born. Groups like Grandmaster Flash and the Furious Five and the Cold Crush Brothers were among the many DJ/rapper (MC) collectives that typified the Break-Beat Period. Within the DJ/rapper (MC) crews, the DJ was the one solely responsible for providing the music that the rappers (MCs) rhymed to.
[64] *Ibid*, 34. Also, see Flash and Ritz, 54-84. During this same period, other DJ techniques emerged like the "scratch" (widely credited to Grand Wizard Theodore, once an apprentice to Grandmaster Flash), and the first form of "pause tape" sampling, done first by Afrika Bambaataa. The pause tape was a technique of using a cassette tape to record a segment of audio (from a record, the radio, etc.). Utilizing the pause button on a tape recorder, one would record the breaks (or desired segments) press pause, then record the same section again in effort to create what could best be described as a crude loop.

who was the undisputed record collection king and the one who also hinted at the future of sampling.

Summary of the Break-Beat Period

The Break-Beat Period of the beatmaking tradition represented the first group of beatmakers in hip hop/rap music. These DJs were all conscious of the fact that what they were doing was certainly not the norm, but something non-traditional and anti-establishment. In fact, in many ways what the first beatmakers were doing was a rebuttal to a lot of the popular, slick and polished disco that was on the radio in the mid- and late 1970s. Furthermore, that all of the first beatmakers were DJs is not a fact that can be taken lightly. For six solid years, the DJ was the sole controller of the music of hip hop. More importantly, in this period, hip hop DJs became the first musicians to use turntables as instruments. In doing so, they became the most non-traditional musicians in America. Finally, as a self-contained music-maker who used non-traditional or non-conventional compositional practices, the hip hop DJ sketched the first outline for the model of the modern beatmaker.

Studio-Band Period, 1979-1982

Prior to the late 1970s and early 1980s, DJs were the main draw. They were the most powerful, most revered, and most imitated figures in hip hop. However, at the same time, rappers were a secondary thought; their main purpose being to introduce the DJ and to provide a level of crowd control. But as lyrical content (subject matter) expanded and the mechanics and language of the art of rapping grew more complex, rappers moved to the forefront, replacing DJs as the center of attention in hip hop. Also during this period, hip hop was going through its first experience with the music industry. Before 1979, there were no studio recorded hip hop/rap songs and/or hip hop/rap acts signed to a record label. Until then, hip hop/rap songs were mostly live DJ/rapper performances that were recorded on cassette tape and distributed (hand-to-hand) throughout New York City. But after the first two official studio hip hop/rap recordings in 1979, "King Tim III (Personality Jock)" by Brooklyn's The Fatback Band and the monster hit "Rapper's Delight" by the Sugarhill Gang, studio recorded hip hop/rap music became a more regular occurrence.

Beginning in 1979, DJs saw their power decrease, as the lane of fame and opportunities further widened for rappers, who were now becoming more eager to cut a record in the studio. And having seen the break away success of the Sugar Hill Records release, "Rapper's Delight," upstart self-described "rap" labels where bent on capturing the same lightning in the bottle that Sugar Hill Records had.

The most noticeable feature of the Studio-Band Period was the replacement of the hip hop DJ (as the sole music provider for rappers) by the studio band (recording studio session musicians). During this period, indie rap labels actively sought out rappers and brought them into the recording studio, where the label's in-house studio bands (who were not part of the hip hop movement of the time) worked up cover versions of the breaks and grooves from the very records that were most popular among hip hop DJs of the time.[65] In effect, the indie rap labels had come up with a way to cheaply manufacture rap records. Moreover, the indie rap labels, most notably Sugar Hill Records and Enjoy Records, figured out how to use the wisdom and influence of the hip hop DJ without having to actually use or *pay* the hip hop DJ. Subsequently, it was during the Studio-Band Period that the DJ/rapper connection began to fall apart; and for the first time in hip hop's history, the DJ and rapper, once a unified force, were separated. It was also during the Studio-Band Period wherein rappers, who had by the late 1970s and early 1980s displaced the DJ as the most visible figures in hip hop, first began to realize that the DJ could not adequately serve as the sole music provider for studio recorded records, which were based on the recording studio environment and model, not the live party one.

Around the same time that hip hop/rap music was finding its way into the studio, there were advancements rapidly occurring in audio and recording technology. Drum machines and more affordable digital samplers were just beginning to hit the market, giving access to an enhanced music-making process not only to DJs, but also to a larger pool of would-be musicians who had missed out (or couldn't cut it) in the first DJ era. Thus, realizing that (A) they no longer had to be attached to one specific DJ, that they were now basically self-contained, independent contractors, and (B) the art of rapping was moving into new levels of complexity and reaching new artistic heights, rappers began to see themselves as any other recording artist in the music industry. Therefore, the need for hip hop/rap DJ-inspired music — *without* necessarily the DJ — soon developed.

By 1981, the studio-band method of music production had all but died out. After getting over the initial novelty of hearing rap on the radio for the first time, there was a huge pushback from those who recognized that the studio band hip

---

[65] It has often been reported that "Rapper's Delight," the first hit rap record, used a sample of the song "Good Times" by the group Chic. The truth is that the Sugar Hill Records in-house band played a cover version of the main riff (a break so to speak) of Chic's "Good Times." That was the rhythm track that the Sugar Hill Gang rapped to, not an actual digital sample of Chic's song.

hop was certainly not authentic hip hop/rap music many had previously enjoyed and observed. In fact, many participants of the hip hop movement began to outright reject the studio-band sound, as it did not represent the essence of hip hop as they'd known it.[66] It was around this time that Kurtis Blow, Grandmaster Flash, and Afrika Bamabaataa (the latter two being among the first architects of hip hop/rap music), emerged as the new leaders and pioneers of the studio recorded rap song.

In 1980, Kurtis Blow, a former b-boy and DJ who went by the name Kool DJ Kurt, tapped into his DJ roots and a lesser-used rap style and form, the "message rap" (yet another development in hip hop that had been overlooked by the recent emergence of the rap music sub-industry), and came up with the seminal hit "The Breaks."[67] Though Kurtis Blow and co-producer Larry Smith used a number of musicians for the making of "The Breaks," they did not merely do cover versions of the breaks of funk records that were popular with hip hop DJs. Instead, they used an original rhythm track that was inspired by both funk and Kurtis Blow's block party DJ'ing days. The other pioneering achievement of "The Breaks" could be heard in both the lyrics and rhyme style that Kurtis Blow employed. Before "The Breaks," most raps were of the bragging and boasting style and form; Kurtis Blow changed all of that. Two years *before* "The Message" (Grandmaster Flash and the Furious Five) would shake up the standard lyrical form and style in the art of rap, Kurtis Blow had already perfected the message rap form and style.

In 1981, for the making of the landmark song, "The Adventures of Grandmaster Flash on the Wheels of Steel," Grandmaster Flash made a triumphant return to his DJ roots. Opting not for any assistance of a studio band, Flash instead chose to do what he had always done best: Serve as the sole controller of the music. Using *three* separate turntables and all of his best techniques, cutting, scratching, blending, punch phasing, and back spinning, Flash weaved together various records into one cohesive tapestry, demonstrating for the first time how, given the chance, the hip hop DJ could translate to the studio recording environment. "The Adventures of Grandmaster Flash on the Wheels of Steel" was pivotal to the advent of the beatmaking tradition for

---

[66] It's worth pointing out that the initial success of "Rapper's Delight," Sylvia Robinson's Sugar Hill Records, and the like was due more to the novelty of rap being heard on the radio for the first time. But the studio band-lead hip hop inevitably died within two years of its inception, as young hip hoppers who had grown up with the real article reclaimed the movement, and brought back the hip hop DJ. This sentiment has been widely expressed and shared by many hip hop/rap pioneers of the time. The rejection of the studio band "hip hop" sound is directly mentioned by Marley Marl in my interview with him, included in its entirety in this study.

[67] Though "Rapper's Delight" was the first big rap hit record, it's worth noting that "The Breaks" by Kurtis Blow was the first big rap hit record on a major label (Mercury Records).

two reasons. First, it established a model for how the hip hop DJ could in fact make it in the studio recording environment. Remember, by 1981, when Flash made "The Adventures of Grandmaster Flash on the Wheels of Steel," the hip hop DJ had been written off as a hip hop element that could not translate well to the studio recording environment. Moreover, it was thought at the time (by the indie culture vultures and exploiters of rap) that the hip hop DJ was naturally a causality of the progression of hip hop into the music industry and, subsequently, the mainstream. In fact, when Sugar Hills Records owner Sylvia signed Grandmaster Flash and the Furious Five to her label, she did so to capitalize off of and use Flash's *name*, not any of Flash's ideas about music-making. "The Message," the biggest hit song credited to Grandmaster Flash and the Furious Five, wasn't even written by the members of the group, save for Melle Mel (Melvin Glover). In truth, "The Message" was the brainchild of Duke Bootee (Ed Fletcher), the leader of Sugar Hill Record's in-house studio band, and Melle Mel.

Second, the making of "The Adventures of Grandmaster Flash on the Wheels of Steel" established the model of the principle (lone) beatmaker in a studio setting. When Sylvia Robinson finally permitted Flash to go into the studio alone and record a hip hop/rap album in the vein of the original (real) essence of hip hop, he took full advantage of the opportunity. Inside the studio, Flash combined his hip hop sensibility and unique DJ style with the recording technology of the time. It was his unique use of both his DJ skill-set and the recording studio tools that paved the way for the beatmaking tradition, as it would come to be known five years later.[68]

Much in the same way that Grandmaster Flash had returned to his roots, Afrika Bambaataa reached back to his DJ and king-of-the-record-collection roots to make a series of critical hit singles between 1981 and 1983. "Jazzy Sensation" (1981), "Planet Rock" (1982), "Looking For The Perfect Beat" (1982), and "Renegades of Funk" (1983), all featured Afrika Bambaataa's hip hop DJ sensibility and examples of his forward-thinking usage of recording studio technology. Bambaataa used his understanding of cutting, mixing, and the use of rupture, and combined it with the recording technology of the time. He used synthesizers and other gear, but in perhaps one of his truest pioneering acts, he reached into his extensive record collection and with the help of co-producer/engineer Arthur Baker, he digitally sampled some of the most unlikely sound sources. Bambaataa called his new sound "electro funk," a homage to both the

---

[68] It's also worth noting that Grandmaster Flash and his "The Adventures of Grandmaster Flash on the Wheels of Steel" is also credited for being the catalyst of the art of turntablism.

funk music that had originally inspired hip hop and to the level of creativity that electronic instruments and equipment was able to uncork.

Summary of the Studio-Band Period

The Studio-Band Period of the beatmaking tradition represented a number of critical developments in the art of beatmaking. First, it's in this period that the DJ is first separated from the rapper. Second, it is within this period that hip hop/rap music gets on the radio for the first time, and, subsequently, gains a national audience outside of New York. Moreover, the Studio-Band Period marks the first time the distribution of hip hop/rap music first began to move from street-sold cassette tapes, to store-sold records. The Studio-Band Period represents the first time that hip hop/rap was snatched from its creators (rightful owners) and exploited commercially. Third, within this period there was a decisive move away from the actual use of breaks from records as the primary (basic) material for making new music compositions. Although most of the in-house studio bands continued to draw inspiration from what hip hop DJs were playing, they never sought the hip hop DJ's input when creating rhythm tracks for rappers. Fourth, it's in this period that we first see the emergence of the lone, self-contained beatmaker (producer). Fifth, it's in this period where we first hear how a limited use of melody can be used in the rhythm and groove-orientated form of music that hip hop/rap is. Finally, it is also within the Studio-Band Period that many hip hop/rap practitioners are increasingly becoming aware of hip hop/rap's ability to distinguish itself as a popular genre in the music industry — in this period, Kurtis Blow becomes the first hip hop/rap artist to ever sign with a major record label.

It's important to remember that the Studio-Band Period did not represent the original hip hop movement. Many people wrongly consider this period to be the original or "real" roots of hip hop/rap music and the beatmaking tradition. This is inaccurate. The roots of hip hop/rap music took shape first in 1973, and consistently developed for six years *before* the Studio-Band Period began in 1979. Furthermore, aside from the isolated developments of Kurtis Blow, Larry Smith, Grandmaster Flash, Afrika Bambaataa, and Duke Bootee, for the most part, the beatmaking of the Studio-Band Period was simply a knock-off of the original hip hop sound. In fact, most of the music put forth by the first indie rap labels in this period was nothing more than poor, ill-conceived, mass-produced and mass-manufactured, superficial renditions of the compositions that the hip hop DJs had been doing in the South Bronx since 1973. Moreover, it was a music that was not in deference to the hip hop sensibility or the underlying hip hop style and sound. Instead, it was a flash-in-the-pan form of music that was designed more for making a splash on national radio than representing authentic hip hop/rap music or hip hop culture.

"Rapper's Delight" was the first single to take hip hop/rap to the mainstream, there is no disputing that; it was also the first single to popularize hip hop/rap music nationally. But it must never be forgotten that the Sylvia Robinson invention[69] (or experiment) was not considered real hip hop/rap by any of the hip hop/rap pioneers and architects of the time. This is why by 1982, the Studio-Band Period, which was really more the result of a business strategy than a musical development, was all washed out. Having no real pipeline to the streets, where hip hop was still emanating from, or to the new rap groups and crews that were rapidly emerging, the Sugar Hill-inspired acts were all displaced, paving the way for a new development in the hip hop/rap music and beatmaking traditions.

Electronic Drum Machine Period, 1983-1987

In 1983, a number of events occurred within the increasingly solidifying beatmaking tradition. Taking a cue from Afrika Bambaataa and his electro funk sound as well as other elements of the Bronx (New York) style and sound, DJ Lonzo Williams (Alonzo Williams) formulated a sound he dubbed "electro hop." Williams is significant for two reasons. First, he is widely recognized as the first person to perform and create any form of hip hop on the West Coast (Los Angeles). Until Williams came on the scene, there was no hip hop in California. And though California had its own funk and dance movements (most notably locking), these artistic expressions, which had some parallels to the funk inspired b-boying, were not quite the same thing. Thus, it was Williams who developed the first hip hop-based music style on the West Coast. Second, Williams served as an early mentor to and group mate of a young Dr. Dre.[70]

By the end of 1983, studio-band hip hop was dead, and in the Bronx as well as all the other boroughs in New York City, there was a widespread resurgence of hip hop/rap DJs and park jams — *"nobody wanted to see the bands anymore."*[71] In

---

[69] Despite the Studio-Band Period's penchant for a less-than-true approach to the South Bronx-born hip hop, Sylvia Robinson and Sugar Hill Records helped crack open the music industry's doors to hip hop/rap music.

[70] It's worth noting that the group, World Class Wreckin' Cru, which DJ Lonzo Williams headed, also included DJ Yella. In 1986; DJ Yella would go on to make beats and produce with Dr. Dre in the seminal hip hop/rap group N.W.A..

[71] See my interview with Marley Marl, located in the Interviews Part of this study.

fact, during this period there was a hip hop renaissance. B-boying (break dancing or breakin') moved to the forefront like never before, due in large part to Crazy Legs (Richie Colón) and the Rock Steady Crew. Also, graffiti writing, which had previously lost its turf battle with NYC subway administrators, began to see a new surge of expression across the city, especially in the Bronx and Brooklyn. This larger hip hop renaissance coincided with further developments in audio and recording technology, specifically in the area of electronic music production instruments (EMPIs). But it was the new focus on rhyme form and style (within the hip hop renaissance, ca. 1983-1985) that was the most pivotal factor in the further development of the beatmaking tradition.

Standing on the shoulders of Melle Mel, Grandmaster Caz, and Kurtis Blow, rappers began experimenting with more complex rhyme schemes. They were now increasingly pushing the boundaries of the rap form and style, offering up rhymes that were more poetically dense and more rhythmically charged. Rising to the challenge of the more extensively developed rhyme form, DJs, who were now becoming more aware of their role as beatmakers (producers) and other recording professionals (typically studio engineers) began creating sparse, drum track-based compositions that were intended to highlight the lyricism and rhythm of the rappers. And the key to this new beatmaking sound was the electronic drum machine.

Among those at the forefront of the electronic drum beat sound were Larry Smith, DJ Jam Master Jay, and Rick Rubin. In 1983, Larry Smith crafted the two beats that would serve as the instrumental tracks for Run-D.M.C.'s first two records, "It's Like That" and "Sucker M.C.s." Following the success of Run-D.M.C.'s debut single, Larry Smith, joined by Jam Master Jay's assistance on occasion, would continue to drum up hit tracks for Run-D.M.C.

Rick Rubin's first officially acclaimed beat was the instrumental he provided for T La Rock's "It's Yours." But it was with Run-D.M.C. (and later LL Cool J, and then later still The Beastie Boys) that Rick Rubin would distinguish himself as a pioneer in the beatmaking tradition. Here, it should be noted that Rick Rubin was clearly influenced by Larry Smith's earlier work with Run-D.M.C. When Smith produced Run-D.M.C.'s song "Rock Box" (1984), he became the first to fuse hip hop/rap and rock, not Rubin as many wrongly insist. Still, Rick Rubin must be recognized for the individuality that he introduced into the beatmaking lexicon. Drawing on his rock music background, Rubin was perhaps most responsible for popularizing the fusion of rock and hip hop/rap music, a feat that not only hinted at the potential range of the beatmaking tradition, but also at the potential appeal of hip hop/rap music in the mainstream.

In 1985, a seminal event occurred that would establish the core model of modern beatmaking. One day, while in Unique Recording Studio sampling sounds with engineer Arthur Baker, Marley Marl, an intern at Unique at the time, made the revelation that changed the hip hop/rap and beatmaking traditions forever:

> My first step was I got my break-beats up. All the songs I used to hear them cuttin' up...I got my break-beats up. And then after that, I would go out into the park and have my crew rhyme over it. After that...I kind of discovered sampling by accident. That's how I got into looping... **I was getting another part of the record, and we didn't truncate it yet. The snare was there and the vocal. I was playing a beat that I made on the drum machine, and I heard the sampled snare playing with it. Then I realized... I was like, "Yo, I can take any kick and snare from ANY of my break-beat records on how rap *should* sound...**
> I don't know if I would call it hunting for a new sound. **I was trying to make rap sound accurate to what I was brought up on.** That's basically it. I wasn't looking for a new sound... Maybe you could call it looking for a new sound. But I know **the representation of what I was hearing [on the radio at that time] was NOT what I grew up on... hearing on these cassettes...and I just wanted to make it more like the rap that I heard before it hit records.** That was my whole premise of everything. [emphasis mine][72]

Soon after his initial sampling revelation, Marley Marl single-handedly took the beatmaking tradition to another level. Before Marley, there was very little examples of actual sample-based compositions. Although DJs of the Break-Beat Period were, for all intents and purposes, sampling, their use of breaks from records was more of a *virtual* form of sampling. Marley was not only the first to realize the full potential of sampling technology, he was also the first to grasp the complete picture of beatmaking. That is to say, he was the first person to recognize beatmaking as a distinct art form and collective musical process that drew on the foundation and understanding of DJ'ing, sampling skills, and traditional instrumentation.

With the combination of his DJ background and his recording studio knowledge, Marley Marl started diggin through his crates of records for drum sounds and all sorts of musical fragments and phrases; and in the process, he developed a number of fundamental standards in the beatmaking tradition. First, he developed the modern practice of using unique drum sounds. Until Marley, the drum sounds in beats were always of the generic, unmodified stock electronic drum machine variety. In pursuit of a more accurate sound, a more realistic sound and tailor-made sound, Marley sampled actual drum sounds

---

[72] Quote from my interview with Marley Marl.

from the records he learned as both a kid and DJ. He followed this up by using his engineering knowledge to further color and customize these sounds, giving him a sound that was (at first) not easily duplicated.

Second, Marley Marl established the modern method for all sample-based compositions. Marley was the first beatmaker to recognize that *any* piece on a record — not just the break near the middle or end — could be converted to hip hop/rap form. Also, it was Marley who first developed the techniques that would come to be commonly known as "chopping" and "layering." The truncation of sounds had been practiced before, but only with the stock sounds of electronic drum machines. Marley took the concepts of truncation and tuning to a new level, instituting the practice of carving up *any* sound so that it worked correctly in the loop and fit into a desired rhythmic and sonic pattern.

It was also Marley Marl who first instituted the use of whole drum breaks as the primary drum track to a beat. Marley was the first beatmaker to sample entire drum breaks and match them or "lock them up" (without any quantizing — the technology had not yet become common place in EMPIs) with a variety of different types of musical phrases and sound stabs.

Finally, Marley Marl perhaps even had both an indirect and direct role in the birth of the "Miami Bass" sound (or "bass music"), one of the biggest sub-developments to emerge during the Electronic Drum Machine Period:

> I brought the bass to Miami… I was with my [TR] 808 drum machine… I used to be on tour with Shanté; this before Miami had bass! Me and Shanté was doing a show for Luke and Ghetto Style DJs, before he even had 2 Live Crew…. This before they even started their sound! There was no 808s out there; there was not. What I did, I brought my 808 to a show, cuz I used to play live beats while she rhymed. I went up there with my 808, and was [imitates sounds] BOOM… Everybody ran over to the booth like, "What is THAT?" Right away, people was like, "What is that?" I was like, "it's the 808." I brought the bass to Miami… This before these niggas even had the bass. At a Ghetto Style DJs show… Even do the research… bass didn't start hitting them until '85… In '84/'83, I brought the bass to Miami.[73]

It was during this same period that DJ Toomp (of trap music and T.I. fame) first came on the scene. Toomp, who admittedly was very much influenced by Marley Marl (see my interview with him included in this study), worked directly with Luke (of 2 Live Crew fame) right out of high school. After spending some time in Miami, Toomp returned to Atlanta, where by 1994/95, he had already played a role in the development of the "Atlanta-Miami Sound" or more appropriately the "Southern bounce" sound. It would be this sound,

---

[73] *Ibid.*

along with the New Orleans version of bass music, that would go on to serve as the foundation for all of the sounds that collectively defined the "Southern rap sound."

Finally, the Bomb Squad (Hank Shocklee, Eric "Vietnam" Sadler, Keith Shocklee, and Chuck D) must also be recognized for their contributions in the areas of sampling. The Bomb Squad were the first beatmakers to approach sampling not merely as a collage of sound, but instead, an almost indiscriminate wall of sound. The Bomb Squad also helped solidify the "booming" sonic impression that had been brewing in New York production, but had yet to completely materialize prior to 1987.

Summary of the Electronic Drum Machine Period

The Electronic Drum Machine Period can be characterized by several key developments. First, this is the period in which individual drum sounds came alive. The drum sounds of this period were characterized (for the most part) by the preset (generic) drum sounds that where stock in the earliest drum machines. But Marley Marl's use of drum *samples* from various records would change that. The Electronic Drum Machine Period can also be characterized as the period in which the matching of drum breaks to other supplied musical components occurs. Mechanic-like drum patterns and sparse sample-stabs typified the kinds of beats (rhythm tracks) that were made throughout this period. This is also the period in which the 808 sounds are prominently used for the first time. Finally, the Electronic Drum Machine Period represents the period in which the foundation for the modern art of sampling is established.[74]

Pioneers/Avant-Garde Period, 1988-1994

The Pioneers/Avant-Garde Period brought an explosion of new developments in the beatmaking tradition. First, this is the period in which the quintessential self-contained lone beatmaker is typified; and it's during this period that beatmakers begin to gain recognition similar to that of rappers. Next, this is the period in which the beatmaker virtually resurrects the role of the DJ as the sole controller of music for the rapper. In fact, not only is DJ'ing seen as a rite of passage for

---

[74] Key/notable beatmakers and other figures who emerge in this period include: Larry Smith, Rick Rubin, DJ Lonzo Williams, Marley Marl, The Bomb Squad (Hank Shocklee, Eric "Vietnam" Sadler, Keith Shocklee, and Chuck D), DJ Toomp, Grand Mixer DXT, Prince Paul, EZ Mo Bee, Steinski, and Mannie Fresh. Key sub-traditons of hip hop/rap to emerge during this period include: Electro-hop and Miami bass or bass music. (Note. Miami bass stems directly from electro funk, electro-hop, and other elements of early/mid-1980s New York hip hop/rap music.) Key gear of the period: Roland TR 808, E-Mu SP, Technics Turntables.

many of the beatmakers (producers) of this period,[75] the notion of "diggin' in the crates" and having a thorough record collection, the original essence and foundation of the first hip hop/rap DJs, becomes paramount.

It's also during this period that there is a celebration of hip hop/rap's underground heritage and subculture roots. More importantly, there's a return to and reaffirmation of the importance of the use of the break and riffs as source material. Also, this is the period where rhythm and groove once again stand out as the guiding compositional principle in beatmaking. And along with the experimentation of filtered bass lines, drum frameworks become more pronounced and designed to create distinct rhythmic grooves, more often resembling the core drum arrangements of early funk records.

In this period, electronic music production instruments (EMPIs) become critical to a beatmaker's methods and techniques. In fact, there are three key EMPIs that stand out during this period: the Akai S950, the Akai MPC 60 (II), and the E-Mu SP 1200. Further in this vein, updated sampling technology points to the potential for a new direction in hip hop/rap music. During the Pioneers/Avant-Garde Period, pivotal strides in sample and arrangement strategies are made. Furthermore, the use of rare and obscure records for source material characterize the middle of this period.

Also, during the Pioneers/Avant-Garde Period, hip hop/rap music experiences a second art-based renaissance. By 1988, the modern hip hop/rap era was two years old, and hip hop/rap had shifted from a mostly dance-based music to an art-based music that celebrated beats as works of art rather than mere rhythm tracks for rappers to rhyme over. This created the new art/dance duality that continues to underscore hip hop/rap music to this day. Further, it was during the Pioneers/Avant-Garde Period that beatmaking began to distinguish itself as an art form of equal weight to DJ'ing and rapping; in other words, during this period, the beat starts drawing even with the rhyme.

This new development in beatmaking was best personified in 15 noteworthy albums that were released between 1988 and 1994: *It Takes a Nation of Millions to Hold Us Back*; *In Control*; *Critical Beatdown*; *3 Feet High and Rising*; *Peoples Instinctive Travels and the Paths of Rhythm*; *Step In the Arena*; *The Low End Theory*; *Mecca and the Soul Brother*; *Breaking Atoms*; *Daily Operation*; *The Chronic*; *Enter The Wu-Tang (36 Chambers)*; *Midnight Marauders*; *Illmatic*; and *Ready to Die*.

Public Enemy's *It Takes a Nation of Millions to Hold Us Back* (1988) featured the Bomb Squad's signature poly-sample, collage sound. Dense and staunchly

---

[75] Marley Marl, DJ Premier, Pete Rock, Buckwild, Showbiz, DJ Pooh, DJ Quik, and many others all have DJ backgrounds.

rhythmic, sonically aggressive and fresh, the beats on *It Takes a Nation...* amounted to what could best be describe as harmonic chaos. Cuts, ruptures, screeches, voices, breakbeats, and sound-stabs were all intricately blended together into lively, often unpredictable, sound walls.

With *In Control* (1988), the first producer album that featured rappers, Marley Marl surpassed his own innovations and created trends that would become hip hop/rap standards, thereby raising the bar for all beatmakers thereafter. One of the album's songs, "The Symphony," stands out for a number of reasons. It was the first beat to feature all of Marley Marl's innovations: It included his talent for beat juggling, mixing/blending, and cutting; it included both individual drum samples layered over a whole drum break; it included a chop of the front end measure of a soul classic; and it included a haunting 808 drum sound that created a powerful sonic impression. Together, "The Symphony" (now perhaps considered by some to be a simple arrangement) was innovative for its arrangement strategy and its overall sonic composite. "The Symphony" also stands out because it was essentially the first posse cut that included multiple rappers — Masta Ace, Craig G., Kool G Rap, and Big Daddy Kane — who were *not* all in the same rap group but in the same crew.

1988 also gave us the Ultramagnetic M.C.'s album *Critical Beatdown*, which marked the first notable appearance of lesser known but influential beatmaker Paul C. Although not credited for the bulk of *Critical Beatdown*, it's widely understood that Paul C. was responsible for the sound of that album. Paul C. would go on to make beats for Eric B. & Rakim, and he was poised to do work for Biz Markie, Main Source, and others. However, in 1989, he was murdered. He was only 24 years old. Even though Paul C.'s production career was tragically cut short, he left an indelible legacy on the beatmaking tradition through his apprentice, Large Professor.

In 1989, De La Soul dropped *3 Feet High and Rising*, one of the most original, enigmatic, and experimental albums in hip hop/rap history. Largely regarded as one of the most important hip hop/rap albums ever (it helped developed the alternative hip hop/rap subgenre; it introduced the proverbial "rap skit"; and it offered a serious crossover hit), the beatwork on this LP was outstanding. The production, which was decadently sample-based, featured a number of sample-based motifs: More deliberate uses of longer musical fragments; a more streamlined arrangement approach; an emphasis on one primary sample and two or three secondary fragments; more original drum machine programming and less reliance on break-beat frameworks as the main drum pattern. All of these sampling motifs would go on to become common stock among sample-based beatmakers. And in particular, Prince Paul's drum programming work (e.g. "Potholes in My Lawn") and deliberate use of longer musical fragments foreshadowed the direction that the art of sampling would go in during this beatmaking period as well as the major sampling era in general.

In 1990, A Tribe Called Quest released its debut album, *Peoples Instinctive Travels and the Paths of Rhythm*. If Marley Marl hadn't yet made it clear how pivotal individual stylized sampled drum sounds could be to a beat's overall sound, A Tribe Called Quest, lead by Q-Tip's production, emphatically hammered this point home. (**NOTE**: Production credit on A Tribe Called Quest albums never singled out Q-Tip, but instead cited the entire group. That said, it's largely understood that Q-Tip made most of the beats for the group with additional production input from Ali Shaheed Muhammad and Phife Dawg. Further, some people will note that J Dilla produced for A Tribe Called Quest. This is true. However, it must be pointed out that Dilla's involvement with Tribe appears to have taken place after Tribe's first three, and perhaps most distinguishable, albums were already released.) It's on Tribe's debut that we first hear their signature crushing and smacking snare drum. And though this album did not have the musical dexterity of their next two albums, it was clear from the start that A Tribe Called Quest would prove to be very influential in the burgeoning beatmaking tradition.

1991 would prove to be a power year in the beatmaking tradition. First up, Gang Starr released its second album, *Step In The Arena*. This is the album that first hinted that DJ Premier would be a mainstay in the top tier of beatmakers. Drawing from a wealth of knowledge shared by other beatmakers (Large Professor's knowledge of filtering and the importance of deep crates; Showbiz's knowledge of sampling, especially chopping; and Marley Marl's use of the break and distinct drums), DJ Premier crafted one of the most influential art-based, beat driven albums in the history of hip hop/rap music. From the chop patterns and arrangements that he developed, to the pioneering of the "scratch-hook" (still to this day a signature of songs that he produces), DJ Premier pushed the art of beatmaking into another stratosphere. And in 1992, Gang Starr released *Daily Operation*, an album in which DJ Premier, seemingly not content with his accomplishments a year earlier, further laid down the drumwork foundations that would soon lead to his distinct signature sound.

One year after their 1991 debut EP, *All Souled Out*, Pete Rock and CL Smooth dropped their first full length LP, *Mecca and the Soul Brother*. With this album, Pete Rock both demonstrated his dedication to soul source material and established himself as a master drum programmer. Furthermore, just like DJ Premier, A Tribe Called Quest, Large Professor, and The RZA, Pete Rock demonstrated his commitment to a signature drum arrangement and a compositional strategy that sought to balance out the original essence of the hip hop DJ with the commercial (mainstream) and technological realities of the mid-1990s. Finally, Pete Rock set the bar for the "art/dance" duality of beatmaking with the song "They Reminisce Over You (T.R.O.Y.)," one the best hip hop/rap songs ever recorded.

Just one month after *Mecca and the Soul Brother* was released and several months after Gang Starr released *Step In The Arena*, Main Source — Large Professor's former group — released its first and only album, the classic *Breaking Atoms*. Large Professor, who produced every beat, save for one Pete Rock-assisted track ("Vamos a Rapiar"), helped further propel the art-first trend that began to underscore the beatmaking tradition sometime between 1988 and 1990. Large Professor's beatwork on *Breaking Atoms* was an explosive demonstration of "diggin' in the crates" (a phrase that would reemerge during this period) and carefully crafted sampling arrangements.

Two months after Main Source released the Large Professor-anchored *Breaking Atoms*, A Tribe Called Quest put out *The Low End Theory*. On this, their second go-round, Tribe was intent on maintaining their smooth, but hard-hitting drum-driven sound. The song "Check the Rhyme" was clearly built off the momentum that they had developed with "Can I Kick It" and "Bonita Applebum" from their debut. But it should further be noted that Tribe were also obviously bent on showing a much rougher production sound. With cuts like "Scenario" (one of the best posse cuts of all time), "Buggin' Out," and "Verses From the Abstract," Tribe created a formula that blended their colorful bounce sound with an edgier (sometimes more funkier) drum arrangement strategy.

At the end of 1992, Dr. Dre released *The Chronic*. With *The Chronic*, Dre, who by this time had already made a name for himself with N.W.A., introduced a new (some might say ambitious) style and sound, one that sought to use distinct melody lines to compliment fundamental hip hop/rap grooves. Admittedly inspired by P-funk (a sound developed by George Clinton and Parliament, who used late 1970s West Coast funk as their basis), Dre created a unique sound that represented the sum of his various musical experiences and ideas. Using a combination of hard-hitting drums, altered funk rhythms, replays of funk samples, and high-pitched portamento — pitch sliding — sine/saw wave synthesizer lines, Dre became the chief pioneer of the budding southern California G-funk sound. While there's some small dispute about who was first to come up with the G-funk sound, there's no debate as to who was the first to popularize it and take it to new heights — that was Dr. Dre. He in effect made G-funk *his* sound, and in the process he helped lay down the foundation for what is now commonly understood to be the West Coast sound. Because *The Chronic* was released in December of 1992, it had a strong shelf life that lasted well throughout the balance of 1993; a fact that further established the West Coast sound as the new national hip hop/rap sound of the time.

In 1993, A Tribe Called Quest released their third album, *Midnight Marauders*. In their third installment, Tribe delivered their most comprehensive album and ground-breaking beatmaking offering to date. With two albums and four years under their belt, Tribe put together an album that summoned both the best of their prior innovations and their obvious recording studio experience. Cuts like "Sucka Nigga," "Oh My God" (ft. Busta Rhymes), and "Steve Biko (Stir It Up)" display both Tribe's commitment to deeper crate diggin' and the new multi-layer chop strategy that they were using to compose their "gut-tough" rhythm tracks. Then with tracks like "Electric Relaxation, "Award Tour," and "Lyrics to Go," Tribe showed off a new artistic polish of the beatmaking craft, much in the same way that Dr. Dre had demonstrated on *The Chronic*. What's more, on *Midnight Marauders*, Tribe profoundly delivered the new "listening pleasure" component to beats and rhymes that had come to personify the Pioneers/Avant-Garde Period.

Near the end of 1993, the force known as Wu-Tang Clan crashed the hip hop/rap scene with the release of their debut album, *Enter the Wu-Tang (36 Chambers)*. On an album recognized as much (if not more) for the individual Clan rappers who appeared on it as the beats it contained, The RZA orchestrated a designed chaos of soul source material, 1970s karate-flick nuances, and perhaps the darkest, rawest underground sonic composite ever heard at that time, and perhaps thus far. As was the case with his beat pioneering peers, The RZA constructed his own signature drum programming style and sound. At the heart of RZA's drum sound was his time-correctless approach to drum programming. RZA pioneered the technique of capturing the natural feel of drum programming and arrangement, *without* relying heavily (if at all) on the time correct function. RZA must also be specifically recognized for his drums because he is the originator of the off-beat drums swing style. But RZA didn't just do off-beat drums for the sake of it (unlike many beatmakers today who seem to force the style to the detriment of the beat). RZA's off-beat swing (and shuffle) never lost sight of the pocket. That is to say, they held the groove together, which was never a stuck-sounding or mechanical concoction. It's worth noting that J Dilla often gets praise for his off-beat drums. Some go so far as to say that he was the first to use the off-beat drum style. But songs like Wu-Tang Clan's

"Clan in Da Front" (which uses a break-beat phrase) and "Tearz" demonstrate that RZA was already making beats with dragging and off-beat drum rhythms as early as 1992. The RZA's experimentation in the area of drum programming, arrangement, and sampling allowed him to explore ideas that took full advantage of the concepts of rupture, rhythm, and groove; and all of this played a role in his creation of what has appropriately been described as the "Wu-Tang Sound" or simply the "Wu Sound." Finally, it's also worth mentioning that it was both DJ Clark Kent and The RZA who first pioneered the use of sped-up soul samples, not Kanye West. Further, RZA's use of sped-up soul samples was more in a complimentary or "sound wall" role rather than a featured role, as was the case for Kanye West and many of those who followed.

By the middle of 1993, most of the nation's attention had been driven to the popularity of the West Coast sound, spearheaded by Dr. Dre and *The Chronic*. But in 1994, with the release of two more classic hip hop/rap albums, *Illmatic* and *Ready To Die*, the overall focus in both the beatmaking and greater hip hop/rap communities abruptly shifted back to New York. For *Illmatic* (1994), Nas assembled what has been commonly dubbed the first all-star team of producers. The beatwork on *Illmatic* was served up by Large Professor, DJ Premier, Pete Rock, Q-Tip, and DJ L.E.S — all were either approaching or at the beginning of their prime. Taken alone, the lyricism of *Illmatic* was a seminal event. But it was the beats on this album that both appropriately helped illuminate Nas' lyrics and make *Illmatic* not just one of the most memorable hip hop/rap albums of all time, but one of the most creative and intensely poetic albums of twentieth-century popular American music. *Illmatic* would have no doubt been *the* album of 1994 for most (it was for many), had another icon not released his debut album that very same year.

Taking a page from Nas (in more ways than one), several months after the release of *Illmatic,* The Notorious B.I.G., AKA "Biggie Smalls," released his debut album, *Ready To Die*. *Ready To Die* also featured somewhat of an all-star line up of beatmakers: Easy Mo Bee, Chucky Thompson, Poke, DJ Premier, and Lord Finesse. Though not as artistically *far-reaching* as the beatwork that permeated throughout *Illmatic, Ready To Die* did feature a sound strategy that was well-designed for radio and national appeal; even the lone DJ Premier produced track, "Unbelievable," featured an R Kelly assist, albeit via Premier's signature scratch-hook. But in no way was *Ready To Die* completely a jaunt for radio. The meat of the album did feature the sharp East Coast drum style that had recently been established; and the sonic composite of *Ready To Die* was dark, hard hitting, and menacing.

Finally, it's important to mention that during the early/mid- 1990s, beatmaking and hip hop/rap music began (necessarily) to fragment in a way similar to how jazz fragmented into big band, bebop, cool jazz, and later fusion.

This fragmentation laid down the foundations for new styles of hip hop/rap music (styles that were based fundamentally off of the East Coast or West Coast sounds). It's also worth noting that during this period, beats were driven — in large part — by "the listening pleasure" aspect. In other words, much how Western classical music was a music meant for *listening* to and not *dancing* to, beatmaking and hip hop/rap became something that was lauded as much for its listening pleasure as it was for its dancing and partying function.

Summary of the Pioneers/Avant-Garde Period

The Pioneers/Avant-Garde Period is best summarized, first and foremost, as the period in which beatmaking (production) first became a nationally recognized art form, sub-culture, and distinct tradition *within* the broader hip hop/rap art form, culture, and tradition. In fact, it's during this period that the beatmaking tradition essentially explodes and becomes more codified, particularly in terms of styles, methods, terminology, and gear usage. This is also the period wherein beatmakers first become more recognized figures in their own right. Also, in many ways, the Pioneers/Avant-Garde Period represents the manifestation of the DJ within the beatmaker. During this period, there's a fundamental return to and reaffirmation of the importance of the use of the break and the rhythm and groove as the guiding principle in beatmaking. Furthermore, this period is also characterized by the extensive development of the techniques first established by Marley Marl. Finally, it should be recognized that the beatwork of the Pioneers/Avant-Garde Period (specifically the 15 noteworthy albums singled out in this section) provided the blueprint for modern beatmaking and hip hop/rap production.

Among all the various developments that took place throughout the Pioneers/Avant-Garde Period, there are six critical developments worth pointing out. First, the art of sampling is explored and expanded way beyond marks previously imagined. In this period, sound-stabs and horn phrases become common place, and there is an extensive use of bass filtering. Second, the scratch-hook becomes a major staple of hip hop/rap songs. Third, Dr. Dre, introduces the first "orchestral-like," broad-based sound to hip hop music production. Fourth, the emphasis on *the mix* as an equally important production process is realized during this period — A Tribe Called Quest, DJ Premier, The RZA, and Dr. Dre stand out in this regard. Fifth, the modern New York sound or East Coast sound reaches its zenith, drawing even with the West Coast sound, which had reached its own plateau earlier during the same period. Finally, it's during the Pioneers/

Avant-Garde Period that beatmaking drum frameworks begin to emulate those of soul and funk records; this move would further increase hip hop/rap music's use of common song structure.[76]

Post-Pioneers Period, 1995-2000

Fresh off all of the strides that were made in the Pioneers/Avant-Garde Period, the Post-Pioneers Period begins in 1995 with the new well-codified New York sound poised to reign supreme. Barely two short years into the period, Mobb Deep, Raekwon, and Jay-Z all release classic albums — each album strongly reinforcing the New York sound and feel. However, by the second half of this period, things would begin to change.

The latter half of the Post-Pioneers Period really represents a period of inevitable change in both the hip hop/rap and beatmaking traditions. The first noticeable change was the dramatic new interest in beatmaking. In 1997, the beatmaking tradition got its first big surge of new interest, due in no small part to EMPI maker Akai. 1997 was the year Akai introduced the MPC 2000, a monster of an EMPI that Akai aggressively marketed to the burgeoning hip hop/rap production world, making beatmaking instantly accessible to more people at one time than ever before. Thus, the new interest in beatmaking, coupled with the advent of the Akai MPC 2000 (an EMPI soon to become an important stable in late-90s hip hop/rap production), the sheer number of beatmakers increased dramatically. By the last quarter of the 1990s, the beatmaking tradition is no longer a small, little-known about subculture, it's a phenomenon that's gaining new steam in the United States and around the world.

The second noticeable change of the second half of the Post-Pioneers Period was that most of the new beatmakers in the late '90s went straight into beatmaking, bypassing the DJ stage, which was once considered a rite of passage in the previous two beatmaking periods. This was a significant change because it assured that for the first time in hip hop/rap's history, there would be a generation of beatmakers that was dominated by those *without* DJ backgrounds, a critical link to the foundation of hip hop/rap music.

The third significant change that takes hold during this period is the beginning of the end of the sampling-major era. After the criminalization of the art of sampling, brought on in large part by the landmark *Grand Upright*

---

[76] Key/notable beatmakers and other figures who emerge or appear in this period include: Marley Marl, DJ Toomp, DJ Premier, Erick Sermon, Prince Paul, Dr. Dre, Buckwild, The Beatnuts, No I.D., Havoc, D.R. Period, DJ Quik, and The Hitmen. Key sub-traditons or styles of hip hop/rap to emerge during this period: G-funk and "hardcore" hip hop/rap. Key gear of the period: Akai S950, Akai MPC 60 II, E-Mu SP1200, Ensoniq ASR-10, Akai MPC 3000.

v. Warner case, the use of sampling as a primary compositional method in beatmaking begins to decline. Furthermore, because many new beatmakers have a lack of interest in or access to DJ'ing, the art of sampling slowly begins to lose ground as a core compositional method. At the same time, there are increasing commercial (pop) influences that are pushing even some of the veteran beatmakers (producers) away from sampling and into other compositional methods.

The move away from sampling led to the fourth significant change of this period: The increased usage of keyboard or synth-based beats that feature little to no sampling. At this time, hip hop/rap music is beginning to become more national than regional, and although it's not as national as it would become by the late 2000s, many new beatmakers are not necessarily deferring to the art of sampling, but rather being drawn to the appeal of two new creative sounds emanating from beatmakers like Timbaland and The Neptunes. Seemingly overnight, this very noticeable shift away from the art of sampling opens up an entirely new beatmaking lane.

Around this same time, hip hop/rap music is beginning to return to its party roots. With the appearance of the Puffy "shiny suits" and the "Jiggy" era, the party trend appears to rise at the expense of the art. However, it should be noted that even though sampling is on the decline and the party scene is on the rise, beatmakers (producers) such as Timbaland, The Neptunes, and Dame Grease all keep the notion of art at the forefront of their production sounds. Finally, by the end of the Post-Pioneers Period, there appears to be a pushback against the tone and mood of the national sound of hip hop/rap music. This pushback sparks a new sampling renaissance that's led by J Dilla, Kanye West, Madlib, and Just Blaze.

Summary of the Post-Pioneers Period

Beatmakers of the Post-Pioneers Period were the first group of beatmakers to directly benefit from the massive blueprint that was constructed by those of the Pioneers-Avant-Garde Period. Thus, it's no surprise that during the Post-Pioneers Period, there were a number of important strides made in the beatmaking tradition. It's during this period that the synthetic-sounds-based style (more commonly known as "keyboard beats") is born. This is important, as it represents the first sound in beatmaking that primarily uses synthetic or so-called "live" sounds, as oppose to traditional samples, while still attempting to remain true to some of the fundamental tenets of the overall hip hop/rap form and style. Production duos and teams become an important new development during this period, no doubt inspired by the success of The Neptunes. Finally, it's during this period wherein the beatmaking culture begins to become one of the most racially/ethnically integrated subcultures in hip hop.[77]

The Southern Bounce Period, 2001-2004

The Southern Bounce Period marks the beginning of the dominance of the Southern rap sound in the United States. During this period, sampling is marginalized more than any other time in the history of beatmaking.[78] Also, although the basic form of rhythm and repetition are left in tact, it's during this period that the hip hop/rap compositional ethic and form undergo their most obviously pop/traditional music-influenced changes yet. During this period, the number of changes or "switch-ups" and "sweeps" in a typical beat increase within arrangements, and bridges, intros, and choruses become more pronounced and elaborate.

During this period there is also somewhat of a diminishing interest in customized or signature drum sounds and drum frameworks. Actually, during the Southern Bounce Period, the use of stock/preset drum sounds become commonplace; and drum patterns, based on the use of claps instead of snares, become rather prevalent. Furthermore, extra heavy syncopation, particularly of the stutter hi-hat, kick drum, and snare variety, coupled with the 808 boom and kick, become somewhat of a standard.

Next, while the Southern bounce sound was clearly on its way to becoming the national hip hop/rap sound, another renaissance, one based on the New York sound of the mid-90s, begins to take shape. Beginning with Jay-Z's album *The Blueprint* (2001), Kanye West and Just Blaze established themselves as both sampling aficionados and commercial realists. Balancing the differences of artistic integrity and commercial viability, the pair go about developing sample-based sounds that are respectfully obscure, but not too terribly arcane or intricate that it pushes away non-fans of sampling. This new sound of theirs is even more conducive to additional live instrumentation. And around the same time

---

[77] Key/notable beatmakers and other figures who emerge or appear in this period include: DJ Premier, Timbaland, Just Blaze, Kanye West, Dame Grease, The Alchemist, The Neptunes, J Dilla, Swizz Beatz, Lil' Jon, Mel-Man, Dr. Dre, Focus, Madlib, Mannie Fresh, DJ Shadow, Megahertz, Erick Sermon, Rockwilder, and DJ Toomp. Key gear of the period: Akai MPC 2000XL, Korg Triton, Korg Trinity, Roland Fantom, and Akai MPC 3000.

[78] This period marks the first time in the history of beatmaking that a number of hip hop/rap beatmakers began to make accusations that sampling isn't creative or original — this is a direct assault on the fundamental roots of hip hop/rap music and the beatmaking tradition. Moreover, it demonstrates a lack of respect for and understanding of the richness of the beatmaking tradition in its entirety.

that Just Blaze (influenced in some ways by Bink) and Kanye West latch on to their new sounds, Swizz Beatz finds his own sound — after perhaps having seen the advantages of the "middle ground" and, more importantly, studying Dame Grease's style and sound and seeing the successful direction of Just Blaze and Kanye West. But unlike Just Blaze and Kanye West, Swizz Beatz's sound is not based upon sampling, but instead ynthetic-based (live) sounds. Still, this push from Just Blaze, Kanye West, and Swizz Beatz can't stop the force that is the Southern bounce at this time. And when it comes to the best of Southern bounce or trap music sound, there is no one beatmaker (producer) more responsible for popularizing it than DJ Toomp. A long-established veteran DJ and beatmaker (producer), DJ Toomp is one of the chief architects and pioneers of the trap music sound, a sound that would come to personify much of what could be described as "the Sound of Atlanta." It should also be noted that this is the period in which Lil Jon comes to major prominence through the use of a three-chord signature synth sound.

Interestingly enough, the Southern Bounce Period also marks the beginning of the all software-based production setups. Even though the mighty Akai MPC 4000 is introduced during this period (2002) and the Roland Fantom series is still in its prime, new software applications like Proellerhead's Reason, and Image-Lines Fruity Loops (now FL Studio) become the chosen production tools of many beatmakers.

Summary of the Southern Bounce Period

The Southern Bounce Period signals the start of three important developments in the beatmaking tradition. First, it is during this period that a noticeably "synth-heavy" sound is established. As sampling is marginalized as a compositional method, many beatmakers take to using groups of synthetic (live) sounds as the basis for their beats. There is debate as to why the synth-heavy sound gains ground during this period. On one hand, the sample clearance issue certainly pushed many veteran beatmakers away from sampling and dissuaded some newcomers from even considering the method. On the other hand, one could argue that the trends of the time influenced many beatmakers to move towards the synth-heavy sound. Still, it might be argued that as a disconnect from veteran beatmakers to new beatmakers broke down, so went the relationship of veterans sharing important knowledge with rookies; subsequently, rookie beatmakers made do with the EMPIs and information that was available at the time. No doubt all three factors (and several more, including the advent of ringtones as a new major source of revenue for music-makers) contributed to the rise of the synth-heavy sound.

Second, during the Southern Bounce Period there are some noticeable changes in composition methods and arrangement strategies. During this period, the increased use of melody begins to stand out. Furthermore, while rhythm and repetition still remain in tact (for the most part), the concept of linear progression starts to gain importance in the work of some notable beatmakers.[79] Again, it is during this period that the number of "changes" within an arrangement increase; and in many cases, other arrangements constructions (e.g., bridges and the like) become more pronounced and elaborate.

Finally, the Southern Bounce Period marks the start (perhaps not ironically) of a somewhat populist return to sampling. In the beginning of 2004, at the end of the Post-Pioneers Period, Kanye West releases his debut album, *College Dropout*. Both a critic's choice and a commercial success, *College Dropout*, which features very pronounced and straight forward sample-based beats (perhaps Kanye's deliberate alternative to Southern bounce), helped spark a new popular interest in sampling.[80]

Retro-Eclectic Period, 2005-2009

The Retro-Eclectic Period is a period marked by an eclectic mix of both a return to some of the elements of beatmaking's earlier periods and the incorporation of a number of non-hip hop/rap compositional influences. Off the success of Kanye West in 2004, sampling gains a new audience, and a number of key sample-based beatmakers capitalize off of the seemingly sudden interest and appreciation for sampling. But whatever strides sampling has been able to gain (or regain) in the Retro-Eclectic Period, the other big development during the same time is that the use of melody has gained a new foothold.

The Retro-Eclectic Period also marks a heightened use of non-hip hop/rap compositional influences. In the past, if and when melody was used in hip hop/rap, it was always used in a subordinate role. But during the Retro-Eclectic Period, melody takes on a more prominent role. Furthermore, in this period, the

---

[79] A lot of the new interest in melody and progession can be attributed to the commercial success of beatmakers like Scott Storch (ex-keyboardist for The Roots), and to an increasing number of new beatmakers who enter into beatmaking with Western classical-trained music backgrounds.
[80] Key/notable beatmakers and other figures who emerge or appear in this period include: DJ Toomp, Lil Jon, Scott Storch, Jazze Pha, Just Blaze, Kanye West, Swizz Beatz, Timbaland, The Neptunes, J Dilla, Mel-Man, Dr. Dre, Madlib, Alchemist, DJ Premier, Mannie Fresh.
Key gear of the period: Akai MPC 4000, Roland Fantom, Akai MPC 3000, Reason (by Propellerhead), Recycle (by Propellerhead), and Fruity Loops (by Image-Lines).

concept of linear progression or material growth is increasingly gaining interest among various beatmakers. This trend is particularly curious (if not alarming), as such concepts are actually *counterintuitive* to the hip hop/rap form and the fundamental tenets of its tradition.

The Retro-Eclectic Period also represents the first beatmaking period where the majority of new beatmakers *start off* with software-based production setups. Prior to this period, the majority of new beatmakers entered into the tradition using hardware-based production setups. This trend began to change during the Southern Bounce Period, and it's reversed in the Retro-Eclectic Period. After beatmaker (producer) 9th Wonder garnered critical acclaim and commercial success working from a software-based production setup (Fruity Loops), many new beatmakers followed his path. (It's worth noting that 9th Wonder switched to hardware, first an Akai MPC and the Native Instruments Maschine). Moreover, software beatmaking tools became even more inexpensive, which made them more accessible to the average person interested in beatmaking. Throw in the fact that software EMPIs are much more mobile, and in some cases more flexible than hardware EMPIs, and it was inevitable that software-based setups would increase in popularity.

Finally, one development that continued on into the Retro-Eclectic Period is the general inclusiveness of the beatmaking tradition. Of all of the sub-elements and subcultures of hip hop, beatmaking, like graffiti, continues to be the most ethnically and racially inclusive. In fact, more ethnic groups and races are now involved in beatmaking (both professionals and hobbyists) more than any of the four original elements of hip hop combined.

Summary of the Retro-Eclectic Period

What makes the Retro-Eclectic Period particularly unique is the amount of cross-fertilzation of styles from the different previous beatmaking periods. During this period, there has been as much of a noticeable return to some of the compositional trends of the Electronic Drum Machine Period as there has been to some of the developments made during the Pioneers/Avant-Garde Period. But things have not all been nostalgic. In fact, in many ways, the Retro-Eclectic Period further confirms the Southern bounce sound (and its peripheral styles), as the national beatmaking sound. And while there's been a return to minimalism, there's also been more development in the area of arrangement, particularly when it comes to the concept of linear progression or material growth. In this period, there was a widespread attempt by many beatmakers to *conform* the hip hop/rap compositional approach — style and form — to the styles and compositional approaches of other forms of popular music, instead of reaffirming hip hop/rap's own tradition. Finally, as these high levels of cross-fertilization persist during a time where audio and recording technology is all but making the beats for some beatmakers, the question remains: What role will beatmakers allow technology to play in their fundamental compositional processes?[81]

Trap Based/Performance-Experimental Period, 2009-2015

In many ways, the Trap Based/Performance-Experimental Period Period, the beatmaking period currently in play at the time of this publication, is a broad continuation of the Southern Bounce Period. In this period, trap based beats — that mostly build off of the trap music tropes and themes first popularized by DJ Toomp and later Shawty Redd — become the dominant sound. And within this trap based continuum, two approaches emerge: The minimalist approach and the broad orchestral approach. The minimalist approach features sparsely made beats that mostly rely on 808 sounds and bare-bones drum frameworks. The broad orchestral approach features the familiar trap sound — i.e. 808 drums and percussion, Synth tubas and other synth brass — along with some sampled elements and additional instrumentation, usually elements found in urban dance or mainstream pop trends that run parallel to this period.

Besides the utter dominance of trap, performance-experimentalism also marks this period. A growing number of beatmakers, notably Araab Muzik and Flying Lotus, take to live performance, demonstrating their beatmaking skills in front of audiences in real time. At the same time, there's a growing number of beat battles and producer showcases, wherein a new type of focus is given to beat instrumentals. Within this climate, an increasing number of beatmakers create beats that are intended for battles and showcases rather than for use in traditional rap songs. In other words, a number of beatmakers in this period take to making beats that have little to no room for vocals.

While the concept of linear progression or material growth continued to be a feature of this period, it should be noted that this concept takes on a deeper hip hop connection. In this regard, traditional sampling approaches remain, but

---

[81] Key/notable beatmakers who stood out or emerged during this period include: Danjahandz, Don Cannon, Jake One, Black Milk, Keak Da Sneak, Droop-E, Alchemist, Marco Polo, Statk Selektah. Sub-traditions to emerge during this period: hyphy. Key gear of the period: Reason (by Propellerhead), Recycle (by Propellerhead), FL Studio (formerly Fruity Loops by Image-Lines), Akai MPC 1000, Akai MPC 4000, Akai MPC 3000, Akai MPC 2000XL.

increasingly beatmakers are using their sampling skills to repurpose stock sounds in software and hardware EMPIs, rather than relying on pre-recorded songs as primary source material. This has created a new kind of diggin in the crates experience for many beatmakers, where one is mining the vast sound libraries of EMPIs and sound packs, which include a number of ever-growing sounds and vintage plug-ins. Right now, Marco Polo is the leading beatmaker (producer) in this vein. But I expect more beatmakers to take up the same charge in future beatmaking periods, especially given the sampling capabilities and sound libraries found in the likes of Native Instrument's Kontakt and Komplete series.

Software EMPIs like Ableton Live, Reason, and FL Studio, and Kontakt and Komplete maintain a high profile in the Trap Based/Performance-Experimental Period, but hardware EMPIs still remain as stalwarts; and hardware/software hybrid EMPIs like the Maschine by Native Instruments and the Akai MPC Renaissance emerge as popular go-to production units for many beatmakers in this period.

Finally, while trap dominates this period and performance-experimentalism carves out its own small niche, what appears on the horizon is yet another sampling revival. With the emergence and popularity of millenial rappers like Joey Bada$$, who conjures memories of '90s style sample-based music, and Mac Miller's early success with '90s style sample-based beats, a number of new, teenage beatmakers have taken to the art of sampling and, for the most part, have rejected the trap based style and sound.

Summary of the Trap Based/Performance-Experimental Period[82]

This period does not stand out for its uniqueness. On the contrary, with so much trap parity and little distinction from one trap based hit song to the next, the Trap Based/Performance-Experimental Period stands out because of how much of this dominant sound mimicks itself. Compare this to the Pioneers/Avant-Garde Period, a period that featured a collective sampling aesthetic as a whole, but nonetheless a period that held for a broader space of interpretation of the aesthetic itself. I believe that one important reason for this is due to the nature of a beatmaker working with different pre-recorded songs as source

---

[82] Key/notable beatmakers who stood out or emerged during this period include: Shawty Redd, Lex Luger, Bangladesh, Harry Fraud, S1 (Symbolic One), Flying Lotus, Boi-1da, Noah "40" Shebib, Mike Will Made-It, Jahlil Beats, J.U.S.T.I.C.E. League, T-Minus, Knxwledge, Metro Boomin. Sub-traditions to emerge during this period: slump, boom trap. Key gear of the period: Maschine (by Native Instruments), Reason (by Propellerhead), Recycle (by Propellerhead), Kontakt and Komplete (by Native Instruments) FL Studio (by Image-Lines), Akai MPC 2500, Akai MPC 1000, Akai MPC 4000, Akai MPC 3000, Akai MPC 2000XL, Akai MPC Renaissance.

material. On the other hand, the core component (the engine really) of the trap sound is the 808 aesthetic, which because of its limited number of sounds and familiar programming, it naturally lends itself to duplication, including everything from arrangement scopes, drum frameworks, percussion structures, and general style and sound. Thus, trap based music benefits from and relies on familiarity — one knows the style, sound, and aesthetic; it's unmistakable. But the very thing that makes trap popular and easy to emulate right now is also the same thing that makes it susceptible to duplication and a surplus of beats that fail to stand out.

As for the performance-experimental component of this period, I believe some conceptual strides have been made. But I don't believe that the live performance of beats alone will be a sustainable model for beatmakers in future beatmaking periods. Finally, as with the Retro-Eclectic Period before it, within the Trap Based/Performance-Experimental Period, there continues to be high levels of cross-fertilization. Yet, there has also been a renewed focus on sampling and minimalism in various pockets of the beatmaking tradition of hip hop/rap music.

Conclusion of the Eight Periods (or Eras) of the Beatmaking Tradition: Three Modern Production Sounds

There are three modern production sounds that have emanated from the first eight beatmaking periods: (1) The East Coast rap sound, also known as the New York rap sound; (2) The West Coast rap sound; and (3) The Southern rap sound (Southern bounce sound).

The traditional East Coast/New York rap sound is best characterized by the art of the dig and the chop. That is to say, the East Coast/New York rap sound features the unique truncation of record samples (usually from arcane records), obscure sounds, and heavy (often dark) drum sounds and heavy-hitting drum patterns. The East Coast/New York rap sound is also characterized by thick filtered bass lines, and straight-forward 2-bar loops. Finally, it's worth mentioning that of the three main production sounds, the traditional East Coast or New York rap sound remains the one sound most dedicated (or conducive) to the use of extensive or complex lyricism.

The West Coast rap sound is an amalgamation of late 1970s West Coast funk and some elements of the East Coast/New York rap sound. The West

Coast rap sound is perhaps best characterized by a collage of heavy moog-like bass lines, live instrumentation, and record samples. Also, in contrast to the heavy chop-and-loop sound of New York, the West Coast Sound is much more orchestral and laid back; it's more open ended than the New York Sound, as it also features melody in a more prominent role than the East Coast/New York rap sound.

Finally, the Southern rap sound, which is based fundamentally on a Miami bass-"Atlanta sound" hybrid with early 1980s New York undertones, is characterized by stutter drums and heavy bass lines. The Southern rap sound actually carries two opposing styles: One style that is sparse with simple keyboard melodies, and another style that is rather dense — conceptually, structurally, and texturally. The latter style includes more extensive melody motives and chromatic harmony accompaniment. Both of these styles, however, still feature the 808 drum aesthetic and heavily syncopated snare, hi-hat, and kick patterns.

Part 2
TECHNICAL BEATDOWN (INSTRUCTION)

DISCLAIMER: **About The Matter of Success or Failure in Beatmaking**
There are a number of reasons that contribute to the success or failure of beatmakers. Truth is, only a small number of beatmakers ultimately reach a high level of commercial success; most have a more real chance at critical acclaim than vast riches. In either case, a beatmaker's development of their own unique style and sound is important. And for this to effectively take place, there are many factors each beatmaker must consider. For instance, what kind of person are you? Are you very organized, disciplined, and forthright? Or are you disorganized, undisciplined, and prone to procrastination? Do you have a good base knowledge of music? Does this knowledge span over multiple music genres and moments in music history? Do you use a hardware- or software-based production setup or? Do you use a classic (vintage) setup or contemporary electronic instruments and pro audio equipment? Do you prefer sampling or utilizing traditional live instrumentation processes? All of these questions are critical aspects of making beats. To that end, this Part of *The BeatTips Manual* examines all of the essential (and not-so obvious) aspects of beatmaking. Finally, it should be noted that the primary aim of this Part of the book is to help beatmakers identify and manipulate the various aesthetics that are critical to creating and developing their own unique production styles and sounds.

Chapter 4

Gear and Sound Fundamentals
Understanding Production Setups, EMPIs, Sounds, and Other Prerequisite Factors

Production Setup Choices and Why They're Made

A Production Setup Defined

A "production setup" or "setup" is simply a wholesale term used to describe all of the gear and equipment that producers use to make their beats; it's where the drums, bass, piano/keyboards, strings, brass, and effects come from. Setups are characterized as hardware, software, or hybrid. They can further be distinguished by all-in-one types of setups, i.e. workstations, production centers, etc. Setups are made up of their base (primary pieces) and their support (secondary pieces). Because beatmakers are self-contained composers who generally create, arrange, and perform all of their music by themselves, we all use a setup of some sort.

The Hardware/Software Debate

Though beatmakers choose hardware- or software-based production setups for generally the same reason: functionality, they often choose a particular EMPI — hardware or software — because of the advantages that each piece potentially presents. Thus, in this section, I'll discuss the commonly expressed fundamental pros and cons of either hardware- or software-based production setups.[83] But before getting into a comparative analysis of hardware- and software-based setups, it's important to point out that the hardware vs. software debate is actually very misleading.

---

[83] There is a timbrel quality associated with hardware units. That is, each unit produces a certain sound (color) that is only characteristic to itself. It's further worth noting that though hardware actually relies on software (i.e., it's internal operating system), it gives the feel and perception of using a traditional instrument. Therefore, hardware EMPIs are non-traditional instruments that give a link to traditional instruments, much like synthesizers and electronic keyboards give a link to the piano.

Regardless of the production setup, no two setups can ever be the exact same for any two people, nor can any EMPI be the exact same to another. But are there some comparable functions in let's say an Akai MPC and FL Studio? Sure. But the functions of a hardware or software EMPI is an entirely different notion than how an individual beatmaker *works* with hardware or software. To be certain, each of our individual musical expressions is pragmatic in nature. And although we often find ways to challenge ourselves, we are still essentially working off of set, subjective ideas about making music. Therefore, musical expression is much more about one's individual feeling about music and the role technology plays in the compositional process; it's less about any allegiance to a piece of hardware or software application. So the more attention we invest in additional (perhaps unnecessary) processes, the less attention we actually pay to infusing the feeling that we ultimately want to express musically.

Another reason why the hardware vs. software debate is misleading is because the decision to use hardware or software should never be about what hardware or software can do (arbitrarily); it should be about how the hardware and software enables you to *react* to and work with it. For example, some beatmakers choose a hardware EMPI because it provides them with a link back to a music-making tradition — a tradition, it must be added, that figures heavily in the psyche of their beatmaking process. On the other hand, some beatmakers choose a software EMPI because it simply makes their musical process more flexible. In either case, the hardware/software debate is mute. The real point is about how effectively hardware and/or software enables you to make the musical expressions that you intend to create. That being said, below is a brief outline of the commonly expressed advantages and disadvantages of hardware and software EMPIs.

Advantages and Disadvantages of Hardware

There are three fundamental advantages that are typically associated with hardware EMPIs: (1) hands-on feel; (2) quick workflow/immediacy;[84] and (3) a link to tradition. Of all the reasons that beatmakers cite as their preference for using hardware EMPIs, the hands-on factor is the one beatmakers raise the most. "Hands-on," an often ambiguous and misunderstood term, simply describes the traditional physicality that hardware EMPIs offer beatmakers. Hardware EMPIs physically give beatmakers the sense that they are not simply programming music, but playing it as well.

---

[84] **Workflow** is the pace, mood, speed, and overall level of efficiency of how a piece of gear and/or production setup enables you to operate. Certain pieces of gear or setups can constrain workflow, just as certain pieces of gear or setups can expedite and ease up workflow.

The quick workflow or immediacy factor of hardware EMPIs refers to how relatively fast hardware allows beatmakers to work out their musical ideas. For many hardware users, the prep-time — the amount of time needed for even the most basic procedures — often associated with software is too much of a hassle. Because of the rather quick workflow associated with hardware, many beatmakers are able to work on (create) multiple beats at just one sitting. But speed of workflow can be subjective, as ome beatmakers are more comfortable working within a software environment.

Finally, for many beatmakers, hardware EMPIs provide a much sought after link to the past, specifically, the classic periods of the beatmaking tradition. Though Software-based setups are no longer relatively new, they don't offer the same sense of connection to earlier beatmaking periods. Thus, for many beatmakers, hardware EMPIs offer a connection to the techniques, methods, and processes of an earlier time; and when it really comes down to it, this connection (real or perceived) plays a significant role in the musical psyche of many hardware users.

As for the disadvantages commonly associated with hardware EMPIs, there are three: (1) cost; (2) less flexibility; and (3) lack of mobility. Hardware EMPIs are often considerably more expensive than software applications that purport to do the same thing. Hardware EMPIs cost gear makers much more to manufacture than their software counterparts, and therefore, they're usually more expensive. Another commonly associated disadvantage of hardware is its supposed lack of flexibility. Although all EMPIs are made compatible through MIDI, Software EMPIs usually have more flexibility, as they tend to include more functions, more sounds, and *access* to more sounds. Finally, hardware EMPIs are less mobile than software alternatives.

Advantages and Disadvantages of Software

There are three fundamental advantages that are typically associated with software EMPIs: (1) accessibility; (2) flexibility; and (3) mobility. If beatmaking is indeed the most accessible gateway to music composition for the ordinary man, then software EMPIs represent the most accessible means to this gateway. Software EMPIs are much more accessible to people for various reasons. First, software programs are usually less expensive than hardware EMPIs. In fact, most software programs offer free downloadable demo versions. Second, the availability of software EMPIs overshadows the often limited availability of hardware EMPIs. Software EMPIs are also quite flexible, and they outshine hardware alternatives in the area of the sheer number of available stock sounds; but hybrid EMPIs like the MPC Renaissance and Native Instrument's Maschine have leveled the playing field. Finally, software EMPIs are more mobile than hardware alternatives; and they can be operated on any laptop computer. This allows beatmakers to make music on the go.

But for all of the advantages that software seems to promise, there are some disadvantages or hazards that are commonly associated with software EMPIs. First, software EMPIs can, for some, present a disconnect from the culture and historical force of the hip hop/rap and beatmaking traditions. Such a disconnect can lead to an overly synthetic sound. Moreover, here, it should be pointed out that software EMPIs are fundamentally designed to simply facilitate (simulate) the mechanical steps of beatmaking. They are not designed to stand alone, or to give the physical instrument dimension that hardware offers. Though beats can be made using software and a computer keyboard alone, most beatmakers who use software-based setups often use hardware gear, such as keyboard controllers and/or drum pad controllers. Perhaps this is because without additional hardware components like keyboard controllers or drum pad controllers, which, in effect, convert software EMPIs to hardware EMPIs, the traditional physical sense of *playing* an instrument is lost.

There is also another type of disconnect that can occur with software EMPIs: Software EMPIs can induce a click-fix approach to making beats. This means that software EMPIs can foster a persona of *clicking* a beat rather than *creating* one. In this way, a software "click-fix" approach can be far too formulaic, placing much emphasis on seeing the digital numeration of music rather than feeling (seeing) the visual imagination of music. Never under estimate the difference between looking at the music on a screen in front of you, as opposed to seeing the music in the wide open space of your mind. It should always be remembered that the musical process is commanded, in large part, by emotion and mood. Sometimes, by the nature of the process of making beats *exclusively* through software, there can be a disconnect from this fundamental understanding. That said, all gear is nothing more than a vessel that serves at the mercy of your creativity and will to express your ideas.

Another hazard (not necessarily a disadvantage) of software EMPIs is the fact that their sound architecture is typically bright, clean, and extremely clear. Most software EMPIs are not designed to account for hip hop/rap's fundamental preference of lower frequencies and vintage sound. However, some software EMPIs have addressed this issue by including sound packs that simulate these types of prioritized sounds. Also, software EMPIs don't "color" the sounds that are input within them; unlike hardware EMPIs, software programs don't carry unique timbrel signatures. The sounds of software EMPIs are primarily stereo quality at 24bit sampling rate. So in other words, the sounds are characterless and flat. But this problem is often addressed through the use of software plug-ins and/or external hardware sound processors.

Hardware/Software Debate Summary

In the final analysis, the hardware/software *question* is not about which is better, but *which is better for you*. Each beatmaker has different aesthetic priorities and, more importantly, different technological and musical sensibilities. These differences are what ultimately determine whether or not a hardware- or software-based setup is right for any us. Plus, the reality is that hardware EMPIs are very reliant upon internal software; likewise most software-based setups actually work best with hardware EMPIs.

Musicians don't deal in infinite realms of creativity. By that I mean, we ALL develop our own fundamental likes and dislikes; from these we establish our own compositional platforms that we use to express ourselves musically. Hence, no beatmaker typically attempts to tap into *100%* of the capabilities of any given EMPI. Why? Because it's impractical and counterproductive to our rather straight-forward musical goals.

Finally, it's worth noting that in moving from hardware to software EMPIs, there is the reference-point factor. That is, those beatmakers who go from hardware to software have an entirely different reference point than those beatmakers who go from software to hardware. Take DJ Toomp, For example; a veteran well-known beatmaker (producer) who can create dope sample-based and non-sampled based beats. What Toomp can do with a software EMPI is different than someone who's only used software EMPIs before. This is because Toomp is *referencing* his own techniques and sound that he's developed over the years through his use of hardware EMPIs (in particular the Akai MPC 60 II, E-Mu SP 1200, and the Roland Fantom). Thus, *starting off* with a software EMPI rather than a hardware EMPI, means you'll lack the same sort of reference to draw upon. This might explain some of the initial distance between some beatmakers who begin with hardware EMPIs and those who begin with software EMPIs. But in either case, eventually experience and knowledge of the beatmaking tradition proves to be the equalizer. Therefore, make no mistake: Quality beats can be made using *either* a hardware or software setup. Whichever you choose ultimately comes down to the type of beatmaker you are or want to be.

BeatTip – Feel, Nuance, Individual Needs, and Approach Holds the Answer

When it comes to the musical instruments or gear that you use, you have to feel good about the instruments that you're using to make your music. Regardless of what anyone might try to convince you of, the way you feel about your gear translates directly (and indirectly) into the music that you make. Remember, creating music is more psychological than it is physical.

As for software gear options, certainly software programs are capable of achieving the technical steps. But achieving the nuances, in this case, a boom bap feel and such, is another dimension. Can the nuances of boom bap be achieved with software-based setups? I believe so. But how are these nuances captured using software as opposed to hardware? That's the critical question. Someone with a background on a storied hardware piece of equipment like an Akai MPC, an E-Mu SP 1200, or an Ensoniq ASR-10 is more likely to capture that nuance differently when they switch to let's say Reason or Ableton Live or Pro Tools (and perhaps even the Maschine) than someone without a background with those standalone hardware instruments.

I have experience with Reason and I understand its flexibility and its appeal. I also think that Ableton Live is a terrific software EMPI that my workflow would translate well to. But I still prefer my MPC 4000 because I like the feeling that it gives me. My production setup makes me feel more like a musician; it also makes me feel connected to history, the present, and teh future. Software, on the other hand, also makes me feel like a musician to a degree, but I can't deny that it sometimes makes me feel more computer programmer than musician (even though my MPC relies on an internal computer and operating system).

Thing is, I just turn on my MPC and I just start playing. That's native to me. I don't get the same feeling with software. But I know that there are many people who do connect with software-based setups in the same manner that I connect with hardware; for them, software is native. Incidentally, that's one reason why the Akai MPC Renaissance and Native Instrument's Maschine is quite popular. Both offer a bridge between a hardware instrument and a software environment. There are tremendous advantages to that setup if you feel you need them for your style and sound. Bottom line: Always go in the direction that you feel, never convince yourself of anything based on flexibility specs alone. Instead, go for the capability/functionality that matches exactly what you need (and will likely use) for your particular beatmaking approach and the style and sound of music you want to make.

Choosing and Getting Your Gear

The production tools of each beatmaker is not only a highly personal choice, it's a major part of their overall technique, style, and sound. The equation goes like this: "The person, plus the device, equals the sum." Translation: "beatmaker, plus production tools, equals sound." No two beatmakers are the same. There are many key elements that distinguish beatmakers from one another. The level of desire or drive to develop skills is a major factor for every beatmaker. Similarly, the practice habits of a beatmaker are particularly important. A beatmaker's base region, that is, where a producer is from or based at (where they live) also figures big into this determination. A beatmaker's historical perspective of music and their overall understanding of hip hop/rap and other genres contributes a great deal to their production identity. And finally, the production setup that a beatmaker chooses is certainly a fundamental determining factor.

Some beatmakers have more desire and professional discipline; thus, they practice their craft on a more consistent, self-disciplined basis. Some are well-schooled in many different music genres, which gives them an added advantage for creating hip hop/rap music. Some prefer production setups that have more limitations, while others prefer setups that appear to have no limits at all. Then there are those who are extremely tech-savvy and steadfastly biased towards technological advancements in the latest gear and equipment. On the other hand, there are those who aren't heavy into the tech-side of things; they are the if-it-ain't-broke, don't-fix-it breed of beatmakers. Some beatmakers favor radio-inspired party-tracks, yet some favor production influenced by the second Golden Era of hip hop/rap production. Point is, *who* you are as a beatmaker is the most significant part in the equation of creating hip hop/rap beats. The second most critical part in the equation is the gear and software that you use.

The question of which gear to choose is not just one for beginners. All beatmakers (whether beginners or pros) at some point deal with this question. As individual skill-sets emerge and musical ideas change and develop, beatmakers tend to choose (or switch) to the gear that they feel better accommodates their current situation (there are certain advantages and disadvantages with whatever setup solution you go with). But ultimately, the decision should come down to which solution gives you the most comfort, and which solution most efficiently enables you to do what you *want* and *need* to do. A fixation on a production solution simply because it's easily accessible is ill-fated because other factors like skill, proficiency, and most importantly, creativity, are things that are not so easily accessible.

Finally, within the beatmaking tradition, there are certain basic formulas for creating particular styles and sounds. For example, dark jazz samples; filtered bass lines; chopped up drum-breaks; horns or strings for hooks; synth-heavy compositions; etc. Therefore, when considering which setup solution is right for you, it's a good idea to identify the sort of style and sound formulas that you will likely employ.

Top 9 Factors to Consider When Choosing Your Gear

#1: Type of Style and Sound

When you know and understand the primary production sounds and specific styles of the beatmaking tradition, it's much easier to determine what kinds of beats and music you want to make. For instance, do you want to make club/party music? Do you want make "art music," the kind indicative of the Pioneers/Avant-Garde Period of beatmaking? Do you want to make West Coast or G-funk-inspired beats, or crunk and trap music? Maybe you want to pioneer any combination of the prominent hip hop/rap sounds. In any case, taking honest stock of the musical sounds that you favor and what you'd like to make is essential in choosing the gear that's *right for you*. Virtually any sound can be achieved with the right know-how and tools within any production setup. But certain setup combinations are more likely to render certain styles and sounds. Specific setups can make certain methods, styles, and sounds more plausible. Also, each individual piece of gear is only capable of producing the sound that is native to its design. Because of this, certain pieces of gear require additional tweaks for certain style and sound types. Finally, keep in mind, your setup is only as good as you *feel* about it. If you're not having success achieving the style and sound that you're looking for, it's usually not you, but the setup you're using.

#2: Functionality: Interface, Operating System and Performance

Functionality deals with the performance and capability of an EMPI. An EMPI's functionality is determined by its operating architecture. This includes a unit's operating system, page or menu layout, and the means for accessing each function within the unit, i.e. knobs, sliders, buttons, menu screens, menu dials, jog (scroll) wheel, etc. When making beats, there are five primary operations that you will find yourself performing and repeating with your EMPIs: chopping, triggering, filtering, sequencing, and looping.

#3: Features: Audio "Ins" and "Outs," Ports, Exclusive Technology, Effects, Computer Compatibility, and Cosmetics

Each EMPI performs according to the class it belongs to. That is, samplers *sample*, sequencers *sequence*, keyboards allow you to play keys, etc. But what often distinguishes one model (brand) of gear from another in the same category is the features that it offers. The features of an EMPI are just as important as its functionality; moreover, the features and functionality of an EMPI are interrelated. The range of things that can be considered features often vary, but the standard types of features are: the number audio "ins" and "outs," ports, exclusive technology, effects, options, computer compatibility, cosmetics, and stock sounds (where applicable).

When it comes to features, it's a good idea to focus first on what you *need*. It's easy to be taken in by all the various bells and whistles of the latest EMPIs. But it's important for you to maintain focus on the style(s) and sound(s) that you want to make and the setups that are most suitable for making it (them). Remember, in beatmaking, the primary operational steps that you will find yourself repeating over and over are: chopping, filtering, looping, triggering, and/or sequencing. So no matter how advanced or sophisticated a setup might be, as long as it can perform the five primary operations associated with making hip hop/rap music, then it's fine.

Audio "Ins" and "Outs"

"Ins" and "outs" (inputs and outputs), determine how an EMPI will receive and send audio and MIDI signals. When it comes to audio, all EMPIs will have either an RCA, a ¼" (pronounced "quarter-inch"), or XLR cable connection option. Some EMPIs have two out of the three of these options, some EMPIs have all three options. It depends on the category of the unit. DJ mixers, for instance, will most likely have all three audio options because they are used as a hub for multiple audio sources. Keyboard workstations almost exclusively carry the ¼" option; while Akai MPC-styled all-in-one drum machines often have an RCA and ¼" option (some units, like the Akai MPC 4000, have all three options). Each EMPI carries a standard number of these options, but the higher the number of ins and outs (regardless of the type) that an EMPI carries can be very advantageous, because it determines the limits or possibilities of an EMPI in receiving and sending audio signals.

Ports

The number and types of available ports can range, but essentially ports refer to MIDI connectivity, digital connectivity (or light pipe), and computer connectivity. There's only one type of port for MIDI. However, for computer connectivity, there are usually two main options: USB or firewire. A standard EMPI with MIDI capabilities will have at least one MIDI in and one MIDI out (two MIDI ins and four MIDI outs are ideal). Just like with audio ins and outs, a variety of ports can be very advantageous. With regards to digital connectivity, one port will do. Likewise, with computer connectivity, at least one USB or firewire port will suffice.

Exclusive Technology

Exclusive technology refers to a unique feature or a "first-of-its-kind" sort of option; for example, something like Roland's skip-back sampling technology — featured on their Fantom keyboard workstations.

Cosmetics

You're setup (and the EMPIs that comprise it) is only as good as you feel about it. And after consideration of functionality and standard features are observed, the cosmetics — the look and feel — of an EMPI can make or break how you feel about it (of course, if you're using software, physical cosmetics is not applicable). A clean design with practical knobs and buttons, ones that feel good to the touch, are a great choice because it makes the production process more comfortable. Beatmaking is a very meticulous endeavor, so it bodes well to use EMPIs that are physically comfortable and easy to manage. As for the color, shape, and size of an EMPI, well, that's kind of hard for end users to decide, as we typically have no say in the color scheme and shape that a gear manufacturer decides to go with. And even though some manufacturers are increasingly offering new color casing options, black, chrome-platinum, blue, and red seem to rival the vintage putty color.

Effects

Effects refers to sound manipulation, things like reverb, delay, chorus, limiting, etc. are typical effects that are offered with most EMPIs.

#4: Ease of Use

Every piece of gear has what I call a "User Degree of Difficulty" (UDD). UDD is the level at which an average or new user could operate an EMPI with the least amount of difficulty. A low UDD describes an EMPI that can be operated by an average or new user without a serious degree of difficulty or without any previous experience with production gear and equipment; a high UDD describes an EMPI that likely requires previous experience with gear and equipment. Choosing gear with a low UDD has its advantages. Beatmaking is not about conquering an EMPI, it's about using effective compositional methods to create quality music — and creating quality music has more to do with beatmaking skills than it does with gear mastery. Most beatmakers can make music using only 25% (or less) of their gear's capability. This is why it's better to focus on how manageable a piece of gear is for you. As your skills develop, your gear will become more manageable and easier to use. In some cases, you might even find that you've outgrown a piece of gear or the whole setup. Either way, when it comes to choosing your gear, try to build your setup with EMPIs that fit the UDD level that you're comfortable with.

What Qualifies As Ease-of-Use?

Ease-of-use refers to the overall straight-forward, intuitive manner that an EMPI operates. Ease-of-use is determined by how an EMPI's menu screen, function dials, buttons, and/or knobs, etc. appear and work together. With any given EMPI, if the manner in which each of these components operates (when you attempt to perform a function) is easy and less-involved, then that EMPI would commonly be considered to have an ease-of-use. The menu screen of an EMPI is perhaps the most important factor that determines whether or not an EMPI is easy to use or not. Menu screens with a low number of function pages and straight forward function terminology go a long way in making a unit easy to manage. Unnecessary, over-burdened menu screens with too much tech-heavy jargon can often be too intricate and time consuming. A low number of function steps is another thing that makes a unit easy to use. When you press or depress a button, turn a dial, or open a new page to perform a function, generally, the fewer the number of chronological steps that must be taken to actually perform the desired function, the easier a unit is to use. A unit that requires too many button presses (or depresses), dial spins, page openings, or mouse clicks can kill your ideas and momentum.

What Qualifies As a High Learning Curve?

A learning curve refers to the typical amount of time it takes and degree of experience required before one grasps a concept, idea, technology, or the like. There are learning curves for every piece of gear and equipment or software. A low learning curve is characterized by a requirement of a minimum amount of time and degree of experience. Gear that has a low learning curve isn't terribly difficult for an average or new user to operate effectively. By contrast, a high learning curve describes the requirement of a very significant amount of time and degree of experience. Gear that has a high learning curve is usually quite difficult for an average or new user (and in some cases even an advanced practitioner) to operate effectively. Take for instance MIDI. There's a relatively low learning curve associated with basic MIDI. That is to say, it isn't particularly difficult to learn the fundamentals of MIDI; for example, using a master sequencer (be it hardware or software) to trigger (control) another piece of gear, let's say a sampler, is somewhat simple. But using a master sequencer to control multiple pieces of gear all at once, like a sampler, keyboard, sound module, and a software program requires a more advanced understanding of how MIDI works. In the latter case, the learning curve is higher.

BeatTip – Taking on High Learning Curves

When choosing gear, it may be ill-advised to take on gear that's associated with a high learning curve, unless you *really* feel that you're a very quick learner. Just like there's gear for every budget, there's gear for every level of experience and understanding. I certainly believe that it's important to challenge yourself; but it's also important to be realistic about your patience level for learning something with a particularly high learning curve. While a high learning curve can pose a challenge, it can also increase the down–time away from actually making beats. An overwhelming amount of down-time, due to an EMPI or setup with a high learning curve, can dramatically slow down your development as a beatmaker. EMPIs with high learning curves can bog down new, less-experienced beatmakers to the point where they're not even getting an opportunity to regularly make beats. And rifling hopelessly back-and-forth through a manufacturer's manual, trying to figure out how to pull off even the most remedial production tasks, can also drain a lot of better-used energy. Therefore, when choosing your gear, try to familiarize yourself with the learning curve that is associated with the gear and equipment that you're interested in. Generally, it's not a good idea to jump ahead, before jumping in. Building up your experience with and understanding of EMPIs, setups, and basic concepts before you tackle more complex gear and equipment can increase your ability to take on gear and equipment that carries a higher learning curve.

#5: User Community

All of the major production pieces of gear, equipment or software have user communities associated with them. When you're deciding on which EMPI(s) to go with, it's very helpful to be able to tap into the user community associated with the EMPI(s) that you're interested in. If there's a high level of common use, like in the case of the MPC series, the Maschine, and FL Studio, then there will be an extraordinary amount of useful information available for you to access. On the other hand, a low level of common use might mean less access to useful information and support; and this can also mean a more centralized, narrow form of available information. In either case, you want to be able to access the user community that is associated with the gear and setup that you're considering. With this access, you'll be able to get an accurate consensus about the gear's ability, which is very important because until you've actually *used* the gear yourself, it's not a bad idea to reference the experience, knowledge, advice, and viewpoints of others who have experience with it.

When I began making beats, I didn't know about the at-large user community that was associated with my setup. As I developed as a beatmaker, I met more beatmakers who used the same setup and/or main piece of gear that I did. What stood out the most about these random encounters were the revelations that hit me. Repeatedly, it was clear that if I had known a few things here and there, it would have led me in the direction of an arsenal of advanced function trends. But back when I first began making beats, the user community surrounding my setup might as well have been non-existent. It wasn't organized, and there weren't any internet production forums to turn to for help or reference. Still, I was able to gain some pointers and indicators that ultimately helped me solidify my style and method of beatmaking.

Also, by tapping into a vast user community, you'll be able to assess a number of key factors about the gear that you're interested in. Things like reliability and compatibility can be ascertained *before* you actually get the gear. For example, let's say you're focusing on one of the big three drum machine all-in-ones and a stand-alone (separate) digital sampler. Technically, since all of these units have

MIDI,[85] they should *get along*, right? Well, yes, MIDI is MIDI, it's a standard language. However, for various reasons, some EMPIs have more of a compatible nuance to one another — they just tend to fit and work better together. And what about reliability? A music store salesperson can tell you that a EMPI is guaranteed to perform in a certain way. But a reliable user community will let you know if something is built like a tank or not. Moreover, they'll let you in on common malfunctions, hiccups, or glitches associated with the gear; and they'll also inform you about features and available options. Furthermore, they'll tip you off to replacement parts that you might need in the future. Usually, you will not get this sort of detailed information from a music store salesman. Hence, a major strength of commonly used gear and setups is the very formidable user communities that surround them. Through a large user community, you will be able to learn some of the important trends, dos, and don'ts, *before* you acquire the EMPI that you're interested in. And it's not to say that you have to follow whatever a particular user community has to say. Once you get your setup, it's entirely up to you what direction you will go in.

#6: Design Intentions

Most EMPIs offer relatively the same functionality. All samplers include functions for sampling and editing those samples; all sequencers include functions for creating and editing sequences; all keyboards include keys to play notes, etc. But all EMPIs are certainly not the same. For instance, let's look at the E-Mu SP 1200, one of hip hop/rap production's most notorious all-in-one units. This powerful sampler, drum machine, and sequencer is known for it's raw, rough, rugged, basement sound — attributes that made it ideal for the early/mid '90s hip hop/rap production scene. However, the SP 1200 is not as warm-sounding as the Akai S950 (another mainstay of the '90s that still finds its place in some of today's beatmaker's setups), and it's certainly not as bright as a Yamaha Motif keyboard workstation. On the other hand, both the Akai MPC 60 II and the Akai S950 are very warm-sounding units. Even still, in the hands of a crafty and knowledgeable beatmaker, the SP 1200 can be manipulated in such a way that it produces a warmer sound. Likewise, the Akai MPC 60 II and the S950 can both be manipulated in a way that produces a raw, rough, and rugged sound. But alone, neither of these two classic EMPIs can replicate

---

[85] **MIDI:** Musical Instrument Digital Interface. MIDI is the standard language by which all MIDI devices (EMPIs) communicate and send data (instructions) to each other. There is no audio involved with MIDI. MIDI is simply the instructional data for audio. MIDI is also what permits one EMPI to trigger another.

the brightness and clear sound of the aforementioned Motif.[86]   So of course all professional production gear has the potential to be manipulated in ways that could produce reverse (adverse) effects. But keep in mind, in many cases this might mean going against the *nature* of the unit's overall design. Think of it like driving a car in reverse, up a one-way street: You can do it, but imagine how much harder you'll have to work just to reach the end of the block; driving against your car's natural design may not always create an effect that you desire.

Hence, for every EMPI that you're considering acquiring, try to determine what each is *designed* to do. For example, it should go without saying that most keyboards are designed first and foremost for *playing keys*. As such, keyboards (with their robust assortment of stock sounds)[87] are usually great for creating and playing out melody and harmonic lines. Likewise, drum machines, which are designed for playing drums, sound stabs and phrases, are great for creating solid percussive rhythms.[88] Finally, samplers are used for sampling and customizing newly sampled sounds. Yet there are some keyboard workstations (for example, the Roland Fantom S or X series, the Korg Triton, and the Yamaha Motif) that are designed to permit users to sample, play keys *and* play drums. Similarly, some drum machines, such as the infamous Akai MPC series, the E-Mu SP 1200, the Roland MV series, and Native Instrument's Maschine are designed to permit users to sample *and* play drums and other sounds. In the case of these three all-in-one EMPIs, keyboard samples can actually be chromatically mapped out across the drum pads, and thereby played out as if it were a keyboard. (For more on sample-mapping and playing techniques, see chapter 6).

#7: Sound Identity: Signature Sound Output/Sound Signature

The development of sampling and sound reproduction technology throughout the 1970s and the late 1990s has led to a countless number of new beat machines, most of which are (overly) capable of performing the core functions required for making beats.   Also, in recent years, beatmakers have become

---

[86] In either case, however, the music produced using the SP 1200, MPC 60 II, S950, or the Motif can be further manipulated with software plug-ins and/or external effects processors. But bear in mind, it's no guarantee that the actual *feel and sound* of one setup can always be completely replicated with another.
[87] Stock Sounds: Pre-edited sounds that are supplied by the production instrument's manufacturer. Keyboards and/or synthesizers come equipped with a library of sounds (pre-sets, patches, etc.) already installed and stored. These base sounds are the default sounds that every user gets when they acquire the units. Drum machines and samplers also carry stock sounds. However, these sounds are not typically pre-installed or stored. Instead, they're usually available in the form of floppy disks, CD Roms, downloadable WAV files, etc.
[88] This doesn't mean that melody and harmony can't be played using a drum machine, or that percussive rhythms can't be established using a keyboard. It's just helpful to know that the design of drum machines and keyboards make certain compositional steps more easier than others.

increasingly recognizable and beatmaking/production itself more popular around the globe. The key manufacturers of the most popular EMPIs have certainly taken notice of this new emergence. They have increased their focus on developing beatmaking tools, rightfully seeing the hip hop/rap crowd as a viable market.

BeatTip – A Note About the Digital Sound Takeover

Although analog sound once ruled in music, digital sound dominates today's recording industry. So one can see why EMPI manufacturers shifted their focus away from enhancing the characteristics (in particular warmth) of their discontinued signature pieces, and opted for more clarity and loudness. Hip hop/rap, a music genre regularly played at high peaking volume levels, had an unexpected adverse effect on professional mixing and mastering. As hip hop/rap began its final climb from its sub-genre status into the mainstream, a parallel trend began to emerge: A demand for a louder overall sound. Mix engineers obliged their clients, and the volume peak level was seemingly irreversibly corrupted, making artful dynamic range a relic from the past.

By 2001, hip hop/rap music had completed its charge towards becoming one of the world's most dominant cultures, and as it could have been expected, other music genres (most noticeably rock) began borrowing some of the recording and production techniques associated with the hip hop/rap music tradition. And as the signals got hotter in the mix rooms, the EMPI manufacturers followed the trend, focusing more of their attention on what I call the "squash-sound," a sound that can best be described as a loud stereo sound with poor dynamic range.

The vintage EMPIs of Akai, E-Mu, Ensoniq, Roland, and Yamaha (the big five beat machine manufacturers) will probably always possess a warmer sound than their current gear offerings; those units were designed and created for a different time and a different breed of beatmaker. Throughout the late 1980s to the mid 1990s, it was more about creating a warm sound collage. And although building a sound collage is still a significant recording practice, in the current music scene, there's more preference given to the maximum loudness rather than the warmth that a sound collage can offer.

Though the vintage EMPIs were (are) great for their warmer sound, it does not mean that they're the only solution for creating a warm sound dynamic. Today, there are loads of plug-ins and external processors that can help you manipulate your sound in ways that may come very close to the sound signatures of the vintage EMPIs. And coming *very close* is all you need to do sometimes, because the average music listener won't be able to tell the difference. The average music listener could care less about *what* gear a beatmaker used to make their favorite song. Their only concern is whether the music sounds good to them or not. Furthermore, the average music listener isn't listening to music in acoustically treated recording studios; yet the trend towards louder music prevails.

To satisfy the hunger and demand for louder music, EMPI manufacturers shifted their concentration from designing units that had superior sound signatures to units that had superior sound quality, as in sample-rate clarity and stronger volume output. Because of this, the "stereo sound" became the norm rather than the option. But EMPI manufacturers didn't want to alienate traditionalists, so they made sure that their newer models contained adjustable sample bit rates and other effects options that could help simulate the sound character of vintage gear. Although these EMPIs were fitted with adjustable sample bit rates, presumably to offer *sound-era* flexibility, the truth is this: A simple switch of a button or lever to a 12 or 16 bit sample rate will not always be able to match the warmth of original 12 or 16 bit samplers, such as the Akai S950 or the E-Mu SP 1200. Likewise, you can't raise (or upgrade) the sample bit rate on units that lack the sound clarity and overall technology of today's EMPIs. Using contemporary EMPIs, you can always match the current volume trends of today, but you will never be able to completely match the unique sound signatures of those early classics. Either way, remember this fact: The average music listener can't always *hear* the difference in sound, but they can usually *feel* the difference. Therefore, it comes down to how you flip (modify) the sound.

So What Should You Look For When It Comes To Sound Quality? (Got Filters?)

Filters are the electronic components within a sampler, keyboard, or the like that are used for emphasizing, deemphasizing, or accentuating a specific range of frequencies. Filters are one of the main determinants of a unit's sound identity. Filter options vary from EMPI to EMPI, but most contemporary EMPIs with filter technologies contain high-, mid-, and low-pass filters (some EMPIs have even more filter capabilities and options than these). When choosing your gear, examine the information about the filters that a unit has. EMPIs equipped with a variety of filter capabilities can be more advantageous, because they offer more sound manipulation flexibility. (Generally, in hip hop/rap production, filters are used to beef up bass sounds, color the mids, and cut down high sounds, or to cut bass sounds and beef up high sounds.)

#8: Price and Availability

Above all, choosing gear should be about you knowing your options. If you place a cap on your research by sticking to a price range, your research will most likely be defective. It doesn't matter how much money you actually have. Money's not complex. With a relatively small budget, you can obtain a setup that's perfect for you. And even with a major lump sum of money you could still buy a setup that's completely wrong for you. It depends more on your knowledge of the options than it does on how much money you have. Also, when money's the concern, your chief consideration should be how much bang you can get for your buck. That is to say, how much quality, how many features, and overall performance you can get for the budget that you have. There are cases in which shelling out additional cash isn't really worth it at all, but there are also cases in which spending a little more money is your best option. After having done your research, you'll know pretty much which features you need. Thus, when given the choice, you'll be able to properly decide whether paying extra for the "extras" is actually worth it or not.

Smart Money is Always Better Than More Money: High-End vs. Low-End Gear

High-end gear is considered as such for three primary reasons: excellent quality, excellent performance, and most notably, an expensive price tag. Subsequently, low-end gear is usually characterized by good to poor quality, average to below average performance, and an inexpensive price tag. On the surface, high-end gear appears to be the way to go *when money is no option*. But be careful, there are some cases where the only thing about high-end gear is the high-end price. In fact, though you might expect high-end gear to crush low-end gear in a head-to-head comparison, it's not always the case. It depends on a number of factors, such as the category of gear, that is, what type of gear is being compared. Are we comparing drum machine all-in-ones? Are we comparing keyboard workstations or synthesizers? Are we comparing mic preamps? Are we comparing turntables, headphones, audio interfaces, tracking (recording) software? With some categories of gear, equipment, or software, there's a dramatic difference between high-end and low-end. Still there are other categories in which there's really no difference at all. (See Figure 2 for a comparison.) If you properly research these differences and then make your buying decisions based upon them, then you'll be spending "smart money." On the other hand, if you ignore these differences and simply opt for high-end gear, simply because it's high-end, then you're just spending *more* money.

EMPIs are not immune to overzealous marketing and promotion tactics. Like all for-profit industries, gear, equipment, or software manufacturers must successfully market their product lines to targeted consumers, in order for them to make a significant profit. So it should come as no surprise that there are pieces of gear, both high-end and low-end, who's popularity can be attributed more to a successful marketing and promotion strategy than to a positive user track record of quality and performance. Hence, more money won't always get you the best setup.

High-End and Low-End Gear:
Where Does It Make A Difference?
When and Where Should You Spend Less or More?

Gear	Major Difference	Minor Difference	Recommendation
Drum Machine All-In-Ones	√		Definitely go high-end, don't mess around.
Keyboard Workstations	N/A	N/A	Personal favorite: Roland Fantom. But the Yamaha Motif is a close second. Price range on keyboard workstations are pretty much locked.
Keyboards		√	So Many options!
Sound Modules		√	Again, so many options.
Stand Alone Hardware Samplers	√		Sound Quality, amount of memory is key here!
Software Samplers	N/A	N/A	Recycle Rules! Combined with Reason it's a beast.
Software Sequencers		√	Cubase
Tracking (recording) Software	√		**Pro Tools is the industry standard,** but Logic will definitely do the trick.
Monitors		√	Depends on your needs and what you're doing. With monitors, you have LOTS of options. For mixing, go as high-end as you can afford. If it's just for playback, you can get by with some low-end monitors, even stereo speakers.
Turntables		√	Technics MK II 1200 are classic. But Numark TT 1600 is top bang for buck.
DJ Mixers		√	Go for one with a graphic equalizer with at least 4 line channels.
Mixing Consoles		√	Just like monitors, it depends on what you're doing. If you plan on mixing, then go as high-end as you can afford. If you're just using it to route multiple audio sources, then you can get by with a low-end, 4 – 16 channel model.
Microphones	√		Try for as high-end as you can afford, but a great mic preamp can do wonders for a low-end mic!
Microphone Preamps	√		As high-end as you can afford!
Headphones		√	The best way to go: Sony MDR 7506, only $99.

Figure 2 High-End/Low-End Comparison Chart

#9: Well-known Beatmaker (Producer) Usage

The notion of getting any music instrument or piece of gear because of a famous user of that instrument or gear is nothing new. Jazz legend Charlie Parker picked up the tenor saxophone because Lester Young, used it (Parker eventually switched to the alto saxophone). Likewise, the music industry is littered with countless stories of musicians, producers, singers, and songwriters who took their professional cues from the well-known music recording artisans of their time. Beatmaking is no different in this regard.

BeatTip – Know The Style of Music You Want to Create

Be clear about what kind(s) of music you want to create. Compare and contrast that with the beatmakers that you admire. With the knowledge of what gear they actually use, you're at least armed with a starting point. Knowing how and where to proceed shaves time off of your production development. The well-known beatmakers who have pioneered the most commonly used production gear and equipment have, in essence, created short-cuts for anyone who's trying to get a grasp of the plethora of EMPI options. These beatmakers have demonstrated how to extract the potential out of even the most limited production setups. By at least examining the road maps that they left behind, you'll undoubtedly have a better understanding of which EMPIs are right for you.

From all of the beatmakers that you listen to, you already have your core favorites. The kind of music production that you favor can be attributed to many different factors. For instance, you may be drawn to the smooth, G-funk sound of classic Dr. Dre; or the synth-soul sound of The Neptunes; or you may like the rugged and rough sampled sound of DJ Premier; or the smooth sample sound of J Dilla; or still you might like the crunk and trap music sounds popularized by DJ Paul and Juicy J and DJ Toomp, respectively; or the modern trap-based sound of Metro Boomin. Maybe you like any combination of the different production sounds and styles that currently exist in today's hip hop/rap music. No matter what style and sound you favor, it's always a good idea to study those beatmakers who make it. By doing so, you give yourself a good starting point, especially if you're unfamiliar with or overwhelmed by all the gear and equipment options that are available.

I don't endorse the idea that the *only* criteria for choosing your gear should be based on which well-known beatmaker uses or used it. On the contrary, I suggest that it should be *one* of the criterions for choosing your gear. When it comes to choosing which production setup to get, it's a good idea to at least strongly consider which production setups are commonly used among well-known beatmakers, because can you afford to ignore the gear options that these beatmakers have proven to be effective? Keep in mind, there are no guarantees that what works for someone else will work for you, but at least in this case, you know what style and sound that a particular production setup is certified and proven to have produced. Having knowledge of proven possibilities is important because it gives you insight on which production setups and individual pieces of gear have been tried, certified, tested, and proven to get the results that you admire most.[89]

Check this out – A Recording Engineer Helped Me Choose

I once asked a recording engineer: "Why do you need a mixing board?" After he paused on the phone, he explained to me that a mixing board allows you to isolate and thereby "mix and EQ" individual tracks and channels. He further went on to explain how and why a mixing board was absolutely critical to the recording process.[90] He then asked me when I would be coming in for a session; he even offered to work the session for a discounted rate; I booked a session while we were still on the phone. *Mind you, at the time I didn't have any money for a session.* So I spent the next eight days raising money, not for gear and equipment, but for the upcoming recording session that I had booked.

It was my first session in a professional recording studio, and I had no idea what to expect, but I had a plan. Through the studio, I had rented an Akai S950 and an E-Mu SP 1200 (because at the time, this was the setup that I had heard DJ Premier and Large Professor used). I brought with me some vinyl records that I wanted to sample and a couple of dummy floppy disks; I say "dummy"

---

[89] Surprisingly, there are some people who disagree with this view. Some argue that you shouldn't be concerned with what a famous well-known beatmaker uses. My response: Every beatmaker that I have interviewed has explicitly said that they chose to get a particular production setup based, first and foremost, on the fact that a well-known beatmaker of their time used it. It's also worth noting that in the beginning of your production career, it's important to acquire a lot of introductory information. The proper introductory information will prepare you for the specific questions that you will inevitably develop with the more beatmaking experience you gain.

[90] This event happened before software and Digital Audio Workstations (DAWs) emerged. So at the time, mixing on a mixing console was the industry standard way to do it. But because of recent technological developments in the software and the DAW realm, it's no longer absolutely necessary to have or use a mixing console. Today, you can mix inside "the box," i.e. Pro Tools, and the like.

because I knowingly brought floppy disks that contained no data. When the session began, I asked the assistant engineer to load the disks for me, while I organized the records that I wanted to use. The truth was, I didn't know how to load the disks. After the assistant engineer struggled to load the disks (*wonder why*), the engineer came over to troubleshoot. He quickly realized that the disks where empty or bad, and he asked me if I had any backups. Of course, I didn't. But I told him that I had a few new ideas anyway. So we proceeded to use the studio's Technics 1200 turntable to sample some of the records that I had brought with me; actually, he did all of the sampling, I just watched, learned, and took mental notes.

Throughout my first recording session — still to this day one of the most pivotal recording sessions that I've ever attended — I was introduced to the basics of digital samplers, drum machines, and sequencers. I got an introduction to what each machine was *designed* to do and how the designs could be *manipulated* to achieve other results. After the session was over, the engineer wrote a page-long list of gear and equipment that I should investigate. From that point on, determining what gear and pro audio equipment to get became a little easier for me. I had received a good introduction of gear-capability, but, I still didn't know what gear and equipment was right for me. In fact, it took me nearly five years before I finally found the production setup that was right for me. Had I known even just 10% of what I know now about gear, its capabilities, and its best or rather most common uses, my beatmaking skills would have developed more rapidly. I can only imagine what I could have achieved, given what I know now and those five years of my production life.

When It's Time to Actually Get Everything, Where and How Should You Get Your Gear?

When you're ready to go and get your gear, take some time to plan out your production space. Clear an area in your home, office, studio or wherever you plan to make your music, and firmly reserve that space as your future production area. Sitting somewhere within that reserved space, write a list of all of the gear, equipment, or software that you are interested in getting. Write down *every* piece that you want. At this point, don't focus on the cost or whether you can get it immediately or not. Where possible, write down both high-end and quality low-end alternatives. The idea is to generate a clear idea on what you <u>want vs. what you actually need</u>. After you've drafted your list, check off each piece in the order of importance to you. Next, mark off a realistic acquisition date for each piece on your list. For most people just starting off, building a setup can be a slow grind. Yet for others, who are fortunate enough to have extensive financial resources, getting a setup can be a one or two-day conquest. Whether your approach to getting gear is going to be a slow or a fast grind, I strongly suggest that you plan and visualize your production setup before you try to acquire it.

Music Chain Stores

Before you make that move to your nearby pro audio megastore, consider a typical transaction that goes down in there. Customer goes in, tells the salesperson he has a budget. Usually, what's the first thing on that salesperson's mind? To get that customer to drop their whole budget, and maybe a little more. Most music store salespeople work on commission, plus big sales often means free gear for themselves. So if this is how the sales game goes in most cases, how is the salesperson going to achieve their goal? By pitching you on the high-end gear, that's how. They're not going to bother showing you bare-minimum, low-end gear. They're going to pitch the high-end stuff; and they're going to try to impress you with their knowledge of "the gear the pros use." Only the savviest of salespeople are going to even dare mention a low-end product; and even then, they're going to do so only to tear down the low-end gear while making the high-end gear appear flawless. So you can see how fast a big budget can easily be blown in your local music chain store when you don't know your options.

So how should you go about buying your gear from the big music chain stores? *Very carefully*, that's how! You have to be crafty in the chain stores. Never show your full hand. If you've come to the store ready to buy your whole setup and you're holding $5,000, tell the salesperson helping you that you only have $1,500 or less. Don't let them know that you're actually trying to buy your whole setup. Instead, see how much bang they can put together for your buck. For example, if you know the centerpiece of your setup is going to be a drum machine all-in-one, ask them to show you their top drum machine production centers. This is a no-brainer for them, because when it comes to drum machine all-in-one production centers, there's really only two games in town: the MPC series or the Maschine. (The E-Mu SP 1200 used to be a mainstay of hip hop/rap production, but finding a new one can be rather difficult).[91] Now having done your research, you'll already know which unit you want to purchase. this

---

[91] Even though it's relatively hard to buy a brand new E-Mu SP 1200 from one of the big music chain stores, you can still find mint or near-mint ones in used music gear stores and at various online retail stores and auction sites.

is where you want to secure your *first* deal (discount).

Music chain stores are in the business of moving big volume (mass quantities). Therefore, they can't afford to just let inventory sit in the stock room. Hence, they're always prepared to take 10-15% right off the top anyway, especially on gear going for $1,500 or more. After you've secured a sizable discount on the drum machine production center (or some other major centerpiece EMPI) of your choice, or the most expensive piece of gear you've come to buy, that's when you inquire about add-ons. For instance, what can you get if you add on a pair of monitors, or headphones, or software, etc.? At that point, you'll probably save 20% to 60% off of what you were actually prepared to pay for your entire setup.

What About A Low Budget?

If you're only holding $500, tell them you're prepared to spend $5,000! Remember the big tipper equation: *the bigger the tip, the better the service.* If a salesperson believes that there's a big tip (in the form of a nice commission) waiting for them after helping you, they'll be more attentive, more patient, and a great deal more informative. You know exactly what you came into the store for, and you know exactly how much money you have to spend. They don't. So here again, you want to get the biggest bang for your buck. But be realistic, you're not going to get a brand new major production center for $500. You can, however, get other critical components of your setup at a great discount.

Is New Gear The Best Way To Go?

New doesn't necessarily mean better. The latest gear, loaded with features galore, won't guarantee you superior beatmaking skills. Further, the vast majority of hip hop/rap music that you've heard in recent years — or that you're currently listening to now, for that matter — has been created and produced using gear and equipment models that are likely *five years old at least.* The biggest well-known beatmakers do not forfeit or abandon their setups every time a new piece of gear comes out. That's crazy. They're cooking with the cookware that helped them make their most famous dishes. This is one reason that vintage gear will always be available; the other reason: Manufacturers will continue to revise, improve, and update their product lines, usally every 6 to 18 months. For these reasons, and many more, you can always find a good deal on the used gear circuit.

Getting the Most Out of Your Production Setup
Understanding The Fundamentals Of Beatmaking, the Drawbacks of Technology, and the Importance Of Mastering Your Routine – Not Gear Mastery

The Fundamentals

The core fundamentals of creating beats and music are pretty simple and straight-forward. The sum of a beat is a series of sustainable loops, with some sort of rhythmic backing, typically drums. These loops can be simply duplicates (copies) of the initial 1- to 4-bar loop created, or they can be modified copies of the initial 1- to 4-bar loop created, as is usually the case. Because this formula is so clear cut and consistent, it makes the mechanics and other key components of beatmaking that much easier to identify and understand. Simply put, the mechanics, both the functional and the technical aspects of beatmaking, revolve around the same aim of creating rhythmic loops. Since beatmaking generally relies on the use of various programmable electronic machines, these loops are designed and created to initiate, duplicate, or change, then repeat *(loop)* automatically, usually with the press of a button or space bar.

All forms of contemporary music employ some variant of repetition or looping. However, there are key similarities and distinctions between beatmaking (traditional hip hop/rap production), which relies on specific kinds of electronic tools (beat machines, software, etc.) and other forms of non-electronic music. The only real difference between the two is procedure and playback. Further, music that is created electronically — using EMPIs — is played and *programmed* to replay *automatically*. In this process, rhythmic music patterns are designed, re-designed, duplicated, then finally deployed over a pre-determined number of bars, which are then programmed to loop on command. On the other hand, traditional instruments (i.e. guitar, piano, drums) must always be *played*. There is no automation when it comes to live instruments, unless of course they are recorded and sequenced into the electronic realm — every hi-hat, every snare, every drum kick has to be *played by someone every time* the patterns (sequences) of a song calls for it, loop after loop until the song is finished.

With beatmaking, after you've crafted out and recorded the core loop, you need only to program it to your liking. You can program changes, bridges, intros, etc., as well as extend the length of the beat. You can even program (automatically) the timing and swing of a song. Naturally, these sort of changes can't be made *automatically* when you're dealing with traditional music instruments. Instead, these changes must be accommodated by skilled musicians, all working in tandem (i.e. a group or band setting). So in many ways a beatmakaer is really a one-person band.

The Drawbacks of Technology in Beatmaking: How an Over Reliance on and Over Use of Technology in Beatmaking Might Affect the Beatmaking Tradition Long-Term

For beatmakers there's really no way around technology. It demands our attention because it's the mechanical conduit through which we make our music; it's the vessel that we use to explore and export the junction of our creativity and imagination as well as our music interests and cultural sensitivities. Moreover, technology dictates the means through which we are able to share our music with others. But considering what the beatmaking and hip hop/rap music traditions are, have been, and may one day be, are there any clear good or bad uses of technology in beatmaking? More importantly, what are some of the drawbacks of an over reliance on and over use of technology in beatmaking?

I'm not sure if there are any obvious good or bad uses of technology in beatmaking, but I do have my ideas about when technology in beatmaking is at it's best and when it is at its worst. I believe technology is at it's best in beatmaking when beatmakers use it thoughtfully, i.e. as a practical tool and as an enabler of creativity, imagination, and originality. I believe technology is at it's worst in beatmaking when beatmakers use it as a crutch, i.e. with little thought for practicality, creativity, or originality, or as an excuse to abandon some of the fundamental aesthetics of the beatmaking and hip hop/rap music traditions.

I embrace technology in beatmaking. I think it's good because it levels the playing field in beatmaking. On one hand, it erases the myths about some beatmaking methods and techniques, and it demystifies the "genius" of some often lauded beatmakers. On the other hand, it illuminates the actual skill and musical sense required to make certain beatmaking methods and techniques soar. This is why I believe that technology should be embraced whenever and wherever beatmakers feel that that they need it and whenever and wherever they believe it can be most helpful to their style, sound, and workflow.

That being said, the idea of keeping up with technology (important as it is) should never trump the creative goals of a musician; nor should the use of technology take precedent over a beatmaker's imagination and skill. Technology should be at the disposal of the beatmaker; the beatmaker should not be at the disposal of the technology. In other words, beatmakers shouldn't use technology to the detriment of their style and sound; they should use technology in the service of their styles and sounds as well as their primary modes for creating beats.

Furthermore, I'm convinced that emerging technologies, particularly in the electronic music production and recording fields, are prompting some beatmakers to expand and explore their creativity and imagination as well as repurpose and refresh some of the fundamentals of the beatmaking tradition. Well-known beatmakers (producers) like DJ Premier, DJ Toomp, Marco Polo, and !llmind (all of whom I've discussed beatmaking with in meticulous detail) have embraced technology — due both to necessity and preference — to degrees that have allowed each of them to expand the scopes of their styles and sounds while retaining the ability to capture the core sensibilities of their music. But while some beatmakers are using technology to climb towards new creative plateaus, there are some who are outsourcing their imagination and creative energy to technology's automation.

Specifically, my concern is that an over reliance on and over use of technology in beatmaking may be creating a disconnect between many beatmakers and the art of beatmaking itself. As many of us migrate further "into the box" for making beats, some doing so out of necessity, others genuinely for convenience, and others solely for the purpose of technology for technology's sake, I wonder what sort of effects this is having on our approach to even the most fundamental processes of beatmaking, like chopping, sequencing, and looping. Are we losing sight of where our tradition comes from — DJ'ing and the use of pre-recorded music or other pre-recorded sounds? And if so, is this leading many of us to ignore hip hop's/rap's canon of music — music largely influenced by soul, funk, disco, jazz, and any other music DJs could get their hands on? Moreover, is this prompting many of us to rethink our views about music elements like riffs, groove, rhythm, harmony, and melody and their role in beatmaking?

And let's not forget that as one becomes more accustomed to relying on technology, the work of remembering how to actually create music gradually falls into disuse. And as beatmaking (and really all music-making) becomes more mechanical and formulaic (than it already is) and less organic or more out-of-the-moment and devoid of feeling, quality standards plunge, rendering the notion of a dope beat obsolete or an afterthought at best.

So, I wonder how many beatmakers are short-changing their creativity because of their use of technology. More importantly, just as technology is allowing for some old traditions to be discovered and on some levels experienced (for example, through new contexts like "e-diggin" for source material and music history), I also believe that an over reliance on and over use of technology may be causing some beatmakers to abandon key stylistic (and sound) aesthetics of hip hop/rap music in favor of those from other music traditions.

And consider the other drawbacks to an over reliance on and overuse of technology in beatmaking. The most obvious drawback being that it's transforming what should largely be a musical process — one steep with reflection and a sense of tradition — into a manufacturing process that avoids tradition in favor of technological brevity. Because of this, some beatmakers are in danger of becoming effectively much more technician than musician. Because of this, there are some beatmakers who think more about technology than they do about music. (Please remember, having a sustained focus on music — its forms, its histories, its common characteristics — plays a large role in the success of any musician.) And also because of the focus on technological brevity, there are some beatmakers who are more enthusiastic about acquiring and mastering new technology than they are about making new beats and further developing their music skills.

Thus when you consider all of the drawbacks of an over reliance on and overuse of technology in beatmaking, it makes you wonder about the future of the beatmaking tradition. If this trend persists, doesn't the beatmaking tradition run the risk of becoming a devalued art form? After all, beatmaking is a sub-tradition of a music tradition that has long been plagued by accusations of illegitimacy or faux originality. In any event, when it comes to technology, in particular the technology that you choose, be sure to think about its advantages, sure; but also be mindful of the ways that a given technology can effect you as a musician. As long as you think music first, technology second, you'll be fine.

Mastering Your Gear vs. Gear Mastery

When it comes to mastering your gear, it's not about mastering every tool in the shed. It's about mastering those critical steps that you regularly use within the fundamental routine of your beatmaking methods. Far too often, so-called gear-masters advise newcomers to "master their gear." This advice is incomplete at best and woefully misleading at worse. To be successful at beatmaking, you don't have to master *every* capability within the EMPIs that you use. You just have to master what you need out of the EMPIs that you use. What I mean by mastering what you need is this. Learn the *key functions* that are critical to your beatmaking aspirations. By doing so, you'll save yourself some valuable time. When the need arises to perform a new function that you've never tried before, it's no big deal to just investigate your gear further. You'll pick up whatever you need quickly, because as you build your skills, your technological intuition will develop right along with it. By getting what you need from your gear, you get the most out of it. Therefore, it's not necessary to break your head trying to know every intricate detail about your equipment.

Truth is, to make quality beats, you'll most likely only need to learn about 25% of what your gear is capable of. Having a considerably high understanding of any particular setup or individual piece of gear will not necessarily translate to a successful understanding of beatmaking. No matter how much you master any piece of gear, the creation of a quality beat still comes down to how well you can craft sustainable, interesting rhythmic backing loops. Too much attention on so-called gear mastery, and not enough attention on mastering the routine functions that help facilitate your imagination, can be detrimental to your beatmaking development.

NOTE: When someone says that they've "mastered their gear," does this typically mean that they know everything about their gear? In the experience of all of the beatmakers that I interviewed (as well as my own experience), this is not the norm. Instead, when someone says that they've mastered their gear, what they usually mean is that they've mastered the key functions that they regularly use. Fact is, as your needs grow, and as your level of creativity expands, you will naturally find yourself exploring and employing gear functions that you never used before. In turn, you'll learn more about the capability of your particular setup.

Remember, your setup is only *part* of the equation. It's the first major technological aspect of the mechanics of beatmaking. That is to say, it's the initial technological means that you use to create the audio results that you're interested in. Thus, the prospect of gear mastery does not, in and of itself, automatically translate into a higher degree of creativity. You can know everything there is to know about the EMPIs within your setup, but that still won't guarantee you a high level of creativity, or even a deeper insight into creating beats for that matter. Consider this hypothetical: If you take away the stable piece of any well-known and respected beatmaker (producer), for instance, DJ Toomp, Pharell, DJ Premier, or Just Blaze, and then supply them with an EMPI which they've never used before, I guarantee you that after they figure out three things: how to sample, chop and record sequences, they will still create quality beats.

Most beatmakers routinely use only about 10% - 50% of their EMPIs' capabilities. When I used my Akai MPC 60II, I *only* used it for triggering sounds from my Akai S950 sampler and programming drums. I never sampled with my MPC 60II (even though it contains a notoriously powerful sampler). Why? Because I didn't *need* to. I use my MPC 60II in the way that worked best for me, the way that was right for me. I used my MPC 60II only in the manner that I needed to, not in the exact manner that it could have been used. On the other hand, when I use my Akai MPC 4000, I do use it's internal sampler; however, I do not always use the plethora of effects that it has to offer.

Consider the analogy of driving a car vs. knowing how a car works. Once you learn how to drive a car, you know, get the basics down, like going, stopping, accelerating, de-accelerating, parking, and just overall maneuvering, you don't spend time trying to figure out how and *why* the car does what it's doing. Though the instrument gauges and gear shifters may look stylistically different from car manufacturer to car manufacturer, the reality is that all cars still perform the same standard functions. No matter what car you step into, regardless which automaker actually manufactured it, you don't have to learn a whole new driving language in order to drive — the fundamentals remain the same: *Park, Neutral, Drive, Reverse*. As you drive more, as you spend more time behind the wheel, you spend more of your time actually becoming a better driver, not a better auto mechanic, right? Learning everything about how cars work in general, and how *your* car works in particular, is not critical to your development as a better driver. However, because of scheduled car maintenance and routine repairs, you'll learn more about how your car works. But this is a by-product of your driving experience, not a necessity for driving.

Likewise, when it comes to beatmaking, it's more beneficial to spend more of your time actually developing and creating new beats and music than it is deciphering how (or why) new production/recording technology works. I certainly urge you to learn as much as you can (when you can) about the gear in your setup. But I don't recommend that you over-burden yourself with the notion that you have to master everything about every piece of gear within your setup. In the time spent trying to learn and master all of the ins and outs and functions and obscure tricks of a piece of gear, you can become void of developing or translating feeling into your music. Perhaps one of the most common and damaging effects of arbitrary gear mastery is the production of cold beats, i.e.

Chapter 5

Drum Sounds and Drum Programming
The Nature of Drum Sounds and Drum Programming in Hip Hop/Rap Music

Drums are the most important part of a beat. –DJ Premier

Without dope drums, you can't have a dope beat. –Marley Marl

I spend a lot of time making sure that my drums are right. –DJ Toomp

Drums are the cornerstone of a beat. Regardless of whatever non-drum arrangement a beatmaker creates, it's always the drums that serve as the foundation, the glue by which all other elements within a beat stick together. Therefore, it's typically the drums that garner the most attention and time from beatmakers. In this chapter, I examine drums in all of their beatmaking glory. From the basics of drum sounds to the various structures that drum programs formulate, I explore both the aesthetic and functional roles that drums play within the beatmaking process.

The Basics: Drum Sound Categories

In beatmaking, drum sounds are divided into four primary categories: kicks, snares, hats, and cymbals. For each category (type) of drum sound there are multiple variants. For example, from among the kick variety there are standard bass kicks, "booms," and 808s. A standard bass kick is your garden variety bass drum, a boom is a more amped-up bass kick sound, and an 808 (name comes from the famed Roland TR 808 drum machine) can be described as a super-powered boom with an additional sustain and broader resonance.

Within the snare drum variety there are standard snares, snare toms, woodblocks, and rim shots. It's important to note that in beatmaking, snare sounds (and kicks and hi-hats) can be anything that *represents* the role of a snare, not necessarily a typical snare sound (more on that later, when I discuss the role of drum sounds and programming).

Among the "hat" variety of drum sounds there are hi-, open-, and closed-hats (or mid-hats). **Hi-hat** refers to the sound of standard hi-hat cymbals in their default position, not tightly closed but resting close to one another. Think of a drum set in which one hi-hat cymbal rests on top of the other, held loosely together by the hi-hat foot pedal. In beatmaking, the sound made when these two cymbals are held loosely together and struck is what is meant by a typical hi-hat. Likewise, **open-hat** refers to the sound of standard hi-hat cymbals in the their maximum open position, and closed-hats refers to the sound of standard hi-hat cymbals in their closed position, i.e. held tightly together.

Within the cymbals variety there are "rides" and "crashes." **Rides** refer to the ride cymbal sound of a standard drum set, **crashes** refer to the gong-like cymbal sound that's created when two cymbals are *crashed* into each other. There are also a number of secondary percussive sounds that beatmakers use as and/or to compliment primary drum sounds. These secondary percussive sounds include shekeres, triangles, blocks, tympanies, sleigh bells, tambourines, and castanets.

Drum Sound Representation, Not Always Actual

In beatmaking, drum sounds do not always necessarily correspond with the actual category of sound that it represents. For instance, snares are not always actual snare-drum sounds. Instead, the term "snare" is used loosely in beatmaking to describe any sound that is used, played, and programmed where the snare drum sound typically would land within a drum pattern. In other words, the term "snare" in beatmaking serves to represent any sound that acts like or carries the purpose and associated dynamics of a snare drum. Hence, snares in beatmaking can be anything from the captured sounds of a hammer hitting a chair to a drum stick smacking the top of a shoe box. It should be noted that this same representational/actual dual understanding in beatmaking applies to all drum sounds as well as bass sounds. For instance, a kick can be any sound that represents the sound and impact that simulates any variation of the sound that a bass drum typically makes. So for example, a kick can be something as creative as a sample of a boot kicking a shoe box stuffed with t-shirts (I've made a kick from that very sound). Likewise, a bass sound doesn't necessarily have to come from a bass guitar or the bass patch of a keyboard/synthesizer; a bass sound can be made from the low-end filtering of an organ patch or something similar.

How Many Drum Sounds Are Enough? Core Set (limited) Drum Sounds vs. Unlimited Set of Drum Sounds

Customizing and Sampling Your Own Drums

The number of drum sounds that a beatmaker should have is debatable. There are some who believe that you can never have enough sounds; on the other hand, there are those who believe that you should have simply a core set of drum sounds. So what is the right amount of drum sounds? Truth is, that's up to each individual beatmaker. However, when deciding upon how many drum sounds to carry, either a core (limited) set or an unlimited set, there are a number of things worth considering. To begin with, you must understand how the *sound* of drums are perceived and valued in the first place. In beatmaking as well as in traditional drumming, the value of drums is predicated more upon *tonal* possibilities than simply *quantitative* possibilities. It's not really the sheer number of available drum sounds that are really important, it's the various kinds of tones (unique sounds) that drum sounds can produce.

Traditional drummers can employ several different techniques to produce different tones. For example, they can tighten or loosen the skin heads on their drums, or they can modify their playing style to manipulate the velocity, attack, and sustain of a drum strike; each technique has the potential to render a unique tone. Likewise, through effects processors and the like, beatmakers can also modify their drum sounds; and just as with traditional drummers, beatmakers in their playing can also manipulate the velocity, attack, and sustain of the drum sounds that they deploy. You should also keep in mind that traditional drummers often do more with less. Celebrated drummers like Bernard Perry, Clyde Stubblefield, and J'abo Starks (the latter two famous for playing with James Brown) did not have an arsenal of snare sounds, yet they were able to carve out very distinct sound signatures. This is because the style, approach, and modification that a particular drummer uses is paramount to their ability to tap the various tonal possibilities of a given drum sound. Because beatmaking is a form of electronic music production, there will inevitably be a larger selection of drum sounds to chose from. That being said, this does not change the fundamental value of drum sounds; the tonal possibilities of drum sounds still trumps the sheer number of drum sounds.

But those who advocate for having an unlimited set of drum sounds have their arguments as well. Some maintain that an unlimited amount of drum sounds leads to a better drum sound library, which in turn makes for more creativity. But if the purpose of a drum sound library is for amassing both a set of standard and customized drum sounds so that one can create and develop their own unique sound, then an *infinite* number of drum sounds actually undermines this purpose and contradicts the creation of one's own unique sound. After all, a unique overall drum sound requires familiarity, and familiarity depends upon a beatmaker's ability to repeatedly use a core set of drums in new (creative) ways.

There are some beatmakers who purport to use entirely new drum sounds every time that they make a new beat. So it would seem that an unlimited amount of drum sounds presents a beatmaker with an unlimited amount of drum sound options. But is such an approach practical or worth it in the long run? I mean, an infinite number of drum sounds doesn't necessarily translate into an infinite amount of quality. For instance, let's say you have a set of 500 separate snares. If you were to critically survey each snare, how many of those snares would truly sound distinct and unique? In fact, how many times would a certain tone be replicated? Furthermore, how many would actually be usable? What I'm getting at is that out of a given set of 500 snares, it's not at all unreasonable for one to expect to find many that are similar, rendering a vast majority of them useless. Finally, there's also the management and real-time use issue of deferring to an unlimited set of drum sounds. Scrolling through thousands of drums sounds just takes something away from the creative process. For one thing, it's rather time consuming. More importantly, it disrupts a beatmaker's workflow, which in turn hampers the creative process.

Check This Out – Core Drum Sounds and Unique Style

Another point I want to make is that a core (limited) set of drum sounds tends to breed a sort of familiarity and personal style and sound, whereas an unlimited set of drum sounds tends to breed an over-reliance on variety for variety's sake as well as a degree of uncertainty and indecision, which typically leads to bad choices. At one point in time, I probably had more than 5,000 drum sounds. I had nearly all of the MIDI Mark drum kits, the Kid Nepro drum kits, Sample Kings drum kits, various drum sound CDs, the E-Mu SP 1200 full drum sound library, the Akai S950 full drum sound library, and, of course, sampled drum sounds from over 14 volumes of the Ultimate Breakbeat Records series. I even had drum sound libraries that were comprised of sounds that I recorded and mixed at Unique Recording Studios and D&D Studios.

Needless to say, I had a major drum sound collection. Then I got real with what I was doing and what I wanted to do. All I really wanted to do was make dope beats, but paying too much attention on building up an infinite drum sound library was actually detracting me from this ultimate goal. Once I made that revelation, I vigorously started purging my drum sound library. I tossed out every drum sound that I wasn't really using. After that, I did another purge, but this time I tossed out all drum sounds that I considered to be just *O.K*. I went on to do even more purges, separating the nice drum sounds from the good drum sounds, followed by a separation of the dope drum sounds from the nice ones. When I was done purging, all I was left with were those drum sounds that I thought were dope, and those that worked best within the style and sound of beats that I wanted to create.

I understand that some beatmakers thrive on having an unlimited set of options at their disposal. Some beatmakers simply like the notion of having unlimited choices. But what often happens in these cases is that you find beatmakers "force-feeding" their beats, using new drum sounds simply because they have them, not for their distinct tonal value or unique character or because they actually work well within their style of beats. For many beatmakers like myself, it's not about spending unnecessary time searching for an arbitrary perfect snare; it's about locating a snare from your library and making that snare sound fit with the theme of the beat at hand.

As I've already discussed, drum sounds can really be divided into four main categories, with additional sub-categories. Of all the aforementioned kinds of drum sounds, I carry about three to five drum sounds of each variety. And if and when I find that I can't make any of those sounds work with a new beat that I'm making, then that means that the new beat is wack, simple and plain. Here's the bottom line: I know my personal drum sound library very well. In fact, I know my drum sounds far better than I know my gear, and almost as well as my favorite records. But when I had 5,000 plus sounds, there was no way that I could realistically ever know all of those sounds. Therefore, I prefer the feeling of knowing that my drum kit is set and ready to go whenever I have a new idea.

Drum Sound Customization and Building a Drum Sound Library

Because the drums are such a prominent feature of the hip hop/rap music tradition, and because beatmaking is set in a pre-recorded-based medium as well as live performance-based medium, beatmaking relies, to a great extent, on extensive sound modification of individual drum sounds (hits). But when it comes to drum sounds, there are only but so many standard sounds that you can have — a typical bass kick, 808 kick, boom kick, mid-pitch snare, truncated snare, shekere, hi-hat, open-hat, closed-hat, ride, and crash. Thus an appropriate number of standard drum sounds (within your choice of sound) should comprise of your base set of drum sounds. And once you've added the appropriate standards (within your choice of sound) to your drum sound library, the balance of a unique drum sound library is usually made up of customized drum sounds. For many beatmakers, the most effective drum customization comes from the manipulation and modification of drum sounds that are already in their base drum sound library. Hence, it's worth examining some of the methods for customizing drum sounds.

There are several somewhat simple ways to effectively customize drum sounds. The easiest way to customize a drum sound is through truncation or the chopping and shortening of sound. Next, you can manipulate the velocity (volume and release) of a drum sound, and you can also manipulate the pitch of drum sounds. There are also a number of complex methods for customizing drum sounds. There are those processes that involve the EQ'ing (sound coloring and leveling) of drum sounds. EQ'ing drum sounds essentially involves turning up or down the low, mid, or high frequencies of a given drum sound. Then there are those methods that incorporate the use of external or software effects processors; these methods include things like adding compression, chorus, or reverb to a drum sound. Methods such as these are considered to be more complex, because they demand a greater amount of experience and understanding of sound frequencies and effects processors, and, of course, beatmaking itself.

BeatTip – Methods for Customizing Drum Sounds

Here are my primary methods for customizing drum sounds. First, it begins with a beat. After I track (record) a new beat into Pro Tools (my tracking/recording software of choice), I pick a drum sound, usually a kick or snare, then I sample it and rename it as a variation of the original. Because Pro Tools allows me to solo (isolate) individual tracks, I solo the drum sound that I want to modify, next I play the track, then I sample (duplicate) the drum sound and rename it as a variation of the original sound. For example, if the original drum sound was "snare 1," I name the variation "snare 1 x." If I want to thicken up a drum sound, I duplicate it a couple of times, then I play the track and sample all three sounds together as if they were one drum sound. For added effect, I EQ each of the sounds separately or modify their pitch before I sample them.

Another way that I customize drum sounds is similar, but it involves first using my Akai MPC 4000. First, I create a basic drum track, or I use a drum track from a previous beat that I made. Next, I take the drum hit or stab that I want to customize, and I layer it on top of itself, by programming the event in the sequence of the beat. But instead of layering the same hits exactly on top of each other, that is, at the exact same step (event) in the sequence, I offset each hit about one or two events in the front and/or behind the original hit. It is then this new "fattened," more resonant sounding hit that I record into Pro Tools. I should note that all of my EMPIs are routed through a Mackie multi-channel analog board (mixing console). So the signal that is ultimately recorded is further "beefed" up (amplified) before it lands in Pro Tools. Once inside Pro Tools, the process can get more complex, as I might do additional EQ'ing or slap some reverb or other effect on the drum hit. Finally, when I'm cool with the result, I sample that sound back into my Akai MPC 4000 — again, it's important to point out that the signal routes through my analog mixing console before it hits my sampler. Once this is done, I end up with a new drum sound that is unique and modified to my desired tonal and sonic spec.

The establishment of one's own sound is mostly about sonic preferences (preferred frequencies), arrangement scopes, types of sounds and tonal preference, individual approach and technique, and an underlying style. Therefore, in this overall scope, drum sounds can, and I feel should, be routinely interchanged and reused. That's one of the fundamental things that beatmaking is about: just flippin' familiar sounds, techniques, and styles in ways that yield a unique style and sound.

BeatTip – Think Outside the Box for Custom Snare Sounds: Presets Get the Job Done, But Customized Sounds Help You Create Your Own Style and Sound

Whether you've made your 10th or 1,000th beat this week, you've learned the importance of dope drum sounds. And when it comes to drum sounds, you can get away with a limited number of non-descript kicks. But without a distinct group of snare sounds, your beats might suffer. Why? Because since the advent of the MPC 2000, widespread sample packs, and software programs galore, many beatmakers have taken to using the exact same stock snares. And, in the process, they've decreased the chance of giving their beats a distinctive sound.

Don't get me wrong, there have been some beatmakers who have been able to get away with using only one or two snares. But in those cases (most of the time), the snares have been cultivated to an ultimate level of distinction, a level in which they work almost with any non-drum arrangement. However, in order to arrive at such snare sounds, some level of customization had to have gone on previously. So in this BeatTip, I want to discuss some different methods for customizing snares. Some of which were taught to me and some of which I developed on my own.

The first set of snare sounds that I ever customized were part of a classic rock kit (on floppy disk) that came with the E-Mu SP 1200, the first drum machine/sampler I ever used. Some of the snares on the kit were OK, but they didn't fit what I was trying to do sonically. So after finally recognizing that none of the snare sounds fit with the feel and style of music that I was going for, I went about customizing them. At the time, I didn't have an analog mixing console to run my sounds through, so I couldn't easily boost up the bass (the low end) of the sounds I wanted to modify. But I did have a dual cassette recorder and a lot of imagination. So here's what I did the first time I customized snare sounds. I recorded every snare sound that I had to cassette tape. Next, I dubbed (duplicated) them. After dubbing the sounds, I sampled them into my Akai S950. Once inside of the Akai S950, I was really able to get creative. It wasn't that I couldn't have chopped or filtered the sounds inside of my old SP 1200, I could have. It was just that the S950 gave me a different sound, plus I felt more comfortable working with its sampling functions than those in the SP-1200.

Next, I went around my room with a Shure SM-58 live microphone sampling all sorts of sounds. I took a hammer and hit the bottom of a metal folding chair. I took a drum stick and rapped back and forth on a Nike sneaker box stuffed with socks (I sampled the sneaker box with and without the lid on; there was indeed a noticeable difference). Switching up between the hammer, the drum stick, and a wooden hanger, I hit the inside of a window pane. Needless to say, I sampled every sound that I could imagine, anything that I thought might be interesting. All of this sampling probably took me 10 minutes. By the way, I would also like to think that this process taught me more about acoustics.

Having sampled this wide assortment of sounds, all in the same room, mind you, I went about "matching" the sounds with the cassette versions of E-Mu's classic rock kit as well as several other snare sounds that I had. Incidentally, this was around the time that I first began to understand the process of layering sounds. Particularly, I was discovering the potential for layering, both as a means for customizing drum sounds as well as other sounds. I was also learning how layering could affect the overall texture and tenor of a beat. Not too long after that, I began applying these techniques to all of the drum sounds that I used. And after while, I stopped buying other peoples' drum kits altogether and I started sampling drums from records and literally making my own drum sounds.

Special Note: Since I first began customizing my snare sounds, I have never used a pre-set drum sound *as-is* again. Although pre-set drum sounds undoubtedly serve a purpose (I have heard some pretty nice pre-set drums), I've always found that customizing your own sounds goes a long way in helping you carve out your own unique style and sound. Still, if I come across a pre-set drum sound that I like, I'll use it. Of course, I modify it to make my own.

Short list of items great for customizing snares:
- Live microphone with an extended chord to allow you to move freely around your space.
- A tambourine. Any percussion instrument you can pick up from a music store will help you customize your snare sounds as well create sound composites that are unique.
- A wood block, mallet, hammer, and a shaker.
- At least one drum stick. You can use two in rapid succession on any hard surface. You'll be surprised at what you can come up with after you filter and adjust the pitch on a sound created by two drum sticks.
- A real set of bongos are ideal but not absolutely necessary.
- A cassette tape player. Yes. They're dirt cheap now, and they allow for connection back to the analog age (if that matters to you). Also, nobody will ever be able to duplicate your sounds if you've used some combination involving a cassette tape.
- Some sort of wooden board, maybe a chef's cutting board, something that you can strike with anything, like a bottom of a shoe, a mallet, a set of keys, a hockey puck, and, of course, a drum stick.
- Some studio foam.

Check This Out – Creating Your Own Customized Drum Signature: Matching Up Certain Sounds and Keeping Them Together

There is perhaps no better way to add continuity to your beats — while at the same time distinguish your sound — than having your on custom drum signature. Just like a typical overall signature sound, a custom drum signature is your own personal drum sound. Various beatmakers have custom drum signatures. Think of DJ Premier, Pete Rock, RZA, J Dilla, Just Blaze, Nottz, 9th Wonder, The Neptunes, Jake One, Metro Boomin, and so on. But how do you create your own custom drum signature?

Building your own custom drum signature starts with a core set of drum sounds. So how do you get a core set of sounds, you ask? Well, the best way (perhaps the only way) that you can develop a core set of drum sounds is through an audition process of the drum sounds that you already have. Whenever you select any drum sound for one beat, you're essentially auditioning it for future beats. Each beat that you make acts as a reference for another. Using this understanding as the foundation for auditioning drum sounds, let me break down how I developed my core drum sounds and my own drum signature.

Strip the Beat

First thing, I stripped down five of my favorite beats to their drum framework, no non-drum sounds. Each beat I had a mid-range tempo of 94 to 97 bpm. Next, I listened to each beat to determine if there were any discernible patterns. Having noticed specific sonic and texture consistencies between the sounds in each drum framework, I then examined the "value settings" for each drum sound (one by one) that I've used. Although I use an Akai MPC 4000, the majority (60%) of my core drum sounds were sampled and modified in my Akai S950 sampler. Therefore, I must spend a brief moment discussing the main "page" in the Akai S950 in which I modify sounds. In "PAGE 08" inside of the Akai S950, each sound — once assigned to a program — can be modified in four ways: (1) Loudness; (2) Filter; (3) Transpose (pitch); and (4) Fine Pitch. (Note: Most contemporary samplers — both hardware and software — have multiple filter options and effects.) For each drum sound that I use, I wrote down the values of "PAGE 08" on a yellow posted note or a yellow legal pad. For example, take a look at Figure 3.

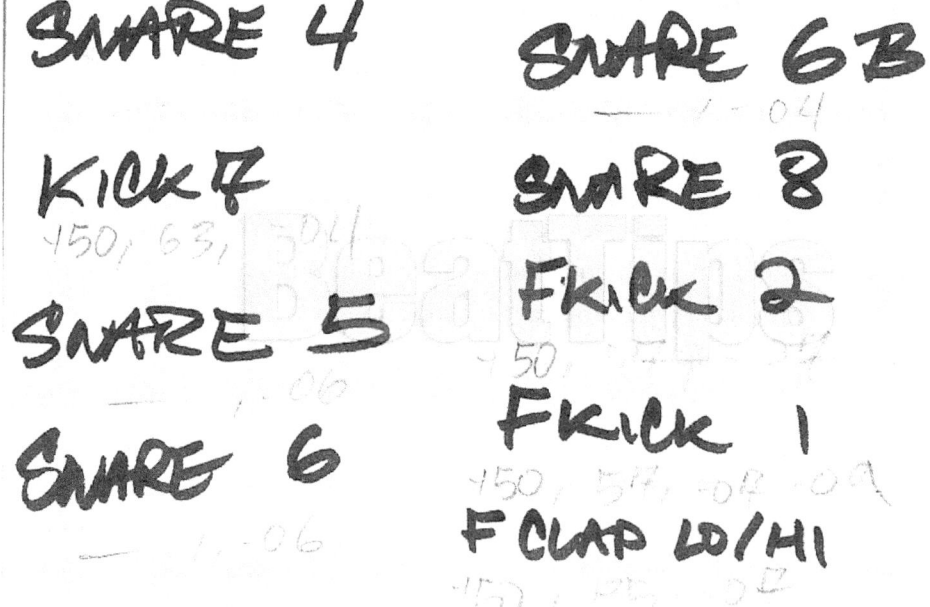

Figure 3 Drum Sounds and Values on Yellow Pad

This allowed me to objectively examine the settings for each sound, which in turn helped me determine the typical settings that I tended to use for each type of sound, e.g. kick, snare, and hi-hat. By writing down my tendencies, I was better able to modify those drum sounds that I was drawn to.

Having found a clear scope of the characteristics that drew me to a particular drum sound, I then auditioned those sounds with each other — pattern after pattern — to see which sounds fit together and which sounds fit with everything. It's worth remembering that for the most part, drum sounds do not play alone; therefore, the true test of a drum sound is how well it plays with and off of other sounds in the drum framework (and the entire beat for that matter). Therefore, auditioning drums sounds together (rather than alone) better helps you identify those drums in your collection that are sure-shot and those that are better used as featured players.

After many drum sound audition practice sessions, I was able to identify roughly 15 sure shot (go-to, dependable) drum sounds and about another 20 feature players (great auxiliary drum sounds) that could be used for special beats and mitigating circumstances, i.e. matching beat styles. As of today, my 15 sure-shot sounds are composed of 4 kicks; 4 snares; 4 hi-hats; 1 crash; 1 tambourine, and 1 ride cymbal. From just these 15 drum sounds, I create the drum frameworks for the bulk of my beats. I should note however that although I always use at least one of my core drum sounds, I routinely use slightly modified versions (e.g. slower pitch) of my core drum sounds. I should also point out that I have another set of 15 "2nd-tier" drum sounds that I use for specific types of beats or for certain layering effects.

When it comes to customizing drum sounds that I sampled and modified in my Akai MPC 4000, the process is similar in terms of writing down my tendencies on a yellow posted note. However, the Akai MPC 4000 has a more extensive filtering editing section than the Akai S950, which leaves room for an expanded area of exploration. That being said, I often work to match the sounds from my MPC 4000 to those made in my S950, the only difference being the level of brightness and perhaps reverb.

Assigning Your Main (Primary) Drum Sounds

Assigning drum sounds to pads (or keys) is every beatmaker's personal choice. Each person's musical inclination and eye/hand coordination directly influences the ways in which they assign sounds to a drum machine's pads. And though there are no wrong or right ways for assigning drum sounds to pads, I do believe that some pad assignments are more practical than others. In the following section, I will describe one of the most simple and practical ways that you can assign your main drum sounds over a standard 16-pad bank of a drum machine.

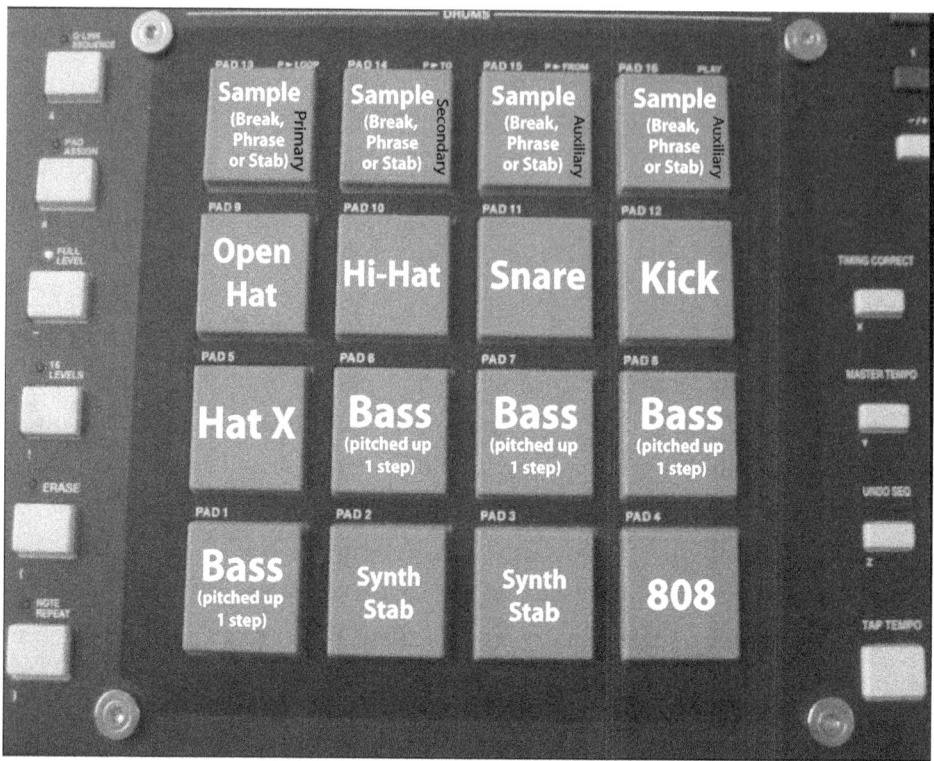

Figure 4 Front 16 Drum Pads—Sa'ids Primary and Secondary Drum Sound Assignment

For your main drums (kick, snare, hat), I recommend that you assign them to the top first-three pads or the bottom first-three pads. There are two practical reasons for this. First, drums are the backbone of a beat, and therefore, they get used more than any other element within a beat. Hence, it helps to have your drums mapped out and assigned in a position that compliments their overall importance. Another reason why it's practical to assign your primary drums to the top first-three pads or the bottom first-three pads is because drums are generally tracked (recorded) into DAWs (Digital Audio Workstations, e.g. Pro Tools, Logic, and other recording software applications) in the same *kick, snare, hat* order.

After you've assigned your main (bass) kick, move over one pad and assign your main snare. The logic behind this? Well, when you're trying to bang out drum patterns from scratch, it helps to have the snare pad as close to the kick pad as possible. Is this a rule? No. I've seen some beatmakers who have their snares assigned directly underneath their main kicks. When I began creating beats, I tried each of these ways and what I found was that it was easier and more effective for me to slide *horizontally* from kick to snare than *vertically* from kick to snare. Moreover, I found that I could make faster pattern progressions. That is to say, with the snare placed one pad over (horizontally) from the kick, I was able to jab my middle finger to the snare pad faster. This in turn improved my drum timing and, subsequently, my overall timing and arranging abilities.

Having assigned your main snare, I recommend assigning the main hat (or ride) to the next pad over from the snare. Hats are funny because at their best, they're actually very subtle, but at their worst, aw, man, they can stab you in the ear. Hence, the importance of hats and their role will vary from beat to beat. Even still, you should give hats (and cymbals) the same positional respect as the kick and snare. Again here, pattern development plays a key role. Here's why hats deserve the same positional respect. Most beatmakers build the main drum framework by starting with the kick and the snare; having successfully created a pattern, they then add the hat in over the top of the drum and snare, creating a basic drum sequence (track). After the individual kick, snare, and hat patterns are programmed and looped, the overall collective pattern becomes the main drum framework. And when a beatmaker plays back the drum framework (sequence), it's the hat that often gives you the most accurate indication of whether or not the pitch of the framework is right for the beat at hand.

I also like to keep the hat within the first three pads for another reason: timing. That is to say, I often use a hat in the same way that most beatmakers use the metronome tone. When I create beats, most of the time I actually don't even use the metronome tone; I pretty much know the tempos I like to work within (usually 84-99 BPM[93]), and therefore, I have a pretty good indication of where things are supposed to land in the measure of the sequence. When the metronome tone is audible, it disrupts my flow and concentration. So if I ever have a timing issue, I simply make a quick 1-bar loop of hi-hat hits; since I know that a standard hi-hat pattern (1, 2, 3, 4, on up to 8) lands on basically every 6th step or event within a 4/4 measure, a simple 1-bar loop of hi-hats helps me get the timing right. After that, I adjust that bar to the desired tempo, using the hat pattern as a guide. From there, I play the kick drum and snare in real time, over the top of the hi-hat.

For the next pad over from your main hi-hat, I recommend that you reserve this pad for your open-hat or even a second hat sound. In fact, the additional

---

[93] **BPM** stands for Beats Per Minute. It's the common terminology used to describe the measurement of tempo in music. It's used to calculate the timing of a piece of music. For example, 60 BPM means 60 *counts* per minute, 1 beat per second. Hip hop/rap music usually uses a tempo of 85-120 BPM, but there are some hip hop/rap songs that carry a tempo as low as 70 BPM.

"hat" on this pad can really be anything from an open-hat, to a ride, to sleigh bells, or a tambourine. These second hats can be either used as layers, or they can be used more sparingly, like every other bar, or every fourth bar, etc., for accentuation and emphasis.

The point I hope to make clear about drum sound assignments is that it's practical to assign your main drum sounds on neighboring pads (or keys). Having your main kick on the third pad, top row; your main snare on the fourth pad of a middle row; and your main hat on the first pad, bottom row doesn't seem very practical for programming your main drum sequences. Such an assignment, which would require your hand position and fingers to move much faster than perhaps necessary. And this factor can increase the probability that your timing will be off, or at least it will make it difficult for you to achieve the timing that you want. On the other hand, if you assign your sounds in relative, pre-determined mapped out groups, especially your main drums, you undoubtedly will gain a number of advantages.

Group Map Assignments (GMA)

The most obvious advantages of Group Map Assignments, hereafter referred to as GMA, is the proximity that it allows and, ultimately, how practical it is. The closer the pads (sounds) that you want to trigger — in conjunction — are to one another, the easier it will be for you to go from one pad (sound) to another. Instead of making distant pad-strikes that force you to go from row 4, then back to row 1, you can simply assign the sounds of an entire *group* to either row 1 or row 4. The idea here is to narrow down your GMAs to three or four pads per group. For example, for drums, this is easy. Kick, snare, hat are already a natural group, so it's practical to keep them that way. And you can add any other drum-related sound to this group to make it a 4-pad group, thereby taking up one entire row of pads — simple, plain, easy, organized, and, above all, practical.

Perhaps the biggest advantage of a GMA is rhythm organization. That is, by mapping your sounds out into groups, you are in essence, turning your sequencer/drum machine into a de-facto rhythm section: the drummer, or rather the drum GMA is on one row; the guitar GMA is on another row; and the piano/strings GMA is on another row.

Finally, here it's important to note that the kind of music production we've been discussing is fundamentally electronic. However, my perspective is that as the beatmaker (composer/programmer/producer) you alone actually make up the rhythm section. A beatmaker's musical understanding is just as relevant as a traditional instrumentalist's understanding. The only difference between beatmakers and traditional instrumentalists is that most beatmakers do not necessarily choose to play traditional musical instruments. Instead, we most often use EMPIs to play, program, and sequence sounds, both in traditional and non-traditional manners.

The Significance of Timing Correct

To beatmakers, timing correct is simply a steady hand and a mistake-proof measure for programming sequences. Timing correct automatically *corrects* time to the preset value that you choose. Here's how it works. Let's say you want to record a musical sequence. First, you set a time correct value, most beatmakers typically set this value to $1/16^{th}$ Note or $1/16^{th}$ TRPLT. Next, you put your sequencer into record mode and compose a pattern. While in your sequencer's record mode, you play sounds (either internally or triggered from an external EMPI) in a pattern of your liking. Each "event-strike"[94] that you program lands anywhere within the measure that you choose. Now what happens with timing correct is that it *corrects* the placement of the event-strikes that you program. That is, it automatically shifts (moves) your actual event-strike performance (placement) to the nearest step in the measure that your timing correct value is set to. This means that a timing correct value of $1/16^{th}$ will shift your event-strike over to the nearest $1/16^{th}$ step in the measure. So for example, within a 1-bar measure in 4/4 time, if you play (program) a snare on the standard 2, then play it again on the 4, timing correct automatically places the hit two beats later, on the exact same $1/16^{th}$ step of where you programmed the first snare. In other words, timing correct not only corrects your timing, for all intents and purposes, it essentially *perfects* your timing. This is why I refer to it as a mistake-proof measure for programming sequences.

Even though timing correct perfects the timing of the events in a sequence that you program, timing correct doesn't always help; in fact, in many cases it actually makes your timing too perfect and unnatural. For example, have you ever tapped in (played) a drum pattern on your drum machine or sequencer and it didn't play back *exactly* how you played it? Well, that's because the timing correct value *corrected* your timing. Remember, timing correct is a "big-brother" style function that automatically corrects your playing within a sequence.

---

[94] Every event that you program within a sequence is what I call an **event-strike**. For example, tapping a drum pad is an event strike, playing a key on a keyboard is also an event-strike.

But timing correct is very helpful when it comes to creating a standard repetitive event-strike, such as a typical hi-hat pattern, which lands on every 6th event (step) within a measure. In a case such as this, you can set the timing correct value to 1/8th, then casually tap out a standard hi-hat pattern, without worrying if your timing is right, because the timing correct function will automatically move each hi-hat event-strike to the nearest 1/8th. But as helpful as this may be, it's important to remember that timing correct does not distinguish between what events that you do or do not want to apply corrective measures to. While you may want to employ timing correct to ensure that your hi-hat strikes are landing exactly 6 events apart, remember that whatever timing correct value you have set will also correct every event-strike that you initiate, which means that you can use multiple timing correct values for different parts of the same sequence.

Choosing the Right Timing Correct Setting (Value):
Depends on the Goal of the Drum Pattern

Timing correct is just that: It's a corrective measure for your timing. Therefore, how you set your timing correct values should be determined by how good (or bad) your general sense of timing is. If your timing is excellent, that is, your drum event-strikes are comparable to the playing of a traditional drummer — meaning you strike *on time*, with little to no mistakes, then you really don't even need to have the timing correct function on. But if your timing is fairly decent and you want to put in some swing, then you're probably better off setting the timing correct note value to either the default 1/16th NOTE or perhaps even 1/32 TRPLT. (If you're using an Akai MPC, you also want to make sure that the shuffle % is set to: 50, and set the Shift timing to: LATER.) If your timing is poor, then you almost certainly want to use the timing correct note value of 1/16th Note or 1/16th TRPLT. The reason many well-known beatmakers set the timing correct to 1/16th and/or 1/16th TRPLT is not because their timing is poor, but instead because their timing is so good, they know how to manipulate the corrective nuances of the timing correct function to their advantage. But when using the standard 1/16th NOTE value, you should be aware that if your timing isn't all that great, and if you're not particularly skilled at note correction and the like, you run the risk of recording drum pattern sequences that sound "stuck" or "robotic" and slow-dragging with an off-beat feel.

Generally speaking though, I recommend setting the timing correct to either 1/32 TRPLT (especially for vintage hardware sequencers like the Akai MPC 60 II or the E-Mu SP 1200), 1/16, or 1/16TRPLT, and leaving it as your default for all of your basic drum patterns. For instance, let's say that you have an arrangement of non-drum sounds looping nicely and you've just added the main kick and snare to the sequence, and everything's really starting to come together. All you need now to complete the drum pattern is the main hi-hat. Why stop the loop, change the timing correct, restart the loop, then play the hi-hat with the corrective *protection?* Forget that, if you've got the loop cooking, and the main kick and snare are already in place, then just play the hi-hat right over the top of the existing pattern, in real-time; in this way, you're forced to trust your own timing rather than merely rely on the time correct function. I also recommended that you get accustomed to programming your event-strikes exactly how your fingers play them in the sequence, mistakes and all; this way, you'll build up your timing strengths and neutralize your timing weaknesses. Finally, though it may be a good idea to keep a default timing correct value for your main drum sounds and patterns, there are occasions where changing the timing correct value makes a lot of sense. For instance, depending upon the rhythmic nature of the event that you want to initiate and drum pattern that you want to achieve (especially additional syncopation like stutter hi-hat, kick, or snare patterns), choosing the most effective timing correct value is essential.

BeatTip – Timing Correct with the Note Repeat Function

Timing correct is a steady hand, but when used creatively with a sequencer's note repeat function, it becomes a stutter and roll sound maker. One of the most popular sound aesthetics in beatmaking is the stutter-drum hit sound (rapid, successive syncopation). This sound aesthetic first appeared in New York in the early/mid-1980s, around the time the Roland TR 808 drum machine started to get its first heavy use in hip hop/rap music. Since then, the stutter-drum hit sound aesthetic has become a major cornerstone of the modern trap sound. There are many methods and techniques for achieving this aesthetic, but if you use an MPC or something similar like the Maschine, the easiest method involves simply adjusting the timing correct value and turning on the note repeat function, and recording the drum-hit (kick, snare, or hat) to spec. For example, in order to achieve the stutter-hat effect, simply set the timing correct value to $1/8^{th}$ or $1/16^{th}$ or $1/16^{th}$ TRPLT, depending on the space and dynamics of the syncopation that you want to achieve.

Drum Programming (Composing)

The Two Basic Forms of Drum Programming: Break-Beat Blend and Hit-Stab Drum Programming

In beatmaking, there are two basic forms of drum programming: break-beat blend drum programming and hit-stab drum programming. Break-beat blend programming, which is characterized by the use of wholesale sampled sections of the break from records, was first popularized by Grandmaster Flash in the early 1980s; it was then further extended by the likes of Marley Marl, DJ Premier, and others in the late 1980s and early/mid-1990s.[95] Hit-stab drum programming, which is characterized by the use of unique, individual one-hit drum stabs and hits (particularly kicks, snares, and hi-hats) that are played (programmed) in traditional drummer-like fashion, was initiated and first popularized by Marley Marl in the mid-1980s. Today, some beatmakers still employ the break-beat blend drum programming form. However, since the mid-1990s, the hit-stab form has served as the unofficial default drum programming for beatmakers.

Basic Concepts of Traditional Drum Programming and Arrangement

The most basic drum structure and arrangement within 4/4 time (the default time signature of most hip hop/rap beats) breaks down like this: kick (bass drum) lands on the "1" and "3" (1st and 3rd beats); snare lands on the "2" and the "4;" and the hi-hat on every half beat. Regarding the placement of the hi-hat, it's worth noting that unlike electronic drum machines and sequencers, live drummers can not play the hi-hat 100% throughout any given drum pattern while they're playing other pieces in a given drum set (e.g. snare, toms, and cymbals), so there are times within any given pattern where the steady hi-hat sound naturally *drops out*. A live drummer has human limitations, while an electronic drum machine or sequencer does not — drum machines play whatever arrangement they're programmed to play, for as long as they're programmed to play it.

---

[95] See my interview of DJ Marley Marl, located in the Interviews Part of this study, for details on how he came up with this form of drum programming. Although Marley Marl is rightfully credited with laying down the foundation for hit-stab drum programming, the form was further developed and extended during the Pioneers/Avant-Garde Period (1988-1994) by the likes of DJ Premier, Large Professor, Dr. Dre, Pete Rock, and RZA. It's also worth noting that the hit-stab drum programming form was again further developed and extended during the Post-Pioneers Period (1995-2000) by the likes of J Dilla, DJ Toomp, Just Blaze, Kanye West, Timbaland, and The Neptunes.

Drum Patterns and How Drums Land in a Pattern/Program

How the main kick, snare, and hi-hat lands

Generally speaking, kicks can either hit *flush* or *off*. A **flush-kick**, hereafter represented by the symbol **fK** on the drum pattern diagrams presented in this section, is the main kick sound. "Flush" refers to a prominent kick sound that lands on a whole or half-beat within a measure (a bar of music). The flush-kick is one of the most pronounced and sonic elements within any sequence and, subsequently, any beat. In fact, it's the lone kick sound that anchors the beat. The **off-kick**, hereafter represented by the symbol **oK** on the drum pattern diagrams in this section, is the kick sound that is the least prominent kick sound. "Off" refers to the less prominent kick sound that lands on quarter and eighth beats within a measure (a bar of music). The off-kick's main purpose is to set up or accentuate the flush-kick.

The flush-kick can be **doubled (paired), stranded, stretched, and/or stuttered**. The off-kick can be *pinched-in* before and/or *wrapped* around the flush-kick. The terms doubled (paired), stranded, stretched, pinched-in, and wrapped all refer to specific event placements — the how and where the events take place. More often than not, the off-kick is pinched-in 2 events (steps) before a flush-kick. When pinching-in the off-kick, it's sometimes a good idea to decrease its velocity. Ordinarily, when you're creating new drum patterns and programs, the velocity level is at its full value for all of the drum sounds. So one way to make your drums sound more real and more natural, and perhaps more like a live drummer and such, is to manipulate the velocity levels of some of the specific drum events within a beat's sequences. Since the flush-kick is more prominent than the off-kick, usually you don't want to tweak it's velocity levels too much. However, decreasing the velocity level (volume and impact of the hit) of the off-kick often proves to be more effective. Remember, the role of the off-kick is to set up, accentuate, and generally, play off of the lead role of the flush-kick. Therefore, decreasing the velocity of off-kicks helps you establish a more real drum texture.

Like kicks, snares either hit flush or off. A flush-snare, hereafter represented by the symbol **fS** on the drum pattern diagrams in this section, is the main snare sound. It's the sound that is commonly known to land on the ***2 and the 4*** — the second and fourth beats of a bar. The flush-snare is the snare sound that is the most prominent and audible within any sequence and, subsequently, any beat.

It's the snare sound that, in effect, *times* the beat — imagine if the metronome played throughout a beat, on every second and fourth metronome tone the flush snare would hit, hence, the meaning of the 2 *and the* 4. The off-snare, hereafter represented by the symbol **oS** on the drum diagrams in this section, is the snare sound that is the least prominent snare sound within any sequence. Like the off-kick, the off-snare's main purpose is to set up, accentuate, and generally play off the lead role of the flush snare.

Hi-hats, hereafter represented by the symbol **H** on the drum pattern diagrams below, are generally all flush. About 10 years ago, hi-hats played a more primary, default-like role in drum patterns. However, since around 2002 they have increasingly been used in a more secondary percussive or featured role. In some beats, beatmakers are even experimenting with leaving out hi-hats altogether (I sometimes make beats with no hi-hat hits at all). Still, basic 4/4 time seems to beg for some sort of hi-hat construction. Thus it's important to know when and where hi-hats land in a typical drum pattern.[96]

BeatTip – Shared Fundamental Foundations of Drum Patterns

No matter what new drum pattern you create from scratch, the reality is that the new pattern will most likely not be that different from any other drum pattern or program that you've already created or will ever create, because all drum patterns share some kind of fundamental foundation. Moreover, there are a number of standard drum pattern clichés in beatmaking; and it is from these standard drum clichés that all new drum patterns emerge. In the diagrams that I've included in this section, I have catalogued what I find to be the four most commonly used drum patterns in beatmaking. And I demonstrate how these patterns break down within a sequence, specifically the ways in which drum sounds land in most beatmaking drum patterns.

---

[96] For an easy understanding of the relationship between drum sounds and where they land in a measure, consider a simple marching band drum pattern. In a typical marching band drum pattern, the kick lands flush on the 1, 2, 3, and 4, and so on, while the hi-hat lands on the 1, 2, 3, and 4; snare on the 2 and 4. Using this basic backbeat of the flush kick, the off-kick, snare, and hi-hat can be syncopated in ways that allow for the creation of an entirely different drum pattern.

DRUM SOUNDS AND DRUM PROGRAMMING

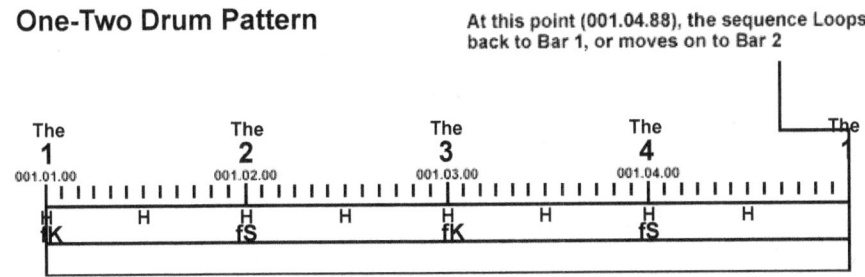

Figure 5 One-Two Drum Pattern

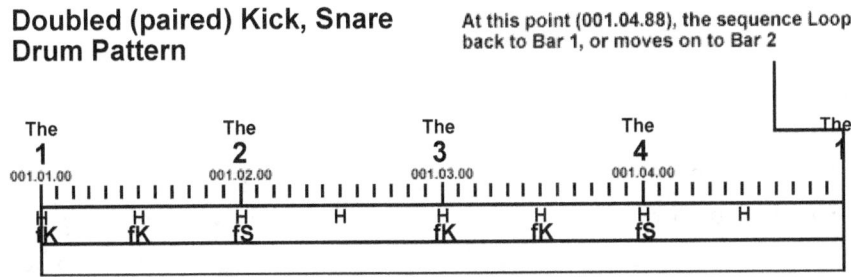

Figure 6 Doubled (paired) Kick, Snare Drum Pattern

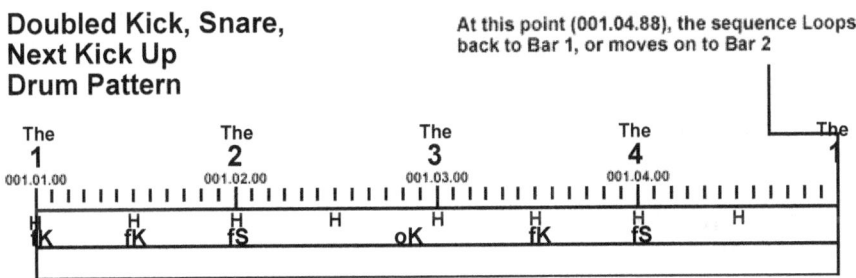

Figure 7 Doubled Kick, Snare, Next Kick Up Drum Pattern

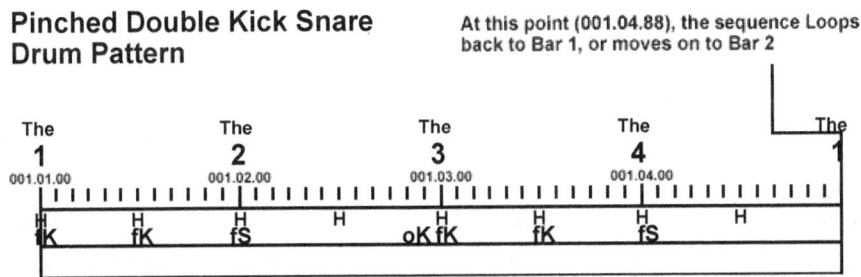

Figure 8 Pinched Double Kick Snare Drum Pattern

From these diagrams, you can make numerous observations about drum patterns and the ways in which drum sounds tend to land in drum patterns (created in 4/4). First, you can see that **a sequence is actually a chronological time line of events** — *a grid of programmed action*. The sequencer grid of each of the diagrams contains measured parameters for which all events must be programmed, played in real time or *placed* in with the sequence stopped.

151

Second, we can see how each drum hit (event) plays off of the other. Looking at Figure 4, One-Two Drum Pattern, we can see how the flush-snare (fS) plays off of the flush-kick (fK). The flush-kick within the bar occurs on the 001.01.00 step and the 001.03.00 step, twenty-four steps apart from itself. The flush-snare falls between each kick, exactly twelve steps apart from each kick, and twenty-four steps apart from itself. This is what I describe as a "long spatial distance," as opposed to Figure 7, where the flush-kick and flush-snare carry a "short spatial distance." Understanding the spatial distance between the kick and the snare helps determine how the drum pattern can be further built up or stripped down. Furthermore, knowing the spatial distances between flush-kicks and flush-snares within typical drum patterns also allows you to identify whether you're working with a simple or complex drum pattern. One of the biggest mistakes that many beatmakers often make is that they mismatch or try to force simple or complex drum patterns to work with the wrong non-drum sounds and arrangements. But the reality is, most drum patterns should *never* be all that complex to begin with. Here, you must remember that the drums are critical to holding the rhythm together and the time steady. Therefore, they can't afford to be too haywire or too active, as this disrupts and undermines the entire flow and feel of the beat.

Determining Simple and Complex Drum Patterns

So how can you determine a simple drum pattern from a complex one? For instance, how do you know that the "One-Two Drum Pattern" is a simple pattern and not a complex one? Simply put, you can identify the "One-Two Drum Pattern" as a simple drum pattern because there are only six total drum-hit events (not including the eight hi-hat events) that occur within one bar. Likewise, how do you know that Figure 7, the "Pinched Double Kick, Snare Drum Pattern" is a complex drum pattern? You can identify the "Pinched Double Kick, Snare" as a complex drum pattern because it contains eight total drum-hit events (not including the eight standard hi-hat events) within one bar. Generally speaking, the higher the number of drum-hit events within a measure, in this case one bar, the more complex the drum pattern will be. Finally, the recognition of simple and complex drum patterns is essential, because not only does it save you time when creating drum patterns, it also broadens your understanding of the ways in which drum sounds can work together as well as the multiple directions drum patterns can potentially take. Moreover, this understanding increases your ability to program in rhythmic samples, melody lines, and other non-drum sounds in a much more creative and efficient manner.

Spacial Differences Between Flush- and Off-Drum Sounds

Knowing the spatial differences between the flush-snares and flush-kicks of typical drum patterns is also key. Knowledge of spatial difference yields a better understanding for where the main drum hit events *should* occur within a sequence; this undoubtedly increases your sense of timing and feeling for rhythm, and thus decreases your reliance on quantizing, time stretching, and other timing correction measures. Finally, although knowledge of spatial difference is important for all beatmakers, it's particularly important for those beatmakers who primarily use software-based production setups, especially those software practitioners who prefer to "draw" in their hits.

Knowing Drum-Hit Event Placements

Another reason why it's helpful to know the event placements of basic drum patterns is because it helps cue in your loop methods. By understanding the most fundamental drum patterns, you increase your looping skills considerably. Furthermore, there is a practical reason for learning the basic drum patterns: corrective editing. When you're building sequences, you tend to quickly get caught up in the creative moment. Good ideas grow in your mind rather quickly, right? So what happens when a drum sound seems to be off-beat and awkward? Well, by knowing where the hits *should* occur, you can isolate the section in the sequence in which the event is in question, then check it out and then quickly correct (or remove) it if necessary. For instance, let's use the "Doubled Kick, Snare Drum." If the event, in this case the flush-kick, starts on the first step of the sequence, then any flush-kick placement not exactly on (or very near to) the 6th, 24th, and/or the 30th step will sound awkward. However, if your isolation of the events reveals that all the flush-kicks are landing where they're supposed to, then you know that it's something else that's generating the awkward sound. This is key because it helps you to troubleshoot your sequences and loops much more efficiently.[97]

Understanding Drum Syncopation

In my examination of how drum hits land in a drum pattern, specifically the concept of flush and off drum-hits, I focused primarily on flush-hits. Here,

---

[97] This usually means that the non-drums music must be further modified. A good example of this would be a sample that needs more precise chopping or a total re-working.

I want to focus on "off" drum-hits, in particular, the meaning of syncopation. In all components of music, not just drumming, syncopation refers to the way in which musical events deviate (unexpectedly) from the established succession of regularly spaced strong and weak beats in a measure. In other words, syncopation could be the result of *stress* (action, a drum-hit event) on a normally unstressed beat or *unstress* (no action, no drum-hit event) on a normally stressed beat. So if a part of the measure that is normally stressed is unstressed, then rhythm is syncopated; likewise, if a part of the measure that is normally unstressed is stressed, then the rhythm is syncopated. By looking at any of the four drum pattern diagrams discussed earlier in this chapter, you can imagine how and where syncopation might occur within any given drum pattern.[98]

Extended Drum Sound and Programming Techniques, Notes, and Tips

How Drum Sounds Are Often Used in Drum Frameworks and Sequences: Kicks, Snares, Hats, and Cymbals Work Together

Drum sounds work together in various ways, so understanding the ways in which the different categories of drum sounds work together in drum frameworks (programs, sequences) is paramount to a beatmaker's ability to insert quality and effectiveness to the overall arrangement of a beat. Below I have outlined a set of parameters for how each sound category can most effectively be used in drum frameworks (programs, sequences).

Kicks

Kicks are the *sonic glue* that hold both the drum framework together and the pulse of the entire beat itself. Therefore, knowing which types of kicks cause which effects within a drum framework and overall beat is critical. For instance, *hard* kicks (heavier frequence and sonic impact) are best used with low bass-filtered driven or synthetic-sounds-based beats that aren't too active. Harder kicks are also very effective with beats that feature simple melodies and minimal changes. On the other hand, *soft* or *medium* kicks work best with more extensive compositional arrangements and sample-based beats that feature highly

---

[98] Syncopation is used in many different musical styles and pretty much all contemporary music, but syncopation is a fundamental component of the African American (Black) music tradition and the styles that stem from it.

creative uses of samples. Softer kicks are also very effective for beats in which the frequency levels range from mostly mid to high.

Snares and Claps
Pitch-Shifts

In the beatmaking tradition, there is a great deal more experimentation with drum phrasing than in other twentieth-century American popular music traditions. One key way that unique phrasing is achieved in beatmaking is through the use of what I like to call snare "pitch-shifts." Pitch-shifts simply refer to alternating pitch values of the same or multiple drum-hits. In the case of snare pitch-shifts, the process of alternating the pitch value of the main snare within a drum sequence not only adds in a subtle but very effective change, it also gives a *push and pull* effect to the various sections within the song structure. This is why snare pitch-shifts work very well within the verse section of a song: they add change without unnecessary distraction — something subtle that true lyricists can use as an additional timing mechanism for their rhyme flow. Snare pitch-shifts also work well in the hook (chorus) section because they offer the level of variety that can further set a hook (chorus) apart from the other sections of a beat/song.

The Genius of the "2" and the "4"

Understanding the *"2 and the 4"* means realizing that once the kick and the hi-hat are laid down, rhythm actually already exists. This is why snares do not necessarily have to be loud or mega-compressed to be effective. With 4/4 time, our minds are already pre-conditioned to hearing *something* land on the "2 and the 4." This is precisely why low velocity claps often work well with high powered kicks. Incidentally, this is why the Atlanta snap sound works. At first glance, the snap sound seems redundantly simple; I mean, musically, the sound appears to be devoid of any real *feeling*. But the snap sound does actually take advantage of the genius of the "2 and the 4." Rather than emphasizing a heavy or unique snare, the snap sound focuses on building the track with a standard *snap* on the "2 and the 4." By restricting the feature component of the snare, and stripping down other musical elements, beatmakers who create the snap sound can then build the track with more percussive collages, 808s, and other bass sounds. And although the snap sound is something primarily meant for the clubs, its philosophy does have its roots in the process of intuitive chopping.

Alternating Snares, Clap-Hits, Chopped Chimes, Velocity Modification, and Delayed-Snares

Another effective programming technique for snares involves alternating the main snare drum-hit with clap-hits, chopped chimes, or other percussive-stabs or -hits. Instead of using the same snare-hit throughout the song, you can program in a clap-hit and alternate it with the main snare-hit. You can let the clap-hit play through for the first 8 bars, then come in with the main snare or any other alternating pattern you can come up with. Also, you can cut up some chimes and layer them over the top of the snare- or clap-hit. And whether you apply this technique throughout the entire beat/song or just in certain sections, it's quite effective because it helps to build ambiance, and it offers a lot of personal nuance to your drum frameworks and overall style and sound.

Modifying the velocity, the attack and volume level or impact-level of each snare- or clap-hit, is a great way to naturally create swing. If you listen to traditional live drummers, you will notice that because of the "human factor," it's impossible for them to ever hit the same drum with the exact same velocity twice. This means that everytime they strike a drum, there is a slightly different attack, sometimes harder, sometimes lighter. To achieve, or rather *retain* this nuance and naturalness in beatmaking, you can simply turn off the velocity function within the EMPI(s) that you use to craft your drum frameworks, or you can record your drum programs with the velocity level at its full value, then afterwards go in and manually adjust (program) the velocity changes on specific drum-hits.

Finally, the use of "delayed-snares" is also another effective snare technique. Delayed-snares describes specific snare-hits that are purposely placed *off-time* within a drum pattern. Delayed-snares can be used to mask awkward pauses and gaps or minor glitches and other unwanted, but otherwise unremovable, blemishes within a beat. Also, delayed-snares can be used to create unique effects in the drum framework. For example, delaying the lead snare-hit for a bridge or a break-down. Furthermore, used correctly, delayed-snares can also conceal the short-comings of a less-than-perfect loop.

Hats

The use of different types of hi-hats can also serve multiple roles within the drum framework and the overall beat. Standard hi-hats (semi-closed), which are high in pitch, work to "push" the flow of the beat. Generally, standard hi-hats have a high pitch. Open-hi-hats are much slower pitched than standard hi-hats, so they can work to drag the pace or rather *temper* the rhythm of the beat. Closed-hi-hats, which are typically faster in pitch than both standard hi-hats and open hi-hats, work like a clear-cut metronome. Sometimes their tightness can make a beat sound too mechanically clean and unnatural. Further, keep in mind that each type of hi-hat can add shuffle and swing to a drum framework; however, that being said, achieving this effect does depend on the actual pitch and tone of the hat being used. Finally, here are some general "rules" regarding hats:

- Standard closed hi-hats help with a tighter sense of time, while semi-closed hi-hats are best for *shuffling* the time along.
- Hats and rides are also great for achieving additional warmth and clarity through unique arrangement and pronouncement techniques rather than using external processors, e.g. reverb, etc.
- The use of alternating hi-hats and hi-hat patterns is a good thing when you want to change the flow of the hook (chorus) section in a song.
- Hats give tracks extra depth; and hats work like the second hand on a clock.
- Unique hat arrangements can shade the loop points in a beat.

Cymbals and Bells

Cymbals play an important role in certain drum frameworks. For example, rides bode well for ambiance; they also help balance out the impact of rumbling (bass heavy, muddy, or distorted) kicks. Bells work well as "treble managers," that is, they're good at meshing with (or rather handling) the high peaks of samples or synthetic-sounds phrases; they're also useful at offsetting the flatness of low-filtered bass-driven beats. Cymbals can also substitute for the role of hi-hat patterns. This substitution carries an array of effects. For certain drum patterns, it can make a drum framework sound jazzier. Then again, with other drum patterns it can make the drum framework sound aggressive and very *hungry*, even haunting. Finally, cymbals can be very effective when they're layered on kicks at specific moments within each section of the beat/song.

Extended Drum Framework Techniques, Notes, and Tips
Uncovering and Taking Advantage of the Open and Hidden Spaces

Every drum pattern has *open* or *hidden* spaces. The "open spaces" of a drum pattern refer to those spots in the pattern where you can imagine (hear) a non-drum sound being placed (recorded) over the top. For example, take a look at the diagram of the "One-Two Drum Pattern" below:

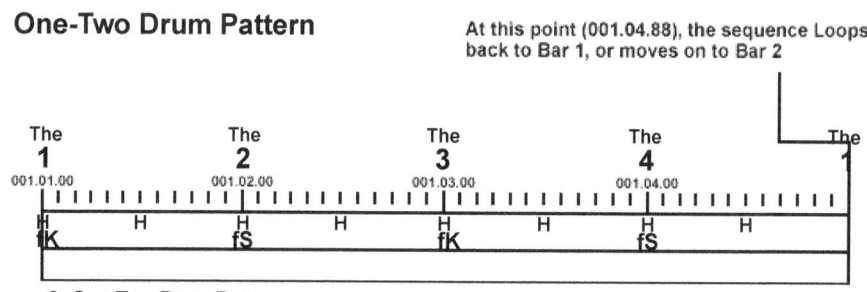

Figure 9 One-Two Drum Pattern

Imagine your favorite kick and snare in this pattern. Because of the spacing dynamics of this pattern, you will notice the *pause* that naturally stands out after each kick and before each snare. These spaces are *open* because they're empty, and therefore, they naturally stand out, and seemingly invite a non-drum sound to be inserted.

On the other hand, "hidden spaces" are camouflaged by the drum pattern itself. That is, the "hidden spaces" are flush with the drum sounds. Look at the same diagram, imagine adding in a sample or bass line beginning on top of the kick, as opposed to between the kick and the snare. The results will be dramatically different for two reasons. First, keep in mind that the way in which a sequence loops is primarily determined by the particular placement of events within that given sequence. So for instance, if you insert a sample or bass line in the open space of the drum pattern, it will overlap in a way that might not coincide with how the sequence loops. However, if you insert a sample or bass line in the hidden space, that is, on top of one of the flush kicks or flush snares, it will more than likely mesh better with how the sequence loops, even if it overlaps.

The second reason the result of the beat will be different when you insert non-drum music in hidden as opposed to open spaces is because these spaces determine the degree to which the drums ultimately stand out or fade back. Remember, though drums indeed play a central role in a beat, they can serve this role in two different capacities: either in a featured capacity or as accompaniment capacity. Take for instance, Jay-Z's "Girls, Girls, Girls," produced by Just Blaze. In that song, Just Blaze uses the drums to *accompany* the samples; that is to say, the drum framework just works to keep the song *steady*. Now consider Amerie's "One Thing," produced by Rich Harrison. In the latter song, Rich Harrison uses the drums in a *featured* capacity, that is to say, the drum framework is really the main component that drives the song.

Drum Fills Require a Different Focus in Beatmaking: Understanding the Fundamentals of Drum Fills in the Beatmaking Process

In beatmaking, there is perhaps no artificial sound event that can be made to sound more natural or more ridiculous than the ubiquitous drum fill (commonly but incorrectly known in beatmaking as a drum roll). Part of the reason drum fills can have such a range in quality is because some beatmakers recognize that drum fills come in an assorted variety, while others inaccurately assume that all drum fills are pretty much the same.

But all drum fills are not the same. For instance, there's the standard classic rock drum fill, where there is a straight-forward progression from snare to tom-toms to floor tom. There's the Southern Bounce drum fill, where the snare fill is augmented by heavy syncopation. There's also the "sweep" drum fill (a type of drum fill native to beatmaking) which is more of a section change than drum fill. Most beatmakers develop their style of drum fills based on some sort of combination of the drum fill types I just described. However, if you listen closely to how different beatmakers use drum fills, you will notice an interesting variation there as well.

Drum fills can be used for a number of reasons. They can be used to setup impending changes in a beat. They can be used to highlight specific events in a beat. They can be used to temper the pace (tempo) of a beat. They can be used to resolve and/or add tension to your music. They can be used simply as a "filler element" when you've exhausted ideas for a dope groove that could stand just something a little extra. Drum fills can even be used to shield or cover up unwanted sounds and loop glitches.

Since drum fills come in a variety of styles and can be used in so many ways, it's important to know several things about creating drum fills in the beatmaking process. First, although some may swear by the time correct, whenever you want to create the most basic, standard, garden-variety drum fill, for example, something like the classic rock style, I recommend turning off the timing correct (if applicable to your gear) or any quantizing value (if applicable to your gear) before you begin. Since it's a simple drum fill style, you can really make it sound more natural without the note correction of your sequencer.

Second, whenever you go for the modern trap drum fill sound, it's best to keep the timing correct on. Moreover, it's a good idea to adjust the value to between 1/8, 1/16 (TRPLT), and 1/32, depending on your use of this style of drum fill. The thing to keep in mind here is, the more stutter syncopation and movement that you want to create within the fill, the more adjustments you may want to make with varying time correction values as well as the note repeat function (if applicable to your gear).

Finally, it's important to remember that when creating drum fills in the beatmaking process, mismatched drum fill timbres (sounds) almost always undermine the overall sound and texture of your music. Therefore, when creating drum fills, be careful of the velocity nuance (tonal feeling generated by velocity) that is created when you play snares and toms in progression and in a rapid succession. When making drum fills, I recommend turning off the default velocity level (if applicable to your gear) and playing the drum fill with velocity levels that match the pressure of your pad hits. If you're not using drum pads, but instead, drawing in your drum hits in a software program, a good thing to do is to alternate the velocity levels of the beginning, middle, and end of the drum fill hits by a level that looks like an arc, that is to say, from low to highest, back to low.

Important note about the terms drum fills and drum rolls. Many beatmakers use the term drum "roll" incorrectly. A regular BeatTips.com commenter, i the t, (Ivan Turner) points out that, "From a drummers perspective…a 'fill'" is a "feature normally lasting from a half to two bars that serves as a transition between sections or simply highlights the quadratic structure of a song." And that "'rolls' are typically where one drum is repeatedly hit (eg. paradiddles) in fast succession to sustain the sound of a drum with a short decay, (like when a magician is building up to the climax of his trick you will often hear a drum roll)."

The Human Touch: A Note About Playing EMPIs Like Various Traditional Musical Instruments

I see the drum pads on my Akai MPC 4000 drum machine/sampler/sequencer the same way a guitarist sees the strings on his guitar; or the same way a keyboardist sees the keys on his keyboard; or the same way a drummer sees the skinheads on his drums. I don't merely *program* my MPC — I *play* it. Beatmakers are not simply a bunch of clever electronic music production *programmers*. Nearly all of us are performance artists, much in the same vein of traditional musicians (instrumentalists). However, what distinguishes beatmakers from traditional musicians is the fact that, by and large, we are not limited to just *one* instrument in the same way that one-instrument-capable traditional musicians are. On the contrary. On every beat, nearly all beatmakers are responsible for playing (or providing) the drums, the string, or wind instruments. So EMPIs represent for us a *multi-instrument* — an instrument that, in effect, allows us to truly play and tap into the essence of *any* instrument that we want.[99] One moment a beatmaker can be crafting the drums, the very next moment he (can be laying down bass lines, and still the next moment he can be *flipping* a sample; or banging out a melodic keyboard phrase. EMPIs are musical devices that virtually give beatmakers endless instrumental and musical possibilities.[100]

Different Ways to Humanize Your Drums in Beatmaking: Maintaining a "Real Drummer" Feel in a Programming Environment

Drums in hip hop/rap music are, more often than not, out in front. That is to say, they are typically arranged and recorded as a feature of the song and placed prominently in the mix. But while most beatmakers grasp this common theme in beatmaking, many execute the practice in a way that makes their drums sound less human and more artificial.

Because most beats are a blend of various drum sounds from any number of sound sources (vinyl records, drum sound packs, .wav files, etc.), I've always believed that much of the value and weight of a beat depends on the "human touch" of the drums. Even though we operate in a programming environment using a palette of sampled and synthetic drum sounds, we can still humanize our drums and maintain some level of a "real drummer" feel. Below are two methods that you can use to humanize your drums and give them that real feel.

---

[99] This is one of the most liberating aspects of the beatmaking tradition. In fact, beatmakers have the potential to be much more versatile music producers than the average traditional musician.

[100] Because EMPIs are indeed instruments, beatmakers who use software-based setups should be careful to remember the "human touch" so that they don't become more *programmer* than musician. One area to safeguard against this is to perhaps use an EMPI with pads (for example a MIDI controller with pads) for triggering their sounds; this gives the feeling of playing something rather than *programming* something. Note: One major characteristic of the African American (Black) music tradition and all of the music traditions that stem from it — most notably rhythm and blues, rock 'n' roll, soul, and funk — was that <u>all</u> instruments, particularly the bass guitar, were played in a percussive manner. Thus, playing samples and other sounds on drum pads harkens back and pays homage to that tradition.

Use Simple Drum Frameworks and Build from There

The easiest and perhaps most effective way to humanize your drums and maintain a more "real drummer" feel is to use more simplified, straight-forward drum frameworks. Overly complex or busy drum patterns not only undermine the feel, texture, and scope of a beat, they also tend to create distractions for rappers (which tend to be especially troublesome for the more skillful lyricists). Simplified drum frameworks and solid, non-distracting drum patterns are in league with a "real drummer" feel because such frameworks and patterns correlate with the physical limitations of a human drummer.

Still, I never overlook the fact that beatmaking, despite some of its live characteristics, is a programmable medium. As such, there are drum frameworks, specifically sub-patterns, that can be created in beatmaking that can not be matched by a human drummer in a traditional setting. But even those drum patterns that go beyond human limitations can still be made to have a more humanized touch and a real drummer feel. In fact, my most complex drum schemes are really just combinations of smaller, simplified drum patterns combined together and arranged in a straight-forward scheme.

Velocity

I rarely make a beat without manipulating the velocity level of my drum sounds. Although I may initially program/record my drums at the full velocity level, I tend to go back and randomly decrease the levels of each drum sound (kick, snare, hat). Note: I typically keep variation of the velocity level of my kicks to a minimum, but for my snares and especially my hats, I tend to explore variation of the velocity level. Sometimes after I've created a drum pattern, I'll replay the snare and hat parts with the velocity "full level" function turned off. This assures that the velocity levels will be random and, therefore, more humanized.

Default Workflow Systems: Default Drum Programs and Sequence Templates

To streamline your creative output, I recommend creating what I call "default workflow systems." A default workflow system can be any stored beatmaking template, like a default drum sequence/pattern. It can also be a default method, style, or technique that you utilize in your personal beatmaking process, like a set approach to sampling, or a set approach to sequencing, etc. The theme of a default workflow system is *recycling*. You want to consistently reuse and infuse those components and characteristics of your beatmaking that are successful. The ultimate purpose of this being that it will help you create new beats much more efficiently, and it will help you customize your own unique style and sound.

A default drum sequence template (pattern) is any pre-made/pre-used/previously programmed drum sequence that you use to create new drum patterns. Default drum sequence templates can be extracted from beats that you've *already* made, attempted to make, or are currently making. Once you've created a beat, you can always scrap the non-drum music material and keep the drums. This left over drum pattern, what I call a "drum shell," can then be saved and used again. This is extremely helpful to your beatmaking process because it provides you with an arsenal of drum sequences that you can tap for ideas everytime you begin to create a new beat. By using default workflow systems you will not only improve your overall beatmaking efficiency, you will also streamline your entire beatmaking output. Hence, every new beat that you make is potentially a template for future beats.[101]

Finally, when it comes to drum shells, I recommend that you always keep at least fifteen drum shells (default drum patterns/sequence templates/programs) stored and on hand. The more drum shells that you have, the more quickly you'll learn to process your ideas. Also, to help increase workflow efficiency, I recommend that you create default sequence templates that include alternating hi-hat patterns.[102]

Check This Out – Use Your Drum Sounds to Improve Your Compositional Workflow: Knowing Your Drum Sounds Makes for a More Efficient Compositional Workflow

Compositional workflow — the collective processes, methods, and time it takes a beatmaker to create a beat — can be improved in a number of different

---

[101] This doesn't mean that you never make any new drum sequences, etc. from scratch. On the contrary, the idea of a default drum sequence (pattern) is to help you generate new ideas, by incorporating some of your most successful old ones.
[102] I maintain 25 default drum sequences, ranging from 1-bar, 2-bar, 4-bar, 8-bar, and 16-bar sequences. This permits me to work much more efficiently; also, it allows me to extract my ideas much more quickly. Consider this: When a live drummer in a band creates a drum scheme for a new song, he recalls on patterns that he's played before in the past, then he makes alterations as the song changes and develops. There's no big deal about making a new drum pattern from scratch, because 70%-90% of it will be something that you've already programmed before.

ways. Depending on the individual EMPI, the steps within most beatmaking processes can be condensed. Likewise, the various methods of achieving particular production goals can be realized, retooled, or retranslated in ways that bring about desired results faster and more efficiently. Even the reshuffling of one's production environment can improve workflow. (Do not underestimate the power of a comfortable chair or a good view.) But among the countless ways to improve compositional workflow, often the most overlooked way can be found in the area of drum sounds and drum sound modification.

Many beatmakers — myself included — take pride in crafting their drum sounds, despite the fact that there are also lots of beatmakers who depend (heavily) on pre-set drum sounds with little to no customization at all. For those beatmakers who see their drums as a major component of their overall production identity, individualized drum sound customization is key. But that being said, the processes of drum sound customization can impede workflow whenever it's overly applied during the making of a beat. This is why knowing your drum sounds is a great way to improve compositional workflow.

Whenever I'm making a beat, I choose my drum sounds quickly because I know them. I know their texture, I know their *color*, I know what types of sounds they'll go well with, I know how they'll sit and sound in the final mix. So for me, selecting the right drums for the right style and sound of beat that I'm working on at the moment doesn't involve a prolonged scroll through my drum library.

And although I may make a couple of modifications to a drum sound during the process of making a beat, those tweaks are minimum and on the fly, nothing too tedious or vibe busting. Again: I know my sounds, so I reach for the sounds that I think may fit with the current arrangement that I'm working on. I do not, however, embark upon some sort of drum-tweaking journey that can shift my focus from the beat — the entire arrangement — to just drum sounds. Moreover, I don't allow my workflow to be disrupted by a prolonged search of a drum sound folder. This is yet another reason why I like to keep my drum sound library tight, i.e. limited to a reasonable number of sounds. In other words, when I'm composing a beat, I'm leery of shifting too far away from composer to drum sound technician, or anything else for that matter.

Compositional workflow determines your ability to harness your creative moments in real time. Therefore, the longer your compositional workflow is disrupted, that is to say, the longer the act of composing is left on hold — in this case, by drum craft or "tech" work — the more you defeat your ability to harness your creative moments. This is why it's just as important to look for ways that improve your compositional workflow as it is to guard against anything that can inhibit it.

Technically speaking, any tweak of a drum sound during the creation of a beat makes you a "drum sound technician," which, in effect, disrupts your compositional workflow. But to what degree? During the live vibe/feel of making a beat, should the arrangement and scope of the beat be placed on hold until you tweak drum sounds to perfection? Or should drum sounds defer to the overall arrangement — with little to no consideration of their fit within the arrangement? What I mean here is, it's easier to find what fits from a well-known personal arsenal of drum sounds than it is from a big box of endless unknown sounds. Further, isn't it better to spend time making major tweaks to a drum sound in a stand-alone context outside of the beat arrangement at hand? I certainly believe there is a time for major tweaks — customization — of drum sounds in a stand-alone context. Hence, I strongly believe that it's important to set aside time for beatmaking sessions that are solely for the purpose of going through new drum sounds, modifying them to specific taste, and creating a trusted core set of drum sounds. But implementing extensive drum sound modifications or a prolonged drum sound selection process during the composition phase of making a beat can disrupt your flow of ideas and severely limit your ability to bring about the beat you envisioned. Simply knowing your drum sounds, particularly a core set of sounds, can improve your compositional workflow and cut down considerably the amount of time it takes you to complete a beat from start to finish.

Chapter 6

Hook A Beat Up, and Convert It Into Hip Hop Form
Composition, Programming, and Arrangement – Getting the Ingredients and Putting them All Together

> Unlike in more traditional music compositional practices, where multiple musicians perform as a group, either under the direction of one arranger and/or bandleader, in beatmaking, the beatmaker is the composer, the arranger, the bandleader, *and* the musician(s). –Sa'id

Programming, Conducting, Performing, and Playing (In Beatmaking, It's All Interrelated)

Even though beatmaking is not a traditional live music medium, it's core compositional processes are programmed (conducted) and performed (played) in real time. In beatmaking, every musical element is programmed/played *exactly* as it is designed by the individual beatmaker (or beatmaking collective). Every pattern, every event-strike of a sound within every sequence requires both programming and performance to be handled by the lone beatmaker (or a beatmaking collective). By contrast, in the more traditional music forms, the musical arrangements (either written or verbal musical instructions) are given to separate musicians. Having been giving their instructions, each musician fulfills the instructions that were assigned to them and their particular instrument. Within this traditional setting, the expectation of the conductor or bandleader is that each musician will play (to the best of their ability) each prescribed note, on time and in complete accordance to the proscribed arrangement, all the way through to the end of the song. In the traditional live music medium setting, there is a lot of room left for chance; everything from unique improvision to poor musical timing to shaky musicianship can occur.

On the other hand, in the compositional processes of beatmaking, not much (if anything) is ever left to chance. Every component of a beat is programmed and sequenced exactly as each beatmaker intends it to be. Once the beat is conceived, composed, structured, and programmed, it's locked in as is. If a beatmaker programs the beat to have changes occur on the 16th bar, there will be no concerns about whether or not the changes on the 16th bar are going to come in correctly and on time. In beatmaking, all of the musical elements have already been programmed, so the changes will occur exactly in accordance with whatever the beatmaker programmed. This does not mean that improvisation does not occur at anytime during the beatmaking process. Even though composition in beatmaking relies on the programming process, the compositional process is still very much a matter of capturing the creative moment.

Improvisation in beatmaking typically occurs at two primary moments: Once during the structural conception of the beat, and then once again after the beat has been created and additional changes are added. But in either case, the final result will still be an electronic program. In this way, beatmakers *give musical instructions* to their EMPIs, not live instrumentalists.[103] And unlike live instrumentalists, EMPIs play their instructions exactly as they were programmed.

Composition, Programming, and Arrangement

In its simplest understanding, composition, as it is in the beatmaking tradition, refers to the process of creating and coming up with sounds (ingredients) and the ideas for using them. The compositional process in beatmaking has no need for, is not predicated upon, nor does it necessarily rely on a *written* composition (as is the case in the classical music tradition).[104] Instead, composition in beatmaking involves the process of developing components and pieces of music that are then combined, arranged, and built into separate *blocks* of music that are then joined together to form one whole musical work. It is through this creation of separate music blocks, sequenced together using hardware or software sequencers, that the character of composition in beatmaking is most realized. Further, in the beatmaking tradition, the overall aim and essence of the compositional process is to come up with a break — the musical anomaly that the earliest hip hop DJ pioneers found on records, and then cut, mixed, and blended together into new compositions. In this vein, not only are beatmakers doing the job of the earliest hip hop DJ pioneers, they are also doing the job previously reserved for traditional musicians.

Finally, in beatmaking, this aforementioned break is usually made up of 2- or 4-bars. This is particularly important to know, as it helps in determining how and where *changes* (motifs) can be applied in a beat. For instance, a 2-bar

---

[103] A number of beatmakers often bring in live instrumentalists to play over their beats. Even still, this instrumentation will only occur where the beatmaker instructs or allows it to occur.
[104] For a detailed comparison of some of the fundamental characteristics of the beatmaking and hip hop/rap music traditions and the Western classicical music tradition, see chapter 10.

break doubled up is 4-bars. Thus the typical spot that an effective change can be inserted is somewhere near the middle or end of the 4th bar. Likewise, 4-bars doubled up is 8 total bars, and therefore, the typical spot that an effective change can be inserted is somewhere near the middle or end of the 8th bar. (These are not rules, but rather guides for common arrangement changes.)

Programming

In the beatmaking tradition, the compositional process is closely linked to the programming process. In fact, in beatmaking, the term "programming" can at times refer to several different processes all at once, it depends on the context. Programming can refer to the technical organization of the compositional components; it can refer to the *technical* organization of the arrangement components; or it can simply refer to the process of inputting technical instructions to EMPIs, like the values for certain functions and the like. Drum programming, which is actually *drum composing*, specifically refers to the program (compositional) approaches that beatmakers take to create their drum frameworks (drum patterns and overall designs). I like to divide drum programming (composing) into three different categories: simple, steady, or complex drum programming. "Simple" drum programming describes the composing approach that renders a bare minimum drum framework — drum patterns and designs that essentially stay the same throughout all sequences of a song. "Steady" drum programming describes the composing approach that renders a drum framework that contains slight changes on alternating bars, perhaps an extra kick here or there, maybe an open hi-hat. "Complex" drum programming is a bit more involved; it describes the composing approach that renders a drum framework that contains more deliberate pattern changes on alternating bars. Complex drum programming may include two or more kicks, snares, and hats, and "double" or "triple" drums. Break downs, custom drum rolls, drum fills, and "stutters" are also common characteristics of complex drum programming. Likewise, a more involved percussion scheme, like the inclusion of a timpani, chimes, bongos, and such are also great examples of complex drum programming.

Finally, if composition is the process of developing components and pieces that form music blocks, and if programming is best described as either the technical organization of the compositional components or the process of inputting technical instructions to EMPIs, then arrangement is the process of creatively organizing the components, pieces, and subsequent music blocks into a conscious thematic order. In simpler terms, arrangement in beatmaking refers to the approach that beatmakers take when *arranging the elements* of their beats. This involves the use of different techniques in basic structure, for example, 2-bar, 4-bar, 8-bar, and 16-bar schemes. It also involves the use of different techniques within arrangement themes and within the sectional structures that make up songs, i.e., simple, steady, or complex transitional developments, and the schemes that make up the verse, intro, hook (chorus), and the build-up (bridge) sections. In the following section, I examine just how the composition, programming, and arrangement processes manifest themselves in the three main approaches (compositional styles) of beatmaking.

The Three Compositional Styles of Beatmaking
Sample-Based Beatmaking (Samples Featured), Synthetic-Sounds-Based Beatmaking (No Samples Featured), and Hybrid Beatmaking (Samples Featured with Synthetic Sounds)

Before examining the three main compositional styles of beatmaking, there are two factors that must be addressed. First, it's important to remember that the beatmaking process stems from two general approaches to making hip hop/rap music: (1) DJ'ing; and (2) live instrumentation "covers" of the main riffs and rhythms of popular funk, soul, and disco songs that were preferred and played by hip hop DJs. The second factor that must be addressed is the fundamental recipe for beatmaking, and how it influences one's own personal style and sound identity. There are many different ways to make a beat, but all beatmakers essentially do the same thing: Combine non-drum sound arrangements with drum arrangements that serve as the backing beat. Together, these two arrangements of core music blocks formulate a solid rhythm and the beat is born. All beatmakers, regardless of style, work from this fundamental recipe. And it is the *way* in which each beatmaker works from or expands upon this fundamental recipe that determines their own personal style and sound identity.

Sample-Based (Samples-Featured) Beatmaking
The High Art of Sampling

Sample-based beatmaking relies primarily on the use of samples of recorded sound. In its most common and fundamental case, these samples (snippets and segments) of riffs, melodies, or sound-stabs are sampled from vinyl records, but today, samples are also egularly accessed from CDs, .mp3 and .wav files, YouTube, and internet streams. Usually, beatmakers who employ the sample-based compositional style try to remain close to the tradition of the second Golden Era of hip hop/rap music (1988-1994). Actually, the most noticeable characteristic of this compositional style is its timeless sound. Practitioners of this approach typically frown upon the mis-perceived laziness and the sometimes lack of commitment to the art of beatmaking that is often associated with the synthetic-sound compositional style, which in its most primitive form involves a low level of creative programming and arrangement. That said, the sample-based (samples-featured) approach certainly does allow room for useful melody phrases, additional percussion fills, and the like.

Another important characteristic of the sample-based (samples featured) approach is that it trains most beatmakers in many of the methods that were initiated and mastered by beatmakers of the first two Golden Eras of hip hop/rap music. Beatmakers who rely on the sample-based compositional style are often masters at complex and unique sound customization techniques as well as the advanced tier of other processes like chopping and looping. Because of this, many sample-based beatmakers have the advantage of being able to create a sound that is on the one hand, reminiscent to a past era, and on the other hand, inline with contemporary trends.

Advantages and Benefits of the Sample-Based Compositional Style

The sample-based compositional style offers numerous benefits, but there are three areas in which it gives beatmakers a clear advantage. First, this compositional style offers the fastest opportunity for setup mastery. Because the sampling process requires you to develop advanced chopping and arranging skills, you stand a better chance at really learning how to *flip* (creatively manipulate) sample source material, sampling methods and techniques, and the EMPIs within your setup.

Second, the sampling process teaches you an understanding of sounds and their relationship to each other — an understanding, I should add, that is not interdependent upon the abstract knowledge of music theory. Whether the possession of a sound understanding of music theory is an advantage to a beatmaker or not isn't the point here, because frankly you don't have to have a theoretical knowledge of notes in order to be a successful sample-based beatmaker. Sampling involves searching through pre-recorded source material for musical fragments that appeal to you. It does not however involve the process of fashioning stagnated preset sounds and tones (notes) into an effective musical arrangement. On the contrary, within the sampling process, you are given the challenge of having to choose brief sections of sound-stabs and collages, based on no criteria other than: *Does it sound good to you, and does it fit within the hip hop/rap aesthetic.*

The third and perhaps most profound benefit of the sample-based compositional style is the fact that this approach helps you to actually teach yourself about note and pitch variations, tonal progressions, and sound frequency characteristics. Incidentally, this is why sample-based beatmakers are often very adept and creative whenever they move to the synthetic-sounds-based style. When most sample-based beatmakers study the basics of the music theory, they usually pick it up quickly, precisely because they've trained themselves to edit and arrange multiple notes and pitches prior to switching to the synthetic-sounds-based style.

Synthetic-Sounds-Based (No-Sample-Featured) Beatmaking
The Art of Synthetic Sound Beatmaking

> This new term "original beats," as it is associated with non-sample-based beats, is not only a grave misrepresentation, it's offensive to all beatmakers who strive to make *original* beats — no matter the style or methods used. –Sa'id

The **synthetic-sounds-based** (no-samples-featured) compositional style of beatmaking relies primarily upon the use of keyboards or hardware or software sound modules (and the like) for coming up with sounds, rather than the use of samples (in the traditional sense). Unlike the sample-based (samples-featured) style, the synthetic sound style features non-samples — usually stock sounds from EMPIs — as the main sound-ingredients for a beat. Within the synthetic-sounds-based style of beatmaking, there are three separate forms: the non-orchestral, the semi-orchestral, and the orchestral or epic form.

The **non-orchestral** form of the synthetic-sounds-based compositional style is characterized by a very basic music theme (or lack there of), a simple or underdeveloped chord progression, sparse percussion, and a general focus on a simple but often strong backing beat that prominently features 808 kick and hi-hat sounds. Examples of this form can be heard in Soulja Boy Tellem's song "Superman," and in many snap music selections.[105] The **semi-orchestral**

---

[105] Many of the popular minimalist trends between 2007 and 2010 helped masquerade many beatmakers' lack of creativity and inspiration as well as many beatmakers' keyboard playing deficiencies.

form is characterized by a moderately developed (but effective and often catchy) musical theme, one or two pivotal changes, some level of sound-stacking, and usually one primary chord progression pattern. Examples of this form can be heard in most Southern bounce beats, which feature typical chord progressions, oft-copied steady chromatic harmony patterns, staccato string patterns, and heavily syncopated drum hits, especially often copied hi-hat patterns, snare and kick fills. The **orchestral** or **epic** form of the synthetic sound (no-samples-featured) is characterized by a well-developed musical theme, multiple chord progressions and melody patterns, multiple changes and "build-ups," an often very distinctive C section (chorus), and heavy "stacking" of sounds. Examples of this form can usually be heard in the more "crossover" hip hop/rap-pop type of offerings.

There are various techniques and approaches to the synthetic-sounds-based compositional style. For the non-orchestral form (the simplest form of the synthetic-sounds-based compositional style), there aren't many techniques to focus on other than the sort of techniques that can be learned from playing (programming) percussive elements and simple sound-stab strikes over a solid backing beat. However, for the semi-orchestral form, beatmakers would be well-advised to focus on chromatic harmony and melodic structures that do not override the theme and impact of the established backing beat. Because the semi-orchestral form is really the closest to the sample-based approach than the other synthetic-sounds-based forms, it almost always includes an advanced level of syncopated arrangements that are designed to accentuate a strong back beat. Finally, for the orchestral form, beatmakers should take a close look at the ways in which chromatic harmony is established alongside the development of more complex melodies and countermelodies and additional (separate) motives. It's worth noting that both the semi-orchestral and orchestral forms often utilize "build-ups" (specific structural changes, e.g. bridges) within their arrangements. Furthermore, the semi-orchestral and orchestral forms of the synthetic-sounds-based style are the beatmaking styles most commonly linked to the use of traditional "live instrumentation."

BeatTip – Anchor Technique: Melody

Although there are a number of beatmakers who have been traditionally trained in music theory, most beatmakers — being the ultra autodidacts that we are— devise their own techniques and methods for creating melodies. For me, such a technique was based on what I call the anchor melody.

I use the term "anchor melody" to refer to the main melody phrase or riff of a beat. Before I understood the basics of music theory or how melody worked in traditional Western music forms, I created anchor melodies by arranging a group of three or more successive tones into a pattern of my liking (usually more rhythmic than melodic), and in a manner that made my drum arrangements shine. Unable to actually play piano, I simply used two or three fingers to find a possible riff or melody. Having found that riff or melody, I established the first note within the phrase as the "anchor point" (or root) to which I returned to, once I played the sequence of keys and/or pads correctly (as desired).

My process of the anchor melody technique was done mostly by sight rather than memorization. Simply put, I looked at the keys or pads that contained the sounds that I was working with and I played out the sequence of arrangements to the best of my *untrained* ability. In time, I got better, and my memorization and finger positioning improved and I found that in order to make the anchor melody sound more complex, or to add an effective change, I could stack the anchor melody with additional phrases. Usually, I simply stacked the anchor melody with the same melodic phrase, in the same key of course, but with a different sound. For example, I would use the timbre of the violin sound stacked over the timbre of a piano or guitar sound.[106]

BeatTip — "Play-'n'-Sample" Technique: Approaching Synthetic-Sounds-Based Beatmaking Through the Prism of Sampling

Another unique technique for effectively manifesting the synthetic-sounds-based compositional style is what I call the "play-'n'-sample" technique. This technique simply describes the process of playing out melodic or rhythmic phrases via a guitar, keyboard, MIDI controller, or a drum machine's pads, then sampling those phrases and assigning them to keys or drum pads and playing them as a sample, as opposed to playing them out *as is*, i.e. "live" — non-recorded — notes. If you're going to employ this technique, it might be more advantageous to use vintage analog keyboards or sound modules, as they offer unique sound color qualities not present in contemporary EMPIs. But if this is not an option for you, then I recommend utilizing the vintage expansion cards or classic sound packs that are available for your hardware and software EMPIs.

---

[106] To hear an example of the sound achievable using this method, check out Ice Cube's "Why You Wanna Murder Me" featuring Soulchild.

Some Key Advantages and Benefits of the Synthetic-Sounds-Based Compositional Style

The synthetic-sounds-based compositional style certainly does have its advantages. First, it's the most accessible style for a beatmaker; it offers a quick entry point into the world of beatmaking. Any person (without even an inclination of soul, funk, or heavy rhythm-based musics) interested in beatmaking can immediately begin using the synthetic-sounds-based compositional style, especially the non-orchestral form.

Second, because the synthetic-sounds-based style doesn't (1) require a beatmaker to spend countless hours digging for and studying source music material to sample, and (2) doesn't require a beatmaker to further spend *more* countless hours meticulously learning the most advanced chopping and looping techniques,[107] it allows (perhaps) a beatmaker a broader range of musical directions to choose from. But then again, some sample-based beatmakers could easily argue that sampling opens a broad range of musical possibilities as well. I'd argue that possessing the ability to work effeciently in both styles is means to the broadest range of musical possibilities.

Third, software setups, which are very conducive to the synthetic-sounds-based style, are much less expensive than hardware setups. In recent years, the pro-consumer recording and audio market has seen an explosion of reasonably priced software programs designed for electronic music production. This alone has accounted for a sizeable increase in the sheer number of beatmakers over the past five years. Finally, the synthetic-sounds-based style offers more opportunity for additional changes, bridges, switch-ups, and build-ups all on the fly.

Check This Out – A Note About the Recent Popularity of the Synthetic-Sounds-Based Style

The synthetic-sounds-based style hasn't emerged from a new found fervor of creative intensity. The popularity of the synthetic-sounds-based style is actually due to two key factors. First, for many former sample-based beatmakers, shifting to the synthetic-sounds-based style was a reaction to the increased scrutiny on the use of samples, sample clearance issues, and the "misperceived" processes of sampling itself. Second, in recent years, the pro-consumer recording and audio market has seen an explosion of reasonably priced software programs designed

---

[107] Sample-based beatmakers consider this to be in line with the most fundamental processes of the beatmaking and hip hop/rap traditions.

for electronic music production, a fact that has significantly accounted for a sizeable increase in the sheer number of beatmakers over the past five years. Because of this recent development, the entry point of the synthetic-sounds-based style is the most accessible (easily learned) compositional style for beatmakers, especially new beatmakers.

The increased use of the synthetic-sounds-based compositional style does not represent "evolution" within the beatmaking or hip hop/rap music traditions, as some commentators maintain. There is absolutely nothing *evolutionary* about the use of keyboards, synthesizers, or sound modules in hip hop/rap music. Moreover, there is nothing evolutionary about composing R&B or rock arrangements with some rap lyrics over the top. Prior to 1979, there were no professional (commercial) recordings of hip hop/rap music. Up until that time, hip hop/rap music was only available on cassette tapes that were sold and shared in the streets of the South Bronx and other areas throughout the five boroughs of New York City. So before 1979, the use of live instrumentation — a precursor to the synthetic-sounds-based compositional style — was not a compositional component used by the first architects of hip hop/rap music. The use of live instrumentation in hip hop/rap music, which didn't began until 1979, was the chief style used by the *imitators* of hip hop/rap. The imitators — who were immediately recognized as such at the time — were not considered to be authentic by the early architects of hip hop. One great example: the studio session musicians like the Sugar Hill Records house band, who did *re-plays* of the breaks of songs that hip hop/rap DJs cut and blended together.

In 1979, the year that "Rapper's Delight" was released, the people who created the instrumentals for hip hop/rap music were actually not DJs or even people in the hip hop/rap community. They were all session musicians and members of the house bands of the first labels to exploit hip hop/rap music as a commercial product. These traditional musicians, who, again, were not DJs, had little to no real contact with the authentic hip hop movement and culture of the South Bronx, let alone any real inclination of what hip hop/rap music really was, or what hip hop culture represented. Instead, under the guise and mass-market inspired direction of the likes of label-head Sylvia Robinson, these musicians created their own rendition or *interpretation* of hip hop/rap music by replaying, mimicking, and altering, the most well-known breaks and rhythms of the records that were made popular by hip hop's earliest DJ pioneers.

In time, those house-band instrumentalists began creating compositions without taking a cue from what the era's DJs were spinning — a development that, right or wrong, helped to broaden the beatmaking tradition. By 1982

('83), this development had helped to usher in a new party-synth sound that was not only a departure from the authentic essence of hip hop/rap music, it was a stretch from the hip hop/rap knock-offs that the house band instrumentalists had previously created.[108]

The Differences Between Creating Beats Using the Sample-Based and Synthetic-Sounds-Based Compositional Styles

When it comes to the sample-based compositional style, originality depends on how well a beatmaker can reference, reconstruct, and more importantly, ***rearrange and reapply***, the source material that they sample. Whereas with the synthetic-sounds-based style, it's more about how well a beatmaker can rearrange a set of manageable, more isolated sound tones. With the synthetic-sounds-based style, the recreation factor that's associated with the sample-based style is mostly non-existent because beatmakers choose separate notes, rather than samples to be *used as notes*. And the samples that most sample-based beatmakers use often contain multiple notes and sounds that can't be removed — whatever's in the source material, stays in the source material. Therefore, like a sculptor, a sample-based beatmaker can only chop and add to a sample, they can not, however, extract the locked-in elements that comprise the sample as is. This is a factor that further distinguishes the sample-based and synthetic-sounds-based compositional styles from each other.

Plus, the underscoring fact is that notes are always the same: Middle C is always Middle C; A Minor is always A Minor. Beatmakers who employ the synthetic-sounds-based approach know beforehand what each note (key) sounds like, or at least they have some inclination of the basic characteristics of tone and pitch and how these characteristics manifest themselves across a keyboard or set of chromatic drum pads. This choice gives synthetic-sounds-based beatmakers a considerable amount of control. On the other hand, however, no record sample is ever really the *exact* same. For instance, most beatmakers, like other composers, "hear" arrangements in their head. So, in the case of the sample-based compositional style, the main challenge then becomes translating those arrangements into an effective, quality sounding program and ultimately a dope beat.

With sampled material, a beatmaker has to bend and re-shape and reorganize an original recording in a manner that matches up with the arrangement that they envision. On the other hand, a synthetic-sounds-based beatmaker is presented with a different — but not necessarily more difficult — challenge. Instead

---

[108] This party synth sound and development is thematically parallel to the synthetic-sounds-based trend .

of re-shaping and reorganizing sampled source material, their challenge is to organize (not *re*-organize) a preset group of sounds (notes) into an arrangement that they too have envisioned. But despite the fundamental differences in the sample-based and synthetic-sounds-styles, within each form there are less difficult, minimal or non-creative approaches as well as more difficult, extensive or highly creative approaches.

Hybrid Approach: The Sample-Based and Synthetic-Sounds-Based Styles Combined

The hybrid compositional style is a cross between the sample-based and synthetic-sounds-based styles. Beatmakers who employ the hybrid approach are not stubbornly focused on using record samples exclusively, nor are they completely interdependent upon the use of synthetic-sounds (and the accompanying methods) as well. The hybrid approach is the most ambitious and often the most rewarding of the three main compositional styles of beatmaking.

The central aim of the hybrid approach is to create musical arrangements that utilize the most effective blend of both record samples and synthetic-sounds. In some cases, practitioners of this approach will create beats that only feature samples; then again, in some cases they'll create beats that only feature synthetic-sounds. But in most cases, they tend to create beats using a unique combination of both record samples and synthetic-sounds.

The hybrid approach is the most prominently used compositional style of beatmaking. On one hand, it clearly offers the most composition possibilities of the three main compositional styles. On the other hand, because it combines sampling — whose roots trace back directly to hip hop DJ'ing — with synthetic-sounds, which is a contemporary force that can not be ignored, the hybrid approach presents itself as the most inclusive compositional style of beatmaking. Plus, the hybrid approach allows for much more experimentation, which often leads to new pioneering ideas and trends.[109]

While the hybrid approach is the most widely used of the three compositional styles, it's also the one approach that carries the greatest risk of the "over-gear syndrome."[110] The "over-gear syndrome" describes the phenomenon of beatmakers who after having acquired far too much gear, feel the need to

---

[109] One unique thing about the hybrid approach is that it allows for the combination of opposing music-making methods that still fit the hip hop/rap form. One such case are beats that are both sparse and developed at the same time. A good example of this type of beat can be heard in 50 Cent's "If I Cant," produced by Dr. Dre and Mike Elizondo.

[110] Over-doing it with gear usually results in the least interesting, least real-feel-sounding beats.

incorporate every piece of it into every beat that they create. Generally speaking, the more gear that you have does not automatically mean the better your beatmaking will be. It's about beatmaking *quality*, not gear *quantity*. But far too often, beatmakers (especially newer beatmakers) add something to a beat that simply isn't needed. In some rare cases, this can be the result of maintaining an impractical perfection level, but in most cases it's because these beatmakers want to flex their *setup muscle*; that is to say, they want to use *every* piece of gear in their arsenal, just because they have it to use. When this occurs, the hybrid approach is always undermined.

Which Compositional Style Should You Choose?

The kind of beats and hip hop/rap music that you want to make will determine the methods that you use. That said, the compositional method that you choose should be the one that gives you the best opportunity to create the kind of beats and overall sound that you like. Still, as I pointed out earlier in this chapter, each compositional style does offer its own unique advantages and disadvantages. Therefore, before you choose or switch from one compositional style to another, consider both the benefits and disadvantages of that style.

The Nuts and Bolts of Composition, Programming, and Arrangement

Group Map Assignments Extended: Triggering Non-Drum Sounds Through Drum Machines, Keyboards, and MIDI Controllers

"Triggering" sounds is simply the process of playing a pre-programmed sound, via a drum machine's pads or the keys from a keyboard or MIDI controller or computer keyboard keys. Whether you sample your own sounds, use preset sounds or a combination of both samples and preset sounds, the way in which you trigger those sounds is paramount to your workflow and personal beatmaking style. In order to successfully trigger your sounds, they must first be placed in an effective position; and by effective position I mean that your sounds have to be assigned to the pads or keys that work best for you and your compositional style. With regards to drum machine pads, it's important to note that the manufacturers of these machines (most notably Akai, E-Mu, and

Roland) issue each individual pad a name, e.g. PERC, HIHAT, etc. However, it should be understood that you don't have to assign the drum sound to the pad name that denotes the sound that you want to assign. For instance, you don't have to assign a percussion sound to a pad marked PERC; you can assign any sound to any drum pad — *you should ultimately develop your own preference for which pads you want to use to trigger your sounds.* But no matter how you do decide to assign your individual sounds, I strongly recommend that you assign your sounds into Group Map Assignments.

A **Group Map Assignment**, hereafter referred to as GMA, is a way of organizing sound categories into groups and then assigning sounds to drum pads and/or keyboard/MIDI controller keys, according to those groups. For example, "main drums" can be a group, "bass sounds" can be a group, "main samples" can be a group, "percussion" can be a group, etc. Organizing your triggering method into a series of GMAs will streamline how and where your sounds are placed and triggered, and it will improve the efficiency of your workflow.

Determining Where to Assign Your Sounds

If you use an MPC of some sort or the Maschine, or any other Drum Machine/Sequencer that uses a similar 16-drum pad design, to sequence your music and gear, take a look at the image in Figure 10. Here's an example of how I map out particular sounds across the 16 pads of a given drum bank. I should note that all of my GMAs are also organized according to the different banks within my Akai MPC 4000. For example, the image in Figure 10 is a screenshot of my GMA for bank A, my "main composition bank." My main composition bank contains an assortment of separate sound categories. However, I use subsequent banks for GMAs of the same sound category; for example, I use bank C as my "percussion bank," it's where I assign my most used percussion sounds.

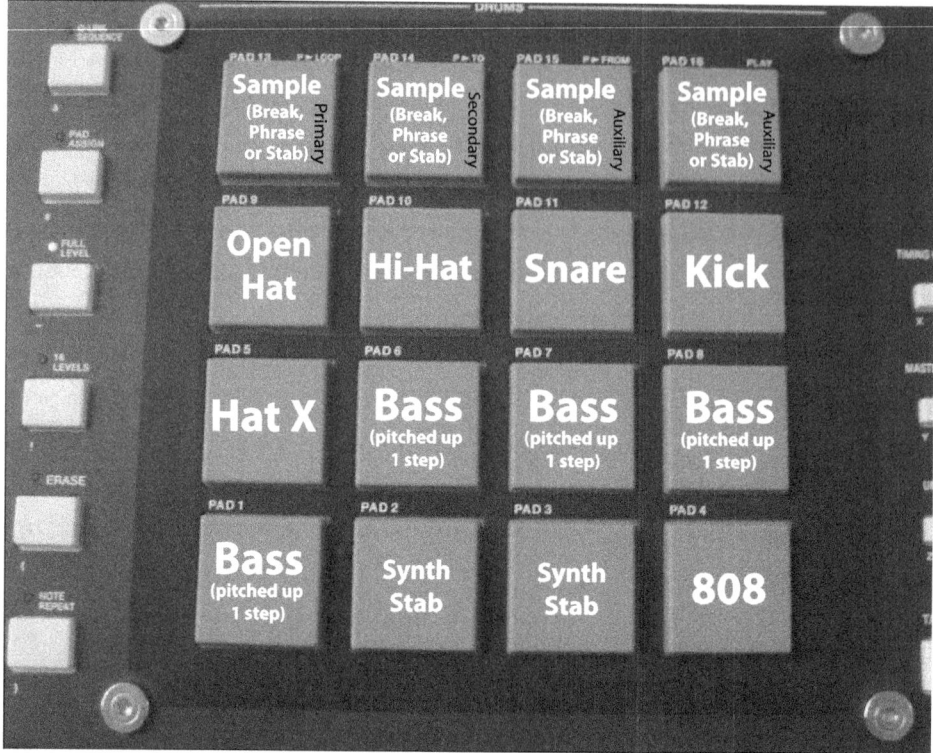

Figure 10 16-Pads of Main Composition Bank

Assigning Bass Sounds, Samples, and Other Non-Drum Music

If it could be said that hip hop/rap music gets its identity from the drums, then it perhaps might be said that it gets its character from the bass. Therefore, when it comes to assigning drum sounds, I recommend that you assign them one row below your main drums. Keeping your bass sounds close to your main drums, in this case one row below, is very helpful for when you're trying out new drum ideas (and beat ideas in general) because it helps you facilitate the arrangement of those ideas quite effectively. Also, although playing the bass on drum pads is certainly a lot different from playing your typical electronic bass guitar, the idea essentially comes down to the same thing: pitch progression. For samples, the notion of the rhythm section should be considered. And in keeping with the scope of the rhythm section in a band, I recommend assigning primary samples to the top row of four pads, just right above the drums. Finally, having assigned your main drums, bass sounds, and samples to the first top three of four rows or drum pads, I recommend assigning synth stabs and/or percussion to the bottom row of pads.

Special Note About Sequencing

Before I go on with a more detailed discussion of the composing, programming, and arrangement processes in beatmaking, it's important to discuss the nomenclature that is associated with the term "sequencing." In beatmaking, the term "sequencing" actually refers to two separate things. One meaning of sequencing deals with the obvious: the sequencing (linking) of multiple EMPIs; it's the linking up of equipment through MIDI. Once linked up, sound generators (samplers, modules, etc.) redistribute their sounds through the main linking device, or better yet, the "master sequencer" within one's setup. In this meaning of the word, sequencing refers to the way that the pieces of your gear communicate with each other; each piece has its own say, but it's the master sequencer that has the final say. Therefore, the goal is to use a master sequencer that *talks* well with all of the gear in your setup. EMPIs use the same language to communicate with each other, via MIDI, but getting multiple pieces of gear to link in the manner that suits your workflow best is an entirely different dialect. For instance, the Akai S950 can be triggered by any Akai MPC as well as any keyboard workstation or controller; however, *how* each unit *links* with the Akai S950 (or any other stand alone sampler for that matter) will vary.

The other (perhaps more prominent) meaning of sequencing deals with beat structure; that is to say, the actual process of *programming* the structure and arrangement of a beat. Under this definition of sequencing, a "sequence" is the arranged and recorded program data within any measure. And simply put, a beat is composed of multiple sequences linked together.[111] Finally, though beatmakers vary in the amount of equipment that they utilize to create beats, nearly all beatmakers strive to sequence everything through one sequencer. This is one of the reasons MIDI is so important. It allows the sequences created in other EMPIs to be streamlined and *sequenced* (recorded) into one master sequencer. This is yet another example that demonstrates how a beatmaker is, in effect, the composer, the arranger, *and* the musician.

Beat Structure: The Basic Components – the Sequence and the Loop

A beat is composed of a series of sequences. A sequence is a program of chronologically arranged events (steps) within a measure of at least one bar. A

---

[111] The use of the term "sequencing" in this manner was popularized primarily by beatmakers of the Pioneers/Avant-Garde Period of beatmaking, ca. 1988-1995.

"loop," the cornerstone time structure of beatmaking, is the perpetual repetition of the same sequence or series of sequences. For instance, a 1-bar loop means that the sequence plays for one bar, having reached its end, it returns (loops) to the beginning of the sequence and plays again. Likewise, a 2-bar loop means that the sequence and/or series of sequences plays for two bars, having reached its end, it returns to the beginning of the first sequence and plays again.

The Main Ingredients of a Successful Loop

The success of a loop depends on four things: the chop (truncation) of the sound; the pitch of the sound; the tempo of the sequence; and the drum framework (pattern and design of the drum arrangement). The "chop" or truncation refers to how the main sound phrase(s), whether samples or synthetic sounds, are chopped. This is to say, how precise the chops (cuts and truncation) are or how *purposefully off* they are; another way of seeing it is how long or short the main sound phrases are.

The "pitch," in this case, refers to the pitch (speed) of the main sound phrases. Often the difference between a dope beat and a wack beat is the pitch of the primary sound phrase. Should you speed the sound up, slow it down, or leave it at the default pitch that you captured it in? The tendency for most beatmakers these days is to speed the sound up. But remember, for every pitch value you go up or down, you affect how the sound will loop in a sequence, as well as how the sound will sound over the drum framework and, ultimately, how the entire beat will sound.

The "tempo" of the sequence is just that, it refers to the tempo, the BPM (Beats Per Minute) value of a sequence, series of sequences, or song. Tempo determines the speed of the sequence and, subsequently, the beat. A deeper examination of tempo reveals that it does more than just determine the speed of the beat; the tempo also determines what I call "the turnover rate" of the loop. The turnover rate is the interval, the time and space, between the ending and beginning again of a sequence. The interval determines what I refer to as the "loop point," the audibly dead point right before the loop *turns over* to the next sequence. The slower the interval, the easier it is to hear the dead space — the loop point. Likewise, the faster the interval (and, subsequently, the faster the tempo), the harder it is to hear or recognize the dead space, which means the loop point is seamless, no glitches. Unless you want to feature the dead point or a space-glitch as a component of the beat that you're making, you should increase or decrease the tempo until the loop point is seamless and indiscernible.

Finally, whenever you're deciding on which tempo to use, always remember: The right tempo can snap or slide the beat into place; the wrong tempo can drag the beat or crack it out of place, making the drum framework sound awkward.

Here, it's important to point out that "drum framework" refers to the pattern and design of the drum arrangement. When designing a drum framework, keep in mind that drum designs that are too active always disrupt the loop, if not the entire beat for that matter; and on the other hand, drums that lack the right kind/level of activity (accents and overall structure) can really *drag* or *drain* the flow of the loop. The right drum framework is critical in beatmaking because the role of the drums is paramount in within a beat. This is because in the hip hop/rap music tradition, the drums are often called upon to maintain various responsibilities simultaneously. In all cases, the drums have to *steady* the beat, ie. keep it running smoothly. And in most cases, the drums also have to knock without overpowering the other musical elements within the beat. Still, in some other cases, the drums have to be balanced and subtle; that is, instead of taking a leading role, they take a supporting role.

BeatTip – A Note About Using Timestretch

At first glance, timestretch is really just BPM matching — matching the tempo of the drum framework with the non-drum music. But a closer look at timestretch reveals the genius of it. Timestretch changes the length of a sound (sample) *without* changing its pitch. Hence, it permits you to mesh together multiple pieces of music that contain slightly off-setting beat patterns; it smooths out the kinks and awkward "clicks." Moreover, it connects music phrases, and it makes audio patterns and textures that otherwise would clash sound as if they're one tight musical composition.

Beat Structure: Creating and Programming Sequences

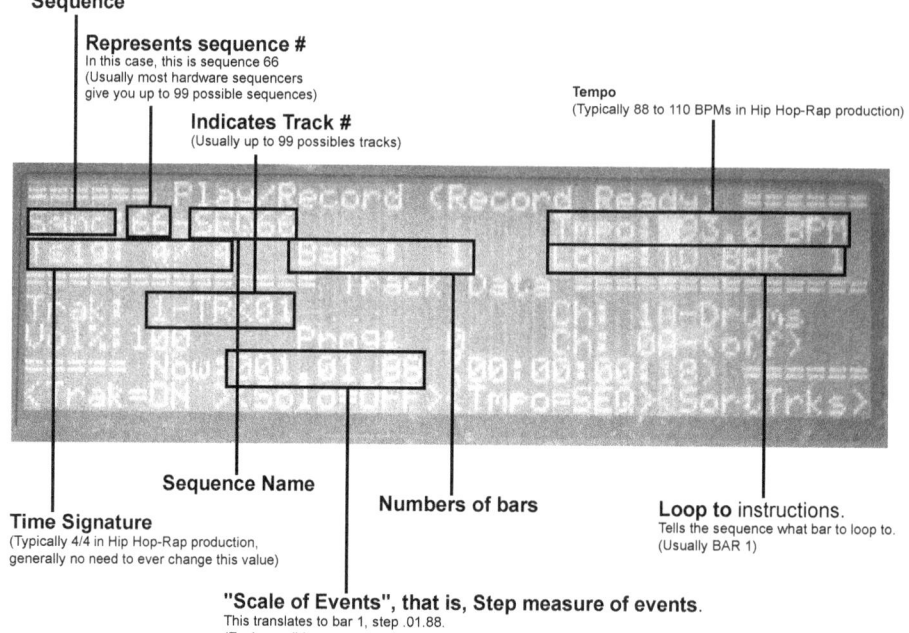

Figure 11 LCD of Main Screen, Akai MPC 60 II

As described earlier, a beat is composed of a series of sequences. A sequence is a program of chronological musical events (steps) within a measure of at least one bar. An "event" or "step" within a sequence is the point at which any programmed *action* takes place. The event serves to represent when and where a piece of specific musical *action* (instruction) takes place within a sequence. An event can be anything. It can be as simple as a kick-stab, it can be a sample of any length. A "track" is an individual channel (file) in which an event(s) is recorded in/on. Most sequencers allow at least 99 separate tracks per sequence. Hence, all of your sounds (events) can be tracked within the same sequence on separate tracks. Which means that you can have your kick on track 1, your snare on track 2, your hi-hat on track 3, your bass on track 4, and so on and so forth.[112] There

---

[112] I understand the reasons why you should assign each of your sounds to a separate track: it makes it easier to modify each track individually or to solo a track within a sequence; it makes it easier to correct mistakes, etc. But if you're using any EMPI with 8 direct outs of audio, along with a mixing console, then assigning sounds to separate tracks is not the only way to go. You can track every sound on the same track, then route the audio to separate inputs on your mixing console or the interface of whatever recording software that you use (that's what I often do). But if you only have access to the main L/R outs, and not 8 direct outs, then yeah, you're better off tracking each sound within the sequencer on separate tracks. In this case, after you've recorded the events into your sequencer on separate tracks and you're ready to track into your DAW, simply pan two tracks at a time, one to the left, the other to the right. Recording two tracks at a time into your DAW takes more time to track an entire beat or song (sometimes 45 minutes to an 1 hour, depending on how many tracks and sounds you're using).

are two basic ways to create a brand new sequence and, subsequently, create and build a brand new beat. You can either start with the drums, or you can start with the non-drum music material. What I mean by the *non-drum music material* is samples, bass lines, melodic lines of synthetic-sounds, etc. Many beatmakers can start a beat either way, so it's really not an issue of which way is better or worse; how each beatmaker begins a new beat ultimately depends on him (or her), their mood, their resources, and their level of commitment to creativity.

You can start beats off by creating drums from scratch (that is, an entirely new drum design and pattern), or you can use your own default (preset) patterns that you've created previously and stored away. But if you're going to create a new drum pattern from scratch, be aware that the new pattern will most likely not be too different from any other drum pattern you've created and/or will ever create. This is because (1) Many drum patterns share the same fundamental foundations; and (2) there are standard *drum pattern clichés* in beatmaking that all beatmakers consciously and subconsciously know. Thus, it is from these standard drum clichés that all beatmakers pretty much create new drum patterns.

The other option for starting new beats is to go with the non-drum music material, i.e. samples, bass lines, melodic synth lines, and the like. The idea here is to get the music into a sequence as soon as possible. Take for example a simple sample, one bar in length. After I've assigned the sample to the pad that I will be triggering it from, I use the sample to create a new sequence in the sequencer of my Akai MPC 4000. The simplest way to do this is to record (place) the sample on the first step of bar 1 within the sequence. I can just go to step edit, then place — record — the sample in. Next, I set a generic tempo, something like 93 BPM, then I play the sequence. As the sequence plays, I pay attention to how it loops. If there is a long pause (interval) between the ending of the sample and when the sequence loops over, then I know that the tempo is too slow. Likewise, if the sequence loops before the sample plays out *to the predetermined length that I've chosen*, then I know that the tempo is too fast. (Remember, when you're looping something, you want to make the loop point seamless, and unnoticeable). Once the sample is looping (turning over) to my liking, without any glitches, then I can go in and add drums, percussion, bass lines, keys, and whatever else. And once I know the tempo of how the sample should loop, I can also go to some of my preset (premade) drum patterns and throw the sample in over the top of one of them.

Beat Structure: Song Form

All beatmakers are commissioned with the same seemingly impossible task: **make a loop not sound like it's looped!** Huh? Crazy, right? But the truth is, that's what it is. In this light, beatmakers are masters of the *misdirect*. We have to know how to misdirect the listener away from the otherwise or seemingly mundane boringness of the loop. But let's not forget that within the hip hop/rap music tradition, progression is based on and advanced by the concept of the loop — repetition. Even though a typical hip hop/rap song may have any number of progressions, the power of the loop is what dominates the song. Other music traditions like jazz and rock 'n' roll are not as emboldened to the loop concept as much as the hip hop/rap tradition.[113] Even though repetition plays an important role overall in those music traditions, there is a premium on adding and advancing as many new changes in the arrangement as effectively possible — so as to progress towards some sort of thematic climax. In the rock 'n' roll tradition, songs return to the core melody (or loop, if you will), but the changes are often so varied that it can not be considered loop-based in the same manner that hip hop/rap music is.[114] Hip hop/rap music is more about returning, that is to say, *returning to the core riff(s)/core grove and rhythm*, returning to the main loop(s). And because the hip hop/rap music tradition is based on cyclical progression (repetition) rather than linear progression (material growth), the arrangement of the musical elements is much more clear cut, but deceptively simple.

The So-Called "Rules" of Song Form[115]

As with all twentieth-century American popular music, the song structure of hip hop/rap music subscribes to a general system of well-defined musical **sections**. In beatmaking, a typical song is composed of two to five different types of well-defined (arranged) sections. Each section is comprised of a series of sequences that are linked together through a program; once all sequences are linked together they are converted into *song mode*. The two most important

---

[113] The Western classical music tradition isn't emboldened to the concept of the loop at all.

[114] There are certain forms of rock music that definitely lend favor to the loop-based medium of hip hop/rap music. For a more thorough understanding of what I mean, check out the following: 1970s power rock, especially Led Zeppelin; 1970s punk, especially The Clash; 1980s Ska, especially The English Beat and The Police.

[115] I used to have lots of difficulty arranging my music. I got past this difficulty by improving my skill for creating and modifying sequences into songs.

sections are the **verse** and the **hook** (or the chorus in other popular music forms). The verse section refers to the *primary* section of the song; it's the instrumental section where the main rap verses (vocals) will ride over; as such it is the section that has the longest duration in a beat. The main purpose of the verse section is to *establish and work the point* of the song. It's like the starting picture in baseball, it's job is to keep the winning momentum going just long enough for the hook — the *closer* — to come in and puncuate the main point of the song.

The **hook** (chorus) is the *secondary* section of the song; it's the instrumental section where the hook (chorus) vocals will ride over. Even though the hook is secondary in terms of the real-time duration of a song, the hook (chorus) is actually the ***marquee*** section — it's the section of the song that carries the most exclamation. This is why I like to call the hook (chorus) section the "pay-off section." Even though it doesn't play nearly as long as the verse section, it's often the section that stands out the most because it carries the hook vocals, the most memorable part of any song. The main purpose of the hook (chorus) section is to *reinforce and punctuate the main theme*, the main point of the song.

The other three types of musical sections that make up a song in beatmaking are the **intro**, the **build-up** or the **bridge** and the **outro**. The **intro**, or what I sometimes like to call the "teaser section," is the lead-in section of a song. It's role is to establish the mood and to engage listeners by giving a sneak preview of the caliber of music that's about to proceed; thus, naturally, in an arrangement, the intro is placed before the first verse section. The purpose of the intro is to draw listeners in, entice them and make them want to hear what's about to come next. An intro is also used for the initial ad lib vocals. I like to separate intros into two categories: either straight-ahead or counter. A straight-ahead intro is one that is made up of some of the same musical components (sequences/sounds) within the rest of the song. This can be the drum framework by itself, it can be the melody and the hi-hat riding, etc. On the other hand, a counter intro doesn't contain any of the components from the other sections of the song, it contains components (sequences/sounds) that won't be heard again in the rest of the song.

The **build-up/bridge** is a catalyst *change*. It's the section that plays between the verse and the hook (chorus). It's like the setup man in baseball, it relieves the starting pitcher, and at the same time, it sets up the hook (chorus). The bridge is unique, in that it can do two things to a beat: (1) It can serve as an interesting intermission or break within the song; and (2) It can serve as a crescendo or the last rising instrumental *statement*, signaling a climax or finale of a verse. The build-up (bridge) is often just an octave or pitch change of the verse melody or rhythm. And just like the intro, it can be counter; it can be an independent section that contains entirely new components (i.e. sequences, sounds).

The **outro** section (which isn't necessary) ties up the entire song. It's the section that advances the final thoughts of a beatmaker, the final touch, the finishing signature of a beatmaker. It also serves as that extra instrumental time, without lyrics, that DJs appreciate for mix blends. The outro, just like the intro and bridge, can be straight-ahead or counter. Typically, the outro is an understated (stripped-down) version of the main verse section, but it can also be completely independent, containing components that are entirely new.

When you're arranging and organizing sequences, remember to be flexible with the final structure because until the beat is actually complete, every created sequence, and subsequent section, can be *rearranged*. This is why it's critical to know the different types of arranged sections, how they work, and their fundamental purposes. When you're creating a new beat, the entire arrangement is subject to change: the verse section can be reorganized to become the hook (chorus) section, and vice versa; the intro section can become the verse; so on and so forth. Embracing this reality gives you more freedom to take intuitive chances when you're building those sequences that will ultimately be linked together into the sections of the song.

From Sequence to Section

By default, the first sequence that you begin is your **core sequence**. From this sequence, you will most likely build the sequences that become the verse section. Most beatmakers do not start off making the hook (chorus) first. The hook (chorus) is usually just the verse section, sprinkled with just enough minor changes to distinguish it as the hook (chorus). This is why it's those changes and modifications that you're able to make to that initial core sequence that enables you to really get ill with the beat.

Earlier in this section, I broke down how sequences are often created, starting with either drums or non-drum music material. Here, I'll discuss more in-depth how beats are made, more *technically* speaking, that is. The technical aspect of how beats are made can be described as: **the composition of rhythm-based musical elements, followed by the process of recording these musical elements into sequences, followed by the process of linking these sequences together in preprogrammed arrangements**.

And how are sequences "linked" together? The most common way that sequences are linked together is through the process of duplication, copying one complete sequence and attaching to itself or to another. You can copy and link as many sequences as you want to. In fact, you can even make a beat from just a 1-bar sequence. All you have to do is convert that 1-bar loop into a song; just copy the sequence to itself until you have the appropriate number of bars, equal to the length that you want the song to be. This is the exact concept of duplication. Once you've established a **core sequence**, the idea is to copy the sequence to itself so that you can increase the length. A 1-bar core sequence copied to itself becomes a 2-bar core sequence; a 2-bar core sequence copied to itself becomes a 4-bar core sequence.[116] The advantage of duplication is that all events, especially the drum framework, remain in tact even though the length of the measure has been increased. The more bars within your core sequence means the more opportunities to program in changes. Conversely, the shorter the number of bars within your core sequence, the less opportunities you have to insert changes. One bar *turns over* faster than two, and so on. Therefore, keep in mind that 1-bar loops also have the potential to restrict your programming and increase the probability of a simple loop; subsequently, it can increase the chance of the entire beat sounding stale or mundane.

Here, I should raise again the point that hip hop/rap music is not dependent upon linear progression, but upon repetition and cyclical progression. Still, some beats that include a number of changes often come off *more pleasing* to a listening public conditioned to favor a more pop sound. On the other hand, rappers with major lyrical skills know how to incorporate their own verbal changes. They can get busy off of any track. But all skillful lyricists favor tracks with *stability*. That is to say, they tend to favor less noticeable changes, because the loop and repetition allows them to take advantage of a solid, continuous groove. Beats with too many changes often restrict a skillful rapper's verbal talents, forcing them to "dumb-down" their lyrical flow and subject matter.[117] Therefore, one general guide you might want to consider for yourself is this: For more *lyrical* rappers, keep the changes to a minimum; for all other rappers, it's O.K. to add more changes; actually, the more changes in beat, the more easily their lyrical *deficiencies* are masked.

BeatTip – The Genius Of 1-Bar Core Sequences

Even though 1-bar sequences can be restrictive, as beats in and of themselves, establishing a 1-bar core sequence is one of the most fundamental ways to start

---

[116] Most hip hop/rap songs are based on root 2-, 4-, and 8-bar loops.
[117] A great example of how a "steady beat" can inspire (provoke) complex lyricism can be heard in Fabolous' "Pachanga." Fabolous, a true lyricist, can "dumb down" his lyrics when he wants to; likewise, he can turn it up when given the right beat to do so.

a new beat. Point is, when I strike up a new core sequence, I already know beforehand that I will be duplicating the sequence either way it goes. So it's important for me to establish a basic core sequence that has a tight drum framework. Once I have a 1-bar sequence looping nicely, I copy it to itself, giving me two bars of a real tight drum framework. From out of these two bars, now I can take the beat anywhere. I can further build the verse section (the primary 2-bar sequences that I initially created from the 1-bar core sequence). I can build the hook (chorus), intro, the build-up (bridge), or outro sections; from this point I can do whatever. After I've auditioned several changes, I make another copy of that 2-bar sequence, then I leave the initial 2-bar sequence off to the side as my default idea to return to if I go too far from the feeling and idea that's driving the beat. Next, I move on, using the copy to sketch out any new ideas.

Song Structure

The bar structure of a typical hip hop/rap song breaks down like this:

- 8-bar intro
- 16-bar verse
- 8-bar hook (chorus)
- 16-bar verse
- 8-bar hook (chorus)
- 16-bar verse
- 8-bar hook (chorus)

Notice how the basis of this song structure is comprised of 8-bar increments. Looking at the above song structure, you can't tell how different one section is from the next, but by seeing the mathematical relationship of the exact number of bars used for each section, you can infer that some sequences were duplicated to create others. Here's another example of a possible song structure:

- 8-bar intro
- 16-bar verse
- 8-bar chorus
- 8-bar verse
- 8-bar bridge
- 8-bar chorus
- 12-bar verse

- 8-bar outro

By making some common modifications to the above song structure, you're able to add more variety to the basic beat. In the second song structure example, notice the changes that I inserted. One of the most difficult concepts for both new and advanced beatmakers to understand is the relationship between the measure of a sequence and timing. Think of the measure of a sequence as being a time-line of clearly defined, highly detailed events that, once programmed, automatically repeat when the end of the time line (i.e. the total number of bars) is reached.

BeatTip – Section Contrast

A "section contrast" is the term that I use to describe an arrangement scheme in which two or more sections in a beat that are not predicated upon one another (based on most of the same elements) are moving in a similar direction and feel. One of the best things about a section contrast is the fact that, when done right, they appropriately add the value of variety as well as a strong sense of tension and release. This in turn makes both the chorus (hook) and verse sections of the song much more climatic, which ultimately keeps the interest of the listener.

BeatTip – Knowing the Right Tempo and Bar Structure for Samples

Most twentieth-century American popular music is predicated upon on 4/4 time, which means it has 4 beats per measure (four "beats" per bar). It doesn't matter if there is any percussion to be heard, because any four-count will give you one complete bar in this time signature. Moreover, most beatmakers tend to build beats using either 2-bar, 4-bar, 8-bar, 12-bar, or 16-bar sequences (basically, some multiple of 2); but *which* numbered bar structure depends on the length of the sample(s) being used. One way to determine the right tempo and bar-count for a sample(s) is to simply determine the length (duration) of the sample(s). What you do is, listen to the sample and run off a 4-bar count by snapping your fingers as if they were a metronome. If the sample(s) is a short phrase or riff, snap faster, if it's a longer complete phrase, snap slower.

An easier way to determine the right tempo and bar-count for a sample(s) is to record the sample(s) into a sequence and set the tempo to something like 89 or 92 BPM. Next, press play and let the sequence progress all the way through. Adjust the tempo as needed so that you can hear the complete sample(s) from beginning to end without the end of it being cut off before it loops. After having played it completely through, when it loops back, without any exaggerated interval, then you've got the right tempo.

BeatTip – Note About Building the Hook (Chorus) Section

Many beatmakers often neutralize the bang (overall quality impact) in their beats by adding elements that simply do not belong in them. This typically happens when beatmakers make the hook (chorus) section of a track. When I'm working on a beat using the synthetic-sounds-based compositional style, I try to build out everything in the beginning. However, when I'm using the samples-based style, my main concern is to establish the rhythm that bangs the most. In this case, finding a change for the hook is a second thought, depending on how tight the primary sample sounds with the drum framework.

For me, the idea is always to create a musical platform that best allows a lyricist to *get busy* on and catch wreck (i.e. have a great performance). Rap lyrics and rhyme form are unlike any other style of lyrics and rhyme form in contemporary popular music. By their nature, there is a lot of rhythm and percussive poetic movement in rap lyrics. Because of this, rap lyrics add another musical element to a composition in a way that often minimizes the need for extensive changes. This is one reason why some beatmakers wait until after the rapper has layed down their vocals to the original core riffs/core groove (base rhythm) of the beat before they consider adding hook elements to the beat.

Check This Out – Overall Note About Beat Structure

Beatmakers used to make beats specifically to be used by rappers only. Today, many recording artists from separate music traditions borrow from the hip hop/rap music tradition. Because of this, many beatmakers have taken to making beats from the vantage point of what is most likely to get them a buyer from a range artists from different genres, rather than what is more likely to be a dope beat. Inevitably, this trend leads to a growing number of beatmakers who try to structure their beats more and more like *pop* songs. If this is your approach, keep this in mind: The more you try to structure a beat like a pop song, the more you actually move away from the hip-hop/rap music tradition.

Chapter 7

Extended Composition and Arrangement Notes
Composition, Programming, and Arrangement – Getting the Ingredients and Putting them All Together

Extended Composing and Sequencing Notes, Techniques, and Tips

Composing Bass Lines Using the Same "Anchor" Bass Sound

When it comes to creating bass lines in the beatmaking tradition, it's first important to recognize that you don't need actual bass guitar sounds to create great bass lines. Bass lines can be created using any sound that represents (i.e. sounds like) a bass sound. You can make bass lines out of anything, just filter out the mid and high frequencies of whatever sounds you're trying to transform into a bass line.[118]

Moving forward with this understanding of how bass sounds can be created in the beatmaking tradition, you next have to examine the dynamics of the bass guitar itself. For example, consider that a typical bass guitar only has five strings. This means you can never really go up higher than four whole pitch levels (whole tones). Therefore, when assigning your actual bass sounds to drum pads or keys on a keyboard, synthesizer, or MIDI controller, there isn't a need to account for more than four or five assignments. That is to say, it's not necessary to assign a bass sound to 16 different pads or 48 different keys and use more than five of those assignments. You can if you want to, but I'm not sure if there's any noticeable advantage, as too much variance in the corresponding pitch values can undermine whatever bass line you create. This is why I simply assign the

---
[118] This sound technique was advanced most prominently by DJ Premier, Large Professor, Pete Rock, RZA, and Kev Brown, who's skill in this area is quite superb. (Application of this same method on horns has a really ill effect.)

same bass sound to four or five pads on my MPC, then I pitch up each pad by one whole tone, then I "walk" (play) up or down to the drum framework I've created, or I match the rhythm or melody that I have going. However, if you use an MPC (or any EMPI with a polynote function), you can also use the 16-note function to automatically slice an individual bass sound into multiple bass tones, which are then mapped out across the 16 drum pads of the MPC. Still, you can also compose bass lines using the stock bass sounds of a keyboard/ synthesizer or sound module. Although this might be the least creative way, it's just as effective, provided you apply some additional sonic modification to the sounds. This helps customize the otherwise generic-ness of the sounds.

Finally, whichever method you use to create your bass sounds (specifically the various pitch levels/tones), the important thing to remember is that it's typically more effective to play out your bass lines in real time with either a drum framework or the established rhythm of the beat.

Composing Bass Lines – An Extended Look at My Process of Composing Bass Lines Using the Anchor Technique

When making effective bass lines in beatmaking, what matters most is how you plan to use the bass line. Let's say you're developing a bass line simply for accentuation or emphasis of some other musical element within a beat. In that case, it's not too difficult to come up with an effective bass line. For example, using the pads of a drum machine or the keys on a keyboard or MIDI controller, you can load up a bass-stab over four separate pads or four keys. Next, you just play out an order of notes (some sort of bass line theme), using just those four sounds; it's almost like mapping a rhyme scheme because each sound represents its own pitch: A B C D — here, everything left of the "D" drum pad or keyboard key is lower in pitch chromatically by one level. So in essence, creating bass lines in the beatmaking tradition is really more about matching the pitch and dynamics of the non-drum elements and the feel and impact of the backing beat.[119]

Composing Bass Lines Using the Anchor Technique

Bass lines are typically three to four steps up or down a scale. *(A scale is seven*

---

[119] Here, the description of pitch and tones is a very crude and simplistic snapshot of the basic pitch characteristics of traditional music theory. But this is exactly how I was able to work it out and make bass lines with no knowledge of music theory at all. Also note: Although possessing a sound knowledge of music theory may give you some advantage when composing bass lines, as with some other musical processes, the possession of even the most advanced knowledge of music theory does not mean that you will automatically make more effective bass lines.

notes all in a row). When creating bass lines using the anchor technique, the idea is to find your "high" and "low points." These are the highest and lowest pitch levels of the bass sound that you're trying to play. Since a typical bass line (sequence) is composed of three to four pitch levels, just find your *anchor*. What I mean is, pick the pitch level that you want to start and end with. Let's say you've already auditioned some bass sounds from your EMPI of choice (keyboard, sound module, MPC, etc.). Start with your anchor, and walk up or down the keyboard using the three to four phrases that you've scoped out. From here, you can experiment with different phrases (lines). The thing to notice is what happens every time you return to your anchor sound.

Here, I should note that when it comes to the sample-based style, as opposed to the synthetic-sounds-based style, it's not necessarily about trying to match the *exact* key of a sample, which in the first place, is very difficult to try and determine with multi-sound/multi-instrument samples.[120] It's much more about trying to match — blend — the bass tones with the overall *tonal mood*, feeling, and sonic texture of the beat. Like a lot of notable beatmakers, when I create bass lines to be used with samples, more often than not I try to extract a bass frequency from somewhere within the primary sample that I'm using. I use the filtered framework of the main sample, i.e. a duplicate of the sample, but only its low frequency. From here, I use this filtered duplicate at the exact pitch and length of the main sample, or I chop it up into pieces and arrange it over four to eight different MPC pads. After that, I match (play) the chopped bass tones to the feel of the beat, using the flow and feel of the main sample as my guide and inspiration. Furthermore, if and when these bass-tone chops lack sonic presence (that certain "umph"), I layer first generation sounds (i.e. synthetic sounds — live keyboard/synthesizer) at strategic points within the arrangement. This adds depth to the initial bass arrangement that I've composed.

When I'm creating beats using the synthetic-sounds-based compositional style, I focus on the anchor point or anchor sound. Again, before I knew anything about music theory (I'm always learning more), I knew that the creation and development of bass lines, melody lines, and the like depended upon an anchor point, or rather some anchor sound. I further understood that my ability to play progressions up or down from that anchor sound/point, in accordance to the drum framework and rhythmic pattern, was essential to whatever beat I was

---

[120] Again, you don't necessarily have to set the pitch of the bass at the exact same pitch of your primary sample. The bass sound is its own thing, it can go off pitch (what I like to call "wildcat") if it works. That's why you can short the measure of a bass melody, while having it at a lower pitch than your primary sample. This is exactly why an 808 can work with nearly anything, without ever having to really be pitched up or down.

working on. I now know that this process is actually akin to using scales (in music theory). Even though I'm armed with this "new" knowledge, I still keep in mind that a standard bass guitar has 5 strings, which leads me to work only with two to five notes. When I trigger bass sounds (either samples or synthetic-sounds), I arrange one bass tone over 16 pads. Next, I pick out what I call a "scale area" to work with. A scale area is just any two to five tones/notes (pads), not necessarily directly ascending/descending but agreeable to the theme of the beat that I'm working on. From here, I kind of give each tone (pad) a mental number, like 1, 2, 3, 4, etc. Then I play out some simple progressive phrases like, 1-2-3...3-2-1... and so on. After I get a good feel for the possibilities, for what I might want to work on, I get a little more advanced with it. The phrases then begin to look something like this: 1-2-3 3-3 2-3-3-3-3-4, 1. After I'm happy with the phrase, I loop it, then after I've recorded and looped that, I lay down another simple phrase based on (playing off of) the first simple pattern that I laid down. Finally, once I've composed a complete phrase that I'm happy with, I let the sequence play out, then I solo and sample it. This allows me to then assign the entire bass phrase to just one drum pad; and thus I'm right back to working from the sample-based compositional style. Another advantage of this final process is that it allows me to store that bass phrase as a default bass phrase, which can be used as part of the musical building blocks for a new beat later on.

BeatTip – Bass Framework Not Predicated on Concept of Bass Line

To be sure, Hip hop/rap music is *bottom-heavy*. In most hip hop/rap beats, bass tones and colors play a fundamental role. But does this mean that most beats contain bass lines, per se? Actually, no. Thing is, in beatmaking, the concept of using bass passages or phrases is more about bass frameworks than traditional notions of bass *lines*. And in beatmaking, bass frameworks are more often than not constructed through the use of individual bass sound-stabs.

Bass sound-stabs — individual bass sounds/tones — typically come from two main sources: (1) synthetic bass sounds, i.e. sound modules, keyboard patches, or VSTs; and (2) samples of recorded source material, i.e. vinyl records, CDs, etc. (A very small minority of beatmakers also play bass sounds from a traditional electric bass guitar.) Regardless of each beatmaker's sonic preference and overall beat style, bass sound-stabs are generally what we use as the building blocks for the bass frameworks of the beats that we create. As such, when it comes to bass, we are not always focused on creating a bass line, per se, but a bass *part* that fits the scope and slant of the beat that we're working on.

In beatmaking, coming up with bass frameworks is mostly about accompanying the overall feel and direction of the beat. In some cases, bass frameworks are made up of traditional bass line schemes. But in most cases, bass frameworks are composed through the use of strategically placed bass parts. Thus, in many ways, beatmaking's bass framework concept is about balancing bass tones with the high and mid textures of a beat. Moreover, bass frameworks are often simply the product of filling "holes" in the arrangement structure of a beat. A great example of beatmaking's bass framework concept could be heard in the song "Keep It Thoro," by Prodigy (of Mobb Deep), produced by Alchemist.

Looping Your Samples or Sounds Through the Sequencer (Using the Tempo As an Additional Chopping Function)

Looping your sounds or sound phrases through the sequencer of an EMPI is often more effective than looping your sounds or sound phrases before you sequence them. By looping your samples (and other sounds) using the sequencer, in real-time, you gain more control over the structure of the beat. Whenever you loop your sounds or sound phrases (especially samples of two bars or more in measure) *before* you sequence them, you forfeit the sample's full potential. What I mean is when you begin to try things out, by having the sample looped already, you can't really hear what it sounds like looped from different **end points**.

The initial chopping of your samples is simply setting the start and end points. So once you commit to looping the sample before you sequence it, you're pretty much stuck with the same **end point** — the point where the sample ends before it loops back to itself. On the other hand, by sequencing or what I like to call **"tempo-ing your loop,"** you can hear how the sample sounds with *unintended* end points, that is to say, the end points that you did not intentionally set when you initially chopped the sample. Therefore, as you increase and/or decrease the tempo of the sequence, you can clearly hear the changes.[121]

BeatTip – Spacing is Fundamental: The Right Element Spacing In Your Beats Is Critical

Sonically, hip hop/rap beats have a "knock" (hard-hitting) factor to them. But Despite the overall sonic characteristics of hip hop/rap beats, the use of space (and often silence) within a beat's given compositional framework can

---

[121] This is an example of the fact that many excellent beats will often be created through a beatmaker's knack and ability for capturing and redirecting unintended accidents.

often make or break the beat.

In my interview with mix engineer Steve Sola, one of the main points that arose was the nature of sound individuality. In particular, Sola stressed to me the importance of each sound being able to stand on its own in the mix. The same sentiment was echoed by mix engineer Rich Keller. These discussions reminded me of my long-held approach to beatmaking. Much like how each sound (track) in a mix has to be able to stand on its own, each element in a beat must also be able to do the same as well as be able to effectively represent its own nuance. And nothing enables an element in a beat to stand on its own and to project its nuance more than the proper spacing of a beat's elements.

Here's the context. All of the elements of a given beat can be broadly divided into two main areas or *grouped elements*: (1) the drum elements — the drums; and (2) the non-drum elements – the non-drums. Inside of these broadly described grouped elements, there are sub-divisional elements. For instance, a drum framework is fundamentally made up of a kick, snare, and hi-hat (or some reflection thereof). In order for one single element (from any group of elements) to play an effective role in a beat, the element's role must be well-defined, more importantly, the element must have its own space.

One thing that all great beatmakers tend to have in common is the spacing of their beats. Inexperienced beatmakers and those who tend to over-produce typically do not share this characteristic. Inexperienced beatmakers are often still working out how to create and merge solid drum frameworks with non-drums, thus their spacing is typically either too wide, too sparse, too full of distance between elements, too shallow, too overlapping, and void of virtually no spacing or room for individual elements to breathe. With regards to those beatmakers who over-produce, their common problem is extremely shallow spacing, which comes from constant overcrowding — which often comes from routinely composing beats with multiple unnecessary elements. Those beatmakers who tend to over-produce often create good core rhythms, but then they proceed to bury those rhythms with layers of unneeded elements, seemingly rejecting the fundamental role that tighter core rhythms play in hip hop/rap music.

On the other hand, great beatmakers never create spacing between their beat's elements that are too wide or too shallow. Instead, their beats tend to have the spacing that always fits the style and sound of the beat they're creating. Whether working from the sample-based style or the synthetic-sounds-based style, great beatmakers establish a core rhythm, isolate it, then add in only those elements that enhance it, which ultimately leaves the entire structure of the beat well-spaced.

3 Safeguards Against Poor Spacing

Silence is golden. Allow for some silence in your beats. Every fraction of every measure does not have to have a definite sound or event. The effective use of silence within a beat's given compositional framework is incredibly important. This doesn't mean create any unnecessary gaps, but it also doesn't mean covering up gaps (especially smaller ones) just because they exist. Certain gaps of silence at specific points in a beat's arrangement adds nuances that can't be easily duplicated by other beatmakers.

Avoid crowding your elements. Don't overcrowd the elements within your beats. Typically, overcrowding occurs when there's too many elements playing at once, rather than taking turns and meshing together in a cohesive cycle. Make sure that each element has its own space and adds its own nuance to the overall structure and texture of the beat. For instance, kicks need space to knock and anchor the pace of the drumwork. But if they're smothered with useless elements, they'll lack depth and purpose. With the proper spacing, kicks are able to breath and play their role.

Avoid unnecessary elements. If an element in a beat doesn't hold its own space and nuance, then it's merely an incidental sound. In other words, if it's an incidental sound, not consequential (i.e. not causing any notable nuance that enhances the quality of a beat), then it's not necessary to the beat. Many beatmakers fall into the trap of adding unnecessary elements to beats because they take a quantitative approach to arrangement. But the arrangement of a beat is determined by its quality, not the sheer quantity of elements that it contains.

Study Examples for Element Spacing: "Fish" by Ghostface f/ Raekwon & Cappadonna (produced by True Master); and "If I Can't" by 50 Cent (produced Dr. Dre & Mike Elizondo).

With "Fish," listen carefully to where the elements of the sampled breaks (primary and secondary samples) fall. In each case, the samples ease through each measure in its own space and at its own pace. And even though the drums are obviously moving at the same time, notice how each element is taking their turn, so to speak. This turn-taking, if you will, is the beat's spacing (it's use of space). Specifically, pay attention to the nuance of the hushed and brushed hi-hat that True Master uses, and how he utilizes a very simple and straight forward kick and snare pattern, which he offsets with various sampled breaks and sound-stabs.

Check This Out – Escaping The Tempo Trap: Exploring Different Tempo Ranges, and How to Avoid Getting Stuck with the Same BPM for All of Your Beats

When it comes to making beats, setting the right tempo (BPM) isn't as easy as it might seem. Some beatmakers prefer to "tap out" the tempo of a beat in real time, while others opt to go for pre-set tempos. Both scenarios are fine, but one problem that tends to plague many beatmakers is the inability to expand the tempo range of their beats. I like to refer to this issue as the "tempo trap."

For most of us, the beats that we make fall within the same general range. And this fact is guided by the style of beats that we like as well as the base compositional style that we work from. Each beatmaking compositional style — sample-based, synthetic-sounds-based, or hybrid-based — offers its own set of possibilities and challenges; therefore, each compositional style, along with the style and sound of beats that you like, plays a big role in the tempo ranges you will ultimately work within.

For instance, with regards to sample-based beats, up-tempo is usually not the norm for most sample-based beatmakers. One reason for this has to do with the pitch limits of sampling. Although sample-based beatmakers (myself included) enjoy utilizing the flexibility of being able to pitch a sample up or down, we're mindful of the fact that drastic pitch moves— up or down — away from the original pitch of the sample can encumber the sample's true potential, and thereby torpedo the chance of a dope beat. For example, if you speed the sample up too much, do you then also speed up the overall BPM of your beat's sequence? And if you increase the BPM rate, do you then have to decrease or increase the number of steps (events) in your drumwork? Sometimes, speeding a sample up (specifically, the primary sample) can be properly reconciled (depending on your style and taste) by slowing down the overall BPM of a beat, and by increasing the number of steps (events) in your drumwork. But of course, that all depends on the type and tone of the sample that you're working with.

With the synthetic-sounds-based compositional style (the so-called "keyboard beats"/synth rap style), there is perhaps more flexibility with tempo ranges. After all, once free of the sometimes inflexibility of samples, synthetic-sounds-based beatmakers can presumably work from a much broader tempo range. Well, in theory that's correct. But in practice, this isn't always the case. Here, the important thing to remember is that contemporary hip hop/rap music is pretty much underscored by a median tempo range. Still, there are certainly slower and faster tempos being used in hip hop/rap. But anything slower than 70 BPM is typically used for today's "R&B" ballads. Likewise, anything faster than 120 BPM is typically used for urban pop dance tunes rather than core hip hop/rap styles and sounds. Hence, even most synthetic-sounds-based beats ascribe to similar tempo ranges that are found among sample-based beats.

Although the three main beatmaking compositional styles defer to the same tempo ranges, the reality still remains that some beatmakers get stuck in a tempo trap, making beats that are consistently too slow or too fast. So how do you break from this? For me, the key to escaping the tempo trap has always been my insistence on practicing making beats within four distinct tempo ranges (BPM ranges): 83 - 87; 88 - 93; 94 - 98; and 99 - 103 BPM (fine tune +/- 5%).

Typically, most of my beats fall within the 86 - 98 BPM range. However, I still practice (experiment) with much slower and faster tempos, because doing so helps me to better understand the subtle vibe and nuance differences between smaller tempo ranges. For example, on the surface, the difference between let's say 96 and 97 BPM is minimal. But depending on all of the elements of the beat — samples, synthetic sounds, arrangement scheme, drumwork, etc. — the slight incremental BPM difference can either push, pull, or shuffle the movement (pace) of the entire beat.

As a rhymer, I can not stress enough the importance of feeling the right pace of a beat. If I feel (know) the beat is pushing, then I know to be quick with my rhyme flow and to truncate more words at certain spots in each measure. If I feel (know) the beat is pulling, then I know to lag with my rhyme flow. And if I feel (know) the beat is shuffling, then I know to increase my word count in each bar, which requires me to be very careful with my breath control. In each case, when I'm creating a new beat, knowing the subtle differences that occur between incremental BPM changes helps me to quickly identify what tempo the beat should be at (especially for me to appropriately rhyme to it). Because of this, I never get trapped in either a slow or fast BPM zone. Instead, I'm always prepared to set the right tempo for the style and sound of beat that I'm working on.

Finally, I should also point out that while I rarely use beats that are north of 99 BPM, there are several reasons that I like to still practice making beats at faster tempos. Using my own tempo and loop exercises, in which I use higher tempo ranges (usually 103 - 125 BPM) with the same primary sample over different drumwork sequences, allows me to work on ideas that I have for new drum structures. It also helps me to audition new snare sounds. Further, practicing with faster tempos also helps me to better understand the different ways that loops can work at faster and slower tempos.

BeatTip – Real-Time Programming and Recording

After you've programmed your main sample and/or collage of sound phrases into a sequence and you have it looping at the right tempo, scrap the drums, especially if they're not clicking with everything else. Next, put the sequence back into record mode and play the drums live, right in over the top, in real time. The result of everything together, moving correctly and at the desired tempo, is what I call the "primary theme loop." In most cases, the primary loop is where the entire beat stems from. This description is also a more detailed explanation of how to create the core sequence that I described earlier in this section.

Check This Out – Programming Improvisation

Since the typical beat is programmed before-hand, improvisation in beatmaking must be accounted for either at the beginning of the composition phrase or in the mixing or re-programming phase of the beatmaking process. After the completion of a beat, any changes that you add or any parts that you subtract is considered as the *re-programming* of the beat. This is one of the reasons that well-known beatmakers often like to get the track back, after the vocals have been laid to the initial beat. This way, they can further embellish the beat, and thereby accent the entire song.[122]

Parts, Components, and Elements, and Progressive or Repetitive Arrangement Schemes

All beats are made up of separate music *parts*; each part contains a variety of music *components*; and each component is comprised of a number of different music "elements." For example, a drum framework is a music part; the particular patterns of each drum sound within a part is a music component; the individual drum-hits (sounds) within a music component would then refer to the music elements. This formula can be used for phrases of strings, keys, and the like. In other words, **arrangement** is literally the creative organization of the separate music parts, components, and elements.

In beatmaking, arrangement can also be split into two broad schemes or

---

[122] In the same vein, once you've completed the initial beat, go back and survey the overall sound of the beat and locate zones where you can throw in changes.

structured varieties: **repetitive** and **progressive**. **Repetitive arrangement** is essentially the organization of music parts in a manner that consistently repeats a primary musical theme.[123] In the repetitive arrangement scheme, the onus is placed on remaining close (in some way) to the essence of the hip hop/rap DJ's musical processes — the earliest compositional roots of the hip hop/rap music tradition. This is to say, the repetitive arrangement scheme is a structure that seeks to represent the processes in which DJs cut or blended the breaks from records together into new compositions. Examples of repetitive arrangement schemes include sample-based beats like those that rely on one lengthy sampled music phrase, or those beats that have multiple chopped samples that are weaved into one cohesive music part. Further examples of the repetitive arrangement scheme include synthetic-sounds-based beats that are based on the use of prominent and oft repeated phrases. A sample-based song that demonstrates the repetitive arrangement scheme quite well is Nas' "Nas Is Like," produced by DJ Premier. A synthetic-sounds-based song that demonstrates the repetitive arrangement scheme nicely is Red Café's (feat. Fabolous) "Bling Blaow," produced by Reefa.

Progressive arrangement is essentially the organization of music parts into several (or more) progressively different musical themes. In progressive arrangement, the onus is placed on structuring a succession of music parts that unravel through a song in linear, rather than cyclical, progression. Unlike the repetitive arrangement scheme, the progressive arrangement scheme is not necessarily predicated upon the repeating of (or consistent returning) to one or two specific themes. Instead, the emphasis is placed on developing multiple themes and, at times, more complex music components.

The progressive arrangement scheme can often be effective, especially when it's used in deference to the hip hop/rap music tradition. For one thing, a progressive arrangement scheme can shake up any monotony that may exist from generic drumwork or a typical loop of a lengthy sample. Also, because progressive arrangement can go a long way in establishing a unique contrast in a beat, it's very useful when you're trying to convey a sense of urgency or seriousness within a song. Furthermore, a progressive arrangement can also be an excellent structural scheme for story-themed songs because the changes within the music components and parts work like chapter accompaniments; plus the changes can provide more acute depth and *distinguished* meaning for each of the rapper's verses. A very good example of a progressive arrangement scheme (albeit a simple one) is demonstrated in 50 Cent's "If I Can't," produced by Dr.

---

[123] It's worth noting that virtually all forms of mid/late-twentieth-century American popular music features some sort of a repetitive arrangement scheme.

Dre and Mike Elizondo.

In recent years, there's been an increase in the number of beatmakers who have moved towards the progressive arrangement scheme as their base arrangement method. There are several reasons for this development. The first reason deals with the hip hop/rap music and beatmaking traditions in their own right. Fact is, some beatmakers are simply unfamiliar with the roots and fundamentals of the hip hop/rap music tradition. And they are particularly unaware of the fundamental aesthetics, tropes, nuances, principles, and priorities of hip hop culture itself and both the hip hop/rap music and beatmaking traditions. But more alarming than that is the fact that there are some beatmakers (mostly new) who do not care at all about the roots and the recent history of the beatmaking and hip hop/rap music traditions (some even show a total disregard for it). In both cases, these beatmakers are prompted to incorporate the aesthetics, tropes, nuances, principles, and priorities of *other* music traditions that are not in-line or consistent with the beatmaking and hip hop/rap music traditions. Incidentally, this is one reason why there's been a recent uptick in the number of beatmakers who have deliberately tried to fuse the "trained musician" nuance into beatmaking. Specifically, there's been a more concentrated (i.e forced) effort to apply advanced concepts of music theory to beatmaking.

The second reason that a sizeable number of beatmakers have turned to the progressive arrangement scheme deals with the lure of the pop music scene. At the time of the publication of this edition, pop music seemingly presents itself as the "safe" music genre for the fledgling music industry to back. And many beatmakers are uprooting their styles and sounds to fit this larger music industry philosophy, hoping that it will increase their chances of a placement. Professional beatmakers have to deal with both the artistic and business realities of beatmaking, so I'm not quick to cast judgement on any beatmaker who has made or is considering making this change in style and sound. But even though trends can offer short runs of opportunity, it is individuality and distinguishable creativity that consistently offer the best opportunities and longevity.

Finally, the third reason that a sizeable number of beatmakers have moved to the progressive arrangement scheme deals with what I can only describe as an identity crises — perhaps caused by either a deep inferiority complex or music traditional self-hate. For years, the hip hop/rap music tradition operated in the shadows of mainstream neglect. But as the American mainstream made room for and, subsequently, co-opted key areas of the hip hop/rap music scene, many beatmakers found themselves in cultural and financial spaces that had been previously inaccessible to beatmakers, DJs, and rappers who had came before them. Thus for the first time in hip hop/rap's history, many beatmakers are forfeiting the pursuit of dope beats and are instead becoming much more preoccupied with how they measure up as music producers against those from other mainstream (more traditional) music forms. Hence, these beatmakers have come to view more elaborate arrangement schemes as a sort of conduit out of and away from the beatmaking tradition. Many of the beatmakers within this group seemingly despise being labeled as "beatmakers" or "hip hop producers." They instead think of themselves — and want to be known — only as "music producers." This despite the fact that beatmaking and hip hop/rap music has been and is paramount to their ability to even compete in a narrow-minded and otherwise non-inclusive music industry.

Creating Arrangement "Changes" in Beatmaking
Making the Task of Coming Up with Changes Less Daunting: Three Things That Can Help You Create "Changes" in Your Beats

Ever make a beat that seems like it's missing something? I mean, the core track is dope; everything is tight and looping correctly, but after 4- to 8- bars, it just seems, well, too redundant? Although redundancy is a good thing in some cases and for certain styles of beats; and although the crux of all hip hop/rap beats is repetition, i.e. frameworks based upon continuously looped riffs/grooves), some beats just work better with effective changes.

In beatmaking, "changes" — embellishments, breakdowns, switch-ups, sweeps, etc. — vary in sound and complexity. They can be as simple as added percussion, something like a mini-phrase of bongo-hits over vocals, or they can be as complex as an entirely new arrangement of sounds and textures, something like dual lines of melody and countermelody played out with a synthesizer.

For many beatmakers, coming up with effective changes (changes that actually fit well) isn't necessarily an easy part of the beatmaking process. On one hand, you have to consider the style and sound of beat that you're making. For instance, to make changes in sample-based beats, many beatmakers simply sample, chop, and insert different parts/pieces of the same source material or even the primary sample. In many cases, this approach is all that it takes to come up with an effective change or two. Still, there are those times when the same source material doesn't have any more pieces that fit with the beat at hand. Therefore, in cases like these, it can be a bit of a task coming up with changes that work. And while there are some who believe that creating changes for non-sampled based beats is a much easier challenge, the truth is, even with non-sampled based beats, creating effective changes can be rather difficult.

But difficulty aside, there are three things that can help you — a great deal or at least make the task less daunting — with your approach to creating (adding) changes to your beats: (1) Knowing if a change or changes are actually needed; (2) Knowing which types of changes typically work well with which types of beats; and (3) Having a good understanding of mood, i.e. the moods that specific sounds and certain categories of sounds invoke and tend to convey.

First, it should always be remembered that some beats simply do not need a change. For example, if a beat is made up of a 4-bar pattern, chances are that complete pattern — from start to finish — is not monotonous; and therefore, it may be able to do without any significant change. Perhaps a few drops (mutes) and solos at various points of the beat can be all the change that's needed.

Second, it's important to gauge which type of changes usually work well with which types of beats. For instance, does the beat need a breakdown or a bridge, an intro or a stacked synth phrase, or just a simple riff pitched up or down? In either case, a change should relate to the basic style, scope, and structure of the beat at hand. Which means everything from style, sound, form, and tempo must be considered before incorporating changes. For example, when working with a sample-based beat, particularly a mid-tempo one (93-96 BPM), I prefer to incorporate changes that feature samples, not synths. If I can help it, I avoid blending samples and synths. But when I do add synth sounds to a sample-based beat, I sample the actual synth sounds/phrases, then I match their sound and feel to style and sound of the beat. However, when I'm working on a synthetic-sounds based (non-sample-based) beat, I take more leisure with the samples that I incorporate because non-sampled based beats tend to absorb — or perhaps feature — samples more effectively than sample-based beats absorb synth sounds. Most of the time, I find that synths either stick out like an obnoxious blemish or they betray the sample style and feel of a beat.

Finally, having a good understanding of mood, i.e. the moods that specific sounds and certain categories of sounds tend to invoke and convey, is the third thing that can help you with your approach to creating (adding) changes to your beats. A big part of coming up with an effective change is being in tune with the core mood and feel of a beat. When you know the moods that particular sounds invoke and convey, you're better equipped to create those changes that work well within the framework of the core structure, form, style, and sound of your beat.

BeatTip – Five Guidelines for Making Changes in Your Beats

The prospect of adding in changes and transitions in beatmaking can be challenging. However, with a number of basic guidelines for adding in changes to your arrangements, you'll likely find that it's not as difficult as you might think. So to help you with making changes in your beats, below I have included five basic (but key) guidelines that I follow when I add in changes to an arrangement.

(1) What kind of rhyme and rhyme voice will go with the beat?

After you've established the main groove of a beat, let it play for a while. Do this for one main reason: You want to really think about what kind of rhyme and rhyme "voice" would go well with the beat. Figuring out what sort of rhyme and rhyme voice would match up well with the beat helps you determine if the beat needs any changes. Remember, even track solos and sound mutes can serve as effective changes. And sometimes, once you've established a great groove, you might not need to add any changes.

(2) Is the arrangement of the beat sample-based or non-sampled-based?

Sample-based beats often allow for fewer and less-complex changes because of their more strict adherence to the groove. Overly complex changes in sample-based beats tend to cause too much distraction throughout the beat. On the other hand, non-sample-based beats typically allow more room for changes. But that doesn't necessarily mean that this room must always be filled up. Changes need not simply occupy space, they should exist to serve some purpose in the beat, for example, to show contrast or to create tension or release. So whether sample-based or non-sample-based, consider the usefulness of a change and its overall effect on the beat's sound composite.

(3) What sort of changes can the beat handle? Minor changes, for example, an slight embellishment, or major changes, for example, a main transition or a broad "switch-up"? And how long should they be?

Having determined that the beat could use a change(s), the next thing you want to assess is what kind of change would work best with the beat. Different types of changes can be added to a beat, but just like with other popular forms of music, the most common change is an embellishment. Embellishment typically refers to the embellishing (decorating) of an existing melody. This applies in beatmaking and hip hop/rap music as well. However, because of the "looped groove" nature of hip hop/rap music, it is the groove — riffs and melodies locked in a rhythm — that is most often decorated. Thus in beatmaking, think of an embellishment as just any musical component(s) that decorates the main groove or any aspect of the rhythm of the beat.

A "switch-up" in beatmaking can be a much more elaborate affair. Unlike an embellishment, which more often than not is simply a musical element based on something already present in the beat, a switch-up is often an independent musical phrase, one that isn't based on something already in the beat, like the main groove. As for how long a change or switch-up should be, well, each beatmaker is different. That being said, a length of 1-4 bars will be quite effective in most beats. If you need to extend the length of an existing change, just duplicate it and take out or add an additional element to the added bars; you can even program drops (track solos and sound mutes) here as well.

(4) Where should you add the changes in at?

Typically, for embellishments it's a good to work them in the hook and near the beginning of the second verse — the second pass (the second installment of 8-, 12-, or 16-bars) of the main groove. But there aren't any hard rules, you can work in changes wherever you like. Just be mindful of a couple of things. First, wherever you place a change, make sure that it doesn't disrupt the feel and scope of what the main groove has established. Even a change that runs counter to the groove can still fit the feel and scope of a beat. Second, when determining where to add in a change, always consider whether or not a rapper would be able to effectively rhyme over the changes. If the core groove of a beat is going in one solid direction for 8 bars, any change(s) worked in on the 9th- 10th-, 11th-, or 12th-bar should not be so disruptive as to hender or break up the rapper's flow.

(5) How many times should you add these changes?

Generally, if you add your changes in too much, that is to say, on every pass (8-, 12-, 16-bars), the beat may sound cluttered, overworked, or too complicated. But again, this is a guide. And even though there aren't any hard rules that you have to subscribe to, do bear in mind that too many changes can disrupt continuity and undermine the feel of a beat.

Sample-Based Compositional Style and Arrangement: Making Beats Using Primary Samples (or Songs) and Derivative Samples

A sample and/or song that serves as the source material for which other samples are then derived from is the **primary sample** or the **primary song**. A sample that is derived *(chopped)* from a primary sample and/or a primary song is a derivative sample. One common purpose of **derivative samples** is to provide a change or progression to the sample from which it was derived. When most beatmakers successfully sample something from a record, and thereby build a new beat around it, they tend to return to that very same record for the *changes* that they want to incorporate into the same beat. Likewise, when you have a sizable complete-phrase, spare-part phrase, or a section-piece, it's somewhat intuitive to chop up the phrase even more, especially for the purpose of finding suitable changes.

Building Arrangements Using Primary Samples Along with Derivative Samples

Whether you build your sample-based beat around your drums or build your drums around your samples, a very effective way of carving out tight compositions is by using arrangements that incorporate the use of primary samples and derivative samples. As I discussed earlier, you can make some quality beats with just one sample by itself. But one-sample beats are typically non-progressive in nature because they rely more upon a central, repetitive loop theme. So, if you're going to use samples and you would like to make more progressive arrangements, then you essentially have two choices: (1) Incorporate several or more different samples from a number of different records; or (2) Incorporate multiple samples from the same record. (This involves the process described above.) My recommendation is to shoot for the derivative approach.

After the drums are created and you have the primary sample laid down, here's a couple of ways that you can work in the derivative samples. First, allow the primary sample to play for 4 bars, then program in one of your derivative samples, beginning on the 5th bar. Since the newly added derivative sample changes the sequence (program), it is considered a *change*; I call this "sample-change 1." When you only have one change, one very effective way to arrange your beats is on the "4" or the "8;" that is, for every 4 or 8 bars, you work in "sample-change 1." If your "sample-change 1" is only 1 bar, double it up to 2 bars before you loop back to the primary sample. If your "sample-change 1" is 2 bars, you can either loop back to the primary sample, or you can double it up to 4 bars before you loop back to the primary sample.

If you intend to make an even more progressive arrangement, using only samples and very minimal synthetic-sounds, then you can add other derivative samples. Naturally, I call the next derivative sample added "sample-change 2," and the next, "sample-change 3," and so on. Multiple sample changes gives you a great deal of flexibility when you're building arrangements. For instance, you can bring one of them in right after the first sample change ends, landing the new change on every 7th and 9th bar that proceeds the primary sample. This technique enables you to *build out* the texture of the beat, using samples in a carefully crafted arrangement pattern. Furthermore, it allows you to build better sound collages for your drum programs.

Here's what the formula could look like, using primary samples and derivative samples. When you apply this formula to the bar structure of a typical hip hop/rap song, it breaks down like this:

- 8-bar intro = 4 bars of "sample-change 1" + 4 bars of "sample-change 2."
- 16-bar verse = 4 bars of primary sample + 2 bars of "sample-change 1" + 8 bars of primary sample + 2 bars of "sample-change 3."
- 8-bar hook (chorus) = (this is where you can get really out there. Mix up the drum program, rotate in two changes while keeping the primary sample moving steady. Or you can drop the primary sample all together and play the changes off of the new drum program).
- 16-bar verse = 4 bars of primary sample + 4 bars of "sample-change 3" (or "sample-change 4 if you have it) + 6 bars of primary sample + 2 bars of "sample-change 1." (This is the middle of the song, so you can really push the envelope more here.)
- 8-bar hook (chorus) = Keep steady.
- 16-bar verse = 4 bars of primary sample + 2 bars of "sample-change 2" + 2 bars of "sample-change 1" + 8 bars of primary sample.
- 8-bar hook (chorus) = Keep steady.
- 8-bar outro = 4 bars of "sample-change 1" + 4 bars of "sample-change 3."

BeatTip – Bumpin' the Sample

There are times when you come up against a sample that has *something* but you can't figure out exactly what that is. Then there are times you come across samples that you know are very recognizable. Situations like these may call for what I' call "bumpin' the sample." **Bumpin'-the-sample** describes the process of neutralizing the main sonic elements of a sample, then using the newly modified sample together with your own enhancement: your own "bump." To bump a sample, first, filter out the bass frequency of the sample. Technically, you can't really *remove* the bass if it's actually within the sample; however, you can neutralize it — make it inaudible — by burying its sonic quality to a level of no distinction. To do this, you have to filter down, or rather flatten the bass. Once you've, *removed* the bass, add in your own bass line (bass parts/framework), either from a set of sampled bass tones or synthetic bass sounds from a synthesizer or sound module or software VST. This bass line (bass part) can be any pattern — when you bump the sample, I recommend taking your bass line (bass part) in a new direction. After you've added your own bass line (bass part), decrease the treble in the sample. Again, here, you want to employ some filtering techniques, but you don't want to kill the treble, you just want to pull it back just enough to let it breathe so that you keep some of the color and character of the sample that you're bumpin'. This is also effective because it enables you to beef up the sample further with your own treble sounds, accents, or percussion parts. Moreover, you can play new high-pitched keyboard parts or high-pitched sample chops right of over the top.

Synthetic-Sounds-Based Compositional Style and Arrangement, and The Use of Melody in the Beatmaking Tradition

Rhythm is king in the beatmaking and hip hop/rap music traditions, and harmony, in the structural sense of the word, is the king's noble servant; melody is the king's ambassador, capable of readily bringing nuances and tropes of other traditions to beatmaking and hip hop/rap wherever effectively possible. Also, melody in beatmaking is characterized more by short, percussive, riff-like phrases than elaborate melodic passages that are further flanked by an extended use of counter-melody or a series of multiple motifs. Because of the unique ways that melody can be used in hip hop/rap music, beatmakers create brief melodic passages in many different ways with a number of different sounds that those outside of the hip hop/rap and beatmaking traditions can't always understand.

Combining Samples and Synths

Samples (sampled breaks, various tones, and sounds) are typically made up of a collage of sounds. As such, the concept of matching synth sounds to the same "key" (pitch) of samples isn't as definite as some would like to believe. In fact, it's a bit misleading. Combining synth sounds with samples is not particularly necessary, but it's certainly useful in some situations. Either way, if you do decide to do a synth-sample blend, remember this: When blending a synth sound with a sample, keep in mind that you are trying to match the synth to the sample, not the other way around. That being said, here are some other important factors to consider when matching, blending, or combining samples and synths.

The Matter of Atonality and Sampling

There are many reasons why the art of sampling is not, nor ever could be, understood entirely under the auspices of traditional music-making practices. But perhaps the most outstanding (and often ignored) reason is the fact that sampling has no partiality to traditional musical tonality. That is, in the sampling process, samples of recorded source material (usually records) are modified and arranged with impartiality to the tones of the chromatic scale. That is to say, in sampling, there is no deference (or reference) to key or a tonal center; on the contrary, sample-based beatmakers are primarily concerned with three things: (1) Whether or not a sample *sounds and feels good*; (2) Does the sample fit with the drum framework (program); and (3) Does the sample and drum framework together ascribe to the aesthetics, priorities, and principles of hip hop/rap music. Sample-based beatmakers are not necessarily concerned with adhering to music theory or concepts and principles of traditional musical tonality.

In fact, it's worth noting that many traditionally trained musician-beatmakers often fail (miserably) at sampling precisely because they attempt to approach sampling through the guise of traditional music practices and the prism of music theory. As such, they attempt to apply the rules of music theory to a compositional process that has no deferential regard for music theory at all. If there is anything that must be understood about sampling it's the fact that sampling seeks, technically and theoretically speaking, to simply use whatever works. If it uses any principles or concepts of music theory, it's not out of deference, but out of prudence.

What Does Tone, Matching, Blending, and Combining Mean?

In beatmkaing, there are a lot of terms that may carry several meanings and, without individual clarification, use of these terms can create some confusion.

Hence, here, it's important to discuss the terms "tone," "match (matching)" "combine (combining)," and "blend (blending)."

When beatmakers speak of "tone," there's two meanings or concepts that we can actually be describing. There's "tone," as in sound; and then there's "tone" as in *feel*. Sound and feel are two different concepts. "Tone," in regards to sound, refers to things like notes, timbre, sustain, etc. "Tone," in regards to feel, refers to variations of mood, like soulful, happy, sad, etc. When beatmakers speak of "matching" something, there's two meanings or concepts that we can actually be employing. There's "matching," as in *matching the sound*, and there's "matching," as in *matching the feel or mood*. Matching sound and matching feel are two different concepts, and as such, each usually requires a different approach. In beatmaking, "matching" is most commonly used to describe the process of working with sounds in the same pitch (key). However, as I've just made clear, it's not the only description, nor is it any more or less important than the other description of "matching." It all depends on the beatmaker and beatwork in question.

When beatmakers speak of "blending" something, there's two meanings or concepts that we can actually be employing. There's "blending," as in mixing or layering two or more sounds of the same pitch (key) together, and there's "blending," as in complimenting or accentuating two or more sounds that are not necessarily in the same pitch (key). Blending sounds of the same pitch (key) is a different concept than the notion of blending sounds that are not of the same pitch (key), as such, each usually requires a different approach.

Finally, when beatmakers speak of "combining" something, we're not necessarily speaking about *blending* something. In fact, we're usually talking about *adding* two or more things (sounds and/or feelings) together, which is different from *blending* something together into one new sound. For instance, you can combine or add a 808 kick drum and basic kick drum to a drum pattern, that doesn't mean that you're *blending* those two sounds together.

Arrangement Scope

The arrangement scope of your beat/song is another important factor to consider when you're combining synths with samples. What's the scope of your verse and hook (chorus) sections? How different is your verse section from your hook section? What about the framework of your sequences? That is, what bar-framework is your verse section based on? Is it a 2-bar, 4-bar, or 8-bar loop? What about the sample scheme that you're using? Are you using just one main sample that is heavily chopped? Are you using multiple samples that are woven together? Are you using a relatively unmodified break of one or more bars? Each one of these factors will better determine what sort of synth combination is likely to work with your samples.

When I use a combo of synths and samples, there's a catch: *I never try to play a synth in the same key as the sample(s) I'm using.* To understand why, you need to know why I use synth sounds in sample-based beats. Whenever I add in synth sounds to a sample-based beat, I usually do so for one or two reasons: (1) To boost or "beef" up the sample, sort of like stacking synth sounds; or (2) To accentuate or emphasize a moment or element of the sample(s) I'm using. Therefore, when I'm making a sample-based beat, I'm not concerned with simply reinterpreting a sampled break with synth sounds of the same pitch. Why? Because then the focus would be more on the synth sounds, and that would essentially make it more of a synthetic-sounds-based beat. (I like to stay consistent to the style of beat that I'm making at the time.)

Also, I should point out that in most cases of a sample-based beat, the sample itself contains multiple instruments; therefore, if you want to match the sound of the synth to the sound of the sample, then sure, you can try to play the synth in the same overall pitch (key) of the sample. However, for me, if I'm aiming to match the sound of the sample, it becomes an issue of manipulating the pitch (higher or lower) of the particular synth sounds that I'm using. More specifically, it's an issue of manipulating the pitch of the synth sounds higher or lower than the pitch of the primary sample and the sample scheme that I'm using.

On the other hand, if it's a matter of matching the *feel* of a sample, then I take a different approach. For instance, if I'm working with a low-pitched sample (something with a bass tone), I usually try to offset its sound with some level of brightness. In cases like these, I'll add in some synth sounds. This contrast makes for a unique, unforced change or accent. Here, one thing I want to point out is that matching the synth closely to the "feel" (not necessarily the key) of the sample typically works better for the overall impact of the sample-based beat. Keep in mind that synth sounds have a completely different sonic quality than samples from recorded songs. So typically, whenever the synth sound is made to match the key of the sample, what happens is that the synth sound winds up *competing with* — if not outright dominating — the sample. In turn, this transforms a sample-based beat into a synthetic-sounds-based beat.

Here's how I combine samples and synths. Either I play a phrase(s) straight up (from my Roland Fantom Keyboard) and record it through MIDI into a sequence on my Akai MPC 4000, or I play a phrase(s), sample it, then assign the phrase(s) to one drum pad or more. More often than not, I do the latter, because sampling the synth phrase(s) allows me more flexibility over the tone and timbre of the synth sound; and once the synth sound is sampled, I can filter it, compress it, add reverb, do whatever it takes to match the feeling (not the pitch) of the sample and the overall beat. For those times where I sample the synth sound, I run my Fantom through my MPC 4000. One more thing. In cases where I'm using synth sounds for slight emphasis or slight accents and changes, I focus on the softest (deadest) part of the sample, then I add in the synth sounds. And sometimes when I have a sample cut off right at the loop point of a sequence, I'll throw some "light" (soft) stacked synth sounds right at the point of where the end of the sample drops out.

Check This Out – Playing Synths in Same Key of Sample?

A member of The BeatTips Community (TBC forums) once asked me the following:

> "I'm kind of confused. You're supposed to make everything in the same key and in tune. If you don't play in the same key as the sample, your beat is going to sound out of tune. So you're saying you play whatever notes on top of the sample?"

Answer: Whoever said that you *have* to play synth/keys in the same key as the sample? First and foremost, when attempting to combine synths/keys with samples, always remember the subtle nuances that samples have (and that synths/keys do not). Samples are "second generational" sounds, meaning that they are pre-recorded composites of music (sound). On the other hand, synths/keys are mostly "first generational" sounds, meaning that they are generated from *sound generators*, etc. They are not pre-recorded composites of sound. This fact alone should indicate to you that matching up synths/keys with samples most likely will never be achieved using the "exact same key." Sure, in some cases it might get the job done. But if you really want to match synths/keys with samples more effectively, and by match I mean timbre, color, weight, and feel, then more than likely off-tuning the synths/keys from the sample will be your best plan of action. The thing is, samples present a sonic quality that can simply never be matched by first generational sounds (this is also why replays of samples may come close, but they're almost never a good substitute). And more often than not, when beatmakers attempt to force an "exact-key" synth-match with a sample, where the exact pitch (in the context of sampling) is actually indiscernible, the sonic dynamics change; this in turn prompts a raise of the volume level of either the original sample or the synth. In such a case, the original feel and nuance of the overall beat changes dramatically.

Whether you combine synths with samples or not, always remember: Each beat is a slave to the style that you made it in. If it's a sample-based beat, the synths that you add in should support the sample-based framework, not dominate it. If it's a synthetic-sounds-based beat, then the samples that you add in should serve to support or accentuate the synthetic sounds. So before you make additions and subtractions to the beat, always give deference to the style and scope of the beat you're making. Also, consider the rhythm quality and structure before you modify the major sonic (sound dynamics) qualities of the beat.

Having considered the "style-deference aspect," as I call it, whenever I use keys/synths I don't view it as playing any notes *over the top*. If I play keys over the top of the sample, I essentially drown out the sample. Instead, I view it as supporting the sample. In beatmaking, since keys/synths are often better used for developing melody as opposed to rhythm, and since samples are mostly used for establishing rhythm and groove, you have to be careful how and when you combine them with samples. Plus, it should be noted that combining synths with samples is not merely a matter of playing notes over the top. However, many beatmakers confuse "playing synths over the top" with simply making a sample fuller or thicker. But the fullness and thickness of a sample is not a melody or rhythm issue, it's a sonic issue. Yet many beatmakers make the assumption that playing synths over the top will make the sample sound better. Wrong! At best, it will neutralize the sample's true impact, nuance, and sonic quality. At worst, it will drown out the sample, both in terms of feel and sound. So there's two things I want to make clear about this. First, if you want to increase the fullness or thickness of a sample, particularly through the use of synths, then I recommend that you sample the synths, chop them down into tones, then use the chopped synth tones to beef up the weaker points of the sample. Second, consider the length of the primary sample that you're using. For instance, if you're working with a 4-bar sequence, how long does the primary sample play for? If it doesn't play for the full 4 bars, you can add in synths on the "free" bars or "free" spots — the bars and spots where the sample is silent. In cases like these, you can play in (add in) synth patterns in whatever key/tune that you like, as long as it sounds good to you. Actually, playing in a different key often works best here because it will give your beat more balance and an increased dynamic quality.

BeatTip – Getting Valuable Clues from Slow Jams

Some of my deepest musical understanding has come from what I've been able to extract from *slow jams*, ie. slower tempo, ballad-like soul songs of the '60s, '70s, and '80s. Although slow jams carry tempos that are much slower than even the slowest beats, I would argue that it is precisely because of this "slowness" that you can more closely examine all of the elements of a song and get a better idea for how each element is woven into a musical structure. Moreover, not only do slow jams typically give off an obvious "good feeling," they also often yield much information about music creation. Slow jams have had a rather profound effect on my musical process. So below, I want to share a number areas in which I've learned a great deal from studying slow jams.

Regarding Arrangement, Tempo, and Movement

Soulful slow jams offer great instruction on what effective, engaging core grooves sound like. The concept of arrangement used to be difficult for me. But slow jams helped me develop a stronger understanding for how to create independent musical sections and then blend them into one cohesive audio composite. Also, slow jams gave me cues on when, where, and how to add secondary musical events to the core groove. For instance, it was through my study of slow jams that I learned how subtle strokes of sound could make a huge difference in the feel and movement of a beat.

So in addition to helping me to better identify the ways in which beats can be arranged (programmed), slow jams have taught me a great deal about the movement of musical parts. For instance, many beatmakers think that the programmed tempo is exact and precise. Well, that's technically true. Fact is though: Two songs of the same tempo never move the exact same way. In other words, songs of the same tempo can actually move and feel slower than one another, depending upon the specific elements of the song. Because of this understanding, whenever I make a beat, I go with the tempo that *feels* right rather than the one that simply *sounds* right.

Regarding Individual Sound Design

Among soulful slow jams you will find some of the most beautifully rich tones and audio *colors* in recorded music. Slow jams, which are delicate audio affairs, require great care to pull off. Because the vocalist is called upon to do more carrying of the song than in the case of faster tempo tunes, the instrumental pallet of slow jams usually calls for softer sonic impressions, which each instrumentalist obliges, being ever careful to stay out of the way of the vocalist. This is one of the main reasons that slow jams sound so incredibly smooth. But remember, these are soulful slow jams; and thus, the instrumentalists who play on these songs typically render some slight embellishments, and it is these boldly-soft, impromptu embellishments that make for some of the most magnificent sound colors. (One of my favorite slow jams to study is "I Miss You" by Harold Melvin and the Blue Notes featuring Theodore Pendergrass. "I Miss You" is a lush, magnetic slow jam that offers a great lesson in studying individual sound design.)

Because most musical parts in slow jams are less deliberate and much more subtle, it's easier to make out the individual sounds. Through my study of soulful slow jams, I learned how to create short harp phrases and unique organ-sound-stabs (truncated and sustained). Furthermore, I developed ways for dissolving horn-stabs into an array of different sounds, making brand new sound textures from otherwise opposing sounds. Finally, with regards to sound design, the harmonizing of backup singers on most soulful slow jams has also improved my musical understanding. The harmonizing of backup singers on slow jams is always warm; it glides and fades in and out, often cradling the song with even more emotional feeling, a nuance I strive to add — in some way — to every beat that I make.

Regarding Drum Frameworks

As for the drums, soulful slow jams have taught me to commit to the core drum framework and to avoid trying to get too fancy or complex with the drumwork. I've learned to just anchor the groove and make sure the drum framework keeps the rhythm steady, no matter the tempo. Even when I add in heavier syncopation to my drum frameworks, I never get caught up in the trend of adding useless snare repeats. Instead, I only use the snare as it fits with the general scheme of the kick and the movement of the other musical elements of the beat.

BeatTip – Quality Parameters: Use the Right Ingredients, But Don't Overcook the Beat

Beatmaking is not only a rich art, it's also a musical science. That being said, some beatmakers get too carried away with the "science" part. (You wouldn't believe all of the different stories that I've heard that describe incredible levels over-production.) The science of beatmaking is a robust one; as mentioned in the Introduction, it contains technical, logical, and creative spheres. This section is about the creative science of beatmaking — more specifically the science of arrangement and how it effects the quality of a beat.

No matter how we all differ with our initial approach to getting a new beat started, we all set out trying to find relatively the same thing: A base (primary) rhythm framework, one that has just the right drums and the right overall sound. Having achieved this framework, through a number of creatively applied musical sciences that are mostly unique to beatmaking, a familiar dilemma sets in: What to add next?

Again within the beatmaking lexicon, these "add-ons" are commonly known as "changes" or "switch-ups." (For those familiar with music theory, a change or switch-up is actually most comparable to a motif or motive, and an embellishment and/or ornament.) Typically in beatmaking, changes are worked in somewhere on 4th, 8th, 12th, or 16th bar, with a significant switch-up thrown in somewhere at the mid-length of the beat. But again, every beat does not requires a significant change (and certainly not a major switch-up) in order for it to sound dope and be of high quality.

Consider this, let's say that you sample a 4-bar measure of any given record from the 1970s — the era of choice of nearly all sample-based beatmakers. Now, depending on *where* on the record that you sample the measure from, you want to remember that contained in just that one sample, there can actually be a wide assortment of individual sounds, each combining to form a wall-of-sound. Think about it: There could be the bass drum, the snare drum, a ride, a cymbal, a hi-hat, an open hi-hat, bass guitar, rhythm guitar, lead guitar, electronic keyboard/piano, tambourine, timbales, horns — it could go on, but that's pretty much the basic sound-wall that you can expect to hear. And since drums are the most fundamental component of standard hip hop/rap beat structure, beatmakers are naturally drawn to those parts of the record that have the least amount of collective sounds. Traditionally, this part in the record is known as the break. However, though I recognize what a traditional break is — the section where all of the music drops out, save the rhythm section, namely the drums and bass, I consider *any* fragmented musical phrase to be a break. Fundamentally speaking, I believe that the quest for the perfect beat is really the quest for the perfect break. That said, after this ultimate break is created, many of us do something very detrimental to the beat itself: We over-do it, by adding in unnecessary or counter-productive changes and switch-ups.

Creating beats is meticulous and very cathartic. And a lot of the time, the way we feel about a beat we've just made has a lot to do with what actually went into the making of it. For beatmakers, *process* matters a great deal. We value the unique processes, practices, and methodologies of our craft in a way that sometimes borders on obsession. And as I mentioned earlier, we take great pride in our particular brand of musical science. Because of this, we're always surveying a beat, thinking about how we can make it better. This (sometimes unhealthy) preoccupation with perfection can sabotage many of the beats that we make. Somewhere in between a beatmaker carving out that ultimate break and officially calling a beat complete is where this preoccupation with perfection tends to go way out of whack.

In much of the beatwork of the past decade, I've noticed that this problem of under- or over-producing is increasingly getting worse. And I think the reason has a lot to do with the shifting concepts of what makes a beat dope, as well as today's loose standards that excludes some beats from being considered wack. In the current hip hop/rap climate, it seems as if there's some *questionable* rules board that renders any criticism as merely "opinion," which, in effect, reduces any negative criticism of one beatmaker to another (after all, nobody wants to be labled a hater). Because the current standards of quality in hip hop/rap and beatmaking have loosened up, what we now have is more uninteresting rhymes and a level of beatwork that either sounds alarmingly incomplete and woefully under-produced, or perhaps worse, too manufactured and over-produced. It's because of this that somewhere between arriving at that ultimate break — the heart of a beat — and completion of the beat, many of us are electing to either stop short or to throw in questionable changes and switch-ups that distract and undermine the main theme or heart of the beat.

I believe that this laxity or lack of concern for quality beatmaking and this over-concern for quantity on the other has been caused by some sort of hip hop amnesia. Throughout every significant beatmaking era from hip hop's inception (ca. 1973) up until the mid to late 1990s, the fundamental principle for when a beat was complete depended on how tight the rhythm was — how dope the ultimate break was. From Grandmaster Flash and Afrika Bambaataa to Large Professor, DJ Premier, and Dr. Dre, on up to J Dilla, Kanye West, Just Blaze, The Neptunes, DJ Mustard, and Metro Boomin, one principle of quality that directly linked all of them was the existence of a complete, solid core rhythm structure — an *ultimate break* that contained no distracting or unnecessary changes or switch-ups. In fact, in the case of Dr. Dre (who's not primarily a sample-based beatmaker), his base rhythm structures were so tight, and his peripheral changes and switch-ups so well-balanced and matched, that one could easily mistake most of his non-sampled structures for samples. However, in the current musical climate, where creativity and non-contrived originality is seemingly less valued, this fundamental approach to beatmaking is routinely being ignored.

As beats are increasingly made much more in a cold, mechanical, assembly-line manner rather than a simple, straight forward *feeling-based* manner, beatwork is moving further away from the base principle of quality that I've outlined above. In order to combat against this unfortunate development and to safeguard against under- or over-producing, I believe that beatmakers should consistently assess the parameters of quality that exist not just seemingly at the moment, but over the last 30 years at best, or the last 15 years at least.

Creating A Signature Sound: One of the Best Way's to Distinguish Yourself as a Beatmaker

Regardless of what approach you ultimately take to make your beats, I can not stress enough the importance of establishing your own sound and style identity. The main reason that so many beatmakers eventually stop and give it all up is because they never develop their own sound and style identity and, subsequently, never establish their own brand of music. Though there are a number of factors that contribute to this, I believe that this phenomenon is mainly attributed to three factors: (1) The lack of thorough practice; (2) The lack of a concrete understanding and appreciation and/or respect for music history in general; and (3) The fact that many beatmakers never really learn how to translate their internal creativity through their production setups. And these days, with so many beatmakers transitioning to a ubiquitous pop radio sound, there's one overlooked option that can offer just as much success or critical acclaim: A signature sound.

Despite what some in the beatmaking community purport, a signature sound is not necessarily a *limited* sound. On the contrary, it's the independent and unique sonic force that is *consciously* created by an individual beatmaker or beatmaking team. Also, more often than not, the signature sounds of beatmakers reflect their commitment to the principle of originality and uniqueness. And whether a signature sound is simple or complex doesn't really matter. A signature sound is a good thing because it allows a beatmaker to distinguish his (or her) music from others within the beatmaking community.

Signature sounds are also a proven phenomenon within the beatmaking and hip hop/rap traditions. From the earliest b-boy inspired DJs of the '70s to the sample wizards of the early/mid-'90s to the synth/synthetic-sounds-based beat crafters of the late-'90s/early 2000s, signature sounds have been more prevalent than some beatmakers may like to acknowledge. Unfortunately, along with the increasing boom of interest in beatmaking, there also came a new level of seemingly acceptable *biting, i.e.* intentional, shameful duplication. In the past five years or so, biting (sucker style) and blatant style rip-offs have become so widespread that it's proving to be more difficult to tell one beatmaker apart from another. And with the apparent tightening up of placement opportunities within the recording industry, many beatmakers, who once would have never considered openly biting another beatmaker's style and sound, have gone over to the darkside. In this light, a signature sound is not only a way for beatmakers to distinguish their beats, it's also an effective means for protecting against wide-scale biting.

The Six Areas of Beatmaking That are Ideal for Creating a Signature Sound: Sound Frequencies, Drum Sounds, Drum Programming, Composing, Arranging, and Mixing

Note: Generating your own unique approach in the six areas that I outline below will inevitably lead to your own signature sound. But keep in mind, the process of creating a signature sound involves the deliberate repetition of many of the unique approaches and methods that you employ. That said, here are some guidelines you might want to follow.

Sound Frequencies

Sound frequency refers to the sound frequencies (color, tone, and character) of the type of sounds — samples, synthetic-sounds, synths, and sound effects — that a beatmaker chooses. This can be further broken down, for example, what kind of samples? Chops, long breaks (2-bar, 4-bar, 8-bar)? What kind of keyboard sounds? Strings, horns, bass sounds? What kind of synth sounds and patches? Mid, high, low frequencies? Each one of these sub-factors can offer a different path to a great signature sound.

More than any other elements of your beats, the sound frequencies that you choose play the biggest role in determining the overall mood and feel of your music. So it's imperative that you identify and develop a range of sound frequencies that you truly favor; that is, a range of sound frequencies that best allows you to make the musical expressions that you seek. After you identify the range of sound frequencies that you like to work with, be true to them. That is to say, try to be consistent to the sound themes, strategies, and ideas that you value, and try to avoid falling headfirst into trends or directions that don't fit your style and sound objectives and goals.

Drumwork: Drum Sounds and Drum Programming

Crafting custom drum sounds are a surefire way for beatmakers to create a signature sound. Remember, it has often been said that a beatmaker is only as good (or as bad) as his collection of drum sounds. Therefore, in order for you to create a signature sound, you must know your drum sounds. Thus it's important to learn what each one of your drum sounds can do individually *and* in tandem. So develop drum combinations and patterns that fit your overall approach to beatmaking. Also, identify what sounds and frequencies interest you. Finally, try limiting the number and types of kicks that you utilize. Re-using the same three to five kicks can go a long way in establishing a signature sound.

The drum framework is the most recognized hallmark of a beat. Therefore, if you want to create a signature sound, your drum programming has to be distinct on some level. Drum programming at its best gets the job done; drum programming at its worst distracts and over compensates. So designing drum programs that defer to efficiency, rather than an obscene level of showmanship, is not only the best path for creating a signature sound, it's also good practice to observe with your beatmaking in general. A distinctive drum sound can be as little as adding percussive elements like elongated rides or bongo stabs, or it can be more, like making your entire drum structure off beat or in a subtle shuffle.

Composing and Arranging

As I note throughout this study, when arranging your elements, make sure that each component makes the overall rhythm tighter and sonically stronger. Also, when considering changes, think in terms of function before form; ie. consider the function of the change — if it's needed and why. After you decide that changes are needed within a given beat, create changes that compliment the main rhythm of the beat.

Mixing: Customize a Sonic Wall in the Mix

Mixing refers to the approach that beatmakers/producers may take to mixing their beats. This describes the sound dynamics that are achieved before, during, and after the beat is made. It involves things like manipulating the dynamics of each sound, through both non-effects processor techniques like tucking and panning, and effects processor techniques like EQ, compression, reverb, and limiting. Mixing offers a great way for you to create your own unique sonic impression. There are many "standard" mixing principles that can be observed, but the manipulation of these standards can often be the best way to establish your own signature mixing approach. The idea here is to establish and regularly work from your own mix settings. This will go a long way in helping you define your overall sound. For good examples of how the mix can be just as much a part of a beatmaker's style and sound, study RZA, A Tribe Called Quest, Large Professor, Bink, Nottz, and Madlib.

Chapter 8
The Art of Sampling

> This is why we sample. We're borrowing from music that was already here and just… like Rakim said, we converted it into hip hop form. Hip hop can take anything and just make an ill beat. It's just about who's constructing it and understanding the science of it and understanding how to listen to it. –DJ Premier

What Is the Art of Sampling?
Consider the Context first, then the Meaning, Purpose, and Conceptual Understanding

By the coldest (non-emotional) and technical definition possible, sampling is described as the act of digitally recording a sound.[124] However, in its most fundamental and traditional context and sense, sampling is the artistic process of extracting fragments of recorded music from old songs for the use of making new beats (music). But even that's the simple definition. The complete and most accurate definition of sampling requires a much deeper examination.

To understand sampling, you must first comprehend hip hop DJ'ing, hip hop culture, and the "hip hop sensibility." In chapter 2, I discussed how hip hop DJ'ing was born from the central use of record breaks. The earliest hip hop DJs were the first to use turntables in ways that transformed their designed technical boundaries. Hip hop DJs cut, blended, and mixed the breaks of various records in an impromptu fashion that was a compositional style all its own.

In chapter 1, I discussed how one prominent result of an isolated and fragmented culture is that its residents learn to make use of their environment; i.e. they salvage practically anything within and outside of their environment for unique use. I further pointed out how the fragmentation caused by the South Bronx Disaster had, in effect, led to a "culture of sampling," a culture which enabled the residents of the South Bronx (and other similarly hard-hit cities across the United States) to take and make use of pieces of culture from both

---

[124] To sample sound, you must use some kind of **sampler**, an EMPI that digitally records sounds. Samplers are most commonly used to sample sounds from other audio devices such as turntables, CD players, computers, and microphones. But they can also be used to sample external sounds that do not originate from other audio devices. For example, the sound of a hammer striking a window pane is a great sound to layer on top of a snare. In order to get this sound, you have to mic the action, that is, you have to record the sound through a microphone.

within their own settings *and* from mainstream American society. Moreover, they learned how to convert those pieces of mainstream American culture in accordance to their own needs, principles, priorities, and values.

In chapter 2, I pointed out how and why the culture of sampling is an important part of the "hip hop sensibility;" how the culture of sampling often manifests itself; and how in a culture of sampling everything is fair game and open to transformation, transgression, and recontextualization (reconceptualization) — music, language, fashion, aerosol paint cans, whatever: If it can be converted and flipped, it will be. In reality, this is not that different than how traditional musicians and artists utilize everything within culture for the source and inspiration of their creative activity. And thus, it is from this context and *perspective* — the culture of sampling context and perspective — that we must continue our discussion about what sampling is.

Sampling is a Special Form of Derivative Art

Sampling is a special form of derivative art. Whether consciously or subconsciously, musicians borrow and incorporate sounds, rhythms, melodies, ideas, and musical frameworks from other artists all the time. Thus the question: What is sampling? is also grounded in the notion of an artist's ability, necessity, and natural inclination to create art based on works that came before. Here, it's important to note that sampling is different than the meaning of creating a "derivative work" in terms of United States copyright law. For example, making an exact drawing from a photograph is what it means to make a derivative work in terms of copyright law. Similarly, a "remix" of a song, where the original is the core, is a derivative work of the original. However, in sampling, only a small piece of a song is used in the creation of an entirely new song. Therefore, the new song is not a derivative of the sampled song.[125]

Derivative art itself is a necessary and an inevitable process; it's also a tradition long-practiced in every major art form. All music, at its core, is virtually derivative, inasmuch as its derived from ideas and works that have come

---

[125] "Thus, 'sampling' could almost never create a derivative work. Section 101 defines a 'derivative work' as one 'based upon one or more preexisting works, such as a translation, musical arrangement, dramatization, fictionalization, motion picture version, sound recording, art reproduction, abridgment, condensation, or any other form in which a work may be recast, transformed, or adapted.' As should be evident from this definition…, one could not create a derivative work in this context unless the original work was used as the main theme of the new work." Quote from Jennifer R. R. Mueller, "All Mixed Up: Bridgeport Music v. Dimension Films and De Minimis Digital Sampling," *Indiana Law Journal*, Vol. 81, Issue 1, Article 22 (2006), 451. Further, in *Williams v. Broadus*, the court noted that "a work is not derivative simply because it borrows from a pre-existing work." *Marlon Williams v. Calvin Broadus* No. 99 Civ. 10957 (MBM), 2001 WL 984714 (S.D.N.Y. Aug. 27, 2001).

before. The intellectual recycling of tropes and elements from older songs is nothing new in music, it has always been a major part of the creative process in music and other art forms. Every musician (every artist) at some point within their creative process *samples* in one way or another. Historically, musicians/recording artists have, in their pursuit to create new music, routinely "sampled" ideas, musical phrases, notes, and/or sounds from each other. There is no such thing as a musician that has or does not intellectually — *virtually* — sample and draw influence and inspiration from other musicians and recording artists or practitioners of some similar artistic medium.

This process of intellectually (virtually) sampling another musician/recording artist is widespread, overtly expected, and accepted as normal creative behavior; in fact, in some musical cultures, it is often celebrated. What is new, however, is the *physical* use — i.e. digital copying — of these elements in a fixed recorded form, which is also what sampling is. But here, we must be careful not to forget that there is no conceptual difference between the intellectual (virtual) copying and the physical (digital sampling) copying of someone's work. Both involve copying and intellectual transformation. Thus, "it is not accurate to say, as the *Bridgeport* court does, that when 'sounds are sampled they are taken directly from that fixed medium. It is a physical taking rather than an intellectual one.'"[126] An artist who samples a song doesn't literally "take" the sound out of the original recording. Instead, sampling technology creates a copy that is transferred to a computer hard drive. An actual physical taking of a vinyl record would mean that after sampling a vinyl record, the sampler would spit out a piece of the actual vinyl record, and the original vinyl record would be missing the piece that was physically taken.

Sampling is a Technique, Method, and Compositional Style

Sampling, or rather sample-based beatmaking, is a music-making technique that relies primarily on the use of samples of recorded sound for the creation of new music. In its most common and fundamental case, these samples (snippets and segments) of riffs, melodies, and/or sound-stabs are sampled from vinyl records. But it should be noted that sampling is not limited to just old songs; for most sample-based beatmakers, *any* sound recording can be sampled and transformed.

Another important characteristic of the sample-based style is that it indirectly familiarizes (often deeply) beatmakers with many of the methods that were

---

[126] Mueller, 450.

initiated and mastered by beatmakers from the first two Golden Eras of hip hop/rap music. Beatmakers who rely on the sample-based compositional style are often masters at complex and unique sound customization techniques as well as the advanced tier of other processes like chopping and looping. Because of this, many sample-based beatmakers have the advantage of being able to create a sound that is reminiscent to a past era while also inline with contemporary trends.

Sampling is Sound Collage

Sampling is part of the broader tradition of sound collage, the art technique that involves combining portions of sounds from previous recordings, including songs. In sound collage, or better stated, musical collage, sound recordings are viewed and treated as sound sources. Thus music collagists extract pieces and snippets — commonly regarded as "found sounds" — from these sound sources to create musical montages, which represent wholly new songs. The sampling tradition of hip hop/rap music fits within the borders of musical collage, as the aims of the musical collagist and sample-based beatmaker are mostly mutual; both seek to create new music from the sound objects of other sound recordings. But the sampling tradition of hip hop/rap music has its own distinct priorities and parameters. And while every sample-based beatmaker is indeed a musical collagist, not every musical collagist is a sample-based beatmaker.

Sampling is Versioning

Sampling is also a natural extension of "versioning." Versioning can best be described as the reworking of popular melodies or familiar folk tunes, songs, catch phrases, and the like. The process of using intellectual (virtual) samples of other works as source material and inspiration, or rather as the model for new works, is nothing new, especially in the African American (Black) music tradition.

Sampling is a Fine Art

Within the beatmaking tradition, sampling is a fine art. Some critics maintain that sampling is uncreative, limiting, or even worse, *lazy*. On the contrary, sampling is a real-time mix of all of one's musical understanding. That is to say, sampling forces beatmakers to identify multiple sounds, tones, and rhythms all at once, in one completed composition. Furthermore, what makes sampling a fine art is the fact that it is also what I like to call "a grid of discovery."

It's substantial training, part intuition, part accident, and a whole lot of diggin' in the crates. Actualy, beatmakers who use the sample-based compositional style are rewarded for their "discoveries," i.e. for what they find and flip. (Flippin' a sample is the process of manipulating and fashioning a sample into a beat.)

Sampling is Digitally Recording a Sound

As a technological concept, sampling is simply the act of digitally recording a sound, then transforming, rearranging, and assembling that sampled sound into a programmed sequence. After that, the idea is to turn this programmed sequence into a new composition. As an art form however, the practice of sampling is quite intricate. Not only does it involve a creative understanding of how sounds, tones, and pitches work, it requires a meticulous method for editing and manipulating sounds.

Sampling is Referential Music-Making

In its most fundamental sense, sampling is also referential music-making. No music is truly independent and free of any references. All forms of music are referential. All musicians create by referencing the elements, styles, themes, sounds, principles, and priorities of music created by others, either before or during their time. The art of sampling builds on this truth and sensibility, as it is a compositional process that uses — *references* — segments of recorded music and other sounds to create new music. And again, *sampling*, in terms of referencing of ideas, has always been going on in music. Borrowing pieces, segments, or varied fragments of songs for the purpose of creating new works is certainly not anything new in the world of music. For instance, jazz giant Charlie Parker is widely considered to be a genius for using — referencing — a little bit of Gershwin's "I Got Rhythm" and recontextualizing (reconceptualizing) it into new music. Are not all of the jazz greats throughout the 1930s, '40s, and '50s geniuses, for using (referencing) pieces of many blues standards in the creative process of new music?[127]

---

[127] "I Got Rhythm" was a George Gershwin song composed for the 1930 Broadway musical *Girl Crazy*. That a song from a Broadway musical was used for the basis of new jazz works demonstrates how critical "sampling" and "versioning" was to the existence and development of the jazz tradition. Moreover, it personifies the importance of sampling and versioning in the African American (Black) music tradition. "These early pieces [of blues songs provided] a basic repertory of stock melodies that have been drawn upon innumerable times by jazz composers." Quote from Eileen Southern, *The Music of Black Americans: A History*, (New York: W.W. Norton & Company, 1971), 339. Within black (African-derived) musical cultures, "the past" has always served as common fertile ground and inspiration for creativity.

Sampling is Musical Recycling

Sampling is also musical recycling, especially as it celebrates the very concept of musical recycling. Recycling is a major component of all contemporary music practices, but for hip hop/rap's earliest and recent pioneers and contemporary practitioners, the art of sampling is the *rightful* recycling of a common heritage. Sampling stems from the art of hip hop DJ'ing, which itself stems from a keen interest in the heritage of the African American (Black) music tradition, specifically the major sub-traditions of soul, funk, and disco. This *heritage music* is an embedded tradition (style, sound, and unique nuance), that can not be easily duplicated. The first hip hop DJs, who were acutely aware of and sensible to this fact, took to recycling this music at a time when it was considered past its prime and no longer usable and/or relevant. The art of sampling extends the tradition of the hip hop DJ, as it makes relevant use of a musical heritage that is considered unusable or no longer relevant. In this way, sampling, as musical recycling, speaks to part of the original purpose of American copyright law: to promote the progress of useful arts.

What's a Sampler and How Do They Work?

Technically speaking, a **sampler** is any EMPI (Electronic Music Production Instrument) that can digitally record sound, usually through the use of external audio sources like turntables, CD players, cassettes, and microphones. Instead of having the ability to simply generate and manipulate tones (like a synthesizer), a sampler deals with the actual digital *recording* of sounds. Once sounds are recorded into a sampler, they can be altered in pitch, duration, and/or sequence, while the unique timbre (tonal qualities) of the sounds within the sample remain intact. The sampled sound(s) can then be triggered (played back) through the use of a MIDI instrument such as a keyboard/MIDI controller or drum machine.

Here, it's worth mentioning how samplers *determine* the clarity of sound. Samplers use something called "audio bandwidth" to determine the clarity of a sound. The general formula states that: bandwidth of the sample signal is usually around half the sampling rate. So 16kHz is = 8kHz audio bandwidth. But clarity does vary from sampler to sampler. The Akai S950, one of the samplers infamously linked to the development of hip hop/rap music and the art of sampling, samples at 12 bit. But it's just as clear as many of the 16 bit samplers that are currently available, but not as bright and clear as let's say a

24-bit sampler. Finally, it's important to remember that samplers can be (and often are) used to sample practically any sound imaginable.

The History and Evolution of Sampling in the Hip Hop/Rap and Beatmaking Traditions

Sampling, as we've come to know it today in the hip hop/rap tradition, finds its roots in the hip hop DJ'ing of the early and mid-1970s. As I detailed in chapters 2 and 3, early hip hop DJs like Kool Herc, Grandmaster Flash, and Afrika Bambaataa normalized the practice of repeating the break in a record; they used turntables to play only the breaks, mostly from funk records and other soul music forms, early disco, and even some late 1960s and early 1970s rock 'n' roll records. Thus, in effect, early hip hop DJs were "sampling" what to them were the *choicest*, most valuable parts of the records.

Pushing the boundaries of the turntables, pioneering hip hop/rap DJs — most notably Grandmaster Flash — transformed turntables into *manual* sampling machines. And under the early guidance of recording engineer/producer Arthur Baker, Afrika Bambatta began experimenting with synthesizers and early samplers. As hip hop/rap music grew both in terms of size and scope, this fact did not go unnoticed by major EMPI manufacturers like E-Mu, Ensoniq, and Akai. By the mid 1980s, Roland and Yamaha had joined the other three major EMPI companies, now making it five big EMPI corporations that were jockeying towards advancements in sampling technology.

At this time, hip hop/rap DJ's — who had steadily been experimenting with all sorts of electronic sound-making devices, and who had spawned an entirely new league of music-makers — were the perfect consumer group for the new samplers that the major EMPI manufacturers were marketing. For the first wave of hip hop/rap DJs (beatmakers), turntables had been their chief instruments, but having seemingly pushed turntables to their limits, these DJs began to incorporate echo boxes, drum machines, synthesizers, and early sound modules into their music rigs. It wasn't long before these music rigs morphed into what we now commonly call production setups.

Again, these new developments in the hip hop/rap DJ world prompted the big five EMPI companies to release a wave of EMPIs that would go on to become classic instruments in the beatmaking tradition. In 1985, Ensoniq introduced the Mirage, a digital sampling keyboard — the first sampler with keyboard control. In 1986, Akai released their S900, which was quickly updated to the celebrated S950, one of the most important EMPIs in the development of the hip hop/rap and beatmaking traditions. Later that same year, Roland introduced their own 12 bit, high-powered sampler: the S50. Then in 1988, two of the biggest sampling classics came to market: the SP 12 by E-Mu, which was soon succeeded by the SP 1200; and Akai's MPC 60, which was quickly succeeded by the much revered MPC 60 II, and later the MPC 3000.[128]

Advents like the E-Mu SP 1200, Akai S950, and the Akai MPC 60 II ushered in a new way of sampling and further extended the compositional process. Before the late 1980s, beatmaking was best characterized by sparsely arranged drums (notably Roland's TR 808) and equally simple keyboard patterns. However, by the late 1980s and early 1990s, the pioneers of sampling — most notably Marley Marl, The Bomb Squad, Showbiz, Q-Tip, DJ Premier, Large Professor, Pete Rock, Dr. Dre, and RZA — used the sample technology of their time to introduce a more dramatic, more aggressive way of making beats. These pioneers went beyond just sampling the break, they explored the entire record and sampled sound segments from practically everywhere. In turn, they would then *flip the samples*; that is to say, they would take these sampled sections and *chop* them, filter them, and fashion them into new musical compositions — compositions that were more challenging and creative than anything previously produced in the young history of beatmaking.

Through an aggressively creative style of trial and era, pioneering beatmakers, particularly those of the Pioneers/Avant-Garde Period (1988-1994) of beatmaking, were able to establish the foundation for which all sample-based beatmakers now build upon. The primary sample-manipulation techniques that were fostered and developed by the aforementioned pioneers *still* serve as the basis for the sampling processes that we now recognize in beatmaking today. Therefore, all beatmakers who sample are forever indebted to these pioneers.

Critical Context: The Impact of the Sampling Pioneers and the Response of EMPI Manufacturers

The new compositions created by the early sampling pioneers were drum-backed re-creations and/or savvy street interpretations of the original recording that they sampled. The process that they formulated was critical to the overall development of the beatmaking tradition for two reasons. For one thing, it allowed a generation of impoverished blacks and Latinos, who had been deprived of instruction with traditional musical instruments, to be reconnected with the

---

[128] The original Akai MPC series was actually designed by Roger Linn, the inventor of the Linn Drum, an EMPI which many rightfully see as the predecessor to the first Akai MPC.

sounds, culture, and a general heritage that they had been mostly stripped of. This connection, which brought about a renaissance for soul and R&B music of the late 1960s and 1970s, helped make beatmaking a legitimate alternative to traditional musical instruction and creation. Today, beatmaking (hip hop/rap music production) is a musical discipline that is appealing to all sorts of people, from all races, ethnicities, and walks of life. Young kids, both impoverished and well-off, who dream of playing the saxophone or maybe the guitar when they grew up still dream of playing those instruments; only now, many of them want to use an MPC, a sampling keyboard, FL Studio, and/or some other EMPI to do so!

The sampling process formulated during the end of the Electronic Drum Machine Period (1983-1987) and the Pioneers/Avant-Garde Period (1988-1994) also had a considerable impact on the technological advancements of the samplers and other EMPIs of today. Before 1995, no manufacturer offered an EMPI with the function name: "chop" or "chopping." Chopping was the jargon used by the pioneers (and other practitioners of the time) to describe the multi-part process of sampling, dissecting, separating, and rearranging of the desired pieces of the original sample. Before 1995, beatmakers had to manually chop up the original sample into sections. After 1995, manufacturers began offering EMPIs with "auto-chop functionality," i.e. chopping functions that *automatically* chopped up samples into sections for you.

Finally, as the sound in hip hop/rap production grew cleaner, brighter, and generally louder, the EMPI manufacturers once again appeased hip hop/rap beatmakers by offering samplers with higher sampling bit rates. From 1985 to 1996, the only available sample bit rates were 8, 12, and 16khz. After 1996, the sample rate in samplers blew up to 24khz. The sampling terminology (mostly created and first echoed by the hip hop/rap beatmakers) and the evolving sound design of the beatmaking pioneers prompted EMPI manufacturers to completely re-structure their design and marketing strategy. By the late 1990s, it was quite clear that hip hop/rap music was the king of all styles of electronic music production. Hence, the big two EMPI manufacturers of the time Akai and Roland — made sure that their product lines were *hip hop/rap production compliant*. And what was the result of the EMPI manufacturer's dramatic re-direction and commitment to hip hop/rap music production? The result was more intuitive samplers, complete with more sampling time, higher sample rates, more critical sampling techniques, and more dynamic processing effects.

So there are several questions that beg answering. Why did EMPI manufacturers continue to develop their sampling technology? And why did they continue to mass market their new sampling product lines? Did EMPI manufacturers anticipate a decline in the interest of sampling and, therefore, a decline in the use of samplers? Or did they expect for the interest in sampling to grow and, subsequently, increase the demand for their samplers? Given their collective advancements in sampling and sequencing technology, then and now, it's clear that EMPI manufactures saw (and continue to see) sampling as a valuable practice that's here to stay.

The Mechanics of Sampling

The Sampling Equation

The Sampling equation is a term that I use to describe the core set of processes that make up the compositional tract of the art of sampling. It also, not coincidentally, describes some of the fundamental factors that ultimately determine the success and effectiveness of the art sampling. There are seven separate but interrelated components that make up the **sampling equation:** (1) the **philosophical approach**, (2) the **sampler's code**, (3) **"diggin' in the crates"** — source material/music, (4) **signal chain**, (5) **chopping/editing** and **sound manipulation**, (6) **triggering**, (7) **arrangement/programming** and **sequencing.**

The **philosophical approach** refers to the overall philosophy of sampling that a beatmaker holds; it also refers to the style of sampling that a beatmaker employs. The **sampler's code** represents the creative and ethical standards of sampling in the hip hop/rap music tradition; each beatmaker's adherrence to this code goes a long way in determining the quality and originality of their beats. **Diggin' in the crates — Source material/music** refers to what the sample actually is, where it comes from (e.g. a vinyl record, CD, mp3, cassette tape, .wav file, etc), and how it was found. **Signal chain** refers to how the source material/music is accessed; that is to say, through which capture media is the source material/music accessed and through what audio connection is it achieved. In other words, the format of the source material/music and where the source material/music goes *before* it's sampled. **Chopping/editing** refers to the "trim" techniques and the other editing processes that sample-based beatmakers use to transform samples through a series of cuts and trims, i.e *chops*. **Triggering** refers to the means through which samples are triggered and played, for example, through the use of a drum pad on a drum machine, a key on a keyboard or MIDI controller, and/or key on a computer keyboard. **Arrangement/programming** and **sequencing** refers to the process of programming/arranging samples into sequences and linking sequences together into fully arranged songs.

The Philosophical Approach

In order to further explain what is meant by the philosophical approach, I thought it would be a good idea to share the approach that I (and many other sample-based beatmakers) use. My philosohpical approach to sampling is this: I look at sampling as a grid of musical discovery with vast creative potential. Unlike a single note on a keyboard or soft-synth (software synthesizer), a sample of a pre-recorded sound recording can give you more than just movement up or down the pitch scale. And aside from the various incidental nuances that samples provide when they're looped, samples often act as cementing agents. That is to say, samples, especially when serving as half of the rhythm section of a beat, *glue* the drums of the beat in a way that makes the whole composition move more organically rather than mechanically. Furthermore, the art of sampling can school (educate) you — on tones and textures, rhythm and timing, function and feeling — in ways that traditional musical processes can not. Whenever I sample a record, I always learn something new about composing and arranging music. More importantly, I gain a better understanding of how to insert a particular mood that I'm feeling into my music.

Whatever your philosophical approach to sampling is, you should always consider three factors when you take up the sample-based compositional style. First, you should seek and fully expect to find something fresh and unique every time you sample something, even if it's just a sound-stab, like a new hi-hat or snare. Second, concern yourself with the mood and feeling of the source material/music that you want to sample. Regardless of what you're sampling, whether it's a complete-phrase or spare-part phrase, focus your attention on identifying the mood and feeling of what you're about to sample. Third, having identified the mood and feeling, shift your attention to trying to get an *audio snapshot* of where you want to go with what you've sampled, like how can you use, and in some cases reuse, what you've just sampled.

The approach that I just outlined is the one I employ, but I certainly encourage you to add your own unique thoughts to it, because it is critical that you identify and incorporate your own approach to sampling. In doing so, you will carve out your own sampling identity and, in turn, you will develop your own healthy approach to sampling. Furthermore, because sampling requires that you devote serious time to mining through source material (mostly vinyl records, CDs, MP3s, or .WAV files) for things to sample, having a clear-cut approach and expectation will dramatically increase your overall beatmaking efficiency. Finally, I should add that the proper sampling approach will train your musical ear, giving you a better indication on what kinds of samples that you're likely to *flip* (transform into something new) more successfully.

The Sampler's Code: The Ethics and Unwritten Rules of Sampling in the Hip Hop/Rap Tradition

The purpose of the sampler's code (or any rule or tradition in an art form) is to help sample-based beatmakers create the best art that they can. The sampler's code is not meant to be a restriction of art; instead, it's meant to serve as a guide to and catalyst for creating the best art possible.

There are a variety of unwritten ethical rules that govern the general beatmaking community, but nowhere are such rules perhaps more clearly defined and adhered to than in the sample-based beatmaking community. For most seasoned sample-based beatmakers, these rules, which are often learned directly or indirectly from other samplers, are well understood and timeless. It should also be noted that the ethical rules of sampling are an extension of the creative, stylistic, and competitive rules that governed over the four elements (main artistic expressions) of hip hop's earlier days. As such, these rules implicitly stress the importance of knowing the fundamentals of the art form as well knowing the work and styles of the art form's most respected artists. Moreover, the ethical rules of sampling are inextricably connected to notions of originality and aesthetic value. What follows below is a list of the most recognized ethical rules in the sampling tradition of hip hop/rap music.

Know the Art Form

Before anything else, a sample-based beatmaker should know the art and craft of sampling. This part of the sampler's code means that you should have a commitment to studying the art of sampling; for this is the first prerequesite for developing a skill and appreciation for sampling. Within this understanding, a serious sample-based beatmaker is expected to know the history and heritage of sampling in hip hop/rap music; the styles and work of the art form's most respected artists and other key practitioners; the aesthetic and technical characteristics of the art of sampling; and the practice of diggin' in the crates (vinyl diggin' or e-diggin'). Also, knowing the art form of sampling in itself underscores the importance of preserving it.

Be Creative and Original

Second only to knowing the art form is the rule of being creative and original. Hip hop culture prioritizes originality in general, but in beatmaking, and sampling in specific, being creative and maintaining an original sound is especially important. For one thing, the most sought after source material (i.e. recordings) in the sampling tradition of hip hop/rap music spans from the late 1960s to the mid-1970s (as I discussed earlier, this is for the aesthetic value of records released in that time frame). This means that sample-based beatmakers are often using the same kinds of source material and, in many cases, the same exact recordings or different recordings from the same album. To be original, a sample-based beatmaker must, necessarily, commit to being creative by using his or her knowledge of the art form along with their own ingenuity and imagination. Further, while being original can mean diggin' deeper for more rare and obscure source material, it can also mean transforming known source material in new ways that thoroughly demonstrate the sampler's code of creativity and originality.

Finally, it's also worth mentioning that the creativity and originality rule in sampling also adheres to the hip hop sensibility's competition dimension. Because sample-based beatmakers aim for creativity and originality, either through a unique blend of their skills or through the use of obscure recordings, they are upholding one of hip hop's driving forces: competition. In my interviews with DJ Premier, Buckwild, 9th Wonder, each pointed out how on a number of occasions they were motivated and pushed by the beats of their peers to come up with even more dope beats of their own. Each maintained that it was "healthy competition." This chain of respectful competition and motivation plays a major role in the sample-based beatmaking community, and being creative and original are important aspects of this competition.

No Biting Allowed

Biting, the overt (sometimes less overt), deliberate copying of another artist's style has never been respected in any of hip hop's four artistic expressions. As I discussed in Part I, style and originality has been prioritized in hip hop culture sense its inception. As two of the most valued and celebrated traits in hip hop, individual style and originality also means that you don't bite! You don't copy someone's style and sound. Instead, you develop your own style and sound, and you always aim for originality. And while demonstrating clear influences of other sample-based beatmakers' (or other artists) works is certainly not a violation of the sampler's code, a total mimic of another sample-based beatmaker is a clear violation of the sampler's code.

Same Sample/Source Rule: Is Using the Same Sample (Record/Source Material) Ever O.K.?

It's generally understood that sampling the same record and using it in the same or substantially similar way is unethical, a clear violation of the sampler's code. However, there are three main exceptions. First, the use of a different section of the same record. Using a different section of the same record, especially in a creative and original ways, does not violate the sampler's code. Second, it's totally acceptable to even use the same section (part) of the record as another sample-based beatmaker, so long as you distinguish your flip of it, i.e substantially transform it, through your own creativity and skills, in a new way. Third, coincidental usage of the same source material does not violate the sampler's code. Many sample-based beatmakers of the early '90s held common cultural backgrounds, and therefore, they shared access to, or at least awareness of, much of the same vinyl records of the 1960s and 1970s. So *coincidental* uses of the same record — even the same part of the same record — have always been inevitable.

But either way, it doesn't matter how many people have used the same sample, because if you can flip it differently, then that's perfectly acceptable within the sample-based community. After all, what is using the same sample and flipping it really all about? Is it not a more transformative form of versioning? So the bottom line is this: Every sample can be flipped differently; it all depends on the ingenuity, imagination, creativity, and skill set of the particular beatmaker.

Using Break-Beat Records (Compilations) is the Norm

Using break-beat records (or compilations) is highly ethical, especially when it comes to drum sounds. Every beatmaker I've interviewed in the past ten years has mentioned their use of break-beat records (compilations), specifically noting the "Ultimate Breaks & Beats" series of compilations. I've seen "Ultimate Breaks & Beats" volumes in the studios of various beatmakers, including DJ Premier, Buckwild, True Master, and Marco Polo. When I first began making beats, the "Ultimate Breaks & Beats" were widely considered an invaluable piece of a sample-based beatmaker's arsenal. (*At last count, I personally own 19 of the 25 volumes released.*) They were used regularly by beatmakers throughout New York City, Atlanta (DJ Toomp mentions his use of them in my interview with him), Miami, and LA. Thus, I suspect that most (if not all) sample-based beatmakers of the Pioneers/Avant Garde Period used so-called break-beat records (compilations) particularly for the creation of new drum sounds. Therefore, to avoid using break-beat records is certainly not the normal stance amongst most sample-based beatmakers, nor is it a purist declaration. In other words, opting not to use break-beat records (compilations) is simply a matter of personal choice, and it should not necessarily be looked at as being aesthetically superior or inferior.

Sampling Source Material: Diggin' In The Crates

The Importance of Mining

There are two basic forms of sampling source material: arcane and familiar. Arcane source material refers to source material that is uknown or unrecognizable (to most) and/or obscure. Familiar source material refers to source material that is recognizable or easily identifiable. "Diggin' in the crates" is a term used to describe mining for source material (usually records). The term comes from the act of DJs storing their vinyl records in milk crates and diggin' through them to find what they need. Since the traditional art of sampling has been about retro-fitting long-abandoned recordings to fit the aesthetics of hip hop/rap, sample-based beatmakers are a special breed of "sound collectors." Sample-based beatmakers mine through used, long-forgotten records for music elements of value. These elements of value are what beatmakers strip down, re-work, and refashion into new works of art. This is why sample-based beatmakers are only as good as their source material. And when it comes to record collections, it's never about quantity, it's always about quality and value.

Records (and other source material, i.e. any recorded sound or sound that can be recorded) are more valuable to a sample-based beatmaker than instruments are to musicians. For sample-based beatmakers, records (and pre-recorded music in any media format) are the primary currency from which the heart of their beats are made, which is certainly not the case for traditional musicians in the West. For instance, a guitarist or pianist has the exact same tool to draw from every time they set out to create something new. They know that musical notes aren't going anywhere; middle C is always *middle C*. In other words, the *framework* which traditional musicians work from essentially remains the same. However, a sample-based beatmaker has to rely on a *new* tool every time out. I mean, one good album might have anywhere from 0 to 10 (perhaps more) interesting segments to sample. Thus, a sample-based beatmaker never really knows what they'll be able to get from a record until they *mine it*, i.e. listen attentively to it. Therefore, the ability to mine quality source material is paramount to a sample-based beatmaker. In this way, mining — diggin' in the crates — is a fundamental part of the music process for sample-based beatmakers.

Diggin' in the Crates as Competition and a Means for Harnessing History

Much of sampling in the hip hop/rap music tradition is about besting other people's (other sample-based beatmakers') source material. Because of this, having a deep record collection or broad knowledge of records is something that is highly respected and regularly celebrated. In fact, in the hip hop/rap music tradition, sample-based beatmakers are often respected for their diggin' prowess — the size and scope of their record collection, their knowledge of records, and their historical music knowledge in general — just as much as they are for their beatmaking skills. In this way, diggin' in the crates is also about discovering and harnessing history.

This is why all serious diggers carefully study the credits and names on the albums that they sample from. Not only is it a widely held tradition that goes all the way back to Grandmaster Flash, it's one of the best ways to enhance your familiarity with the musicians and writers of a given era and genre. I used to spend hours pouring over liner notes and combing through credits. In fact, I still read all of the liner notes and credits of every "new" album that I add to my collection.

E-Diggin' vs. Record Diggin'

Note: The general principles of sampling apply no matter what audio source you're sampling from. The only difference that may exist can be found in the amplification of the original audio source. Further, no matter how you dig for source material, it's important that you listen to music in beatmaking-mode and take time to listen to your music discoveries while doing other things, not just making beats.

Before comparing e-diggin to traditional vinyl record diggin', there are several contextual points that need to be made. First, it must be remembered that hip hop/rap was the first music tradition to be entirely predicated upon the use of previously recorded music. This wasn't an accident, this was a conscious decision by the earliest hip hop/rap practitioners (chief among them, Kool Herc, Grandmaster Flash, and Afrika Bambaataa). Furthermore, the preferred (most important) recorded music came from vinyl records. From the onset of the hip hop/rap music tradition, this wasn't merely some cost-effective necessity, this was the life-force of the entire tradition. Truth is, buying a keyboard — a one-time purchase — would have been much more cost-effective than regularly buying records. In fact, vinyl record diggin' is/was a rather expensive proposition. During the earliest days of hip hop/rap, there weren't any second hand vinyl record stores — records were not yet displaced by CDs (and later downloading and streaming) as the main consumer media format. Therefore, all records were sold at full retail price.

Second, crate diggin' itself was (is) considered to be an important part of the artistic process for those beatmakers who make sample-based beats through the use of vinyl records. Many beatmakers saw (see) the ability to dig for quality source material as a skill, something that required (requires) a unique music education, music research experience, and focused patience.

Third, diggin' for records is not something that is old fashion and/or in danger of being displaced by technology. There's nothing old fashion or outdated about building your knowledge base. Technology serves at the command of the one who uses it. That is, technology is to be used in the manner that each individual deems that it can best be used. And it should be added that one's over-reliance on technology for technology's sake can have a rather negative effect on their creativity. The goal of technology is not simply to replace something, the goal of technology is to facilitate and make easier those fundamental things that we have always done. For instance, shooting a full length feature film with digital cameras is very cost-effective, yet nearly all feature length films are still shot with film. Shooting with film, as opposed to digital, is not considered an old fashion or outdated way of doing things in the movie business. On the contrary, it is an artistic choice, one that still holds tremendous value to filmmakers on both sides of the movie budget extremes.

Although technology has provided a new method for diggin' for source material, we must be careful not to conclude that this new method, i.e. e-diggin', should replace the existing method of diggin' for vinyl records. And consider these facts: (1) Hundreds of thousands of vinyl records — containing jazz, rhythm and blues, rock, soul, and funk — were made between 1969 and 1975; and (2) Most hard core vinyl record collectors own on average just about 1,000-5,000 records; that's not even 5% of the possibilities! So while e-diggin' (which is essentially technology in the form of a search engine) may help one find rare records, technology can not displace the vinyl record search method. Why? Because search technology depends upon *the data that it has access to*; there are 100s of thousands of songs that will likely never be uploaded to YouTube or shared elsewhere online. Thus, for sample-based beatmakers, the only access we will have to some loads of songs released in the twentieth century will only be through vinyl records. That's actually one of the things that makes hip hop/rap so unique: It has always been based on the principle of *unique access*. And being unique, well, that should not ever go out of style.

Finally, diggin' for vinyl records doesn't necessarily determine whether you can be an effective beatmaker or not. In fact, it doesn't even give you an advantage (unless perhaps you really value vinyl and everything that surrounds it). You could have all the vinyl records in the world, but if you don't know how to effectively extract value from them, then you're only taking up space with otherwise useless source material.

As for the process of e-diggin', diggin' for source material on the internet, it should not be seen as an inherently good or bad thing. Instead, it should be considered as a necessary component for many sample-based beatmakers. Fact is, vinyl records are simply not as accessible as they once were.[129] Therefore, diggin' for source material online has become the only reality for some beatmakers. Moreover, it's another legitimate means for finding/discovering new music, often quickly. This is why I strongly endorse e-diggin'. That said, there are some key differences between e-diggin' and traditional record diggin' that are worth noting.

The primary difference between e-diggin' and record diggin' is that the source material found on the internet has a notable difference in sound quality. The sound of a vinyl record is more rich in character, and the nuances of the recording translate better from a vinyl record than an MP3 or .WAV file that has been "squashed" (overly compressed) and flattened.

The other difference between e-diggin' and record diggin' has to do with the processes themselves. Traditional record diggin' is a more extensive, physical pursuit, while e-diggin' is essentially the process of using an online search engine. Record diggin' permits you to actually hold a record, which allows you to get a

---

[129] There are still some vinyl record stores around the country, but for the most part, the used vinyl record industry has been shrinking. That said, there is a noticeable difference between digging on the internet vs. digging for physical records — the musical senses are heightened in a different way when dealing with physical vinyl, as opposed to a digital download, WAV, etc.

feel for the artwork and perhaps the intentions of the artists behind the music; this adds another dimension of creative inspiration. More importantly, the physical record bares critical information such as relevant dates and the ever vital musician, production, and/or studio credits. Such information is generally not provided in the process of e-diggin', and therefore, the potential for a more extended musical education, which traditional record diggin' provides, is usually not afforded with the e-diggin' process.

Check This Out – The Validity of E-Diggin and Why I Support It

As I stated before, "e-diggin'" is simply the process of diggin' for music (source material) on the internet. In and of itself, that should not be seen as an inherently bad or good thing. Instead, it should be considered as a necessary component for many sample-based beatmakers. Vinyl records are not as accessible as they were in sampling's first big heyday. Thus, diggin' for source material online has become the only reality for some beatmakers. Further, it's another legitimate means for finding/discovering new music rather quickly. This is why I strongly endorse e-diggin'. But there are a number of beatmakers (some of them very notable) who view e-diggin' as some sort of bad or inferior process. Inasmuch as e-diggin is, fundamentally, a means to searching for and finding new music, I don't see how anyone can dislike it. It would appear to me that the basis of opposition towards e-diggin' lies in the fact that it does not correspond with the nature and unwritten protocol of diggin' for vinyl records. But let's be clear here: Diggin' for or possessing vinyl records doesn't necessarily determine whether or not someone is going to be a dope beatmaker — knowledge, skill, and creativity determines that.

Therefore, the rants against e-diggin' itself are actually off base. I've been diggin' for records for nearly 18 years. As a result, I, like many music diggers, am a de facto collector of vinyl records. And not just any collector, perhaps you could say that I'm a preservationist preserving otherwise forgotten music. However, I don't allow my slant as a collector/preservationist of vinyl records to cloud or otherwise interfere with my interest in searching for and discovering "new" music, particularly those recordings that I would never be able to find in the rapidly dwindling number of used vinyl record stores.

Spending hours upon end in record shops, flea markets, yard sales, Salvation Army branches, record exchanges, used book stores, and/or the basements, addicts, and storage spaces of friends and relatives — *all of which I have done*

— does not equate to any superiority in the area of musicianship, nor does it necessarily make anyone more skilled at the art of sampling. Instead, it mostly equates to the desire for that particular process and experience. Furthermore, it is simply a reflection of one's "collector's slant," because the reality is this: Most beat diggers with large vinyl record collections will most likely never sample even 25% of their total collection. There are many people (myself included) who have upwards of 2,000 or more vinyl records that they have never sampled. I can assure you, out of my own 3,000+ vinyl record collection, I have yet to sample anything from 2,500 of these. And if those who tout 10,000 and 20,000 vinyl record collections really have sampled even 15% of those records, then it stands to reason that there should have been a much larger number of classic sample-based beats in rotation over the past three decades, no?

Again: Technology serves at the command of the one who uses it. That is, technology is to be used in the manner that each individual deems that it can be used. The goal of technology is to facilitate and make easier those fundamental things that we have always done. Thus, it should follow that the *discovery* of music itself trumps any one method or tradition of discovery. It matters less how I came to discover "new" music; as long as I discover it, I'm fortunate. After all, I can't flip source material that I don't have access to. And whether I prefer to handle vinyl in my hands or stream a cut on YouTube, I still can't ignore the fact that e-diggin' gives me much more access to "new" music than diggin' for vinyl records ever did or ever could. I also can't ignore the fact that the e-diggin' search process generates, on a whole, far more suggestions for similar findings than any cross-credits referencing I've done reading the credits or liner notes of vinyl records that I've acquired.

Still, I certainly do recognize that there is a difference between diggin' for vinyl records and e-diggin'. There are some nuances that come with sampling a vinyl record; perhaps most notably the sound quality of a vinyl record, or the sort of connection to a musical past that a vinyl record can offer, or the connection to the traditional method of sampling in the beatmaking tradition. But that being said, the notion that someone is "lazy" or somehow "uncreative," or that someone is doing it (i.e. sampling) "wrong," merely because they use source material (music) that they've found (discovered) online rather than a vinyl record that they've acquired from a record shop or another place where vinyl records are typically sold, is ridiculous and completely out of tune with the realities of the day.

In most cases these days, e-diggin' is the only choice for would-be sample-based beatmakers; it's the only way many people have access to valuable music from eras gone past. And accessibility to the music (source material) that is to be sampled has always been a key factor of the art of sampling. Because sample-based beatmakers have always been distinguished not only by their skill but by what they actually sample, it should be understood that sample-based beatmakers are also often distinguished by the music (source material) that they actually have access to.

But because of the limited accessibility of vinyl records, the playing field for sampling has been largely uneven. For years, those who lived in or near hot-spot centers for vinyl records, i.e. major cities and towns that contain a healthy supply of vinyl record stores and the like, have had an advantage of access over those who did not live in those centers. But e-diggin' virtually makes an indefinite number of hot-spot centers available to anyone with a working internet connection. In this way, e-diggin' has removed the *advantage of access* that some samplers previously held. Through this new level of access to the same music most privileged by veteran vinyl diggers, e-diggin' has leveled the playing field for sample-based beatmakers. Moreover, because of the scarcity of vinyl record shops and the like, e-diggin' is providing a pivotal link to the sampling tradition, a link that many people might not otherwise be so fortunate to have.

Finally, any capture method — whether it be through the vinyl diggin' or e-diggin' process — that adheres to the fundamental tenets of the art of sampling, while also bringing to light the elements of valuable music from eras gone past, should be embraced, not spurned. Beyond that, we should remember that no one judges sample-based beats according to the original audio format of the music (source material) that was sampled. Besides, there's no way for anyone, other than the sampler who sampled the source material, to be absolutely certain what audio format was actually sampled. One can just as easily say that they sampled a piece of music from a vinyl record, when in fact, they sampled it from a source online. Who's to know either way?

But the truth of judgment remains: The basis for how we judge sample-based beats is pretty much the same for how we judge any style of beat. Our personal tastes, the level of quality of a beat, and the beat's cohesion with the lyricist are all main factors that determine how we rate a beat. Therefore, if e-diggin' plays any role in the creation of a beat that suits our taste and measures up to our individual and collective perceptions of quality, then we have no choice but to support it.

Practicality of Diggin' in the Crates

Vinyl records are also valued for their practical nature. Scanning a record, searching for pieces, parts, and sections to sample, has always been as simple as moving a turntable's needle across the record as desired. The speed and accuracy at which you could locate different parts on a record gives sample-based beatmakers a certain level of immediacy and efficiency. For decades, no other medium could compare to the search speed that vinyl records allow. Today, however, current production software programs like FL Studio and Pro Tools allow beatmakers to import entire songs (digital versions of course), which can than be quickly searched over with a click of a mouse. So with regards to search speed, other mediums have caught up with vinyl records to a large degree. Still, search speed aside, there will always be a difference (sometimes slight, sometimes more pronounced) between the sound of a vinyl record and another format like a digital download or CD. There's also the fact that each vinyl recording has its own subtle differences. Unlike a digital recording, no vinyl record sounds exactly the same because the wear and tear of each vinyl record is unique. Static, hisses, warps, pops, and even scratches make each vinyl record a one-of-kind recording.

Setting the Record Straight About Vinyl Purism: Vinyl Records Are Not the Only Acceptable Medium to Sample

As I've discussed earlier in this chapter, there is an aesthetic value to vinyl records that many sample-based beatmakers prioritize. Further, diggin in the crates, in the traditional sense, will always be linked to vinyl records. Still, we must remember that the underlying idea and motivation behind diggin' isn't just about using one particular audio format or recorded medium, it's about the practice of mining/searching for new material to sample. In other words, diggin' in the crates, both as a traditional idea and practice of hip hop, extends beyond any one audio format or recorded medium. For example, as I discussed in chapter 2, in the early pioneering days (hip hop's first golden era), Afrika Bambaataa became the first to sample television commercials onto cassette tape and incorporate those samples into his DJ set. In doing so, Bambaataa set a precedent: Diggin' for new source material wherever and however you could was the essence of diggin'. And that it was Bambaataa (one of the first three and most important hip hop DJs) to do this first means that diggin' for and sampling any material on any available audio format is just as traditional as diggin' for, sampling, and using vinyl.

Build Your Sampling Ear – How to Listen to Source Material, What to Listen For, and How to Find a "Good" Sample

There are two ways to approach listening to sample source material (music): **spot-listening** and **full-listening**. Both approaches require you to listen or survey the music that you intend to sample; however, the difference is in *how* you listen and survey the source music. Spot-listening is the process of randomly and rather quickly surveying a record. The idea here is to give quick-listens to areas of the record where you might expect the intros, breaks, bridges, and outros to be. For intros, you affix the turntable needle to the beginning of the record. Intros often have a "ready-made loop" that is free and clear without drums. This is why intros are very appealing to many sample-based beatmakers.

When I first started making beats, that's all I pretty much did. I probably spent three years like this. I would buy records and skim over them until something popped out. I would check over the beginnings of songs on an album, looking for ready-made loops. If I didn't find one, I would leave the record alone, thinking it held no value, without ever really listening to each song on the album thoroughly. I assumed that this was how most beatmakers did it. I reasoned, *'Who had time to actually listen to the complete songs on an entire album?'* But as purchasing records became more costly, I found myself going back to my crates for those records that I had once regarded as invaluable. The second, third, and even fourth time that I listened to a record, I increased my patience and discipline until I was able to give each song on an album a full-listen. In the process, I learned that spot-listening was most useful when working with records that I was already familiar with. For example, if I was looking for kicks and I remembered a drum intro or break from a particular song. In this case, it was helpful to target the areas of the song that I was already familiar with. But try to limit how much you spot-listen a record that you've never heard before. There's too much that you will undoubtedly miss. Hence, I recommend that when you have some records that you've never heard before, give each song a full-listen. Don't skim or skip ahead, and don't scrap the record just because you can't *immediately* find anything useful.

The Three Forms of Sampling

When it comes to the various forms of sampling, there are both quantitative and qualitative considerations. Thus, the art of sampling can be broken down into three general forms: (1) **simple** or **"piggy-back" sampling**; (2) **break-beat** or "mix" sampling; and (3) **intricate sampling**. **Simple** (imitative) or **"piggy-back" sampling** is the form of sampling in which a substantial portion of a sound recording is sampled and then "imitated," with little to no significant transformation of the sampled work. Typically, this form of sampling involves looping a 4- or 8-bar break (from familiar or arcane sources), and combining it with a backing drum framework that mimics the drum pattern of the sampled work as close as possible. Usually, the piggy-back form of sampling utilizes known material (popular songs), wherein beatmakers use *sufficient familiarity* so that the listener may recognize the quotation (appropriated work) and may, in turn, pay more attention to the new material as a consequence of that familiarity.

"Break-beat" or "mix" sampling is the form of sampling in which breaks and/or patches of recorded works are woven together in a fashion more akin to a DJ blending and matching multiple segments of records. In this form of sampling, the sampled work can be both minimal and substantial, familiar and/or arcane. Also, in this form of sampling, typically, drum breaks are used as opposed to drum programming featuring individual drum sounds; however, in some cases, beatmakers who utilize this form of sampling will add additional drumming.

Finally, **"intricate" sampling** is the most sophisticated (complex) form of sampling. It involves the deconstruction of the sampled work in an intricate manner, followed by a unique arrangement of the now substantially transformed appropriation. Using the intricate sampling form, beatmakers seek to convert both familiar *and* arcane sources into an entirely new medium, while staying within the aesthetic parameters of hip hop/rap music.

It should be further noted that each of the three forms of sampling involve either a use of *wholecloth, major,* or *partial* sampled elements. Also, each of the three forms of sampling are distinguished by the degree of the transformative nature of the sampled work.

The Five Categories (or Types) of Samples: Complete-Phrases, Spare-Part Phrases, Section Pieces, Sound-Stabs, and Sound-Tones

All songs, regardless of the music genre, are made up of a combination of any number of varying musical phrases and smaller pieces of sound. (Here, I use "musical phrase" to describe any structured musical pattern that lasts for a measure of one bar or more.) Samples themselves can be broken down into five categories or types: **complete-phrases**, **spare-part-phrases**, **section-pieces**, **sound-stabs,** and **sound-tones**.

A **complete-phrase** — a full musical pattern, measuring one complete bar or more — is like a short story; it has a clear beginning, a middle, and an end. As such, it's already conducive for a beat. Think of complete-phrases as "ready-made-loops." Complete-phrases are very easy to identify, and therefore, they are easier to sample and loop, which makes them big targets for many sample-based beatmakers. Most sample-based beatmakers often tend to listen for complete-phrases first and foremost. But the more crafty sample-based beatmakers realize that the more rare the record that you're sampling from, the more rare the complete-phrase, and thus, the better the chance you have for achieving creativity and of avoiding the sample police.[130]

Spare-part-phrases are simply sections of larger complete-phrases. Sampling spare-part-phrases is more challenging because it requires serious patience and a knack for intuitive chopping.[131] The most interesting thing about spare-part phrases is how they stand alone like missing pieces of dialogue; as such, they help signal where the discussion may go. That is to say, each spare-part-phrase helps to determine how the entire beat will flow. Although it's more difficult to identify and sample useful spare-part-phrases, the process is considerably more rewarding.

With spare-part-phrase sampling, you sample the root sounds of complete phrase (not the entire measure of the phrase) of a preexisting recording, then flip it — creatively transform it — into something new and original. Here, the phrases and/or pieces that you sample won't be nearly as easy to identify as the original complete-phrase from which it came. Therefore, when you use spare-part-phrases, it's more likely that you will avoid any sample clearance woes. Another benefit of spare-part-phrase sampling is that it will train and develop your musical ear and overall understanding of rhythm arrangements and drum and loop programming.

---

[130] Sample Clearance, the process of securing the legal right to use samples within a new composition. 20 years ago, sample clearance was a non-issue. Now, it's a revenue stream for the major labels (who generally own the rights to the masters of the songs that are being sampled), the original writers and performers of sampled works, and publishers. Labels and other copyright holders employ people to scan music for any sample that may have been used within the creation of a new hip hop/rap song. Therefore, take heed: If you sample a very identifiable and/or well-known complete-phrase (typical of the *sped-up-chipmunk-sound* variety), beware of a potential sample clearance problem. It used to be that the artist would pay to clear the sample, now, many artists are sticking that tab with the beatmaker (producer). For more information on sample clearance and copyright law, see my book *The Art of Sampling: The Sampling Tradition of Hip Hop/Rap Music and Copyright Law* (Superchamp Books, 2015).

[131] **Mental-Intuitive Chopping** is the ability to hear any musical phrase and formulate a chop-pattern or plan in your head. It's similar to how film directors shoot footage according to the edits that they foresee inside their heads while they're shooting the film. In this way, these film directors are virtually editing the film in their heads.

Note: A number of classic beats, produced by many beatmaking pioneers, were actually recreations (random manipulations) of just one sample. The more experienced beatmakers are skilled at one-sample beats. They know how to chop, copy, and/or manipulate *one* sample to the point where the original sample is unrecognizable, even though the original mood and integrity is in some way still left in tact. The core track[132] of nearly all sample-based beats are composed of, or based upon, one primary sample. The main point with spare-part-phrase sampling is that it always prompts you to create challenging, riveting beats using the shortest or simplest fragments of pre-recorded music and sounds.

Both complete-phrases and spare-part-phrases are comprised of smaller elements called **section-pieces**. Section-pieces are shortened or incomplete musical patterns. Because of their duration, they're often uneven, and therefore, they usually require something else to sustain them, for example, an additional complete-phrase or spare-part-phrase. As with spare-part-phrases, section-pieces offer *source anonymity*. But it's substantially more difficult to identify the source record from which the section-pieces were derived. Because section-pieces are widely uneven, that is to say, heavy or light at the beginning of the phrase and heavy or light at the end of the phrase, they require a great deal of chopping. So as you would expect, beatmakers who hone their chopping skills with section-pieces become master choppers.

Sound-stabs are individual instrumental sounds, single hits, like drum kicks and snares. Mining records to sample is a meticulous, arduous process. A lot of times, one can feel prohibited from sampling something, either because the record doesn't have any interesting phrases or because the "good" (interesting) phrases are trapped (not free and clear).[133] But the fact is, nearly all records can be salvaged for sound-stabs. Everything from short or long horn-hits to keyboard strikes and tambourine shakes make for excellent sound-stabs.

Sound-tones are sustained fragments of section-pieces; they work like sound-stabs, i.e. they are quick single hits. However, sound-tones are slightly different from sound-stabs because they are often made up of multiple sounds, not just one single instrument. Since they are simply chipped off fragments of a larger section-piece, sound-tones are a big favorite among chopmasters like DJ Premier, Pete Rock, and 9th Wonder.

Note: Complete-phrases, spare-part-phrases, section-pieces, sound-stabs and sound-tones can all be used and blended together in a variety of ways, but

---

[132] The **core track** is the fundamental beat framework, consisting of the primary rhythm section.
[133] **Free and Clear**. When sampling sound-stabs and phrases, a sample is considered to be *Free and Clear* when there are no surrounding sounds, particularly drums or vocals, that prohibit it from being "isolated" and sampled clean and clearly.

the two primary types of **sample blends** are: **phrase-blends**, and **stab-blends**. **Phrase-blends** are usually more about connecting one phrase or more to the front or back end of another phrase, whereas **stab-blends** are usually more about layering[134] one sound-stab with another.

Signal Chain

A **signal chain** is the connective audio route between two or more devices. When it comes to sampling, a proper signal chain plays a critical role in the *capturing* of the distinct nuances of a sample. Furthermore, a proper signal chain is paramount to the development of a beatmaker's own unique sound.

For instance, I run my turntable, CD player, cassette player, VHS and DVD players all through my Numark DJ mixer, which outputs an analog signal. From my deejay mixer, I send the master L/R outs to my Mackie 32 channel analog mixing console. From there, I route two direct out channels, which carry the Numark's signal, from my Mackie, to the LINE input of my Akai MPC 4000. I use this signal chain so that I have more control over the EQ's and amplification of the sounds and music prior to me sampling them. When you sample something, the idea is to arm (prepare) the best possible audio signal that you can without clipping. To achieve this sort of amplification, it's best to use some kind of DJ mixer as the hub through which you run all of your audio sources to be sampled.

Editing and Manipulating Samples: Chopping and Filtering

Fundamentally, samples are edited (altered) through one or two processes: "chopping" and/or "filtering." **Chopping** describes the process of dissecting, separating, and rearranging a sample (and other sounds) for use in a beat. It's the process of removing or trimming unwanted sections from a sample. Typically, it involves trimming sections from the start and end of a sample. However, as your overall beatmaking skills develop, you will undoubtedly chop and manipulate various sections of a sample.

When you chop a sample, your main concern should center around an audio snapshot. Let me break it down. When you play a record, you know, move the needle around, what happens when you hear something that you like? You get

---

[134] **Layering:** The process of combining two or more sounds into one. It is typically achieved by taking one sound and placing it on top of the other.

a broad, quick audio snapshot of where you might be able to take that segment. So you sample it. Now that it's sampled, what's your prime objective? To simply tune it (trim it) down to the right start and end points? Not necessarily. Naturally, the first thing to do is to chop (trim) it to the exact segment that you heard. Sometimes this works out just like you imagined it, but most of the time *it doesn't*. So when you chop a sample, you should be prepared to wind up with something that you didn't necessarily see clearly at first. Remember, when you hear something that you like for the first time, before you sample it, it's just a quick, broad audio snapshot; and thus, the photo, so to speak, is not entirely clear. It's only after you've sampled the segment and chopped it and tried it *within* a drum framework that the picture starts to become more clear.

In this way, sampling is like sculpting. What I mean is that you always have to be prepared to shave *more* than you initially intended. On the other hand, you have to be ready to reapply, reshape, and reconfigure those seemingly unwanted shavings. The goal is to make the illest beat that you can; it's not about how many chops you can work in, or how many modifications that you can apply to a sample. Chopping is about extracting the pieces that work best with your drums. It's not just about cutting and truncating something; it's really more about understanding what happens to a sample when a piece of it is removed and/or rearranged and reapplied. In this way, chopping prompts you to uncover the unintended sounds and feeling of the original sample. It let's you survey the texture of the initial sample, giving you a broader pallet from which to paint your beat portraits.

Chopping is also akin to improvisation because it involves embellishing the source material/music on the fly, without little to no musical direction at the onset of the beat. From one recording to the next, a sample-based beatmaker *improvises* how to transform what he (or she) samples.

Finally, there are two broad forms of chopping: basic and complex. **Basic chopping** describes a simple, minimal form of truncation of a sample/sound at its start and end points. The most notable form of chopping within the basic chopping form is loop chopping. **Loop chopping** describes the basic chopping form that is used for chopping loops. **Complex chopping** describes the more extended form of chopping. It includes the processes of cutting sounds down to "tonal chops," that is, chopping samples/sounds down to individual notes for the purpose of being played (often in some chromatic manner), over drum pads or keys, or *drawn* into a beat sequence through the use of a mouse. Within the complex form of chopping, there are two sub-forms: **stab-chopping** and **phrase-chopping**. **Stab-chopping** describes the complex chopping form that is used for chopping sound-stabs, e.g., drum-hits, key-stabs, and tones. **Phrase-chopping** describes the complex chopping form used for chopping phrases.

BeatTip – Precision Chopping: Finger-Point Accuracy

Here's a good rule for precision chopping. In the sample edit mode of your sampler, tap (press) the play back button repeatedly until the sound plays on the *hit* of your fingertip. If the sound is not falling on the hit of your fingertip, then you need to chop (cut) the **start point** of the sample some more until it does. If the **end point** carries over longer than you want it to, then you need to chop (cut) the end point of the sample until it stops where you want it to. The idea is to tap, not hold, the play-back button when you're first chopping the sample. By holding the playback button too long, you will get an inaccurate starting point. After you establish the right starting point, then you can hold the play-back button down. This allows you to play back the sample so that you can capture the right end point.

Here, I should point out that while chopping drum sounds is more straight forward than chopping any other type of sounds, chopping phrases requires you to be much more careful. The reason is because the start and end points of phrases have the power to off-set any drum timing. That is to say, the precision chopping of phrases is critical for a different reason: phrases actually play *over* the drums. So, if the hit of the phrase is off a little, not hitting on that finger-point accuracy, it will make the entire drum program and/or looped sequence sound off.

Check This Out – The Genius of Chopping Before "Auto Chop" Functionality

Technology has long raised questions about musicianship, musicality, creativity, and imagination. And now it would appear that it is reshaping what it means to have "skills" in beatmaking, especially in the area of chopping. Consider the auto-chop function on the Akai MPC (models 4000, 1000, 2500, and 5000). Where does the skill enter into the equation? Is it the source selection? Is it the setting of an automatic 16 to 32-piece, chronological chop, something previously only achieved through a beatmaker's careful selection, good ear, and meticulous manual chopping? I'm not sure where skill begins or ends when this now go-to functionality is used, but one thing's for certain: Auto chop — and it's ability to make some beatmakers appear to be doing much more than they actually are — has become more than just a tool for evenly chopping up samples, for some it's become a creative crutch.

Even worse, some beatmakers are using auto chop as a means of copying the styles and sounds of some the best known sample-based beatmakers. Auto chop functionality has virtually given birth to thousands of DJ Premier sound-alikes. But it's important to make the distinction that at the core of DJ Premier's process and setup (he primarily used an Akai MPC 60 II/Akai S950 setup) does not rely upon auto-chop functionality. His sampling and chopping style is the product of a good ear and his unique manual chopping schemes, not auto chop functionality.

Though I'm an avid Akai MPC 4000 user, I'm mostly reluctant to use one of its most popular features — the 32 region sample divide capability, aka auto chop. Instead of sampling something and automatically dividing it into 32 regions, I prefer to sample something, duplicate it (two or three times, sometimes more, if necessary), then assign it to three or so separate drum pads on my MPC. In doing so, I find that I get a better feel for the many different ways in which the chops of one sample can be used.

But when it comes to auto chop functionality, I have mixed feelings. I was groomed on the Akai MPC 60 II/S950 combo, and before that I'd used the E-Mu SP 1200 along with my S950. Both setups only allowed me to chop samples manually, i.e. there was no 32 region sample divide, push-button architecture that would automatically chop up a sample for me. Thus, because I knew that I'd have to manually chop samples, I found that I listened to source music more acutely. Specifically, I listened closely for possible start and end points of the streams of sounds on a given piece of music. As a result, I was able to develop a better feel for the ways in which sounds, particularly complete musical phrases, could be chopped up and re-arranged in a manner that most favored my style, sound, and sensibilities. On the other hand, the use of auto chop hasn't prompted the same sort of experience. Instead, when I use auto chop, I actually feel — in some ways — like I'm being less creative. The process of assigning multiple regions of a sample for it to be automatically divided into separate parts seems too easy (at times), or at least less demanding of your diggin' and chopping skills, specifically how you hear and imagine chops in your head. Still, I'm not totally against using auto chop.

Auto Chop does has its advantages. For example, if you want to audition specific parts of a sample without having to manually chop each piece that you find interesting, then using auto chop is the way to go. Or let's say you want to quickly sketch out an arrangement idea using a full scale — 12 chromatic pieces — of a sample. With auto chop, you can quickly slice up a sample, then program its parts with pitch adjustments. Of course, as I mentioned earlier, the same idea can be achieved without auto chop. But auto chop allows you to perform this process much faster, with more immediate separate chops per performed function. Because of its robust functionality, auto chop quickly opens up a new level of possibilities that could not otherwise be achieved without it. So when used thoughtfully and creatively, auto chop can certainly enhance your workflow.

But the workflow advantages aside, if you're not careful auto chop can stifle the way in which you approach chopping all together. Auto chop can essentially reduce chopping to nothing more than a scheme of regions and numbers. Which is to say, it can take away a lot of the craftiness or ingenuity that you regularly find associated with manually chopping duplicated samples. Think about it: You load up a sample, assign the automatic splits, then *voila!*: 16 to 32 neatly sliced pieces of the same sample. Because of this, auto chop can prompt you to focus less on the ways in which a given sample can be chopped and more on the prospect of shoving a sample into the "auto chop box". This, in turn, can make you rely more on auto chop functionality and less on your own intuition and ingenuity or your familiarity with the given source material.

Filtering Samples

Filtering refers to the process of boosting or subtracting various EQ levels (i.e. bass, mid, and treble). Filtering is a sound coloring or enhancing technique that is often misused and/or grossly underestimated. Typically, when beatmakers are talking about filtering, what we're mainly talking about is tweaking the low and high frequencies of a given individual sound or sound phrase. The "low" being the *bottom*, like the low frequency in bass lines, bass kicks, low-note piano and organ keys, stuff like that. Filtering is also about accentuating the hi and and mid instrument frequencies, like horns, strings, and hi-hats. The effects and enhancements that filtering can offer are tremendous. Creative filtering can *fatten up* or bring out a weak bass line. At the same time, it can push down unwanted high and mid frequencies, or it can vitalize weaker high and mid frequencies. Furthermore, filtering can tuck or *hide* unwanted sounds (sometimes even vocals) deep inside the sample.

There are a couple of good filtering techniques that are commonly used. For your lows, the process is fairly straight forward, so long as your sampler has effective low and hi-pass filtering functions. Both of my samplers — the Akai S950 and the Akai MPC 4000 — have filtering functions, yet each are very different. The Akai S950, a vintage sampler, has the simplest filtering function that I've ever used. Essentially, it has a filter value of 0 to 99, 0 being the lowest level and 99 being the highest level. Via the S950's menu dial, the value can be adjusted up or down until you reach the desired tone, feel, and texture. The Akai MPC 4000, on the other hand, contains a rather extensive filtering function that is comprised of a series of filtering *pages* that are designed to color the frequency of a sound in various ways. In order to filter samples on the Akai MPC 4000 (and many other contemporary samplers and keyboard workstations with sample engines), you have to tweak both the low and hi-pass filters separately. But whether you use a vintage sampler or a contemporary one, in either case the idea of filtering is universal: Bring down the lows to kill the high and mid frequencies, and turn up the high frequencies for brightness. To achieve this with contemporary samplers, you actually have to increase the value of the low-pass filter and decrease the value of the hi-pass filter if you really want to fatten up low-end sounds. You also have to adjust the level of resonance, which essentially smoothens out the *scope* of the filtered bass line.

Check This Out – My Process for Filtering Out Bass Lines On The Akai S950 and/or the Akai MPC 4000

Before I break down my process for filtering samples on the Akai S950, I should note that the technique which is used is, in theory, pretty much universal, and therefore, it can be applied to any hardware and/or software sampler. However, it must further be pointed out that the sound quality, feeling, and warmth will vary from EMPI to EMPI. So here's what I do, as well as the most notable masters of the Akai S950. *(Big respect to Peter Panic for teaching me this technique. And much respect to DJ Premier for confirming and thoroughly explaining it to me.)*

- In the EDIT PROGRAM mode, I locate the sample that I want the bass filtered out on.
- Then I go to the Keygroup page (page 03).
- Where it says Copy (+), I initiate the (+) sign.
  This will copy the entire Keygroup, the sample, the filtering parameters, the assigned output channel, and all.

- Next, I locate the *new* Keygroup and assign it to a different channel, preferably the channel/output on my mixing console that is next to the channel/output of the high part of the sample. (Note: I use all eight individual outputs of my Akai S950, and each are assigned to their own channel on my 32 channel mixing console.) Then I set the filter on the new Keygroup to 0.
- Now, when I strike the assigned pad on my MPC, I will actually trigger *two* sounds simultaneously. Thus, I'll have both a mid to hi sound of the sample and a low sound of the exact same sample.
- On my mixing console, I simply mix the low part with a little more bottom, being mindful to keep it warm. On the other hand, I mix the mid to hi part with some hi, a little more mid, and nearly no low at all. And thus the proper blend will effectively filter out *(bring up)* the bass.

Note: If you do not have an Akai S950 sampler or a mixing console, essentially what I just described above is the practice of duplicating a sample, then treating it as left and right stereo sound — the left being the low, the right being the hi. So the idea is just to copy the sample and EQ the duplicate in a manner that contrasts the original. To achieve this using a Hi-Pass/Low-Pass filter combo, make sure you *ground* the Low-Pass filter, that is to say, boost up the low. At the same time, you want to pull back on the Hi-Pass filter until you decrease the distorting "rumble" of the bass sound.

Pro Tools (or any DAW such as Logic), really makes this process easier and more effective. Regardless of whatever sampler you're using, if you have access to Pro Tools and the like, then all you need to do is duplicate the audio track for which you want to filter. From there, just EQ the duplicated track until the bottom is out in front where you want it.

Filtering Out Bass Lines On The MPC 4000

My process for filtering out bass lines on the Akai MPC 4000 is different, but it's *easier* in it's own right and much faster than my process with the Akai S950. Here's how I do it. In the Program mode, I go to Edit page, then to the Filter page. Within the Akai MPC 4000, there are 35 different types of filter modes (options). When I want to filter a sample to sound *comparable* to the sound that the Akai S950 generates, I use the "Lo<>Hi" filtering option. There, I set the default cutoff frequency somewhere between 15-23, and I set the Resonance value somewhere between: 10-17. Keep in mind, increased resonance increases the presence and "thickness" of the bass, but it also induces *rumbling* (distortion) the higher you go up the value dial.

Using Your Chopped and Filtered Samples To Make Beats

After you've collected and chopped your sample(s), you basically have two different ways to incorporate them into a beat. You can "paper clip" (blend and fasten) your samples to a preset drum beat that you've already created, or you can build a drum beat from scratch that is based around the arrangement of your sample(s). **Minor paper-clipping**, the most common way in which beatmakers use samples, is the process of taking a sample and *attaching* a backing drum beat to it, or vice versa. It usually involves sampling a complete-phrase, i.e. a ready-made loop or a similarly long musical phrase. Essentially, it's just clipping one finished piece of music, i.e. a sample, to another finished piece (or pieces) of music, like a drum pattern. For example, let's say you have a preset drum beat playing on your EMPI. With the drum beat sequence in record mode, you trigger the sample right in over the drum beat. With the primary sample successfully recorded into the sequence, the sample (complete-phrase, etc.), along with the drum beat, becomes the rhythm section; and as such, it serves as the **core track** from which the entire beat's design (arrangement) will be based upon. The core track, composed of the core riffs and groove, is the main framework of a beat. (The core track is the initial foundation of rhythm and groove and perhaps a simple melody. It provides the basis, the "core" of the beat.)

Major paper-clipping, or what I like to call **"B 'n' P-building,"** employs the same process, but in this case, you're using smaller samples (segments that have been put through a complex chopping process). Unlike minor paper-clippin', which tends to be characterized by complete-phrases and ready-made loops, major paper-clippin' is best characterized by its use of "bits and pieces" — **B 'n' P** (smaller segments of sounds). Major paper-clippin' requires a beatmaker to meticulously fashion both a backbeat *and* an air-tight rhythm while using non-ready-made loop samples to do so. Thus B 'n' P-Building requires a beatmaker to have highly creative and advanced chopping skills.

Drum Frameworks and Your Samples

As I discussed in chapters 6 and 7, building drum patterns from scratch is pretty much rhetorical. What I mean by that is, no matter how *differently* you arrange your drum pattern, it will always be some variation of a drum pattern that you've already created or heard before. Even if you interchange the pattern with new drum sounds, the reality is that the patterns stay relatively the same. Hip hop/rap music — like jazz, blues, and rock 'n' roll — builds upon its clichés. Therefore, rarely will you ever hear a drum pattern that you've never heard *some variation* of before. When you're building a drum pattern from scratch, based around a primary sample, your goal should be to compliment that sample, not disrupt it or distract attention away from it. In other words, when you use samples, then let the sample shine! The drums that you blend in should hold everything down. When you have a dope sample looping, in readying yourself to play in a drum pattern, keep your focus on building a drum framework that lets the sample *breathe* properly. Don't overpower the sample with drums that cloud or distort the sample. Drums can still bang without having to sacrifice the sound and feeling of the main sample. I believe drums bang the most when the blend between the sample and the drum pattern is straight-forward and not too busy or overly loud. When it comes to creating a drum framework with your sample(s), a proper balance of well-grounded power and subtleness is the key.

Important Note About Sampling and Arrangement

To really understand the concept of sampling, you must understand how arrangement works, more specifically, how to weave samples (fragments of recorded music) into a montage of sound. There's two ways you can look at arrangement. You can look at it as the order and measure (length) of sounds and sequences within a song (composition), or you can look at it as the pattern in which sounds correspond sequentially within any song (composition). The length (measured in bars or seconds) and sound of a sample determines the way in which the backing drum pattern is going to be arranged. Until the backing drum pattern is established, which gives you the core track (the basic rhythm track), the arrangement of the composition can not be completed. Understanding how standard drum patterns work with varying sample arrangements (e.g. 2-bar loop beginning on the downbeat), allows you to map out how you will be able to manipulate your samples. This is critical because it teaches you how to break samples into multiple sections, i.e. the intro, verse, chorus, and bridge.

BeatTip – Choosing Audio Bandwidth Settings

Before I sample anything, especially drum sounds, I come up with a short name, usually no more than 5 to 7 characters. If I do not readily have a name to associate with the sound, I simply use a "default" name. For instance, if it's a snare and I can't relate anything to what it sounds like, I simply name it "snrx1" — "snr" for snare, and "x" for whatever number. If and when I use the snare again, I rename it more descriptively, then I store it with my library of drum sounds. I avoid using elaborately descriptive names because it takes up too much time scrolling and assigning long names. Bottom line: When it comes to naming samples, I try to keep it as simple and as relative as I can. Also, I should point out that I never name anything a "loop." Why? Because complete-phrases are not actually loops, they are "breaks" that are *programmed* — made — to loop. Records do not come with loops per se.[135]

Whatever sampler you use, I recommend that you use a default audio bandwidth setting.[136] More specifically, I do not recommend using dramatically different bandwidth settings for everything that you sample. Don't get me wrong, you won't really disrupt anything that you normally do when you use varying settings. To me, it's just more time consuming, and it goes against customizing your sound. But if you do ultimately decide to use different audio bandwidth settings, I recommend that you at least make those the default settings for the types of sounds that you sample. For example, always use the same audio bandwidth setting for deep, hard kicks, or thick bass lines, etc. One benefit to having a default audio bandwidth setting is that it saves you a lot of valuable production time. Moreover, it enables you to sample new sounds more rapidly and efficiently. It also familiarizes you with what works, like how certain sounds might best be sampled and, subsequently, edited. Finally, another reason that I utilize a default bandwidth setting for nearly everything that I sample is because it allows me to customize and uniform my sound.

---

[135] When a beatmaker says that they got a loop from a record, what they actually mean is that they sampled a complete phrase, usually 2 or 4 bars, and then looped it. This is why the notion of *looking for "loops"* in pre-recorded music is a misleading proposition...

[136] It's worth noting that a higher Audio Bandwidth setting, or rather higher frequency response level, will make the sample sound brighter. The frequency response level is one of the things that separates the Akai S950 from the E-mu SP 1200. Although both units are 12-bit, the Akai S950 has a higher (range) frequency response level, therefore, sounds have a bigger, warmer overall sound.

Extended Sampling Notes, Techniques, and Tips

Sample Blending, Multi-Sampling, Spot-Note Sampling, and Shading Samples

There are four commonly used sampling techniques ("tricks" or methods) that go a long way in shaping a beatmaker's sampling abilities: (1) **sample blending**; (2) **multi-sampling**; (3) **spot-note sampling**; and (4) **shading samples**. Like it sounds, **sample blending** is simply the process of blending samples together. There are a couple of ways to go about this. You can *splice* two or more samples together, e.g. splicing a snare and tambourine so that the snare strikes, followed by the sound of the tambourine. You can also do manual blends, similar to layering,[137] where you actually play in (*program*) the samples to play together or in chronological variations.

Here, it's worth mentioning that "front" and "end sample-fades" (created through the use of the Attack and Sustain functions of a sampler), help make the sample blends even more effective. A front sample-fade refers to how a sample begins after it's been chopped. This means how much of the very beginning of the sample is audible? Does it come in hard, heavy, and/or flush? Does it slide in? Does it blend in? An end sample-fade refers to how a sample ends after it's been chopped. This means how long does a sample *sustain* itself after it reaches its end? Decreasing the sustain of a sample gives the effect of a fade. Thus, the right decrease of sustain at the beginning of a sample and the right decrease of attack at the beginning of another sample allows two (or more) samples to blend together more effectively, sounding as if they were just one sample.[138]

Sample blends can be complete-phrases and sound-stabs that are fused together by your sampler's splicing function. They can also be two spare-part-phrases played together with sound-tones and other pieces of sound. Chopping samples and then blending the "new" samples (the remains minus the cuts) together into one cohesive measure of music is one of the most creative ways of developing your own production style and sound.

Multi-sampling is the process of sampling the same sound (phrase, instrument, stab, etc.), multiple times, each at a different pitch. This neutralizes

---

[137] I use the term **layering** here to describe the process of combining two or more sounds into one. It is typically achieved by taking one sound and placing it on top of the other.
[138] Sample-blends composed of sound-stabs are an excellent example of how "front sample-fades" and "end sample-fades" can be used. For an example of a great sound-stab sample blend, listen to "The Owners" (Gang Starr) produced by DJ Premier. That song has a bass-stab underneath a baritone horn-stab.

the awkwardness of short semitones. Here, the idea is to then assign the samples to the same limited area of drum pads or keys. Once assigned, you can play the various "versions" of the same sample.

Spot-note sampling refers to the process of sampling pieces of a musical phrase that *can* be sampled, while replaying the minor tones of the phrase that can not be sampled. For instance, the notes of a phrase that can not be sampled clean because vocals are running over them. Using the spot-note sampling method, you can sample the part of the phrase that *can* be sampled clean, then you play the "spot notes", using a keyboard, synth, VST, or sound module (*as close as audibly possible*) that can't be sampled. For example, if it's a bass phrase that's cut off by vocals, drums, etc., simply replay (duplicate, emulate) the spot notes, the bass parts that you're not able to sample.

Finally, the process of layering samples with matching and/or non-matching notes, tones, frequencies, percussion, voices, etc. is what I like to call **"shading samples."** It's an extremely valuable sample editing technique that can be used to *disguise* a sample without having to forfeit the feeling and mood of the sample being disguised. Shading a sample can also be used to accentuate and/or punctuate the depth, texture, and feeling of a sample.

Making Samples Sound Thicker: Fattening up Samples

Two of the most common questions regarding the sound of samples are: 'How do you make a sample not sound *thin*?' and 'How do you add "umph" to a sample?' To answer these questions appropriately, you must first consider the sound source that you are using. Are you sampling from vinyl records? Are you sampling from a CD? Are you importing an .mp3 or .wav file? This matters a great deal because the potential modifications of a sample are only as good as the *sound* of the sample when you first sample it. The brighter the sample, the thinner it will sound, and therefore, the harder it will be to make it sound "warm." And *umph* is a separate issue that I'll discuss later in this section. But in both cases, the fundamental thing to understand is that the approach that you take in this matter is really determined by the sound and source that you *start* with. Typically, vinyl will always have a more thicker (warmer) sound than a CD. Likewise, a CD will always sound thicker than an .mp3 or .wav file. In fact, though .mp3 and .wav files may be cleaner and brighter, they're thin (cold) to begin with. On any given recording, each format produces an aural response that sounds as if 1/4 of the sonic quality has been shaved off (compressed) and flattened. Therefore, when you work with an .mp3 or .wav file, the first thing you might want to do is *re-sample* it into your own sampler. This way, you have more room to play with. Once you "recapture" the sound into an environment that you control (i.e. a sampler that you know), you can go about modifying the sample into a thicker sound.

With vinyl and CDs the process is a little different. Instead of *re-sampling* the sample from the vinyl or CD, just duplicate it (make an exact copy of the sample) then focus in on the lower tones and frequencies. The **duplicate and layer** method allows you to build up the sonic quality that you're aiming for. Many beatmakers will sample something and just let it be. Then, after they throw in some drums and percussion, they believe that the sample is *thin*. Most of the time, it's not even an issue of the sample being thin, it's just that the drums are texturally and sonically stronger than the sample. Thus, in a situation like this, I recommend that you "boost" (enhance the sonic impact) the sample with a lower frequency version of itself.

The other thing that you can do is program in low and low-mid sound-stabs. Here's what you do, check out the sample that you want to use, identify the parts in the sample that you hear thinness. Next, determine which sounds in the sample (instruments) are causing that thinness. The majority of the time the thin-spots will be either a guitar, bass, or keyboard. After you've determined the thin-spots in the sample, make and play sound-stabs that match the tone and timbre of the thin-spots. To get the sound-stabs to match the thin-spots, you'll have to modify either their velocity, sustain, attack, overall volume, or all of the above.

Incidentally, adding *umph* to a sample is very similar to what I just described. If all you want to do is add umph to a sample, you need not always duplicate and layer the sample. Instead, you can simply accentuate the sample with a combination of percussive elements and short or medium bass-stabs.

BeatTip – Adding Bass Fill-Ins

Aside from the organic rhythms, that were typically underscored by funky drums and smooth bass lines, the other appeal of the music of the 1970s is the way in which it was recorded. Though the recording and mixing techniques of the 1970s may seem quirky, compared to today's common industry recording practices, the reality is that they produced perhaps the warmest, most organic music ever recorded. Certainly, this fact has not been lost on many beatmakers. And truth is, more often than not, it's the *sound* and its accompanying *feeling* that most beatmakers are after. But while that 1970s sound shines, typically when it comes to overall warmth and feeling, it often doesn't suit the sonic demands of today's audible standards. More specifically, it lacks the level of bass amplification that is typically associated with hip hop/rap music. Therefore, in order to maintain the warmth of a sample, while at the same time satisfy that deep bass sound that hip hop/rap music warrants, beatmakers often attach bass fill-ins and/or accents to their samples.

A **bass fill-in** is any bass phrase, tone, and/or sound that is deliberately blended into a beat. Bass fill-ins are usually added to beats in which the framework-sample — the main sample in which the beat is driven around — is devoid of a *fat* enough bass line (or bass part). For example, let's say you sample a mean guitar lick that dissolves into a crazy organ sound. You loop that sample, maybe one bar, maybe two bars, then add in a nice backing drum beat. Now, the framework might be good to go as it is. But remember, we're talkin' hip hop/rap music: It's a bottom heavy genre. So most of the time, you're going to need some sort of bass element, e.g. 808 kick drum or a bass line. Hence, you throw in a bass fill-in right on top of the gaps, the parts in the loop where the sound is *skinny*, where the musical events are diminished and lower in sound.

Typically, beatmakers use the bass sounds from their keyboards and sound modules as bass fill-ins. But this is a very tricky process because when you attempt to combine synthetic-bass sounds that adhere to today's audio standards with samples that adhere to the audio standards of more than a quarter century ago, the sonic nuances of the sample can be diminished, if not outright destroyed. If the bass fill-in is too thick and dominant, it will disrupt, if not totally consume, the warmth of the framework sample. Remember, the wrong bass sound, or the wrong pitch and texture of the bass sound, can result in the entire beat sounding uneven and overpowered by an awkward bass element. To guard against this, tweak the resonance of the bass fill-in that you've added. This will smoothen it out and warm up its ambiance.

Sampling Live Instrumentation or First Generation Sounds

Sampling live instrumentation is an extension of sampling records. The major difference being that you're sampling "live" instruments. Whether you're a trained musician or a keyboard finger-stabber, you can still sample some effective riffs. In hip hop/rap music, it doesn't take much for something to bang, provided you know how to flip it. There are a wealth of hip hop/rap songs that carry only one and/or two chord piano (or guitar) licks. Point is, once you have the drums and the drum programming down stone cold, there's no limit to the ways in which you can sample live instrumentation.

Here's where studying music comes into play. The more you study and listen to music, the more you will subconsciously and consciously pick up things. Music, like all art forms, is predicated upon on a number of fundamental themes and clichés. Take for instance note progression on a piano. The right side has the *highs*, higher pitched notes; the left side has the lows, the bass, the lower pitched notes; and the middle has the *mids*. The further to the right that you progress on the piano, the higher the notes will be. Likewise, the farther left that you progress on the piano, the lower the notes will be. Get it? Right high, left low.

Granted, my example here is a crude one, to say the least. I'm not stating that someone *without* piano lessons or a strong understanding of traditional music theory has the same chance of mastering the keyboard as someone who takes a regular regiment of lessons. No, I'm not saying that at all. I'm a realist. Hip hop/rap music is a fast medium. Beatmakers who opt for taking music lessons, more power to them; it's certainly not a bad thing to do. But the fact is, at the end of the day, those beatmakers will still be competing for production work with other beatmakers who have *no* formal training at all. Beatmakers who have been fortunate enough to have music lessons will always run the chance of being passed over by beatmakers without training. Sounds funny? Hear me out.

Take this scenario: Let's say two people decide that they want to go into the beat trade at the same time. Beatmaker X gets a keyboard and an MPC, and he signs up for piano lessons. Beatmaker Z gets the same keyboard and the same MPC but doesn't take any piano lessons. One year later, by chance, they both submit beats to the same rapper. Whose beats do you think that the rapper is going to pick? If you said beatmaker X, then you missed the point; and if you said beatmaker Z, then you missed the point. Are you saying, "huh?" The point is, the rapper could care less if you took lessons or if you know how to play the piano, or any instrument for that matter. The only thing that trumps process, method, and the like in hip hop/rap music is the overall result of the final product. Simple and plain: It's about does it sound *good* for whom you want it to sound good for.

Let me further clarify what I'm saying. Can piano lessons (or guitar, etc.) help you step up your live instrumentation game?[139] Of course they can! Matter of fact, incorporating the ability to play a traditional instrument, especially the piano, will definitely add to your entire beatmaking skill set. But remember this:

---

[139] For those who are not trained to play the piano or any traditional instrument for that matter, and who are not intent on taking any lessons, I recommend that you at least try looking at the keyboard like a mixing board, with varying EQ and volume dynamics that are controlled by knobs. The keys on the keyboard act as knobs, if you will, agents that work to speed up and/or slow down sound expressions.

There will always be beatmakers who bang out beats on the keyboard *without* any formal musical training, or without any prerequisite requirement for beat completion other than *does it sound good*.

Some of the dominant sounds in hip hop/rap music do not require that beatmakers actually *know* how to play Western classical music, let alone rudiment chord structures. And what about someone like Scott Storch, you might ask? Well, Scott Storch is *Scott Storch*. He's a trained keyboard player. If I had to estimate, I'd say he's had more than a few music lessons as well as some kind of consistent study in traditional music theory. But whether he did or didn't, doesn't matter. His music is polished and controlled; he's obviously not just a finger-stabber. He doesn't simply "hit" the keyboard, he *plays* it; and it's evident that he's been playing the keys for *years*.

So in the broader picture, *anyone* can sample live instrumentation. It certainly helps to know how to play, but it doesn't hurt you in beatmaking if you don't. Either way, sampling live instrumentation is about sampling the sound-stabs and riffs that you (and/or your hired musicians) play. The method adheres to the aforementioned process of sampling. But where sampling live instrumentation differs is in the texture and feeling of the source being sampled. Unlike records, which present second generation sounds to be sampled — second generation in that they have been played within the context of a recorded song and mixed in accordance with the RIAA mix standards of their time. However, live instrumentation sounds are *first generation* sounds, i.e. they're the original source. Hence, the management of these sounds give you more control. But this control comes at a price of several obstacles, namely the signal chain question.

In order for first generation sounds — like those that emanate from keyboards, VSTs, sound modules, guitars, drums, etc. — to hold their full sonic value, they must be routed and/or mic'd appropriately. This is the first obstacle that you face when trying to sample live instrumentation. If you do not have an elaborate assortment of microphones, you can still route instruments in a way that will enable you to sample them directly into your DAW. Essentially, you just record what you want to sample onto a track as if you were tracking a sound from a beat. This is actually another instance where having a mixing console comes in handy. The signal chain: *instrument to mixing console, mixing console to sampler*, gives you a greater flexibility over the sound of the original source instrument than the signal chain: *instrument to mic, mic to sampler*. Here, even the smallest mixing consoles (for example, an 8-channel model) gives you an edge, because a mixing console offers you tremendous amplification and sound coloring capabilities. Moreover, it gives you the opportunity to further color the sound of the original instrument source.

BeatTips Standards and Best Practices of the Sampling Tradition of Hip Hop/Rap Music

There are no written rules of creativity. All sample-based beatmakers can make beats in whatever manner that they choose. Nevertheless, in the sampling tradition of hip hop/rap music, a set of **standards and best practices** have evolved over the years. Although these standards and best practices have been informally shared and well understood among many beatmakers, they have never been formally organized or properly promoted. Thus what follows here is a discussion of these standards and best practices.

Standards and Best Practices – Transformation:
High Transformation, Reconceptualization, and Recontextualization

Creative, well-conceived chop arrangement schemes (no-matter how many or how little chops are made and used), constitutes best practice and standards. Chop arrangement schemes that effectively enhance the overall arrangement of a beat constitutes standards and best practices. Excessive chop arrangement schemes that sound overly forced, particularly cases where the multiple sample triggers can be heard (i.e. where the beatmaker is punching in the chops in the arrangement), fall below the threshold for standards and best practices in the sampling tradition of hip hop/rap music. Chop arrangement schemes that serve no musical purpose (rhythm, melody, harmony) or sonic purpose (layering, sound design) also fall below the threshold for standards and best practices. Chopping that relies more on the beatmaker's own ear and creative sense of arrangement and less on auto-chop functionality constitutes best practice. Chopping that relies solely on auto-chop functionality, rather than the beatmaker's ear and arrangement skills, falls below the threshold for standards and best practices.

Although transformation may be subjective, when considering how transformative a beat is or isn't, ask yourself these three main questions: Is the way in which the sample(s) is used conceptually different from its source? Is the way in which the sample(s) is used a change in context from the original? How much does the sample(s) used sound substantially similar to the sound recording from which it came?

Standards and Best Practices – Amounts Used
(Sound-Hits, Sound-Stabs, Parts, Phrases, and Low Number of Bars)

Sampling less and doing more with it constitutes standards and best practices. Sound-hits and stabs, which are both de minimis (insignificant) usages by default, are well within standards and best practices. Short music phrases and parts there of (e.g. riffs, drum fills, drum rolls, parts of melodies) used in contexts different from their source, constitutes standards and best practices. The lower the number of bars sampled and used, for example, 1 - 4 consecutive bars (the best practice), the deeper the sampling and use fall within the parameters of standards and best practices. However, a higher number of bars sampled and used does not automatically disqualify the sampling and use from standards and best practices. For example, 5 - 8 consecutive bars sampled and used constitute standards and best practices when substantial transformation takes place, or when the sample is used in a substantially different context. Though not likely most of the time, the sampling and use of 9 - 16 consecutive bars may possibly fall within the parameters of standards and best practices, provided transformation is significant and the new context of the sample is different. The sampling of 17 consecutive bars or more is not best practices.

What's important to remember when considering amounts is that the less that is sampled and used, the more highly regarded the instance of sampling. Further, creative transformation, reconceptualization, or recontextualization should always be a central aim of a sample-based beatmaker. No matter the amount used, the level of creative transformation, reconceptualization, and recontextualization determines whether an instance of sampling qualifies as standards and best practices or not.

Standards and Best Practices – Significance of Sample(s) Used: Using the Heart of a Recording or Parts Less Significant?

The sampling and use of less significant parts of a sound recording fall well within the parameters of standards and best practices. Sampling the whole or parts of the heart (the main theme) of a sound recording constitutes standards and best practices only when the use of the sample is highly transformative, or when the sample is sufficiently reconceptualized or recontextualized.

Standards and Best Practices – Original Drum Work or Drum Breaks in New Contexts?
(Original Drum Patterns and Transformative Uses of Drum Break Samples)

Drums are a cornerstone in the beatmaking tradition, thus original drum patterns created using individual drum sounds, especially a beatmaker's own customized drum sounds, constitutes standards and best practices. The use of drum breaks (either from break-beat compilations and other songs) instead of or in addition to individual drum sounds, constitute standards and best practices, especially when drum breaks are used in new contexts.

Standards and Best Practices – In the Matter of Loops
(Obscurity, Familiarity, and Transformation)

Typically, transformation always falls deeper within the standards and best practices. However, *ready-made* loops should be considered by a different transformation metric. For example, obscure ready-made loops (e.g. a couple of bars of a sample from a lesser-known soul recording) with less transformation to the original sample but added original drum work qualifies as standards and best practices. However, ready-made loop samples of very familiar songs (well-known hit songs) are less likely to meet the standards and best practices thresholds. But ready-made loops of such familiar songs that effectively transform the context of the use may fall within standards and best practices.

Summary of the The Art of Sampling

If anything, the examination in this chapter should dispel the notion that the art of sampling is simple, easy, or void of its own compositional system. Within the mechanics of sampling, there are many different dimensions. Collectively, these dimensions underscore the *science* of the art of sampling. This science, better stated as *the Sampling Equation*, encompasses a unique system that includes philosophical, technical, and compositional spectrums as well as a code of ethics. Thus to truly understand (and appreciate) the mechanics and compositional tract of the art of sampling in the hip hop/rap music tradition, one must first understand this robust equation.

Chapter 9

Practice Makes Better

Talent is the desire to practice. –Malcolm Gladwell

In beatmaking, practice is paramount. Actually, because of the collective demands of the three spheres,[140] it's absolutely necessary, and it's one of the most pivotal factors in the development of a beatmaker's skill set. Thus in this chapter, I discuss some of the most effective forms of practice in the beatmaking tradition.

Philosophy of Practice (The First Goal)

Each time you make a beat you are, in effect, practicing. Therefore, rather than merely focus on creating beats, I recommend that you also concentrate on practicing beatmaking. This philosophical approach to practice can have a profound effect on your overall approach to beatmaking. Not only will it enhance your overall understanding of the various processes, techniques, and styles of beatmaking, it will undoubtedly increase your efficiency in actually making beats.

So how do you *practice* beatmaking? Well, what I began doing (and still do) is I set aside certain days and times specifically devoted to practicing beatmaking (much in deference to the practice regiment that jazz artist John Coltrane maintained). Although the exact day and time of my practice may change, the process always stays the same: I commit the time to practice, then I practice. And here, I note that at the beginning of each practice, it is rarely my *first goal* to make a new beat; my first goal is to improve my beatmaking skills. Moreover, when I practice, my aim is to explore new ideas, then use my intuition to incorporate those ideas with my style and sound of beatmaking. Thus, I consider any quality beats that I create — during the midst of practice — as the residual benefits of the practice itself.

---

[140] In the introduction of this study, I pointed out that, as a musical process, beatmaking can be divided into three separate, but equally important, spheres. The "three spheres" of beatmaking include: the technical, the logical, and the creative spheres.

Scheduling Practice Time

The best practice is regular practice. It doesn't really matter how long each practice is. But it's important to maintain a consistent practice schedule. I recommend that you make, and rigorously maintain, a regular, realistic practice schedule. If you can, devote at least 2 to 4 hours a day, at least 3 days a week. If you can't commit to that, then at least shoot for 30 minutes a day, two days a week. Everyone has responsibilities outside of beatmaking, so it's important that you determine before-hand the times of the day and/or night that is best for you to practice. I practice either late at night, usually between 11:00pm and 6:00am, or in the early afternoon (2:00pm - 6:00pm). For most people, the daytime is occupied with work or school, which means that practicing at night is the only real option. I'm comfortable practicing either late night or in the day, but late night practice sessions can sometimes offer better isolation. Whatever time you choose to practice, stick to it. And be sure to clearly let your family and close friends know your schedule, because if they know and respect your schedule, they'll be less likely to interrupt you.

Establish Consistent and Realistic Practice Goals and Practice Sessions

Be honest about your level of beatmaking and quality of beats, then begin improving it. Determine how much you want to improve your level on a daily, weekly, and monthly basis. Within these practice sessions, devise a direction for where you want to go with your style and ideas.

Next, every time you practice, aside from what I like to call "MusicStudy" (and specific area-aimed practicing, like chopping practice), create at least one beat. Each week, strive to make *at least* five new beats; every month strive to create *at least* fifteen new beats; then, every month, have your own "battle of the beats" with the fifteen new beats of the month. The beats that lose, just toss them into the garbage. When you make a new beat, if the quality of it is too far off from your goal, just scrap the beat. However, if the beat is wack, *but* there's still something grabbing you about the beat, then hold on to it. Keep in mind, however, the more self-admitting wack beats that you keep, the slower the development of your overall beatmaking level will be.

Truth is, you have to forfeit a lot of "O.K." beats in order to create some dope beats; it's part of the developmental process. Forfeiting low-quality beats is actually a big part of maintaining quality control over your beats. And to that end, to organize your quality control, I recommend that you do a quality check of your beat catalog (all of your collective beats) every two weeks. The top five beats from each of your catalog beat battles will clue you in to what your style and sound is, or at least it will give you a clear hint as to where it's headed. These are the beats that you want to keep and study. Moreover, you should strive to surpass the level of the previous month's production output, or at least match that same level of quality.

It's also important to establish dedicated practice sessions. I recommend that you map out key areas for your practice. These should be the areas that are vital to beatmaking and, more specifically, tthose areas that you have deficiencies in *and* areas that you consider to be strong in. After you've mapped out areas for practice, divide your practice into two kinds of practice sessions: skills-based practice and knowledge-based practice. I use the term "skills-based practice" to describe those practices in which you work on skills like looping, chopping, drum programming, layering, etc. I use the term "knowledge-based practice" to describe those practices in which you enhance your musical knowledge through focused study and examination; i.e. through reading books, listening to music, and/or watching relevant movies, shows, and documentaries.

Finally, I want to make a note about down-time management. When you're not practicing, you should be practicing. In your down-time away from your production setup, there are a number of ways to continually improve yourself as a beatmaker, including cataloging your development, reading, organizing your practice notes, and most importantly, conducting MusicStudy.

BeatTip – Beats Made Per Week vs. Regimented Practice: Which is the Better Developmental Path for Beatmakers?

Making a set number of beats per week has long been an activity well-represented among beatmakers. (Many of the beatmakers that I've interviewed have told me about the sheer number of beats that they used to (and in some cases, still do) make or attempt to make per week.) The beats-made per-week quota has become so commonplace among beatmakers that it is now widely seen as a natural link to the development of beatmaking skill. But does the sheer maintenance of a specific quantity of beats made per week actually guarantee a deeper skill for beatmaking?

I suspect that a commitment to such a formula does generate a legitimate level of proficiency — not necessarily great skill — in beatmaking, particularly in terms of actually completing a beat. However, I wonder if this proficiency in beat completion, if you will, actually translates to a higher quality of beats. For some, I think so. Still, for most, I'm not entirely convinced that it does.

Let's say you make 20 beats per week. If you maintain that level of output, by year's end, you will have made over a thousand beats. Does this mean that at year's end, your sum total of beats made is an accurate measurement of your development as a beatmaker? I've never been comfortable with evaluating my development based on the quantity of my production output, but rather the *quality* of my production output and, more importantly, the individual breakthroughs (conceptual understanding, method mastery, etc.) that I experienced amid regularly scheduled practice sessions.

In regards to a developmental path for beatmakers, I believe that maintaining a strict per-week beat quota raises more questions than it answers. For instance, does a rigorous schedule of beats made per week correct your beatmaking deficiencies? Let's say you have difficulty with programming drums. Will making 20 beats per week correct that problem of yours? It might, but then again, not necessarily. For me, the most effective way to correct any deficiency, whether it be drum programming or any other process, is to hold isolated practice sessions wherein you work on nothing but correcting that deficiency. Such a dedicated drum programming practice session, for example, could be 30 minutes of studying the drum programming (patterns) of those beatmakers (producers) whose beats you admire. This could be followed up by another 30 minutes of sketching out your own drum patterns, using the ideas and understanding that you've gleamed from your study. To me, this kind of dedicated practice offers more promise than arbitrary beats-made-per-week quotas.

And what about those things that you do well as a beatmaker? Does a beats-made-per-week quota help you recognize the things that you do best? For some, I'm sure it does to a certain degree. After all, one advantage of completing an arsenal of beats each week is that it allows you to survey, study, and audit your own style and sound. Still, I also believe that regular regimented practice sessions also help you to identify the better elements and characteristics of your beatmaking style and sound.

Thus in my final analysis, I'd say that there's value in both approaches. I do believe that maintaining some sort of beats-made-per-week quota is beneficial. However, I caution that the maintenance of any such quota, without regular regimented practices, is far less beneficial. Practice in beatmaking, as with any other music process, is always necessary. No matter how developed you may be as a beatmaker, it's important to continue to sharpen your skills. And by this

I mean, practice without the intent of always creating a new beat, but rather the intent of further developing your skill and understanding of the multiple processes of beatmaking as well as music in general.

Check This Out – Some Areas of Practice Worth Conducting: Loop Practice, Chopping Practice, Sound Practice, Cataloging, and Studying

Loop Practice

Looping sequences and sounds is one important area of practice that I recommend that you focus on as much as possible. What I recommend that you do is set aside time for practicing and developing your loop technique. Practice looping both sample-based and synthetic-sounds-based style sequences, everything from up-beat bass lines to heavily syncopated drums; from slow-pitched organ tones to sound effects, like alarms and such. Also, practice manipulating endpoints and tempos. Use both complete-phrases and spare-part-phrases. Discover what happens to sounds when you program them to begin on the downbeat as opposed to the up beat, or when you program them to begin in the mid-section or end of your drum-framework. Find out what happens to the loop when you do this to your sounds, especially samples: Do your sounds sustain or get clipped? Also, see what nuances occur when you drag or speed up the tempo, while keeping your sounds at their initial pitch. Understanding loop patterns and the characteristics that occur with tempo changes (like pitch changes and varying melody changes within your drum frameworks) is critical to developing and creating your own sound. Finally, with loop practice, you also want to get to the point where you can cleanly loop any sample-based or synthetic-sounds-based sound framework rather quickly (for me the goal was usually three minutes).

Chopping Practice

If your chopping skills are not up to par, practice sampling and chopping drum kicks. When I had trouble understanding chopping, I shifted my attention from trying to chop the largest segments of music to the smallest segments of music. This improved my chopping skills dramatically. How did I do it? I took the 75 drum kicks that I had (you really only need about 5 to 15) and tried them

ALL out in different drum frameworks (sequences), just so I could hear how well they were chopped. In addition to learning how to cleanly chop sounds, I weeded out a lot of similar sounding kicks, thereby making my arsenal of kicks more leaner. These chopping practice drills also helped my timing.

Sound Practice

Too much reliance on "effects" or "plug-ins" *before* you even understand how certain sounds work together will actually take away from your development. Practice working with your sounds *without* using effects. That is, get really familiar with the three main "zones" of sound (hi, mid, and low), and take one zone of sound at a time and dedicate practice sessions to making beats with one pre-determined zone of sound as the center of the beat. For instance, make some beats that all feature strings or some other high-pitched sound. Practice sessions like these will not only teach you more about the "hi" zone of sound, they will teach you a great deal about high-pitched strings and how they blend with other sounds and how they create new sound textures. Incidentally, exercises like these will also inform you more about which of your drum sounds work best together.

BeatTip – Creating Your Own Moods/Sounds Chart: Understand the Link Between Moods and Sounds, and Help Make Composing Beats More Manageable – the Benefits of a Moods/Sounds Chart

It's impossible to listen to music without being emotionally involved. Plus, the appreciation of a given piece of music often depends a great deal on the moods that it evokes. And specific sounds can evoke certain moods. So for musicians, it's important to have a strong sense of the link between moods and correlating sounds. But for beatmakers, musicians who fundamentally rely on the use of pre-recorded sounds, a solid grasp of the mood/sounds link is critical.

Although people experience emotions in different ways, some basic emotions — like happiness, sorrow, fear, etc. — can be categorically represented in music. I use categorically in a generalized sense of course. For example, happy/festive moods can often be evoked by maracas and kazoos; likewise, sadness can be evoked by a bugle horn playing the song "Taps." Or how about chaos? Can it not often be evoked by sirens, broken glass, car crashes, and the like? But moods are not exactly the same thing as emotions. Moods tend to contain a wider, deeper meaning. While an emotion may represent the snapshot of a feeling, a mood represents the snapshot and its surrounding story. Thus, matching the sounds to the moods you're going for isn't always easy, especially in beatmaking. That's why I created a mood/sounds chart to help me catalog sounds that correlate with specific moods.

The image of my Moods/Sounds chart (pictured in figure 11) include some mood descriptions that might be obvious to some as well as some mood descriptions that are entirely subjective; i.e. they work in terms of how I personally feel and hear the moods. Therefore, when creating your own moods/sounds chart, use the language — the mood descriptions — that work best for you.

Finally, I should point out that my Moods/Sounds chart helped me to find the style and sound that kept me engaged the most, the sound that I felt the most. Note: The highlighted sounds are the sounds that form the core of my sound and the "mood" and "sound" that I strive for.

Sa'id Mood/Sounds Chart 5

Moods ("feels")	Correlating Sounds
Suspense	Reverse crashes, bongos, Wood Guiro
Sinister '70s	**Dragging horn-stabs**, sustained big brass sounds [mid- and low-pitch], bongos, **walking bass riffs, wah wah guitar riffs**
Mellow	rhodes
	Rise
Scenic	broad violin phrases,
Revenge	dragging pitched-low violins
After Hours Lounge	bongos, flat guitar,
Tension 2nd Level	ascending high-pitched violins
Chaos	sirens, broken glass, screeching tires
Joyful/Happy/Festive/Celebration	maracas, **tambourine**, bells, kazoos, bright horns, C-Major riffs
Doom	kick booms, slow triangles
Mystery	harps, chimes
Solemn/Somber	ambient cymbals (brush-hit)
Despair	soft strings, dragging mid-pitched violins
Dreamy/Surreal	**harps/rising**, (filtered) strings, chimes,
Spring/New Dawn	flutes, birds, high-pitched flutes,
Tension	reverse crashes, rising strings, wood guiro, cabasa

Figure 11 Sa'id's Mood/Sounds Chart 5

BeatTip – Modifying the ADSR Sound Envelope Pattern: Changing the ADSR Settings to Get the Most Out of Your Sounds

After you've chosen your samples/sounds and chopped them (established their start and end points, etc.), there is another series of modifications that you can perform to enhance and customize the character of your samples/sounds: Tweaking the ADSR sound envelope pattern. But to effectively modify the sound envelope pattern of a sample/sound and, subsequently, unleash even more flavor from your samples/sounds, it's important to understand just what sound envelope refers to.

Every sound (dynamic tone) has three components: **Attack**, **Decay**, and **Sustain**. Taken together these three components (parts or dimensions) are known as the sound envelope. (I should also point out that I like to extend the definition of sound envelope to mean: the entire span — from start to go — of a sound.) With regards to synthesis techniques (synthesizers/samplers) there is a fourth component, **Release**. Collectively, these four components are known as the ADSR envelope. When you modify or remove any one or a combination of these ADSR components, the sound's properties change, rendering an array of different effects. So it's important to understand what each component within the ASDR envelope represents if you're to modify them in ways that best serve your beats' arrangements.

Attack

Attack refers to the time/distance between a sound initiated — first struck or pressed, via a pad strike or a key pressed, etc. — and when it reaches its peak, the highest level/intensity of a sound. A sound's attack can be fast or slow. This means that the closer the attack of a sound is to its peak, the faster its attack. Conversely, the further away the attack of a sound is from its peak, the slower its attack. Further note that sounds with a fast attack reach their sustain level quickly, while sounds with a slow attack take longer to reach their sustain level. For example, a sound like a kick or snare has a fast attack, while a sound like a multi-toned sample phrase has a slow attack. A sampled phrase without drum sounds (particularly kicks and snares) at its start point has a slower attack than a sampled phrase that does have drum sounds at its start point. As such, sampled phrases without drums at their start points often tolerate adjustments of the attack value very well, usualy producing interesting results, depending on the sound of the sample and the overall scope of the beat that you're making.

Decay, Sustain, and Release

Decay (or "decay time") refers to the time it takes for a sound to fall from its attack level to its sustained level. "Rate of decay" describes how gradual a sound decays. Sustain refers to the span of a sound that's audible just after or nearest a sound's peak (the highest level of a sound). In other words, sustain is what I like to call the "plateau level" of a sound; it's the level where a sound assumes and maintains its steadiest level or main intensity. Although the sustain actually represents a slight drop off in level from the peak of a sound, it's the "meatiest" (steadiest, most sustained) part of a sound. So for instance, think of a 2-bar sample. The sustain is the level that is reached and maintained the longest during the duration of the sample. Release refers to the time it takes for the sustain level of a sound to diminish to silence. In other words, it's the rate at which a sound fades to silence after it's played.

Modifying the ADSR Envelope

Modification of the ADSR settings not only affects the tone quality of a sound, it also affects how sounds "sit" with each other within a beat's arrangement. This is an important point to consider with any sound, but when it comes to sample arrangements, it's even more critical. Why? Because the more instruments/sounds within a sample, the more dynamic tones it will contain. And the more dynamic tones that exist, the more potential for customization/stylization.

Modifying the Attack

Because my style and sound calls for a lot of blending and rupturing of samples/sounds, attack is the most critical ADSR setting that I use. Hence, whenever I modify the ADSR settings on my Akai MPC 4000 or Akai S950, I always begin with the attack, using a method I call "pinching the attack." Pinching the attack of the sample is the process of setting the attack value so that the very front end of the sample is ruptured or cut into a beat's arrangement. Because I use the common technique of assigning multiple sampled phrases to various drum pads, I prefer to have more stylistic control over the ways in which the samples I use sound and move within and throughout an arrangement. By pinching the attack, I can make samples/sounds spring, rupture, or fade into my beats' arrangements. For me, this is important because I like to protect the spaces of the samples/sounds that I use. By that I mean, I make arrangements wherein the harsh parts do not drown out or slam the subtle and smooth parts.

Something to Keep in Mind

In addition to the definition of attack that I offered above, I also think of attack in the sense that it controls the value of fade at the beginning of a sound. Therefore, the higher the attack value (up from 0), the less presence (force, impact) that the head (front part) of a sound makes.

Effective Uses for "Pinching the Attack"

Pinching the Attack is a great method to use when the start point/front end of a sample has a harsh beginning, like a kick drum beneath the non-drum sounds. In a case like this (which is common, because you can't remove kicks from a sample that contains them), an increase of the attack value can affect the sample in a way that allows it to represent its tonal essence without having it's kick slamming with your own kicks and snares.

Why not just chop (truncate) more of the head of the sample? Well, I could do that, and whenever suitable, I do. But if I were to simply chop further into the start point, removing the part of the sample that has the kick in it, I lose part of the character of the sample's beginning. Pinching the Attack allows me to retain the character of the sample (or as much as substantially possible), while neutralizing the disrupting kick. Modifying the attack level to the needed value (it's different for each beat) allows me to hear exactly how much of the unwanted dynamic — in this case, the kick in the sample — fits with my beat's design.

Pinching the Attack is also a great method to use when you want to create the effect of multiple samples/sounds spliced together. Remember, also think of attack in the sense that it controls the value of fade at the beginning of a sound. Therefore, the higher the attack value (up from 0), the less presence (force, impact) that the head (front part) of a sound makes. Just as this understanding allows me to slam sounds together or rupture and cut them into an arrangement, it also allows me to create spliced effects as well.

Modifying the Sustain and the Decay and the Release

Modifying the sustain value allows you to affect how long you want the sustain — the main intensity of a sound — to carry on. Normally, I make very little adjustments to the sustain setting. In fact, I modify the sustain only when I want to do a quick fade of the tail (back end) of a sample/sound or when I want to fade the tail of one sample/sound out so that another sample/sound can be faded in or spliced. In conjunction with the sustain modification, I often tweak the decay when I want a sample/sound to fade out of a beat's arrangement.

I modify the release to help prevent a sample/sound with harsh tones (e.g. kicks, snares, peak points of bass parts, etc.) from slamming or distorting the drum pattern of the beat I'm composing. In other words, I always modify the release along with the sustain in ways that make the beat's elements mesh together and sound smoother.

Special Note

All of the modifications that I've described in this section are circumstantial ADSR modifications that I make of samples/sounds that are already part of an arrangement. Although these tweaks can be performed on stand-alone samples/sounds, i.e. sounds that are not yet incorporated into an arrangement, keep in mind that those samples/sounds will not sound the same as is, in their default state. For instance, you can increase the attack on a kick drum within a drum pattern, so as to decrease its punch/impact within a particular beat. But chances are, that kick drum, as a stand-alone sound with the tweaked attack, will sound thin and not much like a kick at all. This is why it's always important to know the default properties of your samples/sounds as well as the particular types of customizations, i.e. ADSR modifications, that work for your style and sound.

I should further point out that I view the processes that I've described in this section as an extension of the chopping process in beatmaking. Also, remember that different sample/sound spans (scopes) work best with different ADSR modifications. For instance, sound-stabs, 1-bar, 2-bar, and 4-bar sampled phrases will undoubtedly require different ADSR tweaks, depending on the drum patterns being used and the style and feel of the beat you're composing.

Document and Catalogue Your Development

Write down what you've improved on and/or struggled with each month. If you felt that you made a major leap in the level of your beatmaking, write it down. If you feel that there are areas of your beatmaking that are not developing as fast as you think that they should, document that. If you regularly preview your beats for rappers and other people, document the responses that your beats receive. By cataloging your development, you give yourself a great opportunity to reflect on your accomplishments *and* disappointments. In turn, this reflection ultimately helps your overall development as a beatmaker.

Study Music Books and/or Music Films and Documentaries

Read as much literature on music, electronic music production, and audio technology as you can. I specifically recommend that you read the biographies of acclaimed musicians, singers, songwriters, music producers, entertainers, and other music industry insiders. Reading about the experiences, the trials and triumphs, of these people can be very beneficial because it provides a wealth of information and valuable insight. This type of literature gives you a good indication of what it may take to reach your beatmaking goals, both creatively and professionally. Moreover, you will be able to more adequately gauge the stages of your own career and development.[141]

Guard Against Beat Block – Shifting Interest to Practice is Key

Beatmaking is a meticulous process, and needless to say, it can often get intense. Therefore, repeated extensive sessions of making beats will undoubtedly take its toll on a beatmaker. Plus, throw in dealing with life outside of music, and what we usually get is the infamous "beat block." So how *do you* deal with beat block when it happens? For me, I take an aggressive approach: I defend against even having beat block in the first place by actually factoring in routine breaks and "time outs" from making beats. When I didn't have a set plan or routine for making beats, I used to always run into beat block. But it was only after I shifted my scope to practicing was I able to conquer the beat block issue.

I elevated the process of practicing making beats above the notion of making beats itself. Instead of worrying about making beats, I concentrated on practicing making beats. That had a profound effect on my approach to (and efficiency in) making beats. By setting aside certain days and times specifically devoted to practicing making beats, the issue of beat block never arose again.

Decide on the Styles and Sounds That Are Right for You

Who's In Charge of Your Creativity?

Music, like any art, should never have to be, by default, a compromise. Nor should it be the act of catering to an abstract client or the perceived whims of the day. Aside from being an artist, a beatmaker is an independent music contractor who mostly creates work prior to being commissioned — we make beats, stash them, and when the opportunity arrives, we present an assortment

---

[141] One of the most helpful music books that I ever read was *Bob Marley* by Stephen Davis (Schenkman Books). Perhaps the two most insightful music films that I've ever seen are *Wild Style,* and *The Harder They Come*, starring Jimmy Cliff, directed by Perry Henzell (Xenon Entertainment Group).

of them to interested parties. In this context, a beatmaker has a tremendous amount of freedom in the choices he or she makes. This means that a beatmaker is free to choose and pursue individualized goals in everything from style and sound to quality and impact. Yet none of these goals need be tempered by the idea of simply catering to the desires of someone else. Moreover, in the current era, where a sold beat doesn't translate to "in-the-studio" work with the buyer, the purchased beat is sold as is, meaning that there was no creative direction given by the buyer.

First and foremost, you should make the music that pleases you. Focus on the style(s) and sound(s) that move you. Learn them, practice them, absorb them, and you will discover and develop your own unique way of interpreting them. And it is this interpretation, your own signature, that you should, by default, ultimately be after. Does this mean that you shouldn't make "the flavor of the month?" No. But it also doesn't mean that you should outright ignore those trends that genuinely interest you. Either way, beware of chasing trends for money. You might earn some money on someone else's terms, but you stand to earn a greater reputation and make money more consistently working from your own terms. Always remember: You can commission rappers for your own projects. Marley Marl, Large Professor, J Dilla, Marco Polo, Gensu Dean, just to name a few, have all had success with producer-based albums. You don't have to focus solely on selling beats or trying to land placements.

Whether you're a professional or hobbyist, you should be guided by the convictions of your imagination and talent as well as the scope of your true creative interests. Don't follow some arbitrary anticipation of what you think the commercial market bears. Instead, think in terms of the unique musical tapestries that you provide. Think in terms of your particular craftsmanship, not the unknown demands of someone else. This will help lead you towards making the music that you want. And if that music is consistent quality, you'll not only fulfill a creative commitment to yourself, you'll also be able to attract more listeners and buyers for your music, which can only grow demand for your style and sound.

Boom Bap Can't Die; It's in the DNA: If You're Planning on Abandoning Boom Bap Because You Think It's Less Viable, You May Want to Reconsider

Tripmaster, a regular BeatTips.com reader, left a great comment for me one day. In his comment, he mentioned a debate that he had with a friend regarding whether or not boom bap is dead. He argued, and rightfully so, that "boom bap will never die." Still, he also wondered if he was perhaps "out of place" for maintaining his connection to boom bap.

My mantra: Make the music you want! Every music form has its own tradition and sub-traditions, and it's up to each musician to determine what they will embrace. That being said, conformity, particularly the kind that leads one to simply abandon the core aesthetics of the tradition that they're working within, is also a choice.

You should never question yourself for adhering to styles, sounds, and principles that helped make hip hop/rap music the great tradition that it is. In the case of boom bap, in particular, the notion of it ever dying is counter intuitive. Boom bap is a concrete style and sound of hip hop/rap; it's not a fragile fad piggy-backing off of hip hop/rap. Boom bap, in its broader meaning, encompasses a distinct approach, similar to the ragtime (style) associated with jazz. But unlike the once popular ragtime, a style that is all but non-existent today, boom bap is so embedded into beatmaking's lexicon and hip hop's/rap's lyrical dimension that it can never die.

Although there are, and will continue to be, "off-shoots" of hip hop/rap music, these derivative styles will never overtake the fundamental styles and approaches of hip hop/rap. That we still honor particular rhymers and beatmakers, that new beatmakers and rhymers admittedly echo the sounds, styles, and approaches of beatmakers and rhymers from 20 years ago is something that speaks to the durability of hip hop/rap's core aesthetics. By comparison, it's worth noting that ragtime did not remain as a go-to style and form for 20 years; however, its chief practitioners, Jelly Roll Morton and Scott Joplin, continued to be revered by jazz musicians long after the form was displaced as a go-to style. Boom bap has not been displaced as a style and form of hip hop/rap; there are simply other (some new) styles and forms that beatmakers can choose from. Today, boom bap still exists as the chosen go-to style and form of 10s of thousands of beatmakers around the globe.

With regards to dubstep, trap, EDM, etc., I think they're all cool for what they are. (And just like with any style and sound, you can expect differences in quality.) But those styles and sounds are not mutually exclusive to boom bap; all can be enjoyed or fused with something. But the overall reach of dubstep or EDM isn't necessarily rooted in a hip ho/rap lineage. And while Dubstep and EDM rely mostly on the same electronic music production tools as boom bap (i.e. drum machines, samplers, turntables, etc.), they are a different beast altogether; each with its own direction, popularity, and lease on life. So a consideration of the death of boom bap, based on the fondness of the life of any other style or sound — hip hop/rap or otherwise — is misguided. Point is, boom bap, as an approach, outlook, stylized slant, is intertwined with hip hop's/rap's identity in a way that assures that it will be in use for as long as there is something known as hip hop/rap. In other words, boom bap is transcendent; no one era after the 1980s can contain it, but all can claim it.

Finally, remember this: The "mainstream" music climate says more about what the purported major media gatekeepers (on radio, broadcast television, print and online publications, etc.) and major record labels feel can safely be pushed and sold to the masses than it does about quality music, or what beatmaking styles and forms that are prioritized by beatmakers around the world. So make the music that you want, using the styles and forms that you want, in the way you want. If for you this means sticking with boom bap, go for it. You're in good company, and there's an audience that prefers it.

Should Beatmakers Listen to "Club Music" At All? Perhaps Not Doing So Is Akin to Production Malpractice

Even before hip hop/rap's current trap/club-pop driven mainstream music scene, DJs and beatmaking pioneers (most notably Marley Marl) made their names in radio by spinning the records that were popular in local clubs. But it should be noted that in this capacity, DJs are not only charged with giving the people what they want, they are also responsible for breaking (introducing) new records to the masses and/or leading the people, if you will. Therefore, beatmakers (the direct descendents of DJs) who outright dismiss all contemporary popular themes and/or the popular mood and tastes of the time, are perhaps ignoring one of their fundamental responsibilities: To survey both historical and contemporary trends in music.

Now of course, I'm certainly not advocating that beatmakers should make an immediate mass exodus towards the typical contemporary radio-style music (i.e. the cliché club-pop sound aesthetic). On the contrary, I'm making the point that by ignoring the ethos of popularity, on perhaps its most dominant level, a beatmaker runs the risk of missing the opportunity to get the pulse for what's happening now all across the music landscape. And without a pulse on what's happening now, a beatmaker is subject to fail in the prospect of combining some of the best historical elements of hip hop/rap music with some of the best elements of current trends. If a beatmaker can't reconcile some of the most important elements of hip hop/rap music and beatmaking of the past with some of the most important elements of the present, they will be less likely to come up with any "new" style or distinguishable sound.

Point is, just as most quality beatmakers study the beats of other quality beatmakers, it's also important for beatmakers to at least audit (survey and listen to) some of the most celebrated hip hop/rap music of the past as well as those musical developments that are generating the most buzz at any given moment in the present. And this audit should not be carried out just to see if the music is good or bad, but rather to determine exactly what sort of musical components that average music listeners are and are not strongly responding to. By doing such audits, you're in a better position to change those things that you may deem to be wack, as opposed to simply turning your back to the problem and offering no solutions.

Versatility Is Cool, as Long as It's Within Your Own Style and Sound: No Matter How Broad Your Beatmaking Range, Your Individuality Is Still Key

When it comes to the concept of versatility in beatmaking, there are two widely held notions: (1) multiple-style versatility; and (2) single-style versatility. Multiple-style versatility describes the ability of a beatmaker to make beats in a variety of common styles and sounds, using applicable beatmaking methods and processes. Single-style versatility refers to a beatmaker's ability to create style variation within one set style and sound.

Both multiple-style versatility and single-style versatility have their advantages and their disadvantages. Having multiple-style versatility means that a beatmaker has a broad understanding of and unique sensibility for the common hip hop/rap production styles and sounds. The advantage here is that a beatmaker who possesses multiple-style versatility is likely to have knowledge of a higher number of beatmaking techniques. Having single-style versatility means that a beatmaker has a broad understanding of and unique sensibility for one specific beatmaking style and sound. The advantage here is that a beatmmaker who holds single-style versatility is likely to have an increased comprehension of the intricate nuances that underscore the single style and sound that he makes.

Presumably, multiple-style versatility presents a beatmaker with the best opportunity for the most placement opportunities. On the surface, the more style versatility that a beatmaker has, the more valuable he will always be, right?

Well, not necessarily. Although some beatmakers (producers) like DJ Toomp, Kanye West, and DJ Khalil, have benefited (and continue to benefit) from multiple-style versatility, many beatmakers don't. Why? Because most rappers and A&Rs (prospective beat buyers) have traditionally sought out beatmakers (producers) for their specific style and sound. When rappers look for beats, they are typically not looking for one beatmaker who can do six different beat styles. Instead, rappers are more likely to reach out to particular beatmakers for their particular styles and sounds. For instance, no one ever sought out The Neptunes for soulful sample-based beats. Likewise, no one ever sought out DJ Premier for keyboard beats. If the beatmaker (producer) who's sought out happens to have range and versatility, that's a huge plus, depending on what the rapper or singer is looking for.

As for single-style versatility, perhaps the biggest disadvantage is the fact that no one style and sound is always in demand. For instance, if trap is hugely popular, then a hardcore or East Coast sound will likely not be in as much demand. Therefore, beatmakers who only possess single-style versatility can run the risk of being on the outside of current trends. But given some contemporary trends like ultra-minimalist beats, being on the outside isn't such a bad thing. That said, how versatile a beatmaker can be within a given style and sound will determine how much demand they can create for themselves. For instance, Marco Polo, who's primarily a sample-based beatmaker (producer) has continued to expand his sound without giving up his feel or style. Thus, the way in which you practice your versatility can go a long way in your overall development.

Warning About Multiple-Versatility

If you do decide to go the multiple-versatility route, then be careful not to try and master too many styles and sounds. Thing is, beatmaking is not exactly like martial arts. That is to say, there isn't necessarily a premium on mastering multiple styles. While a martial artist certainly benefits from mastering let's say, Judo, Samurai sword fighting, and Tae Kwon Do, a beatmaker will not automatically benefit from mastering the East Coast style, the West Coast style, and the Southern Rap style. Don't get me wrong, knowledge of multiple beatmaking styles and sounds will enhance your understanding of the art of beatmaking, and it will likely help you develop a higher beatmaking skill-set. However, with multiple-versatility, there's always the risk that you may not ever develop your own distinct sound, but rather a mish-mash of common sounds. And a beatmaker who doesn't have his own unique style and sound is less likely to stand out and, subsequently, less likely to have any sustainable success. This is why I recommend that you practice and work within those styles and sounds that genuinely appeal to you.

Mainstream, High-Concept Approach to Beatmaking Scuttles Hip Hop: Creative Appeasement Undermines Hip Hop's Core Focus on Style and Originality; Beatmakers Better Served by Less Compromising

Under the guise of mainstream demands (or perhaps mainstream aspirations), some beatmakers ignore the core aesthetic preferences and characteristics of beatmaking, aiming instead to use compositional styles that they believe will accommodate the greatest number of listeners. This mainstream strategy, or rather "high concept" approach to beatmaking, which in and of itself isn't inherently a bad thing, often leads to a cycle of mediocrity, or perhaps better stated, pseudo-hip hop/rap music.

On one hand, this cycle of watered-down hip hop/rap music appeases the consumption demands of club-going and less-scrutinizing pop masses. But on the other hand, by offering up a false dominant hip hop/rap ideology, this grade — perhaps lower or just different, depending on your perspective or vested interest — of hip hop/rap music works to mis-inform people about hip hop/rap music and the encompassing hip hop culture. Unfortunately, this often carries with it the side-effect of undermining the efforts of those hip hop/rap music makers who seek to represent a more balanced composite of what hip hop/rap music has to offer.

While hip hop culture's fundamental ideology has in many ways (and for many reasons, far too many to analyze here) moved into the mainstream, it still remains in its original sub-culture context. And this cultural duality inevitably affects how individual beatmakers approach music concepts such as rhythm, melody, form, texture, theme, scope, feel, arrangement, etc. A fact that's illuminated even more when you consider how individual interests and tastes, as well as class and ethnic backgrounds, manifest themselves in particular notions of creativity and originality. But should mainstream considerations, or perhaps even what is or should be considered mainstream, be privileged more than the basic concept of one's own sense of creativity?

Aside from the aforementioned benefits of a high concept approach to beatmaking, the dangers of such creative appeasement (or unreasonable compromise) are many. But the most pressing concerns that I have are threefold. First, as I mentioned earlier, the act of favoring a mainstream approach to beatmaking over valuing the core/fundamental aesthetic concepts, principles, and priorities of the beatmaking tradition often leads to a cycle of mediocrity, which yields pseudo-hip hop/rap music. In turn, this pseudo form of hip hop/rap music establishes — and simultaneously reinforces — a false dominant hip hop/rap ideology, an ideology that in many ways downgrades or ignores some of the most important tenets of hip hop/rap music and the broader hip hop culture.

Second, this creation of and deference to a false dominant hip hop/rap ideology strangles creativity and undermines hip hop culture's fundamental focus on and notion of style and originality. When this happens, a disconnect is created between the music and the culture that spawned and nurtures it. As a result, much of the nuance, formal and informal elements, and sensibility that makes up hip hop/rap music dissolves, damaging, perhaps irrevocably, the entire music tradition.

My third concern with the mainstream, high concept approach to beatmaking deals with how creative appeasement (at this alarming level) diminishes the overall value and power of hip hop/rap music in contemporary music culture. When hip hop/rap music is watered down, it loses its bite, weight, and overall affect. And although hip hop/rap currently enjoys a hefty influence over contemporary music, what will be the level of this influence in the future? Even more pressing, who will be the beatmakers most responsible for maintaining this influence as well as moving hip hop/rap music forward? Does this mean that future beatmakers — co-leaders and gatekeepers of the hip hop/rap tradition — will be urban pop sympathizers, who are mostly ashamed to even use the "beatmaker" moniker? Does it mean that future beatmakers will be those who merely dabble in something that, at best, echoes hip hop/rap music?

In retrospect, over the past 25 years, most of hip hop/rap's biggest mainstream successes did not come about due to beatmakers having a subdued sense of style and originality, or a warped deference to mainstream compositional conformity. On the contrary, in the period between the early 1980s and mid-1990s, the period wherein the beatmaking tradition witnessed (absorbed) its most formal strides, it was pioneering beatmakers, not an abstract mainstream, who dictated compositional style and direction.

This is not a simple commentary on, or an exhausted, romantically nostalgic look at, the mid/late1980s and 1990s eras of hip hop/rap music. Sure, there were classics in the '80s and '90s, many of which were rightfully added to the canon of hip hop/rap music. But I also recognize that there were a great deal of absolute duds and disturbingly poor knock-offs of hits during these eras as well. So I'm not hypnotized by hip hop/rap's past golden eras (ca. 1973-79; and ca. 1988-95). Instead, I value, embrace, and revere the foundations of hip hop/rap music, particularly its beatmaking tradition and the developments that have occurred within the aforementioned periods. That being said, I'm also deeply concerned about the current era of hip hop/rap music, specifically the beatmaking tradition, as well as future eras to come.

Therefore, within this context, my focus is narrowed to the compositional choices of those beatmakers most responsible for the classic (well received, "mainstream")material of both of those heralded eras of hip hop/rap music. In each of those golden eras, you find many (nearly all) beatmakers helping to shape and define what mainstream hip hop/rap is, rather than seeking to be shaped or defined by it. Today, however, there seems to be far more beatmakers actively aiming to be defined by a hip hop/rap mainstream (one that currently is woefully unbalanced) than there are those seeking to help rehabilitate and/or continuously redefine it.

Finally, it should be remembered that the ubiquitous hip hop/rap underground emerged as a response to a burgeoning hip hop/rap mainstream that increasingly grew unbalanced. Prior to, let's say, 1990, the line between what could be considered underground or mainstream hip hop/rap music was blurry. Or another way of looking at it: The hip hop/rap mainstream was more balanced. So will mainstream hip hop/rap music ever contain the level of balance that it once did? Perhaps not. But I believe if it does, it will be because of the help of those beatmakers who utilize the core aesthetic preferences and characteristics of beatmaking for their compositional style and direction, rather than take dictation from abstract mainstream demands.

MusicStudy
The #1 Ingredient and Form of Practice for Quality Beatmaking and All Music-Making

MusicStudy is the most important form of practice for all musicians. Because practice is one of the most vital factor's to our individual development, I believe that before you can even begin to really understand the whole craft of beatmaking, you must first develop a respectable knowledge and appreciation of music and music history. Whether you favor soul, rock, or hip hop/rap, you should possess a respectable knowledge of music in general. A familiarity with the basic kinds and forms of music, in particular the *gateway* music traditions and forms, can only have a considerably good effect on your development as a beatmaker.

When considering hip hop/rap music, the four music traditions — within the grand African American (Black) music tradition — that are the most hard to ignore are: the blues, jazz, soul, and funk. Familiarizing yourself with the blues, jazz, and soul will increase your appreciation for and improve your knowledge of music history. It will also enhance your overall grasp of contemporary music, and this will undoubtedly help make you a better beatmaker.

If your knowledge of American music history is shaky, I recommend that you take a one-month sabbatical away from the contemporary music scene. Just block out the radio *(if you already haven't)*. Don't tune into any music videos, don't listen to your heavy rotation music, just take a break from all of that and research the blues, jazz, and soul. After you've secured great examples of the blues, jazz, and soul, set aside at least one full practice session a week for MusicStudy. Dedicate that session to listening to music from at least one of the aforementioned music traditions. Once you've familiarized yourself with each one of these music forms, start taking detailed notes. When you move from one tradition to the next, you will naturally begin to draw comparisons and see patterns, and there, it becomes important to actually write those comparisons patterns down. Below, I've included a number of comparisons or patterns to look for and characterize:

- In a typical blues song, how many bars do you hear before the first change?
- Are there frequent melody changes in blues?
- Does the blues rely more on rhythm or melody?
- Do you notice how the blues is based on bent pitch levels and emotional vocals?
- Do you notice the vocal phrasing connection between the blues and soul?
- In jazz, how significant is the drummer's timing?
- In jazz, what other time signatures, other than 4/4, are routinely used?
- Do you see how a combination of the blues, jazz, rhythm and blues, and soul lead to funk? Specifically, do you see how funk grew directly from soul?
- Is the bass thick or somewhat flat in jazz?

- Are there frequent melody changes in Jazz?
- In blues, jazz, and soul, what role does repetition play?
- Does soul sound more rooted in jazz or blues and why?
- How did starting on "the 1" in funk revolutionize soul music?
- Why are the lyrics in soul songs so urgent and real?

Making meticulous observations like these, then writing your findings down, will give you the extra edge that the overwhelming majority of beatmakers will never have. Once you've gained a respectable understanding of the blues, jazz, and soul, continue to have regular MusicStudy practice sessions. But it's a good idea to include music from other genres as well (and remember to continue to take notes on those comparisons as well).

After your one-month sabbatical from the contemporary music scene is over, go back (albeit slowly) and listen. Then ask yourself this question. How well does the current music scene hold up against music from the past 30 to 50 years? Is the quality the same? Is the appeal the same? Are there any comparable or parallel developments, patterns, or trends? Are lyrics more poignant now than they were then? Are there any recurring themes?[142] By these questions, I'm not saying that all good music is behind us; nor am I advocating that anyone should be stuck in the past. Here, my point is that music is a *continuum* — it's a continuing process that utilizes the fundamentals of previous traditions to either prolong specific tropes of those traditions, or to create new music traditions altogether. Moreover, by "continuum" I mean that music is a revolving, recyclable activity wherein quality is found, again and again, through both a subconscious and conscious emulation of, and a sincere study and appreciation for, the music that came before.[143]

Studying Beatmakers (Well-Known and Otherwise)

When it comes to studying well-known beatmakers, stick to the beatmaking style that you *feel* the most. After that, then consider these factors. What style of beatmaking do you favor the most, the sample-based, synthetic-sounds-based,

---

[142] Consider this: There are entire libraries and museums (funded both by wealthy philanthropists and the United States government) that are named for and devoted exclusively to the study of particular American musicians and singers such as Louis Armstrong and Duke Ellington. Furthermore, artists like Curtis Mayfield, Aretha Franklin, Donny Hathaway, The Delfonics, and The O'Jays were inspiration for each other. Fortunately, they will continue to be inspiration for those beatmakers and other recording artists that have an aim for that level of quality music.

[143] The neglect of, or in many cases the lack of respect for, the music and level of quality that came before is in many ways responsible for the "sound-a-like," downward trends in 2010s hip hop/rap music.

or hybrid style? If you like the sample-based style, then you should more often than not study beatmakers that use that compositional style. Don't get me wrong. Studying beatmakers that feature the synthetic-sounds-based style won't hurt you. But you'll be hard pressed to match or surpass their sound if you do not intend to incorporate that style into your *own* beatmaking approach.

Regardless of your approach, I do recommend that you more aggressively study all three of the primary compositional styles of beatmaking by beatmakers that you respect and admire. But in the early beatmaking stages, you should primarily study the beatmakers that create the kind of beats and music that you *want* to make, as well as those who incorpoate the methods that you envision yourself using. So if you are into the sample-based style, your focus should be on those beatmakers that use the kind of samples and arrangements that you favor. Study how sample-based pros incorporate samples into their programming. Do they feature it, do they use it sparingly? Do they simply snatch large complete-phrases and loop them, or do they borrow sections from arcane (rare and/or obscure) records? Each sample-based beatmaker uses samples to a different degree. Some use wide open, easily identifiable sample material (well-known records), while some cleverly chop up samples into pieces that reserve the original feel of the initial sample material, without actually revealing the identity of the sample source. And if you're into the synthetic-sounds-based style, study how the beatmakers of that style actually *use* synthetic-sounds within their approach to beatmaking. Do they employ simple, two-finger key-strikes, or easily predictable, re-worked sound patterns? Do they use complex chord arrangements, indicative of someone who's professionally trained or self-taught to play the keyboard? Do they *play* the keyboard at all, or do they use an alternative technique like the "anchor technique" I discussed earlier?

Emulation

Here, I want to stress that the idea is not to *copy* another beatmaker. NEVER COPY another beatmaker's style or sound; it will ultimately leave you creatively bankrupt. However, in your early stages of beatmaking, you will undoubtedly try to *emulate* the beatmakers that you favor. And perahps in the beginning, you should! It's a natural part of the development process for all artists. In every artistic or creative medium, especially music, emulation always takes place. And in hip hop/rap music, the most well-known beatmakers are consistently emulated. Everything from their format, approach, technique, style, sound, and their choice of EMPIs is mirrored.

Every beatmaker has borrowed a piece of some other beatmaker's sound, approach, style, method and/or technique. No beatmaker is an island unto himself — no beatmaker is completely influenced by their ideas alone. For instance, look at the late 1980s/early 1990s. Once Marley Marl began sampling James Brown records and the like, pretty much every other beatmaker of that era began exploring the same avenues. This is not to say that most skilled beatmakers are *biters* or trend-followers; on the contrary, I would argue that the most effective beatmakers are trend*setters*. But you have to examine this more closely.

In order for a beatmaker to be a trendsetter, they have to first be able to incorporate both past and current trends (to some degree). Likewise, in order for a beatmaker to develop his own skill and style, he or she must be able to access and incorporate the developments, pioneering techniques, and/or inventions advanced by both those beatmakers who came before them and those who currently stand out.

The more skilled — and the more critically acclaimed and financially compensated — beatmakers are masters at borrowing what they admire, then incorporating it into their individual approach to beatmaking. Hence, there is nothing wrong with taking your initial lead from the beatmakers that you admire. Remember, every accomplished recording artist (within *all* twentieth-century American popular music traditions) got their initial lead from someone else. And as with any art-craft, you build your own unique style and presence by first using the tools and techniques of the experts you admire.

Finally, it's worth noting that most (if not all) beatmakers get their cue, initially at least, from other beatmakers (their styles and sounds) that they like. Then, through our own unique discoveries, observations, and developments, we strive to take it to another level. From there, we create our own style and sound; ideally, a style and sound that is considerably distinguishable from where we first got our cues.

Understanding Musical Boundaries and Borders

Hip hop/rap music is truly capable of transcending all musical borders. Even still, it's important to know and respect the boundaries and borders of the main traditions of twentieth-century American popular music. To that end, it should first be understood that boundaries are not rigid barriers. The boundaries of a given music tradition are the well-understood (conspicuous) aesthetic, procedural, and emotional parameters of that given tradition. In all cases, these parameters, which define a given tradition, must first and foremost be upheld. This doesn't mean that these parameters can't be *explored*. They can, and in certain cases they should be. Experimentation with other music forms and the styles that they possess can stretch the boundaries of a given tradition. But it should also be understood that when the boundaries of a given music tradition are *pushed and stretched*, the music can go somewhere "else." Thus a proper understanding of musical boundaries means recognizing the fact that when this occurs, that is, when the "else" emerges, the new music, if it can sustain itself, should be recognized as its own thing, liked or disliked on its own merits.

Every music genre has its own tradition — its own sound, its own pioneers and auteurs, its own aesthetics, principles, methods, ideologies, priorities, and predilections; and thus its own set boundaries. If they didn't have clear and often well-defined boundaries, how could anyone determine or describe one music tradition from the next? Crunk, trap music, hyphy, chop n' screw, West Coast, and East Coast are all hip hop/rap because each style (sub-tradition) resides *within* the boundaries of hip hop's tradition. On the other hand, techno, electro, drum and bass, house, jungle beat are NOT hip hop/rap. Even though each borrows from and shares some similarities with the hip hop/rap tradition (specifically, the beatmaking tradition), they do not reside *within* the boundaries of the hip hop/rap tradition. So, it must be clear: Every music tradition is determined first and foremost by the boundaries that encompass it.

But even though these boundaries are fixed, can they be explored, even pushed? Yes, absolutely. Bob Marley infused black American soul and traditional African rhythm arrangements into his unique style of reggae, clearly pushing the boundaries of the reggae traditions (and later within the broader West African traditions). Yet throughout his career, Bob Marley was deliberately careful to work from *within* the boundaries of the reggae and broader Jamaican music traditions. But the vast body of his work comprises a *reggae* composite, not a world beat template. And consider classic rockers Led Zeppelin. They pushed the boundaries of late '60s rock 'n' roll perhaps to its brink. Their music was conspicuously underscored — instrumentally and lyrically — by the blues (Mississippi-Delta) tradition, yet they deliberately worked *within* the then established rock 'n' roll tradition. John Coltrane and Ornette Coleman pushed the boundaries of jazz and helped to develop a new style and form of jazz commonly known as "free jazz." But Coltrane and Coleman both worked well *within* the jazz tradition. Certainly no one today could confuse what they did with the rock 'n' roll of Led Zeppelin or the reggae of Bob Marley.

The boundaries of any musical tradition can and should be explored and pushed. But once a practitioner of a musical tradition firmly exceeds (goes beyond) the boundaries of said tradition, they must concede that they are no longer working from within the boundaries of that tradition. They must at least acknowledge, or at best embrace, the fact that they are entering into a new space, and that they are developing a new musical tradition, one who's proximity is fixed well outside of the tradition it began in. When this occurs, it becomes necessary that the *new* tradition become recognized and appropriately labeled, for risk of neutralizing and further diluting the integrity of the base tradition from which it was spawned.

The analogy that perhaps works best is the relationship that states have with other states and nations, in particular those that each shares borders with. That is, music traditions are like individual states (or nations). Each state has its own methods and nuances, and each state borders another. When one journeys out of the center (or heart) of the state and then on past the borders of the state, they are no longer in the state from which they began their journey. This is not a critique of anyone who presumably wants to push or challenge the boundaries of hip hop/rap, it's just a fact. Rhythm and blues and rock 'n' roll share a distinct lineage to the grand blues tradition, yet each were spawned from different sub-traditions of the blues. Rhythm and blues grew from a gospel/blues hybrid, whereas rock 'n' roll sprouted up from boogie woogie, rhythm and blues, country, and rockabilly — all spawns of the broader blues tradition.

Song Structure: Shared Music Boundaries

In some cases, the boundaries of one tradition will overlap with the boundaries of other musical traditions, such is the case with song structure in twentieth-century American popular music. Here, I should note that song structure is simply a platform that can be used for all popular music traditions in America. For example, on his version of "By the Time I Get to Phoenix," Isaac Hayes worked well within the parameters of the standard American song structure. The fact that he extended the length of the song (a practice and tradition long upheld in his and other artists' live shows) was simply his unique arrangement and an extension and attempt to recreate a live feel in the studio. Isaac Hayes didn't throw song structure out the window, he worked well *within* it. Thus, again, song structure serves as a basis from which all musicians work when they create songs. This structure can be reversed, re-arranged, minimized, and/or extended, but it can not be *abandoned*, otherwise there wouldn't be a song. This is why song structure is one of the most clearly shared boundaries in all of twentieth-century popular music.

Again, every art form has its own clearly defined fundamental (paramount) components and some marginal components. No one individual can redefine an art form that is already clearly defined and set. Once individuals innovate within it, and once that innovation takes hold and goes in a different direction, then the result is something new, perhaps a new *dimension* of the tradition, or even a new tradition altogether. This doesn't mean that it's bad, good, better, or worse; it's simply *new*. There were some distinct innovations made within the blues traditions, which begot rhythm and blues, which begot soul. And of course, there were some innovations made within soul, which begot funk.

BeatTip – MusicStudy: How Elvis Helped Me Become a Better Beatmaker: Homage to Black American Music Tradition, Part of the Secret to Elvis' Success

For the better part of the last 15 years, I've encountered people who either adore Elvis or hate him. This has always struck me as an odd scheme of understanding. I mean, how and why can one individual cause so much polarization? Of course, you never hear anyone say (publicly at least) that they hate The Beatles. And Michael Jackson's *Thriller*, one of the greatest selling albums of all time, still draws strong favorable consensus. So what is it about Elvis that causes such disdain, especially among purveyors of hip hop/rap music?

Maybe it's because Chuck D declared him a racist two decades ago. Remember the Public Enemy song "Fight the Power," where Chuck D rhymes, "Elvis was a hero to most/But he never meant shit to me you see Straight up racist that sucker was simple and plain..." Or perhaps the disdain for Elvis by some in hip hop/rap stems from the misperception of Elvis as a culture vulture who stole his sound from black American musicians in the Mississippi Delta. But that's a bogus argument even on the face of it. Lest one forgets (or doesn't know), Elvis is from the Mississippi Delta. Therefore, he has as much a native claim to any and all musical developments that occurred there as anyone else who was born and raised in that region. Moreover, it's been widely reported that the teenage Elvis spent considerable time taking in the blues scene of Memphis' Beale Street. Add to that the fact that he grew up listening to the regional radio stations like Memphis' WDIA, the nation's first radio station to feature an all-black format and on-air staff (1949). (Stations like WDIA played what was then known as "race records".) So by all serious accounts, it's obvious what Elvis' early musical influences were: blues, gospel, rhythm and blues, and rockabilly; all components of the Black American music tradition. Thus these early musical influences from the Black American Music Tradition were largely a part of Elvis' success.

So when hip hop/rap aficionados (or any other group) reject Elvis, they are actually rejecting a musical icon who earned his stripes through the serious study of the musical tradition that laid the foundation for all American popular music in the twentieth century. Moreover, those who reject Elvis's musical validity also, in effect, turn their backs on the musical scholarship that he provides. Every musical artist is a gateway to others, and the more critically acclaimed the artist is, the more enriched the gateway is.

By listening to and studying Elvis, I was prompted to listen to and study Big Joe Turner, the iconic bluesman who helped create the template for rock 'n' roll. Perhaps I would have studied Big Joe Turner even if I didn't take a more serious look at Elvis. But listening to Elvis' earlier work prompted me to compare his style to Big Joe Turner's style. MusicStudy of this nature has been and remains important to an understanding of all music, not just hip hop/rap music.

Certainly, Elvis doesn't need any marketing help; you don't get much higher than him in the scheme of American pop culture. And there's no doubt that his career benefited tremendously from the fact that he was white. Many of the Black artists that influenced him could never access the platform that he was afforded, or gain anywhere near the same level of popularity or financial success that he obtained. But Elvis, who I at one time refused to listen to, does represent the complexity and beauty of how music traditions and cultures can, at times, transcend negative racial attitudes. But all of this aside, "What can his music teach or do for me," I once asked myself. Well, it taught me a lot, and it did more for me than I could have imagined. Ironically (or perhaps not), through an honest MusicStudy of Elvis, I discovered Sister Rosetta Tharpe; I became more interested in Big Joe Turner and B.B. King; I meticulously traced the business roots of rock 'n' roll, and I became even more aware of the importance of rhythm in American popular music.

Bottom line: If you're going to contribute to any music tradition or culture, if you're going to go after a career in music, the more musical understanding that you can draw from, the more enriched your own music will be and, subsequently, the better your chances at having a career in music.

NOTE: here are a couple songs worth giving the MusicStudy treatment to:

- Elvis Presley – "Shake, Rattle and Roll" (Elvis's first televised appearance.) "Shake, Rattle and Roll" was originally recorded by Big Joe Turner.

- Big Joe Turner – "Shake, Rattle and Roll"
This is the original recording of "Shake, Rattle and Roll."

- Elvis Presley – "Heartbreak Hotel"
The song is unmistakably blues.

- Sister Rosetta Tharpe – "Didn't Rain"
Sister Rosetta Tharpe had a seminal influence on Elvis.
Elvis Presley – "A Little Less Conversation." Although it's from Elvis' later catalog, it's my favorite Elvis recording. If you know Mack Davis (singer-songwriter), you can hear him in the lyrics. Also, peep the drumwork at the intro of the song.

BeatTip – MusicStudy: Johnny Pate's "Bucktown" and the Drum Lessons of Soul, Funk, and Disco: To Understand Key Elements of the Drums in Soul, Funk, and Disco, It's Important to Be Familiar with those Music Forms

While many beatmakers might be aware of the connection between hip hop/rap and soul, funk, and disco, it's not always so clear to see, or better yet to hear, exactly how soul/funk set the foundation for hip hop/rap music and beatmaking. Within the overall rhythmic influences of these musics lies the most glaring connection: the drums.

Johnny Pate's "Bucktown (Main Theme)" a song from the 1975 film *Bucktown* is a great song for studying drums. This song straddles soul, funk, and disco all at once — a sound that, in 1975, sat as a unique mix of the three music forms right before the complete onslaught of disco. For the purposes of better understanding this style of drumming, with this song what you want to focus your attention on is the drum framework, which you can hear best between the 0:17 - 0:49 marks. You will notice that if it were just the drums playing, most people now would describe it as a hip hop/rap drum beat. And therein lies the point.

Which brings me to this: I receive a number of emails and private messages in The BeatTips Community (TBC) from people concerned about making their drums "funky," "funkier," or "more soulful." Invariably, I always ask, "Are you listening to any funk or soul?" In every case that I've replied back with this question, the answer has always been the same: "No." Further, in every case, the answer has also included this statement: "I want my drums to sound like..." Usually, it's the same — DJ Premier, Pete Rock, RZA, J Dilla, and so on.

Imagine wanting to talk (sound) like a supreme court justice or a successful corporate lawyer without ever studying law — its theory or philosophy. Although the art of beatmaking and making music in general is altogether a different practice and culture, I find it just as ludicrous to want to make "funky" or "soulful" drums without ever studying or listening to funk or soul music. When someone says that they want to make drums that sound like some of beatmaking's most notable pioneers, I get it. For many, it's just a reference point for the style and sound that they like; it's the zone in which they'd like to work in. Understandable. But what's usually lost in this oft-repeated statement is the fact that all of beatmaking's notable pioneers, prior to the early 200s, studied and listened to funk, soul, and disco. Though each pioneer ultimately emerged with their own unique style and sound (of course, they are all collectively representative of the same fundamental understanding), they did not arrive without clear guidelines from funk, soul, and disco drum arrangements. But beatmaking pioneers notwithstanding, it's misleading to believe that one can understand how to inject soul music's influence into their beats or make something funkier or add a disco backbeat, while being completely unfamiliar with soul, funk, or disco. How can one know to include key elements and stylings of musics that they've never listened to before? Such a prospect is so fundamentally flawed that it can produce a false sense of musical understanding — something that can certainly disrupt the development of any beatmaker.

And while some beatmakers can perhaps clone a DJ Premier or Pete Rock drum pattern, this type of mimicry does not serve as a substitute for the original thing. For one, obviously mimicked styles and sounds stand as clear and unabashed cheap knock-offs of someone else, just mere shells of ideas without the essence or subtle nuances of the original creators. But worse, this form of mimicry mostly exists devoid of the caliber of knowledge, understanding, and general music appreciation that produced the original benchmarks.

This is why it's important that beatmakers not lose a sense of the fundamental connection that hip hop/rap music and the art of beatmaking has with soul, funk, and disco, especially when it comes to the drums. With a strong sense of this connection, your production repertoire, no matter how varied, will always retain its link to hip hop/rap's foundational elements.

Part 3
MUSIC TRADITION, CULTURE, AND THEORY

Music Theories and Hip Hop/Rap Music, and the Cultural Metrics that Comprise the Hip Hop/Rap Music and Beatmaking Traditions

The power of music is that it always celebrates the commonalities of mankind. Yet we can not accurately decipher and highlight these commonalities if we examine any music tradition from an improper context. Therefore, to truly understand the nuances, priorities, and other fundamental elements of the hip hop/rap and beatmaking traditions, we must always be mindful of its place squarely within the broader African American (Black) music tradition. By examining the hip hop/rap music tradition from within the framework of both its parent tradition, the African American (Black) music tradition, and its own distinct tradition, my aim is not to insist and/or imply that hip hop/rap music is a tradition wholly owned by any one racial or ethnic group. Having already thoroughly discussed the origins of hip hop/rap music and the subsequent development of the beatmaking tradition, it's clear that hip hop, despite or because of its origins, became the most inclusive music tradition and culture of the twentieth-century. Therefore, my goal in this part of this study is to carefully, accurately, and more extensively explore the existence of the hip hop/rap music tradition within the context of both its immediate and somewhat distant musical ancestry. Moreover, my purpose is to show how this existence plays a role in hip hop/rap's place in twentieth-century American popular music.

Further, one of the main purposes of this Part is to help beatmakers gain a better grasp of the nuances of the hip hop/rap music and beatmaking traditions. Just as a keener understanding of the origins of hip hop/rap music can lead to better beatmaking, an enhanced understanding of the nuances of the hip hop/rap and beatmaking traditions also directly correlates to a beatmaker's ability to make higher quality beats.

Finally, in keeping with my commitment to make this study a "gateway book" to more MusicStudy, I have also included the following chapter to explore how hip hop/rap traditions often inform popular culture. Also, it is my hope that the discussions that follow will motivate readers to explore (in greater detail) many of the concepts, notions, and ideas that this part (as with all parts of this study) raises.

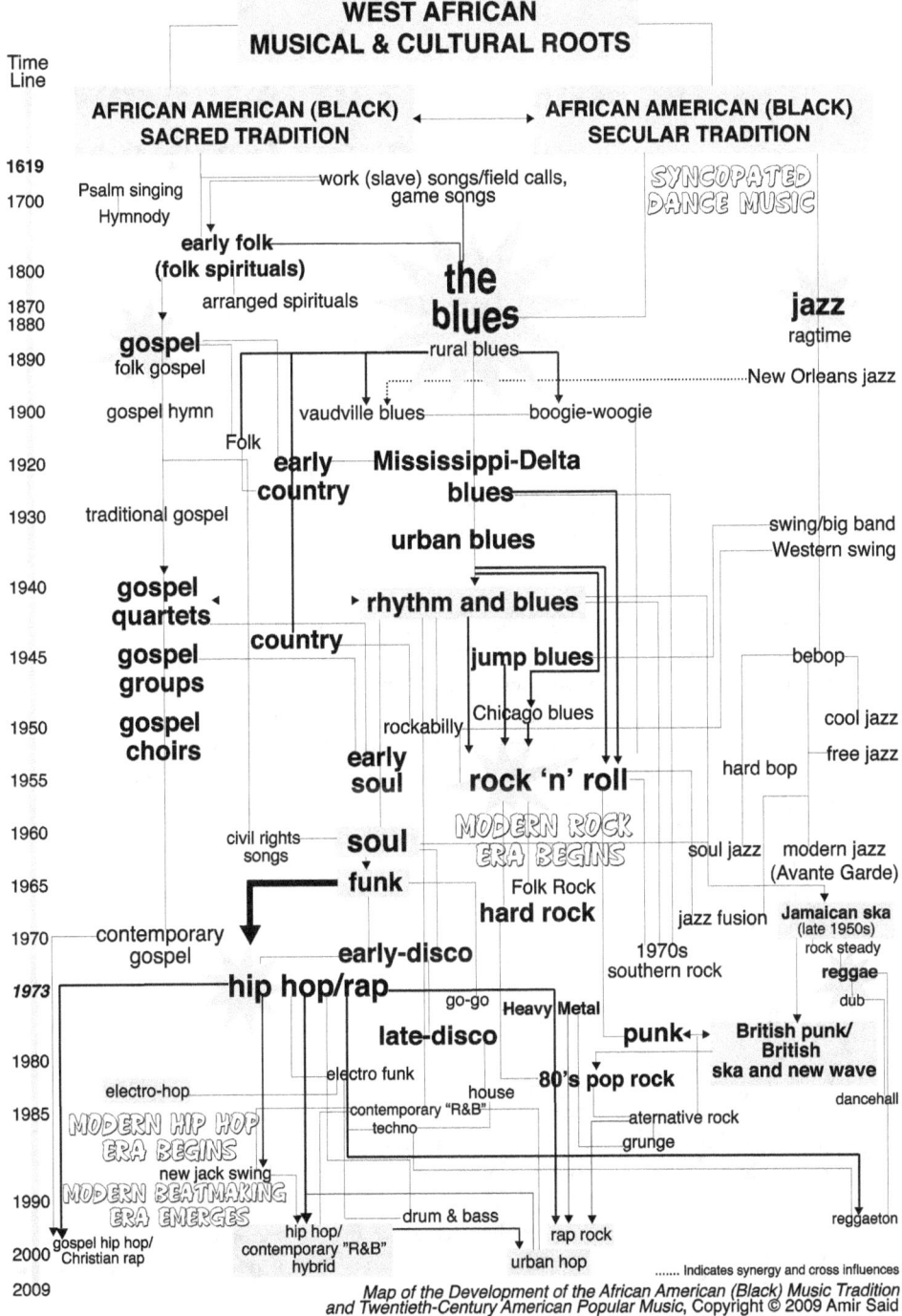

Figure 11 Map of the Development of the African (Black) Music Tradition

Chapter 10

Flash Battled Mozart at the Fever, and Mozart Got Burned
The Hip Hop/Rap Music and Beatmaking Traditions, Its Theory, and How It Does and Doesn't Jive with the Western Classical Music Tradition and Its Theory

In the field of music, perhaps more than in any other field, the black man's pre-eminence was acknowledged by the nation…His contributions not only made a decisive impact on the existing style of music in the western tradition, but also gave birth to a new style of music. –Eileen Southern

Much African music features rhythmic patterns that make it sound almost childishly simple, but since nobody is called upon to write them down or read them the music is labeled "primitive." –Christopher Small, *Music, Society, Education*

Leonard Bernstein spent several summers staging operettas with friends, foreshadowing his great interest in theater. During the summer of 1934, for example, they staged a version of Bizet's *Carmen* with sexes reversed in the roles and lyrics full of local jokes. In the fall of 1935 he entered Harvard, where he majored in music, and began piano instruction with one of Boston's finest teachers, Heinrich Gebhard. His teachers at Harvard included Edward Burlingame Hill for orchestration, A. Tillman Merritt for harmony and counterpoint, and Walter Piston for counterpoint and fugue. Another professor who influenced Bernstein was David Prall of the philosophy department.
–Paul R. Laird

When I knew him, Jelly still had a whorehouse complex—sang dirty songs and thought they were great. I remember inviting him to dinner one evening after a rehearsal or recording date and having him decline because he had two suckers waiting for him down the street. He was a shark all right! Often he and I used to rehearse together at the Melrose office. Morton was a tremendous worker. If he was working on something, he would sit there for four or five hours at a stretch.
–Volly DeFault, Chicago clarinetist and friend of pianist Jelly Roll Morton, the first serious composer of jazz.

Many saw him [Jelly Roll Morton] as an anachronism, an embarrassing holdover from the distant days of New Orleans when what would become jazz music was inextricably bound up with brothels, card cheats, and the tall tales of the carny.
–Marshall Bowden

> A work of art is not and cannot ever be free from the conditioning imposed by history, class and market conditions....We shall judge him [the artist] by what he makes of the conditions of his time and place in the continuum of history, but we shall not ignore those conditions. –Gerald Moore

> When ragtime pianists from all over the country gathered for the Ragtime Championship of the World Competition held at Tammany Hall in New York City on January 23, 1900, it was Ernest Hogan's song that was recommended for the final test. The three pianists who had reached the semifinals were asked to demonstrate their skill in ragging a song by playing *All Coons Look Alike to Me* for two minutes. –Eileen Southern

> Man, listen…Motherfuckers wasn't trying to emulate Beethoven, Mozart, or Bach! Cats were trying to emulate Grandmaster Flash, Marley Marl, DJ Premier, and them. In a battle in the street or a club in the hood — I'm not talkin' Carnegie Hall or the Metropolitan Opera, you dig — beatmaking and hip hop/rap would destroy classical, cuz we got the vicious beat! –Sa'id

For many musicians, music scholars, and music critics in America, Western classical music represents a superior intellectual frontier, while hip hop/rap music represents an inferior horizon. In fact, there are those who do not even consider hip hop/rap to be music at all. And then there are those who regard hip hop/rap as just a lowly form of music that can only be "elevated" through an extended use of Western music theory and/or the processes and practices associated with rock 'n' roll and the like.

The so-called trained musicians, music scholars, and music critics, who claim (or imply) that hip hop/rap music represents a primitive sphere of music, are completely off base. Whenever this claim is leveled against hip hop/rap music, it is inevitably leveled on the terms and from the perspective of music traditions *outside* of and not closely related to the hip hop/rap music tradition. Therefore, the "primitive" accusation against hip hop/rap is ill-founded and misguided. That's why in this chapter, I'm gonna flip the script! I'm not going to compare key elements of the hip hop/rap music tradition to the Western classical music tradition on the Western classical tradition's terms, or from Western classical music's cultural and philosophical perspective. No, we can't go for that. I'm going to compare key elements of the Western classical music tradition *to* the hip hop/rap music tradition, on hip hop/rap's and beatmaking's terms and from its perspective.

But before I begin this comparative analysis of some of the core components of the hip hop/rap music, beatmaking, and classical music traditions, I must note that the aim of this chapter is not to mock, attack, or otherwise attempt to undermine the Western classical music tradition, but rather to make four critical points. First, I want to further extend upon the detailed discussion of the beatmaking tradition and how it manifests itself within the broader hip hop/rap tradition; the ultimate aim being to provide additional evidence that the hip hop/rap and beatmaking traditions are independent (and often interdependent), distinct, and both creatively and commercially legitimate music traditions that are worthy of such description. Second, I want to point out how ideological presuppositions about music, in specific, certain ideologies of composition, performance, and authenticity have driven the dominant culture's view of what constitutes *music* and/or legitimate musical processes. Third, I want to provide further evidence that the beatmaker represents what I call "the common composer." Finally, I want to why it's impossible to *objectively* designate one music culture and tradition as superior to another.

In this chapter, I also will show how the classical music tradition and culture — the pinnacle of musical expression in Western culture — does not subscribe to the fundamental aesthetics, principles, nuances, predilections, presuppositions, predispositions, and priorities of the hip hop/rap and beatmaking traditions. In doing so, I will demonstrate that the *presumption* that the Western classical tradition is superior to the hip hop/rap and beatmaking traditions is really more of a reflection of the peculiar bias of the dominant culture in Western society than a fair and objective examination of simply another independent and legitimate music tradition and culture. Though I concede that one might be able to objectively ascertain whether one music tradition and culture contains a more complex series of processes than another, the judgment, support, and criticism of one music tradition and culture over another is entirely subjective and based on one's familiarity and knowledge of the music traditions and cultures being compared. A music tradition is appropriately *judged*, first and foremost, by its chief constituents, that is, the community from which it was born, exists in, and/or functions for. Moreover, the value of a music tradition and culture is determined by the functions it serves for its constituents. If the given functions are met, then the music tradition is thereby considered to be successful, in the eyes of the constituents of the encompassing culture. Sure, music traditions and cultures may vary in their compositional processes, principles, properties, practices, and priorities. But no one music tradition and culture can hold more meaning and/or a level of supremacy over another.

Furthermore, whenever we consider established standards from two separate music traditions, we must remember that our tendency to uphold one standard as superior to the other is always rooted within the philosophical *insight* — worldview slant — of the dominant culture in which the larger, more extensive standard was formally and firmly codified. In the case of the hip hop/rap music tradition, and dare I say its own *theory*, and the classical tradition and Western (European) music theory, there is no question whether or not music theory is the more extensive, more formally and firmly codified standard. But here, it is also important to point out that in music, as with all arts and philosophy, that which the dominant (extensive, codified) culture establishes as *the* standard shall simultaneously be held as the bar of excellence for which all *new* standards are measured against. Hence, it will ultimately follow that the established standard will then have an air of superiority about it.

Also, we must be mindful that the upholding of Western music theory as the standard set of musical principles of "intelligent," "great" music serves as insurance against any threat to that very assertion. Therefore, to the gatekeepers of music theory, the hip hop/rap music and beatmaking traditions — which do not necessarily rely on music theory to a great extent — can't simply be *different* from the Western classical music tradition, they must be considered *inferior*. As such, it is more likely that the values and fundamental aesthetic choices of the established standard, in this case, Western classical music and its use of music theory, are predictably preferred — without any need for legitimization — by members of the established standard culture. And equally predictable, these same members see the values and fundamental aesthetic choices of the hip hop/rap and beatmaking traditions as irrelevant at best, or non-existent at worse. Thus, in any head to head comparison of two or more music traditions and cultures, one should expect the host culture and tradition to prevail on its own terms — its own sensibilities, principles, ideologies, and aesthetic priorities. So following this pattern of thought, in a head to head competition between the Western classical tradition, on its own terms, and the hip hop/rap and beatmaking traditions, the Western classical tradition wins, hands down. However, and this is the critical point here, in a head to head *battle* (competition, comparison), on hip hop/rap's and beatmaking's own terms, the classical tradition gets burned.

Finally, before we begin the battle, I should point out that this chapter is by no means intended to be a definitive study of or an extensive survey on the full scope of Western classical music and culture and/or Western music theory, hereinafter referred to simply as music theory.[143] A thorough study of the Western classical music tradition and music theory would be exhaustive and would not adequately serve the purposes of this present study. Music theory and the western classical music tradition are too large of subjects to be thoroughly covered here. But I'm confident that some of the key components of music theory and the classical music tradition that I present in this chapter will permit readers to better understand the contrast between two separate musical traditions and cultures — one music tradition and culture that spans 400 years, and the other that stretches roughly 40 years. But it's important to note that today both traditions enjoy a level of dominance around the globe.[144]

Hence, in this chapter I have chosen to discuss what is commonly recognized to be the most basic (fundamental) elements of music theory. It should also be noted that the information in this chapter is provided to serve multiple purposes, but with regards to music theory there are two primary aims: (1) To formally introduce music theory to those beatmakers who have yet to grasp the basic understanding of it; and (2) To demonstrate, to both those new to and very familiar with music theory, how hip hop/rap music distinguishes itself from other music traditions that are governed by and/or rely on music theory.

Why Compare The Western Classical Music Tradition to the Hip Hop/Rap Music Tradition?

Every music culture has its own so-called "classical" tradition, that is, a tradition that represents the highest form of musical expression within a given culture. Such a musical expression is predicated upon four fundamental things: (1) a set of well-understood aesthetics, principles, and priorities; (2) a set of distinct and well-defined compositional methods (and approaches); (3) a core philosophical approach to music-making; and (4) a well-recognized canon of works. In Europe and the United States (Western culture), Western classical music is widely considered to be the highest form of musical expression. And though rock 'n' roll, generally speaking, may perhaps be the most popular musical

---

[143] In the interest of accuracy, it should be noted that it is often forgotten or ignored that there are multiple "music theories" around the world. However, *Western* music theory is most often referred to simply as "music theory," as if there are no other prominent and/or relevant music theories around the world. There are other music theories; for example, there are Asian music theories, take for instance India's music theory, which by the way is widely considered to be more complex than Western music theory. I concede that I am no more qualified to discuss Western classical music than a Western classical music composer is to discuss hip hop/rap music and/or beatmaking. But since it's commonplace for many *outside* of the hip hop/rap tradition to offer *their* analysis (critique) of hip hop/rap, I'm more than comfortable with exploring the contrast between the hip hop/rap and beatmaking traditions and the Western classical tradition

[144] It must be distinguished that hip hop/rap is more representative of popular culture, whereas Western classical music is more associated with highbrow or elite culture.

expression in Western culture, in this study there's no point in comparing it to hip hop/rap music for two reasons: (1) Rock 'n' roll itself was not too long ago treated like the bastard stepchild of American popular music;[145] and (2) Rock 'n' roll, like hip hop/rap, emanates from the African American (Black) music tradition, and therefore, it too does not subscribe to the compositional ethic of the Western classical tradition.

Finally, it should be noted that hip hop/rap music is American *street culture's* "classical" music. Therefore, it is from this vantage point that one must approach hip hop/rap music if one is truly committed to understanding its full magnitude. Who or whatever you are — rich or poor, highly or poorly educated, traditionally trained or self-taught, from the city or the suburbs — if you want to create quality hip hop/rap music, and I'm not talking about a sham off-shoot, then at some point you will inevitably have to reconcile your station in life and presuppositions about music with the fact that hip hop/rap music is fundamentally a street culture music.

Does this mean that hip hop/rap music, American street culture's "classical" music, is exclusively for those who come from the street? Certainly, not. As I have maintained throughout this study, hip hop/rap is actually the most *inclusive* music tradition in the history of American popular music. And I should add that throughout the world, street culture is perhaps the most inclusive culture within society; membership within it is not based on one's acquisition of abstract knowledge, but rather on sensibility to and knowledge of the ubiquitous "codes" of the street. For if one can handle themselves in the streets, regardless of race, ethnicity, and even gender, they are welcome. And should one rise up the hierarchy of the street, through mastery of (or even efficiency with) the codes and rules of the streets, they are ultimately respected. Much in this same context, the hip hop/rap music and beatmaking traditions do not demand that its members pass some sort of bar of abstract knowledge. Moreover, no one is considered privileged or thrusted to the top of hip hop/rap's and/or beatmaking's hierarchy merely because they can play a traditional instrument, read music, and/or comprehend advanced concepts of music theory. These elements are not

---

[145] When rock 'n' roll first came on the scene, it was hated by the dominant culture. In fact, it wasn't even considered music at all. Between the mid-1950s and late 1960s, rock 'n' roll was often described by established musicians and members in the media as "noise." And some of the major record companies of the time, like Columbia Records, were very reluctant to sign any rock 'n' roll acts. However, as the economic and social realities presented themselves, record companies soon adapted the rock 'n' roll format as their main stable. The parallels and similarities between the rock 'n' roll and hip hop/rap traditions are numerous, therefore, a specific contrast of their key differences isn't necessary for the purposes of this study. Furthermore, In showing the stark contrast, and in some cases similarities between the hip hop/rap music tradition and the Western classical music tradition, I hope to demonstrate the fundamental parallels that hip hop/rap music actually has with two of America's biggest music revolutions: the blues and rock 'n' roll.

necessarily prioritized in the hip hop/rap and beatmaking traditions. Instead, the hip hop/rap and beatmaking traditions make one simple demand: That all those who participate within it demonstrate a respect and understanding for its fundamental aesthetics, priorities, and unique musical features. So while it's a fundamentally a street culture music, it's barrier to entry more accessible — to anyone, from anywhere — than the Western Classical music tradition.

I have also chosen to compare and contrast key elements of the Western classical music to those of the hip hop/rap and beatmaking traditions for several other important reasons. First, both musical traditions are on opposite ends of society as well as various spectrums of culture. The western classical music tradition is now widely regarded as high-brow culture, while the hip hop/rap music tradition is broadly considered to be low-brow. Of course, implicit in the notion of high-brow culture is the idea of strong intellectual activity. Likewise, the notion of low-brow culture implies little to no intellectual activity. Second, for nearly four hundred years, the Western classical musical tradition has served as the musical culture *par excellence* for the Western world, and thus, it has become the supreme musical culture for which, presumably, all musical cultures are measured against. Finally, the third reason I've chosen to compare and contrast key elements of the Western classical music tradition to those of the hip hop/rap and beatmaking traditions is because Western classical music represents the ultimate manifestation of music theory.

The number of traditionally trained musicians (and others on the fringe of hip hop culture) moving into hip hop/rap music is steadily increasing. And paramount to this phenomenon is the fact that, by and large, they are naturally bringing with them their presuppositions, ideologies, philosophies, and priorities about the musical process. This is important to point out because, for better or worse, those presuppositions, ideologies, philosophies, and priorities are well-grounded in and guided by the principles of music theory, *not* the principles of the "hip hop sensibility." And despite the apparent wishes of some traditionally trained musicians who *flirt* with the hip hop/rap form, beatmaking is not in need of an increased usage of music theory. This does not mean that the hip hop/rap and beatmaking traditions seek to be at odds with music theory. Hip hop/rap theory utilizes music theory whenever and however appropriate; likewise, it ignores it whenever and however appropriate, without even giving it a second thought.

My goal is certainly not to malign the magnificence of the Western classical music tradition and/or the brilliance of music theory, but instead to bring attention to and highlight the magnificence of the hip hop/rap music tradition and the brilliance of beatmaking, the chief compositional practice of hip hop/rap music. The hip hop/rap music tradition is no more or less greater than the classical music tradition. As I maintained earlier, to compare the "relative greatness" of both traditions is actually the wrong analytical approach. Both traditions are rich and hold entirely different meanings and purposes for the communities that enjoy them. But I'm compelled to point out that hip hop/rap music, and the beatmaking tradition that emanates from it, are not orphan music traditions that are in want or need of rescue by any other music tradition. Hip hop/rap and beatmaking shines it own light; it does not stand in the shadow of the Western classical music tradition. Hip hop/rap and beatmaking has its own autonomous tradition and culture — a tradition and culture that contains its own logic and language; its own aesthetics, properties, and principles; its own values and priorities; and its own distinct history.

Music "Defined"

Often people confuse the definition of what music is with their own particular music tastes, preferences, and/or prejudices. And, technically speaking, what *is* music really? Can it not be simply defined as "the organization of sound?" So then, what is it that distinguishes music from other forms of organized sound, for instance, the sound of a telephone ringing? One useful definition of music describes it as being "the art, the craft, and the science of organizing sound and silence in the framework of time."[146] To that definition I would add that music is distinguished by the conscious and willful intent to *make* music through the use of pre-established musical elements and properties. And it is in the area of "pre-established musical elements and properties" where the biggest discrepancies — about what exactly is or isn't music — have often been found. In fact, what actually constitutes an established musical element or property? Perhaps a more important question is, who decides which musical elements and properties are important and which ones are not? Fundamentally, the answer is determined by one's background: their cultural sensibilities, values, and prejudices; their musical training and orientation; and the range of their knowledge of music history in general.

---

[146] Michael Miller, *The Complete Idiot's Guide to Music Theory, Second Edition*, (New York: Alpha, 2005), 3.

Western (European) and African Perspectives of History, Time, and Repetition and Their Influence on Music

The Western (European) perspective of history and time, which finds its roots in nineteenth-century Western (European) philosophy, is *linear*. In the Western (European) perspective, progression is seen as something that is linear, hence, the term "linear progression." Also, unique to the Western (European) perspective is the notion that growth is something *new*, something non-cyclical and non-repetitive. In fact, within nineteenth-century European culture there stood the belief "that there is *no* repetition in culture, but only a *difference*, defined as progress and growth."[147]

The African perspective of history and time, which predates nineteenth-century Western (European) philosophy by centries, is *cyclical*. In the African perspective, history and time is seen as something that occurs in a cyclical, repetitive manner. Also, unique to the African perspective is the notion that growth, and the process thereof, is an instance of repetition, or *a series of repetitions linked together* (sound familiar?). This explains the roots of the African American (Black) music tradition's emphasis and priority on repetition.

As nineteenth-century Europeans "were defining themselves over against other European nations, they were also busy defining 'European culture' as separate from 'African culture.'" Moreover, "Black culture" was a "concept first created by Europeans and defined in *opposition* to 'European culture.'" For instance, Hegel, the influential nineteenth-century European philosopher, "saw 'black culture' as the lowest stage of that laudable self-reflection and development shown by European culture whose natural outcome must be the state or nationhood. In his by no means atypical nineteenth-century view, **Hegel said that black culture simply did not exist in the same sense as European culture did. Black culture (as one of several non-Western cultures) had no self-expression.**"[148] From this context, we can also see how cultures, particularly dominant ones, project themselves as superior to all others that are different. Thus, in the West, it is no surprise that the European perspective of history, time, and repetition is more highly regarded than the African perspective.

---

[147] James A. Snead, "On Repetition in Black Culture," *Black American Literature Forum*, vol. 15, no. 4, 147, 1981.

[148] *Ibid*, 147, [emphasis mine]. Snead examines how and why repetition is a major component within black culture (specifically in the arts). Also, he examines how European culture has a long history of both denying the existence of and suppressing repetition in culture. In the reference that I cite here, Snead does a wonderful job of pointing out how cultures (particularly dominant ones) project themselves as *superior* to all others that are *different*. Also, I use this Snead reference to reinforce my argument that Western classical music is not only widely viewed as simply different than hip hop/rap music but superior to it.

The distinct differences between the Western (European) and African perspectives of history and time have been, for the better part of the last three centuries, contentious, albeit unknown to the casual music listener. However, because of the *peculiar institution* of American slavery, this contention has, on the one hand, been neutralized (to a considerable degree) in America; for clearly the origins of a specifically *American* music certainly includes contributions by both African and European descendents. But on the other hand, this contention has still worked to establish Western (European) music as the standard of music superiority the world over. Usually, when one says *classical* music, it's widely understood that they're speaking about a European music tradition that was most personified by seventeenth, eighteenth, and nineteenth-century Europe.

Although the hip hop/rap music tradition was created in America (obviously a segment of the broader Western society), we must not make the mistake of forgetting that hip hop/rap, like all other twentieth-century African American (Black) popular music forms, prioritizes — and relies on — the African perspective of cyclical progression and repetition.[149] And even though hip hop is an art-based cultural phenomenon of American culture, it falls under the rubric of post-modern Western culture.

Finally, for further cultural context, it is necessary to point out that it is precisely because of the fact that the hip hop/rap music tradition is grounded *within* the African American (Black) music tradition that it has, throughout most of its history, received a negative bias in the American mainstream. Only recently has hip hop/rap music began to be "accepted" (tolerated) as a legitimate art form by traditional music institutions and the gatekeepers of American pop culture alike. But let's be clear: This acceptance is due more to the pop-culture co-option of hip hop/rap music than it is to a true acknowledgement or recognition of hip hop/rap's sovereign creativity and/or its canon of compositional methods and aesthetics.

Lest We Forget the Architects and Pioneers of the Hip Hop/Rap Music and Beatmaking Traditions

Before I get into the crux of this discussion, it's important to remember that the pioneering DJs and early beatmakers were surrounded by people (family members, friends, neighbors, etc.) who played traditional instruments and new music theory. Also, hip hop's earliest architects went to school at a time when

---

[149] It also must be understood that the roots of the African American music tradition firmly emanate from the larger African concept and framework of time and music.

music and band were still public school educational requirements, hence, they were familiar with traditional instruments, and they were likely introduced to music theory on some level. But the first architects and pioneers of hip hop/rap and beatmaking consciously rejected traditional instruments and most of the advanced tenets of music theory. The big myth (pushed by those who love to romanticize hip hop's roots) is that the first hip hop architects couldn't afford instruments, so they had to go into DJ'ing as an alternative. This is inaccurate.

Fact is, choosing electronic music production gear was certainly not a choice prompted by poverty. The gear and equipment that hip hop's earliest architects used to create a new music form was much more expensive than traditional instruments; indeed, the cost of traditional instruments in the early 1970s pales in comparision to the cost of the complete DJ rigs that the early architects and their immediate descendents desired. Moreover, in the '70s and early '80s, traditional instruments (guitars, horns, etc.) were much more accessible and cheaper than complete DJ rigs and the first wave of digital samplers. Even still, the pioneers, and their direct apprentices, consciously chose to acquire DJ gear and other electronic music production instruments.

When they made the conscious decision to focus on making a new music form through the use of recorded music, hip hop's earliest architects were fully aware that they were going in a different musical direction. They knew very well that they were doing something that had never been done before; and they embraced the fact that what they were doing was certainly something that was not easily comprehensible by those who were outside of hip hop culture, or those who were otherwise non-appreciative of hip hop/rap music. Thus, these conscious decisions, and many others, lead directly to the development of hip hop/rap's own way of composing music and, subsequently, it's own music "theory."

Music Theory Defined

The following section is not intended to be an exhaustive discussion of music theory, but rather it's a brief (but detailed) examination of the key concepts, principles, and terminology that is most applicable to hip hop/rap, beatmaking, and common forms of twentieth-century American popular music.

A "music theory" is a system that organizes and distills the elements, properties, language, mechanics, and parameters of music; it's a study that deals with how music works; and it's also a means for notating musical "instruction." Because a music theory may include any belief, statement, conception, or presupposition of or about music, I also like to consider music theory as the "grand approach" of a particular music tradition. All music uses some sort of music theory, that is, a way of expressing how and what musical events have occurred. When most people say "music theory," they typically say so as if there is only one music theory in the world. While European music theory is perhaps the most well-known music theory in the world, it certainly isn't the only music theory on the planet.[150]

The Basic Properties and Elements of Music Theory
Harmony, Melody, Rhythm, Timbre, Texture, Structure, Form, and Dynamics

Before discussing the basic elements of music theory, a few words about tones, semitones, pitch, notes, intervals, chords, and scales are necessary for readers not entirely familiar with their definitions. A **tone** is any sound of distinct pitch. A **semitone** is a "half tone" or a half step in pitch. **Pitch** refers to the frequency (speed) of a note. High pitch translates to "fast frequency," low pitch translates to "slow frequency." A **note**[151] is a tone of a particular (definite) pitch and duration. An **interval** is the relationship between the pitches of two notes. Intervals are described as either "linear" (or melodic), i.e. if the notes sound successively, or "vertical" (or harmonic), i.e. if the two notes sound simultaneously. A **chord** is three or more notes sounded simultaneously. The notes of the chord may be played at the same time ("block chords"), or may be played separately with some overlap, or may be played separately but in a quick enough succession that they will be "heard" as a chord or understood to imply a chord (**arpeggiated chords** or **arpeggios**). Chords are either major, minor, or diminished.

A **scale** is a progression of seven notes all in a row, upwards or downwards in steps. Scales are defined by their starting point/step or, more precisely, their starting note. Scales in Western music generally consist of seven notes and repeat at the octave. In Western music, there are four specific seven-note scales: "major," "natural minor," "melodic minor," and "harmonic minor." Other commonly used scales in Western music are: the *chromatic scale* (twelve notes), the *whole tone*

---

[150] For instance, there are a number of Eastern music theories. Indian (India) music, for example, has its own theory, it's own grand approach. Indian (India) music theory, which is based more on rhythmic structures than melodic structures, is more rhythmically complex than Western music theory.

[151] Sample-based beatmakers use samples similar to the way traditional musicians use notes. However, in this process, sample-based beatmakers are not governed by the abstract knowledge and/or rules that the use of notes follow in music theory. Instead, sample-based beatmakers are focused on what sounds good or what "works" according to the priorities and values of the hip hop/rap music tradition.

scale (six notes), and the *pentatonic scale* (five notes).[152] Notes in the commonly used scales are separated by whole and half step intervals of tones and semitones. Finally, it's important to note that scales are used to create melodies.

Major and Minor Scales

To understand what "major" or "minor" means, one must recognize that music in a particular key tends to use only some of the many possible notes available; these notes are listed in the scale associated with that key. **Major scales** all follow the same interval pattern, for example: whole step, whole step, half step, whole step, whole step, whole step, half step. Each major key uses a different set of notes (its major scale). In each **major scale**, however, the notes are arranged in the same major scale pattern and build the same types of chords that have the same relationships with each other. Therefore, music that is in C major, for example, will not sound significantly different from music that is in D major. Major chords also have a **tonal center**, a note or chord that feels like "home," or "the resting place," in that key. **Minor scales** sound different from major scales because they are based on a different pattern of intervals, and so the notes in the minor scale have different relationships with each other; for example: whole step, half step, whole step, whole step, half step, whole step, whole step. Music in minor keys has a different sound and emotional feel and develops differently harmonically. So you can't, for example, transpose a piece from C major to D minor (or even to C minor) without changing it a great deal. Major chords are used for happy, up-tempo moods; "minor chords" are used for sad, tragically reflective moods; and "diminished chords" are often used for darker moods.

The Three Primary Elements of Music Theory: Harmony, Melody, and Rhythm

Harmony

Harmony is the most highly developed aspect of Western music; as such, music theory tends to focus almost exclusively on harmony and melody. In music, harmony is the use of simultaneous pitches or chords. That is, when

---

[152] "Jazz and blues use scale intervals smaller than a semitone. The "blue note" is an interval that is technically neither major nor minor but "in the middle," giving it a sound and feel that is unique to jazz and the blues. In blues, a pentatonic scale is often used. Moreover, in jazz many different modes and scales are used, often within the same piece of music. Chromatic scales are very common in modern jazz. It's worth noting that scales translate well to the basic concept of building a loop in the beatmaking tradition.

you have more than one pitch sounding at the same time in music, the result is harmony. This does not mean that harmony has to be particularly "harmonious;" the important fact to be understood is that notes are sounding at the same time. Harmony can be the subject of an entire course on music theory, but for the limited purposes of this section, here are eight basic terms and/or concepts associated with harmony that are helpful to know.

First, it's important to know that there are different "harmony textures." There's an implied harmony texture. A melody all by itself (monophony) can have an **implied harmony**, even if no other notes are sounding at the same time. In other words, the melody can be constructed so that it strongly *suggests* a harmony that could accompany it. For example, when you sing a melody by itself, you may be able to "hear" in your mind the chords that usually go with it. But some melodies don't imply any harmony; they are not meant to be played with harmony and don't need it to be legitimate music. **Parallel harmony** occurs when different lines in the music go up or down together (usually following the melody). **Homophony** is a texture of music in which there is one line that is obviously the melody; the rest of the notes are harmony and accompaniment. (See Homophonic in *Texture* sub-section.) **Polyphony** refers to a harmony texture in which there is more than one independent melodic line at the same time, and they are all fairly equal in importance. (See Polyphonic and Counterpoint in the *Texture* sub-section.) I should also mention drones. A **drone** is a note that changes rarely or not at all. The simplest way to add harmony to a melody is to play it with drones.[153]

Next, it's important to briefly discuss chords and their relationship to harmony. In Western music, most harmony is based on chords. Chords are built on major or minor triads. **Triads** are simple three-note chords. "In traditional triadic harmony, there are always at least three notes in a chord (there can be more than three), but some of the notes may be left out and only "implied" by the harmony. The notes of the chord may be played at the same time (block chords), or may be played separately with some overlap, or may be played separately but in a quick enough succession that they will be "heard" as a chord or understood to imply a chord (arpeggiated chords or arpeggios)."[154]

A discussion of **harmonic analysis** is also important here. Harmonic analysis refers to the understanding of how a chord is related to the key and the other chords in a piece of music. There are a number of reasons why harmonic analysis is useful, especially to those who have not studied music theory. First,

---

[153] Catherine Schmidt-Jones, CNX.org (Connexions), "Harmony," http://cnx.org/content/m11654/latest/.
[154] *Ibid.*

many standard forms (for example, a "twelve bar blues") follow very specific chord progressions, which are often discussed in terms of harmonic relationships. A **chord progression** is a series of chords played one after another.[155] Second, if you understand chord relationships, you can transpose (change the key) of any chord progression to any key you like. Third, let's say you're searching for chords to go with a particular melody (in a particular key). Knowing what chords are *most likely* in that key, and how they might likely progress from one to another, is very helpful. (Incidentally, this is a basic example of how abstract knowledge works and guides a composer in the Western classical tradition.) Finally, understanding how a chord is related to the key and the other chords in a piece of music, specifically the chord progression of a piece of music, is paramount to improvisation.[156]

The concept of consonance and dissonance is also important to this discussion of harmony. **Consonance** and **dissonance** are musical terms describing whether combinations of notes sound "good" together or not. Notes that sound pleasant, i.e. good or stable when played at the same time, are **consonant**. A **dissonant** note may sound unpleasant, i.e. harsh, jarring, and/or unstable.

It's also necessary to mention cadence. A **cadence** is a point where the music feels as if it has come to a temporary or permanent stopping point. In the Western classical music tradition, cadence is tied very strongly to the harmony. For example, most listeners will feel that the strongest, most satisfying ending to a piece of music involves a dominant chord followed by a tonic chord.

Accompaniment is another term and concept important to this discussion. **Accompaniment** refers to all of the parts of the music that are not melody. This includes rhythmic parts, harmonies, the bass line, and chords. Accompaniment contains inner parts or inner voices. **Inner parts** or **inner voices** describes accompaniment parts that fill in the music in between the melody (which is often the highest part) and the bass line.

Another basic concept of harmony that is helpful to know is functional harmony. **Functional harmony** is harmony in which each chord functions in a specific way in the key, and underpins the form of the piece of music. It's worth noting that harmony can simply be more than one note sounding at a time, providing texture and interest to a piece.

Finally, the last basic concept of harmony that is helpful to know is harmonic rhythm. The **harmonic rhythm** of a piece refers to how often the chords change.

---

[155] *Ibid.* Musicians may describe a specific chord progression (for example, "two measures of G major, then a half measure of A minor and a half measure of D seventh," or just "G, A minor, D seventh"), or speak more generally of classes of chord progressions (for example a "blues chord progression."
[156] *Ibid.*

Music in which the chords change rarely has a *slow* harmonic rhythm; music in which the chords change often has a *fast* harmonic rhythm. Harmonic rhythm can be completely separate from other rhythms and tempos. For example, a section of music with many short, quick notes but only one chord has fast rhythm, but it has a slow harmonic rhythm.[157]

Melody

Melody is technically defined as a linear succession of musical notes which is perceived as a single entity. A melody is a sequence of pitches and durations that consist of one or more musical phrases or **motifs**, usually repeated throughout a song or piece in various forms. The melodic line of a piece of music is the string of notes that make up the melody. Melodies move in three ways: up, down, or repeat. This is referred to as "direction." The way in which notes move gives the melody its "shape," and the shape of a melody is called *contour*. As the melody progresses, the pitches may go up or down. "Compass" refers to the difference in pitch between the lowest and the highest notes of a melody. Melodies are distinct and clear, i.e. even without words, the phrases in a melody can be very clear.

There are a number of other important characteristics associated with melody. A musical **phrase** is a measurement of a musical line; it's a short musical passage — usually of four bars, sometimes less, sometimes more — that has a complete musical *sense* (character) of its own. A musical phase is composed of one or more "motives" (figures, cells) and usually consists of a single idea, which is then repeated, complemented, or added to by the next phrase. **Theme** is a complete melody fragment, a section of melody that reappears in the music of a song. A theme can also be described as a recognizable melody upon which a part or all of a composition is based.[158] **Counter-Melody** describes the sequence of notes, perceived as a melody, written to be played simultaneously with a more prominent melody. In other words, counter-melody refers to a second but subordinate melodic line. One common basic principle of composing a counter-melody deals with moving the counter-melody while the "main" melody is least busy and vice-versa. Essentially, this can also be described as the process of creating variations upon a similar theme.[159]

---

[157] *Ibid.*
[158] Aside from melody, a theme can refer to any prominent musical idea that is established in a piece of music. In beatmaking, a theme can be used to describe the sense or mood of a beat. A theme can also be used to describe a prominent structural component that reoccurs within a beat, like a heavily syncopated drum roll proceeded by a bouncing bass line. Also, in beatmaking a theme can be used to describe the style of a beat; for example, a hardcore beat, a party track or club banger, etc.
[159] A great example of counter-melody led by rhythm can be heard in the song "Heartbreak Hotel" by The Jacksons.

A **motif** (or **motive**), also commonly referred to as a cell or a figure, is a short musical ideal — shorter than a phrase or theme — that occurs often in a piece of music. In the Western classical music tradition, a motive must consist of at least two notes to have purpose (usually a motif is made up of three, four, or more notes). This short "melodic idea" is a scrap of melody that can be pieced together and formed into main melodies. When a motif returns (reappears) in a piece of music, it can be slower or faster, or in a different key. It may return "upside down" (with the notes going up instead of down, for example), or with the pitches or rhythms altered. In order to make up a line of music, a motive must lead somewhere and must link to the next motive and from the previous motive so that the piece flows well.[160]

Finally, extra notes, such as **trills** and **slides**, that are not part of the main melodic line but are added to the melody (either by the composer or the performer to make the melody more complex and interesting) are called **ornaments** or **embellishments**.

Rhythm

The term rhythm has more than one meaning, but generally **rhythm** means the placement of sounds in time. Music cannot happen without time. Because music must be heard over a period of time, rhythm is one of the most basic elements of music. Rhythm is comprised of four elements: the beat, accent, meter, and tempo. The term "beat" also has more than one meaning, especially depending on the context. Fundamentally, **beat** refers to (the speed of) the underlying "pulse" in music; it's the basic time unit of music. Therefore, one description of rhythm is that it's the pattern of regular or irregular pulses caused in music by the occurrence of strong and weak melodic and harmonic "beats." Beats are grouped into measures or bars. The first beat is usually the strongest, and in most music, most of the bars have the same number of beats. This sets up an underlying pattern in the pulse of the music. "Beat" may also refer to a distinct or recognizable (specific) repetitive rhythmic pattern that maintains the pulse (as in "it has a jazz beat").

In a rhythmic pattern, it is also important to understand the differences between the "downbeat," "upbeat," or "off" beat. The **downbeat** refers to the moment when the pulse is the strongest; the downbeat is the impulse that occurs at the beginning of a bar of measured music. The **off-beat** is in between

---

[160] Symphonic music uses motives all the time. With just four little notes Beethoven created one of the most famous motives ever written. In his piece "Symphony No. 5," he repeated four little notes and made them grow into a big symphony.

pulses; and the **upbeat** is exactly halfway between pulses. (Think of the upbeat as "and": 1 *and* 2 *and* 3 *and* 4.) Here, it's worth noting that James Brown's signature funk groove emphasized the downbeat, the "one" — emphasis on the first beat in 4/4 time measure — rather than the upbeat. However, in rock 'n' roll, like early rhythm and blues, the upbeat is emphasized. In hip hop/rap, a descendent of funk, the downbeat is emphasized.[161]

A meter is a division of a composition into units of equal time value called "measures." **Measures,** synonymously known as **bars**, simply refers to the notes and rests between two bar lines; more specifically, it's also described as a segment of time defined as a given number of beats of a given duration. A **bar line** is a vertical line which separates measures. Also, it's worth noting that the word "bar" comes from the vertical lines on the music staff, which separate one measure from another.[162] I should further add that a more specific description of **meter** in a piece of music is that it is the repetitive arrangement or "grouping" of strong and weak pulses (beats) in the rhythm. It is on these pulses, the beat of the music, that you tap your foot, clap your hands, dance, etc. Also, the meter of a piece of music is the arrangement of its rhythms in a repetitive pattern of strong and weak beats. This does not necessarily mean that the rhythms themselves are repetitive, but they do strongly suggest a repeated pattern of pulses. The concept of meter emanates in large part from the rhythmic element of poetry or song, where it means the number of lines in a verse, the number of syllables, and the arrangement of those syllables as long or short.

Time signature, also commonly known as "meter signature," is the notational convention used in Western music to specify how many beats are in each measure and what note value constitutes one beat. Meters can be classified as either "simple" or "compound." In a simple meter, each beat is basically divided into halves. In compound meters, each beat is divided into thirds. The length of the meter, or metric unit (usually corresponding with measure length), is usually grouped into either two or three beats, being called duple meter and triple meter, respectively. If each beat is divided by two or four, it is simple meter, if by three (or six) compound meter. In fact, there are four different categories of time signature or "meter signature": simple duple, simple triple, compound duple, and

---

[161] For a more extensive understanding of rhythmic features, in particular, the "beat," see: Southern, 206: "The modern scholar Richard Waterman has used the term metronome sense to refer to the African tradition for 'conceiving music as structure along a theoretical framework of beats regularly spaced in time...whether or not the beats are expressed in actual melodic or percussion tones...Since this metronome sense is of such basic importance...it is assumed without question to consideration to be part of the perceptual equipment of both musicians and listeners and is, in the most complete way, taken for granted.'"

[162] There are different types of bar lines, each with a specific instruction. However, I have not included the various descriptions of bar lines because it is not critical the purposes of this study.

compound triple. Again, if the beat is divided into two, the meter is "simple," if divided into three, it is compound. Likewise, if each measure is divided into two it is "duple," and if into three, it is "triple." In other words, **simple duple** describes two or four beats to a bar, each divided by two, the top number of the signature being "2" or "4" (2/4, 2/8, 2/2...4/4, 4/8, 4/2...). Note: When there are four beats to a bar, it is alternatively referred to as "quadruple" time. **Simple triple** describes three beats to a bar, each divided by two, the top number of the signature being "3" (3/4, 3/8, 3/2...). Compound duple describes two beats to a bar, each divided by three, the top number of the signature being "6" (6/8, 6/16, 6/4...). **Compound triple** describes three beats to a bar, each divided by three, the top number of the signature being "9" (9/8, 9/16, 9/4). For example, if the meter of the music feels like "strong-weak-strong-weak," it is in duple meter; "strong-weak-weak-strong-weak-weak" it is triple meter, and "strong-weak-weak-weak" is quadruple.

Tempo is the speed or pace of a given piece of music. More specifically, the tempo is a measure of how quickly or rather how slow or fast the pulse in music *repeats*. Tempo is usually measured in "beats per minute" (BPM); for example, 60 BPM translates to a speed of one beat per second. Rhythms are usually arranged with respect to a **time signature**, partially signifying a meter, and set to a tempo. Tempo is a crucial element of music composition, as it can affect the mood and difficulty of a piece. Finally, tempo is also described as the interval of time between beats. Therefore, the closer the beats, the faster the tempo; the farther apart, the slower.

Finally, rhythm can also mean the basic, repetitive pulse of the music, or "a rhythmic pattern" that is repeated throughout the music (as in "feel the rhythm"). It can also refer to the pattern in time of a single small group of notes (as in "play this rhythm for me"). There are also different types or kinds of rhythms. For instance, **syncopated rhythms** are rhythms that accent parts of the beat not already stressed by counting. Syncopation occurs when a strong note happens either on a weak beat or off the beat. Then there's **polymeter**. Polymeter is different rhythms played simultaneously in more than one time signature.

The Primary Sub-Elements of Music: Texture, Dynamics, Timbre, and Form/Structure

Texture in music describes two areas of musical phenomena: (1) melodic and harmonic relationships; and (2) the density of the simultaneous layering of different musical components. With regards to the melodic and harmonic relationships, texture is used commonly to describe the construction of music. That is, it refers to the number of melodies (or rhythms on percussion instruments) played at a given time in a piece of music. There are three typical texture constructions: monophony or monophonic texture, polyphony or polyphonic texture, and homophony or homophonic texture.[163] In a **monophonic** texture, a single melodic line (one melodic voice) is played without harmonic accompaniment. A single musical instrument playing a melody or many instruments playing the same melody is monophonic texture.

Polyphonic texture describes a texture in which two or more melodic lines (voices) of relatively equal complexity (considerably independent from one another) are played simultaneously. Melodic lines in a polyphonic texture are complementary to each other, they sound well together and do not interfere with each other sonically. It should be noted that the craft of combining two or more melodies of equal complexity that occur in music at the same time is known as **counterpoint**, that is to say, point against point. Music that has a polyphonic texture is said to be contrapuntal. Each melodic line in a **contrapuntal** texture occupies a separate sonic range, and their rhythm activity compliment each other. Note: **Simultaneity** describes more than one complete musical texture occurring at the same time rather than in succession.[164]

A case in which a single melodic line plays with an accompaniment of harmony is called **homophonic** texture. In homophonic texture, there are actually multiple voices of which one, the melody, stands out prominently and the others (clearly less important melodies) form a background of harmonic accompaniment. Most songs and much instrumental music is composed in this texture. Also, homophonic texture represents the classic idea of simplicity and balance.[165]

Finally, there are two musical techniques or styles that are often associated with analysis of texture: heterophony and antiphony. **Heterophony** describes a "shadow" or "echo" effect in music, wherein two or more voices simultaneously perform *variations* of the same melodic material. In the **heterophonic** style, one performer plays the basic melody while other performers "shadow" or "echo" the melody notes by playing slightly after the basic notes. In some heterophonic styles, the "shadow" performer not only "echoes" the basic

---

[163] There are two other broad types of texture: simple and complex. **Simple** texture is a texture in which the same rhythm is played by all musicians. A **complex** texture is one in which a different rhythm is played by each musician.
[164] Southern, 209. Also, see: Danlee Mitchell and Jack Logan, Ph.D, "Four Combinational Operations of Music: Texture," *Cartage.org*, http://www.cartage.org.lb/en/themes/Arts/music/elements/four.
[165] *Ibid.*

melodic tones, but also ornaments them as well. **Antiphony** describes the stereo or quadraphonic effect achieved by placing two or more groups of performers at different locations in a performance space, such as a large church or performing hall. When each antiphonal group alternates its musical material in succeeding phrases this "effect" is known as antiphony or the music is said to be antiphonal. Another term for this technique is **call and response**.[166]

Texture is also a term used to describe the overall quality of sound of a piece of music, most often indicated by the number of "voices" — the number of different instruments and their timbre (unique sound and color) — in the music, and by the relationship between these voices. Many composers often use more than one type of texture in the same piece of music. The texture of a piece of music can be affected by the number and character of parts playing at once, or the timbre of the instruments or voices playing these parts, or the harmony, tempo, and rhythms used. This is what contributes to the "thickness" or lack their of in a given piece of music.

Dynamics

Dynamics refers to the selected "levels of volume" of the voices in a given piece of music. More specifically, in the Western classical tradition, dynamics describes the range of sounds from barely audible to very loud. Dynamics has its own distinct terminology and instructions used for achieving each range or *style* of sound. **Dynamic markings** (terminology) used in the Western classical tradition are based on Italian words. The two basic dynamic indications are: *piano* or *p*, which means "soft," and *forte* or *f*, which means "loud" or "strong." From these basic dynamic indications, subtle "degrees" of loudness or softness are indicated as: *mezzo-piano* or *mp*, which means "moderately or medium soft," *mezzo-forte* or *mf*, which means "moderately or medium loud," *fortissimo* or *ff*, which means "very loud," and *pianissimo* or *pp*, which means "very soft." For *pianissimo* and *fortissimo*, there are still further indications: *pianissimo possibile* or *ppp*, which means "softest possible or very, very soft," and *fortissimo possibile* or *fff*, which means "loudest possible or very, very loud." Sudden changes in volume also have specific dynamic markings: *sforzando (sforzato)* or *sf, sfz,* or *fz*, means a "strong, sudden accent. Finally, gradual changes in volume also have distinct dynamic markings: *crescendo* or *cresc.*, which means "get gradually

---

[166] *Ibid.* The **call and response** technique described here is not to be confused with the tradition of "call and response" of West Africa or African American slaves and/or the Black Church.

louder," and ***decrescendo*** or ***diminuendo*** (***descresc.*** and ***dim.***), which means "get gradually softer."

Dynamic indications are relative, not absolute. For example, an entire orchestra playing very loudly is louder than a single pianist playing very loudly. Hence, dynamic indications do not indicate an exact level of volume, but rather the dynamic instructions for a music passage in a given piece of music.

Timbre

Timbre (pronounced as "tamber") is the term used to indicate the distinctive properties — characteristic, quality, or substance — of a sound or sound produced (made) by a particular instrument or voice. Timbre, commonly referred to as "tone quality" or "tone color," describes all of the aspects of a musical sound that do not have anything to do with pitch or duration. Timbre speaks to the fact that each individual instrument or voice has its own distinct sound. For example, there is a timbral difference between a saxophone, a piano, a trumpet, and a guitar. Each instrument playing the same note at the same pitch and volume will sound differently because each instrument conveys its own distinct "character," "tone quality," or "tone color." Timbre is also relative to amplification and harmonics, that is to say, the timbre of an electronic guitar is recognizably different from that of an acoustic guitar. Also, because of the attack of each note or sound, the timbre of *two different* electric guitars is also recognizably different. Thus, various musical instruments have different musical colors.

Form/Structure

Form is the basic "structure" of a piece of music. Form is a musical blueprint that helps the composer put his sounds together in different ways. Every piece of music has an overall plan or structure, *the big picture*, so to speak. In the Western classical music tradition, musical forms offer a great range of complexity. Therefore, in this sub-section, I will briefly go over some of the most familiar and commonly used forms in the Western classical music tradition.

The simplest musical forms that composers use are the **binary**, **ternary**, and **rondo** forms. The **binary** form consists of two sections (complementary and of roughly equal duration) that are commonly known as the "question section" and "answer section." Note: these two sections are often repeated to highlight the differences between them. In the binary form, the first section, "A," will start in a certain key, and will usually modulate to a related key, while the second section, "B," begins in the newly established key. To achieve the "question" and "answer," section A ends in a different key to the one in which it starts. Section B then goes through a series of modulations into different keys until it ends up at the "home" key once again. Thus, the binary form is usually characterized as having the form AB. The **ternary** form is simply an A section, followed by a contrasting B section, and then the A section repeated. Finally, the **rondo** form is just a progression of ternary form: the A section is often itself in binary form and the B and C sections are deliberately contrasting.[167]

Some of the more commonly used complex forms include: **canon**, **fugue**, **sonata**, and **concerto**. The canon form is contrapuntal, which means a lot of emphasis is placed on the melody and its structure. In the **canon** form, the instruments play the same melody but at different times in relation to one another; in other words, the melody is imitated by various parts at regular intervals. So one instrument will begin and another will start playing the *same* melody a few bars later.

The **fugue** form or style incorporates "imitative counterpoint," that is to say, it involves the overlapping of several melodies, beginning with an initial theme or subject. This subject is developed and repeated becoming a counter-subject, at which point another instrument enters and "imitates" the subject, often transposed into the dominant key so that the parts sound different but stay in close harmonic relation.

The **sonata** form consists of three parts: the exposition, the development, and the recapitulation. The **exposition** is where the main "themes" are introduced. The **development** is where the material from the exposition is "developed" to a climax. Throughout the development, tension builds steadily. In the **recapitulation,** tension is "relieved" by the repeat of the exposition. However, this is the *appearance* of the exposition, as the familiar motives of the beginning are actually slightly modified in the recapitulation. Finally, a sonata is a piece of music that consists of many movements, whereas a **concerto** is a piece of music for a solo instrument accompanied by a full orchestra.[168]

---

[167] "Structure In Classical Music," http://www.bbc.co.uk/dna/h2g2/A8379219. "Rondo Form," Capistrano School, http://www.empire.k12.ca.us/CAPISTRANO/Mike/capmusic/form/rondo%20form/rondo.htm.
[168] *Ibid*. It's worth noting that the Western classical tradition tends to encourage longer, more complex forms which may be difficult to recognize without the familiarity that comes from study or repeated hearings.

Compositional Ethic of the Western Classical Tradition

Every music tradition has its own compositional ethic, i.e. its own guiding philosophy. In the Western classical music tradition, its compositional ethic (guiding philosophy) emanates, above all, from five things: (1) The reliance upon music theory — abstract knowledge; (2) The importance of logical (clearly understood) form or structure; (3) A strong emphasis on harmony; (4) The principle of linear progression (material growth, horizontal forward movement); and (5) The use of rhythm as only an *aid* to progression, and the opposition to the use of repetition.

In the Western classical tradition, music theory is the fundamental apparatus (mechanism) through which music is made. One might say that it is the "life force" of the Western classical tradition. *But one must remember that music theory is a very complex system.* In the previous sections of this chapter, I surveyed the basics of music theory and described how complex even the most introductory aspects of music theory can be. In fact, music theory is an incredibly dense framework that incorporates a range of components, including, but not limited to, physics, mathematics, Western philosophy and notions of logic, Italian terminology, and even the Western literary tradition. As a rigid set of logical rules, music theory achieves a number of things: It provides an orderly system for music-making; it reinforces Western presuppositions about harmony, melody, and rhythm; it maintains harmony as the most highly developed aspect of Western music; it governs the "approach" of composers; and finally, it dictates the elements that inform composers of the Western classical tradition and other Western musicians on how music supposedly *should* work.

In the Western classical tradition, form/structure is an entirely literal and logical concept. That is to say, there is a premium on the written score or a set of instructions that make logical sense, in relation, of course, to the directives, sub-theories, and principles of music theory. Thus, what "works" in the Western classical tradition is absolutely defined by the tenets (rules) of music theory. This means that within the Western classical music tradition, everything in the form or structure of music must make *literal* sense. In the Western classical music tradition, composers approach music in a literary sense. In fact, some of the most important *language* of music theory makes this connection quite clear: "theme," "sentence," "structure," "verse," "bar," "phrase," etc. In this way, the written score in the Western classical music tradition is akin to a narrative in a literary work. A composer from the Western classical tradition need not *hear* the score to know if it makes sense, they can *read* the score and *comprehend* that it makes sense. Incidentally, this is precisely why the notion of musical "questions" and "answers" is a pivotal component to the Western classical music tradition.

Finally, it's worth noting the fundamental presuppositions of form or structure within the Western classical tradition. In the Western classical tradition, a "good" structure is one in which the music takes the listener on a musical journey, through a clear *beginning, middle,* and *end*. Moreover, the common view within the Western classical tradition is that music, without structure, is merely a random set of ideas that leaves the listener completely unsatisfied. Certainly such a view implies, at the very least, that the *full* enjoyment of Western classical music requires that a listener understand music theory. Composers in the Western classical tradition are quite concerned with conveying to the listener his or her musical ideas, which implies that the common listener actually understands his or her ideas. Also, the goal of Western classical composers is to create "interest" in a piece. However, it would appear then that what is interesting can only be "understood" by those well versed in the abstract knowledge of music theory. Moreover, this also seems to suggest that the listener's level of enjoyment is dependent upon their ability to see the big compositional picture, that is, to see the given form that a composer is using. Thus, this all raises an important question: Who is Western classical music actually meant for? Is it meant for the common listener, or is it ultimately really meant for those who understand music theory?

Next, because harmony is the most highly developed aspect of Western music, music theory tends to focus almost exclusively on harmony and melody. Thus, **tonality**, a system of music in which specific hierarchical pitch relationships are based on a key "center" or tonic, is central to the compositional ethic of the Western classical composer. Since the mid-eighteenth century, tonal music has increasingly been composed of a 12-note chromatic scale in a system of equal temperament. As we've already learned, tonal music makes reference to "scales" of notes selected as a series of steps from the chromatic scale. Most of these scales are of 5, 6, or 7 notes with the vast majority of tonal music pitches conforming to one of four specific seven-note scales: major, natural minor, melodic minor, and harmonic minor. Hence, in the Western classical music tradition, there is a strong priority on definite tones, pitch relationships, and on constant "shifts" in melody.

It must also be remembered that Western classical ideology is completely invested in the notion of linear progression, and that linear progression in music theory is actually a representation of European (Western) culture's perspective (philosophical slant) of history and time. What's most illuminating about this perspective is that on the one hand, it views history and time as a matter of "material growth," "progression," and "newness." On the other hand, it views repetition as *regression* when it repeats what has come before, and it views repetition as *progression* when there is a quality of difference to it.[169] Because of this, the Western classical compositional ethic, which emanates from European (Western) culture,[170] considers music as a *logical* process that seeks to move forward in time through a series of "new" *developments*. No surprise then that progression and material (differential) growth are prioritized in the Western classical tradition. Since rhythm both implies and *requires* repetition, it is the least prioritized of the three main elements of music theory. Because the Western classical tradition places such a premium on linear progression (material growth), rhythm is necessarily reduced to a secondary role:

> **European music uses rhythm mainly as an *aid* in the construction of a sense of progression** to a harmonic cadence, **repetition has been *suppressed* in favor of the fulfillment of the goal of harmonic resolution.** [emphasis mine][171]

Rhythm is valued in the Western classical tradition only inasmuch as the beat, accent, meter, and tempo relate to linear progression or "forward movement." Thus, the drums — a fundamental characteristic of African and African derived musics — are *not* a priority or a fundamental aspect of the Western classical tradition. Furthermore, what also stands out about the role of rhythm and repetition in the Western classical tradition is the fact that actual occurrences of (natural) repetition are often covered up or ignored, as if they do not exist:

> Although the key role of 'recapitulation' in the ABA or AABBAA sonata form (often within a movement itself, as in the so frequently ignored 'second repeats' in Beethoven's major works) is undisputed in theory, in live performance, these repetitions are often left out to avoid the undesirability of having 'to be told the same thing twice.' Repeating the exposition, as important as it no doubt is for the 'classical style,' is subsumed within and fulfilled by the general category called 'development.'[172]

---

[169] *Ibid*, 146.
[170] Here, I use "culture" in the same way that James A. Snead, Raymond Williams, and Tricia Rose all do: Culture is a "whole way of life, which is manifest over the whole range of social activities but is most evident in 'specifically cultural' activities — a language, styles of art, kinds of intellectual work; and an emphasis on a 'whole social order' within which a specifiable culture, in styles of art and kinds of intellectual work, is seen as the direct or indirect product of an order primarily constituted by other social activities." Tricia Rose, *Black Noise: Rap Music and Black Culture in Contemporary America* (Hanover and London: Wesleyan University Press), 198. Tricia Rose actually quotes Raymond Williams, *The Sociology of Culture* (New York: Schocken, 1981), pp. 11-12.
[171] Snead,152
[172] *Ibid*,152

INTERMISSION

Hip Hop/Rap Theory

Again, all musical cultures use some sort of music "theory," that is, a way of forming and expressing (describing, explaining) how and what musical events have occurred. However, not all musical cultures use a written notation to express their theories. (Some areas of hip hop/rap music can be analyzed and understood by some of the basic language and concepts of music theory.) But music theory, as a whole, is an inadequate means for surveying and truly understanding hip hop/rap music and beatmaking.

We must also not forget that hip hop/rap music is a different musical convention altogether — the hip hop/rap music tradition is an amalgamation of a number of things. It's a music tradition that is well embedded within the African American (Black) music tradition; it's obviously not a descendent of seventeenth, eighteenth, or nineteenth-century European music traditions. Also, hip hop/rap music is a hybrid of pre- and post industrialism, coupled with dramatic advancement in recording technology. Even more telling, hip hop/rap music is the born product of urban American street culture and neglected lower class blacks and Latinos, not privileged whites. Finally, and perhaps most importantly for the purposes of this study, hip hop/rap music is the first music in the world to be created exclusively through the use of recorded music and other electronically pre-recorded sounds.

Hip hop/rap theory is further distinguished by the fact that it governs and speaks to two different, but co-equal and interdependent, layers or dimensions of musical activity: the beat and the rhyme — the instrumental and the vocal. In the hip hop/rap music tradition, the "rap" or the "rhyme" describes the chief (native) form of vocalization, while the "beat" is used to describe the entire instrumental.

Order and "Rules" and the Hip Hop/Rap Theory

Music theory depends on *order*, that is, a set of rules and logical equations that must at all times be accounted for and respected. This is a major area in which hip hop/rap theory differs from music theory. "Logic" in hip hop/rap theory does not defer to a set of "rules," but rather a set of flexible aesthetic *parameters*, which don't always have to be strictly followed. Where music theory seemingly demands, above all, the pursuit of *perfection* — based, of course, on the logic of music theory — hip hop/rap music theory demands, above all, the pursuit of the *right* sound and feeling, as determined by the individual beatmaker, not abstract knowledge. In hip hop/rap, the pursuit of perfection is secondary to the pursuit of a particular sound, feeling, and/or impact. Hip hop/rap music is less concerned with rigid and rudimentary notions of accuracy; it's more concerned with capturing the naturalness and energy of the creative moment. This is one reason that hip hop/rap theory accounts for, and seeks out, mistakes; even going as far as to manufacture mistakes in the form of cuts, scratchin', distortion, and, of course, looping. Because of this, the factors that determine what "works" in hip hop/rap are largely outside of the realm of music theory and the Western classical music tradition. What works in the hip hop/rap traditions depends on its own distinct aesthetics, principles, ideologies, priorities, and what *sounds good*. But let us not forget that what sounds good or not is certainly relative to the tastes and musical ideologies of a given musician working within the parameters of a given music tradition.

How the Primary Elements of Music Theory Translate to the Beatmaking and Hip Hop/Rap Music Traditions

Rhythm, Repetition, and Groove in the Hip Hop/Rap Music Tradition

Unlike the Western classical tradition, where harmony rules supreme, the organizing force which underscores the hip hop/rap music tradition is **rhythm**. As with all of the core African American (Black) music traditions, rhythm is the most perceptible thing. Rhythm has long been recognized as a focal constituent of African music and its American descendants — slave songs, spirituals, hymnals, blues, gospel, rhythm and blues, soul, and rock 'n' roll. In the hip hop/rap tradition, rhythm also serves as what I call the "vibe of timing," the *feeling* of an established pace. Contrary to this, in the Western classical tradition rhythm is employed inasmuch as it helps in the pursuit of precision, "order," and linear progression. But in the hip hop/rap tradition, rhythm (and then melody and harmony) is always used to help in the pursuit of capturing the *groove*,[173] the locked-in rhythm section, the natural *feel, pulse,* and main rhythmic moments where the rapper rhymes. This is because in hip hop/rap music, the development of the groove takes major precedent.

---

[173] The **groove** is the sense, feel, and sound manifested through rhythm and created by the rhythm section: the drums, bass, and rhythm guitars, etc.

Although there are "rules" for harmony, there are no rules for rhythm.[174] And rhythm, in the hip hop/rap and beatmaking traditions, completely lends itself to the lyrical style, syntax, and syncopation of rapping, hip hop's native form of vocalization — the **2nd dimension** of the hip hop/rap music tradition. Actually, it should be understood that in the hip hop/rap tradition, the more harmony and melody, the looser the rhythm, the weaker the repetition, and thus, the less room and space, which leaves a smaller "groove" for the rapper (lyricist) to settle in on and key off of. Likewise, the *tighter* the rhythm, the stronger and more effective the repetition and, therefore, the more "room" and space and the larger the groove for syntax and the unique syncopation of rapping. In contrast, the more harmony and melody, the less space for vocal style, syntax, and syncopation. Essentially, this also means that the more harmony and melody is added to a beat, the less space or room for extensive rapping styles. This is because the more harmony and melody that a piece of music has, the more rhythm is overshadowed and relegated to a secondary role. And in hip hop/rap music, rhythm is always primary, it is *never* secondary. As I previously discussed, hip hop/rap music emanates from the use of the break — the rhythm at its rawest point — and *not* from the use of harmonies and melodies of songs.[175] Finally, it should also be noted that rhythm and repetition in all African American (Black) music traditions is not only a "priority," it is at once both a *necessary* and *beautiful* thing:

> "In black culture, repetition means that the thing *circulates* (exactly in the manner of any flow, including capital flows) there in an equilibrium. In European culture, repetition must be seen to not just circulation and flow, but accumulation and growth. **In black culture, the thing (the ritual, the dance, the beat) is 'there for you to pick up when you come back to get it.' If there is a goal (Zweck) in such a culture, it is always deferred; it continually 'cuts' back to the start, in the musical meaning of 'cut' as an abrupt, seemingly unmotivated break** (an accidental da capo) with a series already in progress and a willed return to a prior series. *A culture based on the idea of the "cut" will always suffer in a society whose dominant idea is material progress* .... The greater the insistence on the pure beauty and value of repetition, the greater the awareness must also be that **repetition takes place on a level not of musical development or progression."** [emphasis mine][176]

---

[174] Christopher Small, *Music, Society, Education: An Examination of the Function of Music in Western, Eastern and African Cultures With Its Impact on Society and Its Use in Education* (New York: Schirmer, 1977), 20. Small drives home the point that "harmony," in the post-renaissance musical tradition, is the "logical element par excellence," and that it is the "most systematically taught and most bound by rules." He further adds that "in teaching melody writing, instrumentation, rhythm, the teacher may give advice and criticism, but there are 'rules' only for harmony."

[175] Even when harmony and melody are used in hip hop/rap music, it has always been typically percussive in nature. For example, in hip hop/rap music, it's not atypical for bass lines to be used as the only form of melody. Also, in hip hop/rap, harmony and melody are usually better suited for singing and simple rhyme schemes and strategies.

[176] Snead, 150.

BeatTip – Rhythm, Time Correct, and Natural Feel

It's important to remember that rhythm isn't merely a mathematical concept, it's a "time" concept; it deals with how musical elements move through time. When you attempt to narrow the scope of rhythm to simple mathematical principles, you actually subtract away from the natural essence of time in music. As I pointed out earlier, timing correct is the mechanical correction of time. It "corrects" the value of timing that a beatmaker programs. But another way of looking at it is that it disrupts (in some cases destroys) the natural — *live* — sense of timing by making time more artificial than it already is, thanks, of course, to the looping that takes place in the framework of a beat.

It's also necessary to note that when beatmakers make beats, we are essentially moving between artificial and natural (live) realms. Still, the more artificiality we incorporate into our beats, the more likely they are to sound mechanical, stiff, stuck, or just plain lifeless. On the other hand, the more naturalness that we are able to incorporate into our beats, the more likely they will have a "real" feeling to them (more "vibe"). Hence, hi-hats (and other percussive elements) are ideal for incorporating a more natural feel and rhythm to our drum patterns and our beats overall. Therefore, the less corrective measures you take with hi-hat programming, the better the chance that you'll retain some naturalness and vibe in your beats.

Melody and Harmony in the Hip Hop/Rap Music Tradition

Despite the increasing use of melody in recent years, melody has never played a major role in the hip hop/rap music tradition. Hip hop/rap music does not use melody in the same way that other forms of music does. Rather than feature or build the musical framework *around* melody, in the hip hop/rap music tradition, melody is often used to support and/or accentuate the rhythm of a beat. Also, in the hip hop/rap tradition, sounds of less than two notes in length can indeed have purpose (e.g., 808, chimes, sound-stabs, etc.). And unlike in the Western classical tradition, hip hop/rap motives do not necessarily have to lead somewhere, i.e. to other melodies, nor do they necessarily have to link to the next motive (if there is one) in order to ensure that the beat (piece of music) flows well. Also, the rupture (abrupt cuts) of musical phrases of various lengths is common in the hip hop/rap music tradition, especially considering the pivotal role that the loop plays in every hip hop/rap beat. Because of this, hip hop/

rap songs often exhibit varying types of melodic contours that are not always consistent with other music forms. For instance, melody lines in hip hop/rap music are often short and less developed, not because of a beatmaker's inability to develop the sense or range of a melody, but because the longer (larger) the melody line, the more rhythm gets overshadowed. When this occurs, a beat moves away from the quintessential hip hop/rap form, and it goes towards other music forms, presumably with some hip hop/rap *flavor* underneath it.

There are however some parallels that can be drawn between the principles of melody in the Western classical and hip hop/rap music traditions. For instance, the term "change" or "changes" in beatmaking translates well to "motif" or "motives." Also, where the Western classical tradition typically features constant melody shifts, the hip hop/rap tradition commonly features "phrase shifts," or rather well-developed changes. And just like motives are used in the Western classical tradition to form larger melodic lines and various movements, in the hip hop/rap tradition, changes are used to create what is commonly known as "switch-ups," "build-ups" (crescendos), and bridges. Also, "heterophony," the "shadow" or "echo" effect created when two or more voices simultaneously perform *variations* of the same melodic material, is akin to the process of "stacking" in the hip hop/rap music tradition, where melody lines are shadowed with additional instrumentation and varying timbre, usually strings, synths, and/or bass.

As for harmony, well, for starters, the hip hop/rap tradition recognizes two separate meanings for harmony: (1) The use of simultaneous pitches or chords — the traditional meaning in music; and (2) The combination of sounds considered "pleasing" to the ear. In the traditional sense of harmony, there are some parallels between the Western classical and hip hop/rap music traditions. First, chromatic harmony is a common feature of the synthetic-sounds-based style. Here, chromatic harmonies (scales of ascending or descending pitches proceeding by semitones) are used within the basically diatonic (major scale) coloring. Second, consonance and dissonance — musical terms describing whether combinations of notes sound "good" together or "stable" or not, or rather "pleasant" or "harsh" — is not necessarily in-line with the Western classical tradition's view. In hip hop/rap music, consonance is relative to the aesthetic values and priorities of the tradition itself, which for the most part, favor rough, rugged, raw, and harsh tones. In other words, what is often harmonically "stable" in hip hop/rap music is considered to be "unstable" in the Western classical tradition. That harshness is often embraced in hip hop/rap is one of the key distinctions between the Western classical and hip hop/rap music traditions.

If I had to translate hip hop/rap's relationship to dissonance, I would say that dissonant phrases play a fundamental role in many beats. In the Western classical tradition, unstable tone combinations, which are said to be harsh, are used to express (themes of) pain, grief, and conflict.[177] However, in the Western classical tradition, unstable tone combinations have to be *resolved*. This is not so in the hip hop/rap music tradition, where the focus on dissonance does not necessarily have to be resolved, and where breaks and loops, by their nature, do not resolve but instead repeat. It must also be remembered that Western classical music is centered on a "wholeness" and a "*new* completeness" that reinforces the European (Western) perspective of history and time: linear progression. In contrast, the African American (Black) and African music traditions are centered on a "returning *newness*," that is, repetition, which reinforces the African perspective of history and time: cyclical progression.

In the hip hop/rap tradition the second meaning of harmony is not merely a matter of aurallity but of philosophy. That is to say, like many concepts in hip-hop/rap music, harmony, in this other sense of the word, is ultimately concerned with the end results and not necessarily the means to them. In beatmaking, whatever sounds good *together* — no matter what the actual sounds are or whatever beatmaking compositional style is used — is what matters. In other words, whatever works to *make it* sound good together is the key; **there are no rules of abstract knowledge to follow.** In this way, the hip hop/rap music tradition is less restrictive about harmony because it does not necessarily have to subscribe to any system and/or rule about harmony to achieve harmony. Here, the concept of harmony mostly refers to *cohesion* and *agreement*, as it is understood under the aesthetics, values, and priorities of the hip hop/rap form and sound. It does not refer to a strict scheme of tones that logically fit together. In the hip hop/rap music and beatmaking traditions, there is no tonal litmus test that must be passed; if it works, it works. Moreover, in the hip hop/rap music tradition, the second meaning of harmony really serves to denote *feeling* more than a "correct" sound equation.

BeatTip – Regarding Tonal Progression in Hip Hop/Rap Music

I strongly recommend that all traditionally trained musicians really get to know the hip hop/rap music and beatmaking traditions *first*, before you

---

[177] For an interesting look at dissonance in the African American (Black) music tradition, particularly a discussion of "blue notes" in blues music, see Cornell West's segment in Astra Taylors documentary, *Examined Life*, 2009.

explore ways for incorporating traditional practices such as tonal progression methods. Many traditionally trained musicians who become beatmakers often attempt to do two things that are actually contrary to the tenets of hip hop/rap music — things that often lead to the creation of hip hop/rap-*like* beats at best, or just plain wack beats at worst. First, many traditionally trained musicians try to apply methods of tonal progression to hip hop/rap music — irrespective of the fact that hip hop/rap has its own notions of form and harmony; irrespective of the fact that hip hop/rap beats are predicated upon rhythm; irrespective of the fact that hip hop/rap emanates from the use of breaks in a *looped* strategy. Second, many traditionally trained musicians carry out such musical exploration with little to no concern for, nor aim to, preserve the cultural flavor, nuance, and other crucial idioms of hip hop/rap music.

Still, methods of tonal progression can be applied to *certain* forms and styles of hip hop/rap music. In some cases, I even encourage that sort of exploration. However, I do not favor applying — often forcefully — methods of tonal progression when such methods are used to displace, supplant, and/or usurp the fundamental parameters that gave rise to, and still maintains, the hip hop/rap music tradition.

Texture in the Hip Hop/Rap Music Tradition

In the area of texture, there are some parallels in the Western classical and hip hop/rap music traditions. Specifically, the concept of "simultaneity" is fundamental in hip hop/rap music. Typical hip hop/rap beats have at least two different textures going at the same time. For instance, in hip hop/rap music, "the drums," i.e. the entire drum framework or pattern, comprise one musical texture and rhythm, while the "non-drums," i.e. rhythm riffs, tone-stabs, ruptured chords, short melodies, and/or other musical phrases, form other complete musical textures and rhythms. Also, the way in which the "recapitulation" in the Western classical tradition is comprised of variations of the subjects and motives that appear in the exposition, structures in hip hop/rap music (particularly drum frameworks) are similarly created by adding variations or "changes" to the frameworks and patterns and other musical phrases introduced within the first 4, 8, or 16 bars of a beat.

However, the hip hop/rap music tradition is not necessarily engaged in the process of establishing elaborate expositions and extensive recapitulations. This is because there's no premium (or real need for) on creating extensively (overly) dense sound textures. In the hip hop/rap music tradition, beatmakers create sound walls for the purposes of rappers to rhyme over. These sound walls, regardless of the number of musical layers, can never be too dense as to clash with the syncopation and rhythm of a rapper's rhyme flow (stylistic vocalization). Also, these sound walls or beats are typically just three minutes long (usually never more than five minutes); therefore, a beat's typically short duration, as compared to the duration of a Western classical piece of music, and a beat's typical (fundamental) form, i.e. looped break-like textures, actually make beats less adept to the same type of melody shifts and various movements in a typical Western classical piece of music.

Form or Structure in the Hip Hop/Rap Music Tradition

Before analyzing form and structure in the hip hop/rap music tradition, it is first necessary to spend a few words on the notion of "conversion" in the hip hop/rap music and beatmaking traditions. Like hip hop culture in general, hip hop/rap music is predicated upon conversion. Nothing starts out as hip hop/rap music. Instead, beatmakers *convert* pre-recorded sounds *into* hip hop/rap form. A music form, you will recall, that is driven by rhythm, repetition, and an upfront, syncopated drum beat, which is fused together into a tight "sound montage" that is then looped for a pre-determined number of bars (measures). There is no permanent source of hip hop/rap "notes," there is no "blue note" equivalent waiting to be arranged to spec. For beatmakers in the hip hop/rap music tradition, *any* pre-recorded or available sound — raw notes, electronic or acoustic included — can be modified to *fit* within the hip hop/rap aesthetic. Thus, in the hip hop/rap process of "conversion," any ingredient that works goes into the musical pot that ultimately manifests the general hip hop/rap form.

The general hip hop/rap form is predicated upon the use and creative manipulation of repetitious loops, fragmented sounds, sharp drums, and solid bass lines. Beatmaking is embodied by the use of fragmentation. And as the hip hop/rap music and beatmaking traditions further developed over the years, a series of structural patterns emerged. Many of these patterns have been streamlined and emulated to the point where they are now more like *structural clichés*.

Within the general hip hop/rap form, there are two basic forms, i.e. compositional structures and styles: sample-based and synthetic-sounds-based. Within each basic form there are distinct forms or styles. For instance, as I pointed out in chapter 8, the sample-based form can take on three varieties. First, the **simple sample-based form** describes a form of sampling in which a substantial portion of a recorded work is sampled and then imitated, with little to no significant transformation of the part that was sampled. Second, the **break-beat sample-based form**, which describes the form of sampling in which breaks and/or patches of recorded works are woven together in a fashion more akin to a hip hop/rap DJ blending and matching multiple segments of records. Third, the **intricate sample-based form**, the most sophisticated form of sampling, involves the deconstruction of the sampled work in a meticulous, intricate manner, followed by a unique arrangement of the substantially transformed sampled work.

There's also the synthetic-sounds-based (no-samples-featured) form, which also has several sub-forms. First, the **non-orchestral synthetic-sounds-based form**, which is a very basic music theme and/or an underdeveloped chord progression with sparse percussion is used. Second, the **semi-orchestral synthetic-sounds-based form**, which is a moderately developed, but effective and often catchy, musical theme is used. Often the theme that takes shape in this form is characterized by one or two pivotal changes, some level of sound-stacking, and usually one primary chord progression pattern. Third, the **orchestral or "epic" synthetic-sounds-based form,** which is distinguished by well-developed musical themes that incorporate multiple chord progressions and melody lines, multiple changes and "build-ups."

Dynamics in the Hip Hop/Rap Music Tradition

Just as in the Western classical tradition, dynamic (volume and velocity) changes occur in hip hop/rap music composition as well, and for similar reasons: Namely, to effect the mood of a piece of music, to color the overall sound, and/or to serve any number of structural possibilities. The big difference in the hip hop/rap music tradition is that dynamics are not regarded as being part of a highly instructive process (as is the case in the Western classical tradition), but ra, a straight-forward process that depends on one's imagination and creative use of particular dynamic "functions" of a given EMPI.

Dynamics in the hip hop/rap music tradition work quite differently than in the Western classical tradition mainly because the way in which beatmakers change sounds from one dynamic level to the next is through the use of various "dynamics functions" (velocity, sustain, fade, chorus, filter, etc.) of EMPIs. In the Western classical tradition, the realization of a composer's dynamics instructions depends on the individual ability of each performer. By contrast, in the beatmaking tradition, the realization of a beatmaker's dynamics ideas is made through his or her knowledge and use of multiple dynamics functions within a given EMPI. For instance, in beatmaking, **velocity** is the term most associated with the manipulation of the volume of individual sounds during the initial composition process. All EMPIs have default velocity levels which can be adjusted, thereby giving beatmakers the ability to create sudden changes in sound and the overall sonic impression of a beat (piece of music).

It's also important to note that most words or phrases used in the Western classical tradition to indicate changes in dynamics has a corresponding "function" in the beatmaking tradition. For example, **al niente**, which means "to nothing" or "fade to silence," and **calando**, which means "becoming smaller," are dynamic effects that are achieved in the beatmaking tradition through the modification of the "sustain" function on most EMPIs. Similarly, **da niente**, which means "from nothing, out of silence," and **perdeno** or **perdendosi**, which means "losing volume, fading into nothing, dying away," is a dynamic technique (style, effect) that is achieved in the hip hop/rap tradition through the "fade," "sustain," and "chorus" functions of EMPIs. Finally, **marcato**, which means "stressed, pronounced," **sotto voce**, which means "soft, subtle," **crescendo** which means "becoming louder," and **decrescendo** or **diminuendo**, which means "becoming softer," are sound techniques (styles) that are easily achieved in the beatmaking tradition by using the velocity function of EMPIs. Also, **accents**, the increased volume of one particular note (sound) above the rest, can also be achieved through velocity function manipulation as well.

The "Lack of Music Theory Knowledge" Argument is Wrong

In recent years, there have been murmurs about the "lack of music theory knowledge" of some the most well-known beatmaking pioneers. This argument has been lobbied into the hip hop/rap musical process debate as some sort of answer as to why many principles of music theory were *not* used in the hip hop/rap music and beatmaking traditions' developmental years. Here, I want to set the record straight.

By the time Marley Marl, Dr. Dre, DJ Premier, Prince Paul, RZA, DJ Toomp, and notable others garnered their first level of critical acclaim, there was already a well-defined approach to creating beats. So the concept of "lack of music theory knowledge" is woefully inaccurate and, more importantly, irrelevant. All of the aforementioned beatmakers were extremely knowledgeable of *their* particular music tradition, the hip hop/rap music tradition, which is all they really needed to be knowledgeable of. One wouldn't say that a Western classical composer's "lack of hip hop/rap knowledge" weakens his understanding of the Western classical tradition, would they? A Western classical composer is expected to be thorough in their own music tradition — the Western classical tradition. While knowledge of other music traditions might be helpful to Western classical composers, such knowledge is certainly not necessary for them to be successful within the Western classical tradition. But all Western classical composers must have a solid understanding of music theory. Likewise, beatmakers from the hip hop/rap music tradition must have a solid understanding of the fundamental aesthetics, concepts, practices, methods, presuppositions, and priorities of the hip hop/rap music tradition. Thus, to imply that beatmakers who lack a knowledge of music theory have a musical deficiency is bogus, misguided, and completely unmerited.

Another related point is the notion that *none* of the earliest pioneers of the hip hop/rap music tradition even knew how to play a traditional instrument. Not true. Many of those involved in the development of hip hop/rap music and beatmaking did play traditional instruments; and a majority of them also knew music theory, or were at least familiar with its basic tenets. Remember, from 1930 to 1970, New York City was one of the epicenters of music in the United States. Much of the top blues, jazz, rhythm and blues, soul, and certainly, funk, was played in New York city during that time. Thus, for proper context on why or why not music theory is used, one must concede the fact that many of the first practitioners of hip hop/rap music were the children of traditional instrumentalists and musicians. And as we've learned in Part I of this study, the hip hop/rap music tradition was built upon the *conscious rejection* of more traditional compositional methods that typically rely on music theory.

Finally, I should note that herein lies the reason why so many trained musicians have difficulty actually creating, dare I say, "authentic" hip hop/rap music: They try to think of hip hop/rap music in terms of music theory and its principles, when the reality is that, for the most part, hip hop/rap music can not — and should not — be thought of in that context. Although I have tremendous respect for music theory (I use it whenever applicable), I also recognize that it is just *one* music theory out of many that exist throughout the world. As such, I don't consider music theory to be a grand musical converter that has ominous powers to conform *any* music that it touches into something greater. But there can be no denying that hip hop/rap music is an entirely different musical convention altogether precisely because it *converts* and can not be converted in quite the same way.

Sound and "Sounds" in the Hip Hop/Rap Music Tradition

The hip hop/rap music tradition's conception and use of sound differs than that of the Western classical tradition. For example, within the fundamental compositional methods of the hip hop/rap music and beatmaking traditions, there is a predilection for the use of pre-recorded and/or electronic–generated sounds. No such predilection exists in the Western classical tradition. But where hip hop/rap's conception and use of sound differs the most from the Western classical tradition's conception can be seen in the area of harmony.

Beatmakers — hip hop/rap music composers — and Western classical composers are both concerned with the way in which individual sounds render collective audio composites. However, Western classical composers are more concerned with the "collectivity" of sounds, inasmuch as they are juxtaposed in harmonic relation. This is not the case in hip hop/rap music for several reasons. As I've pointed out before, in the hip hop/rap music tradition, harmony isn't always about the combination of simultaneous musical notes formed into different chords. Instead, for beatmakers in the hip hop/rap music tradition, harmony is actually more about the *arrangement* of sounds, irrespective of the logic and rules of music theory. The point I'm making here is that the very practice of creating chords isn't as significant in the hip hop/rap form because hip hop/rap music is fundamentally predicated upon the use of pre-recorded (electronic) sounds and music, rather than the use of raw musical notes. In the hip hop/rap music and beatmaking traditions, individual components, i.e. sounds or instrument voices, are valued more for the unique audio result that it will produce *in conjunction* with other sounds. That is to say, beatmakers place a premium on the role and position an individual sound will play in a collective audio imprint (i.e. sound wall). So when it comes to the question of sound(s), beatmaking is fundamentally about creating a unique collective timbre through the use of individual pre-recorded (electronic) sounds in arrangement styles that don't necessarily defer to the rules (abstract knowledge) of music theory. Still, I concede that the Western classical tradition is also similarly concerned with achieving a unique collective timbre.

Sound Rendition and Timbre

The two types of recorded sounds that are most valued in beatmaking are: (1) Self-sampled sounds, in particular those sounds sampled from vinyl records; and (2) Stock or preset sounds, like the ones typically found in keyboards, sound modules, and music production software suites. Both stock sounds and sampled sounds change according to their source, i.e., vinyl record and/or EMPI. Raw musical notes never change; middle C is always middle C, it always sounds the same. However, how middle C is *rendered* (the audio representation of middle C via a given instrument) and the timbre of middle C changes dramatically, depending on the EMPI (keyboard, synth, sound module, etc.) that produces it. This factor of sound rendition is paramount in beatmaking. Again, beatmakers are not driven or motivated by the logic behind linear progression or the rules of music theory in general. Beatmakers are fundamentally concerned with how something sounds, and the way in which specific tapestries of sounds make a collective audio composite. And thus, for beatmakers, having "unique" sounds is critically important because the use of non-unique sounds is in many ways tantamount to biting — unmotivated, rampant "copy-catting" and duplication.

Sonic Properties

Here, it's necessary to point out the obvious: Hip hop/rap music is *funky!* Western classical music is not. Hip hop/rap music, even when it includes comedic lyrical matter, is often gritty and always sonically formidable. Further, hip hop/rap music is meant to be *felt* and heard; it is not meant to be *understood,* literally, through the prism of abstract knowledge. In the hip hop/rap music tradition, rhythms and sounds are chosen as much (if not more) for their impact as they are chosen for their unique sound. This is one reason that explains why the hip hap/rap music tradition often features bass lines and bass frequencies for melody. And from hip hop/rap music's inception, sonic *force* has always been a key aesthetic. Also, just as with all twentieth-century African American (Black) music traditions, the notion of capturing *feeling* within the music has always been a critical component of hip hop/rap music. Thus, for beatmakers in the hip hop/rap music tradition, the sonic properties of sounds, not notes, hold the most value. This is a key aesthetic that most traditionally trained musicians have a hard time grasping when they venture into the world of beatmaking.

Rapping: The 2nd Dimension of Hip Hop/Rap Music

Afro-American music is primarily a vocal music. –Eileen Southern

Rhymes overflowin', gradually growin', everything is written in code so it can coin…cide… –Rakim

There can be no serious discussion about the hip hop/rap music and beatmaking traditions without an analysis of the art of rapping. "Rap" or "rapping" is a unique form of vocalization that truly helps distinguish the hip hop/rap music tradition from all other forms of vocal music. And though some of the vocal habits of rappers can be easily traced back to the African American traditions of "toasting," "signifying," and radio DJ raps, there are other factors (as you will see in the following section) that help make rap the most percussive and rhythmic of all African American (Black) music vocal sub-traditions. Finally, it must be pointed out that rapping, like the art of beatmaking, is yet another component that greatly distinguishes the hip hop/rap music tradition from the Western classical tradition.

Before I begin my analysis of the art of rapping, it's important to again point out that the beatmaking tradition developed in part as a direct response to the development of more complex rhyme flows. The art of beatmaking grew, necessarily, as rap schemes, styles, and flows grew more advanced, more poetic, more syncopated, and more rhythmic. Also, rhyme verses gained a new level of density and grew longer in duration; and subject matter became more varied. Such complex advancements in the art of rapping could no longer be adequately serviced by DJs backspinning breaks live or on cassette. Hence, the beatmaking tradition emerged as a means of both representing the DJs music-making role, and as a means to accommodate the new complexities of rapping.

Fundamental Characteristics of Rapping

The art of rapping, which shares a similar depth and complexity with beatmaking, is an amalgamation of many different cultural components. It's a manifestation and extension of black vernacular; it's a vocal style heavily grounded in African American (black) dialect and street slang; it's an American "pat-tois" done over music; it's also a highly developed form of vocalization and poetry.

The poetics and musical metrics of rapping are unlike any other vocalization style in popular music. On one hand, rap's "verbal rhythm" bends, cuts, and reshapes combinations of standard languages with slang and other common language nuances, illuminating words with new phonetics and metaphorical meanings. On the other hand, its percussive sensibility and vocal *attack* and *release* projects a poetic dexterity that is both dense and astonishingly fluid.

"Yo, Kick That Rhyme" – the Mechanics of Rap: Improvisational Writing, Performance, Delivery, and Flow

Rappers, unlike typical songwriters/lyricists, use more words to fill up the instrumental space and time on a common 4/4 measure. And in doing so, rappers also use a more rapid rotation of words in an improvisational style. This improvisational style allows rappers to respond to and accentuate the pulse of the beat (the instrumental), using vocal inflection, non-verbal sounds, and emotional tenor. In this way, rappers are charged with the job (goal) of writing more words per bar and more bars per stanza. Thus, in the art of rapping, each bar can either be its own story or serve as the basis upon which other storylines emerge. Moreover, these multiple words, lines, and bars are often *connected* (strung together) to accommodate one central lyrical theme, while at the same time they merge and mesh with the beat.

Finally, rapping also stands out because of the style and level of declamation that it requires. Rappers not only play off of the unique timbre of their individual voice, they take great pride in developing their **delivery**, the unique personification and enunciation of their rhymes, and their **flow**, the rhetorical and rhythmic pace, pitch, tone, and volume of their rhyme performance. And it is through the creation and mastery of one's own unique delivery and flow that rappers are truly able to make a beat come alive. In this light, rappers are vocal virtuosos.

Rapping and Form – Dense Measures: More Words Per Measure

Rap rhymes contain dramatically more words per measure than your typical song. Because of these dense measures, the writing/performance style of rapping relies heavily upon the ongoing recurrence of the beat. Below, consider part of the first verse to rapper Nas' song "Memory Lane (Sittin' In Da Park)":

> I rap for listeners, blunt heads, fly ladies and prisoners/
> Henessey holders and old school niggaz, then I be dissin a/
> unofficial that smoke woolie thai/

> I dropped out of Cooley High, gassed up by a cokehead cutie pie/
> Jungle survivor, fuck who's the liver/
> My man put the battery in my back, a difference from Energizer/
> Sentence begins indented… with formality/
> My duration's infinite, moneywise or physiology/
> Poetry, that's a part of me, retardedly bop/
> I drop the ancient manifested hip-hop, straight off the block/
> I reminisce on park jams, my man was shot for his sheep coat/[178]

In the verse above, even without any accompanying music, one can *read* and *hear* the verbal rhythm it embodies. This verse presents a series of "cuts," "ruptures," and precise transitions that could *only* fit in a framework of rhythm and repetition. Such poetic dexterity could never fit with linear progression or constant material growth. Thus, rappers — especially those who use the complex lyrical rhyme style — *depend* on points of return, or in other words, the start *restarting*. It is the rhythm, the repetition, the cycle of the groove that allows for the nature of rap's orality to properly manifest itself.[179] Rappers *respond* to the rhythm and the repetition. And from the drums of a beat, they take their cue and internalize the proper tempo — rappers never rap to the set tempo of the beat, but instead to their own internal tempo that the beat's tempo inspires. Therefore, the weaker the rhythm, the less opportunity for a rapper to *respond* to it. So it must be understood that rappers (for the most part, complex lyricists) naturally count on the repetitive nature of the looping of a break. The loop returns the *new* starting point in strategic repetition, which supports and encourages the multiple starting points within rap rhyme stanzas. It is this response by the rapper to the rhythm and repetition that actually completes a song in the hip hop/rap music tradition.[180]

---

[178] Nas, "Memory Lane (Sittin' In Da Park)," produced by DJ Premier; from the album *Illmatic* (Columbia Records, 1994).

[179] "The growth of emotional force also serves to better connect the audience to the sonic world and communal feeling created in the context of repetition," quote from Guthrie P. Ramsey, Jr., *Race Music: Black Cultures From Bebop To Hip-Hop*, (Berkley, Los Angeles, and London: University of California Press, 2003), 129. "The repetition of a well-chosen rhythm continually affirms the power of the music by locking that rhythm…," quote from John Miller Chernoff, from *African Rhythm and African Sensibility: Aesthetics and Social Action in African Musical Idioms*, (Chicago and London: The University of Chicago Press, 1979), 111-12.

[180] In recent years, there's been a move away from a focus on lyrical acumen and extensive verses to "hook singing," "melody-rhyming," and sparse lyricism. Today, it has risen to the point where the oxymoronic phrase "lyrical rap" is often used to describe rappers who actually rap. Among the many reasons for this development, including the easily and often mimicked minimalist trap sound, there can be no illusion that the increased usage of melody, harmony, and other "traditional" music priorities has played a major role. As the importance of harmony and melody rise in the hip hop/rap music tradition, the role of rhythm declines, causing the overall quality of lyricism in hip hop/rap to suffer; and as a consequence, the hip hop/rap music tradition weakens.

The Function of Hip Hop/Rap Music ("Gonna Make You Move")

Above all, music in the African tradition is functional. –Eileen Southern

Since it's inception, there has always been five fundamental functions or purposes of hip hop/rap music: (1) To make people *move* — dance and provide "party music;" (2) To entertain; (3) Inform and teach; (4) To serve as an "art music;" and (5) To provide a coping mechanism for some of the trials of daily life.

The original function or purpose of hip hop/rap music was to make people *move*, i.e. dance at parties. The proverbial "park jam" was a major cornerstone in the early development and spread of hip hop/rap music. And when the pioneering DJs moved from the parks (and rec rooms) and into to the clubs, the park jammers migrated with them. Thus, the park jam era subsided and gave way to the club era that still exists today. Fittingly, hip hop/rap clubs are still ruled by the DJ, who still has the essential task and purpose of "movin' the crowd."

Next, as hip hop/rap music developed, spread, and grew more complex, it also became a form of entertainment, a powerful means for teaching listeners (effectively providing listeners with an array of needed information), and a form of art music. In addition to providing the vibe for dance parties and social gatherings, songs in the hip hop/rap music tradition were/are used as much to chronicle everyday life, give "street reports," and even decipher political information as they are to serve as art music to be listened to and appreciated for their artistic merit.

But of all the functions and purposes that hip hop/rap music serves, perhaps the most critical one is the function of providing a "coping mechanism" for some of the trials of its listeners' daily lives. All of the independent music traditions within the broader African American (Black) music tradition, have always been primarily *function*-based. For instance, to African slaves in America, music meant a cultural and kind of psychological survival; it was a companion of sanity. The very presence of music allowed these slaves to hold out for hope, even in the face of incredible despair. Hence, music *functioned* as a means to deal with the daunting experiences of a tragic daily life. Fast forward to the twentieth-frist century, and we still see a similar *function factor* in hip hop/rap music.

Throughout the 1970s, on up until the present day, hip hop/rap music has functioned in much the same way that it always has for oppressed blacks and Latinos and other minorities. Of course, the conditions of slavery cannot be appropriately compared to the conditions of contemporary America; even the worst oppressed blacks, Latinos, and other minorities do not live in the horrendous social and legal conditions and environments of slavery. Still, it's important to note that by today's living and social standards, many blacks and Latinos and other minorities do indeed live through the rigors of other peculiar institutions such as poverty, institutional racism, unemployment, inadequate social services, defacto segregation, and disproportionately high unemployment, and the like.[181]

Hence, while the hip hop/rap music tradition serves the five aforementioned functions for its primary constituents, there aren't many comparable functions that the Western classical tradition serves. Western classical music is not meant for partying or dancing (at least not in the same sense as hip hop culture is). Furthermore, Western classical music isn't meant to make people *move*— dance — in the manner that hip hop/rap does. Also, Western classical music doesn't have the function of providing news and information in the way that hip hop/rap music does. Moreover, Western classical music isn't intended to serve as a coping mechanism for the harsh daily realities of its constituents daily lives. And though I concede that many of those who enjoy Western classical music also find it theraputic, I maintain that the function that Western classical tradition has most in common with the hip hop/rap music tradition is in the area of art music.

Compositional Ethic of the Hip Hop/Rap Music and Beatmaking Traditions

There are a number of core factors that distinguish the compositional ethic of the hip hop/rap music and beatmaking traditions. First, in the hip hop/rap music and beatmaking traditions, the use of electronic pre-recorded sounds (music and synthetic-based) is the fundamental apparatus (mechanism) through which music is made. Unlike the Western classical tradition, in the beatmaking tradition, beatmakers are not necessarily concerned with using raw musical notes; instead, they're focused on using unique electronic sounds to compose their musical ideas.

Next, we already know that in the Western classical tradition, the compositional ethic is grounded on the use of abstract knowledge with great emphasis on harmony and the concept of linear progression (material growth).

---

[181] Certainly, one can understand where much of the underlying anger that exists in hip hop/rap music comes from: it is actually the manifestation and expression of the collective frustration of a consistently oppressed community. Likewise, one can also see where much of the fantasy rap and escapism that manifests itself in hip hop/rap music is generated from. Escapism not only helps one to ignore the present reality of one's ill fate, it also serves as a means to redefining a life that society at large deems worthless.

By contrast, the compositional ethic of the hip hop/rap music and beatmaking traditions emanates from the use of electronic pre-recorded sounds (music and synthetic-based), with great emphasis on rhythm and repetition (cyclical progression). And in the concept of cyclical progression, the ultimate aim is not material growth, but instead, a willful return to a prior series of musical ideas.

Another core factor that distinguishes hip hop/rap music and beatmaking's compositional ethic can be seen in the area of structure. In hip hop/rap music, structure is not about grappling with the "pure physics of tone" or manifesting linear logic. Structure in the hip hop/rap music and beatmaking traditions is more about creating cuts and rupture in a way that emphasizes strong rhythmic and repetitive activity and powerful (overbearing) sonic impact. In the Western classical tradition, a "good" structure is one in which the music takes the listener on a musical journey, through a clear beginning, middle, and end. Fundamentally, in the hip hop/rap music tradition, the notion of a clear beginning, middle, or end is quite different. The origins of hip hop/rap music are predicated upon the use of the break (a cut section of recorded music), overtly repeated for the rhythmic effect that repetition produces (cyclical rotation). So it's not that the notion of "taking a listener on a musical journey" isn't a priority in the hip hop/rap music tradition, it is. But the musical journey is made possible by an instrumental structure that is cyclical-based rather than linear-based. Further, in the hip hop/rap music tradition, the "journey" is also moved from the beginning, middle, and end by the rhymes of the rapper.

Drums, specifically, the creation of drum frameworks (drum programming), is another core factor of the compositional ethic of the hip hop/rap music and beatmaking traditions. In the hip hop/rap music tradition, the drums are fundamental to hip hop/rap's musical architecture; in fact, they play a paramount role in the overall compositional ethic of the hip hop/rap music tradition. This is in stark contrast to the Western classical tradition, where drums (think of a modern drum kit) are certainly not prioritized, mostly because they are said to have no *definite* pitch. Furthermore, it is well-understood that drums play a key role in the development of rhythm and groove; therefore, they actually necessitate the use of repetition. Finally, drums also offer a powerful, in-your-face sonic impression; a characteristic that is not a priority in the Western Classical music tradition.

The "hip hop sensibility" is another core factor that distinguishes the compositional ethic of the hip hop/rap music and beatmaking traditions. The "hip hop sensibility" is a sensibility that highly values and prioritizes competition, individual style, syncretism, a "culture of sampling," transformation, and the transgression of musical rules. Also, the "hip hop/rap attitude," which is fundamental to the "hip hop sensibility," is an attitude that carries a straight-to-the-point music philosophy, an attitude that is decidedly anti-establishment, ultra competitive, in-your-face, and often confrontational.[182] Though competition and individual style exists in some areas of the Western classical music tradition, it certainly does not engross the entire tradition in the way that competition and individual style underscores and encompasses the hip hop/rap music and beatmaking traditions. "Battles" (both rap and beat) are fundamental in the hip hop/rap music and beatmaking traditions. Obviously, battles are not a characteristic of the Western classical tradition. And although the Western classical tradition does indeed host its own forms of competitions, these competitions are not a main part of the fabric that makes up and informs the compositional ethic of the Western classical tradition.

Finally, the hip hop/rap compositional ethic is also distinguished by the unique process and relationship that beatmakers and rappers find themselves in. Although beatmakers are concerned with conveying to listeners their musical ideas, they are equally focused (if not more) on forming their musical ideas into a beat, i.e. an instrumental layer, that will ultimately be used, first and foremost, to inspire a rapper to provide the rhyme (vocal layer) for it. This is certainly unlike the Western classical tradition, where composers are more often concerned with conveying to the listener his or her musical ideas. And although some composers in the Western classical tradition do provide music intended for vocals (for instance, the opera), they are not assigned with the fundamental charge of providing one half of the total dimension of an entire music tradition.

Tale of the Tape
Key Differences Between the Western Classical and Hip Hop/Rap Music and Beatmaking Traditions

The hip hop/rap music tradition doesn't abandon music theory altogether; it can't, particularly because it necessarily uses some of the basic elements and language of music theory *within* its own compositional ethic. But the point here is that the hip hop/rap music tradition does not prescribe to, use, and/or have *need* for most of the rules of music theory. More importantly, the hip hop/rap music and beatmaking traditions do not subscribe to the core concepts, practices, principles, or priorities of the Western classical tradition,

---

[182] Without the "hip hop sensibility" and/or the "hip hop attitude," hip hop/rap *music* is incomplete. Without the "hip hop sensibility" and/or the "hip hop attitude," *attempts* at hip hop music are only superficial at best.

most notably, the hierarchy of harmony, melody, and rhythm, and the notion of linear progression (material growth). In the hip hop/rap music tradition, the hierarchy of the basic elements of music are reversed: Rhythm is dominant, melody is secondary, and harmony is the least important. And as I mentioned before, in the hip hop/rap music tradition, repetition (cyclical progression), *not* linear progression (material growth), is the guiding philosophy on the issue of time and space in music.

The "Hip Hop Sensibility" and "Hip Hop Attitude" Factor

Obviously, the Western classical tradition does not incorporate the "hip hop sensibility," nor does it rely on the "hip hop attitude" to manifest its musical ideas, presuppositions, and predispositions. And while the Western classical tradition may inform one about the principles, ideas, presuppositions, and predispositions of European culture in the seventeenth-, eighteenth-, nineteenth-, and early twentieth centuries, it can not inform one about the "hip hop sensibility" or the underlying "hip hop attitude." In other words, a better understanding of the Western classical tradition and/or music theory, no matter how advanced, does not provide one with the "hip hop attitude" or the "hip hop sensibility;" nor does it give one a greater understanding of the hip hop/rap music and beatmaking traditions.

"Logic" in Each Compositional Ethic

"Logic" is something that is always open to interpretation in music traditions. Any objective analysis of logic must recognize two important questions: (1) *Who's* point of view of logic is being considered? and (2) In what context is logic being considered? Logic that is based on the laws (properties and elements) of music theory is quite different than logic that is based on the idioms, tropes, properties, and principles of the hip hop/rap music tradition. Logic is certainly at work within the Western classical and the hip hop/rap music and beatmaking traditions; however, how logic is *interpreted* and *used* differs from tradition to tradition. In the Western classical tradition, the notion of logic is more literal and attached to Western rules about harmony and tonality. But in the hip hop/rap music tradition, the notion of logic is based on hip hop/rap's own aesthetic priorities. Moreover, logic in the hip hop/rap music and beatmaking traditions is rooted in a pragmatic approach: To beatmakers, if it works, then it's logical, regardless if it makes literal sense or not.

Significance of the Written Score

As beatmakers, the fact that we do not write our compositions down on sheet music does not, in any way, disqualify us as composers. The arrangements (the sequences of consciously placed musical events) created in our EMPIs serve as our de facto sheet music; and the capture media that we record our beats in/to serves as our score. Taken in a creative and technical context, this is no different than a traditional composer inputting musical directions into a sheet-music computer application. Furthermore, the non-use of traditional compositional techniques also does not disqualify beatmakers as composers, especially in the most fundamental sense. Electronic music production tools have made it possible for beatmakers and traditional composers to bypass using separate performers, which allows beatmakers to truly be both composer *and* performer simultaneously.

Function and Accessibility

Western classical music is primarily an art music; it's something on display where the listeners and onlookers do not, nor are they expected to, participate. The music of the Western classical tradition is typically something that is experienced *apart* from everyday life. In fact, the Western classical tradition really has no participatory function, other than the concert hall-going experience. And even within that setting, audiences do not *move* along with the music, nor do they echo (outloud) anything familiar to them. Instead, they are expected to remain silent, clapping (as is custom) only at the end of the symphony or opera.

By contrast, hip hop/rap music is both a function music *and* an art music. Hip hop/rap music, which is highly participatory in its functions, has several functions or purposes. It's original function is to make people dance as well as to serve as party music. Hip hop/rap music, like Western classical music, also functions as a form of entertainment. However, the difference here, again, is the level of involvement by listeners and patrons. And although hip hop/rap and Western classical music share a somewhat similar art music function, hip hop/rap music also serves as a powerful means for teaching listeners and providing an array of information. The Western classical tradition has no such function and serves no such purpose, especially when you consider the fact that the works that are performed in front of audiences are from the tradition's greatest canonical works, which are centuries old in most cases. Finally, as I've pointed out in this chapter, hip hop/rap music provides a coping mechanism for some of the trials of its listeners' daily life. Western classical music serves a parallel function in its listeners' lives, but certainly not to the extent of the hip hop/rap music tradition.

Here, it's also worth mentioning that the Western classical tradition does not have a *common-man* accessibility. To even begin to have the remote resemblance of a career in the Western classical tradition, one must have a solid grasp of the abstract knowledge of music theory, as well as be familiar with the canonical works of the Western classical tradition. By contrast, the hip hop/rap music and beatmaking traditions, which also prioritizes the value of study and knowledge of its canonical works, do have a common-man accessibility.

Instrumentation and Vocalization in the Western Classical and the Hip Hop/Rap Music and Beatmaking Traditions

The fundamental purpose of hip hop/rap beats, in their native context, is not to remain as an instrumental, the "1st dimension" of hip hop/rap music. The purpose of a beat is to be paired with the lyrics of a rapper, the "2nd dimension" of hip hop/rap music. It is the bringing together of these two dimensions that makes the hip hop/rap music and beatmaking traditions whole. By contrast, the Western classical tradition is a mostly instrumental tradition. And although opera[183] is a part of the Western classical tradition, it does not play the same primary role that rapping does in the hip hop/rap music tradition.

Final Analysis of the Battle

The Western classical and hip hop/rap music traditions are both formidable traditions. Each tradition has its own systems and grand approaches, and each tradition has its own encompassing culture. But when it comes to a battle between the Western classical music tradition and the hip hop/rap music tradition, on hip hop/rap's and beatmaking's turf and terms, the Western classical music tradition gets burned!

The Western classical music tradition has music theory as its greatest compositional apparatus; the hip hop/rap music tradition counters with beatmaking as its greatest compositional system and achievement. And while music theory may be the more well-known, more complex, and presumably more advanced compositional device, it can not convert the advanced or even

---

[183] Opera, which includes the arts of solo and choral singing and declamation, is not purely a vocal tradition; it also includes acting, and dancing in a staged spectacle.

most basic processes of beatmaking for its uses. However, the hip hop/rap music and beatmaking traditions can indeed convert and use much of music theory, *at will*, throughout its basic and advanced processes. Finally, while the Western classical tradition is completely and rigidly bound by the abstract knowledge of music theory, the hip hop/rap music tradition is not bound just by beatmaking. It is best translated and *enhanced* by the unique processes and nuances and pragmatic logic of beatmaking just as much as it is informed by the cultural metrics of the encompassing hip hop culture.

Furthermore, while the Western classical tradition has the opera as its chief form of vocalization, the hip hop/rap music tradition has rapping as its native form of vocal expression. But unlike opera, rapping is truly a "2nd dimension" that makes the entire hip hop/rap music tradition whole. Opera does not make the Western classical music tradition complete; rapping does make the hip hop/rap music tradition complete. And although rapping represents its own separate sub-tradition within the broader hip hop culture, it is widely considered to be indispensable to the hip hop/rap music tradition.

Finally, while the function of the Western classical tradition may be to serve as entertainment and an art music that prompts listeners to literally *comprehend* a composer's musical instructions, the function of the hip hop/rap music tradition is not only to serve as an art music as well, but to inform, teach, serve as a coping mechanism, and, of course, to make people move and get up and dance. And, it must be remembered, listeners of the hip hop/rap music tradition need not "understand" the musical instructions of beatmakers (composers) to fully realize this function.

More Insight and Perspective that We Can Take Away from the Battle

The Usefulness of Music Theory in the Hip Hop/Rap Music and Beatmaking Traditions

Music theory doesn't necessarily *unlock* the creative potential of beatmaking and/or hip hop/rap music. Actually, because of the additional set of rules that music theory applies to the beatmaking process, it often works to inhibit beatmaking. In many ways, applying some of the rules of music theory is like calling out cues and counts to a b-boy, as he battles in a cipher. Stripped from the freedom of his tradition, he's led to focus on nailing cues rather than doing dope moves and catching wreck on the dance floor. As with b-boying (hip hop's original dance), the hip hop/rap music and beatmaking traditions prioritize staying *true* to the rules of its own tradition, while recognizing the freedom of exploration of those very rules at the same time. Therefore, it is with this understanding of the "rules/freedom duality" of hip hop culture that music theory can be used most effectively. In other words, I see nothing wrong with using music theory in beatmaking, so long as the essence of the hip hop/rap art form isn't compromised and/or diluted in the process.

Here, let's remember that the South Bronx disaster created a heightened level of urgency that was predicated upon daily survival. So it should come as no surprise that hip hop culture and hip hop/rap music has an underlying urgency to it. This urgency manifests itself in different ways in hip hop/rap music, but one notable way is that it outfits hip hop/rap and beatmaking with a straight-to-the-point musical philosophy. Such a philosophy tends to have little use for drawn out conceptions based on a rigid set of abstract knowledge.

Still, the fact remains: Music theory is one of the most magnificent systematic musical inventions in the world. So a working knowledge of music theory *can* be of great help to some beatmakers, particularly those who are interested in making the "pop-hop" sound. But a working knowledge or understanding of music theory is not critical to a beatmaker's ability to make dope beats! The pursuit of beatmaking through the lens of music theory is actually a major detriment to those who aim to make beats in the most fundamental/traditional meaning of the entire art form. Again, hip hop/rap music is *not* reliant upon the laws of music theory in the way that the Western classical tradition is. Moreover, the displacement of the use of pre-recorded music — the core component that gave rise to, and is the fundamental definition and essence of, the hip hop/rap musical form — is not some modern example of the "evolution" of hip hop/rap music. It is something separate and different altogether.

Finally, because some laws of music theory are actually used within the hip hop/rap music tradition, I recommend that you at least acquire an understanding of the basics of music theory. The advantages of having even the most remote understanding of music theory are plentiful. For one thing, it will undoubtedly help the scope of your arrangement, which will in turn increase your overall production capabilities. Also, an understanding of music theory will help you learn how to "play things out more," instead of only sampling. (Of course, not that there's anything wrong with sampling.) And perhaps the biggest advantage of possessing *some* knowledge of the basics of music theory is the fact that it will help you recognize and analyze structures and patterns in existing music works outside of the hip hop/rap music tradition. This is key because the more that you're able to identify common music structures and patterns, the more effective you will be in determining how to convert them into hip hop/rap form.

Compositional Ethic and the Seven Periods of the Beatmaking Tradition

There have been a number of developments that have occurred throughout the past four decades of the beatmaking tradition, but perhaps none have been as interesting and more responsible for the state (good or bad) of beatmaking than the development of what I call the "pusher/resister compositional dialogue." What I mean by the "compositional dialogue" is that there are essentially two compositional sentiments that now underscore the hip hop/rap music and beatmaking traditions. One compositional sentiment can be best described as the "push," by some beatmakers, for conformity. That is to say, the push to use more traditional compositional schemes that are *outside* of the hip hop/rap music and beatmaking traditions. The other compositional sentiment is best described as the "resistance" to conformity. That is to say, the resistance to use more traditional compositional schemes that are *outside* of the hip hop/rap music and beatmaking traditions.

The push for conformity in beatmaking has resulted in beats that feature melody and harmony in much more prominent roles than rhythm and groove, two musical elements that are prominent in the hip hop/rap music and beatmaking traditions. Those who push for conformity have widely attempted to create beats that are more in line with other popular genres of music rather than beats that speak to the fundamental tenets and priorities of the hip hop/rap music and beatmaking traditions. On the other end of this spectrum, those who resist conformity have consciously attempted to create beats that rely prevalently on the use of compositional schemes that are well within the hip hop/rap music and beatmaking traditions, which means a reliance on rhythm and groove in the fundamental manner that hip hop/rap music was characterized, especially prior to the Post-Pioneers Beatmaking Period.

To be certain, there have been obnoxious choices made on both sides of this compositional dialogue. On the "push" side of this conversation, there has been far too much movement away from what actually distinguishes hip hop/rap from other music forms. And on the "resistance" side of this dialogue, there has been, at times, too little openness to the benefits of compositional exploration and experimentation. Debating which compositional sentiment is better or worse for beatmakers is perhaps a useless endeavor, mostly because of the realities that come into play when a *sub*-subculture like beatmaking moves into the mainstream.

If we look at the way in which the compositional ethic of beatmaking was governed over the past 40 years, we can see that this governance fundamentally comes down to either the use or non-use of some form of the break as the guiding compositional process for beatmakers. And we already know there's no dispute in the matter of the break: The use of the break is the core compositional tenet that the hip hop/rap music and beatmaking traditions were founded upon. By its definition and how it was used by the earliest DJs (beatmakers), the use of the break emphasized the importance and priority of rhythm and groove. It did not however place any emphasis on the use of harmony and/or melody, tropes fundamental to American popular music traditions *outside* of hip hop/rap. This compositional ethic of beatmaking governed supreme for approximately 15 years, or as long as hip hop/rap music remained a subculture and not a major part of American mainstream culture. But although the break is a core compositional tenet of the hip hop/rap music and beatmaking traditions, it can't be forgotten that once hip hop/rap music hit the mainstream, it was inevitable that the compositional ethic would expand for two reasons: (1) Mainstream access warrants it; and (2) The addition of different cultural influences assures it.

An objective look at the mainstream reveals that what constitutes "mainstream" is almost never anti-establishment and/or particularly cutting edge. But anti-establishment and cutting edge is exactly what hip hop/rap music was in its initial state and what hip hop/rap music remains in its fundamental form. Moreover, the mainstream of American popular music is mostly *safe*. That is, it's not risky; it's designed to appeal to the greatest common denominator. And when it comes to the musical tastes of the listeners who make up the greatest common denominator, these are mostly people who are persuaded by, and more familiar with, tunes and songs that are in a more traditional song form and style, i.e., inclusive of a definitive melody and definitive harmony. Likewise, the listeners who comprise the greatest common denominator are not expected to be persuaded by, and certainly not familiar with or in favor of, the "non-traditional" priorities and processes of a non-traditional music form like hip hop/rap music, or for that matter, beatmaking, its chief compositional process. Therefore, as hip hop/rap music became a major part of the fabric of the American mainstream, many beatmakers (producers) saw conformity (once something considered to be terribly bad in hip hop/rap music), as not only a means to success but also as a means to *separating* themselves from the beatmaking pack.

Furthermore, as the hip hop/rap music and beatmaking traditions spread, more people inevitably joined in the dialogue of its development. And as hip hop/rap and beatmaking garnered more attention, each new person who entered into both traditions brought along with them the presuppositions of their own personal background. Their age, their ethnicity, their cultural and socio-economic background, and, of course, their city, region, and state of origin all factored into what they brought to the dialogue. Each one of the factors in one's personal background collectively defines one's *sensibilities* about the creative compositional practices and processes they ultimately choose to rely upon. More importantly, it is these sensibilities that also serve to inform how each person chooses to interpret the roots of the hip hop/rap music and beatmaking traditions.

Parting Shots
The Soul and Essence of the Hip Hop/Rap Music Tradition

Regardless of what side of the music theory or sampling issue you're on, there can be little debate as to whether or not the majority of contemporary hip hop/rap music offerings lack much of the "soul" and essence of the original, fundamental tradition.[184] There are a number of combined factors that have contributed to this, notably the over-commercialization of hip hop/rap music and the illegalization of sampling. However, I consider the single biggest contributing factor to be the emergence of a negative slant towards the art of sampling and the subsequent widespread move away from sampling — the use of fragments of old recordings — as a major part of the compositional process of hip hop/rap.

It bares repeating that the architects and pioneers of the hip hop/rap music tradition had access to traditional instruments, some were even as talented on the drums, keyboard, and guitar as they were on two turntables and a mixer, or a sampler and a drum machine. The architects and pioneers did not separate their talents with traditional instruments from their talents with non-traditional ones. Instead, like the pioneers of b-boying — who did not separate their "power moves" and acrobatics from the rest of their b-boy repertoire (or the dance form on a whole), the architects and pioneers of beatmaking maintained all of their talents as one collective skill-set. But today, the true essence of beatmaking (and hip hop/rap music in general) is being overshadowed by an

---

[184] The majority of hip hop/rap music between 2005 and 2015 is best characterized as brilliant examples of what I call "popularism" songs, songs that have a decidedly "pop" slant rather than a "rap" slant. Hence, my earlier "pop-hop" description of this new hip hop/rap-based genre.

over abundance of, and reliance on, live instrumentation (i.e. no sampling) as well as concepts and methods that are clearly contrary to the essence of the hip hop/rap music tradition.

This is by no means an attack on such concepts and methods outside of hip hop/rap; truth is, live instrumentation has often played some (minimal) role in beatmaking, be it a keyboard harmony fill, a live bass line, or perhaps even a live drums program. That said, this presents a rather simple question. If the fundamental tropes, aesthetics, predilections, principles, and priorities of the hip hop/rap music tradition are neutralized, ignored, and ultimately *replaced* by those of another tradition, is not the resulting music something "other" than hip hop/rap music?

Although I embrace, and in some cases encourage, the intermixing of musical genres, I also recognize that "intermixing" hip hop/rap with other musical forms is quite different than *converting* other musical forms *into* hip hop/rap music. The reality is too much intermixing of other musical influences (like contemporary pop-rock or pop-R&B or even Western classical) with hip hop/rap tends to dissolve hip hop/rap's structure, and ultimately dilutes, if not destroys, its fundamental identity. This doesn't mean that the "other," i.e. the hybrid results of intermixing, is better or worse. It is merely a recognition that an "other" *exists*. But classifying this hybrid other as hip hop/rap music is really a misrepresentation of the hip hop/rap music tradition. This is why, inevitably, a new name (genre) will have to emerge. It's the only way to distinguish the hybrid "other" from the original base essence of the hip hop/rap music tradition. And what name this new hybrid-based "other music" takes going forward is certainly open for discussion, but I'm convinced that neither "hip hop/rap," "hip hop," or "rap" can carry its weight any longer.

This is not the stance of a purist — I'm certainly not a purist. Nor am I concerned with or focused on to taking hip hop/rap music back to its so-called golden days. I like hip hop/rap music from the 1970s, 1980s, 1990s, and the 2000s. Moreover, as far as the "hit song"/to release ratio, I believe the 2000s have produced far more, and from a larger number of artists. Although there were undoubtedly some timeless works of art made during the 1990s, it's not like *everything* created in that era was pure gold.

I also want to be clear that this isn't an attempt to quantify "good" or "bad" hip hop/rap music; nor is it a condemnation of the new or a boost of support for the old. My only goal (concern) is to present the facts that the history of the hip hop/rap music tradition overwhelmingly support. In other words, this is about recognizing and upholding what hip hop/rap music *is* in its fundamental essence and in accordance to what its chief architects and pioneers have consistently maintained that it is. It's also about how change inevitably happens within music traditions, or more specifically, how changes and new developments are reconciled with the core tenets of a given music tradition.

Although there may have been new techniques and styles incorporated into hip hop/rap's musical lexicon over the past decade, the base tradition itself can not be *revised* or *redefined* no more than can the blues be revised and redefined; or jazz be revised and redefined; or rhythm and blues be revised and redefined; or soul and funk be revised and redefined. And with regard to those other aforementioned well-defined music traditions, no one has dared to loft a generic (wholesale) misguided claim of "evolution" against them. Each of those music traditions — the blues, jazz, rhythm and blues, soul, and funk — are forever locked in *as is*. Whatever new flavor someone wants to add to them is perfectly fine and perhaps even encouraged, but it should be well-understood that such an addition can never *change* and/or *reverse* the base tradition itself. The facts that comprised the history of a music tradition, and the culture which produced it, can not be undone. Thus, no matter who attempts to add to it, the fundamentals of the hip hop/rap music tradition, like the Western classical tradition and music theory, are permanent.

The fact remains that no new group of musicians (no matter how well "trained" they are), nor any new legislation (no matter how much backing it has from the RIAA, or how recognized it may be within intellectual property circles), can revise or redefine the autonomous and socially codified musical tradition and culture that is the hip hop/rap music tradition. Likewise, no group or legislation can reorganize, neutralize, and otherwise discard the fundamental aesthetics, principles, and priorities of the hip hop/rap music tradition and culture.

However, it is also important to recognize that there is no way to restrict one music tradition and culture from influencing and/or serving as the basis for the creation of a *new* music tradition and culture. After all, the blues begot rhythm and blues, and the blues and rhythm and blues begot rock 'n' roll; and yet today, no reasonable person would refer to rock 'n' roll (especially as we now know it) as the blues, despite rock's actual musical kinship. Hence, a fixed musical tradition and culture can not be overhauled simply because new musicians discover it. Moreover, if the outer fringes of a well-codified music tradition and culture begins to move in a new direction, via the fusion of other music traditions and cultures, then that new direction deserves to and should be recognized and even celebrated as its own movement, as something new and distinguishable from the tradition(s) which spawned it.

This is why the oft-heard "hip hop has evolved" claim is consistently misapplied. The hip hop/rap music tradition has indeed evolved in a number of areas; for instance: In the area of the modern rhyme style, in the area of more meticulous sampling and more intricate production processes, in the area of an increased usage of technology, and, of course, in the area of pop culture exposure and commercialism. But what fundamentally defines the essence of the hip hop/rap music tradition has not evolved, it's the same. The only thing that has consistently changed are the waves of new practitioners who have migrated to the hip hop/rap music and beatmaking traditions.

The underlying fundamentals of the hip hop/rap music tradition and culture can't change. The only thing that can change are the people who migrate to the traditions and their subsequent interpretations of them. There are those who, with great care and patience, take the time to learn about the hip hop/rap and beatmaking art forms and cultures. In turn, they interpret the hip hop/rap music tradition in the way the art form and the culture was intended to be. Then, there are those who either haven't made enough effort to learn the art form properly, or lack the resources to do so; thus, they are unfamiliar with the root structure and nuance of beatmaking and hip hop culture in general. In this case, it should be expected that they will not likely interpret the art form and culture in the way that it was intended. Therefore, when these alternative interpretations manifest themselves, in ways that are foreign to the hip hop/rap music and beatmaking traditions and cultures, what you have is not the wholesale "evolution" of the hip hop/rap and beatmaking traditions, but rather the makings of a *new* tradition and culture altogether.

What made — and still makes — hip hop/rap music and beatmaking so powerful (and alluring) is its level of non-conformity. Hence, the more practitioners of hip hop/rap music and beatmakers seek to conform to the "accepted norms" and concepts, methods, and structures of other musical forms rather than holding fast to hip hop/rap's and beatmaking's own nuances, the more hip hop/rap music and beatmaking actually loses its power, impact, and overall allure. But for whatever it's worth, I acknowledge the fact that, naturally, conformity to a dominant culture does present a more broader appeal. But hip hop/rap music wasn't founded upon the idea of broad appeal or on the idea of being safe or pleasing to everyone. Hip hop/rap music was founded upon the idea of being hip on its own terms, not on the terms of outside musical or cultural forces. Here, I'm neither co-signing or condemning whether a beatmaker stays close to the fundamental tropes and nuances of beatmaking and hip hop/rap or not. I'm merely presenting the fact that this is a choice that each beatmaker must ultimately make. A choice, I should add, that determines whether or not they are actually being guided by the hip hop/rap music tradition or another one.

Finally, one of the primary points that I've hoped to get across in this metaphorical battle between Grandmaster Flash and Mozart was that each music tradition and culture has its own ideology and distinct aesthetics, common elements and priorities, principles, presuppositions, and dispositions. Though one music tradition and culture may be compared to and contrasted with another, one music tradition and culture can not be appropriately *judged* by another, because in the final analysis, such judgment is, despite all attempts at objectivity and fairness, always one-sided. The hip hop/rap music and beatmaking traditions and cultures can no more be judged (appropriately) by the Western classical music tradition and culture than can the Western classical music tradition and culture be judged (appropriately) by the Eastern classical music tradition and culture. Music traditions and cultures can only be judged (appropriately) by its constituents and the metrics of their own unique devices. Thus, while the metric for superior classical music may be based on the mastery of music theory (Western or Eastern), the metric for superior hip hop/rap music is based on the mastery of beatmaking and the execution of a dope beat and an ill rhyme.

Part 4
THE BUSINESS OF BEATS

Important Note About This Part

One of the reasons that I wrote *The BeatTips Manual* was because I wanted to create a formidable platform that beatmakers and rappers (and others in the hip hop/rap music community) could rally around. This book, in and of itself, is a direct link to every beatmaker who has ever aspired to make it — *on their own terms* — in the music business. Therefore, one of my goals with this chapter is to present knowledge and information that is relevant not just to beatmaking, but genuinely important concepts and issues within the music industry in general.

Business is no less important than it was half a century ago. And given the fact that beatmakers are mostly self-contained and free to make their own moves, business acumen plays an even bigger role in the success of a beatmaker. But dread the day when you find yourself taking care of music *business* more than you're actually creating music. Be mindful of as many music business matters as you can; more importantly, continue to increase your understanding of how things *really* work in the music business. But, if at all possible, never allow your business activities to overshadow your creative artistry. Though I can not stress enough how important it is to know the "business" of the music-business, I also can not stress enough how important it is to retain your sense of creative artistry, because once you lose that, you've lost the most important form of leverage in actually creating good business situations for yourself. However, your aspirations and concerns are your own. So I recommend that you use the knowledge and information in this chapter to help you make more informed business decisions.

Finally, remember that music is not just an art, it's a form of show business; which means its both a creative and business endeavor. In other words, all of the decisions or choices that professional beatmakers (producers) make are governed by both creative and fiscal considerations. Always keep that in mind no matter what creative-business path you ultimately take.

Chapter 11

Know Where You Stand
Understanding Your Own Genius:
Beatmaker or a "Producer"?
The Differcence Makes All the Difference

In the hip hop/rap music and beatmaking traditions, the term "producer" is often synonymously used to describe a beatmaker. But is that always appropriate? Whatever one ultimately considers themselves — either a beatmaker or a producer — is one of the key factors that will determine one's professional beatmaking/production opportunities. In recent history, there has been a push by some beatmakers (producers) to distinguish and separate themselves from the ubiquitous hip hop/rap "beatmaker" pack — as if being a beatmaker is something to be ashamed of — by declaring themselves to be "producers," not beatmakers. And therein lies the true origins of the beatmaker vs. producer debate.

But before I decipher the beatmaker vs. producer debate, it is first necessary to spend some words on defining what hip hop production is as well as what a (music) producer has traditionally been considered to be. Simply stated, hip hop production is the creation of hip hop music. Although this description broadly covers every dimension of hip hop/rap music, the term, "hip hop production," is used most commonly to refer to the making of a hip hop/rap instrumental, i.e. a beat. So technically speaking, a beatmaker, one who makes beats, is a hip hop producer; ergo, a beatmaker is a producer.

Then there's the the term "producer" itself, which has often been tossed around in the music industry. "Producer" can be used to describe a musician and/or songwriter. "Producer" can also be used to describe a total hands-on music person, someone with complete audio and recording technology understanding and a serious appreciation for music. A "producer" can be the person ultimately responsible for the final sound of a recording, much like a beatmaker/producer is in hip hop. But let's not stop there. A "producer" can also be someone who finances and/or secures the financing for a music project. A "producer" can be someone who organizes and manages recording sessions, someone who hires musicians and songwriters. A "producer" can be someone who picks the songs that make an album. A "producer" can be a marketing wiz or tastemaker who polishes the "look" of a music act. "Producer" can even be used to describe someone who orders food or arranges specific vices (alcohol, drugs, etc.) during the recording of a music project. Certainly, the term, "producer," and the concept of music production is nothing new.

However, the term "beatmaker" is indeed something new and altogether distinct from the *multiple* meanings of a "producer." A beatmaker is a truly unique and new breed of music-maker, what I call the common composer. But more simply put, a beatmaker is someone who makes beats! Me, personally, I'm first and foremost — and will always be — a beatmaker. Having produced two of my own albums and various music projects as well as the projects of other recording artists, I'm also a producer. And to be sure, there can be a valley of difference between making a beat and producing a record. But that doesn't mean that being a beatmaker is inferior to being a so-called producer. In fact, within the hip hop/rap music tradition, I find (for many reasons) the beatmaker moniker to be quite noble.

One way to highlight the differences between what a beatmaker and a producer does is to do a comparative analysis of well-known producers who are not known for any beatmaking ability. Here, I'll use Diddy (aka Puff Daddy), and Quincy Jones, the producer of Michael Jackson's *Thriller*. First, it should be noted that although both Diddy and Quincy Jones are both "producers," they are certainly not in the same league. (However, both have successfully produced albums for at least one decade). Prior to Michael Jackson's two breakout solo albums, *Off The Wall* (1979) and *Thriller* (1982), Quincy Jones was an accomplished and very well-respected musician (trumpeter), arranger, conductor, *and* film and television composer. Quincy Jones, in every sense of the term, is (was) a music-maker. On the other hand, Diddy had (has) no such pedigree when he "produced" Notorious B.I.G.'S *Ready To Die*, one of the most popular and successful selling albums he's produced to date. Neither Quincy Jones or Diddy likely played any instruments or wrote any songs on each album, respectively. But this does not disqualify neither as "producers."

In each case, both Quincy Jones and Diddy applied some of their best production talents. In the case of *Thriller*, Quincy Jones ran the show. Over a six-week period, he oversaw the recording process, which included several days of three separate high-powered studio sessions. He hand-picked the songwriters for Michael Jackson, in some cases, based on the song themes and concepts that he (Jones) came up with. Quincy Jones, like famed producers Gamble & Huff, contained the ability *to do* a lot more than just hum a tune. He could write a tune, sing a tune, arrange a tune, and, of course, *play* a tune. Quincy Jones could readily write the arrangements for a brass section and then comfortably turn around and sit in with them and play. This is to say that Quincy Jones could play within the established norm of his field (brass instruments, particularly).

By contrast, Diddy did not run the show for *Ready To Die*; if anybody did, it was really the Notorious B.I.G. (aka Biggie Smalls) who did. It was Biggie who chose the beatmakers; it was Biggie who chose the beats; it was Biggie who came up with the themes and concepts for each song; and, of course, it was *only* Biggie who wrote and performed the rhymes. This does not subtract from Diddy's role in the release of *Ready To Die*. After all, it was Diddy who signed Biggie; it was Diddy who put up the funding through his record label, Bad Boy; it was Diddy who provided the recording studio where Biggie recorded his hip hop/rap classic; and perhaps it was Diddy who gave some coaching or motivation during the recording sessions of *Ready To Die*. Thus, Diddy is a "producer," certainly one of the best, according to various definitions of producer in the common hip hop/rap era.

Although Diddy is a quintessential music "producer," he is not a quintessential music-*maker*. Diddy could not improvise and come up with a beat idea and/or structure, then get in a room with other quality beatmakers and hold his own in the beatmaking craft — the established norm of his field. Diddy could not use an EMPI and create a beat — from start to finish — completely alone (a fact he's never hidden); nor could he write an entire three verse rhyme and chorus for himself, let alone an interpolation for another recording artist. This is no disrespect to Diddy; remember this: You don't have to be able to make a beat in order to be a "producer;" but you do however have to be able to make a beat to be a beatmaker. And note: For the last 50 years, major label executives have routinely signed artists to contracts that included provisions which granted them producer credits, no matter how much actual production work they did on a project. So I'm not taking anything away from Diddy; but I'm also not giving him any undue credit either.

Having established some of the main capacity in which producers typically work, it is now necessary to describe those things that do and do not make one a producer or a beatmaker. First, if one merely submits a beat to a rapper, and the rapper uses it to create a song, it doesn't necessarily mean that the one who merely submitted the beat is the "producer" of whatever song emerges. That said, the song, should it be made using said beat and placed on a commercially released project, will be credited as: "produced by: *insert the name of the one who submitted the beat*." This credit will be given even if the beat submitter wasn't present at the recording session (with the rapper) which resulted in the complete song. Second, if one makes very small "suggestive changes" to the beat that someone else made, the one who suggested changes is neither a beatmaker or producer, but he still may receive a "co-producer" credit.

Let's remember, in the traditional sense of the word, "producer" can loosely stand for many things. However, it is almost always associated with someone who oversees the completion of a record. That means, overseeing or managing the process from its inception to its completion: hiring session musicians, songwriters, and engineers; booking studio arrangements; making travel and lodging arrangements; making payment arrangements to vendors and workers alike; clearing samples; finding source materials; coaching vocalists; being the most critical "ears;" all sorts of things. Therefore, "production," in its most common sense of the word, is the process of assemblage: It's the process of putting multiple components of a project together. A producer need not possess *any* artistic, technical, theoretical, and/or financial skill whatsoever. And, as I mentioned earlier, a producer can be anybody who has contact with artistic people; people with audio/recording knowledge; people with theoretical understanding; and yes, people with financial competence. Hence, a person who puts — assembles — all of these people together in an effort to develop, create, and/or polish a product is a "producer." Fact is, a producer need not know a thing about drum sounds; or about chopping; or sequencing and looping; or even about hip hop/rap music for that matter. A "producer" can simply be someone who puts together the people who do know about those things.

Thus, in the final analysis, the concept of a "producer" really shouldn't be compared to the concept of a "beatmaker." Beatmakers are a new and special breed; a vanguard that did not exist (in their current form) prior to the early 1970s. As you already know, hip hop/rap is the first music tradition that is primarily predicated upon the use of pre-recorded music and/or sounds. Prior to hip hop/rap music, there was no music tradition that was exclusively based on the actual use of pre-recorded music material as its chief compositional method and process. With the emergence of the beatmaking tradition (which is still relatively new) came the advent of the "beatmaker," not the advent of the "music producer" (again, producers have existed long before hip hop/rap music and beatmakers came to town).

So what makes beatmakers different from producers? Beatmakers, by the nature of what they do, are embodied with the task of: (1) composing; (2) performing/playing; (3) mixing; and (4) various other similar meticulous editing practices that have been extensively explored throughout this study. And much like the primary music-makers of all cultural traditions (for example, drummers in Africa) and everyday musicians as well, beatmakers actually make (create) the music and provide the "musical frequencies" for rappers to rap on. This is not the job description that is synonymous with the proverbial "producer."

Furthermore, beatmakers belong to and come from a lineage of music-makers, whereas some producers belong to and come from a lineage of project managers. And regardless of the methods individual beatmakers use (i.e. the use of pre-recorded music and/or sounds), Western classical composers like Beethoven and Mozart share more of a lineage with beatmakers than they do with ambiguously named "producers." Beethoven and Mozart were commissioned (hired) by others (typically persons best described as "producers"), to create new musical pieces. But in their time, Beethoven and Mozart usually still got the proper (*full*) credit for their work; a reality that escapes many producers today.

Here, it's worth noting the sentiment of some well-known beatmakers (producers) on this matter. I've interviewed a healthy number and variety of well-known and/or critically acclaimed beatmakers (producers), and the most common thing that I hear is: "Producers produce and beatmakers **just** make beats." Huh? To me, this is simply nonsense. The implication here is that a "producer" is superior to a beatmaker. This has always struck me the wrong way, because on one hand, many so-called "producers" are denying the one thing (that they are a beatmaker) that actually makes them more unique than any other form of music-maker. And on the other hand, this denial is, for many, deeply rooted and hidden within the subjective standards of what actually qualifies as music — subjective standards that still view hip hop/rap as a primitive form of music.

Perhaps it's also the case that some of those who prefer to be called "producer" rather than beatmaker have a serious inferiority complex. Far too many of these self-described "producers" adopt the idea that established "producers" and people on the outside of the hip hop/rap tradition look down on beatmaking and beatmakers. Therefore, they desperately aspire to rid themselves of the beatmaker tag. In this way, they feel that the "producer" moniker elevates them above being a beatmaker. Nonsense. If one wants to separate themselves from other beatmakers, all they need to do is make doper beats. And consider this last point: Every dope beatmaker has the ability to *produce*, if he (or she) so chooses. However, every music "producer" does not have the ability to make dope beats.

Establish Your Own Unique Body of Work – Build a Music Catalog

A music catalog is a portfolio of completed music works: songs, instrumentals, and other similar projects. Think of your music catalog as your music résumé. As an organized body of work, it stands as proof that you are well-experienced and serious about your beatmaking (production) endeavors. Without your own body of work, how can you prove that your beatmaking services are worth someone's time and money? Thus, a solid music (beat) catalog is absolutely essential to any beatmaker's plan for earning a living off of their music.

So how do you make your own beat or music catalog? Well, there's actually two parts to that: there's the beat CD part (though few people make physical beat *CDs*, beat CD is still the common term today), then there's the completed projects part. I will discuss the beat CD aspect of a music catalog in this chapter, and I will discuss the completed projects part in chapter 13. Finally, I should note that in order for you to build a solid music catalog, there are three fundamental things that I recommend that you do: (1) Consistently create as many quality beats as you can; (2) Attach yourself to and complete as many projects (that you believe in) that you can; and most importantly for our purposes here, (3) Always keep an up-to-date beat CD, or online page where you showcase your music.

How to Create An Effective Beat CD*

Today, "CD" is more of a figure of speech, as most people showcase their beats on Soundcloud, Bandcamp, and other similar sites. Also, submissions are sent via email or delivered on a thumb drive. Still, the steps for assembling a beat CD generally apply to how you should assemble your music pages and beat submissions.

The way that you should assemble your beat CD is like this. First, gather together twenty of your best beats. If you don't have twenty beats, don't worry, go with what you have, but you should at least have ten. These beats should be the ones that you and your "trusted ears"[185] really feel. If you've previewed some of your beats for rappers and other people before, that's fine — provided

---

[185] **Trusted Ears:** They are the people whose musical opinion you truly value. "Trusted ears" should not be people in your crew who simply tell you that every thing that you do is "hot!" Those who do so are "yes men." Be very careful of "yes men," because they will give you a bad ear! On the other hand, trusted ears are not people who simply shoot down everything that you play for them. I've always liked letting non-beatmakers hear my new beats and music. I've found those opinions to be the realist, most gut-feeling and straight forward. Other beatmakers tend to critique the elements within the beats, rather than simply listen to the music and see if they like it. Far too much stuff Like: *'Oh, I like that snare'*… *'The hi-hat is nice'*… *'You should have used a different kick'*…*'Where did you sample that from?'*.

you received honest, constructive (hopefully good) feedback. Next, spend three to five days having these beats "battle off," i.e. competing with one another, until you reach your best fifteen. Once you've done that, you're ready to begin assembling your beat CD.

Which Type of Beats Should Go on Your Beat CD?

Your beat CD or online music page should be a demonstration and representation of what *you* do *best*. If you are a devoted sample-based beatmaker, don't throw a clumsy attempt at a synthetic-sounds-based track on your beat CD. Likewise, if you're a strong synthetic-sounds-based beatmaker, then you shouldn't add any awkward rendition of a sample-based beat. But if you are seasoned in making both sample-based joints and synthetic-sounds-based bangers, then you should indeed add your best demonstration of both kinds of beats to your beat CD. And though the idea may be to add as much variety to your beat CD as possible, you also want to be careful to maintain a consistent level of quality on your beat CD. Moreover, keep in mind that this variety should be within the context of what you do best.

Further, when you send submissions to artists, avoid populating your submission with beats that contain ridiculously long-winded intros. Great intros can be a magnificent draw, but some intros can be more distractive than helpful. Long intros are better served when the song is complete, that is, when the lyrics are added and the music is mixed. Point is, when your music is submitted to someone, you have a very brief amount of time to persuade them that your beat(s)is worth investing in. Thus, you don't want to blow the deal and turn potential clients off before they even get a chance to really hear your music.

Finally, if you have beats with hooks, you're at an advantage because you're not just pitching a beat, you're pitching a concept and a song. Pitching a concept and a song is always better than merely pitching a beat, particularly because it gives a rapper a more direct *cue*; moreover, it helps assure that you receive a writing credit. There are numerous writer/beatmaker teams who send off songs, complete with reference vocals, both verses and hooks. Again, in those cases, they are not simply shopping a beat, they are shopping an entire song. If this applies to you, you want to keep the demo down to no more than five songs.

How Many Beats Should Go on Your Beat CD?

There are no concrete rules for how many beats should go on a beat CD. But you never want to overburden your beat CD with too many beats (especially if there is a wide gap in quality), nor do you want to have too few beats on your CD. Therefore, when deciding how many beats to put on your beat CD, go with quality over quantity. Remember, a beat CD should be a demonstration of what you can do. It should not be a CD full of as many beats as you can fit on a CD or USB drive. Generally, somewhere between ten to twenty beats — no more than two minutes per beat — is the norm. However, some well-known beatmakers (producers) put only five beats on their beat CD. Finally, it should be noted that many beat submissions are made through email as well. In this case, you may not want to send more than three beats/songs at a time.

Should You Put Your Best Beat First?

"Put your best beat first" is generally the mantra echoed by most in the music industry, but I don't necessarily agree with this strategy. The thing is, the "best beat first" philosophy actually emanates from the "best *song* first" philosophy, which refers to the song that has the best chance of appealing to the broadest section of people upon the first immediate listening. A lot of beatmakers and so-called music industry insiders will tell you that you should always put your best cut or beat first. What they won't tell you is: If you're not an established, name brand beatmaker, your beats will be listened to from a different perspective.

Music is very saturated right now; it's been this way for the past decade. Today, when most A&Rs (at least the ones who still have jobs) listen to a new beat submission, they seemingly expect to hear nothing impressive, because "everybody's a 'producer' now," or at least that's often their cynical belief. Furthermore, the A&Rs who are still left are often so jaded that they actually believe that they are the only people qualified to pick out good music. But to their credit, most A&Rs who actually receive beat submissions will check to see if there's at least one good beat. I've seen A&Rs listen to the opening track of beat CDs and demos for about 15 or 20 seconds, then quickly scan to track 2, before quickly moving on to track 3. In fact, many A&Rs will actually listen to track 3 *longer* than they will track 1. Why? Remember, they're already pre-conditioned with the "Great, another 'producer'" syndrome. Thus, many A&Rs assume that most of the material submitted to them is wack, or at best the same thing they've been hearing. Therefore, they are subconsciously looking for a surprise, something that will knock them out. This is why I recommend the strategy of leading off your beat CD with a 40 second snippet of your *third* best beat and/or song, followed by a 40 second snippet of your best beat and/or song, followed by a 90 second snippet of your second best beat and/or song. All songs after that should be a variation between 60 to 90 seconds if you're trying to shop a song complete with hook. The thing about *not* leading off with your best beat is this: If your entire beat CD/catalog is good, it really won't matter what order your selections are in. To most A&Rs, there's a good chance that your third best will sound like the best, so they'll rewind to the first two tracks to see if they missed anything. So it's important to remember that you're not trying to showcase the fact that you can make *one* good beat; you want to demonstrate that you are capable of consistently making quality beats and music.

Shopping Your Beats

"Shopping beats" is the phrase that is most often used to describe the process of pitching or showcasing beats to perspective buyers. In this rather precarious process, beatmakers (and beat brokers, producer managers, lawyers, and other music insiders and affiliates) pass on beat CDs and Soundcloud links, etc. to different interested parties, including recording artists, record labels, publishing houses, media networks, music production companies, and music licensing companies specializing in instrumentals for commercials, film, and television. When A&Rs ruled the day (just under two decades ago), the big thing was "meetings" between beat shoppers — usually beatmakers themselves — and A&Rs. But as the industry downsized and advancements in recording technology leveled the playing field for beatmakers outside of the industry network, "shopping beats" took on a new form. Some A&R beat shopping meetings still occur, but nowhere near the scale that they once did. These days, beatmakers (especially brand name ones) shop their beats directly to rappers, bypassing A&Rs and other middle-men altogether.[186] But whatever path you take to shopping your beats, there are a number of factors that I recommend you consider along the way.

First, before you begin shopping your material, be honest with yourself about the quality and level of your beats. If you really feel that your beats are ready, then, by all means, proceed. But if you're not sure of your sound or overall production level, then you're probably not ready to shop your material

---

[186] In the past, A&Rs had more control over the beats used by the rapper's under their supervision. In many cases, this was counterproductive, as the A&R, not the rapper, was responsible for securing beats. In situations like these, many rappers were often paired with beats that weren't always great fits for their styles and concepts, but rather the calculated sales projections of A&Rs who thought that they knew best what beats worked for the rappers under their supervision. As Marley Marl describes in part of his interview (located in this study), such a situation almost tanked LL Cool J's hit album *Mama Said Knock You Out.*

yet. Second, if at all possible, aim for pitching complete songs; this will almost certainly assure you credit and, more importantly, a share of the publishing rights (provided you don't give these rights away if and when you sign a producer agreement). Again, I can not stress this point enough: Pitch concepts, do not simply try to sell beats, shop your beats with hooks and concepts. If you can't rhyme, find someone who can, and have them express your ideas. And if you can't find a suitable rapper for your beats, affix a line or two describing the theme you envision for each beat.

Submitting Your Music to Rappers and Other Beatmakers (Producers)

When it comes to shopping beats, your best chance for getting heard, recognized, and, subsequently, securing production work, will come from either an established rapper and/or an established beatmaker (producer) *not* an A&R. Rappers are often very visible. And aside from the fact that most of them like to hang out and be seen, many of them thrive on the celebrity, and nearly all of them know that their job actually demands it. So they don't really mind mixing it up with the people; they understand the demands of their chosen profession. Further, many rappers are also not terribly discrete about the recording studios that they record in. That is to say, it isn't that difficult to find out who's recording where. Hence, most rappers are actually very approachable, provided you catch them at the right time and the right place.

Shopping your beats directly to rappers increase your chances of at least getting a call back. Right now, budgets are tight, and they're never going back to pre-industry crash levels. Plus, there are more beatmakers submitting beats than ever before (*there are also more rappers than ever before*). Therefore, rappers — who have historically received lower budgets than other recording artists — are aggressively looking for ways to cut cost and keep as much of the budget for themselves and/or marketing and promotion. These days, rappers are taking unsolicited beat CDs (demos) very serious because they know they'll have more leverage and control on price, should they want to use any beat they find on a beatmaker's Soundcloud or Bandcamp page. In fact, rappers know that in some cases, there's a good chance that they can get quality beats for free, just production credit and no payment. Better still, most astute rappers see promising new beatmakers as an opportunity for new music endeavors.

Shopping a beat CD to established beatmakers (producers) is also a great idea. Established beatmakers (producers) have the unique freedom to work on multiple projects simultaneously. A top producer can be involved with as many albums or projects that he wants; he is not limited by the number and/or type of projects, nor is he confined to any particular music genre. One producer can have beats and music on three or four albums, a film soundtrack, a television show or commercial, and a department store soundtrack all at the same time. In a case like this, not only does the producer get his or her base payment (the pre-determined price for their beat or production work), they receive additional revenue in the form of publishing, licensing, royalty payments, etc. Also, a producer's base fee isn't dependent upon the success of a project for which they've produced. That is, established producers get their base fee upon delivery of their production, directly from the client's budget or some other pre-arranged agreement, whether the project is a hit or not. In fact, producers actually do business like general contractors.[187]

Check This Out – Ghost Production, In-House/"Staff" Production, and "Farming Out" Beatwork

In the music industry, it's common knowledge that a number of well-known producers do not actually make the beats that they are credited for. In fact, a lot of times they have a number of *unknown* beatmakers, employed as "staff," who create beats for them; this is known as ghost production.[188] These well-known producers, who are often in demand, then make minor "edits" or "changes" to the initial (original) creations — *most of the time, they make no changes at all.* Next, these well-known producers use their powerful name (brand) to sell the final product (beats) to well-known recording artists. So in a case like this, who do you think gets the production credit, the publishing points (percentages) and the producer's paycheck? The well-known producer, of course. The reality is this system has been a routine way of doing business in the music industry for more than 60 years. In the music business, time is absolutely critical; therefore, it is not at all abnormal for some producers to have other beatmakers make or "jump-start" beats for them.

"Farming Out" beatwork is also another practice that occurs in the world of beats. Check out the following hypothetical (but realistic) scenario. Let's

---

[187] On the other hand, the average rapper (who, these days, really only makes about $20,000.00 to $40,000.00 a year off record sales — and that is if everything's somewhat of a success) has to wait until their quarterly royalty checks arrive.

[188] Typically, it works like this. A well-known, established producer has an agreement with other beatmakers who are unknown and out of the picture. These out-of-the-picture beatmakers agree to a one-time fee per beat, plus a co-production credit; or they receive a salary. Thus, the credit reads like this: "produced by established producer x and co-produced by unknown producer y." Agreements such as these are so common place that it makes you wonder who's *really* creating and who's just attaching their name in front of the talented people underneath them.

say a top-level producer gets 10 project requests. That is, 10 separate artists/projects, due out over a four to six week time frame, all running consecutively. Understand, most rappers tend to preview (listen to) at least 10 - 15 beats before they find one to write to. So let's say each artist wants to preview at least 10 beats. Is it *possible* for this top-level music producer to kick out 100 *quality* beats in this short amount of time? Sure, it's possible but not likely. How difficult do you think this would be? Keep in mind, this is a top-level producer, so they were likely already working on other projects before they accepted these additional 10 new ones. They're not going to turn down a huge pay day, so in a case like this, a top-level producer is definitely going to farm-out or even turnover some of the production work, entirely, to the producers within their network (i.e. in-house/"staff" producers, friends, affiliate beatmakers). Aside from shedding light on how and why farming out beatwork becomes necessary, one other point that I hope to make here is that if a producer respects the quality of your beats, they are 100 times more likely to point you in the direction of paid production work than an A&R is, or any other music industry insider for that matter.

Submitting Your Music to A&Rs

Some A&Rs are actually very valuable. One of the biggest myths in music (especially hip hop/rap) is that artists choose all of their own beats. Though some artists actually do, many artists still have to rely on what they receive through the channels of their A&R reps. But the problem with this practice is that A&Rs don't always know what kind of beats that the rappers they represent need or want. Thus, this is one problem that faces beatmakers shopping their beats to A&Rs: You might think you have the "right" beats for a rapper, but if the A&R doesn't think so, chances are the rapper who he represents will never even hear them.

Another issue with many A&Rs is their devotion to playing it safe and riding the trends (often until those trends die). For certain, a lot of A&Rs are quick to say that they're always looking for "new material" or the "next big thing." What they're really always looking for is two things: (1) New material from established producers, at bargain prices; or (2) "Copy-cat" beats at basement fire-sale prices. Contrary to what they are actually supposed to do, most A&Rs typically do *not* seek out any new sound or creative unknown beatmakers. Most A&Rs give off a persona like they're always looking for new artists, new producers, and new material. That's nonsense. Today, most A&Rs are not looking for the next new thing; they're looking for the *same thing* — whatever's out — at a cheaper price.

These days, most A&Rs are five minutes away from losing their jobs, so they don't have room for error. They're looking for surefire names to fill the bill, or cheap knock-offs they can hopefully get over with. Also, if and when they do employ the services of an unknown beatmaker, you can be sure that they're going to try and stiff 'em on the front end and back end of the price.[189] Moreover, most A&Rs are not *music* people. By and large, they are desk-job, wanna-be industry moguls who are not motivated by innovation, creativity, or uniqueness. Instead, many are more often inspired and influenced by money, greed, and/or status. And what's more, this kind of A&R is typically not aggressive in finding new talent or new kinds of production material.

But, to be fair, there is a small handful of A&Rs and other music industry insiders who actually do pursue new talent and new production material. If presented correctly, these A&Rs will give some fresh material a quick listen. So how do you submit material to the "right" A&Rs? First, make a list of at least five A&R reps.

BeatTip – Submitting Beats to Beat Brokers: The Bad Odds and Low Probability of Beat Placement Success

Here's where most people get blackjack wrong: They believe that blackjack, one of the world's most popular casino games, is a game of chance. But the truth is, blackjack is a game of skill that carries good odds. Understand the rules of the game, as well as the cards and their probabilities based on all the players involved, and you reduce your losses. More importantly, you increase the probability that you will win, certainly more often than the average unskilled player. On the other hand, if you don't understand the game or the cards and the probabilities involved, and you simply drop down money on a "chance," you might win, you're certain to lose a great deal more.

This is how I feel about anything that requires skill and understanding. Increase your skill and understanding, and you increase the probability of your success. But, put your faith in the whim of chance, and you decrease the probability of your success. This philosophy tracks across all industries. Trust me.

In the music industry, as with any other sector of the entertainment industry, there are no guarantees, only high and low probabilities. There are no surefire approaches to making it or getting on. Every strategy, every chosen path comes

---

[189] **Front End** and **Back End**. These terms refer to fees that producers receive for their services. Front End money is the initial, up front money that a producer receives. Back End money refers to any and all money that a producer receives after the song has been released. Back End money can be a percentage of the Front End that was deferred or it can be publishing royalties, incentives, and the like.

with its own risk and its own probability of success. And when it comes to placing beats and using beat brokers, the probability of success is low, very low.

Entry-Margin Service Providers

Before I discuss beat brokers and the role that they play (or don't) in placing beats, it's important that I spend some time explaining entry-margin services and products. Entry margin services and products are the sub-industry products or services designed to help people gain entry into any given industry. From the tech industry to the publishing industry, there is an assortment of sub-industries that are focused on helping people navigate to and within their chosen industry.

Some entry margin service providers are top notch; these are the specialists. People like the film industry's Dov Simens or Syd Field, whose products and services have helped and continue to help countless screenwriters, producers, directors, and the like break into the film industry. There is a host of reasons as to why these two entry-margin specialists have been able to help so many people crack the film industry code, but I suspect that their success is most attributed to three things: (1) Their deep and up-close understanding of the history of the film industry as well as its creative and business processes; (2) Their commitment to being brutally honest about the film industry; and (3) Their very thoughtful and timely instruction, advice, and general counsel.

Below the top-notch entry-margin specialists, you have a mix of service providers. There are some entry-margin service providers who are perhaps O.K. The ones that usually fall into this category are those who maybe have a few legitimate low- to mid-level connections in a given industry. Although this group of entry-margin service providers may have a basic understanding of a given industry, they usually have an incomplete view, as they typically lack considerable knowledge of that industry's history as well as its finer creative and business processes. Still, even with limited understanding and sometime B- and C-list contacts, this group of entry-margin service providers are often able to secure fees for their services or products.

Finally, there are those entry margin service providers who are, at best, barely helpful, and at worst, absolutely terrible! These are the middle-men types that present (or try to, at least) themselves as highly knowledgeable industry insiders with great connections to, and close relationships with, key or otherwise known decision makers of a given industry. This group is a real toss up, as within their ranks you will find some who are somewhat knowledgeable of the industry they provide services and products for; and you will also find some who do not really understand the industry they purport to know. Furthermore, from this group, you will often get the most narrow (sometimes intentionally misleading), self-serving advice.

Broadly speaking, the entertainment industry is filled with people who earn a living off the entry margins. But the music industry is notorious for middle men who earn money off the margins by "selling the dream" or, "selling the secrets" of the industry, or "selling their contacts," or even "selling their feedback." This is not to say that all middle-men types in the music industry are bad, some are useful in specific situations. But when it comes to using an entry-margin service provider, you have to ask yourself if a middle man is actually needed. I never recommend seeking out or working with a middle man if you don't have to. But that's the unfortunate issue with many beatmakers: They believe that they have to go through middle men to make it, or more precisely, to get beats placed.

Beat Brokers and the Beat Market Exchange

Beat brokers, one of the newest class of entry-margin service providers to emerge in recent years, purport to broker beat placements for aspiring music producers. Although some may have secured placements for acclaimed producers, most beat brokers generally focus their time and energy on attracting so-called up-and-coming producers (particularly those beatmakers who view beat placements or sales as their primary or only idea of success in music). Some beat brokers are self-described producer managers, some are not. (Don't confuse a producer manager with a beat broker, they're two totally different positions.) Finally, most beat brokers tend to push for non-sample-based beats over sample-based ones. This is usually for either one or two reasons: sample clearance concerns or personal taste.

Beat brokers work in a tremendously flawed and counterproductive cottage industry that I call the **beat market exchange**. In the beat market exchange, the only focus is to get beats placed. So beats get shopped, either through direct contacts with recording artists and key decision makers, widespread email submissions, or impromptu chance meetings, etc, and hopefully somebody buys them. Although the beat market exchange does render some results for a small minority, I view the beat market exchange on the whole as a highly flawed industry, I'm talking bad odds here. Remember what I said earlier about blackjack? Good odds?

Making music to be submitted into some black hole of an exchange just doesn't sit right with me. I find it highly counterintuitive, especially when more evidence supports building your own group/platform is the better way to go. The whole concept of the beat market exchange is so far removed from the organic approach to making beats and coming together with a rapper to form something truly collaborative that I find it difficult to see why anyone chooses it as their number one option.

What about simply being practical and pragmatic? When you think about it, most things can be broken down to a basic set of variables. The more practical and pragmatic you are able to view these variables, the easier it is for you to understand them and, therefore, predict a given outcome. So in the case of an open call for beat submissions, via a beat broker's beat submission email address, it's worth examining the numbers. In other words, all we need to do is look at the math.

For example, let's say beat broker X accepts submissions from any beatmaker that knows how to use to email. You know what, in fact, let's be fair and say that beat broker X only accepts submissions from a list of beatmakers that are either signed up with them or following their Twitter timeline or some other social media access point. Now, let's say that this amounts to 10,000 total beatmakers. Let's cut that in half and say that 5,000 of those beatmakers actually email at least one submission every three months. All right, so that's one beat broker and 5,000 submissions.

One beat broker + 5,000 beat submissions, via email? These numbers don't appeal to my practical and pragmatic side, as they raise a number of questions. First, who's going to actually listen to all 5,000 of those beat submissions? I receive a lot of emails, including beat feedback requests, on a daily basis and I have trouble checking them as soon as they come in. But with organization, structure, and diligence, I'm usually able to read (and respond to) all my important emails within 2 hours to 2 days (some times not for weeks if I'm traveling) of receiving them. So let's say beat broker X is highly organized, diligent, and has a solid structure for listening to 5,000 beat submissions. Can they even listen to all 5,000 beat submissions in three months, let alone properly evaluate them all? Perhaps. Maybe they have a team of assistants, who knows. So is it possible? Sure. But is it probable? I don't think so. But I'm practical and pragmatic.

Point is, numbers usually never lie. If you dramatically decrease the size of the entry post, that is, where people have access, and you dramatically increase the size of hopeful entrants interested in that particular access point (i.e. beat placement), then you create a very low probable success rate. In other words, the more beat submissions that a beat broker gets does not improve those beatmakers' probable success rate. But it does improve the beat brokers' success rate. The more beats a beat broker can funnel into their network of prospective beat buyers, the more likely they will be able to get at least one placement; and that's really all they need each year to advertise their rate of success.

And for every successful placement that a beat broker's efforts lead to, either directly or indirectly, the more credits they can point to. This, in turn, allows them to expand their profile as a successful beat broker (or "producer manager"), which then, of course, attracts more beatmakers and more beat submissions. Great for the beat broker who actually is able to place beats; good for the handful of beatmakers who perhaps get a placement through the beat broker; not-so-good for all the others who emailed submissions. But as I said at the start of this section: There are no guarantees, only high and low probabilities. Each individual decides for themselves how they want to weigh those probabilities, based upon their own understanding and unique circumstances. But why bother playing the daily lottery when your own blackjack table is right in front of you?

My biggest concern with regards to beat brokers and the beat market exchange is the common misinterpretation of beat placements. Many beatmakers, new and old, chase the foggy dream. They believe in something they can't see clearly. They believe that a beat placement is the only entry point to a career in music. And while some may not see it as the only entry point, they still see the coveted beat placement as the #1 means to music related revenue or a thriving career in music. They believe, even in the face of clear evidence that says otherwise, that a placement automatically leads to another even bigger placement, or at least some semblance of a career in music. In some cases, this can happen. It has happened for some, and I'm sure it will continue to happen for a handful of others in the future. But the probability of it happening will always be low. (Everyday, *somebody* wins playing the daily lottery, and everyday, 10s of millions more lose.) And because so many beatmakers do not properly understand beat placement or the beat market exchange and how it works, they do not correctly understand the probability of beat placements through a beat broker (or anyone else for that matter). As such, they run the risk of allowing themselves to rely more on a bad-odds racket than on the development and use of their own music-making skills and understanding of how things really work.

Create Your Own Platform, Expand Your Opportunities

Let's say you make dope beats, and through your own dedicated journey, you find and partner up with a rapper. Together, you make dope songs. You build sincere relationships with other equally talented music makers. They dig what you're doing. At the same time, you build respectful relationships with people in the online music press, and one of your songs gets some shine on a blog… then another…then another. While there are certainly no guarantees that this would happen, is this scenario not a more proactive, realistic, and meaningful scenario than throwing beats at a beat submission email address?

Again, I'm not saying that the scenario is automatic, or that it will play out overnight. But then again, neither is the beat broker scenario; and the beat broker scenario has much longer odds and not even the same sort of payout. What I'm getting at is the *odds*, the *probability*. If you make dope beats and combine forces with someone as or even more talented, and you cultivate authentic relationships with people who care to put others on to your music, you will eventually win. How much and for how long? Well, that all depends on how you play the cards.

Finally, consider this. No matter what approach you ultimately take, beat broker, self-platform, or both, if you contribute to solidifying the prestige and importance of the beatmaking tradition, you not only help raise the profile of the entire tradition, you position yourself as one of the tradition's leaders. This, in turn, leads to multiple opportunities for your music, which improves the odds and probability of your success. So perhaps what it really comes down to is you thinking about the ways in which you want to contribute to modern music and your best means for improving the probability that it happens.

BeatTip – Don't Market Your Beats Like a Pack of Cheap Steak Knives in a Cheesy, Late-Night Infomercial
If Beatmakers Don't Respect the Trade Value of the Beatmaking Tradition, Who Will?

Despite what some outside (and, unfortunately, inside) the beatmaking tradition may think, beats are music. Of course, as one-man (usually) orchestrated instrumental composite, beats are a unique kind of music, but music they are still the same. Yet in recent years, a growing number of beatmakers (producers) have been given over to treating beats as less than music, devaluing and marketing them in a cheap, cheesy manner and peddling them as gadgets rather than music.

Certainly you've seen adds online like, "Beats for Sale;" "Buy Hot Beats Now;" "Buy Two Beats, Get One Free;" "Lease Beats for $9.99;" etc., etc. I cringe when I see these type of adds and promotions. I'm turned off by the "As Seen on T.V." marketing approach that many are using to peddle their beats. I dislike seeing the dignity of any music tradition being undermined by such practices, but it pains me the most to see the beatmaking tradition being brought down by the intentional devaluing of those beatmakers (producers) who push beats for sale as if they were anything but music.

I understand that there is a business component to making beats. Since hip hop/rap music leaped into the world of commerce more than 30 years ago, the making of hip hop/rap music has been a desired commodity worth paying for. And because beats are the chief instrumental bedrock for rappers (and increasingly vocalists from other genres), I can completely understand why. But it's the demeaning approach that I can't stand to watch. Whether it's the "As Seen on TV" approach or the standard "$50" (or lower) beat sale platform, it doesn't matter. Both approaches devalue the work and ingenuity that goes into developing a serious skill for beatmaking. Both approaches demean the tradition built up by beatmaking's pioneers and most respected practitioners. Both approaches effectively bring beatmaking down to a third class music citizenry, where beats are thought of as a dime-a-dozen, rather than skillfully crafted individual works of art. Unfortunately, some may simply be too far gone to understand that whatever short-term financial gain they may be making is dwarfed by the likelihood that they are losing sustainable respect and support at the very same time. No sustainable career in music can be built by a delusional beatmaker (producer) who pushes his product with little consideration for trade value.

At the height of his career, jazz giant Charlie Parker reportedly did numerous impromptu recording sessions for woefully low pay, just to support his drug habit. That he was already under contract with one label or another mattered little to him, or to those eager to take an advantage of his condition and cut a rare Charlie Parker record. By practically giving his talents away, Charlie Parker, then the seminal figure in be bop, summarily undercut his own trade value. Certainly, one can understand why he did it. Being caught in the throws of a bad heroin addiction can cause the best of us to compromise our integrity and sell our talents far below their true worth. But it's important to understand that Parker's actions only undercut *his* trade value; they didn't undermine or impact the trade value throughout the entire jazz community.

Leap ahead to the present-day beatmaking community, where many beatmakers regularly, and sometimes rather aggressively, aim to sale beats — to anyone — for $25 and lower. Some in the beatmaking community are comfortable with this tactic; they simply see it as a means of getting paid. Others find it ridiculous and shameful; something that's not befitting of anyone who takes the beatmaking tradition seriously. Whatever side you fall on, one things for certain: $25 or less beat pricing undermines trade value throughout the beatmaking community.

I recall a conversation I once had with a then somewhat rising beatmaker (he would eventualy land a large television commercial placement, followed by a career fade that could have been avoided) about his beat-selling activities on MySpace. He wasn't at all concerned with whether or not he was caving on his integrity; nor did he give any thought to how he was representing the beatmaking community at large. He was making upwards of $300 (allegedly) per month selling beats for $25, $30, and $50 to *anyone* who found his MySpace page and was interested in buying a beat. Notwithstanding that there once was a time when beatmakers would never give a beat out to or work with anyone who's music they didn't personally like or respect, this particular beatmaker could care less who was buying and using his beats. His stance: *Why should I sit on the beats that I make, hoping to get thousands of dollars for them from big placements, when I can sell them on MySpace and get paid now?* My reaction: If your'e selling beats for $25, beats that you crafted and believe in, why not just give them away for free to rappers who you believe in and try to build something great? He didn't see it the same way. And since that conversation almost 10 years ago, plenty of others have shared the get *cheap*-rich now scheme, or the basement blowout beat pricing sentiment.

Hip hop/rap music enjoys a global audience, so there's literally 10s of millions of people who are interested in hearing an individualized version on the music that they love. To gain even a sliver of 1/1000th of a half-percent of this grand audience, you will have to earn their ear. How do you do this? Well, there's no surefire way for any one music maker, but I believe that for beatmakers, in specific, it comes down to quality music that skilled rappers (and other vocalists) and other parties want to use. And, of course, this depends on some degree of promoting yourself and your music, which is part of the overall point that I'm making: If you devalue yourself as a discount peddler of beats, why would you expect for anyone else to see you any differently?

There are better paths to take, if music truly is how you'd like to earn a living. For instance, forming a rap group, something that I've long been a strong advocate for, has greater potential for sustainability than selling beats — to anyone — at $10-$50 a pop, or spamming Twitter feeds with "Hot Beat Sales." Building genuine, solid relationships with people who share your enthusiasm for the same style and sounds of hip hop/rap music bodes much better than "As Seen on T.V." infomercial tactics that most people dismiss, anyway. Also, offering up a well-designed and well-executed beat tape, that doubles as both a release that can be reviewed and auditioned for prospective beat buyers, is much more noble and potentially rewarding. And I'm sure there's any number of other unique (more respectful) ways to gain an audience for quality beats; in this regard, everyone's limited only by their own imagination and drive.

But either way, I understand. There are lots of people who want to make money off of their beats and make name for themselves. I understand that "people have to eat," that people have to make money how they can. I find nothing wrong with the fundamental premise of selling beats. It's the "discount-beat" and the low-grade marketing approaches (which too many have drafted in recent years) that concerns me. Forget for a moment that the widespread devaluing of beats (through cheesy marketing and near-sighted, quick-cash mechanisms like $10 beat sales and leasing) reflects poorly on those beatmakers who take those paths. What does it say about the beatmaking tradition as a whole when you have large numbers of beatmakers carrying on in this way? Further, is the small promise of money (or lack their of) causing some in the beatmaking community to see beats as something that is less than music? Something to be pushed to phantom buyers with less consideration than a hot pretzel in Times Square?

Remember, this isn't the same thing as someone taking a gig in a tiny after-hours night club for small pay. It's not someone forgoing payment to land a placement with a talented indie rapper. No, this is intentional cheesy marketing and deep discounting. While such approaches and hard-sale methods often work for gadgets sold on TV, when such tactics are applied to beats — music — they carry the stench and stigma of desperation and needless compromise. Of course, this is not to say that there aren't some beatmakers that are making dope beats at discount prices. I've surveyed thousands of "$10" and "$50" beats that sounded great. In those cases, my main gripe is that those beats would have been better used for free in the hands of capable rappers, or on a free beat tape, not sold off at bargain basement prices, only to never be heard of again or, worse, leased out to too many incapable rappers.

In other words, this is a trade issue. The beatmaking community, as a whole, is responsible for setting and maintaining our trade value. When we lower that floor, why should we expect others to raise it? So here's the main jewel: If you market your beats like a pack of cheap steak knives on a late-night infomercial, you might grab a few dollars here and there, but don't expect to earn much respect for your music, or any sustainable money from it, or any legitimately long career in music.

Expanding the Concept of Placements: The Who-Gets-to-Make-Music Dimension of Placements and Why Self-Placed Producer Projects Are the Most Viable Alternative to Chasing Placements

Music is one of the most important, influential parts of life. Most people in modern society desire, need, and consume large daily doses of music. Plus, when it comes to pop culture, most of us are unavoidably attached to music one way or another. Thus, music must be made, it needs to be made, and broad demand ensures that it will always be circulated. This continuum is both inevitable and perpetual.

It's equally important to understand that there is no one industry or group of people who decides who gets to make, publish, or distribute music. Yet, to a large degree, the placement structure — like the top-down music industry that encourages it — feeds on the idea that there is only a select group or limited number of people who get to make music. This is one reason why beat brokers and some other folks often claim that music, in general, is over crowded; that there is too much beat supply and very little demand for beats; and that there are too many beatmakers (producers) and not enough placement opportunities. But beat brokers, and others who tow this line of thinking, are either unaware of, or conveniently ignoring, two important facts. First, there is an unlimited number of music listeners around the globe, all with unprecedented choice and various devices to consume music. This means that there are literally hundreds of millions of music consumers who are actively in control of their music consumption habits and not necessarily guided by a monolithic music industry. Further worth noting, none of us share the exact same taste in music, nor do any of us have identical purchasing or concert-going habits. Second, every beatmaker has the ability to be his or her own placement opportunity. This means that every beatmaker has the power of self-placement.

The notion that there is too many beatmakers or that music is over crowded is ridiculous. There could never be too many music makers because the number of potential music listeners (hip hop/rap fans alone) is limitless. But coming from those who defer to, and are seemingly enamored by, the music industry (particularly the old music industry system), the "over-crowded" sentiment is no surprise. In recent decades, the major record labels, the wounded kings of the music industry food chain, have consolidated and further narrowed choice (i.e. availability of a diverse mainstream product) in attempt to guarantee a high hit-to-release ratio. (Remember, for every hit record/artist, there are a number of less successful records and outright busts.) In the 1950s, '60s, and '70s, there was less consolidation and narrowing of choice, more independent record labels doing their own thing, and a wider variety of music product on offer to the public. But along with major label mergers and creative consolidation came a deep narrowing of choice, centralized marketing and promotion channels, and the illusion that there were only a limited number of professional recording artist slots available to serve the world — a world full of 100s of millions of music listeners, mind you. Combined, all of these factors gave the major labels an almost exclusive level of access to music listeners.

Many of today's beat brokers (and similar music industry consultants) entered the music industry between the early 1990s through early 2000s, the precise time major label mergers and creative consolidation were at an apex. Naturally, these music industry insiders absorbed many of the common industry views and perceptions about who gets to make music, artistry, production, and distribution. As such, many beat brokers tend to want to cement the placement and access systems that have been in place for a long time. But things have changed dramatically. Today, technology has democratized music, the tools of production, the channels of distribution, and even the channels of marketing and promotion. This means that access to music listeners is no longer something reserved for major labels and their marketing channels. So while the major labels still sit (far less comfortably) at the top of the music industry food chain, the democratization of music, along with the tools of production and distribution, has created a new reality. A reality where music artists are no longer shackled to, or encumbered by, the rigged major label system or many of its antiquated methods and processes. Thus, the music industry, which was once a staunchly exclusive club, operating from a centralized piece of real estate, has now become more of an open-ended and loosely inclusive league, functioning from wherever, as anyone with music-making tools can bypass the major label system altogether and still be in the music industry.

Given the fact that each beatmaker represents their own placement opportunity, it stands to reason that most beatmakers should be more focused on producing their own projects than chasing down placements on someone else's. I certainly don't want to discourage anyone from going after a successful placement or using a beat broker to get it. If you have a real shot at placing a beat through your relationship with a beat broker, go for it. But my aim is to help change the default psychology associated with beats and placements, and to encourage beatmakers to take a more proactive philosophical approach with their music. As I mentioned earlier in this chapter, nothing is guaranteed, but you can increase or decrease your odds of a successful career in music, depending on the path(s) you ultimately decide to pursue.

Unfortunately, far too many beatmakers see chasing placements as the first and only path. This is problematic for a number of reasons. First, as I pointed out earlier, the odds are lower going the beat broker-placement route. Remember, the more beats a beat broker has to submit, the more their odds increase of getting a placement. But this works the opposite way for beatmakers who submit to beat brokers. This has nothing to do with one particular beat broker (individual or service) vs. another, it's just simple math and industry shenanigans. As the pool of people submitting beats to one person or service increases, the odds of each person within the pool getting a placement decreases. Second, by focusing squarely on the placement/beat broker path and thus, restricting the distribution of their beats to long-shot beat placement opportunities, many beatmakers are not only curbing the flow of their music and its contribution to the beatmaking community, they're taking away their best chance for the world's unlimited number of music listeners to find it. Finally, while submitting beats for placement through a broker may fulfill some notion of taking charge of your career, the truth is it can foster a false sense of action and build up a wall of discouragement, due to actual inactivity and response limbo.

So if I haven't been clear enough, let me again make it plain: I believe in the philosophy of placing yourself first before anything else. In the next chapter, I discuss forming groups as one way to do this, but here, I want to talk about another way: self-placed producer projects.

In 1998, Pete Rock dropped *Soul Survivor*, not just one of the best producer based albums, but one of the best albums in hip hop/rap music, period. In 1988, ten years before Pete Rock's *Soul Survivor*, Marley Marl dropped *In Control*, his first producer based album. In 2001, J Dilla dropped *Welcome to Detroit*; and in 2006, he followed with the vastly influential *Donuts*. Marco Polo dropped his first *Port Authority* in 2007; and the follow-up, *Port Authority II*, in 2013. Statik Selektah has released a number of self-placed producer projects in recent years, and his two most recent albums *Extended Play* and Lucky 7 (2013 and 2015 respectively) were well-received. I mention all of these albums (and to be sure, there are more) to make the point that the self-placed producer album isn't a new idea, it's a proven one.

Self-placed producer projects cut out the placement chase, as they empower beatmakers to essentially place themselves. Recruiting rappers (a verse or two at a time) for features and putting together self-placed producer projects allows beatmakers to independently forge projects, which affords them greater creative control, a much larger and immediate stake in the songs produced, the final say in the promotion and marketing of the resulting projects, and creditable exposure for their music, which can ultimately lead to more placements on other projects. Even still, most beatmakers are not exploring this option. And although some have taken to releasing beat tapes (beat tapes are not producer albums in the same vein as the aforementioned projects by Pete Rock, et. al), there's a sense that it's difficult to bring self-placed producer albums to market. This is because (A) Most beatmakers are locked into the concept of chasing placements and are, therefore, unaware of this option; and (B) The handful of beatmakers who are aware of this path wrongly believe that landing decent features, particularly for albums by unknown music makers, is virtually impossible. But this is simply not the case. Most rappers — some of A-, B- and, C-level, notoriety — *are* for hire, and are more than willing to get on new album projects if the price is right, or if they feel it's a good look for them.

Obviously, Pete Rock, Marley Marl, J Dilla, Marco Polo, and Statik Selektah have all certainly benefited from their own notoriety in the hip hop/rap music scene. So it perhaps goes without saying that such notoriety made it easier for them to get decent features for their albums. But lesser and unknown beatmakers are not without recourse for making similar projects. Just as access to music listeners is no longer something reserved only for major labels, access to music makers, rappers in particular, is no longer something reserved only for managers, other handlers or industry insiders, or even notable producers. Many acclaimed rappers have made it known that they're available for hire. For instance, in the heyday of Myspace, Kool G Rap reportedly had a price of $500 - $1,500 for a verse. Now, lots of rappers are taking full advantage of the promotion power that social media sites like Twitter and Facebook offer. Rappers like Sadat X (always a safe bet for a dope verse and decent media coverage) and others have taken to Twitter to directly promote their rhyme services and rates. And on both Twitter and Facebook, most rappers post their business, contact, and booking info right in their bios. In most cases, this contact info is an email address that they personally check — no middle man, no beat broker. (Don't be surprised by how far an email with a rates request or a direct payment offer can take you.)

So it would appear that the only real obstacle to getting decent features from rappers comes down to price. And depending on your situation, network of connections, and skills, you may even be able to barter for features. But in my own non-scientific survey and research of various rappers who have in the past five years made public their rates for verses, the price range is between $140 on the low end to $2,500 on the high end, with $400 being about the median rate. Of course, each rate is negotiable on a case by case basis. And while you may not have the money for an entire project, you might be able to afford at least one song. In either case, you're still placing yourself. When you consider that popular online beat-selling sites like PMP (Production MarketPlace) charge around $275 for their annual membership, which does not guarantee a placement, is it not worth considering paying as much or a little more for a guaranteed placement? All things considered — from access to rappers, to the ability to guarantee your own placement, to ownership, to marketing and promotional control — self-placed producer projects are the most viable alternative to chasing placements.

Chapter 12

It's Yours; Nothin' to it But to Do It
Know the Angles, Because You Have the Control

> Musical artists are some of the most resourceful people in the world. —David Sherbow

> Forget a "placement!" The whole "submitting beats" game is messed up. You're better off starting your own thing and rockin' with that. I mean, in a game this wide open, if you lose, you can't blame the next man for what *you* didn't know, or what *you* didn't do. —Sa'id

DIY: Do It Yourself – Independently

Despite the various means of distribution, beatmakers and other recording artists have the ultimate control over the *creative path* that they choose — not the labels, not the A&Rs, and certainly not the so-called tastemakers in the music industry. Right now, the music industry is wide open. Advanced technology, widespread and long-practiced industry mismanagement, and product over saturation has all made it more possible than ever for independent recording artists to liberate themselves and aggressively compete for reasonable market share. In today's music scene, anybody with the right know-how, the right skill-set, and the proper drive and ambition can carve out a fair living, outside of the fledgling major label system.

Thus, **DIY stands for Do It Yourself.** More broadly speaking, it means take control of your own destiny, by managing your own unique product. DIY is about being your own boss and calling your own shots. Moreover, it's about recognizing that you are a professional the moment you take your product seriously and bring it to a market. DIY doesn't mean that you have to do everything. It simply means that you are the Chief Executive Officer (CEO) of your products and services. As the CEO of "Your Products & Services, Inc.," if you will, it is your job to make sure that your product or service ultimately gets the best chance to perform well in the marketplace. In other words, there are some steps in the DIY process that you should do alone; there are other steps that you should do along with someone else; and then there are also other steps that you must (necessarily) contract-out to other professionals.

Context of the DIY Artist

Right now, it's never been better to be an indie artist. Today, music listeners know that they have immeasurable access to massive choice and variety. Therefore, they're seeking out and finding new music and related products that cater to their own unique interests and tastes. Moreover, today's music listeners are not sitting back and waiting for the radio or other traditional tastemaker channels to tell them what they should be listening to. This context is of particular importance to beatmakers (producers), who are, by the nature of the music business, self-contractors. Point is, why chase down placements for well-established acts, or veteran acts with declining fame, when you can use your time and effort to establish your own projects and acts?

The largest advantage to any new artist in any new artistic medium is unfiltered choice. Today, there's an infinite menu of music. And in the web age, where radio and TV no longer serve as the chief channels of taste, ALL artists compete in the same space, with the same ground rules: *He who wins a presence on the internet, wins indeed.* In fact, "winning" is no longer measured by the metrics of enormous (hard to repeat) record sales, but often by the amount of space you create and expand online. And the sobering truth for recording artists (not the A-list acts) is this: Record sales are just a residual effect of the space that you're able to maintain.

BeatTip – What is a DIY System?

A DIY System is an organized plan of action that an artist uses to do it for himself. There are a number of factors that contribute to a successful DIY system, but I believe that there are eight key factors to any artist's DIY system.

The BeatTips DIY Checklist: 8 Points of an Effective DIY System

(1) Assess Your Current Situation

Assessing your current situation means honestly and objectively analyzing where you currently stand. This includes an analysis of your products and services, your talent level, the level of your contacts and alliances, and the city and region that you currently reside in.

(2) Create Your Own Style/Brand

In a wide open music market, the best way to really compete is by offering your own unique style/brand. Although you may not make the sort of music that falls into one broad category, in order to separate yourself from the rest of the pack it's a good idea to create a sound and style that is truly distinguishable.

(3) Get a Website/Blog and Create Your Own "Web Space" and Marketplace

Without your own website/blog and social media identity, it is virtually impossible for you to build a following for your products or services. Bottom line here: You must consistently maintain your online footprint; and you do that by (1) recommitting yourself to the task of making your web property (or properties) the best experience(s) that it (they) can be; and (2) by building up social equity with the people you encounter, especially the people you interact with in social media networks.

(4) Create your own Sales & Distribution System

Traditional distribution channels, such as large retailers and major/indie distributors are no longer the only game in town. In today's music sales environment, there are a plethora of options. Aside from the many digital download options, you can also sale and distribute your product or service directly from your own website. In this case, the easiest way to take online payments is through an all-in-one payment gateway system like PayPal.

(5) Build a Solid Fan Base

No matter what product or service you offer, there is no group that will consistently support you more than a solid fan base. But how do you start a fan base? Well, first of all, the oft-repeated notion of starting a fan base is flawed. You don't just one day decide to "start" a fan base like it's the push of a button. You have to *earn* a fan base. And once you earn a fan base, you have to continue to maintain it. So then, how do you earn a fan base? In order to earn a fan base, there are three things that you must do above all: (1) Consistently create new product; (2) Regularly offer something for free, whether it be content or your side exclusive product; and (3) Always engage with your fan base.

(6) Create Your Own Word-of-Mouth Chain

In a global consumer market, one that is increasingly being powered less by mass media and more by niche-based consumption, word of mouth is even more crucial to the success of your products or services. Word-of-mouth marketing is not new, but within the old music industry and traditional media, word-of-mouth strategies were nearly always considered a secondary marketing apparatus. Things have changed dramatically. Because of the rapid emergence and direct influence of social media, word-of-mouth marketing is now the premier marketing strategy for all forms of entertainment, especially music.

So in order for you to compete in this climate, it is essential that you come up with your own word-of-mouth strategy. The best way to do this is to create what I call a "word-of-mouth chain." A word-of-mouth chain is a network of people that is comprised of your core supporters and their closest peers. It's important to note that every person in your word-of-mouth chain is essentially an independent marketer for you.

To assemble your word-of-mouth chain, begin with your most ardent supporters. Identify those people who repeatedly support you and take the time to have thoughtful exchanges, via message boards and/or through email. As these people make themselves known, be sure to trade updated contact information with them. Next, let them in early on all of your upcoming products or services; and even grant them access to much of your past works (if you have any). Also, whenever possible, directly invite them to help you market your products or services. If you follow these basic steps, you will inevitably build solid relationships (perhaps even friendships) that you'll be able to count on for your word-of-mouth campaign.

(7) Manage the Rights of Your Music

Even if you make a song/beat and upload it to your own site, your music is not as protected as you think; you still need to have evidence that you are the copyright holder of that music. Sending your music off to the U.S. Copyright Office is important, and at some point, you may need to do that, but perhaps an even more efficient way to "manage the rights" of your music is by joining a performing rights Society (e.g. ASCAP or BMI) and filing your music with them each time you create something for commercial release or even for a mixtape.

(8) The Music Business System and Its Relevant Sub-Systems

The "music business system" is a phrase that I use to describe the fundamental framework by which the music industry is organized. Up until now, the music business system was defined by the formulaic manufacturing of a few clear hit records, whose channel of distribution was controlled by a few major companies. Today is quite different, mainly because there's no longer a dominating mainstream that dictates what music listeners hear. Actually, "mainstream" is mostly a relic notion of the old music industry — micro-streams of shared interest is the new way. Having a clear understanding of this fact, is essential to your bid to do-it-yourself music-making.

Frame it the Right Way, Aim for A Career in Music: Opening Up Music-Related Opportunities by Broadening Your Scope

Many beatmakers put themselves in a trap. For most, the goal is to have a music career rather than a career in music. What's the difference? Isn't that the same thing? Isn't that just semantics? Well, no, it's not the same thing, and it isn't just semantics. Once you unpack the philosophical approaches that lie beneath the framing of each of these phrases, you notice that there are glaring differences.

As a framing, "music career" usually evokes the understanding of the traditional recording artist/label dichotomy and music industry architecture. For most people, this is the idea that "music career" triggers. So as it follows, a music career is typically understood as a vocation that is squarely rooted in, and otherwise connected to, the parameters of the music industry. Thus, a music career is something that is inevitably measured by or against, for better or worse, the metrics of the major label system hierarchy and the mainstream infrastructures that secure its place in both commerce and popular culture. And although the music industry as a whole contains a number of distinguished areas of concentration (production, songwriting, performance, licensing, publishing, etc.), to have a music career commonly implies that one's livelihood is inextricably tied to the music industry.

A "music career" embodies a philosophical approach that fundamentally sees the music industry as both the chief means (if not the only means) of employment and as the primary arbiter of success. This deference to the music industry is warranted, given the scope of what a music career implies. But such deference can be detrimental, inasmuch as it often curbs how most recording artists/musicians think about their possible career opportunities. When recording artists/musicians limit the scope of their career opportunities to those traditionally only found within the music industry, they cut off a world of other industries that could use their musical talents. Similarly, when beatmakers narrow their idea of a music career to simply landing placements on a rapper's album, they shrink the modes by which they can earn a living from their music-related talents.

A Career in Music Signals Something Broader

As a framing, "a career in music" implies much more than the traditional recording artist/label dichotomy and music industry architecture. It embodies a philosophical approach that fundamentally sees one's musical talents, not the music industry, as the guide for opportunity and the chief metric for success. Moreover, "a career in music" signals something broader, something less restrictive and hierarchical. While the "music career" framing seems to imply something singular, something that's attached to the music industry and its sub-industries (e.g. session work, tour support, etc.), "a career in music" conveys something much more multi-dimensional and spacious. "A career in music" works as an umbrella framework that's not deferential to any one spectrum. For instance, it treats the traditional recording artist/label dichotomy and music industry architecture as one dimension. And so, there's infinite room for a league of other music-related dimensions as well. Further, as a framing, "a career in music" leads recording artists/musicians to expand their ideas about how they can earn a living from their music-related talents. Inevitably, the "a career in music" framing opens up new possibilities for them; at the same time, it removes a dependence upon the music industry architecture.

What Does this Mean for Beatmakers?

Far too many beatmakers look at beat placement with romantic eyes; they see it as the single "big break" that can make their career. As such, these beatmakers focus all of their attention on getting their beats into the hands — or email inboxes — of any rapper or other vocalist, or A&R, or so-called music industry insider that they can. At the same time, they ignore or choose not to explore other ways to earn a living from their music-related talents. Is this singular strategy wrong? Not necessarily, depends on the situation and the people involved. Each person brings their own advantages — i.e. know-how, expertise, and connections — to the table. But if this is the only strategy that a beatmaker has, then I believe that the odds of them having a sustainable career in music are extremely low. Still, can one placement trigger a music career? Of course. But that's more long-shot exception than it is the norm. So is it reasonable or practical to follow such a course? And even with a number of acclaimed placements, a beatmaker can still be on the short end of a music career.

If this "one-shot" placement strategy describes the approach and course that you've been taking, I strongly urge you to stop and transition to a more diverse way of thinking about your music-related talents. You are the commodity, not your beats. Beats are an extension of your music ability, but they should not be considered the extent of your career capability. I am in no way suggesting that beats hold little weight or that they're inferior to other recorded music compositions; beats have their own distinct value, both in terms of their art and in their financial value. What I am saying is that in addition to the traditional use and scope of beats, that is to say, for use by a rapper (or other vocalist), you have to think broader and more deeply about the new uses and commercial scopes for your beats and your music-related talents.

How you frame your goals are just as important as the goals themselves. So goes your framing — the philosophical context from which you approach something — so goes your thinking, so goes your opportunities and actions. For many beatmakers, transitioning forward from the "one-shot" placement strategy will depend on how committed they are to seriously studying the art of beatmaking and music in general. To be certain, the only way to unlock new possibilities for your music-related talents is to be aware of their existence in the first place. If your equation is: "make a beat + shop it + get placement = music career," then you need to learn new math.

In addition to helping beatmakers better understand the art and craft of beatmaking, my goal is to encourage and help beatmakers think in terms of having a career in music, rather than having a music career. To that end, below I've listed some music-related opportunities that you can create for yourself that you may not have thought of before. To be sure, there are more opportunities, but the following brief list will help you get started in how to think them up.

Museum projects. Museums of all kinds put on new exhibitions each year. Most try to involve local artists and creatives whenever they can. Visit local museums and come up with music ideas that you can pitch to them. Is it a long shot? Not really. You're not competing against millions of other people shopping their beats for the exact same slot on an album or a free mixtape.

Art Galleries. Like museums, art galleries rely on their ability to put on new and interesting shows. I've been to a number of art shows in New York. Some have had non-descript DJs; some have had the radio playing; some have had iPod playlists; etc. Never have I seen a show with a mix of beats crafted exclusively for an artist's work. I suspect that this market will blossom in the future, especially as upstart galleries continue to vie for attention.

Film Schools. I've seen some pretty decent student films that were undermined by poor quality music. There's a market here. Maybe not the most lucrative one, but you can get the experience of using your beats in new ways, not to mention the valuable experience of working with an artist from another medium. Offer your services to film school students. Better yet, see about getting your name onto a film school's registry of services.

Performance Poets and Other Spoken Word Artists. Offer beats to those artists that are "rappers" outside of the traditional hip hop sense.

Sneaker Stores and Boutique Shops. Sneaker stores and hip boutiques are art galleries, well, to some at least. These are places that thrive on an edgy, "hip" vibe. Capitalize off of this and pitch stores on custom beat tapes. At worst, you play a hand in setting the mood of the place for eager shoppers. At best, your music is an ad for you work.

Don't Make Placements Your Sole Focus

The mad dash by some beatmakers to capture big name placements is an exercise in futility. With casino-style odds, music industry shenanigans, and infamously flawed hip hop/rap business practices, why chase after placements when you can build your own group? In fact, most of the time, capturing a placement can be a trap. Here's how it works. A beatmaker lands one to three key placements. After they land these placements, they then gain (naturally) a new level of confidence and, subsequently, they subscribe to the idea that more placements will come regularly. Truth is, the placements do not come regularly, even for some established brand name beatmakers (producers). Making matters worse, many of these now marginally successful beatmakers seemingly forget the level of "placement competition" that exists in the formidable beat market exchange.

There's no secret anymore that beat prices across the board have gone down, way down. Furthermore, the *distance* between submitting a beat and getting a placement is terribly far. Thus, chasing down music placements are *not* what most people think, or what some producer managers might want you to believe. This is why I strongly encourage beatmakers to go it alone and start their own outfits. Of course, this doesn't mean that I suggest that you should entirely ignore submission requests and placement opportunities; placements — *if* you can get them — do have an upside, but they also have a down side as well. For example, there can be low pay, delayed pay, and even no pay. Furthermore, placements are tied to the success of someone else's project, which beatmakers have no control over. So if you land a placement on a project that sells poorly in the marketplace, there is very little residual income you can expect to receive from that project. The only payment you might get is the initial fee for the beat that you sell. Thus, what I hope to stress here is that in an ad-hoc and over-saturated beat market exchange (submission environment), making a placement your #1 option is career suicide. Chasing placements should never be your first option; *you* should be your first option.

Check This Out – The Frustration of Placements

One great beat placement *can* make a beatmaker's career. But you also have to recognize that landing such a placement is a long shot. Further, for the most part, placements represent a new kind of frustration. To see what I mean, consider the following scenario.

You're in the lab (your production environment), making a new beat. You have the drums knocking just right, the rhythm is tight, and the beat, overall, is driving you to nod your head. It's official, you have a dope beat! But what do you do now? How do you get that dope beat into the hands of someone who can really catch wreck on it, and/or to someone who can cut you a check? Well, for 10s of thousands of beatmakers across America, this is the $62,000 question that typically leads to the $2,500 frustration.

Right now, the going industry rate for a beat by a "newcomer" is roughly $2,500 (typically, much lower for unconnected and lesser-known beatmakers). Sure, there are some beatmakers who are getting more than that for their first placement, but they are very few and far between. The list of beatmakers that make above the unsanctioned minimum of $2,500 includes the so-called "super producers" and the marginally successful beatmakers who were able to piggy-back off a placement or two. But for the rank-and-file beatmakers, if they do land that sought after placement, they can expect to be paid $2,500, *at best*. So what's wrong with that? $2,500 is twenty-five-hundred dollars, you say. Well, let's take a closer look at that amount.

Let's say it's you who sold the beat for $2,500. First question. Who's the manager of the recording artist that you "sold" your beat to? You might have to pay a small fee to him or her for having your beat actually used and making the album. This "manager's tax," as I like to call it, is just your typical kick-back.[190] The manager's tax (kick-back) can range anywhere from 10% to 100% of the beat price. But let's just say in this case, your beat is so ill, so game-changing that the manager waives his special tax. Cool, so you escape with $2,500. Still, not bad, right? Wrong, there's more.

Now, let's examine more closely that banger of a beat that you made. Does it contain any recognizable samples? If it doesn't, you can skip the rest of this paragraph, but if it does, read the next sentence very carefully. Any beat that contains recognizable samples will be subject to sample clearance, or run the risk of being exposed to a potential copyright infringement lawsuit. In other words, if your beat does contain recognizable samples, unless those samples can be cleared, the song containing your beat will not be used (placed) on the typical major label release. Major labels (and some indies) are terrified of potential litigation against them, so they do their best to properly clear samples on any release that they plan to bring to market. Furthermore, sample clearance fees come out of the rapper's recording budget. And guess who the rapper passes the cost on to? Yep, you, the beatmaker (producer). It's important to note however that sometimes "super-producers" are absolved from "eating" (i.e. absorbing) the sampling clearance fees.

If your beat doesn't contain any samples (or at least any that could ever really be identified), you're almost home free. But there's one other thing: timely payment. Up until about 15 years ago, payment came with *delivery* of the beat, regardless if it was used on a project or not. But things have changed. Today, it's common for beatmakers (producers) to hand over the beat, complete with all audio files, *without receiving any payment.*[191] So after you've handed over your beat, and it's been used to generate a new song, when do you actually get paid? Well, the true answer is somewhere between maybe soon and perhaps never.

Finally, let's not forget the rapper who did use your beat to write some great new lyrics and a catchy hook. Guess what? He can use those lyrics and hook — inspired by your beat — on another beat. If that beat sounds better with his/her lyrics than your beat does, who do you think gets the coveted placement,

---

[190] There are many types of "kick-backs" (money kicked backed to someone as payment for a *favor*) in the music industry, this is just one that a beatmaker may be expected to pay at some point or another.
[191] So-called "super-producers" and some marginally successful beatmakers/producers are usually able to secure 50% of their fee upfront. Some super-producers command 100% upfront; but super-producers are increasingly making concessions on upfront payment.

and who do you think gets paid for the usage? And let's not forget that it can be months before you hear any word as to whether or not your beat was used. Which, in effect, means that bangin' beat that you created is in limbo. So do you shop it to anyone or do you wait for a green light that may never come?[192]

4 Reasons Why You Should Start Your Own Group

The first reason you should start your own group with a rapper and/or rapping yourself (if you can) is peace of mind. Having your own group and doing it yourself means that you have complete creative control; your career and success is in your hands. You get the chance to build your own unique brand identity, which in turn, assures more longevity than constantly waiting for others to choose your beats.

The second reason you should start your own group with a rapper and/or rapping yourself (if you can) is touring. As the member of a group, you get to go on tour, continuously earning revenue that you do not have to pay back to a label or an A&R rep who got you a placement. Most recording artists usually make more money from live performance tours and shows than they do from record sales. But beatmakers (producers) who land placements do not get a share of the tour/show money of the recording artists whom they placed beats with.

The third reason why you should start your own group: Faster payment. Doing it yourself, when you're part of a group, means you see the check. Payment when you're part of a group or solo, or doing it yourself is far less precarious than the situation that involves a beatmaker waiting for payment on a beat sold.

Finally, the fourth reason you should start your own group (or going solo) and doing it yourself is that *you* neutralize the beat placement issues. Having your own group assures that you choose which beats and songs make an album. Beat submissions are certainly no guarantee, and even if and when you land a placement, you have no say about the actual roll-out of that placement.

---

[192] There have been cases where some beatmakers have shopped the same beat to two or more different rappers and, subsequently, there have been cases where the same beat from one beatmaker has appeared on two separate albums. When this occurs, a beatmaker's reputation can take a serious hit, as it goes against the ethics of business.

Get on Someone's Radar: Louis C.K., Why You Should Form a Beatmaker-Anchored Group, and Build Your Own Platform

In the late fall of 2012, I learned about comedian Louis C.K.'s self-distributed one-hour online comedy special, *Louis C.K. - Live at the Beacon Theater*. At that time, I didn't have all the details; I hadn't heard of C.K.'s show until two months after he had initially released it. But as a casual fan of his work, the murmurs and word of mouth about the show peaked my interest. As a DIY advocate, I was also interested in hearing more details about how the show came about. Was it really independently produced and released? Was it really released from his own website? What payment options did he make available to consumers? And, was the show a success or not?

In early 2013, I listened to an interview that Louis C.K. did on the talk show "Fresh Air with Terry Gross." In the "Fresh Air" interview, C.K. confirmed that he produced the special with his own money, edited it entirely, and released it independently from his own website. In exchange for two streams and two downloads of the unencrypted, high-definition show, fans were asked to pay just $5 directly to him via PayPal. C.K. explained that he went this route because he wanted to see if releasing a video of himself could make money. But he also revealed that TV comedy specials he had done in the past had netted him no money at all. "I've never seen a check from a [TV] comedy special," he said in his interview with Gross. Clearly, another reason why C.K. went the D.I.Y. route was because he wanted to eliminate the middle man. Finally, C.K. expressed that the project was a success, revealing that he "made all of his money back and then some."

Before I go on, I want to make a couple of points of context about the anatomy of a sale. Louis C.K. independently released *Louis C.K. - Live at the Beacon Theater* in early December, 2011. It got on my radar in February, 2012, nearly two months later, *not the first week* of its release. I first heard mention — word of mouth — of Louis C.K.'s special on Twitter, not a paid advertisement on television or radio. Because Louis C.K. was already on my radar, when I heard that he had a new special, I was interested in learning more. I was able to learn more about Louis C.K.'s special by listening to an *archived* episode of the talk show "Fresh Air," a show that is heavy on my radar. After listening to Louis C.K.'s interview on "Fresh Air," I wanted to purchase his special, which I did less than 24 hours after listening to his interview on "Fresh Air."

It's important to note that the way in which Louis C.K. rolled out his special exemplifies, in both broad and specific ways, how music projects are now sold. Although the instant-hit, first-week sales paradigm is still widely in play, most music releases, especially those from independent recording artists, make their sales over an extended period of time. This difference is in how core fans and casual fans of large and smaller acts make purchases. For the major label backed releases, especially those from the biggest artists in music, there's typically a heavy push to attract both the core fan and the casual fan alike within the first week of release. In these cases, first-week sales (good or bad) often narrate the level of success or failure of the music release.

For smaller, independent releases, first-week sales aren't as critical. For one thing, core fans of independent artists don't always go for the first-week sales crunch. Core fans already have a fluid connection with the artists that they support; and in most cases, core fans maintain an unwritten, revolving commitment to buy their favorite artists' releases at some point. This revolving commitment is understood to mean that, while the core fan may not buy the album in the first week — or even the first month — of it's release, he or she will indeed buy the album at *some point*, usually within the first 6 months of the release, sometimes longer. Also, because smaller, independent artists lack a major national/international marketing and promotion push, the rate of casual fan discovery takes longer for them.

While bigger, major label-backed artists rely on a heavy push for their releases, most smaller, independent artists simply build something that they trust (or hope) people will gravitate to. In other words, smarter independent artists know how to follow the "Build it, and they will come" maxim. Louis C.K. followed this maxim, too. He built his brand and offered a project directly to his fans, and they came. He didn't wait for approval or validation; he just built it. With his own imagination, wherewithal, and money, he put together his comedy special and released it to the world on his website. I'm not sure how much emphasis C.K. placed on first-week sales. I know he did some press in the weeks leading up to the release, but that was minimal, and it was certainly not a 4-month, full court marketing blitz. Either way, I get the feeling that he believed that his "Beacon Theater" project was the sort of thing that would scale over time.

The Radar: Why Most Music Releases Now Scale Better Over Time

Right now, there's so much music, so much information in general, that today's average music listener can't find the time to get through as many new releases as they'd like to in a calendar year, let alone trying to keep up with the first week that those albums drop. Actually, when you think about it, in an age of ultra accessibility and abuncance of choice, the idea of buying or listening to music projects in the first week of their release is an antiquated practice that has outlived its usefulness.

I don't know about you, but throughout the year, I find myself playing catch up. Each month, I miss a number of potential great releases, not because of a lack of interest but because of the overwhelming number of new releases. Add to that the sheer amount of noise that's tossed around, and the task of keeping up with new music becomes even more daunting. But that's the problem. Discovering great music shouldn't be about keeping up with mounting release dates; discovering great music shouldn't be a task. Discovering great music should be an enjoyable, rewarding journey. And I've found that the only "new" music that I can check is the music that makes it on to my radar. (Louis C.K. made it on to my comedy radar around 2008, yet it wasn't until 2013 that I purchased something from him.)

I tend to circle back to the "new" music that stays on my radar with a strong signal. For me, and I suspect many others, hearing music as soon as it's released is less important than hearing it at all. With more choice than ever before, I can tune into "new" music on my schedule, not the arbitrary release schedule of 10s of thousands of different artists. So for me, and I believe most others as well, the probability of me hearing "new" music and buying it (or something else from the artist) depends on whether or not the music/artist can get a strong signal on my radar. The greater the artist's signal is on my radar, the more likely I will purchase their music, eventually.

The Instant Success Problem, the Similarities Between Comedians and Beatmakers, and Why Forming Groups Might Be the Best Way to Go

There is no such thing as instant success. Peel back the curtains on any success story, and what you'll find is a more humbling set of facts. Everything from arduous practice hours, to tons of money spent (and lost), to creative failures, to opportunities that fell through, to lost and made business connections. It's all there behind the curtain of instant success.

Louis C.K.'s story, like most comics, is a story of endurance. Countless hours of practice in the form of doing shows, writing bits, and honing his style. Long and late nights. Numerous dead-end gigs. False-starts. Rejections. You name it, he's gone through it. And through it all, like other comic success stories, he carved out a lane for himself in the form of his hit television show, "Louie," and his aforementioned comedy special.

There are plenty of stand-up comics chasing after success. For most of them, the idea of success is divided up into a series of reachable plateaus. Develop your own style and type of bits, get noticed, earn a following, get noticed again by "TV people," get a TV special, land a writing gig, land a television show. Of course, the order of some of these plateaus could be rearranged, but you get the picture.

Like stand-up comics, there are loads of beatmakers. And, like comics, serious beatmakers spend countless hours practicing, studying, and developing their craft. Beatmakers drop long, late nights without a second thought. They optimistically field dead-in beat sale offers and collaboration pitches that never take off. They absorb false career starts and fast-talking music insiders and posers. And they endure rejections on a multitude of levels. Yet with all of this, why is it that most beatmakers fail to simply carve out their own lane?

The main reason is that most don't even try to carve out their own lane. Why? Because in beatmaking, the idea of success that most beatmakers envision centers around two things: A beat placement or a beat sale. For nearly two decades now, the dream of landing coveted placements has given off the illusion that all one needs to do is make a beat (quality debatable), get it placed, and success instantly follows. In lieu of successful beat placements, a number of beatmakers have turned their focus to selling and leasing beats at unprofessionally low prices, often dragging down their brand and profile rather than raising it. Finally, a small number of other beatmakers have gotten into music licensing, but that's a different thing altogether. Still, what you haven't seen much of, and what I strongly advocate for, is beatmakers forming their own groups.

The music business is different than the comedy business. Hundreds of comedy clubs exist all over America. There aren't any beat clubs. And stand-up comedy, like the movies, sports match, or a music concert, is an event that people pay money to go out and see or watch at home on television. Beatmaking, by itself, can't make such a claim. Live beat showcases and battles don't move the needle much at all. Those events, the best of which sometimes tout acclaimed A&Rs and "celebrity" beatmakers as judges and offer some level of placement/career assistance, are usually populated by some music insiders but mostly by the participants and their friends and family. In other words, these aren't shows in the traditional sense; those beatmakers who participate are not being paid. In fact, in some showcases, they're actually paying the showcase organizers to participate in the showcase. Perhaps this is a legitimate investment for some beatmakers. But what if beatmakers just formed groups (or became solo rap acts) and bypassed the song and dance of beat showcases and the precarious world of beat placements?

During the 2010 CMJ Showcase in New York, I took in a great show. Among those on the bill who I had come to see (and would have paid for, had I not been comped at the door with a press pass, thanks to Michelle over at Audible Treats) was Diamond District and Nottz. Formed by Oddisee, a beatmaker (producer)/rapper, Diamond District is made up of solo rappers XO and YU. And Nottz, one of the most prolific beatmakers (producers) to date, rocks solo. Both performances were worth the attendance (Diamond District's set was especially impressive). More importantly, both acts proved the point that I've been making for years: That beatmakers could form rap groups and put themselves on.

Rather than limit the idea of success to placing beats with artists (which often attracts unnecessary middle men), or selling beats for less than their true value, beatmakers should expand their focus to include building new music groups. As a basis for success in beatmaking, beat placements are, for the most part, not sustainable. Being a part of your own group, with control of your music and direction, offers a far better chance at a sustainable career in music than chasing after beat placements.

There is, and will always be, room for a dope new rap group. Music consumers thrive on a fresh slate of new music. And there's never been more music consumers in the world than there is at this moment. So instead of tossing your best beats into a bottomless pool of other beat placement chasers, why not use them to start a new group? A new group that you're a central part of, not a marginal character. What's the worse thing that can happen, a few shows, a tour, and some record sales? Either way, whether you build a new group or create a series of beat tapes, the idea is to build something of your own, then get on someone's radar. If you do so, eventually the success will come.

Get Around: Marketing and Promotion, and the Keys to Branding Yourself

In order for beatmakers to actually carve out a name for themselves, they have to do more than just make beats; they also have to market and promote not only their product, but *themselves*. The beatmaking trade has emerged as its own cottage industry inside an industry. Therefore, it's more important than ever for beatmakers to have their own brand.

There are many elements that go into creating a distinct quality "beat brand." First, obviously, one has to have a decent level of beats. Fact is, a beatmaker doesn't necessarily have to make top-quality beats to build an effective brand. For better or worse, many prominent beatmakers have built their brands more off of strategic self-promotion, pivotal contacts, and key relationships than off of a catalog of dope beats. So be mindful that there are other factors at play when it comes to brand names. In the following section, I will examine some of the most important keys to marketing, promoting, and ultimately, branding yourself.

GA Stands for "Get Around"

You have to get around. As I pointed out in the History Part, graffiti writers were not only separated by talent but by whether or not they "got around." Those that didn't get around were labeled with the DGA tag: "Doesn't Get Around." I think this same principle is useful to beatmakers interested in developing their own brand and carving out a career in music.

There are two relatively easy ways for beatmakers (and rappers) to "get around": (1) Get involved with as many worthy collaborative projects that you can; and (2) To push out as many free *quality* music projects into the atmosphere as you can. In both scenarios, if the music is dope, you'll get exposure and your brand will begin to solidify. The idea is that "free" is often the price you pay for getting paid work in the future. Think of it like an internship, with each level of exposure comes a chance for you to move up into paid work. Also, sometimes the exposure of free quality works brings an assortment of music-related opportunities, for example: ringtones, commercials, infomercials, sponsors, and, of course, even other beatmakers (producers). Finally, consider the fact that the more beats that you make, the more opportunities you have to connect with others, as well as make new projects ("demos") of your own work. Point is, the more projects that you are attached to, the more exposure *your* work ultimately gets. And the more exposure your work gets, the more promotion it gets and the more your music catalogue swells. The more promotion you get and the more your catalog swells, the better chance you have for establishing your own distinct brand, which means the better chance you have of getting paid and earning a living from your beatmaking (production) services.

And when collaborating with others, quantity is a good thing, but you also have to focus on quality as well. That is, only get involved with collaborative projects under two primary conditions: (1) If the project is well-suited to your scope and style of beatmaking; and (2) If you really believe in the overall worth of the project. Point is, do projects that you're pleased with. If you try to please everybody — the music press, record companies, other artists, etc. — you'll end up with a watered-down product and an undistinguished brand.

Also, it should always be remembered that there are a countless number of rappers (far more than beatmakers, although the gap is closing) who have little to no access to original beats (rather than instrumentals of well-known hip hop/rap songs). A lot of these aforementioned rappers are forced to hone their skills to the instrumentals of popular hip hop/rap songs, which often do not fit their own unique (developing) styles. Given the opportunity, these rappers would gladly write to original material. Therefore, take advantage of this fact and create your own situations. Rather than "sit" on your beats, or chase down major labels and well-known artists for non-guaranteed placements and marginal, often uncredited work, why not aggressively locate and link up with these new "unknown" (highly motivated) rappers and offer your beats on a full credit basis? That is, offer to construct their demo for non-pay, but full production credit. Remember, an artist demo produced entirely by you is also *your* demo. And it's a demo, I should add, that proves that you can work with a recording artist and handle the duties of more than just one song. I should also add that when approaching new rappers for collabs (i.e. collaborative projects), if you're in a position to cover studio costs, you should do so. If not, stipulate that either you and them split costs, or that they pay for all studio time.

Finally, when you do engage in collaborative work, I also recommend preparing an invoice (if applicable) and a simple written agreement (contract). The invoice should be a dated record of the particular beats and music and other services that you've provided, along with the name of the rapper(s) that received those services. You will also want to have a written agreement between you and the rapper(s) that you provide your production services for. If you're not familiar with drafting a production agreement, don't worry, just remember to include two main things in your agreement. First, make sure the full and legal names of all parties involved are represented. Second, get the full details of all the terms of the agreement down on paper. These terms should include: recognition of full and complete production credit; start and end dates of the project, whether it's a "one-off" (one time thing) or not; fees and penalties (if any); and any incentive clause that you may think of. For example, an incentive clause for the agreement could be one that stipulates that in the event that the rapper(s) obtains a record deal as a result of using your beats and production services, 3-10% of their recording budget goes to you. And you certainly want to stipulate that in the event that the rapper(s) desires to use the "demo beats" you provided for a commercial release, the artist must pay a pre-determined price for your beats and production services. The point here is that covering all expenses for talented rappers not only allows you to build your beats and music catalog, it presents you with the tremendous opportunity for potential exposure and extended revenue.

Marketing and Promotion

Creating Your Own Market

Creating your own market begins with creating your own sound. Every time a "new sound" is born, a new market is created. This is why it's so absolutely important for beatmakers to create their own unique style and sound. Understand, when you develop your own quality, unique (i.e. signature) sound, there is a market waiting for you. Think about it: With you at the forefront of a new emerging music market, you will be able to brand both yourself *and* your unique style of music. After you've worked out your own sound and you're comfortable with the level of its quality, the next important thing to do is identify your target audience; that is, locate the audience that you suspect would appreciate the style and sound of music you bring. It is absolutely critical that you identify the right audience for your brand of music. If you know the kind of music that you like to make, then you should also be able to identify the audience that will likely appreciate it as well.

Creating and Developing Your Marketing Plan

A marketing plan is a pre-designed strategy for effectively promoting and, subsequently, selling a product, service, and/or brand to a specific audience. Typically, a marketing plan is formally written and distributed to all persons working on the marketing team of a product or service. A good marketing plan contains clear themes and objectives as well as detailed actions for implementing those objectives. A theme and/or objective of a marketing plan can be a sales goal or any other similar benchmark. An action of a marketing plan can be a scheduled advertisement placed on websites or in magazines; it can also be show performances and/or a variety of promotions.

In order for a marketing plan to be effective, it must be as creative as the product that it's trying to promote and sell. Servicing records — the typical music industry practice of supplying DJs and/or radio stations and retailers with inventory and promotion materials) — is the run-of-the-mill promotion approach in the music business. But have you ever seen someone without an album or even a single get major promotion and publicity? Of course you have. How was that achieved? More often than not, it was achieved through a very carefully designed marketing plan. The important thing to remember here is that consumers do not only buy a product or a brand, they buy into the person(s) behind tbe product or brand. Understanding this marketing philosophy is the ultimate key to designing a successful marketing plan, achieving its objectives, and ultimately branding yourself.

Brand Yourself – Putting Your Marketing Plan Into Action and Building Your Fan Base

The key to branding yourself is all about the overall design of your marketing plan and how much of it you're able to execute. Whatever the main theme and objective of your marketing plan is, your ability to effectively brand yourself will rest on how well you pull off the detailed actions within your marketing plan. And there will be no bigger detailed action in your marketing plan than building your own fan base.

If you want to be successful in the music industry, you're going to need a solid fan base. Having your own fan base means that you have a regular group of highly devoted supporters, a group that is always enthusiastic about your brand and the list of products you have to offer. A great marketing plan always has detailed actions for building a fan base. Thus, what follows in this section is a list of the four main actions that I recommend you include in your marketing plan. If implemented properly, these actions will help you build your fan base and promote your brand at the same time.

Your Own "Web Space"

First, you have to build your own "web space." An online presence is paramount to the success of all recording artists, but it's absolutely critical to all independent recording artists, especially beatmakers. To create your own online space there are essentially three things you must do: (1) Create your own website; (2) Maintain at least two social media profiles, ideally Facebook and Twitter;

and (3) Maintain an active membership in at least one beat/production-based forum (message board).

Your own website is critical for two reasons. For one thing, your own website gives you complete control over where your music catalog is stored online. Furthermore, your own website serves as the "home site" or hub of your online presence. The more involved you are online with other sites and social communities, the better it is to have your own site that your other "web spaces" link back to. It is your own website or rather "home web space" where you really get to shape your overall online presence.

Social media refers to those specific online communities that allow for people to freely interact with one another. There are various types of social media sites or online communities, but all require you to sign up, register, and create a profile. Currently, the four social media and music sharing sites most critical to the exposure of independent recording artists include: Facebook, Twitter, Soundcloud, and Bandcamp. Each one of these sites are free to join, and each allows great potential for interaction and word-of-mouth promotion, a cornerstone of any good successful marketing plan. Maintaining a profile on at least one of these sites (if not all four) is essential to your ability to get your brand (name) out into the atmosphere. Social media sites permit a "leveled playing field" type of interaction. That is to say, on sites like Twitter, users can freely exchange ideas and information, without the interference of tastemakers *filtering* everything. In social media communities, the truly interesting and sincere users easily find that they have a powerful voice. And it is this voice that you can use to drive traffic back to out your home site. Also, online "friends" or acquaintances tend to be supportive of the products and services of the people they regularly interact with. So developing social media networks are crucial, as they will help you to formulate a fan base and a regular source of sales.

Finally, maintaining an active membership in at least one beat/production-based forum (message board) is key. There are many beat/production-based communities online, each offering their own slant. Most are helpful, some less so, and the good ones act as a communal space for beatmakers (producers). As a practitioner of an art form and member of a global community, it is important for you to interact with others in this community, not only for the purposes of establishing your brand, but also for improving your skills and understanding of the beatmaking tradition and community. And just as with other social media sites, online beatmaking communities tend to be very supportive of their members. Therefore, if you're an active member of a beatmaking forum(s), you will undoubtedly garner support for your products and services.

Identify Your "Fan Pools"

Another important factor in building your fan base deals with identifying the right "fan pool." A fan pool is similar to a target audience, only it's bigger and broader. For instance, a fan pool can be teenagers or adults; it can be only men or women; it can be novices or experts within in a given field or profession. Knowing which fan pools to target and tap is essential to building a solid fan base.

Capitalize on "Indie Towns"

Another important factor in building your fan base deals with identifying those areas or cities that qualify as indie towns. An "indie town" is a city or locale that is conducive to independent music, arts, and business. For example, cities like New York, Miami, Atlanta, Houston, Los Angeles, Oakland, Chicago, and Seattle are all truly "indie towns." Each of these cities are conducive to almost any kind of independent business that you can imagine, but because they are all important "hubs" for hip hop/rap music and beatmakers, they are particularly well-suited for an independent hip hop/rap music enterprise. Each of these cities also have access to multiple college radio stations; college radio stations are very favorable to indie hip hop/rap. Also, most of these cities, particularly New York, Miami, and Atlanta, contain a number of local or mid-level venues for hip hop/rap performances.

In the last two years, there has been an uptick in the launch of city venues that feature hip hop/rap music as the main ticket. Moreover, all of these venues are distinctly concerned with providing a balanced, more honest hip hop/rap music experience. That is, these venues are not underscored by a rotation of "radio hits," but instead, they are predicated upon offering a more authentic reflection of hip hop/rap music, a reflection that stands to offer new acts chances that they might not otherwise get.

Power Alliances

Another factor that can be key, not only to a successful marketing plan, but also to your production output and opportunities, deals with what I call power alliances. A power alliance is an alliance/relationship with other like-minded individuals which benefits the careers of all parties involved.

Production Teams

Like all popular music compositional practices, beatmaking requires a great deal of time and attention. But unlike other popular music composers, hip hop/rap beatmakers tend to work in a rigidly self-imposed solitary environment. Though some beatmakers choose to work in production teams (usually as a duo), most work alone. This self-imposed creative solitary confinement has its advantages. On one hand, a beatmaker who works alone doesn't have to answer to other band mates or a partner; every critical creative decision is theirs alone. In this light, hip hop/rap beatmakers have more in common with Western classical composers than they do with contemporary pop and rock outfits. Also, since beatmakers are essentially one-man bands, they are perhaps the most self-contained of all contemporary music-makers. But while this self-contained environment may go a long way in determining the level of creative control and freedom that beatmakers ultimately have, it does not offer many social and networking opportunities that are inherent within a band or collaborative environments. Therefore, beatmakers who are able to form power alliances with other individuals tend to be at an advantage.

The most common power alliance that beatmakers can join (or form) is a production team. The term "production team" actually carries multiple meanings. Previously, I described the many types of jobs and different descriptions associated with being a "producer." Here, I'll discuss the meaning of "production team" in two different situations. The first meaning of production team is in regards to hip hop/rap music production only and in the most common meaning of the term, that is to say, the creative sense. Thus, a production team in this sense describes the situation in which two or more beatmakers combine forces to put together (create) music (beats) and, in turn, promote, market and sell it as the work of one collective, one production team. When analyzing a production team, bear in mind that each beatmaker (producer) need not play a role in the actual creation of every beat that comes out of the collective. What I mean is, in many production teams, the beats are composed individually, separately by each beatmaker on the team. However, each member of the team agrees to come under the same banner and split the rewards appropriately.

The other meaning of production team deals with "production team" in the broader, perhaps more traditional business sense. "Production" in any business actually refers to the design, creation, and mass production of a product. Well, for a hip hop/rap beatmaker, that product is beats; and in the earlier stages of this "product development," the design and creation is typically handled by one individual, while the later stages (think additional playing and programming, mixing, mastering, mass CD duplication, etc.) are designed, created, and facilitated by other individuals. Hence, one way or another, beatmakers actually work in a "team" capacity anyway.

So think about the two ways of approaching a production team. Ask yourself this question: As an individual beatmaker (producer), how do your trusted ears rate your production? If the consensus on the level and quality of your beats is high, then maybe you shouldn't be thinking about building a creative production team. Instead, you might want to consider building a business production team; think administrative assistant, promoter, financial investor, and perhaps a manager. If you already have the talent and skill, then a team of business professionals (especially those with a marketing, law, or finance background) is the way to go. Remember, although creating beats may be a solitary process of creativity and imagination, marketing and selling beats is really a mass production process. Therefore, the more dedicated individuals that you can bring to help you mass produce your product, the better. By embracing the fundamentals of mass production, you do two things: (1) You maximize your time and effort by targeting it where it's needed most — the design and creation of ill beats; and (2) You assign a great deal of the business process to those who can handle it best.

Finally, if your beat skills aren't quite up to par, let's say, for instance, you lack drum programming skills, but you can play the keys. In this case, linking up with another beatmaker (producer) or group of beatmakers who possess drum programming skills (and other techniques and skills that you lack) might be a great idea. However, the bottom line in each type of a production team is this. In order for your product to ultimately be successful and reach the people you've targeted, you will undoubtedly need a team. And how that team is broken down depends entirely up to you.

Pivotal Partnerships

Pivotal partnerships describes yet another type of power alliance. Beatmaking or hip hop/rap music production is an entertainment *services* profession. Beatmakers are artisans who provide a unique and highly sought after service; and as such, the success of a beatmaker's career depends on strategic business and creative relationships. Therefore, it's critical that beatmakers seek out and build as many key relationships as they can. This does not mean simply trying to meet well-known, well-established recording artists, producers, A&Rs, label executives, and other music industry insiders. Although such meetings do present the potential for high returns, if you do not have the right connections, the probability of such meetings are so low that it's not even worth devoting much of your time. Instead, I encourage you to be as independent as you possibly can. Which doesn't just mean do your own thing; it means finding other like-minded, independent beatmakers, other recording artists, and related professionals. In this case, the probability of such meetings are much higher. Furthermore, the returns are much greater. Should any of those persons — with whom you hold strong alliances with — become the next major players in the music industry, think about where that might put you.

Selling Your Own Commercial[193] Releases: Singles, Mix Tapes, Albums, and other Relative Music Products

If you and your trusted ears believe that you have quality music, then chances are there's a market somewhere in the world that's ready to hear it. This is why I strongly believe that it's better for unknown beatmakers (producers) to commercially release their own product than to just shop a demo and/or a beat CD. When you commercially release your own material, you level the playing field for yourself. The world isn't made up of just a handful of talented beatmakers and rappers; there are scores of beatmakers and rappers who are as talented (if not more) as some of the well-established figures in hip hop/rap music. But what is it that separates these two groups, the have-made-its and the have-not-made-its, from one another?" Certainly some people catch breaks and some don't. Some people are in the right place, at the right time. But aside from individual drive, desire, and financial backing, what's left? Luck? No. I don't believe in luck. To me, "luck" is simply the scattered, left-over residue from proper planning and preparation, the right know-how, good intuition, strong endurance, and perseverance. Which is why I'm convinced that beatmakers actually have an unprecedented amount of control over their careers. Beatmakers provide the frequencies for rappers, and as such, each beatmaker can potentially generate the careers of an unlimited number of rappers. Thus, when beatmakers commercially release their own material, they have a better shot of joining the ranks of the have-made-its.

Throughout this chapter, I've pointed out that the three main keys to success for a beatmaker in the music industry (on both the indie and major levels) is

---

[193] Here "commercial release" refers to legal commerce, bar codes, retailers, etc. It does not refer to a form of "selling out" or compromising one's artistic integrity.

a combination of three factors: (1) The development of a strong and unique product; (2) The marketing and promotion of that product; and (3) The building of critical, straight-forward, real relationships and alliances with other people within the industry. So in the following section, I'll focus on two pivotal areas of your marketing plan: the budget and the press release.

How Budgets Work

One of the most underestimated and woefully mis-managed features of doing an independent commercial release is the budget. A budget is a financial war chest that is priced and designated to cover all of the associated costs of a proposed project or structured endeavor. Typically, music related budgets are composed of funds that cover two main areas: (1) recording; and (2) marketing. When drafting a budget, consider these primary factors: fundamental needs, probable upgrades, miscellaneous/petty cash, and unforeseeable emergencies. A budget (the financial parameters in which a project will be executed) is also critical because it helps frame and organize the methods in which the project will be carried out. Proper planning and organization increases the chances of a project being executed and marketed successfully.

Send A Press Release

Once you've made the bold (necessary) decision to put yourself on, you have to immediately go to work on your plans for getting your name and brand out. Keep in mind that the difference between two equally talented beatmakers (or other recording artists) can be found in the circumstances of each. As long as talent isn't a question, other intangibles are in play. Money, marketing prowess, inside connections, and the like are all different types of intangibles that can ultimately determine the success of any recording artist. But the one intangible that trumps all others — even money — is press.

Thus, whenever you complete a project, such as your own album of beats or a collaboration with an artist/producer of *any* note, I strongly recommend that you send out a press release to the people within your network and to the publications that you believe might cover your project. A press release is a public relations announcement, a news story that is issued to the news media and other targeted publications for the purpose of demonstrating the newsworthiness of a particular person, event, service and/or product. *Any* newsworthy development, such as your new product, is worth sending out a press release.

Although traditional print mags and internet news media portals are both similar in scope, the latter is much more flexible and willing to give you press. Therefore, when it comes to sending out your press release, your main focus should be internet publications. Traditional print magazines require a significant amount of lead time. "Lead time" is the amount of time needed for a journalist to complete a story for a particular issue of a magazine or episode of a TV news program. Typically, the time frame is two to four months, but it depends on the publication. Online magazines do not require a long lead time; their lead time is immediate. And their viewers have come to expect new content everyday. Hence, online magazines have to rapidly find newsworthy content to publish more consistently than print mags. Because of this, online mags are much more willing to throw some press your way, provided your project and press release draws their attention.

Critical Pointers About Writing an Effective Press Release

There are three critical pointers for an effective press release. First, keep it simple. Make sure that you have a catchy and informative headline. You want to hook people. Publications receive tons of press releases everyday, so they don't have the time nor desire to sift through an ego-tinged rant about how "unique" or how "hot" or how "great" something is. Their only questions are: Is it newsworthy, and will their readership find it interesting? Second, keep your press release to 200-300. The shorter and the sweeter, the better. The idea is to pack a powerful punch, not an epic beat down. Third, make sure to send your press release to as many outlets as possible, especially your target news outlets.

Chapter 13

The "Business" of Business

> It's sad that you still have cats in the basement, trying to be the best beatmaker or programmer, but the minute that somebody gets one of their tracks and it's the hottest song in the world, they don't even know what the next step is! Like, you really need to put more energy into learning this business. If you're doing it as a hobby, let it be a hobby. If you wanna get in the music business, you gotta learn about the business. –DJ Toomp

Management and Representation: When is a "Producer Manager" Needed?

Representation, such as a manager or a lawyer, is an essential asset to any recording artist trying to succeed in the music industry. But for hip hop/rap beatmakers, representation takes on a new meaning. For one thing, the role of a beatmaker is different than that of a typical recording artist. Beatmakers provide beats for other recording artists to write and perform to. Moreover, unlike other recording artists, who sell their persona and image to the public just as much as they do their music, beatmakers sell their music to other recording artists, and they usually don't have to worry about their persona or image being in the public eye. Instead, their primary concern is pairing their beats with recording artists who need new music. Thus, this unique music-matching process is one reason why beatmakers could use (but don't always need) representation. For instance, beatmakers can use someone who can help them find recording artists and other comparable parties who are seeking new beats.

Beatmakers could also use someone who can help flush out opportunities for music placements. But then again, as I've mentioned throughout this study, beatmaking is a very meticulous and often arduous craft that is usually orchestrated in a solitary environment. It is this solitary dimension of beatmaking that often prompts the need for some form of representation. Beatmakers need a representative, someone to pitch and/or broker the sell of their beats. So as with the music-matching process of the beat-selling world, it's easy to see why a representative might increase the chances of a beatmaker landing a placement on a commercial release. Finally, although representation can be quite varied, there are three kinds of "representers" that hip hop/rap beatmakers can consider: (1) beat brokers; (2) producer managers; and (3) lawyers.

A beat broker is someone who simply shops (promotes) the beats of a beatmaker. A beat broker, not to be confused with beat broker service websites, etc., can be a friend, a music insider, or anyone that has access to a network of recording artists, in particular, recording artists who are likely to be in the market for new music material. A beat broker's only responsibility is to shop the beats of the beatmaker that they represent. They need not be skilled in negotiating the terms and sale of the beats that they're shopping; an entertainment lawyer privy to beat/instrumental placements can handle that. Because of this limited (but critical) scope, an agreement between a beat broker and beatmaker can be simple, straightforward, and short in duration. A beat broker can be commissioned for a 10% finder's fee, worked out on a per-beat or per-situation agreement.

A "producer manager" is perhaps the most ubiquitous type of representer that a beatmaker can have. Normally, a manager is someone who manages the entire career of a client. But as noted earlier, a beatmaker's career is based primarily on their ability to make and sell beats. Beatmakers are not expected to perform, make public appearances, and/or maintain a public image, unless they do DJ shows like DJ Premier, Just Blaze, Metro Broomin, and the like. Thus, a producer manager's responsibilities can fall anywhere from simply shopping beats, to negotiating the terms of beat sales to arranging pivotal meetings with prospective beat buyers to setting up beat showcase meetings with key decision makers at record labels. But because of the scope of the role of a typical manager, it is likely that a beatmaker will have to enter into a more lengthy and more detailed agreement than they would with a beat broker. A typical producer's management agreement will stipulate that a manager receives 15-20% (in some cases more) of all music-related revenue that a beatmaker earns. A producer management agreement also maintains that the representation occurs (usually) between two and five years or longer, depending on the individuals.

The role that an entertainment lawyer usually plays in the career of a beatmaker is very different from both that of a beat broker or a producer manager. Shopping beats is not the primary role of a lawyer; although, in some cases, lawyers do pass on the music of their clients to individuals in the music industry. But for the most part, entertainment lawyers are responsible for drafting and/or reviewing the legal agreements of their clients. It is in this capacity that entertainment lawyers can ultimately be more important than beat brokers and managers.

What Kind of Representation is Right for You?

Though the kind of representation that you choose depends on your individual situation, I believe that most beatmakers only need either an assistant, beat broker, or lawyer, but not always a producer manager. Beatmakers are already self-contained, and most are usually very organized. Furthermore, even though the "right" person or contact is always a plus, given the nature of the general openness of the beat shopping process itself, it's not terribly important *who* gets your beats into the hands of decision makers. Fact is, recording artists are accepting and actively soliciting beat/instrumental submissions through other outlets, like social networking sites and national contests.

Another important thing for you to consider before you sign with a producer manager is the fact that once the agreement is signed, the producer manager is entitled to at least a 15-20% cut of all the music-related revenue you earn, typically for a period no less than two years. And bear in mind that a producer manager gets this cut for essentially doing exactly what a beat broker could do; but, of course, the beat broker does it for a much cheaper rate and a less restrictive representation period. That said, I think that as your career grows and as you become a more sizeable figure in the recording industry, then it may not only be advantageous but necessary for you to get some sort of manager. After you reach a certain plateau of success, you will be eligible for opportunities outside of selling beats, and a manager (of some sort) might be quite helpful at that point.

But if you're a beatmaker who's just starting out, well, the decision to get a manager can go both ways. It's important to remember that beatmaking is a relatively new and rather unique phenomenon in the recording industry, and as such, many recording artists are still trying to navigate their way through the current model of obtaining beats. Moreover, because of the aforementioned solitary factor of the beatmaking craft itself, beatmakers do not typically need the guidance of a producer manager. While a well-known producer manager can help a beatmaker gain access to recording artists as well as perhaps general exposure in the music industry, there are two important points that shouldn't be overlooked: (1) A producer manager's access to some key recording artists and/or major record labels does not guarantee a placement, it doesn't even guarantee a submission; and (2) Once a beatmaker is established on any significant level, the task of successfully shopping their beats *themselves* (as many well-known beatmakers now do) actually becomes more efficient and cost effective. Should you reach a point of acclaim, people interested in your brand of beats will often reach out to you.

Thus, if you're a beatmaker just starting out, the question of whether or not to go with a producer manager is really a question of exposure. So if you feel that the exposure a producer manger can get you is above and beyond what a beat broker can provide or what you can provide for yourself, then getting a producer manager might be the way to go. However, if you do go the producer-manager route, just make sure that the producer manager's responsibilities and obligations are well-defined in writing. It's also a good idea to include benchmarks (predetermined goals) within the language of any agreement that you enter into with a producer manager; and you also want to have fair "exit" clauses in your agreement, as well as caps on compensation when the deal is over.

Getting Paid

Determining Beat Prices: Price Is Always Relative to the Situation

The common industry standard payment range for a beat (intended to be used on the commercial release of an established artist) usually ranges from the low end of $2,500 to the high end of $35,000 — higher, of course, for bigger names. Prior to 2002, the median was perhaps around $10,000 per beat for an established beatmaker (producer). But today, because of the wickedly fast pace of today's hip hop/rap climate, the democratization of production tools, and the plethora of hungry new beatmakers (who are all-too willing to take less pay in exchange for production credit), the median for most well-known beatmakers has dropped down closer to the $5,000 range. But since price is always negotiable, this price can easily deflate or inflate in a moment's notice.

There are many factors that go into determining how much beatmakers should charge for their beats. Notoriety is perhaps the most important factor for a well-known beatmaker (producer). But notoriety isn't a luxury that lesser-known beatmakers (producers) rarely get the chance to experience. Beatmakers "on the come-up" have to use a different set of factors in determining how much they ultimately should charge for their beats and music services. In the following section, I discuss four important factors that you should consider when determining how much you ultimately charge for your beats and music services.

When it comes to determining beat prices (how much you charge for beats and music services), the first factor that you should consider is the overall quality of your production catalog. Do you honestly feel that you have quality, competitive production? It doesn't matter if you think any given well-known beatmaker (producer) is wack. What matters more is whether or not someone else will think *your* beats are dope. In other words, of the beatmakers that you respect and admire, how would you honestly rate your production in comparison to theirs? If you feel that your production can compete, then I recommend that you be willing to come down (substantially) off your price. Let's say in fact, your production does rival some of the best. In the beginning, until you build some notoriety and get your name heard, it's important to recognize the fact that you will not get paid like some of the best. So proceed with humbleness, and keep this in mind: If the situation presents itself, at least you can aim for a high minimum.

The second factor that you should consider is the artist(s) and/or person(s) interested in your beats and music. How do you feel about the artist for whom your beats and music will be used? If you believe that they're very talented, then be prepared to come down off your price. If you think that they're extremely talented, and I'm talking like on a level with critically acclaimed rappers, then be prepared to let go of your beat(s) for free. The thing is, if they are as talented as you believe, then you should do everything possible to make sure that your production plays a part in such a phenomenon. The upside to a situation like this is tremendous. For one thing, you can simply *defer* all payment until some agreed upon future date; this date can be months, even years after the commencement of the project. More importantly, you can secure future production work with this artist; and future production work with any artist is the real prize. It's that work — especially should it be critically acclaimed — that will undoubtedly help garner you more production opportunities in the future.

On the other hand, if you think that the rapper is really not talented at all, I would then suggest that you reconsider doing production work for them. Never waste your beats on rappers who neither keep pace with or enhance your beats. Going this route once or twice is perhaps O.K. if you have to; you should be able to recover. But if you repeatedly go down this road, wasting your beats at random, you will drain yourself of creativity, and in some cases, you'll lose the drive and desire to even make beats. Remember, quality rappers regularly help inspire and motivate beatmakers to go into more creative, more advanced musical directions. Untalented rappers often do not understand and/or appreciate your efforts, skill, and dedication. So they often have a reverse developmental effect on your production.

The third factor you should consider is whether or not you will actually get the opportunity to work in the recording session of the song, that is, will you get to be present for the initial tracking and/or to assist the rapper. In most cases these days, beatmakers sell their beats and do not hear from the rapper and/or label for months (sometimes years). If you know before hand that you will not be participating in at least the initial recording of the song, then your beat-price should be somewhere towards the low end of the standard price range. Point here is to not price yourself out of serious consideration. But if you know before hand that you will be very much involved in the shaping of the song, then stand firm around the mid-price range; charge your full worth, not just the beat price. In a situation like this, you want to establish what you think your beats and production services are worth, then go about proving it through your studio session management skills and creative ideas.

Finally, when trying to determine the price you should charge for your beats, the fourth factor that you should consider is the situation of the rapper and/or persons interested in your beats and music. This factor can be divided into four different areas: (1) Is the rapper signed or unsigned? (if the rapper is signed, is s/he signed to a major record label or an independent record label?); (2) What's the size (overall amount) of the rapper's recording budget; (3) Your gut feeling about the rapper's potential; and (4) Your personal financial situation at the time.

If the rapper is signed to a major record label, proceed with caution. It's O.K. to feel good about your accomplishment, but never appear over excited or too indebted to the point that you're just happy to be at the session. If your beats and music got you there, then continue to demonstrate why. Remember, you're a professional, so never forfeit your personal and/or business integrity for anyone. And Even though it may be in your best interest to forgo payment in certain situations, make it clear that you are doing so of your own free will and not because someone shrewdly duped you out of a payday.

If the rapper is signed to an independent record label you might have a better chance of getting cash upfront, if that's what you're really after. Indie labels operate on smaller budgets and rigid time constraints, so they like to handle as much as possible for as little as possible. Hence, they often use upfront cash to get better terms from the beatmakers that they work with. Major record labels also use cash in a similar fashion, but on a much grander scale, and usually only among a select group of people that they regularly do business with. On the other hand, many indie labels relate rather well to the independent nature of beatmakers, so they often like to negotiate cash and pay on the spot. In most cases, because they are paying cash (a lot of the time 100% upfront), they will get you to come down off your price. So don't feel like you were taken advantage of if and when this happens.

Regarding the question of whether the rapper is unsigned and *really* talented, I strongly recommend that you try to do one of two things, either: (1) Form a group with them; or (2) Sign them yourself and offer your beats for free as an incentive. These days, there are a lot of just *O.K.* rappers. I believe there are far too many so-called "hot" rappers that are benefiting from a weak talent pool. So if a quality unsigned rapper approaches you about your beats and production services, do whatever you can to formulate a power alliance with them. After all, two quality music professionals is more powerful than one. Plus, you double your chances for success and exposure.

When it comes to the size of the rapper's recording budget (even if you know the rapper's budget), you still have to be careful when negotiating price. Again, if the rapper is of high caliber, the most important thing is the production work, not the immediate money you might get. The more quality credits you acquire, the more production work will come your way, provided you market your brand well. So instead of seeing how much of the budget you can get, maybe offer multiple beats for the price of one. If the rapper has a sizeable budget, as long as your asking price is reasonable, you'll most likely get it. But keep in mind that all prices are negotiable.

Your gut feeling about the rapper's potential should always determine how much you charge for your beats and production services. Think about how you honestly feel about the rapper. Aside from getting paid, is the whole project really going to be worth your beats? There are many cases of talented but obnoxious rappers who have a penchant for making sessions long and disastrous. Before you commit to such an artist, make sure you've got a good gut feeling about them.

Finally, what's your personal financial situation at the time of the negotiation? Your personal financial situation should play a role in whatever price you ultimately decide to charge someone for your beats and production services. If your financial situation is strenuous, be careful not to reveal it. As I mentioned earlier, keep your integrity at all times. With reasonable beat prices, not only will the beat prices that you name be respected, but you will also stand to gain more production work with the rapper(s) in the future. And on the other hand, if you're doing fine financially, you certainly don't want to overemphasize price. Again, the main goal is additional production opportunities.

To sum it up, when it comes to determining how much you should charge for your beats, keep your price range for your beats and services from between $0 and $8,000, depending, of course, on the types of circumstances I outlined in this section. Also, recognize that there may arise many situations wherein it's advantageous for you to defer payment in exchange for other benefits. Likewise, there may be a few situations where it's necessary for you to set a very high asking price. But whatever you to be flexible.

The New Beat Market Exchange: Celebrity Beatwork Solicitation Means Your Favorite Beatmaker is Now Competing with You

Once, there was a time when most critically acclaimed beatmakers were in demand. It was a time when $15,000, $25,000, and $40,000 beat prices were attainable for proven beatmakers. It was a time when the most recognizable names in beatmaking were flooded with work. That time is no more.

The ruling party of beatmakers have been, through no fault of their own, unceremoniously stripped of their power; this has resulted in a level playing field for new contracted beatwork. With the emergence of new technology (specifically, new music production tools), the explosive growth of a new class of beatmakers, the advent of the "new music industry," the presence of social media sites like Twitter and Facebook, and music streaming sites like YouTube, Soundcloud, and Bandcamp, the terrain for paid beatwork has become tumultuous, making it seemingly possible for any beatmaker to have access to the very same beat users/beat buyers that only the beatmaking pros formerly had access to.

In an interview I did with DJ Premier, he told me about his beat prices in the 1990s. Although he did have what he called a "sliding scale," he didn't have to, it was his choice! He was in demand, and the artists who wanted to work with him, that is to say, those who needed his beats and co-sign, simply paid whatever price he set. But that sort of want-and-need structure no longer exists for most beatmakers in the new beat market exchange. Certainly, quality beats and celebrity co-signs still remain valuable, but quality beats are no longer the products of just a small elite group of beatmakers. Anyone with the right know-how and access to the right music production tools can put the practice and time in, and come up with quality beats. Just look at what happened with "Panda," the runaway 2016 hit song by Desiigner. Reportedly, Desiigner bought the beat for "Panda" off of YouTube for $200 from it's producer Menace. Combine the reality that anyone with beats to sell and an internet connection with the front-door access to rappers (the chief buyers and users of beats) that social media offers, and what you have is a new beat market exchange, one that is vast and open, where truly any beatmaker can compete. So while some beatmakers may have once had the comfort zone to successfully operate using a sliding scale for their beat prices, today, no such luxury exists. In the new beat market exchange, every beatmaker — acclaimed and lesser-known — must have a sliding scale, because inflexibly in beat prices in the current climate is akin to professional suicide.

Background Context of the New Beat Market Exchange

Beatmaking is a new musical phenomenon, as such, the price parameters and ceiling for beats were being set — in real time — in the 1990s. And what was the price parameters and ceiling for beats based on? Well, in many ways, the price was based on the model for previous music producers, those prior to the advent of professional beatmakers. By 1999, it became clear that not all beatmakers were actually in the studio with rappers "producing," i.e. helping out with song ideas, vocal coaching, mixing, etc. Thus, quite naturally, beat prices necessarily had to go down. Think about it: If a beat goes to a rapper, without the beatmaker's presence, well, then what you have is a situation where the instrumental — the beat — is being bought wholesale, which is to say that the beat, without the beatmaker's direct input (post beat sell), the beat should be less expensive. Add to that mix the fact that the number of capable beatmakers grew exponentially over the past 10 years, and what emerged (naturally) was a dramatic drop in beat prices. In other words, the beat market prices corrected themselves; it was inevitable.

You Can't Blame This One on Poor Music Sales and Illegal Downloads

There's only so much that can be blamed on poor music sales and illegal downloads. Poor music sales or illegal downloads are really not the reason that beat prices have gone down. High beat prices, for example, $25,000 and above, were unreasonable and unsustainable in the first place. It just took little more than a decade for the market to correct itself. Fact is, by 1995, beat prices were steadily going down for most acclaimed beatmakers. Only a specific few were able to command exorbitant beat prices and fees. The likes of Dr. Dre, Timbaland, and The Neptunes saw their prices go up during the mid- to late 1990s, but by the end of the '90s and the early 2000s, they would eventually see their workloads go down. Reason why? Their price points became too high for too many artists; pluts lots of artists were looking to tap new (and cheaper) production talent. As great as all of these beatmakers (producers) are/were, none of them could guarantee hits in the hard-pressed environment the music industry was increasingly having to cope with. And thus, with no guaranteed hit, there were very few takers willing to absorb the risk that accompanied high beat prices.

All things considered, the true market price range for quality beats has, in reality, always been roughly $2,000-$7,000 per beat. And consider this. In most cases, between 1989-1999, the bigger beat price tags for most acclaimed beatmakers typically covered multiple flat-rate beat deals, usually 3-8 beats (plus in-studio work), depending on the beatmaker and the specific rapper or other artist involved.

Even still, there wasn't a level playing field in the 1990s. However, in the new beat market exchange, there is a level playing field. Still, it should be noted that this level playing field is "upside down." That is to say, there's no protection against one beatmaker underbidding another beatmaker. For every one beatmaker who commands $10,000, there's another one equally capable who will accept $5,000; and there are thousands more just as good who are willing to take $1,000; and there might be tens of thousands more who are almost as adequate and willing to forgo any payment, in exchange for production credit. Therefore, even though there is a level playing field, the only real choice that any career-worthy beatmaker has for long-term beat-placement survival is to unionize.

Finally, I believe that too much attention has been misplaced on beat prices rather than on guaranteed residuals (royalties) for beatmakers. The focus should mostly be shifted away from beat prices, and placed squarely on beat royalties. As suppliers of the instrumental music, beatmakers should be entitled to receive royalties for the beats that they sell, just like any other composer of music material. Fortunately, considering the realities of the new beat market exchange and the increased level of more informed beatmakers, I believe that statutory beat royalty rates will soon become standard.

Understanding Publishing Splits

It's important to note how publishing splits (percentages) work as it pertains to beatmaking. There is a music industry standard regarding publishing splits. Publishing splits for a song are broken down into two shares (areas): (1) the music; and (2) the words. The "music" refers to the composition, i.e. the rhythm, melody, or harmony of the song. The "words" refers to the lyrics of the song. In beatmaking (hip hop/rap production), since the beatmaker (producer) is considered the composer, the beatmaker (producer) is entitled to 50% (1/2) of the song; while the rapper (lyricist) is entitled to the other 50% (1/2) of the song. This means that if there is more than one beatmaker (producer, composer) on a song, each will have to split the 50% "composer's share." Likewise, if there is more than one rapper on a song, each will have to split the 50% "writer's share" of the song. So if there's one beatmaker and two rappers on a song, the beatmaker owns 50% of the song (the song's publishing), and each rapper owns 25% (and if there's *eight* rappers on a song, like for instance a classic Wu-Tang song, each rapper owns 6.25%). As is most often the case, there's only one beatmaker (producer) who's credited on a song; so typically, one beatmaker (producer) is entitled to the *entire* composer's share. However, it's common for some new beatmakers (producers) to forfeit a percentage of their publishing to someone, usually an A&R or a recording artist, in order to get placements. My advice: You typically don't want to forfeit your publishing rights under any circumstances. However, there are some situations where it may be advantageous to you to do so. For instance, if you receive a large up-front fee and/or guaranteed future production work.

Join a Performance Rights Organization (Society)

A performance rights organization or society (PRO) is an organization (typically, not for profit) that protects its members' musical copyrights by monitoring public performances (uses) of their music. Public performances that are monitored by PROs include radio and television broadcasts and stadium broadcasts and the like. PROs collect licensing fees from users (those persons who wish to use copyrighted works publicly) of music created by its members (copyright holders), then distributes them back to its members as royalties. This arrangement is not to be confused with the royalties that are generated from the record sales, as this describes private performance rights, something that is handled separately by record labels and music publishers.

I recommend that all beatmakers (producers) join a performance rights organization, either ASCAP or BMI, the two biggest performance rights organizations in America. By joining a performance rights organization, you're able to register all projects (songs) that you create, even those mixtape projects with established artists. Should a project that you're connected with really take off, i.e. it becomes a big hit, registration with a performance rights organization safeguards against beat-jacking (the stealing and unauthorized use of beats) and non-compensation or non-credit.

How Beats Are Typically Sold

Before examining contracts and how legal agreements work, it's useful to outline how beats are typically sold. Producers often sell beats outright. This means that for an up-front free, usually $50 to $5,000, a buyer, i.e. an artist/company buys the beat from the producer and the artist/company owns the beat free and clear — ALL rights, including copyright and right to use the beat again. Under this paradigm, any compensation that the producer receives *after* the up-front free (i.e. royalties) is determined by whatever the producer and the artist/company negotiate in the contract. If the producer and artist/company do not sign agreement stipulating further compensation, the artist/company is not obligated to pay the producer a royalty or any other compensation. This is important to note, as many producers sell beats online or to artists in their neighborhood for $50-$200 without any agreement. *If you sell beats online or informally to artists in your neighborhood, make sure you have an agreement.*

Some producers also license their beats. Licensing a beat is not a "sell" in the same way that selling a beat outright is. When a producer licenses a beat, the artist/company have a non-exclusive right (major and independent labels typically will not buy a license to a beat unless it is an exclusive license), which means the producer retains the copyright to the beat and can use it to make other deals. In cases were a beat is licensed exclusively to an artist/company, the producer owns the copyright to the underlying composition, i.e., the beat, while the artist or company (usually the label) owns the copyright to the sound recording.

Understanding Contracts/Legal Agreements

Contracts are the written, legal manifestations of all informal and formal negotiations that comprise an agreement between any number of parties. The terms of a contract refer to the details of an agreement, for example, the terms of payment, obligations, commencement, durations, benchmarks, notices, and the like. Before you sign any agreement, have an entertainment lawyer thoroughly look it over. It is not terribly difficult to find a qualified entertainment attorney who could examine a contract for you, and such a service is not as pricey as you might think. Sometimes it costs as little as $200 (even less for some lawyers in New York City), and usually it can be done within 24 hours. Having a qualified attorney even glance at an agreement is well worth the price, especially when you consider the fact that it will likely help you gain the best possible agreement and, more importantly, help you avoid entering a considerably bad deal.

Contracts can be as creative as a beat. Even though there are industry wide standards, these standards can be, and often are, altered and manipulated to address the specific interests of all parties involved in a given agreement. Many recording artists, especially in hip hop/rap, routinely get taken advantage of simply because many of them are unfamiliar with contracts or how the negotiation process works. Specifically, recording artists are often unfamiliar with the way in which unique terms and clauses resonate within various legal agreements. Thus, too often the end result is a recording artist entering into a one-sided, unfair agreement. One of the biggest reasons that many beatmakers enter into unfair agreements is because they simply do not understand that, in reality, there is no such thing as a "standard" contract. Sure, I concede that there are standard *frameworks* from which all music recording contracts are drafted. However, understanding how and why these contracts are typically altered, manipulated, and/or totally remodeled is critical to a beatmaker's bottom line.[194]

The Main Types of Agreements Involving Beat Sales: Work for Hire vs. Non-Esclusive

In a work-for-hire agreement, the producer forfeits all rights to their beat, including the copyright and the right to use the beat again for any purpose. If an agreement is work for hire, the producer usually receives an up-front fee and a royalty based either on net profits/net receips from sales (independent labels) or percentage of the artist's royalties (major labels — usually 2%-5% based on the artist's royalty). Note however that even when an agreement is work for hire, it may be possible for the producer to retain the copyright in his contribution to the underlying musical work, as opposed to the sound recording. In that case, the label or artist will require the producer's permission to use that contribution so that they can exploit the recording. Always aim for this with any producer agreement that you sign, especially when the beat is non-sample-based.

Building a Contract

Here, I'm discussing how to incorporate those things that you would want out of a contract and agreement. That being said, if you draft your own contract,

---

[194] A beatmaker's "bottom line" describes the net compensation that a beatmaker receives for his production services. The bottom line doesn't always have to be money; it can be equipment vouchers, future work, staff positions, and a variety of other things.

make an effort to at least have it looked at by a qualified attorney.

If you have the skills to get into a contract negotiation, then you have to believe that you have the skills to do it again. Therefore, when building your contract(s), I recommend that you aim for particular tangibles, not just money. That is, whenever possible, try to cover as many non-recoupable costs as possible. For instance, let's say the contract stipulates that you will get paid $5,000 for one beat, with 50% — the first half — being paid at the signing and another 50% — the second half — at the completion of the project. You can either accept this standard format or you can get creative. For example, you can forfeit meal costs and/or local travel costs, and up to 25% of the first payment due to you, in exchange for a gear and equipment voucher. (And once you get the setup, you can always liquidate it.)

Finally, in this section I have included four sample contracts. Carefully examine each contract, and be sure to notice their similarities as well as the specific language (wording) of each agreement, and the order of the terms. Also, notice how each agreement is fashioned and shaped in a way that is more suitable for the beatmaker (producer).

SAMPLE CONTRACTS

PRODUCTION FOR HIRE AGREEMENT 1

This agreement made on ____/_____/_____(date) is between the Producer and the Undersigned Artist. The Artist has either signed a recording contract with the following Record Company: _____RECORDS and the date of the contract was ____/_____/_____(date), or is an unsigned/ independent Artist.

TERMS AND RECITALS

The effectiveness of this Agreement shall commence with its execution by all of the parties. Please note the following:

a.   The Producer specializes in recording, and musical production of musical Artists, background recordings, music drops, etc.
b.   The Producer is familiar with the musical abilities of Artist.
c.   The Artist performs under the name_____ *(if no other name, leave blank)*.
d.   The Producer and the Artist wish to enter into this agreement to complete the music production of the songs recorded.

1. PAYMENT

1.1. The Artist/Company, *(whichever applies)*, promises to pay the Producer the following payments in the amount of $_____ per beat *(track or song can be inserted here if you prefer)*. The Artist promises to make payments to the Producer before the pre-production recording phase ___% *(usually 50%, but negotiable)* and as soon as all production is final and approved ___% *(usually remaining balance, but always negotiable. For instance, you can defer payment for other incentives, such as guaranteed future production work)*.
This agreement hereby requests, instructs, authorizes, and empowers the Artist/Company to pay the Producer all amounts agreed upon. The duration of this agreement commences as of ____/_____/_____(date).

2. PRODUCTION

2.1. The Producer agrees to produce masters of recordings consisting of songs performed by Artist (hereinafter referred to as the "Songs"). The resulting recording (hereinafter referred to as the "Recording") shall be of a quality that is equal to master recordings normally produced for commercial distribution. The Artist will also give production credits (full or Co) to the Producer(s) in both written and verbal formats. (i.e. Album credits, or person-to-person inquiries).

3. CONTRIBUTION BY ARTIST

3.1. The Artist agrees to fully cooperate with the Producer, in good faith, in the production of the Recording; to contribute to such production the music and lyrics embodied in the Songs; to arrange, direct and perform the Songs in such a manner as to facilitate the production of the Recording; and to otherwise strictly observe the remaining duties and obligations of this Agreement.

4. ARTISTIC CONTROL

4.1. The Producer and the Artist shall be jointly responsible for all decisions regarding the artistic content of the Recording. The Producer *(or artist, depending on the situation)* shall maintain final decision rights in the event mutual consensus is not reached.

5. TITLE

5.1. The title of the Recording shall be chosen by agreement between the Producer and the Artist.

6. DATES AND LOCATION OF RECORDING SESSIONS

6.1. The recording sessions necessary to produce the Recordings will occur at studios and facilities chosen by the Producer. (Or Artist, depending on the agreement).

7. ADDITIONAL MUSICIANS

7.1. The _____ (Artist) or _____ (Producer) shall provide and compensate sufficient and competent musicians to properly perform the Songs, as arranged and directed by the Artist and the Producer.

8. COSTS

8.1. The Producer and the Artist will be responsible for deciding in advance who will pay all of the costs that will be incurred in the production of the Recording, including the prepayment of all travel, hotel and meal costs incurred by the Artist and/or the Producer in attending the recording sessions.

9. COMPLETION AND RELEASE

9.1. If the Artist or the Company plans to release and distribute the Recording(s), the Recording(s) shall be completed and prepared for release and distribution on or before ____/____/_____ (date). The Artist or the Artist's Company will be responsible for the release and distribution of the Recordings. If the Artist or the Artist's Company isn't ready to release and distribute the Recording(s) by the date previously aforementioned, the Artist will notify the Producer and will continue to give frequent updates concerning the status of the recordings. The Artist will also inform the Producer once the final release and distribution dates are determined. The Producer and the Artist acknowledge that time is of the essence in the completion of the Recording, and they each agree to exercise all reasonable means to achieve such completion.

10. COPYRIGHT

10.1. Upon the Artist's assignment of the Songs pursuant herein, the _____ (Producer) or (Artist) or (Company), whichever applies, shall proceed to obtain and secure a copyright for each of the said Songs. Each such copyright shall be the sole property of both the Producer's *(designate your publishing company, i.e. ASCAP, BMI)* and the Artist/company, **(whichever applies)**, 50/50.

11. SAMPLE CLEARANCE

11.1. The Artist understands that the Producer may have utilized a sample from another artist's (s) recording, which was previously copyrighted, to create the beat (music, track, song, etc.). The Producer will give the Artist full disclosure of the origin of all samples. In the event that the song from the recording is published, utilizing the beat (music, track) the Artist/Company, *(whichever applies)*, will assume all responsibility for clearing any samples utilized. In the event that there's a lawsuit, the Artist/Company, *(whichever applies)*, and NOT the Producer, will assume all responsibility for settling the copyright infringement and the Producer will not be liable. If the name of an artist sampled for the beat (music, track, etc.) is required, the Artist will consult with the Producer and will get the information concerning the origin of the sample(s) utilized in the song. In the event that the Artist is not able to retrieve the name of a sampled artist(s) from the Producer, the Artist will be responsible in obtaining the names of any sampled artist(s) and getting the sample(s) cleared. The Artist/Company, *(whichever applies)* will accept total responsibility and liability for any changes made to the tracks after the Producer has delivered the master track(s).

13. UNDERSTANDING

13.1. The Artist/Company, *(whichever applies)* and the Producer understand that this written agreement is a legally binding document. In the event that either the Artist/Company, *(whichever applies)* or the Producer violates any of the above clauses, each understands that they will be liable for damages and attorney fees.

By signing their signatures below or executing the purchase online, both the Artist and the Producer agree with all the terms and conditions written in this agreement.

Print: X_____   Date_____/_____/_____

Sign: X_____   Artist/Company, *(whichever applies)*

Print: X_____   Date_____/_____/_____

Sign: X_____   Witness_____

PRODUCTION FOR HIRE AGREEMENT 2

This is a Production Agreement made this day of ____, 200_,
between the Master Producer (You/Your Production Company) _____ and the Undersigned Artist_____. The Artist has signed a recording contract with the following Company _____, and the date of the contract was _____ 200_, or the Artist is unsigned and/or independent. All references to the Master Producer, Producer, "Us", "We", and/or "I", and the like will hereby refer to the aforementioned Master Producer and/or Producer employed by the Master Producer, only. All references to the Artist/Company, and/or "You" and the like will hereby refer to the aforementioned Artist/Company, only.

1. SERVICES AND OBLIGATIONS

1.1. In this Production Agreement, the Master Producer is a work for hire for only ___ recording(s).

1.2. PRODUCTION

1.2.(a) The Producer agrees to produce masters of recordings consisting of songs performed by Artist (hereinafter referred to as the "Songs"). The resulting recording (hereinafter referred to as the "Recording") shall be of a quality that is equal to master recordings normally produced for commercial distribution. The Artist will also give production credits (full or Co) to the Producer(s) in both written and verbal formats. (i.e. Album credits, or person-to-person inquiries).

ARTIST CONTRIBUTION

1.3.(a) The Artist agrees to fully cooperate with the Producer, in good faith, in the production of the Recording; to contribute to such production the music and lyrics embodied in the Songs; to arrange, direct and perform the Songs in such a manner as to facilitate the production of the Recording; and to otherwise strictly observe the remaining duties and obligations of this Agreement. The Artist shall be responsible for booking all associated recording sessions, and shall be responsible for notifying the Master Producer/Producer at least ___ hours prior to the commencement of any recording sessions.

3. PAYMENT

3.1. Artist/Company, *(whichever applies)*, promises to pay Master Producer/Production Company the following payments in the amount of $_____ per beat *(track or song can be inserted here if you prefer)*. The Artist/Company, *(whichever applies)*, promises to make payments to the Producer before the pre-production recording phase ___% *(usually 50%, but negotiable)* and as soon as all production is final and approved ___% *(usually remaining balance, but always negotiable. For instance, you can defer payment for other incentives, such as guaranteed future production work)*.

3.1.(a) This Production Agreement hereby requests, instructs, authorizes, and empowers Record Company (in your case the artist) to pay Master Producer (or production company) all producer fees agreed upon.

4. COSTS

4.1. The Artist/Company, *(whichever applies)*, will be responsible for paying all of the costs that will be incurred in the production of the Recording, including the prepayment of all travel, hotel and meal costs incurred by the Producer in attending the recording sessions. Costs that are NOT prepaid shall be recoupable by the Producer within ____ business days, from the time the Artist/Company receives receipts of such legitimate costs.

5. MISCELLANEOUS

5.1. This Production Agreement can and will be used in a court of law (city, state) in the event that there is a breach of these contractual provisions.

6. COPYRIGHT

6.1. By signing this Agreement you (Artist) hereby grant our publishing designee 50% of your share of world-wide copyrights for this recording.

The duration of this agreement commences as of the date of the contact between the Artist and the Master Producer(Production Company) ____ ,200_.

By signing their signatures below or executing the purchase online, both the Artist and the Producer agree with all the terms and conditions written in this written agreement.

Print: X_____   Date____/____/____

Sign: X_____   Artist/Company, *(whichever applies)*

Print: X_____   Date____/____/____

Sign: X_____   Witness_____

EXCLUSIVE PRODUCTION AGREEMENT 1

This agreement is made by and between Master Producer (You/Your Production Company) _____ and the Undersigned Artist_____, for the exclusive, non-transferable right to use the musical composition known as (the "Composition") for all commercial recording, performing, broadcasting and distribution purposes ("Exclusive Rights").

1. SERVICES AND OBLIGATIONS

1.1. This license permits the exclusive use of the Composition ("the beat") or any portion thereof in particular recordings made in connection with the Composition, including the exclusive right to perform, broadcast and distribute any derivative thereof. This license is non-assignable and any attempt to reproduce, share or re-sell the Composition itself is strictly prohibited.

2. FEES

2.1. The Exclusive Rights are granted for and in consideration of the sum of ("price")_____ and other valuable consideration, receipt of which is hereby acknowledged.

3. ROYALTIES

3.1. Royalties for the sale, distribution, broadcast and performance of any derivative of the Composition shall be allocated as follows: Sales: 3% of gross sales to Master Producer.

4. CREDIT

4.1. All distributed works must show the following music credit: Produced by (name of Master Producer).

5. WRITING SPLITS

5.1. 50% - Master Producer BMI or ASCAP #, 50% - Artist.

6. PUBLISHING SPLITS

6.1. 50% - Master Producer BMI or ASCAP #, 50% - Artist.

7. COPYRIGHT

7.1. Master Producer to retains the copyright in his contribution to the underlying musical work, not the sound recording.

8. WARRANTIES

8.1. Unless otherwise agreed in writing, Master Producer offers the Composition as-is and makes no representations or warranties of any kind concerning the work, including, without limitation, warranties of title, merchantability, fitness for a particular purpose, non infringement, or the absence of latent or other defects, accuracy, or the presence or absence of errors, whether or not discoverable.

The duration of this agreement commences as of the date of the contact between the Artist and the Master Producer(Production Company) ____ ,200_.

By signing their signatures below or executing the purchase online, both the Artist and the Master Producer agree with all the terms and conditions written in this written agreement.

Print: X_____   Date_____/_____/_____

Sign: X_____   Artist/Company, *(whichever applies)*

Print: X_____   Date_____/_____/_____

Sign: X_____   Witness_____

Master Producer: (You) _____

EXCLUSIVE PRODUCTION AGREEMENT 2

(Used for the purpose of signing other producers to your Production Company)

This is a Production Agreement, (hereinafter referred to as the "Agreement") this day of _____ 200_, between the Master Producer, ("You", producing under the pseudonym, "_____") and the Production Company, ("Us"). Hereinafter the company shall be referred to as "the Production Company" and/or the "Company" and/or "Us".

1. <u>SERVICES/TERMS</u>

1.1. The term will commence on the date hereof and will continue, unless extended as provided herein, for _ years.

1.2. During the term of the Agreement, you will render your personal
production services exclusively to us, as the producer of Pre-Mastered Recordings, hereby referred to as "Beats". The company has the Full and Exclusive right to negotiate price and payment for all of your beats and production services.

1.2.(a) Your beats shall be produced and used for any one and/or combination of the following:

1.2.(a1) For the purpose of creating songs, backgrounds, interludes, intros, outros, and the like for all of the Company's recording artists and producers.

1.2.(a2) For the purpose of creating songs, backgrounds, interludes, intros, outros, and the like for any artist(s) and/or other like person(s) NOT signed to the Company.

1.2.(a3) The producer agrees to give the Company the Full and Exclusive right to stipulate and negotiate any and all terms of agreements associated with your beats produced for any artist(s) and/or other like person(s) NOT signed to the company. This DOES NOT mean that the company is, nor shall ever be, the producer's manager. The producer shall have the right to enter into a Management Agreement with whom they choose. However, it is understood that all terms of this agreement shall remain intact, throughout the term specified in section 1, sub-section 1.1.

1.3. Your production role in the studio:

1.3.(a) In regards to the beats that you produce for _____ and other Company Artists, it shall be no less than your assistance with the tracking of your beats. That is, you are required to be present at the recording session, whenever the initial tracking of your beats are being performed, unless otherwise noted in writing by us. ALL final mixes and/or master recordings of your beats and/or songs is the sole responsibility of the Company.

1.3.(b) In regards to the beats that you produce for anyone NOT signed to the Company, you shall be required to perform or assist in performing the initial tracking of your beats.

1.4. In the event that you can not be present for an initial tracking recording session, you must give us at least 3 days notice. You must also deliver any beat in consideration for any Company related project, within 48 hours of said notice.

1.4.(a) The following formats of beats shall be deemed suitable for delivery to us:

1.4.(a1) Audio CD.
1.4.(a2) Pro Tools data CD, with two additional backups.

1.4.(b) The time length of each beat that shall be deemed suitable for delivery to us:
5 minutes or more, but not too exceed 8 minutes, unless otherwise expressed by us in writing.

2. PRODUCTION CREDITS AND RECOGNITION

2.1. For beats produced for any recording artist signed to the Company: You will receive Full Production credit, in regards to any and all beats that you produce. Production credit for the song (single or album) shall read like this, "Produced by "You" for the Company (Us). For beats produced for artists NOT signed to the Company, you will receive Full Production credit.

3. OBLIGATIONS

3.1. Producer Obligations:

3.1.(a) You are obligated to submit at least 3 brand new beats to us every week.

3.1.(b) You are obligated to perform such services as are customarily performed by a record producer, including but not limited to, editing/sequencing, tracking, and the initial recording of your beats.

3.1.(c) You are obligated to produce and perform under the pseudonym, "_____" and/or "_____".

3.1.(d) You are obligated to report any and all inquiries about your production services to the Company.

The "Key Man"[195] in this clause is _____.

3.1.(e) You are obligated to assist in the promotion and marketing of your production services.

3.2. Company Obligations

3.2.(a) The Company is obligated to identify, seek, find, and foster Artists for your production services. These Artists shall be of a talent level approved by both the Producer and the Company. Though the Company has final say over which Artists the Producer can produce for, the company must inform the Producer of any and all inquiries, in regards to the Producer's beats

---

[195] The "Key Man" is the contact person. Key Man clauses are very important. People routinely move around in the music business. Pressures run extremely high, which often translates into a strange culture of impulsive promotions and terminations. Because so many people are fired, hired and/or relocated, the changes essentially jeopardize the situations of everyone directly associated. "Key Man clauses" makes it clear which company representative will be dealing directly, (the majority of the time), with the producer/artist. Key Man clauses also give producers/artists a way out of an agreement, in the event that the Key Man (contact person) departs from the company.

and production services.

3.2.(b) The Company is obligated to promote and market your beats and production services, worldwide, via customary promotional practices and channels, including but not limited to, industry contacts, online promotional campaigns, business cards, flyers, etc.

3.2.(c) The Company is obligated to negotiate and secure price and payment for your beats and production services with any artist and like persons NOT signed to the company.

3.2.(d) With regards to artists and the like NOT signed to the Company, the Company is obligated to secure a purchasing price for your beats and production services that is NO LESS THAN $_____ per beat. After _ *(number of)* credits from the date of this agreement, this minimum amount shall increase to NO LESS THAN $_____ per beat produced by you.

4. PAYMENT PER BEAT

As full consideration for all of the rights granted to the Company hereunder and provided you have fully complied with all of your material obligations, hereunder, the Company will pay you, subject to all the terms and conditions hereof, a payment sum of:

4.1 On your beats used for any artist signed to the Company:

4.1.(a) Not less than $_____, no more than $_____ for any number of beats up to 3. Whichever amount is at the sole discretion of the Company.

4.1.(b) Not less than $_____, no more than $_____ for any number of beats between 4 and 6. Whichever amount is at the sole discretion of the Company.

4.1.(c) With regards to beats used by any Artist signed to the Company, the Company will pay _% of the payment up front, at the commencement of the initial tracking session. The Company shall pay the remaining _% of the payment to you within two weeks of the completion of the final mix of the song(s), in which your beat(s) was (were) used.

4.2. On your beats used for artists NOT signed by the Company, in particular, Artists and the like whom the Company has secured and entered in with an agreement for your production services:

4.2.(a) _% of the purchasing price paid for your production.
Please note. _% of the purchasing price shall be retained by the Company, as its percentage.

4.3. With regards to beats purchased from artists and the like NOT signed to the Company, All payments owed to you shall be paid to you within two weeks of the Company's receipt of such applicable payments.

5. EXPENSES

5.1. With regards to Costs incurred in the Production of the Recording:

5.1.(a) As full consideration for all of the rights granted to the company hereunder and provided you have fully complied with all of your material obligations, hereunder, the Company will pre-pay for all of your costs incurred in the production of recordings for Artists signed to the Company, and Artists NOT signed to the Company—provided they have entered into an agreement with the Company for your beats and production services, and have agreed to pre-pay us for your costs incurred, during the use of your production services.

6. ACCOUNTINGS

6.1. The Company will render statements on October 31 and April 30 of each year of all royalties due and owing to you at the end of the semi-annual periods ending on the preceding June 30 and December 31, respectively. Such statements shall be accompanied by payment of royalties shown to be due and owed to you, if any, after deducting any and all un-recouped Advances and chargeable costs under this agreement.

6.2. We will maintain books and records which report the sales of the Phonograph Records, Compact Discs and/or Cassette Tapes. You may, at your own expense, examine those books and records, as provided in this paragraph only. You may make those examinations only for the purpose of verifying the accuracy of the statements sent to you under paragraph 4.1. You may make such an examination for a particular statement only once, and only within two (2) years after the date when we send you that statement under paragraph 4.1. (We will be deemed conclusively to have sent you each statement on the date prescribed in 4.1 unless you notify us otherwise, with respect to any statement, within thirty (30) days after that date.) You may make those examinations only during our usual business hours, and at the place where we keep the books and records to be examined. If you wish to make an examination you will be required to notify us at least thirty (30) days before the date when you plan to begin it.

7. MISCELLANEOUS.

7.1. Neither party will be entitled to recover damages or to terminate this agreement by reason of any breach hereof by the other party, that otherwise entitle you to recover damages or the right to terminate this agreement, unless the latter party has failed to substantially remedy such breach within a reasonable time following receipt of your notice thereof. For the purposes of this paragraph 8.1 and solely with respect to our obligation to make payments to you under this agreement, "reasonable time" shall be forty-five (45) days, it being understood however, that you shall not be entitled to recover damages or terminate the term of this agreement if the breach of our payment obligation cannot be remedied within thirty (30) days, and we have commenced to remedy it within that time and have proceeded with reasonable promptness.

7.2. <u>YOU WILL BE CONSIDERED IN BREACH IF YOU:</u>

7.2.(a) Negotiate ANY production agreement with any Artist and the like signed or not signed to the Company, without the expressed, written consent of the Company.

7.2.(b) Provide ANY of your beats and/or production services to any Artist and the like, for any project, whether it be for free or payment, without the expressed, written consent of the Company.

7.3. <u>TERMINATION</u>

7.3.(a) This agreement may be terminated by the Company at any time, for ANY reason. The Company's desire to terminate the agreement must be presented to you in writing. However, any and all monies remaining due to you must be paid to you within forty-five (45) days of the termination of the agreement. If you do not receive monies owed to you within forty-five (45) days of the termination of the agreement, the agreement is automatically reinstated.

7.3.(b) You may remove yourself from this contract at any time with a one-time buy-out fee of $_____. If you buy out of the agreement with the Company, any and all payments owed to you shall be forfeited, immediately.

7.4. This agreement contains the entire understanding of the parties. No change of this agreement will be binding upon us unless it is made by an instrument duly executed by us. No change of this agreement will be binding on you unless it is made by an instrument signed by you.

7.5. This agreement will be governed and construed pursuant to the laws of the State of _____ applicable to contracts entered into and performed entirely within the State of _____, and any disputes or controversies arising hereunder shall be subject to the jurisdiction of Courts of the State of _____ or of the U.S. Federal District Court for the _____ District of _____. Any process in any action or proceeding arising under or relating to this agreement may, among other methods, be served upon you by delivering or mailing the same by registered or certified mail, directed to the address first written above or such other address as you designate by notice to us. Any such delivery or mail service shall be deemed to have the same force and effect as personal service within the State of _____.

7.6. All notices hereunder shall be in writing and shall be given by personal delivery, registered or certified mail, return receipt requested, or by Federal Express, at the addresses shown above, or such other address or addresses as may from time to time be designated by either party by notice. Notices shall be deemed to be given when mailed, except for a notice of change of address which shall be deemed to be given on the date of its receipt.

7.7. You may not assign this agreement or any of your rights hereunder to anyone.

7.8. This agreement shall not become effective until executed by all proposed parties hereto.

7.9. You have read and fully understand this agreement. You have either consulted with an attorney regarding any questions you may have or have voluntarily elected not to do so.

IN WITNESS WHEREOF, the parties have executed this agreement on the date and year first written above.
Witness_____

_____
Producer

My social security number is_____. Under the penalties of perjury, I certify that this information is true, correct and complete.

By_____
   (Capacity)   The Company

<u>YOUR ASSENT AND GUARANTY.</u>

To induce the Company to enter into the forgoing agreement with the Producer, "_____", (the "Agreement"):

1. _____ (Producer)

1.(a) represents to us that he has read the Agreement and has had the legal effect of each of its provisions of it relating to the Producer, and the Company, and artists NOT SIGNED to the Company.

1.(c) acknowledges that we will have no obligation to make any payments to the Producer in connection with the services rendered by the Producer or the fulfillment of the Producer other obligations under the Agreement, except for the payments specified in paragraphs 4, 5, and 6.

2.(a) "_____" (The Producer):

_____   Date____/_____/_____

Part 5
INTERVIEWS

A Note About the Interviews Part

When I set out to conduct the series of interviews that follow, I did so with the aim of achieving five things. First, I wanted to show the full gamut of beatmakers. That is to say, I wanted to interview elite beatmakers (producers), pioneering beatmakers, and beatmakers on the rise. Second, I wanted every beatmaker that I interviewed to tell it like it is, in their own words. Third, I wanted to demonstrate any areas of major consensus among successful beatmakers. Fourth, I wanted to dispel myths, while at the same time, prove commonly held beliefs about beatmaking (hip hop/rap production). Fifth, I wanted to gather and preserve rare, accurate, first-hand professional insight to and historical analysis of the art of beatmaking and the aesthetics that surround it.

I should further point out that the following interviews are candid, and they are presented here as is. To preserve the actual words and sentiments and overall aunthenticity of each interviewees words, I have not attempted to correct or censor any of the slang or profanity that each interviewee used during my interviews with them. Finally, I use "Sa'id" — my music performance pseudonym — in the question column, as that is the name all interviewees know me as and are familiar with.

INTERVIEWS

MARLEY MARL

Marley Marl is the father of modern beatmaking. Indeed, he is to beatmaking (hip hop/rap production) what Kool Herc, Grandmaster Flash, and Afrika Bambaataa are to hip hop/rap DJ'ing and hip hop/rap music in general. Many of Marley Marl's innovations have become fundamentals in the beatmaking tradition. And his long list of song credits with some of the most influential rappers in history are too many to name here.

Sa'id: In the beginning, DJs were the central figure to hip hop/rap. How and why do you think that changed?
Marley Marl: I don't think it changed too much because the DJ still is one of the key figures of the survival of hip hop. You go up in the clubs, the DJ is still throwin' on joints. It's not how it was when there was a DJ and MC. The DJs breakin' the records in the club; the DJ plays the records on the radio. And I think the DJ is still very essential in the creation and in the movement of hip hop. The DJ still holds a very sacred part in hip hop.

Sa'id: When rappers started realizing that they no longer needed the DJ, and, essentially, that they could go to anybody and get music, why do you think that happened so fast?
Marley Marl: At one point, the DJ did get kind of x'd out… But the hip hop DJ had to evolve itself into something where the hip hop DJ is needed…the guy making the beats. The DJ had to evolve into another role… even radio… the DJ was there, the mix show was there.

Sa'id: Speaking of radio, what was the difference between now and then? When you were with Mister Magic, did the two of you have the same type of say?
Marley Marl: Some radio stations, some program directors and some music directors, they let some of their tastemaker DJs taste make, basically… I mean, if you're on prime time you can't really do what you would really want to do on your own… You have to stay in a certain zone; they have a certain format. Like if a station is looking for 18-35 year old females. If that's who they shop for, you have to base your programming and your music around attracting those people.

Sa'id: But that's now. Back then, rap was protected, it was kind of insular…
Marley Marl: Cuz it was too new! So they would let us do more of what we wanted to do to break that music and that genre to everybody. Yeah, it was more leeway.

Sa'id: How did you take advantage of that leeway?
Marley Marl: Just by bringing the streets to the radio, bringing what the people like, what they was vibing to in the streets. What we were doing was bringing what was popular in the streets to the radio. At that point, a lot of radio guys weren't really going out, so they didn't have an idea of what people really loved.

Sa'id: Let me take you back to when you were first deejaying. What was the name of the park in Queensbridge where all of the park jams were poppin'?
Marley Marl: Queensbridge Park. I can't remember the date that I first rocked a jam, but I remember the day I first touched a turntable in Queensbridge. It was on the 41 side of Vernon.

447

They had music out on the block; that's before they even took it to the park. It was like a little thing on the block. It was like a block party, everybody was out. Those block parties became so big and legendary, you know, we had to take it to a bigger place. The big park was across the street. I remember when we took it to the park, it was incredible. EVERYBODY came, even people from different projects [public housing projects] came.

Sa'id: Who led you into that, who led you into the music in that way?
Marley Marl: My brother. My older brother, Larry La, he was in a group called High Fidelity. They were the first DJs out of Queensbridge, they were the first DJ crew…It was a DJ CREW! And what they used to do, this is funny, this was BEFORE rap, they were a DJ DANCE crew! So they used to go and dance. It was like a freestyle dance that they used to do. Kind of like break dancing, mad movement. This is when everybody used to dress up, they used to kind of dress up like Shabba Doo and them and do their break dancing, poppin'…They were like a break dance crew with DJs. ALL of them could dance and DJ. They use to all dress alike… marsh mellow shoes… As a kid, that's what I used to look up to, that's what I used to see… They [High Fidelity] were Gas, Jappy Jap, Larry La, and T Tom, the founder. That was my early beginnings in getting into the music. And what was great for me is that they used to keep the equipment up at my house. They use to keep the stuff in the living room, and they used to go out, I used to go and toy around with the equipment. Of course they'd unplug it. I use to find the plug and plug it back in. Soon as I see them walk out the building, I'm trying to get on the 1 and 2s [two turntables] and mimic what I saw them do; play some of the records I saw them dance to. That was my early beginnings.

Sa'id: You taught yourself?
Marley Marl: Yeah.

Sa'id: It got to the point where you got your own rig?
Marley Marl: Well, it got to the point where my brother went to the service [military], and it kind of just disbanded. Cuz a lot of people was encouraging him like, "Ah, that's that music stuff, that DJ stuff, ain't no money in it." People didn't know where it was going. And actually, my stepfather told my brother, he was like, "You gettin' to old to be runnin' around doin' these parties, you ain't really gettin' no money. You gotta think about your future." My brother was like 18 years old, so that made him go to the service. He went into the air force.

Sa'id: Damn, 18 years old? How old were you at the time?
Marley Marl: I was like 8 years old. Believe me, I was watching them from the inception. I would say by the time I was 13, I was already nice on the 1 and 2s. I put in my time… I was exceptional. By the time I was 13, I was better than all them, I'll tell you that.

Sa'id: So you saw at that age where the music was going?
Marley Marl: Right.

Sa'id: You were also with the Sure Shot Crew. Describe how it was "crews" then vs. the cliques of today. Talk about you putting together a crew and what a crew meant.
Marley Marl: Basically, my crew came together because I was the guy in the park, and there's always guys who wanna rhyme. So I would let some people get on the mic sometimes, I'd throw on "To Be Real" [by Cheryl Lynn] or somethin' like that and let them rhyme over it. So what happened, I would keep coming out and the same people kept coming to the mic. And that's how my crew really started. And I was like, "O.K.!" One of my rappers, he had ties to the Bronx. His name was Bar'Shon. He used to hang out with Melle Mel and them. Rapper Bar' Shon…and he's actually the guy that named me. He was on the mic, and he had a rhyme

talkin' bout, [starts rappin'] "Miss Shirley had a baby, she claimin' to be a star, when he came out with two pioneers, they named him Marley Marl." I was like, "WOW!"

Sa'id: Ha… and you was like, "I'm keepin' it."
Marley Marl: I'm KEEPIN' IT. [Laughs] My name before that, actually, I was Marvelous Marlon. I had one of those names. But when he came out with that rhyme and said it on the mic, it stuck. People started calling me Marley Marl after that.

Sa'id: See that's how organic hip hop is… One thing everybody talks about is, O.K., hip hop as a culture, and rap music, it all started in the Bronx. But what is never discussed and is seldom known is that rap beatmaking (hip hop/rap production) — a lot of what we commonly know it as today, i.e. looping, chopping…it more formally first developed in Queens.

Marley Marl: Oh, no doubt!

Sa'id: Why do you think that the actual rap "production," beatmaking trade developed with you in Queens, and others like Paul C., and then Large Professor? What made that more conducive in Queens rather than in the Bronx?
Marley Marl: Because the earlier records that came out… My whole premise of getting into production was because I didn't like the representation of rap that was on wax [ca. 1979-1981]. Once rap was on cassettes, and everybody was runnin' around with the latest Flash tape, that was DOPE! Because there was cuttin', there was scratchin', there was echoes, and it was original beats they was rhymin' off of. That's what…as a kid, that's what I was brought up on, you know, the scratchin' element, the echoes, the break-beats, the RAWNESS, the rub-a-dub scratchin'. But I noticed, by the time rap hit records, it was BANDS…It was bands re-playin' break-beats! [Laughs]. I remember the first record I heard with a rap on it. I was so disappointed, because as I was growing up, I was always hearing all of these Breakout cassettes from the streets; the Grandmaster Flash tapes, and [starts to mimic a popular break-beat]… the echo, the energy. Aw, man, what a disappointment when rap records *first* came out. I was like, "NO! This is not what it is…This is not a great representation of what I was brought up on." That wasn't what rap was. That's not what everybody used to go up in Harlem and in the Bronx [and] get the tapes and for.

Sa'id: So how did you go about changing that, what was your first step?
Marley Marl: My first step was I got my break-beats up. All the songs I used to hear them cuttin' up…I got my break-beats up. And then after that, I would go out into the park and have my crew rhyme over it. After that…I kind of discovered sampling by accident. That's how I got into looping… I was getting another part of the record, and we didn't truncate it yet. The snare was there and the vocal. I was playing a beat that I made on the drum machine, and I heard the sampled snare playing with it. Then I realized… I was like, "Yo, I can take any kick and snare from ANY of my break-beat records on how rap should sound."

Sa'id: When was this?
Marley Marl: I would say, '84/'85-ish…

Sa'id: Were you at Unique [famed NYC recording studio]
Marley Marl: Yeah, I was interning at Unique.

Sa'id: Describe that setting. Were you purposely hunting for a new sound?
Marley Marl: I don't know if I would call it hunting for a new sound. I was trying to make

rap sound *accurate* to what I was brought up on. That's basically it. I wasn't looking for a new sound… Maybe you could call it looking for a new sound. But I know the representation of what I was hearing [on the radio at that time] was NOT what I grew up on hearing on these cassettes. And I just wanted to make it MORE like the rap that I heard before it hit records. That was my whole premise of everything!

Sa'id: You speak to DJ Premier, he'll tell you how he was influenced by Marley Marl. But who came before Marley Marl? Who was it that had that direct influence on you? Where did you take your cue from? Who was it that you were under, who was it that you were watching?
Marley Marl: I was…hmmm… I would say my production… I was heavily influenced by radio mixers. Like back in the day, I think it was Shep Pettibone on Kiss FM. There was a guy, Ted Curry, on BLS (WBLS). These are like… Yo, the funny thing about me with this whole music, I wasn't even a rap believer in the beginning! And my skills came from me basically connecting records from the clubs. I was like a club DJ first… I came in hip hop at a point when people wasn't even blending records or connecting them. Yeah, they was just like, throwing records on; they was just like, cuttin' them in. It wasn't about putting two beats together and matching them. They wasn't doing that. Only the club DJs was doing that or the disco DJs; that's like a disco mix. So what I did is, I took the disco mix and brought it to hip hop. Because disco used to blend the next record in on time. And I knew how to do that real well, cuz I used to play in a club. Matterfact, when I was 15, I was playing in a club. I wasn't even old enough to be in the club, but I was the DJ of the club, a club called Pegasus, off East 63rd Street and 2nd Ave [in Manhattan]. I was the DJ there. There was a guy named Lindsey, he used to let me get on on Thursdays… I was able to seamlessly blend records. I think that was my superiority over the average hip hop DJ, cuz they wasn't doing that. By the time I got to Magic [Mister Magic radio show] and started doing it on the radio, I started doing blends, putting songs together, making smooth transitions. [Without timestretch, just matching them up.]

Sa'id: You kind of single-handedly started the whole James Brown sample craze. Then, when everybody got up on the James Brown style, you went in a completely different direction with that. I remember the first time I ever heard "Road to the Riches" [Kool G Rap & DJ Polo, beat by Marley Marl] I was trying to make a pause tape. I was trying to break down where that break-beat came from. I think it took three years before I realized it *wasn't* a break-beat. There was one element here; then there was another element here; then there was the 808 [booming bass drum] coming in. What prepared you to be able to break multiple components down and then put 'em together into one cohesive thing?
Marley Marl: It was the fusion of where I was trying to take the music. I guess it was the fusion of hearing break-beats, and scratchin', and echos, and all of that on earlier tapes that came to my attention. So I think the fusion of all of that. And the reason I even used, went back to the break-beats was because I remembered. When I went back and started making records, after what I realized with sampling what I could do! They made me go back to my brother and them records. I started diggin' in my brother and them crates. Like "Nobody Beats the Biz" beat, [starts beat box imitation of the "Nobody Beats the Biz" beat], that was a beat they used to play. But they didn't rock the beginning, they used to rock the bass part. But I was remembering, and I was like, "Yo, hold on. This African music today!" The beat was dope! So I would go back to my brother's crate. That was in my brother's crate…" Fly Like An Eagle" [the song sampled for "Nobody Beats the Biz"], all those elements was in my brother's crates. Even the James Brown stuff, I would remember that they used that… "Funky Drummer" [James Brown] was dope. Then I started going back to every song that I remembered people used to dance to. And that's why my selection was always something hot. And by me putting elements together, once I learned about tracking [cuts a serious look], it was over!

Sa'id: When did you learn about tracking, who showed you?

Marley Marl: That? My boy Andre Booth showed me about tracking. He's the guy that definitely put me in the "game" game. You know, even though I was messin' around at the place [night club]. And it's funny how I met him, because I was jammin' in the park. And this was when musicians was going out, and DJs was coming in. The band was down there, down this side of the park, playing with no crowd. I was down this side with the DJ set, with the crowd. There was no crowd over there, everybody was like, "The DJ's exciting." The bands was like, [in mocking voice] "DJs ain't real music, so why everybody…" And I was like, "Let me bridge the gap right now." [I said to them] "When I take a break, do ya'll wanna plug your band equipment into my systm? When I take a break, ya'll can get down for an hour…" I did it to make the peace, and that's how I got cool with the musicians in Queensbridge; and that's how I started producing. The very next day after I did that, I got musicians showing up at my door. I got guys coming with guitars to my crib…with they keyboards…and I'm plugging it in in my house, and I'm learning how to make them sound good. Then I realized that I needed a 12 channel mixer. Not the up and down fader mixer like I had, I needed something with more inputs. That's when I went out and bought a little 12-channel redboard, I think it was called Mavis or something. And at that point, that's when I started learnin' how to EQ keyboards, EQ drums, guitars, EQ the mic better… That's how I went to the studio with Andre, he took me to Unique [Unique Recording Studio]. It was funny, because around that time, he knew Arthur Baker. So he got me into a Jazzy Jay session. It was way back. I was like, wow, the studio atmosphere. Because I had like a little Jr. version of it at my house. And that's when I realized, I have to get rid of all my DJ equipment, all my big speakers, because this is what I wanna do. I don't wanna lug speakers around no more." I was like, "Yo, I'd rather do this!" And that's when I took an internship at Unique. Well, first, it wasn't even an internship [Laughs], I was just showing up. They saw me so much and they saw me with Andre, and they knew Andre; he got me in. I was able to get in sessions, "Yo, what you need from the store?" I was running to the store for people, just to be in the mix. And from there it turned into an internship. I learned the fundamentals of making something "sound" good. That's how it all got started.

Sa'id: Given all these dynamic qualities that you now have, at that point, what would you have considered yourself to be, were you more of a sound organizer or a sound creator?

Marley Marl: I would say DJ! Cuz, to the last minute, I was DENYING to myself that I was a producer! I actually argued Fly Ty down the first time I saw my name on a record, "produced by Marley Marl." I was like, "Yo, I'm not no producer, man!" In my brain, I was a DJ, a sound manipulator. I didn't really consider myself as a producer. I guess that's not what I was going for, and it just happened. I was a DJ, and I was like (to myself), "What are you doing? You're messing up my brand." [Laughs].

Sa'id: When was it that you embraced the producer moniker?

Marley Marl: After the success of a few records. Because I started seeing myself in a whole 'nother light.

Sa'id: How so?

Marley Marl: I was a producer! [Laughs] It's funny, cuz I used to work for BLS (WBLS) but Kiss FM was playing all of my shit. That's when it really hit me. I had the longest internship at BLS; it was like a 2-year internship. Already on the air, DJ'ing for Mister Magic. I had worked for Sergio Jeans at that point. And my side hustle was to buy jeans from them at wholesale and sell at a retail price, and that was how I was making money. And I still was on the radio.

Sa'id: You would sell the jeans to regular people?

Marley Marl: Yeah, regular people. People around Queensbridge knew that I worked at Sergio. That's actually how I met Shante (Roxanne Shante), I was selling jeans and she wanted to buy a pair of Sergios off me. That's how I met her, that's how I got acquainted with her on the block, by selling them jeans. I was still working there and I had a record on the radio. And I was starting to get interviews and stuff that pertained to my musical career. And my boss at the jeans company was like, "Look, you're getting hot out there... I'm starting to see interviews with you. I'm starting to hear about you. Do you still really wanna work here?" Then he said, "What I could do, I could lay you off, and say that you made this amount of money. So when you go to unemployment, you'll still be getting what you were getting here. And you should pursue your career, because it looks like it's kicking in for you." I was always the person that said, "Never quit your day job." Because it was at the point when I wasn't getting any money in rap; I wasn't getting no money in producing. I was still doing my internship at BLS, on the air with Magic — but I was on unemployment! So people use to see me on unemployment [on the unemployment line], and be like, "Wasn't I just jammin' to you on the radio?" Cuz my face was already known. It wasn't a paid internship, so I still had to make money. That was like one of the most awkward times in my life. I was rockin' for Mister Magic on the weekends, but finding myself up at unemployment, going to sign for my check on Wednesday.

Sa'id: Describe the social and financial atmosphere of that time, what was going on?
Marley Marl: My financial background was grim... It was GRIM! Crisis [the NYC 1970s fiscal crisis]... [then the] Reagan Years... [When] I had my job at the jean company, I always had some like DJ job at some club. I used to DJ at the local after hours club in Queensbrige. So that kept money for me to buy records, so I could next week DJ with something new. The funny thing was, they [the proprietors of the club] were in the music business. And I would beg and plead to try and go into the studio with them and mix one of their records. They would never let me go into the studio.

Sa'id: Why do you think hip hop, which came from such dire circumstances and poverty, became so dominant.
Marley Marl: It became the alternative. Like I said, the bands were going out. When the groups of the 60s started going out, and the DJs and the rappers started coming in, that was the new. I think the reason why it was accepted so well was because it was different and new. And whatever's different and new and making noise is usually picked up by the masses.

Sa'id: You mentioned several times the bands going out. I remember in the 4th/5th grade it was mandatory to have to take music...
Marley Marl: Yeah, to have to play a trumpet, or something!

Sa'id: But when 7th grade came around, all of that was gone. Was that a situation that happened with you, or were you able to get out of school before the music cuts came?
Marley Marl: I was already out. At my school we had flutes, trumpet, violin. I used to play the violin. I used to play the clarinet. I don't remember nothing now.

Sa'id: How much of a role do you think the cuts in music contributed to the bands dropping out?
Marley Marl: It was a real major factor in people not playing anymore. That was definitely a major factor, because most of the bands that were out, they were teenage guys that had formed bands from around the school thing. That was part of the economy that made rap happen. The economy and what we was in. And people wanted something different. They got tired of the bands. Rap was new, it was different, it was energetic. And there was a lot of non-believers. Believe me, cuz I was a non-believer at first. I was so ANTI-RAP after it got on records. But I was a rap ADVOCATE when it was out on tapes. That was the authentic rap! I just didn't like the way it was done [when it was first on records]. The live bands? I didn't like King Tim

III, I didn't like [the live band-based rap]. I used to hear the 12-minute records and the super rhymes and all this other stuff —[emphatically] IT WASN'T WHAT RAP WAS SUPPOSED TO BE! I hated that [so-called] "rap." Even in the Vapors movie, there's a scene in there, I was reading in the script, and there's a scene in there where I'm in the studio with Magic, and I turn the music down and I'm like, "Yo, why we gotta play this bullshit!" It wasn't a representation of what rap was.

Sa'id: When you look at rap as a whole, what you were doing — and the pioneers before you was doing — is what it would become: which is a focus on rhythm, a beat, and bass. There wasn't so much attention focused on melody. Why was that?
Marley Marl: Cuz I was a beat guy! When I first started sampling, it was the beat. The beat made everybody dance. The beat made everybody like rap! When that beat hit you… ooooh…

Sa'id: Even listening to you describe it, saying "When the beat hit you." Rap is so different than any other music form. Your descriptions right now emphasize that rap had a lot to do with feeling and contact…
Marley Marl: Right!

Sa'id: Now, there's a lot more melody going into rap. Do you think that that's one of the reasons that the quality of rap music has gone down?
Marley Marl: Yeah… I think what's missing is what made the whole genre what it is, which is basically the beat. Once you try to cloud up the music with more melody, it makes it more melodic, and you're taking away from the foundation. Believe me, the whole foundation of hip hop is the beat! You know, break dancing was first — people breakin' and poppin' to the beats. The foundation, that's what carried rap on to this day. If the beat is whack, you're not going to get into the rap. You're not going to hear it, if the beat is not strong. I think what happen is that people took the emphasis *off* of the beat, trying to be more melodic. You can always be melodic, you can always have a melody, you can always have a great bass line, but the beat (the rhythm) is the life of the beat!

Sa'id: Yo, when I first heard "The Symphony," I remember trying to study it from every angle. Then when I saw you in the video, I was like, "Damn, he can play the piano, too. And he knows when to stop." I didn't know anything about sampling and chopping. Then I heard that, "Marley Marl said you have to get break-beats." That's how it was with us, we were all coming up trying to figure out what *you* were doing. I had a little crew, we used to go to Down Stairs records in the City [Manhattan] and get break-beats. And I remember thinking that all I needed to do was this and that. But it didn't sound right. I didn't have ANY concept of sampling! What do samplers do for you?
Marley Marl: Woo… Samplers became my world. Samplers changed my life. From the first mistake I made when I accidentally sampled that snare. The way my face lit up and the way I realized the importance of it. And I realized it before the engineer that I was sitting with. When I told him to sample that, and I walked out of the room and came back, and he hadn't truncated it yet. I hit the keyboard and the snare played first. He didn't realize what was going on. He's the person that put it into the machine.

Sa'id: What sampler was it?
Marley Marl: It was one of those big 'ol Stevie Wonder samplers with the big computer floppy disk. It was a big, mono, 12-bit, keyboard, nasty looking one.

Sa'id: For you, what was the essence of drum programming? What were you trying to achieve?

Marley Marl: What I was trying to achieve? That's funny, cuz like you had mentioned earlier the James Brown era. Funny thing is, I was never in the James Brown era! Everybody THOUGHT I was in the James Brown era. See what I used to do was I used to take the "Impeach the President" kick and snare, and listen to James Brown records, and program it the same as the beat.

Sa'id: Wait, the individual hits?

Marley Marl: Yeah, I used to take the kick, the snare, and the hi-hats. That's why on "Eric B. for President" it goes [demonstrates drum pattern from "Eric B. for President"]. That's supposed to be "Funky President," but I tapped out "Impeach the President" beat to the same pattern as I heard on the record. That's why nobody could ever find the record [they thought I was using]. This is two myths I can clear up right now: I wasn't using no 1200 (E-Mu SP 1200), so anybody who went out there and bought a 1200 cuz they thought I was using it, I WASN'T!

Sa'id: What were you using?

Marley Marl: I had a Roland TR-808 that was triggering off of three separate samplers. You know, I was already an engineer, so the toms, the three toms on the 808, I used to use those to trigger my samples. And that's back in the day when a pulse would trigger a sample. So sound coming from there would trigger my sound over there. I was a brainiac. I was lke, "Hmmm, there's this sampler, and oh, this sampler's got a pulse on it? Boom, give me the sampler with the pulse." Cuz I already knew from working at Unique that the pulse would trigger the sample to go. So when I was putting my rig together, I couldn't afford no Emulator, so I bought the cheap little samplers, the one-shot bullshit. I had a Korg SDD -2 [2000], it had a sampler and digital delay. I had three of those [samplers]. That was important to me to have a sampler with a pulse. So I knew I could use a drum machine and go from there and trigger the samplers. I would put my kick in there and snare in there, and I would [sometimes] use the hi-hat from my drum machine. Now, if I wanted to sample something like [starts imitating the sound] "The Bridge, the, the, the Bridge…" I would put like a chorus in my other sampler. I would just program the 808 and make my tom 1 be the snare. That's why a lot of my earlier productions always had drum rolls in it. That's AUTO FILL on my 808. So at every two bars, it would go back to the AUTO FILL.

Sa'id: Were you printing [assigning] all of this through your 12-channel mixer?

Marley Marl: Yep, going through my 12-channel mixer into my 4-track. Putting kick and my snare. I was a frequency dude, so I knew what frequencies could work with each other. So in the middle frequencies, I would put the snare and the hi-hat on one track, under the same frequency, so I could EQ those in there. Then, I'd put my kick and my bass line in the same channel [on one track]. For a lot of those 4-track records I made back in the day, that's how I did it. I put the same frequencies on the same track. And that's how I made my beats. Any drum rolls or fills would come up on the snare track.

Sa'id: Being that you were an engineer, I assume other engineers were telling you that you were breaking the rules?

Marley Marl: Right… Right… I was [breaking all the rules]… I was right in my living room. Matter fact, this is what happened. I noticed other engineers was picking up my stuff at the studio — seeing what I was doing. So I stopped going to Unique. I started noticing engineers looking at what I was doing; now I'm hearing records coming out with other engineers, you know, with people trying to take a sampled snare, like from [the group] Art of Noise or something. So I was starting to hear that and I was like, "Oh, everybody's biting what I'm doing." Cuz before I started doing that, you have to think about that, it was just Linn Drums, DMX drums and all of that; those were just regular [drum machine] drum sounds. Those [sounds] was the foundation of those [machines] but they weren't really the shit! And that's why I was like, "Oh, let me get 'Impeach the President.'" I remember I had an assistant, he used to work with me. He actually was security, working with me back in the days. His name was Claudio. He was like, "Yo…" He saw me getting into my sampling, I was sampling all of these other drums, and he was like, "Yo, you know what's dope? I notice every time you play that 'Impeach the President' record at a party, it gets the party jumping. You should fuck with THOSE sounds." I was like, "Yo, You're right!" I went and got that and sampled it out. I made so many records off of that kick and that snare. Then I would take those sounds and listen to my James Brown records. The premise of me sampling was to make my own beats, my own "sounding" beats, my own patterns of records.

Sa'id: When you were sampling your drum sounds, were you sampling them dry or with effects?
Marley Marl: Nawgh, I was sampling them straight dry, no effects. I had bullshit mono samplers, so it was like a mono sound. It was nasty, it was a 4-track, it was ashy… oooh it was so scratchy and nice.

Sa'id: When you finally switched your rig, what did you switch to?
Marley Marl: I tried to get an SP-12, I tried to use it, but there wasn't enough sampling time so I put that back on the side. Then they came out with the SP-1200; still wasn't enough sampling time for me. I was used to my 4 seconds on each of my other samplers. And my rule was to never sample too much. My rule was to get snippets, pieces, fractions of seconds cuz that's all the time I had to work with. My rule was to not sample too far, to just get little segments and seconds of snippets and manipulate it into my own pattern. That's what I told the engineer as soon we did it, I was like, "Yo, you know what this means, I can take kicks and snares from records and make my own patterns." He's looking at me like, "What, what do you mean?" He didn't get it! I went home that day, DJ'd, made some money, and I went back to Sam Ash and asked them "Which samplers do you have?" They said they had a digital delay sampler, so I was like, give me that. That was that Korg SDD.

Sa'id: After that what did you switch to.
Marley Marl: At that time, Akai came out. I got an Akai S900. Somebody showed me how to break down the samples in there on the keyboards. I was using that for a minute. Then when the MPC 60 came out, the first one, I had my Akai S900 with my MPC 60. My engineer at that point…I was already making money at that point, so I started taking engineers from Unique, "Come work with me up at my crib."

Sa'id: Were you still living in Queensbridge at this time?
Marley Marl: Nawgh, by that point I had already moved upstate [upstate New York]. I moved upstate in '88. By then, you know, I had bought a console [mixing console] for my crib. I bought a 2-inch machine. I put like a real full blown studio in my house upstate, when I first moved up there. I wanted my house like Unique, and I actually had a room built just like that one [at Unique]. Yeah, it had the sliding door in the front, vocal booth over there. Monitors up there, speakers in the wall. I had somebody come and build me a smaller version of the same…replica of that room.

Sa'id: So did you rock out with the MPC 60 and the S900 till this day?
Marley Marl: I rocked with that, then I got an Akai S950. Then I got an Akai S1000, once it got stereo. Along the way, I started using my Akai rack. When the '90s came in, I was fucking with Akai. Akai all the way up until…'95…I moved up to the Akai MPC 60 II; I became an Akai person. As they started coming out with stuff, I started believing in what they were doing.

Everything they came out with. That became my primary sampler! The whole Akai rack. I had the S900, the S950, the S1000, I had EVERYTHING in my rack. Whenever I had to go to the studio, I would just have them cart my rack to the studio. I started getting bored with producing after '95. Because my brain wanted to do things that the equipment couldn't do.

Sa'id: Such things as what?
Marley Marl: My brain would hear things, you know beats that I wanted faster, but it was already locked to that speed. I was way, way ahead of the technology [at the time] in my brain.

Sa'id: As a *beatmaker/producer*, you started the most notorious crew ever. People can say what they want, but there will never be another crew of the magnitude of the Juice Crew All Stars. It was like putting together a basketball team with the best skill players of the time — all in their prime!
Marley Marl: Dream Team!

Sa'id: Dream Team [First USA Olympic Mens Basketball "Dream Team"] don't even compare, because a couple of the players were on that team because they had earned it, but they weren't in their prime. So as far as some of the crucial building blocks of modern MC'ing, you had Kool G Rap and Big Daddy Kane in the *same* crew! How did the Juice Crew All Stars come about?
Marley Marl: [the] Dimples D [record] that was the first record I ever made. After Dimples D what happened, and this was even before I met Magic, I was already…me and Andre had went and produced Dimples D, the "Sucker DJs" song. Me and her [Dimples D] started doing shows. But this was when I had met Magic. One day I had a show with Dimples and I ain't have no manager. And Tyrone was working at LIB [WLIB] doing some board stuff. He was like a straight nobody. I used to see him at the station all the time. I knew he was a college guy, so I was like, "Yo, Tyrone, I got a show in Baltimore and I don't have a manager. Would you mind coming out there with me?" And he was like [imitating in an indifferent voice], "O.K., I'll come." So you know we go out there. It was me, him, Magic and Dimples, we was on the train going out to Baltimore. And Magic was being *Mister Magic* (laughs), making Dimples not like him. You know, being so arrogant. And she was like, "You know, I don't think I wanna do this rap shit, if people are like him." You know what I'm sayin', cuz he was really rude to her. She didn't like him, and that's when she…After that trip she was like, "Look, my parents are talking that I should go to college… I don't know about this rap stuff." So I needed another MC. Because I did that song and we was already doing some tours, and I had gotten a taste of the light. I kind of liked going to other states and DJ'ing for somebody MC'ing, with like 2,000 people screaming, that's dope to me. At that point that's when I met Shanté [Roxanne Shanté] on the block. I remembered that there used to ALWAYS be rhyme ciphers on my block. I used to always see a crowd, you would think it was a fight, but it wasn't a fight. It was people rhymin'; battlin'. And Shanté used to always take everybody out. I remember I'd be standing over there, and she'd straight take people out. That's when we made the "Roxanne" record; and the Juice Crew started from Shanté! It actually started from Dimples quitting. And then Shanté was the first member that I got. Then, Shan and Shanté used to always win on the block. Later on I met Shan, and he hit with a Marley rhyme, a Marley scratch rhyme; it was written on tissue. And after that, I met Biz hangin' out in Queensbridge. He was impressing everybody with his beat-box skills, then everybody brought him to my house. I met Kane through Biz, cuz Kane was writing his rhymes on the low.

Sa'id: Writing Biz's rhymes?
Marley Marl: Yeah, writing Biz's rhymes on the low. But nobody really knew. Cuz I knew Biz was a great beat-boxer, but I was like, Where you getting these rhymes from? I met Kool G

Rap through Polo. Polo used to go to school with me, and I remembered he was one of the DJs in the area. He used to be in the after hours club; we was in like an after hours club network. Polo told me that he had an MC that was dope, which was G. Rap. Masta Ace (from Brooklyn) had won a contest at USA.

Sa'id: At the roller skating rink?
Marley Marl: Yeah, USA Roller Skating Rink. Craig G., his brother, used to be in the Sure Shot group. Craig was always trying to tell me that he rhymed. Masta Ace beat Super Lover Cee. Super Lover Cee came in 2nd place. DNA took Super Lover Cee, and I took Ace.

Sa'id: Do you think how you as a DJ/beatmaker/producer putting a crew together is still a viable way to success?
Marley Marl: It's viable right now, *IF* everybody's talented! Cuz what seems to have happened throughout [these last] years, putting a crew together became putting a crew of untalented people together, with maybe one talent. That's not how we did it. Everybody was able to stand on their own. You had to be able to rock the crowd on your own! What happens these days.... I think the next crew after the Juice Crew era...the only crew that was able to sustain and had [individual] talent was Wu Tang. Everybody from Wu Tang was able to stand on their own, as a single artist and *within* the crew.

Sa'id: Wu Tang patterned everything that they did after Juice Crew.
Marley Marl: Yeah, because RZA used to be signed to Cold Chillin'. He was in the building: Prince Rakim [RZA's forme rap name]... "We Love You Rakim."... He watched [smiles].

Sa'id: At Cold Chillin', you had say [creative control, power, influence]. I've always said that if you put music people in executive positions, you'll have better music and a better label situation.
Marley Marl: Right! Oh, yeah. Oh, yeah. Why Jay-Z failed up at Def Jam is because he's not a "music" man, he's a lyrical man. O.K., you can write lyrics, BUT, you have to RELY on people to bring you music. You have to rely on people bringing you the shit. Somebody like Jermaine Dupri, he can go make the shit. He can sit there and be like, "Oh, this is what everybody's liking right now? I'm up in the lab!" And he'll be right there with it. That's why consistently, he keeps coming out with songs that make you dance. His stuff always does well because he's a music guy. He knows how to go in there with his hands and create; as opposed to waiting for somebody to give you songs or that hit. Even as a DJ that's why I think I sustained so long as being a DJ, cuz I do remixes. I don't have to rely on looking in my email or having somebody coming to me with shit. NO! I can sit there and be like, Oh, this worked last week? Let me go in the lab and cook this up.

Sa'id: Yeah, you were doing remixes heavy. But you were doing them before the Pro Tools era. With Pro Tools and the like, anybody today can do a remix.
Marley Marl: Yeah, you can do 'em on Garage Band.

Sa'id: How were you doing remixes then? A lot of people often rate the "Marley Marl Remix" better than the original song.
Marley Marl: I was able to do remixes from my training with fucking with the bands from earlier; as opposed to people doing blends, where they happen to take an instrumental that somebody made and all this stuff. I was able to go grab my musician friends, get the a cappella of a song, and be like, Here let's go remix it. That's how I was able to sustain the test of time. Basically by my training earlier. That's how I was able to sustain later on. I used to do a damn remix every week. When I was working at BLS [WBLS] every song on their rotation was one

of my remixes. That came from the training of my internship at Unique…that came from the training of learning how to EQ my band friends from the neighborhood. I would get the vocals [a cappella] off of the records, then I would just make my own tracks. It's different being that person who can make what you need; as opposed to that person sitting back waiting and relying on somebody to bring you what you need. I was that hands-on person. That's what makes me real.

Sa'id: How would you actually take the vocals and use them?
Marley Marl: I would sample the vocals one verse at a time, then put them back into the track.

Sa'id: What was the most difficult business situation you ever had to go through?
Marley Marl: It was actually two. My first was leaving Cold Chillin'. That was pretty difficult, because when I left Cold Chillin', my last, very, last, last song I made with them was "Just A Friend." I made the song at my crib, recorded Biz Markie, erased out…I didn't have automation, so I erased out where the beat wasn't never suppose to play, like in the beginning when he sings, and then the beat drops, I had to erase the beat. So you know wherever the beat dropped in the song, I erased it. We had "ghetto automation;" just erased what we didn't want and it will never play [Laughs]. It was a little nerve-wracking when you missed it, so you had to pay attention. I think my hardest thing was leaving that label and not getting credit for that hit. You know, they gave the credit to Biz Markie, cuz I was leaving the label. I guessed they didn't wanna promote me anymore. That was kind of hard for me… BUT the upside to that was, I didn't give them a track that became "Jingling Baby!" By me not giving him that track and giving it to LL [LL Cool J], that made my career explode on another level, somewhere else.

Sa'id: Let me say this. Now, people say that Run-DMC really put rap on the map. I don't necessarily disagree with it. But that LL Cool J *Mama Said Knock You Out* blew it open for everybody!
Marley Marl: Right.

Sa'id: And it's very telling that LL came to you for that! "Jingling Baby" was crazy… A hard song that people could dance to… You knew what you were trying to do with that track?
Marley Marl: Yeah, actually, that track was Biz's track. It was for that album that "Just a Friend" was on. But when that happen to me, and I let them hold the 2-inch so they could do the vocals over at Power Play. And then for some reason, I never got the 2-inch back. Then I'm hearing this song on the radio that I know I produced. I didn't give him that other beat. Then when LL came, I had it in the back of my brain that I had a hit beat. I knew it was a hit. Once I put that together and orchestrated it, I knew we was gonna make history. The funny thing, even with LL, I didn't do nothing extra special for LL that I wasn't doing for the Juice Crew. It was kind of like the same thing. But since Cold Chillin' was over here, we was trying to prove ourselves. We wasn't down with Russell and them [Def Jam]. Here, I had the "golden boy" [LL Cool J]. And they had a bigger machine, so they were able to take my work much further. So it made it look like, BOOM, like I did this [big thing] for LL. But I was doing that all the time, anyway, you know that. Anybody that's followed my career. The beats on *Mama Said Knock You Out* were Juice Crew beats. That was LL in Juice Crew mode. And we was separated from Russell at that point. The funny thing about that LL album is, Russell told LL don't fuck with me. [Imitating Russell Simmons] "Don't fuck with Marley. We don't fuck with him! He's over there…" But LL heard that shit and was like, "Yo, I don't know what you talkin' about, holmes… This beat got the f-dunk!… You want me to go in there with Rick Rubin, and me and Rick Rubin just made an album…" *The Walking With A Panther* album. He came to my BLS show and I was like saying in my mind, "That shit is garbage, it's whack!" But there was one record that stuck out to me. There was a record where he said, *"Running over niggas like a redneck trucker."* That was the original "Jingling Baby" for that album. And I said, "Yo, that track, that record is dope,

you need to let me remix THAT." And you know, he gave me a shot, he gave me a shot to remix it. And when I hit him back with it. That ONE remix created the whole next album. He went to Russell like, "Boom, look what Marley did!" But Russell was still on, "We don't fuck with Marley." But you know, the single came out and it did what it did. But LL was on some other shit, "Yo, fuck that…" LL was coming to my house everyday, "Yo, let's make an ALBUM!" [LL said] I wasn't even thinking about getting paid, I didn't give a fuck about it at first. I had something to prove to these guys over here, that LL needs to be fucking with me. So we went and did the whole album on the side. They still had him going in the studio, fucking with other producers and all this other shit. But he would come to my house in the evenings and we'd knock out like one or two joints [songs]. Boom, and he'd go back to the city. We was knockin' out JOINTS! [songs] Them shits was crazy!

Sa'id: How many of your joints actually made the album?
Marley Marl: Oh, I did the whole album! THE WHOLE ALBUM!

Sa'id: They credited you for the whole album?
Marley Marl: Yeah.

Sa'id: That's right, that's how you caught the Grammy!
Marley Marl: Right, right… But that was a gift and a curse. The gift was, I was able to show the world my production skills and how sharp I was getting *after* the Cold Chillin' years, because after I left Cold Chillin', I was supposed to be straight over, done, done with, you know, as far as their eyes. But the gift was that I was able to show the world that I was still here. The curse was that Russell [Simmons] Didn't want him [LL Cool J] to fuck with me. And that curse followed me all to this day. Because now we had a very successful album. That's the biggest album that Def Jam ever put out in they whole career. Yes, I was down with the other people, not down with ya'll [Def Jam] so I was kind of like…being down with Cold Chillin', being down with the Juice Crew was their enemies. So that's when all the bullshit started. When we made "Boomin' Systems," the promotion department over at Def Jam was like, "Yo, that's a hit. That's the shit!" And Russell was like, "No, uh, I don't get it." He was so anti… You now how it goes in business. The nigga wasn't down with us, so [he's like] I'm not feelin' nothin' he do. If a nigga invented the Ferris wheel, and motherfuckers was riding on it, screaming, having fun, Russell would be like, "I don't give a fuck, I don't like that bastard, fuck that shit." [Laughs]. That was Russell's stance, "I don't give a fuck, I'm not feelin' [it/him]" And everybody was like, "You are BUGGIN', THIS IS A HIT!" And it was, right after "Jinglin' Baby." He didn't like us. He spited us by putting it out. He was like, "I'm-a put it out and show ya'll that it ain't shit." [Laughs] Because it wasn't that "rock n' roll" hip hop he was doing with his partner Rick Rubin, his partner, you know what I'm sayin'. This was something totally opposite, this was some street shit. This ain't rock 'n' roll hip hop! This IS SOME STREET BOOM BAP SHIT!

Sa'id: What led to you leaving Cold Chillin'?
Marley Marl: One year I did… I think I did four albums in one year. And my salary was only $200,000 a year. So in my mind, I was like, I'm only getting $50,000 for each album I'm doing. HELL NO. I was like, I had to get up outta here.

Sa'id: Cold Chillin' was killin' it with album sales…
Marley Marl: Oh, Yeah… When I finally left and got some of their paper work and saw the kind of money THEY was making, I was like, come on man, NEVER AGAIN… But back to the Russell thing, he didn't want LL to fuck with me, so he spited us by putting it ["Boomin' Systems"] out. And it did well, it blew up in his face. That put LL back on the map. And they HAD to do a video. That's why the video was so cheesy, they had to just rush a video out real

quick, right. So they did that... and LL goes up to Def Jam and plays them the stuff we been doing. [LL was like] "Yo, I got an album done with Marley already." [They was like] "What!" So really that album was a piggy back off of that successful single. Russell was still like, "No, that's not the shit!" all the way down to the last... But then the promotion guy got "Around the Way Girl" [another single that would be on the album], and was like, "Yo, this is a SMASH! What are you talking about!" And Russell fought it... He fought it all the way to Grammy day... He fought it all the way to it come time for me to get paid. Then that motherfucker jerked my shit, and never gave me my money to this day. Cuz he was so against it... He was so against LL fucking with me, cuz I wasn't in his camp. He wasn't managing me... [so then] he was sending out people trying to manage me, and I was like, No! In a sense, he fucked me over ROYALY!!! Those are my two fuck ups — the two most heart-aching things that ever happened to me in my life. Two of my greatest successes, making "Just A Friend" and not getting credit, and working with LL and helping him grow up, and the President of the company wasn't in my corner. And they [Def Jam] was doing so bad at that point. They were about to lose their deal. LL's album put new fire in them like they had the answer. "Boomin' System" went platinum, I got the plaque at the crib. [Marl speaking to Def Jam at that time] "Ya'll artist went platinum off of a street record, and ya'll thought it was the rock way!" And I defied what they did, and made them look like they was the shit. Now [meaning at that time] Columbia [Columbia Records] throwing all this money at them. Russell's giving everybody labels, but I didn't have a label. It was because of me ya'll [Def Jam] got that budget. Ya'll was about to lose your fucking deal. Public Enemy wasn't even doing good. LL was they're last stand. And it blew up for ya'll. But everybody got a label up there, except for me.

Sa'id: You never sat down with Russell and spoke about that?
Marley Marl: He never wanted to sit with me. At that point, he become a little a nervous of me... Still to this day... He's not comfortable in the same room with me... Still to this day. Cuz he don't know...what I'm thinking about... He don't know what I know. He don't know that I'm smarter...as I backtrack... I got royally fucked! You know there's no one man that made the WHOLE album that sold 8 million [copies]. People be on one album that sells 1 million [copies]... You got people that got one or two songs on an album that sells 2 million [copies], they own cribs.

Sa'id: So you were never able to go straighten that out?
Marley Marl: It was some bullshit; lawyer bullshit. Every lawyer that you get, you know...they [Def Jam] have such a monopoly where they'll [Def Jam] hire somebody else from that law firm to do some other dumb shit for them. And makes your shit look like... it becomes a conflict of interest, so you can't get shit done... it gets locked!

Sa'id: You never really tried again, cuz even if you were getting your mechanicals; just the 5 cents for each joint...
Marley Marl: Yeah, I know, that would've been nice! But they threw so much shit up in the game... That's the downside of the music business. It's hard to fight "City Hall." You know what the lawyer told me... there's a fund out there where... See, my whole deal with Def Jam, from the gate, was a little funky. Cuz the main lawyer that worked for Def Jam, the year he broke out from Def Jam, he started working for me. After that success, he broke out of Def Jam. So in Def Jam's eyes, it's like I took him from them. But what became the conflict was, how can this guy do your contract but was working here? It was funky from the gate. So I think to save his ass, he threw some bullshit up in the game — the lawyer, cuz I wasn't fucking with him no more. And that one lawyer told me that there was a fund where lawyers sit there and split my money, EVERY royalty! Every royalty period, they would go and get my money and it's not coming my way. You know it's people protecting their licenses, protecting their livelihood, you

know, it's kind of fucked up. And that's why around '95, I got fed up with producing. Look, I'm here, at the time, I produced a 6, 7 million seller! I outsold everybody in the music industry [at the time] by doing the whole album. How am I pigeon-holed? How I can't get a deal? How Russell's influence doesn't let me get no where?

Sa'id: What makes sampling an art form rather than a simple case of thievery?
Marley Marl: The creativity of it is the art form. Cuz believe me, Puffy [Diddy] was not creative when he fucked up sampling in the '90s…the way he took certain old songs, certain instrumentals…the way he did it, he stunk up sampling; he gave sampling a bad name. After that point, if you were a sampler, people looked at you as a joke. You know that was bad for the Premiers, for the… EZ Mo Bees…it was bad for us. He gave sampling a bad rap, because of the un-creativeness of how he used it. The real samplers, we was creative with it. We took things, changed the note, chopped it up, made our own beats, made our own patterns or did our own thing.

Sa'id: So when you were doing all those things on Cold Chillin' before you left, did they clear all of those things?
Marley Marl: Nope. That was the wild west.

Sa'id: What's your [fundamental] take on the music business?
Marley Marl: This business…to me I look at it like, blocking out the real. The real dudes in the industry ain't really making it as they should. Even with Jay-Z and Premier. I put Jay-Z on the spot. He was at Power 105… I was a fan of Jay-Z and Premier together. Jay-Z was on the radio talking about how his new album was all dope; and they're playing songs. I called up, like, Jay, I like your album, it's going in the right direction, but you're better than that. He got quiet. I've been a fan since day one, I seen your career go, I've been a producer… And he was like, "If you ain't like the way my album was going, why you ain't send me beats?" Come on, duke, you're the President [of the Def Jam label], you're not taking people calls on my level; even though you should be. I'm like, Come on man, where the Primo [DJ Premier] beats? You and Primo make magic together. You're playing Primo instrumentals from your other albums in the background, making ya'll sound hot talking about your new album…

Sa'id: How did you first get an 808 machine?
Marley Marl: That was off my Dimples D, off my first record I went and bought and 808.

Sa'id: Didn't the 808 cost a lot?
Marley Marl: Mine cost $650, I remember… I bought it…it was the drum machine that I used to see at Unique. That's why I bought an 808…I was like, Yo, I gotta get that. I brought the bass to Miami… I was with my 808 drum machine… I used to be on tour with Shanté; this before Miami had bass! Me and Shanté was doing a show for Luke and Ghetto Style DJs, before he even had 2 Live Crew; this before they… this before they even started their sound! There was no 808s out there. There was not. What I did, I brought my 808 to a show, cuz I used to play live beats while she rhymed. I went up there with my 808, and was [imitates sounds] BOOM… Everybody ran over to the booth like, "What is THAT?" Right away, people was like, "What is that?" I was like, "it's the 808." I brought the bass to Miami… This before these niggas even had the bass. At a Ghetto Style DJs show. Even do the research…bass didn't start hitting them until '85…'84/'83… I brought the bass to Miami.

Sa'id: How did the movie, *The Vapors*, come about?
Marley Marl: The movie came about because, basically, I was tired of seeing rap award shows, and things that's giving props…all types of shows that's given props to people that was in hip

hop... I've yet to see, other than Kane being in *Hip Hop Honors* — that was cool, but I've yet to see anybody mention the Juice Crew — like we didn't exist. I'm like, "Hold on..." We helped shape this into what it is — the crews, the R&B hip hop, the sampling; there's like so much that came from what we started, and I've never seen nobody representing us in nothing. And I started realizing, these shows are what go down in history. These shows are what people are gonna watch ten years later, 15, 20 years later, and do their research on how hip hop was. So I was tired of getting slighted. Like we didn't make ya'll niggas go out there and make better records. [Laughs]. Like we wasn't the blue print...like You, Russell, wasn't in the studio screaming at Doctor Dre [the New York Doctor Dre, not famed producer Dr. Dre], cuz he told me — screaming at Doctor Dre: "What? You can't make records like Marley Marl? This motherfucker is in the fucking living room playing with $100 equipment; ya'll in a million dollar studio, this motherfucker's making better records than ya'll?" You know, he used to tell me that's what Russell used to say to him. When Russell used to be in there cracking the whip on 'em, trying to make them make better records. So you're trying to tell me that we weren't influential enough to get an honorable mention or anything at none of the shows? So I started feeling like this: History is slipping by us. Because these shows are references for the people later on! And I know I was relevant; I know I changed hip hop. I know we had the dopest crew in hip hop history. Why nobody's mentioning that? We're getting *lost* in history. So my way of us not getting lost in history...I can't rely on the haters to pump us. I can't rely on the people that blacklisted us out of the business to promote what we did. There has to be a way. O.K., let's make a movie, stating what we did. What's a better title than *Vapors*? Make motherfuckers catch the vapors. That's the whole thing: Catch "the vapors" again. So that was my whole premise of putting it together. So I got with Biz and Kane, you know the two biggest stars from the Juice Crew era. I was the producer, Kane was the big star, and Biz...We was the top three of the whole crew. So I got with them and started expressing it...People pitted us against each other, and that's fucking up our history. It's strength in numbers...we need to get together and do something big. So we got together, and that's basically where it came from.

Sa'id: So did you reach out to a film producer and director?
Marley Marl: Basically, how it happened for me, I was scoring Wendy's [Wendy Williams] movie, cuz you know, I got into scoring. So basically what happened was, I was telling the director about that, I was like. Yo, I got an idea... I have a title first... a title of a movie called *Vapors*. I told him what it's about, and he was like, "Yo, that's dope. Why don't you let me do that movie. So I gave him a shot. I'm like that, you know how some people are haters and don't wanna give people a shot and all of that. I gave him a shot.

Sa'id: So he wrote the script with you?
Marley Marl: Yeah, well, basically, we sat with him, told him a few things that happened; funny things, sad things, real life story stuff.

Sa'id: How are you going to be officially affiliated with the film project?
Marley Marl: I'm executive producing it; of course, I'm scoring the track, you know, scoring the movie.

Sa'id: How did you get into scoring?
Marley Marl: It was a natural progression. It's something that I always wanted to do. I always wanted to score movies or do music for commercials. I always wanted to do that. And then technology; right now, technology made it feasible for me. Because you know, Pro Tools...Pro Tools is great for scoring movies. Pro Tools is like the wonder drug... you can put the movie in Pro Tools. And then you just put your sounds and waves up against the movie, where you want it to start and end. Just drop the movie in Pro Tools. You'll see your movie on the screen

but you'll have your wave screen, too; you got two screens. That is my future. My future's not producing songs; it's not being on the radio. My future is films.

Sa'id: What makes a song a "Future Flavor?"
Marley Marl: Um, Great… What makes a song a Future Flavor? Future Flavors, of course, the history of it, as you know, we started it at Hot 97, back in the day, me and Pete Rock. And the whole premise of Future Flavors was New York underground hip hop. And that's what makes a song a Future Flavor. We're not looking for bounce tracks. We not looking for nothing out of the region; it's regional music. And what makes Future Flavors "future flavors" is, while everybody went bounced out and started all types of other genres and intertwined with the music scene, Future Flavor keeps it New York. So what makes a song a Future Flavors song? Tri-State underground hip hop. Which is seeming to come back in… We stayed in it. I didn't go bounce, I never went left, I just kept right there. And people looking at us like we're crazy. No, that's New York music.

BUCKWILD

Buckwild burst on the scene in 1994, during the tail-end of hip hop/rap's second Golden era, with the song "Time's Up," O.C.s wake-up call to the hip hoppers who had strayed far away from the essence of rap music. Over the next 11 years, Buckwild produced some of the most memorable and well-known rap songs of all time. From O.C. to Nas, from The Game to 50 Cent, from Faith to Black Rob, all of Buckwild's beats always stayed true to his sound and, more importantly, his love for hip hop/rap music. His comprehensive grasp of hip hop/rap music and the hip hop/rap production movement is first rate.

Notable Credits: "Time's Up" – O.C.; "These Are Our Heroes" – Nas; "Whoa"- Black Rob; "I Don't Need 'Em" – 50 Cent; "I Got a Story to Tell" – The Notorious B.I.G.; "Lucky Me" – Jay-Z; "Like Father Like Son" – The Game

Buckwild's Setup: Akai MPC 4000, Akai S6000, Yamaha Motif 6, Pro Tools TDM running on an Apple Mac G5.

Sa'id: When did you first come to the Bronx and where in the Bronx were you at?
Buckwild: When? When I was like 4… [before that] I lived in Manhattan. We was on 141st Street and Cypress. Then from there, we moved to 138th, between St. Ann and Cypress.

Sa'id: What was your family life like when you moved to the Bronx?
Buckwild: How can I put it, you know, single mom, brothers, sisters. I was the youngest. I had five brothers and sisters; two brothers and three sisters.

Sa'id: What type of kid were you when you were coming up?
Buckwild: Well, I could never say I was a street kid. I mean, I was a little rebellious, here and there, you know, but I was always was into music. Music was always in the house. Everybody says that, you know, but it's a difference. I think my type of music in the house was different from everybody else.

Sa'id: How so?
Buckwild: When I first wanted to start DJ'ing, taking the records that we had in the house. We had like, The Meters in the house. So even hearing my brother and them who had the hand clap song and all that other stuff like that, "Devil's Gun," all that other stuff. We had a variety.

Sa'id: Who brought The Meters and all that other stuff into the crib?
Buckwild: My sisters. My sisters had wild [a lot of] records.

Sa'id: How much older were your sisters than you?
Buckwild: Oh, they're way older than me.

Sa'id: That time was the tail end of the Street Gang era in the Bronx.
Buckwild: Yeah, I don't think it was that. I think it was people bought records for what they like. You could tell people's taste in music. Like, one of my sisters used to listen to the Beatles. So it's like, when you have all these different types of music just around, it's like— people always tell me that I have an ill [great] sampling ear. But it's like, put in you from that. If this is what you're used to, then the type of music that you really— you can listen to something differently than anybody else.

Sa'id: Were your sisters and brothers the ones that put you on to that music?
Buckwild: Nawgh, it was just in the house. Then growing up on the block, you know, every young dude wanted to be a DJ. So me, and a couple of dudes on the block, we used to DJ. We put shit together. We ain't have Technics, but we'd take some ol' school turntables, take off the spindle, and break off a pencil and put it in the middle and use the balance to cut back and forth.

Sa'id: How were you in school, what kind of student were you?
Buckwild: I was always smart. I used to get bored with school. As I got older, I did dumb shit cuz I got bored with school. I excelled in every subject.

Sa'id: How did you get into DJ'ing?
Buckwild: It was the thing to do. It's like a fad, when you see everybody is into it, and it seems like the cool thing to do, you know. And if you already like music, DJ'ing is just the next step.

Sa'id: Who did you directly see that influenced you the most in DJ'ing?
Buckwild: I won't *say who did I see,* or what did I hear. Really, I used to always hear the jams in the park from my window. When you hear the jams in the park and you're too young to be there, it's a whole 'nother element. I used to try to tape 'em — the music from the jams — from my window. I would put the ol' school radio on the window and I would try to tape what I could. And you know, as a kid, if you already have that fascination…I was hungry for it.

Sa'id: How did you get the name Buckwild?
Buckwild: From my man, Joe Sets, my man, Joe. But that's later. I DJ'ed, I got bored with DJ'ing, did dumb shit, then got back into to DJ'ing.

Sa'id: You first started DJ'ing when you were 14, 15 or what age?
Buckwild: Nawgh, nawgh, I was like 8! I told you, I had the box in the window! [Laughs]

Sa'id: So at 8, what DJ did you have a close eye on?
Buckwild: You mean like Flash [Grand Master Flash] and them?

Sa'id: You was into Flash when you were 8?
Buckwild: You gotta remember, when you're coming up. Right now it is a different mentality. Some people are fascinated by it early. Most people, they wait till they get older and they see the money in it. We came into it when it was just the love. You know, you weren't looking at it like, "Yo, I'm going to get paid from this." It was just, "Wow, I like that!" I got into DJ'ing because it was something that I liked doing.

Sa'id: So when was it that you got heavy into DJ'ing?
Buckwild: Ever since I first started. I died for turntables until a couple years later. Then my moms bought me a couple of B-10s. That was a Christmas gift! That was that, and it went from there.

Sa'id: What were your skills like, were you more into blending or scratching?
Buckwild: Nawgh, I was into cuttin'! I could cut, I could blend, I could do whatever. I can't cut like Raider [DJ Roc Raider] and them, but I can cut.

Sa'id: How soon after that was it before you made your name as a DJ?
Buckwild: That was in the early 90s. I was in the neighborhood, I was known for DJ'ing. Everybody knew me; cuz like, when you a young dude, and all the other dudes are 15, 16, 17, and you barely hitting 10, everybody want you down with them. I used to DJ on the milk crates, I used to stand on the milk crate and DJ.

Sa'id: Did you ever shoot for the regular club look or something bigger?
Buckwild: Nawgh, I wasn't really thinking of that. It's how you look at it. Like, say all the dudes who were really there, like Flash, Theodore [Grand Master Theodore]. I don't think they were like, "Yo, we gonna make this and this is going to be the biggest business." It was just something that they probably liked to do. Like a lot of people who were DJ'ing who I was cool with. We just did it cuz it was crazy fun. Number two: While people were doing, you know, *negative things* on the block, we were doing something constructive. It keeps you off the street.

Sa'id: Tell me about the lessons you learned from DJ'ing that you incorporated into beatmaking, which helped you become a better producer.
Buckwild: Really, the appreciation of the music, the records. Back in the early days of DJ'ing, every DJ was known by the breaks they had. Same thing with production. Producers would have their own sound, their own originality. And I think later on, after those doors was broken, you know, when hip hop started turning into "pop-rap," it was more like, "O.K., cool, well, if he used that record I can use it, too." And then he can use it, and he can use it, and it does matter, and then to the consumer it's nothing special.

Sa'id: When did that unwritten rule of not using the same record that somebody else used break down?
Buckwild: The late 90s. You gotta remember, going into Tribe (A Tribe Called Quest), like sometimes with certain dudes, you would have a couple people that would use the same record, but it was not intentional. Like "Soul Clap" and Cypress Hill. I think Cypress Hill used the same James Brown thing Show and them (Showbiz & AG) used. I don't think that they set out to do that. Also, when Cypress Hill and Tribe used the same Grant Green record, it's not like they were all in the studio. You know, people would dig to find new breaks. That's the thing about hip hop, what makes it evolve is when you keep bringing something new into it. And based on it being from DJ'ing, you know, cutting the break back and forth, that's what keeps it going. So right now, you could say its lifeline is dying because people aren't really into that.

Sa'id: What did DJ'ing specifically help you to understand more about making beats?
Buckwild: Number one: The break and what you could put with it, how you can enhance it. As a DJ, when you're DJ'ing for a dude to rhyme, you're cuttin' that one part back and forth. It may be a break that's a little long, you may be like, "Cool, I can scratch this in, and throw this in while he's rhyming, and then take this and keep going back and forth." Or you could be like, "Yo, we could use three turntables," which really is the evolution of mixing.

Sa'id: When a lot of people try to describe what you're saying, they always use the word "loop." People with a DJ background say "break." For people that really don't understand that when you say "a loop," what you're not talking about is that a *break* is a specific section; that it denotes something else.
Buckwild: Yeah, exactly. It could be the part that you just like to cut, the best part of the record that you could have a dude rap on.

Sa'id: In your words, describe what a break is.
Buckwild: All right, take "Hand Clapping Song," it goes into just a kick, snare and hand claps. You can have that, or you might have a song that's...you might have a song like, "Funky President," that's just a kick, snare and a guitar. It's different things; it's the part of the record where, musically, certain things (instruments) are dropped out and other things are featured.

Sa'id: Did breaks encourage you to start going around a whole song looking for other sections?
Buckwild: Yeah. Just knowing that. That's the musical appreciation. Listening to a whole record. You're always looking for the Holy Grail, the ultimate beat. Looking for the ultimate beat, that's what I think kept hip hop alive. When you heard all of these great records that came out. Like when you heard Public Enemy, EPMD, then you heard A Tribe Called Quest, Mobb Deep. When people heard "Shook Ones" [by Mobb Deep], people were like, "Damn, what did they use?" That's what hip hop is, hip hop is a part of that. Most people's misconception is when you don't live in New York, cuz like when you first heard "Rapper's Delight," that's your first insight into hip hop. Because you hear people rhymin' off a [live] sample of "Good Times." So imagine, people were like, "Wow, this is funky, dudes rhymin' over some live stuff." While in New York, we was down with the greatness. That's a part of New York hip hop culture.

Sa'id: People sometimes incorrectly think that when you sit down to make a beat that that's all you do. They forget the part about actually listening to music.
Buckwild: You have to!!! Creatively, if I'm doing a beat, competitive wise, you have to bring your best forward. If you sit down and you get a record and you just listen to whatever's at the beginning— I mean whatever's at the beginning, it might be hot, but in the latter part of the record there may be a hotter part. In New York, we have a record shop called Sound Library, which I call the McDonald's of record shops cuz you can get what you want. Ten niggas can go in, get the same break. If me, Just (Just Blaze), Lord Finesse, L.E.S., and a whole bunch of other producers get the same record, now it's all about who flips it the best. So you have to listen hard to what you have. If you don't— the best beat wins. So if you don't put your foot into what you're doing, you're not going to have the best; you treat every beat like it's your last.

Sa'id: How often do you dig for new records?
Buckwild: It depends how I feel when I get up. When I get up, I might feel like, "O.K., let me go to the record shop." Or I might be like, "O.K., let me call one of the dudes who I know got records." And you know, there's times I might feel I want to go to record conventions. It can be maybe 1/3rd of the year!

Sa'id: Right now, what's the size of your record collection?
Buckwild: Too much. Probably way more than 10,000.

Sa'id: Talk about how hip hop production evolved between 1991 and 1993.
Buckwild: My first record was in 1993, "Shit Is Real" Diamond D. That song came about, well, Diamond was doing a song and needed a remix. Being around Diamond, Finesse, Sadat, just listening to music, Diamond was like, "Yo, I know you're doing beats, let me hear what you got." I was doing beats for O.C. already. I wanted to DJ. I met Lord Finesse through DJ'ing, let's start from there. I met Finesse like in '90, '91, from DJ'ing, mixtapes. And from there we became cool. Finesse is the dude. If I never met Finesse, we wouldn't be here talking right now! First of all, you gotta put that with it. For him to be who he is, he's one of the dudes who never gets the credit he deserves in anything. For *me*, he's like the seed for the whole thing. Without Finesse, a lot of us wouldn't be here. Through him you know, he brought me around Show (Showbiz), Diamond. I met Show, Show welcomed me with open arms. The only person I

already knew was A.G., cuz we was from the same hood. From there, seeing Show when he was making "Party Groove," before that evolved, not "Party Groove," it was another record similar to "Party Groove," that was right after "Party Groove." And seeing that, I was like, "Wow, he got the 1200 (E-MU SP 1200)." I already knew about the 1200, so I was like, "Cool." And you know, he showed me certain things. And there's another dude that used to be with Finesse, it was this dude, Chilly D. When I first got enough to buy a 12 — I scrapped up some money, I bought a SP 12. It had short time. Show had a sampler laying around and he let me hold that. So you know, they were busy with their thing, so man Chilly helped me, Chilly helped me with a lot. Really everything, like you know with the 12 speeding up the sample. How to chop certain things, he showed me a lot of that. Yeah, Chilly D, he used to be with Ice T and them, he used to be down with them. After that, Diamond was doing his album, Joe [Fat Joe] was doing his thing, Showbiz & A.G. was doing they thing;. So being in Diamond sessions. I tell people: Before you get in, YOU REALLY GOTTA STUDY WHAT YOU'RE DOING. I used to go to Diamond sessions, go to Lord Finesse sessions. Everything that you can do to soak up knowledge, you do it! That's how you learn. So Diamond heard one of my beats and he liked it. And he was like, "Yo, I'm-a use this for a remix."

Sa'id: One good thing that you touched on is that during that era, a lot of producers and other artists you mix-it-up with visit each other's sessions. Also, producers used to be in the actual sessions with the artists. Speak about that.
Buckwild: Now, we don't have that. Now we got *Beat Donors!* Back then, you had to earn your keep. In the 90s, even before I came about, Pete Rock was the dude. Everybody wanted to be Pete Rock. When you put the horns in your shit, when you was making beats, it was like, you're going to copy Pete Rock. I guarantee you anybody that came up around the same time is going to tell you the same thing. After that, you're like, "O.K., I've learned how to do a beat like Pete, now, I gotta distinguish myself!"

Sa'id: Back then, how would you say the communication was amongst fellow producers?
Buckwild: Communication was all love because it was friendly competition. No one thought about like, "Yo, I gotta be bigger than this dude." Dudes heard what you had. Even though it was very competitive, people respected each other. It wasn't as much money then, but people were like, "I heard such and such, he's crazy with it." Back then, one thing I can say is people earned the title, *producer*, because most, if not all, of the album was produced by one dude. One dude would shape the sound. You can't have a hot album without having your own sound or your own identity. So if you have to rely on having 20 different people on your album and 15 different producers to give you a sound, you're not going to have a hot album.

Sa'id: How did your connection with O.C. come about?
Buckwild: It was on *The Source [The Source Magazine]* tour. It was Finesse, Organized Confusion, Red Hot Lover Tone, Roxanne Shante, RSO, which was Benzino and them. And it's cool you know, because one thing I learned, when we went on tour, it was when a lot of these dudes had like no bread. And everybody came home tight, close friends. That's when I made all my first remixes. That's how I got tight with O (O.C.), how I got tight with Organized, how I got tight with Tone from Trackmasterz, Benzino, Roxanne Shante. Everybody that was on that tour, I got tight with.

Sa'id: When you did [the song] "Stress" for O.C., what equipment did you use?
Buckwild: The 1200 [E-Mu SP 1200] and the 950 [Akai S950].

Sa'id: In an interview from 1995, you were quoted as saying, "Even if you don't make crazy money, you might have longevity." Were you able to live out that statement?

Buckwild: I think so. I'm still here, I'm still relevant. Even now, I'm working with artists I've never worked with. I'm working with Snoop now, Redman, Jadakiss. And still being in demand, I lived that statement out. Like Finesse used to say, "When all else fails, you work hard at what you do." I think I have more passion for the music than anything else. When you have that rush, that same love that you had as a kid. When you have that, that's what makes the music dope. I've seen a lot of dudes come and go. And I've seen a lot of dudes that are very much respected. Take dudes like Bomb Squad (Hank Shocklee), they opted out, like, "We're not doing this no more." But those dudes you gotta really respect them for what they brought to the game. Marley Marl, Howie T, Larry Smith. A lot of times a lot of these producers don't even know who came before them. So before you can be the person you are, you have to really appreciate all these guys who came before you.

Sa'id: Going back to the quote that you made in 1995, let's put this in proper context. The year before, in 1994, O.C.'s Word...*Life* came out; Biggie's *Ready to Die* came out; Nas' *Illmatic* came out. Then in 1995 Mobb Deep came out with *The Infamous*; and Raekwon & Ghostface dropped *Only Built 4 Cuban Linx*. So there was nothing that indicated — at least not on the surface — where hip hop/rap music was going to go. At that time, the state of hip hop/rap was real strong. So what prompted you to make a statement like that in 1995? What were you seeing at that time that indicated to you where music was going to go?
Buckwild: Let me put it this way. In 1995, *Illmatic* wasn't even gold! And we felt Nas was... we felt nobody in the world was better than Nas! So when you see that, when you have that substance in you, even if you not crazy paid. For Nas to be the greatest rapper alive, then. We put Nas on a pedestal where Rakim was. Everybody said Rakim was the greatest rapper. Between Rakim, Kane, Kool G Rap, KRS One and those times. Then after that when Nas came around, we said Nas was the next coming of Rakim. Then when Nas didn't sell 500,000 — instantly — with Columbia, Columbia questioned that. So even if Columbia questioned Nas— For us we questioned it, like, "Yo, this dude here is one of the greatest out right now. So when you look at that, he didn't have the success — instantly — you know, like Biggie [Notorious B.I.G.] had. Biggie sold a million and half, whereas *Illmatic* was probably like 350,000. People felt that Biggie and Nas ran New York. In that critically acclaimed album, *Illmatic*, he had a lot of people looking forward and a lot of eyebrows opening. Then you can fast forward to Rae and Ghost and the next shit. And Nas being the artist that he is, because you have that talent, that's where the longevity goes. When you have talent, people are always going to check for the talent.

Sa'id: So at that time were you thinking that things weren't going to last? Remember how things turned out. In 1995, at The Source Awards, Biggie beat out Nas and won Best Album of the Year (1994) *and* Lyricist of the Year (1994). Then Mobb Deep comes right out in 1995; *Only Built 4 Cuban Linx* in 1995. There was no reason for anybody to believe that all of this was going to end—
Buckwild: I don't think that we thought it was going to end, either. Dudes was looking at us like— You can understand that there's money in the game, but dudes weren't seeing the vision like a dude like Puff (Diddy) had. Puff had a bigger vision than anybody, you know, cuz he seen what rap and hip hop was: masses. Whereas, we looked at it like, what we were doing was acceptable for us, and we weren't getting paid from it. And it's like, you're never thinking from within, until things dry up and you don't have the quality. To me, I think the last level of great artists that we had to come out from New York was '97, '98. We had Pun, we had Canibus, we had Nature, Cam'ron, The Lox. When you look at that, some of them artists is still here. This is why I say your talent will give you those future years. Because while everybody else who comes out is a gimmick, to have the talent, that's what keeps you going.

Sa'id: Did you see the transformation of power, the dominance being transferred to the South, before it happened? And if so, when did you see it?
Buckwild: Yes. No Limit! [Master P's label] And the one thing that I can say that really gave New York up is when New York DJs stopped supporting New York artists, and would support artists from other states even more.

Sa'id: When did that first start happening?
Buckwild: No Limit. Matter fact, right after Cash Money, so that would be like 2000. And you can see. Our artists were more on the decline and the majors (major labels) started picking people who *looked* like they were selling records, that's one thing. But then you have the emergence of *Radio One*. Even for me, I'm a cool person, I'm cool with everybody. when I'm talking to the dudes who I know who do radio, and they tell me about this *Radio One* thing, about this one big conglomerate that controls all the stations — that's when you see the change. So once you lose your grip, it's like, once we didn't have all of these artists coming out, I mean even adding on, we had DMX, we had Eve, The Rough Riders. '95., '96, '97, '98 was the last years we had our stars coming out. After that, no one knows what happened. Matterfact, I believe it was because no one wanted to put anybody else on, who probably was coming up.

Sa'id: So when you made "Whoa" was "Whoa" your reaction to the Southern Explosion, or were you already tinkering with your sound before that?
Buckwild: I didn't really care about the Southern Explosion. I looked at it like this: Everybody needs their sound. Like you can say, in '90, '91, '92 the West Coast was winning. And it was cool! Cuz when you have dudes like King T., you had The Alkaholiks, you had Dre, you had Snoop, it was all cool. But the one thing that people can't get twisted is that's them, they're doing they're thing. You have to appreciate them. But us living in New York, we have to do us, too. And right now, when you're looking at it now, we don't have that. New York has lost their identity. Dudes don't know what to do, as far as making records. The level, the bar of production is down. When you look at it, you got people who think it's not really cool for artists like Kanye to sell 3 million, why not? Tribe (A Tribe Called Quest) used to sell 2 million; you know before all the gangsta records kicked off. The whole game is so one-sided, it needs a complete overhaul.

Sa'id: Now, go into "Whoa." Again, is that sound something you set out for? That type of beat?
Buckwild: Nawgh, it's just another extension. For me, all my beats— People say that I really need to produce albums because I don't just make one type of beat. They say that my music has a spectrum to it. A lot of it has emotion. And you get good rappers, you could bring out a lot of different things. So even doing "Whoa," having that on a beat CD, it was just one morning. That came at a time when he had came into a *single*-driven industry. It was hard to get the beat off. People were like, "Hey, I need an up-tempo record, this is too slow, blah, blah, blah," and all that hoopla. People don't understand that singles are just records that people like! When you look at it, to me, there's no set sound for a single!. The greatest group to ever do that is Outkast. They change their sound all the time, they're one of the most creative groups out. A lot of times people don't give The Dungeon Family their props on producing. They have to be one of the greatest set of producers out!. For you to change your sound every album, no other producers can do that. And for the sales to elevate, and to also be respected.

Sa'id: Describe in your words the difference between '90s production and production now, the 2000s. In specific, how it lends itself to the rapper, like how they write and the concepts they develop. What was '90s production and what did it do for rappers? And what is 2000s production (today's production) and what is it doing for rappers?
Buckwild: '90s production, I think the artists were more challenging. And in the 2000s, the

artists are more lazy; and you can tell, they make *sing-songy* hooks. These dudes aren't really challenging the music. A lot of them look for beats that are bigger than they are. They want the beat to save their life. The beat isn't going to save your life. Because if you get a beat that's hotter than you, the beat is gonna fizzle out. So when you look at it in the past 10 years, for us to have about— What was the latest hottest beat we had? "Lean Back?" Before that, name another one. Joe [Fat Joe] had a couple, but out the 10,000 records that was dropped, you can only remember about three of the beats? It has no replay value. So when you look at it, it's a big difference between '90s production and production now. That's a whole 'nother thing. Like a lot of these dudes now, they get a keyboard and a MPC 2000, and they figure, "Yo, I can make beats!" Anybody can make a beat. My daughter's 11, I can teach her to make a beat. I could be like, "Yo, hit the snare on every two, and hit the kick on every one, and you got 16 doubles, and you can go from there — anybody can do that. Hit the hi-hat on every eight: 1,2,3,4, 1,2,3,4. But the difference is bringing life to it. There's no life in a lot of the music that's out. It's just like, O.K., it sounds *different* or it sounds like they're trying to make something that will rock in a party.

In the '90s, you had a different array of records that would rock in a party. You had Luke (Luke Skywalker), you had Snoop and Dre and 'em, you had Geto Boys, you had dudes from all over. And it wasn't like everybody was trying to be like, "Yo, we gon make this certain sound." Dudes were doing what they *felt!* Like Luke was into the bass music, so he made his music sound like it was more stripper music. And in the '90s, maybe people didn't really know about strip clubs down south, you wasn't like, "O.K., this record is for the strip club." But it was like, if you threw "Doo Doo Brown" on in the club, people lost their mind. No one was biased. But nowadays, people they have to have a certain stature, or they have to be a certain type of person to make records. And it makes the music suffer. You got all these artists that are cardboard. They're one-dimensional. They have no life; and when they have no life, they're trying to sell records, instead of trying to sell themselves as artists. People buy into artists, not just records. People are following this record company mumbo-jumbo. Like people always say, "New York people don't sell records." But I remember in '98, '99, DMX, Ja Rule, and Jay-Z ruled the charts. So while they was telling us they don't sell records, DMX sold almost 5 million records in one year. So people keep listening to the record company. This is where the artist fell. And now what we have, we don't have artists, we have puppets. Like no one wants to go against the grain and be like, "Yo, I'm-a sell my art, and people gonna feel me!"

Sa'id: What is the major distinction between a beatmaker and a producer? Before you answer that, let me say what I think of you. I think you're a beatmaker at heart, who knows how to produce? Would you agree with that?
Buckwild: I agree with that, 'cuz I love beats. Hearing a beat, that's what makes me wanna work. I can get stuck, and I can go visit another dude who makes beats and hear his beats in a raw form, and get inspired. It doesn't mean like copying off of him or doing the same thing.

Sa'id: But when you use the term "producer," that's when you get into the gray area. How do you view the difference between a producer who actually does the drum program, who actually does the chopping and comes up with the ideas vs. a Quincy Jones-*Thriller* style of producing where someone is hired to do those sort of things?
Buckwild: Yeah, well, a producer is only a person with the vision. So if you have a vision for something, you know, from start to finish, that's the part of production that's not just like, "O.K., put some drums in the MPC and chop up such and such." What about after it gets across? What about after the artist drops his lyrics? What are you going to say, like, "Oh, I need something in the chorus, I need I to do this," or "Yo, I think you need to do the chorus like this, or "Let's change these words and change this around like this." All of these things are

part of production. And today, let's be real, most of these dudes are not in the studio with the artist producing records. Like all them producers on 50's (50 Cent) album, how many of those producers do you think were really in the studio with him? But they can say, "Yo, I produced for 50." No, you didn't *produce* for 50!!! *You're a beat donor!* With The Game's first album, that was a different story. There were a lot of producers who were in with him. I was in with him, I remember being out there, I can remember Just (Just Blaze) being out there, I can remember Hi Tek. But most of these guys, beside those guys that I named, most of these guys aren't really in the studio with the artist producing records.

Sa'id: What piece of equipment would you say had the most influence on your development?
Buckwild: I'd have to say Pro Tools. Pro Tools has been around. Like doing a beat in the MPC, you can get it, but sometimes It's not tight. But you can take it in Pro Tools and you can fix what you want. Not only now do I not have to sit there and sequence a whole beat into song mode. But I can do it inside of Pro Tools, and I can have a dude come in and do what I want him to do. And I can sequence everything in there, and do all the drops.

Sa'id: So have you reconstructed how you put together beats? You no longer sequence in the MPC, then dump it into Pro Tools?
Buckwild: Yeah!!! I still sequence in the MPC and dump it into Pro Tools. But I can do beats in the MPC with my eyes closed. To me, sometimes I figure that's not enough.

Sa'id: Getting back to the art, describe what you do, from step 1 to step 4, before you get to Pro Tools. You don't just get a record, slap it— Describe that, describe what you do.
Buckwild: I go dig, and I find the best records I can, listen to the records, find the best part in the record, put it in the drum machine. I might chop it, I might just add drums to it. Right from there, I go to Pro Tools, Pro Tools is where I make everything happen. Sequencing, like if I'm adding instruments, etc. You know, we're in a different time now. I look at it like, I love the '90s, but we're not in the '90s anymore. So many producers I know are stuck in the '90s. The only way to make a difference is that you have to be in the front line and you gotta help change with people. So by helping change with people, where it's like, cool, even if I'm sampling, now I got somebody to play this. So when I get it to the labels, instead of being like, "O.K., here's my song…," when they're negotiating I can tell my lawyer like, "Yo, we need a fair shot!" Because I think all of this stuff got out of hand, because no one cares. For example, if I was like, "Sa'id sampled me', and I'm like, "O.K., damn, everybody else is asking for 5 ($5,000)… I WANT 15!" and the labels be like, "O.K.!" Then I'm like, damn, I can ask for whatever I want. Because once it got to the point like you said, where no one is fighting for it, everything did get out of hand.

Sa'id: All of that though, we agree on some of the issues. But my whole thing of it is, it's the art of it. If we focus too much on the business and money, the art will get lost.
Buckwild: With certain people, the art will never get lost. Even for me, the art never gets lost 'cuz I'm thinking art first! I'm not thinking about— For number one, I don't look for a lot of these dudes who are very recognizable or don't clear samples.

Sa'id: When *you're making* tracks I know you're not making tracks with the understanding from start to finish that you'll be done in 5 minutes.
Buckwild: Oh, nawgh. Sometimes it happens, but that's the difference, I'm not looking to finish something in 5 minutes. Say certain producers put out 100 songs in a year, how many songs do you remember at the end of the year? There's a quality control issue, like you said. And it's like, no disrespect to anybody else, but sometimes even if I make 3 beats a day— I can make 10 beats a day, but my 10 beats is not made that one day, cuz it might take me a month to get those 10 hot loops. You see what I'm sayin'. So I could be like, "Yo, I made 10 beats today." So

when you look at it, even for me to find 10 hot records to fuck with, that's the damage control. Shit, if I was doing 7 beats a day, I might have like a million beats! It might be 7 for the *month*. You know, it just depends on how I feel, and what's going on. See people think that if you can do 10 beats a day, it makes them an ill producer. No! If I put out 100 records in a year, and nobody remembers all 100 at the end of the year, what does that say about my beats? I'd rather do beats that people remember. If I play my last 10 records and you know what they are, then obviously I must have a good batting average. If I'm 10 for 10, that's good. If I'm 8 for 10 that's good. So you have to look at it, that's good quality control.

Sa'id: How do you deal with a dead ear? Like if you've been listening to music all day, you can't tell, you really can't distinguish, either shit sounds hot to you or they all sound whack. How do you deal with that?
Buckwild: I just leave it alone. I just go do something else. You know, you do the family thing. You bug out with your peoples, you go on the internet.

Sa'id: Everything you make you save?
Buckwild: Nawgh! If I ain't feelin' it, I delete it.

Sa'id: Scrap it immediately?
Buckwild: Yeah.

Sa'id: How many of your joints were near scraps that became something?
Buckwild: None! Everything that I made that became something that I liked. You could look in my Pro Tools, if I switch the screen [switches screen on] I might have 500 beats in there. But there's like 20 that I really like right now. But then there's others where I'm like, "I like this, this is cool, but I'm not lovin' it.'" But if I save it, I like it. If I track a beat, then I like it.

Sa'id: In those cases, what are you lookin' for then? What's that pinnacle point?
Buckwild: I just gotta feel it. I'm a hip hop dude. The same way I listened to another dude's record and be like, "I don't like this," I listen to my beats and say the same thing. I look at it like as if I'm somebody else. That's why a lot of times when people hear beats, they be like, "Yo, I ain't really feelin' this." I'll keeping shopping a beat because I'm confident with it. Like even with "Whoa," it went through certain people, I was confident that it would get a placement.

Sa'id: What do you mean it went through certain people? Artists?
Buckwild: Yeah, Artists.

Sa'id: They passed on it?
Buckwild: Yeah, some laughed at it. Some was like, "Oh, it's too slow," or "It sounds like an album cut." But I've grown to learn that a beat is only as good as what the artist does to it. So when you look at it, even "I Got A Story To Tell," Foxy. Tone and them wanted it for Foxy, but Foxy was like, "The beat is whack!" Then Big [The Notorious B.I.G.] was in a session, and it was one of the best beats on the album. But it's only what the artist does with it. So when you have something you believe in, you shop it.

Sa'id: When did you switch from the 950 and why?
Buckwild: I started usin' the 3 [Akai MPC 3000] after that. And that was during the time of O's [O.C.] second album. Different machines allow you to do different things. And I always believed that you need to grow, you know. And it's like changin' with the times. Different machines give you different sounds. Sometimes you gotta switch with the times. As time grew, the sound [in hip hop/rap music] started to get a lot cleaner. I always look for change. It's like,

the drum machine does what you want it to do. I used to think, O.K., I got a 12 [E-Mu SP 1200] and a 950 [Akai S950], but then I thought, O.K., if I get a 3 [Akai MPC 3000] it has more time, so I can keep everything inside the 3. Instead of going with two machines. Then my 3000 got stolen, and I bought a 2000 [Akai MPC 2000]. That was around the time of Rob's [Black Rob] album. That was like '99. I liked that. The only thing that I didn't like about it was that it couldn't cut everything off like the 12 and 950. That was the only problem I had with the 2000 and the 3000. But the sounds with the drums, I loved the sounds.

Sa'id: What do you mean by cuttin' off?
Buckwild: Like you know, a poly thing, where's it like no matter how many sounds you got— With the 12 and the 950, you could take five different sounds, and chop 'em differently in different places and make one loop. You can have a kick, snare, hi-hat, hi-hat, snare, hi-hat. It's like different parts. If you listen to *"I Gotta Story To Tell,"* that's an example of how you can take three, four different parts of a sound, and chop 'em into one loop. Like if you listen to *"I Gotta Story To Tell,"* and you listen to *"What's Beef,"* it's the same drums, but the pattern is extremely different. So that shows right there the power of the machine.

Sa'id: So how did you get around that [the problem of cuttin' off]? You went from the 2000 to the 4000. There was nothin' in between that, right?
Buckwild: After the 2000, I went back to the 3000, the 3000 and the 6000 [Akai S6000]. The 6000 does everything the 950 does. I just used the 3000 as the *sequencer*. Once I did that, I could doctor [edit and manipulate] samples. I was able to do various things in the 6000 that you couldn't do in everything else.

Sa'id: Do you use timestretch?
Buckwild: Yeah, I do. Some songs, some beats I have it where I can stretch it. That's the one thing a lot of cats don't understand. Sometimes you buy records, and the time progression changes. Like the song starts going faster, or starts going slower. So if you got a song going and it starts off at like 80 [BPM], then it goes to 81 and 82, you can't loop that. So you have to figure out a way to make it all relevant. And that's where the 6000 (Akai S6000) came in. The 6000 was one of the best machines that they invented for just straight hip hop.

Sa'id: Let's say you take a record and you throw it into the 6000, how did you make it the way that you wanted to, if a problem like that occurred. You know, if you wanted to throw it to a drum backbeat?
Buckwild: I would take the parts that I need, and I would do a BPM match. There's so many things that the Akai S6000 does. I could take this one part right here and make it one part of the tempo that I need. It has a lot of little secrets, but you just have to have the patience to get into it.

Sa'id: So what if somebody says to you, "listen, you're usin' the 6000 and you're usin' somethin' else to sequence. Why don't you just throw everything in the 4000?" The 4000 [Akai MPC 4000] is a monster!
Buckwild: The 4000 is a monster, but if it's certain things that I need to doctor up with the 6000, I'll go back to the 6000. But everything now, I use with the 4000. The 4000 is ridiculous. You can put so many different programs in there and change up so many ways that people don't even understand. Like I know a lot of people who don't use the 4000. Only people that I know use the 4000 right now might be me, Just Blaze, Lord Finesse, and Rsonist from Heatmakerz. Not too many people. Everybody uses the XL [Akai MPC 2000XL] or they use Reason and all this other stuff. But the best thing about the 4000 is that you can doctor your sounds how you need to.

Sa'id: So the 4000 allows you to do everything you need?
Buckwild: Everything! And like for me, I sample. I'll sample my joints, NO EQ, right into the 4000. And everything I need to do with the sample, I'll do right inside the 4000. And then from the 4000, I'll go to Pro Tools.

Sa'id: When you produce, who do you have in mind?
Buckwild: I'll have the artist, but it has to be a vision for me. Because even knowing certain things, and the way production is, you always gotta change. Like people will get a hold of something, it's like— Even when I first came in, I might hear a Pete Rock beat and be like "Yo, I like that beat Pete did. I'm-a do a beat like that." So what happens is now is that back then, you might've had 10,000 people wantin' to do beats. Now you have a million! So if you got a million people wantin' to do beats— I'm going to give you a perfect example, right now. We take soul records with the sped-up sample, etc. You had a couple of hits with those. So now it's 10 million people, who's doin' beats, who's going to submit the *same* type of beat, who might find the *same* record, because it's very common. You might take Aretha you know, the Isley Brothers, any thing that might be very common that you could find in your mom's house, your grandma's house, etc. Now you got a million people with the same record, the same type of technique, etc., the same machine. How do you differentiate yourself from them? So for me, I do what I feel is gonna be somethin' people will know *me* for. Like I'm into to obscure records. I wanna have things that will make you be like, "Yo, what was that he used?" Even right now with the record shops online, you can basically get records on the menu now. And then on top of that, production has gone to another level. You have to be able to do other things that people can't do. So a lot of times now, I fuck with live musicians, and I can produce records where it's like it will sound like a sample, but it's not.

Sa'id: You have them come in here and play your ideas out?
Buckwild: Yeah, see [he points] got the keyboards, bass guitar, Pro Tools, sound modules. The dudes that I work with, they know how to play what they need to play. These are real musicians. They tour with people. So when it comes to playing records, they play. They don't just pick up a Triton and go *berp, berp berp!* They got groove, they got melody. So whatever I need, I can either recreate or create right from that.

Sa'id: A lot of producers say that your sound is balanced. It never seems like the beat gets away from the artist, you understand what I'm sayin'?
Buckwild: Yeah, I dig what you're saying. I'm a person like this. I'm a fan, before I'm-a producer. So when I make records, I'll make records that I think that I wanna hear if I was drivin', or if I got an iPod on the train, you know, or if I'm on the plane goin' cross country. CDs cost money. $17 a CD? I wanna make the songs that keep people listenin'. And that's what's missing right now. You can party and do whatever-whatever, but it's like in our time, when we was comin' in the game, if you buy a CD with 14 songs, you want at least 12 hot songs you can relate to. And it's like to me, that's what I think is the perfect balance. Like when you have a variety of different music. I came in listening to Tribe (A Tribe Called Quest), *Ready To Die* [The Notorious B.I.G.], *The Chronic* (Dr. Dre), *Doggystyle*, you know, all those albums, De La Soul, any De La Soul album. To me De La always had the perfect balance when they did their albums, too. And for them, their job to produce was bigger because they were making a whole album. For me, if I'm on somebody's album, I might have one song. Like Mobb Deep, it's a balance to have the whole album. You need everything to be cohesive, but nothing really sounding the same. Those dudes like that. That's how I learned. I've learned from that! Those are the things that I want to emulate. So when it's time for me to do an album, I will have a sonic style to it, but I will try to have a balance. That way if you buy the album, you're getting your money's worth. And not somethin' that you're going to get tired of after the third or fourth listen.

Sa'id: How do you sample drums? Do you process your drums? Do you sample dry?
Buckwild: I sample all of my drums dry. But I doctor [tweak] all of my drums in the 4000. The one thing that dudes gotta understand is that, we all pick machines, even Minnie [producer, Minnesota], Minnie use the ASR [Ensoniq ASR 10], but we all have a certain technique for what we do. You can give 10 dudes the same record, that don't mean we all are goin' to do it the same way. Like we all have a vision of how we like our drums. I like my drums tight. So I'll do whatever I need to inside of here [MPC 4000] so that way when I get my record to an engineer (if I can't mix my record), at least everything is there. I've known a lot of engineers that have been like, "I love mixing with you because you make my job so easy, everything sounds the way it should be. I may have to put on a little reverb, but everything sounds good." Hearing that, that's a blessin'. I'm like "Cool." That let's me know that I must be doing something right.

Sa'id: Do you sample your drums from vinyl?
Buckwild: Vinyl. I'm Ol' School [Laughs]. Vinyl!

Sa'id: But what about companies that sell sounds? Many people are going online, downloading waves [.wav files], and such. But a lot of drum sounds now stand out too much.
Buckwild: Yeah! You know what it is. You know what people forget to realize? When you're tuning instruments, you also have to tune your drums to your music. And a lot of dudes don't understand that. So sometimes you hear drums and they may stick out, you know, [somebody might say], "I want this right here to be dominant." But I think when you're mixing your records, there needs to be a balance, but sometimes that's on your engineer also.

Sa'id: Do you have individual rules, you know, how you approach your kicks, how you approach your snares, how you approach your hats?
Buckwild: It depends on if I'm using a loop, or if I'm using a lot of live stuff. Every beat is different. Like on some records, sometimes I put reverb on a kick just to give it an effect, but I'll put something behind that kick to still make it knock. I'm not saying that you want to try to be so different, but you want to try to be *creative*. It's like, O.K., I'm taking a loop but I'm making this loop *my* record.

Sa'id: So what do you say to a beatmaker who say's that they have 500 drum sounds?
Buckwild: What do you say to them? <u>KNOW YOUR SOUNDS?</u> If you have 500 drum sounds, *you can't use 500 drum sounds!!!* Like even dudes tell me "Yo, I made 20 beats today." If you make 20 beats, that's cool. But how many of them are extremely hot? I'd rather do 2 beats in a day — that's flames — then say I did 10 beats, and 5 of them are just O.K., and I got 1 hot one. Because that means I'm putting my time into that one hot one, which, hopefully, will please the public. It's better to know what you have than to just have abundance. So if I got 50 drum sounds, and I know all 50, then I can be like O.K., cool I'm using this loop over here, this the perfect sound for it. I'm from the school where instead of just the [typical] kick, snare, hi-hat, they want their drums to play like a drummer would play. So you know it's like, you take pride in your music. It's good to see sometimes dudes who have that same mentality, where they love the music. They take pride in what they do. Then it's some people who just do it, who are like 'O.K., only thing I need is a kick, snare, hi-hat and I can do this, and I can get a check.'

Sa'id: In '93, '94, when was it before you realized that you knew what you were doing, that you knew you had the skill, as opposed to when you were just feelin' your way through?
Buckwild: I ain't gonna lie, for me to get into the game when I did was luck! With O's (O.C.) album, I had timing, right place, right time. The *game* is more luck than skill. I know a lot of *nice* dudes on the beats, and rhymes. But it's just, they don't have a break. You think it's that easy just to get a spot on Jay-Z's album? Jay-Z flourished a lot of producers. Because you know,

you do a beat for Jay-Z, it makes everybody check for you. That's a stamp! So can you imagine what would happen with some people if they didn't do a record with Jay-Z? You know, they still might be in the same melting pot as 100,000 other producers. But once you do somethin' like that, it pulls you out of that pot and puts you on a certain plateau, regardless of anything. Jay can get a beat from anybody.

Sa'id: Outline a typical session for you. How do you do it? Do you listen to some music first? Do you work with a drum sequence that you already have?
Buckwild: I listen to the music, or I already have something in my mind. It all depends on who I might be trying to do a beat for. You're trying to find a balance. And sometimes trying to find that balance [in your music] is harder than anything. See, people who sample, sometimes dudes will pick up anything and be like "Yo, I just chopped this." Sometimes it might be hot, it might not be. Sometimes it might take two minutes, sometimes it might take you a day to make a hot beat.

Sa'id: So you don't have a rigid time frame?
Buckwild: Sometimes I'll sit there, I might do a beat for 6 hours, then scrap it, be like "Nawgh, this ain't it." Some dudes might be like "That's crazy!" But you know, if it's missing something, it ain't it! If I'm listening to it I wanna be like, Can I listen to this shit over and over again? or if I got an M.C., you know, that's another thing. Producing and rapping go hand and hand. A dudes beat is only as good as the rapper that gets on it! So right now, if we're making dope beats, are the rappers who we have in the game equally dope? Right now, a lot of dudes beats out-shadow the artists.

Sa'id: Who was it again who originally showed you how to work the machines?
Buckwild: My man, Chilly D. I started off with an [Akai] S01 and a SP 12 1200.

Sa'id: An Akai S01? Damn! That's what I started with.
Buckwild: Yeah! No sampling time! [Laughs]

Sa'id: You didn't have any filters on that.
Buckwild: Nothin!!! So you learn to chop stuff the right way. You know, you get lazy when you get time (extra sampling time). Back then, I'd have to put something on 78 [BPM], then I'd have to chop what I need, then I'd go from there. So it helped me to become inventive with certain records. Like with the 12, doing beats on the scale, not too many people was using the scale. That's why I say O.C.'s album, doing *"O Zone."* When Q Tip heard it, he was like "That's hot right there." You take a certain record and you play it out you know, like you would a keyboard. But it's not a keyboard, it's a filtered-up SP 1200 sound.

Sa'id: So you can filter sounds on the 4000 the same way you would on the 6000?
Buckwild: Yeah, you can filter on the 4000, but it's not like the filters on the 950. None of the Akai drum machines/samplers have the same type of filters like the 950. You know those have the best filters!

Sa'id: So when you do go into a session, are you involved in the mix?
Buckwild: I always mix my record. Only record I ain't mix was The Game's record and the 50 Cent record, you know, because they requested Dre to mix it.

Sa'id: Who taught you all of that?
Buckwild: It's a learning experience. I use to be around Lord Finesse when he was in the studio. I was in a lot of dudes sessions. Red Hot Lover Tone, Biggie sessions, early on. You know, being

477

around certain people you can look and you learn certain things, talking to the engineers. The engineers teach you certain things, they'll tell you if you ask questions. It don't just come to you, you gotta ask questions. And also with EQ'ing, being able to EQ my own sounds came from knowing the EQs as a DJ.

Sa'id: What was the music that you listened to when you were coming up?
Buckwild: Public Enemy, EPMD, BDP, Slick Rick. Anything by Marley Marl!!! Back then, I don't think Marley Marl or Bomb Squad could make whack records, you know. So as a producer, you're like, "O.K., cool, these guys made whole albums that were dope, not just a hot record." And that's where producers now get it twisted. They think that you gotta have the club record that plays on BET and MTV, but right now the labels got them really confused. It's like right now, we need like a school. A school for producers and a school for M.C.s — to teach them what's really right. So that way, you take the culture back and you can sell records. It's too much instant gratification, where it's like, [people think that if] you get a hot record on the radio and MTV, you going to sell records. Well, you know right now, look at the Soundscan, and look at who's getting crazy spins and look who's selling records.

Sa'id: So does this compare to schools like Scratch Academy and Full Sail? I think Scratch Academy offers a course, Hip Hop 101.
Buckwild: All right, but think of it like this. If you go to Scratch Academy or you go to Full Sail. *Who are your teachers?* [pause] Who was *my* teacher? And it's like, I'm a dude who learns from listening, too. But learning how to make the machine do what you want it to do comes from within.

Sa'id: Some dudes are like "I give you a beat machine, talk to me in 5 years." It's producers who have said this. Like, "Don't talk to me until you've spent at least 5 years with a machine." What do you think about that?
Buckwild: I think that that's kind of a cold statement to tell somebody. I've known dudes who just got a knack, a natural knack for it. Like one of my man's, LV, he DJs, and Roc Raider. When I first heard their beats, you could tell from their drum programming that they was gonna have it. The drum programming is what's gonna show, it's gonna make you or break you. Your drum programming, your programming is the ultimate key for doing beats. So if you're a dope drum programmer, you can become a dope producer. It just depends on your ideas that you put on top.

Sa'id: Do you feel that people are limited if they do their drums on an MPC or Roland MV vs. software like Reason, etc.?
Buckwild: My man [Lou] does it on Fruity Loops. And when I heard his beats, I was like "Yo!" It doesn't matter, the programs do what you want it to do. So if you can program, if you got a good general idea of what to do and a good choice of sounds, that's how you can tell about a good producer. Their drums are distinctive, their drum programming is always tight. The longer you produce, the tighter your programming becomes.

Sa'id: How much music outside of hip hop do you listen to?
Buckwild: I listen to everything outside of hip hop. I listen to rock, jazz, I listen to different things. Right now, I can't say I really listen to hip hop because it's like, honestly, there's not too much that really makes me be like "Oh, shit, did you hear that?" Not unless I make my own compilation of songs, or I just buy mix tapes.

Sa'id: As far as business goes, another thing that keeps coming up is how producers have to chase people down for payment.
Buckwild: It's even worse now! Every year it gets worse and worse. The lower the record sells

go, the harder it is for you to get paid. And what makes it harder too is Pro Tools. Dudes will Pro Tools 10, 12 beats [forward the Pro Tools files of beats to rappers], and they got their album. You have to wait until they O.K. everything. You really don't get paid until after the album's out. And sometimes, there's albums that are out that I still haven't gotten paid on. I could put it on blast, but you know. But that's a good example. The artist is doing their music so fast because of Pro Tools, but the paperwork isn't getting done at the same time.

Sa'id: Is it left up to the producer or his manager to send the P.O. [purchase order] in?
Buckwild: Yeah, it is. But you have to be on top of that. The producer, the manager, and the lawyer. If you're a good producer, you're going to need a strong team, if you wanna be successful. And that's another important thing. Not only do you have to have control inside the studio, you have to have control outside the studio. That's why to me, the greatest producers are those who always control their destiny. Like Dre, he controls his destiny. People come to him. Like Dre probably won't go in unless he got the whole check!

Sa'id: Knowing that, are you a producer that only talks to well-known artists? Or can anybody get at you for a beat?
Buckwild: Nawgh, I talk to everybody. If you can't talk to me, you can talk to my people. It's like, if I think you got talent, you hot, I'm like, "Yo, we can rock." Because the one thing that a lot of producers fuck up in the game, and it's been a slew of them, they get to a certain level where they forget about how it was for them when they was coming up. So you got dudes that's always hot on the street. So you might have to throw a mercy beat [a beat for free]; you know, let's do it, we can work something out. That's the thing about me, I've always liked being on an artist's first album. A lot of producers won't really deal with that until they've been co-signed where you got different producers on the album. Like "Oh, you got The Neptunes, Timbaland?" Then dudes wanna rock. Take The Game, he was fortunate, he had a lot of nice producers on his first album. And I'm pretty sure on his other albums, he's got more producers who didn't fuck with him, who are gonna wanna' fuck with him now because he's proven himself.

Sa'id: You've proven yourself, both with street credibility quality, beats and commercial viability, but do you find that you still have to make beat CDs and go after people?
Buckwild: Some dudes, yeah. And then sometimes, we'll just book time in my studio and work from there. I'll give them the benefit of doubt — "All right, well, let's book time and we'll do songs." That way, I hold the Pro Tools. So if I got the Pro Tools, I'm not worried about it.

Sa'id: I've seen well-known producers out with beat CDs, like a producer just starting out!
Buckwild: Yeah! Right now, it's going back to that because you got a lot of hungry dudes coming in. And artists are like, "Why should I pay this producer $80,000, when I can pay Jon Doe, over here, $2,500?" So what happens is the dude who's getting $80,000, yo, you can't forget where you came from. Just because you getting $80,000, or $125,000 or $250,000, whatever-whatever, it's a dude over here getting $2,500, or even less, making beats just as hot as you! Therefore, the artists are like, "You know what, you gotta submit just like them, because even though you're getting $100,000, $200,000, I'm not going five times platinum with the record that you're giving me, so that means I'm not making no money. So I can take that same record from him and go gold, and that way I'm going to make money."

Sa'id: Is it important to have a team early on, or is it something that you shouldn't be concerned with, not until you have the money?
Buckwild: I think as a producer you need to come under an umbrella. This is the problem we have right now. Everybody coming in want to be the boss. You can't be the boss with no workers, and you can't be the boss if you don't know what you're doing! So therefore, your best bet is to

get under an umbrella. So you can come under another company, so you can learn and grow.

Sa'id: Do you suggest going with another producer?
Buckwild: More than likely. Who else you gonna go with to learn? If you don't know the game, how are you going to learn? You're going to be learning on a trial basis and you're going to make mistakes, and you're going to be listening to the labels. And the labels don't know, only thing they want is a quick fix; they're like dope fiends.

Sa'id: So do you think that what's on the radio is a reflection of what's really going on or is it a reflection of what the labels are putting out?
Buckwild: It's a reflection of the labels. If you listen to radio, think 10 years ago, you had mix shows that would play dope album cuts. Nowadays, everybody's just focused on that one radio record and they don't really care about the rest of the album.

Sa'id: But do you think that producers share in the blame with that?
Buckwild: Yeah, they share blame, because instead of trying to make dope music, they just trying to make a club record that plays on the radio. I've seen it. They wanna emulate whatever's hot. Whatever is the flavor of the day, they wanna emulate that.

Sa'id: Do you think that the overall sound lacks quality or is it getting' back to where it was?
Buckwild: It's creeping back to where it was. It's a slow movement. Think about what makes a person wanna retire. What makes a person wanna retire is when the game is no longer exciting. Go back to 2002, 2003, you could tell it was going down hill because all of the producers who would look to the people coming in for the hot records, there were no hot records coming in. All the records were regurgitations. So a lot of the top people are like, "Yo, it's not a lot of hot M.C.'s or a lot of hot producers impressing me." So therefore, they get tired. So then those people who helped the game move start playing the back. So if you don't have good teachers, how can the dudes who come in now be even more successful?

Sa'id: You talk about teaching new producers. What would you recommend…
Buckwild: What I recommend? I recommend that they go pick up some CDs. Pick up Slick Rick, pick up BDP (Boogie Down Productions), A Tribe Called Quest, De La Soul, Public Enemy. Pick up *The Chronic*, pick up *Doggystle*. It's a lot of records that you could pick up that you could see that a lot of people was diverse. It was a lot of originality. Run-DMC, Third Bass. [Now] there's no originality.

Sa'id: So are you saying study the music, before you study the beat machines?
Buckwild: Yeah, it's like, yo, you gotta have a love for it before you make it happen.

Sa'id: Do you still practice? Anything. Let's say like a jazz musician, someone like John Coltrane, who was known for having days where he set aside time for practicing.
Buckwild: Yeah, you might come in— It's like practice makes perfect. Sometimes you have to take a day, you know. Like I was just here with some of my boys the other day, I took some drums and chopped them into a loop. And they was like, "Yo, how did you do that?" And I'm like, "This is what we used to do." You do those things to keep you sharp. It's some dudes out here that do that, but they're not getting their shine. That's what I mean by there's a lot of people out here that's really dope, and they're creative, but they're not happening because they are not what BET, MTV and Hot 97 is looking for right now. So they're not looking for creativity, there just looking for an instant hit.

Sa'id: How were you able to maintain your relevance from the time that you started until now.
Buckwild: You know what I think? It's the love of the music. Still finding the love for the music. You have to have it in your heart. I know a lot of producers who still love the game like that. You can't say that everything that comes out is trash. But you always have songs that come out where you're like, "Wow, that shit is crazy. I gotta do something better than that or just as equal." We all raised the bar for each other, little by little, between all the producers that are out. That's what I mean by having a genuine love for it. Because when you have love for something, you treat it with care!

Sa'id: But you didn't zigzag. Some pioneering producers are not where they should be. I don't know if it's because they are on some purity thing or something like that—
Buckwild: It's being humble. If you're not humble, if you're always cocky, no one wants to deal with somebody who's cocky and always holdin' they dick! They wanna deal with the person that they can always relate to, like *you're* reachable. Some dudes priced themselves out of the game, and they was always holdin' they dick and they not reachable. So they might've had bad dealings with people. So people be like, "Yo, he's a dickhead!" When you meet people, your first impression is the lasting one. So for dudes to be like, "I met Sa' (Sa'id). Yo, Sa' is mad cool. And though he may charge $100,000 for a beat, I once had a small budget and he did a joint for me for 5 grand." I learned that from Premier (DJ Premier). Premier was like, "Yo, you can't always get the big check. But you may have records that'll keep you goin'." And I've had a lot of records where I've gotten almost nothing for it, but they were great records that kept me going. So it's like, you have to stay relevant somehow, someway.

Sa'id: Speak about tossin' work around, what does that mean?
Buckwild: You know like, say, my man, Sa'id doing his album. I could see LP (Large Professor), Minnesota, whoever, dudes in my clique that I rock with. And I could be like, "Yo, I'm goin' over here, you got a CD, a beat tape, whatever? Let's go over here, there's work over here." Like we tossin' work around! That's how you keep your ties with dudes. That's how you make the game fresh. Because even with that, it's not one person trying to control everything. Yo, you can't be insecure. I'm secure enough to bring a dude with me. Some dudes are insecure because they feel like, "Damn, I don't want you to get a track and I don't." Well, guess what, if *I* walk in and *I* lose, then it's a lose/lose situation. But if *we* walk in and *you* win, then at least we still got that outlet. Because when we come in, they know we peoples. And we can still come back! But dudes don't think like that, they just think like, "me, me, me."

Sa'id: What's your last words?
Buckwild: Yo, stay humble, do good music, and keep good relationships. If you got all three of those, you'll go very far.

D.R. PERIOD

D.R., (the D.R. stands for Divine Ruler), stays amped up; Brooklyn is in him. It's in his actions, his thoughts, and his music. His career began long before his classic M.O.P. opus, "How About Some Hardcore." D.R. has worked with Jay-Z, The Notoriaou B.I.G. (Biggie Smalls), Tupac, Nas, AZ, Smooth Da Hustler, and countless others. He's done scores for films like *The Nutty Professor, Brown Sugar, Briggin' Down The House*, and *State Property*.

Notable Credits: M.O.P, "How About Some Hardcore," "Ante Up;" Cam'Ron, "Hey Ma;" Smooth Da Hustler feat. Trigger Da Gambler, "Broklen Language;" AZ feat. Nas, "Mo Money Mo Murder (Homicide);" Cormega, "The True Meaning."
D.R. Period's Setup: Akai MPC 60 II, various *hard-to-find* analog synths, Reason, Pro Tools TDM

Sa'id: In a word, describe your production.
D.R. Period: GUTTER! I describe my sound as gutter! Or unique, 'cuz my sound is universal. I'm not like one of those producers who are stuck with just the records and the drum machine. I'm a musician first. I know how to play bass, guitar, piano, drums — self taught. Only thing I didn't teach myself more or less is how to read music. That was something that was taught to me by Stick Evans, James Brown's drummer.

Sa'id: From off the bat, was your sound something that you were aiming for? Or is it something that as you grew, you grew into, realizing this was the type of thing you do?
D.R. Period: Nah, what happened was…when I started producing— see, I think like a band. I didn't even realize what I was doing, you know what I'm sayin'. I was always taught that the drummer leads the band. *Without the downbeat, you have no band!* So everything I did I built around drum patterns. That's why my drums was always so heavy and hard, because I was thinking like a drummer. Like you ever notice a band playing live on stage? There's nothing soft about that. So that's how I started producing tracks. So when the bass line come in, its got to ride with the drummer, and when the guitar comes in, its got to ride with the drummer, and when the keyboard comes in its following the groove. So that's how my style of production came about. It was coming from the state of mind of a band.

Sa'id: When did you start, when did you first start hitting the machines?
D.R. Period: Probably around about when I was 12, 13. My first drum machine was a Sosonic Drum. And how I got that Sosonic Drum, actually, it's a crazy story. There was this kid on the block, named Peter Pan. On Christmas, his moms bought him a Sosonic Drum. And my moms bought me a sheepskin coat and a pair of Pumas. So when I went over to his crib, I'm shinin', *geared up*. But he's mad because he got a drum machine, you know what I mean. It was like a vibe thing, he was hyped over my coat and my sneakers, really more my coat! I fell in love with his drum machine. I had never heard a drum machine until I turned on that Sosonic Drum. I was like, "Yo, this is incredible." Everyday I kept calling him and calling him about his drum

machine. Then one thing led to another and I was like, "Yo, you can *have* this coat, kid. Just give me the drum machine!" He was like, "Yeah, right." I told him, "Yo, you can have this coat and the Pumas!" So I went home without a coat and a pair of Pumas. But I came home with a drum machine. My moms was mad as hell, 'cuz she worked hard to get me that. But at the end of the day, that's what it was. And that started D.R. right there producing.

Sa'id: What kept you going? How did you keep taking it further?
D.R. Period: Then I started to DJ. I started messing around with the turntables. 'Cuz I always had mad records. My moms was like a manager. She was a manager for like Crown Heights Affair, BT Express, she managed a lot of acts. She used to manage a lot of groups. And records was always coming in the crib. And we had an old school record player. And this cat named Mario on the block used to try and blend records. He ain't have no mixer, but he used turn one on and turn one off. And I was like, "Yo, this is incredible!" Then I started copying off him. One thing led to another and I started replaying melodies that were on the records. You know, practicing my skills as a musician. The next thing I know, I did a record called Bad Boys "Inspector Gadget." Me and my man, MJ, we in the studio, just playing around; one thing led to another and it's a record. Next thing I know, I did Force MDs. Then C & C Music Factory. But mind you, I'm young, not having a clue of what I'm doing! Because like if you say, "Let's go to the studio and make some music," I'm making music. I'm not making any copies, I'm not taking anything home. I'm not doing no contracts with you, nothing. I was just happy to be in the studio making beats. That's how crazy it was. I started working with Color Me Bad, when they first came to New York. It's crazy, I've worked with so many acts. I've worked with Sting, I've worked with The Jacksons, I've done so much work, like, not knowing what I was doing. But I was real good at what I did. I was one of those cats that was built for the studio. Because I knew how to connect sounds. And the machines was real easy for me to learn. Every studio I went to never had the same machines. They always had something different. And the engineer that sat there would be like, "Well, this is how you record and this is the sequence page." I learned just that fast. Song modes and all that, I was flipping machines.

Sa'id: Do you feel that you have an advantage because you know before hand that you're going to be the one mixing it?
D.R. Period: Not really. Nah, nah. Because certain stuff you make, you gotta get away. See, I always like creative ears and creative opinions around me. I want to make sure that my say-so is more correct. I hate to be just the only judge of it, and then at the end of the day it was kind of wrong. I've learned that you make better records when you have creative people around you.

Sa'id: So in regards to the mix process, how much do you save for mixing, versus how much you do complete production?
D.R. Period: If the record is in flow mode, if it's just like moving a certain way, sometimes I mix the whole record right then and there. Sometimes I get tired of a record, then I don't even want to come back to the record. That's when I know I need another creative ear to come in. I can't say that every record I make, I wanna mix. 'Cuz every record don't give you that same vibe. Like certain artists take too long on vocals, they kill the session. And when they kill the session, they kinda kill the record for me, you know what I mean. 'Cuz if it took them three days to make the vocals right, I'm like, "Damn, I don't even wanna touch this record." Because I'm so stuck on mistakes. I can hear every punch. Even though the punch was right, I still hear it and I know where it was punched in at, and I know all the wrong parts of the record. So as I'm mixing, I'm focusing on everything that I knew was wrong about the record, that's not really wrong *now*. But I get stuck in that zone. So what I do is get away from that and let another creative ear come i. Music is weird, man. You have to be open for constructive criticism. That's the only way you grow in the game. Without that, you can't grow. You can't have all the answers.

I don't care how dope you are, I don't care how many hits you made, you just can't have all the answers and all the solutions to the game. So you gotta leave room for other people.

Sa'id: You know what's bugged? Most cats who use vintage gear consider themselves musicians. On the other hand, most cats who use newer gear never really even mention the word musician. Do you think that vintage gear is the reason that your sound is so full, as opposed to being thin?
D.R. Period: You know what I think it is, experience vs. wisdom. You see what I'm sayin'. You got a lot of cats that are inexperienced. They don't know how to take an 8-track— My first record on Select Records, "How 'Bout Some Hardcore," (M.O.P), we did the whole album on an 8-track. We didn't have the budget to go into the studio [and use the big SSL boards]. So I had to go in my little studio in the basement, with my little 8-track mixer and my little 8-track recorder, and then I bought a Tascam 24-track and connected it. It was the weirdest sound, but I connected them together, and Laze [M.O.P. associate] is on the other end, he got the drums, I got the base and the chords and the vocals are just playing. That's why if you notice every time you hear an M.O.P single from *back then*, none of the passes were the same. All the mutes were different, all the drums were different. Because we had to do it manually. So that's experience. You know, coming from that era of making records up to now, learning how Reason works. I'm glad they made Reason. I'm glad they made Pro Tools.

Sa'id: As far as classic pieces of equipment, do you think that it is an advantage for a producer using that vs. somebody who started off with later gear?
D.R. Period: It is an advantage for cats who use more of analog gear vs. digital gear. 'Cuz with digital, it's like, all you gotta do is know how quick-punch works and how to cut and paste — and you've made a record. Back then, it was a different way of training a producer. That's why you got cats that sit around and make beats all day but can't deliver a record. If you notice, all the cats who are really makin' the hits are really producers. Like The Neptunes. They're musicians first, before producers. So they understand when they come up against a brick wall what to do to fix it. You got a lot of cats now that are just beatmakers. Everybody got a 2000 (MPC) and a bunch of downloads and stuff like that. They don't even have vinyls; they got a collection of CDs! I'm not mad at that. But at the end of the day, you got to understand the value that vinyl can give you. They don't really understand. So everybody figure if they speed it up and change the pitch and get this real chipmunk sound, they really killing the sample. That can only carry you so far.

Sa'id: How do you feel about software setups?
D.R. Period: I'm loving it. Like right now, 59% of my beats is made on Reason! I make beats in my car. I drive, I pull over, take my laptop out, plug my keyboard in, and boom: I'm making tracks, you know what I'm sayin'. Then when I get here [studio] I'm on the MP (MPC), rockin' the MP. Going back and forth.

Sa'id: So what you're describing is that you haven't left this?
D.R. Period: NO! Never! One thing about old equipment is that there's only one way to make music. Sometimes when you make music with older equipment, your sound stays the same and you dig yourself— You become a *has-been*. If you don't grow, you can't change your sound. And if you don't change your sound, then you become a *has-been*. So I learned how to work with different programs just so I could grow with my sound. A lot of producers can't do what they do in the dirty South. But not D.R. D.R. make those tracks in his sleep. I'm working with Killer Mike and them. I'm down there working with Lil' Flip and BG, you know what I'm sayin'. And you can't tell that that's a D.R. Period track. Musicians know how to adjust to time. And that's the advantage to being a musician. Because when I was going to school, we had to

go to band class. We had to go to music class. There wasn't no computer class. We had to go to typing class. That was the closest thing to learning how to use a computer. So that experience vs. the experience of a music class in a digital world now, it's like I'm glad I was forced to go to music class, as opposed to going to a Pro Tools class. You understand what I'm saying. The difference is that with learning how machines work and learning how they break down and how they get fixed is the dopest. Because that helps build your sound. And a lot of beatmakers now don't know nothing about sound. They only take whatever the machine offers them and they making beats.

Sa'id: How do you make your drums? Do you sample dry, then add effects in the mix? Or do you process them before?
D.R. Period: I have a library. I have what you call the "D.R. Period library of sounds." [Laughs] I have a library that a lot of producers need to give me a call. [Laughs] I have kicks that were made from like five different kicks. I have drums that were made from live drum sets. Every new drum machine that comes out with internal sounds, I buy it. I take it in the studio, put all the sounds on disk, sample everything, then I go back [take the unit back] and get my money... A lot of these new producers don't think like engineers. It's like they don't have any control. 'Cuz everything is left and right. Even in Reason they give you the option to use the mixing board, still EQ everything.

Sa'id: But did you build the bulk of your drum sound library from vinyl? Or did you snatch it from CDs?
D.R. Period: I snatched from wherever I heard it at. 95% of my stuff came from vinyl. Break-beat records. Drum machines give you a bunch of sounds, but they don't give you different drum sets.

Sa'id: So what do you think about downloading sounds?
D.R. Period: The reason why cats are sitting around downloading sounds all day is because it's something to do. A lot of producers need to start getting more involved in the community of production.

Sa'id: So are you saying that producers should start playing a heavier role in influencing new producers?
D.R. Period: Yeah! They got to!!!

Sa'id: Who influenced you?
D.R. Period: Well, when I came up, everybody on the block did something. Either they beat boxed or they rapped or they was ill with everything. As soon as I seen somebody on the block doing something, I wanted to do it. Like break dancing. I see a new move, I wanted to learn that move. So I'd go in the crib and practice that move. That's the same thing that came with production. It's like every record I heard that came out from some rap group around the way got me amped. Like, "Yo, where did ya'll get that sound from?" and they like, "Oh, well, we was listenin' to James Brown's 'Funky Drummer' and we got this sound right at the end of the record." So then I'd go in the crib, 'cuz I got the record, and I'd be so amped when I found the sound. I'd figure out that these dudes took the sound and they flipped it. And that's what would motivate me to find a record that I know they ain't got that I have. And I flip. A lot of producers, they need to get involved with that. Because now they hatin'. "The only reason why they sellin' is because..." [In sad, mocking voice] Nah, dog. Give duke his props. You don't know how far he came from to get to where he's at now. You know what I'm sayin'. Like, I don't understand the era now. <u>The era now. It's so much hate going on, and it's not enough communicating.</u> Cats is not getting together. Dudes used to share sounds.

Sa'id: That's one of the purposes of this book: To share. If we help each other, we raise the entire game.

D.R. Period: Right, There you go!

Sa'id: You coach, you mix, you direct. Is this something that new producers should focus on?
D.R. Period: They got to!!! That's what takes them from being a beatmaker to a producer. The first level of becoming a producer is knowing how to catch the beat, how to make the beat, how to mix the beat. The second level is learning how to communicate with the artist. The third level is letting somebody else to come in and take your sound to another level. Now you're a producer. A beatmaker is stuck in his world. He'll sit there play a thousand and fifty beats for you. A producer don't really have to do that. A producer could play like ten beats for you and get you to love him within *four* beats! He'll be like, "There's ten beats on this CD, but I'm only going to play four." And the music already sounds like its got words on it because it's already arranged. A lot of beatmakers don't even know about bars. They don't know how many bars there are for an average verse, what works for an average verse. And what's too short for an average verse.

Sa'id: Elaborate on that.
D.R. Period: If you're doing hip hop, there's three types of bars you can use. You can use 16s, 18s, and 20s. 16s, you need three of those (three 16 bar verses). 18s, you need two of those and a bridge. So now we're up to a 3-4 minute record. 20, you just need two. When you're doing 16s, you can either do freestyles or stories. When you're doing 18s you can do like a story, or some kind of like, skillful thing. Two 20s *definitely* gotta be a story. It's gotta keep you focused on what's goin' on. You gotta know the difference of bars. And if you're doing R&B, you gotta know the 8-bar verse, Intro, 8-bar verse, hook; or Intro, 8-bar, then if you add another 8-bar, then bridge, you gotta add a pre-bridge before the bridge. You know what I mean. You gotta understand structure. And a lot of producers and beatmakers gotta understand what role a beatmaker plays in the game and what role a producer plays in the game.

Sa'id: We all start off as beatmakers, until we evolve. But what's the trigger? How does somebody go to that next level, especially if they don't know anybody?
D.R. Period: Right!!! That's the thing. The day you're about to transfer from a beatmaker to a producer is the day somebody says, "Come in the studio, let's make records." Now you're forced to become a producer. Because now you have to walk in with a producer's state of mind. They already love your beats, that's what got you into the studio. Now you gotta figure out how these vocals and your beat gonna work together. Or is the drums, the kicks and snares matching the artist's voice. You gotta know the tones of things. Like some snares might have too much of a ring, and the artist's voice is thin and the snare is thin, and the record is sounding all whack, 'cuz everything is thin. And that's the mid. The snare plays the mid end of the beat. So you might have to get a darker snare.

Sa'id: Right now, do you think it's more of a producer's game or an artist's game?
D.R. Period: It's more of a producer's game. It's always been a producer's game because without a producer, there's no artist. You can throw an instrumental on without no vocals and still move a crowd. Let's see you try to throw on a cappella and do that!

Sa'id: How did "Ante Up" work?
D.R. Period: "Ante Up" cut through because it was an aggressive record. It was a different kind of record. The music sounded like warrior music. The horns were aggressive. The music was almost like an old Public Enemy record. It demanded respect. When I first did the track, I knew the track was crazy, but I didn't know what these dudes was gonna do with it. But when they [M.O.P] went back and revisited the state of mind that they had on their first album on

that track, it was over!

Sa'id: Did that beat take you a long time [to make]?
D.R. Period: Nah. I make beats so quick, it's ridiculous. That beat was done in like, say no more than 15, 20 minutes.

Sa'id: Are there ever times when you make a beat, walk away from it, come back a couple days later?
D.R. Period: If I gotta walk away from a beat, I don't need the beat, 'cuz it just ain't happenin'. 'Cuz tomorrow, it's going to be a different feeling. If it ain't doing it, I'm forcing something to work that ain't working. Creativity is something that's gotta be natural. It's gotta flow. It's like if you're writing as an artist, the words gotta flow. If you're taking four or five days to write the song and then when you finally lay it down it ain't a hit? You played yourself. Music shouldn't be hard to do, when you love it!

Sa'id: When you produce, who do you have in mind?
D.R. Period: I like to think about the artist, but I can't think about the artist if I ain't dealing directly with him. If me and the artist didn't build on what he wanted— Like, Cam'Ron, prime example. Before I did [the song] "Hey Ma" for Cam'Ron, he was like, "Ay, yo, D, you remember that old t.v. show *The Facts of Life*? Yo, nobody never touched that shit. I want somebody to flip it." So I went home, I did my research, found the *Facts of Life*, played the shit over, flipped the beat, did all that shit and took it back to Cam'Ron. And he did what he had to do. So people in the streets liked it. So now, I'm in Cam'Ron mode. He's already told me what he's thinkin', what he's liking, you know. So then I go and do "Easy Like Sunday Morning," flip it, brings it back to him, and he's like "Yo, this is what I'm talkin' about." And that's exactly how "Hey Ma" came about. So that's what I mean about if I'm dealing directly with an artist. Then I can think for the artist and make beats for him. When I'm dealing with an A&R, who's just sitting behind a desk, who think he knows the artist — when the artist don't even talk to him, don't even invite him to studio sessions or don't even respect him!

Sa'id: How often does that happen?
D.R. Period: It happens all the time!!! It's a trouble-shooting game. Right now, I got a lot artists that call me. Yo, they come and pick the beats from me. So it makes life a little more easier. But when I gotta go sit in they office and deal with an A&R dude, that's when the problem begin. Now, I'm not going [to the office] with beats. I go with like three tracks! 'Cuz I gotta get past him [the A&R]. Out of the three tracks, I'm gonna play a real crazy, hard core, gangsta joint. Then, I'm-a play some hip hop shit. Then, I'm-a play a commercial record. And I'm gonna see which of the three he picks. If he picks anything out of those three, then I know where his ear is at. So if he pick the hard core shit, then I'm gonna go in my bag and pull out three more hard core joints to play for him, especially if that's where I think the artist is at. So if I feel the A&R is on the same page as the artist, I play more joints. But if I play all three of those joints [initial three beats] for him and he don't pick none of them, I don't ever come back to his office. Because it's a waste of time. Because what he's going to pick – 95% of the time — the artist is not going to take.

Sa'id: So how often do you have to deal with A&Rs who are trying to run the shots, as opposed to the artists?
D.R. Period: They call me all the time, man. I don't dis nobody, but I can count on my hand the A&Rs that I would love to go sit down and take a meeting with. And then I got like a book in the cabinet of those I would not like to go sit down and take a meeting with! A lot of A&Rs are just homeboys, put on because they man is in position. They're not music dudes. Just 'cuz you know what you like as a person doesn't mean you're a music dude. Right now, a lot of

these A&Rs— That's why everybody rhymin' on they own shit now. Producer's are like, "Fuck keep trying to submit beats to A&Rs and never getting a check." Because they [A&Rs] rather say, "Yo, I got this new 17 year old kid with beats." Remember what they just said: *"This new, 17 year old kid, with beats!"* That don't mean he's gonna give you a hit. And that don't mean he *can't* give you a hit — you know 'cuz a beatmaker come off [makes a quality song], too, sometimes. But 95% of the time it don't happen! So you got this new 17 year old kid you just signed, who makes 50 beats a day, you all hyped over the dude. But you can't go in the studio and get a single out of your artist. And your artist has recorded 30 records and you ain't got a single? You [A&Rs] wouldn't have that problem if you just put him with two producers who know what they were doing.

Sa'id: What's the name of your production company?
D.R. Period: Next Level Entertainment

Sa'id: Is that what forced you to start your own production company? The fact that you had to go to a business level?
D.R. Period: No, I always had a production company for years, 'cuz back then it was the shit to have one. Now, it's to show a lot of these new A&R's, just stepping on the scene, who are the producers to deal with. So even though I may get a hit record, it's still just a record to an A&R. He'll knock it. [In many cases] He don't even like the artist. So he ain't even paying attention to the producer if he don't like the artist. So the key to it is to show them D.R. as the artist. If I can take myself out of producer mode and make myself sound like the hottest artist of the year, it opens up an A&R's whole outlook of you. They be like, "Oh, I didn't know you could rhyme." How hard is it to put words together? Either you got a vivid imagination or just brag and lie a lot. That's all these niggas do. Like what the fuck. Like they sayin' something real? Just 'cuz they got guns on they block; and everybody sold drugs on they block; they been doing that shit for years. I mean, like, what makes that the truth, you know what I mean. It's something that's in the hood. That shit is just furniture. It's just there, you know what I'm sayin'. It ain't ever leaving, we all know. So when I shop my music I show my artist skills and a lot of A&Rs are like, "Yo, you need to work with my new artist."

Sa'id: What about somebody that doesn't have a name but they got some fire?
D.R. Period: Those dudes need to go up under somebody, like they need to work for free! If you make 6 or 7 beats a day and you have to lose 12 of those beats, and you make between 400 and 1000 beats within a year, and you only lost 12 free beats! Yo, those 12 free beats is going to be the beginning of your whole career, especially if you get a hit. Now once you get a hit, now everybody gotta pay you. Like everybody talk ridiculous money. Just because you got beats and you think they hot, nobody's gonna give you no 15, 20 Gs [$15,000 or $20,000] and you don't have a track record, and you haven't proven yourself. They *might* give you like a G [$1,000]. There's a lot of producers now that make beats for $700! And that's what a lot of the artists are going for now. Sometimes this shit work, sometimes it don't. That's why their albums be all over the place because they're using producers who just don't have what it takes.

Sa'id: As far as somebody that wants to produce, what type of gear setup would you recommend? Should they start with a vintage setup or should they go with the software first?
D.R. Period: Whatever they feel they can learn fast, that's what they should start with. Because everybody's mind is different. Some people relate to certain things quick. Some people take months, some people take years. Like I know somebody that just got a drum machine. Nigga still don't know how to sample, and he had the shit for a year! And I told him a thousand and fifty times how to sample, he just don't get it. But he's a computer wiz. So I was like, "Why didn't you just get Reason?" He'd probably be better off with software because that's his thing.

So my thing is to say to a lot of new producers is, whatever machine do it for you, that's the machine for you.

DJ TOOMP

There is no beatmaker (producer) more responsible for the Atlanta Sound (and perhaps the Southern bounce) than DJ Toomp. In a career that spans five of the seven major beatmaking periods, Toomp has always been at the head of the pack. Relevant and consistent and, more importantly, a true hip hop/rap pioneer, DJ Toomp is indeed one of the most important figures in the history of beatmaking.

Notable Credits: T.I., "U Don't Know Me," "24s;" Kanye West, "Big Brother;" Jay-Z, "Say Hello;" Ludacris, "Two Miles an Hour;" Nas, "N.I.G.G.E.R. (The Slave and the Master);" Young Jeezy, "I Luv It"

DJ Toomp's Setup: Akai MPC 60 II, E-Mu SP 1200, Roland Fantom S-68, Propellerhead Reason, Mackie 32 Channel Console, Yamaha NS-10 Reference Monitors, Pro Tools running on an Apple Mac G5.

Sa'id: I want to show what really goes into being a music person, not just a beatmaker (producer)—What really "scopes" a person, what influences them, why a person is doing what they're doing—
DJ Toomp: Un hungh…

Sa'id: That being said, get into where you were born?
DJ Toomp: I was born and raised right here in Atlanta, GA., East Park Medical Center, 8/2/69, [born to the parents] Mary and Al Davis. Grew up in Southwest Atlanta, where everybody know it as S.W.A.T. Southwest Atlanta is a popular location when it comes to the music business. You got a lot of artists and people from the old school who lived in South West Atlanta, like Millie Jackson, Hamilton Bohanon, Curtis Mayfield, Brick, Jean Carr. It's a long list. It's just something about that Southwest Atlanta area. S.O.S. Band, few of their people stayed over there. So it was just that area, man. Then you got me, Sleepy Brown, which his dad was in the group Brick. There's a whole lot of people coming out of that Southwest Atlanta area, you know, Polo.

Sa'id: So when you were born, did your parents say anything, tell you anything about the time and era in which you were born, that they knew something was going to happen for you?
DJ Toomp: You know, I don't know, man, I do so much, but they knew I was interested in music, 'cuz my dad was in a singing group called the MVPs. They were signed to Buddah Records, you remember that label with the Buddah?

Sa'id: Yeah, Buddah Records—
DJ Toomp: Yeah, they used to tour with Gladys Knight, The Impressions and all of them. They had put a single out. They had about one or two joints, but they really didn't make it to the album level. It did all right, they were able to tour. For him, he'd just got a little taste of it, but I'd gotten a BIG taste of it just watching them practice and rehearse. And I was like 4, 3 or 4 years old, just watching them sing down stairs in my house. And I mean during that time, you gotta think, in the '70s if you wanted to be in the music business, you had to sing

or play an instrument. There wasn't really DJ'ing. DJ'ing is a part of music business now. It wasn't rapping, you know what I'm sayin'. It was either you play an instrument or you sing. So I learned how to sing at an early age. I used to sing. My dad taught me how to sing at an early age. I was never on stage with no microphone. [Laughs] But I was always singing. I was taught a lot about harmony and stuff like that at an early age. I used to tap on the piano every now and then when I didn't go to school. But I just never thought that I would really get into it. But they [parents] even noticed that when I was a kid I just used to sit down and watch them practice all the time.

Sa'id: Was it just you or do you have brothers and sisters?
DJ Toomp: Yeah, I got two brothers and one sister.

Sa'id: Older?
DJ Toomp: My brother and sister are older, and I got one younger brother. My sister actually named me Toomp. Yeah, when I was born she was like 5 years old. She just looked in my carriage and started calling me Toomp.

Sa'id: No reason?
DJ Toomp: Just Toomp. Come to find out, it's a name in Africa, it's an African name. And what was wild is that it was spelled "T-o-o-m-p." So I just took it and we rolled out with it. Real name, Aldrian Davis. But everybody know me as Toomp. Used to be Toompy with a "y" when I was younger. As I got older it was just Toomp. I went through a whole lot of flashy names: Special T, Cut Master T, Special D, all kinds of joints, man. Spin Master, Tad Ski, crazy names. Then I kept it simple. I was like, You know what, I'll just be DJ Toomp!

Sa'id: Being that your father was in this group, how much did your parents stress music in the household?
DJ Toomp: It really wasn't even stressed. It was just a natural thing. Like I can almost paint the picture, man. Just imagine 1975. Between '73 and '76, or just the whole '70s and '80s era, mostly '70s. Man, we were the type of family, you know, me, my mom and dad and my sister, we'd jump in the car on a Saturday night or a Friday night and go to this big record store, Peaches Records and Tapes, they used to stay open real, real late. Man, whatever record I'd been listening to on the radio, they'd buy me a 45, and whatever my sister had been loving, she'd get her a set of 45s. My dad would get his albums, Earth Wind and Fire and all that, and my mom would get her Minnie Ripperton. So if you got a family of four people in the '70s going to the record store on the weekends, just kicking it. And I used to— My sister had a little record player in her room and my mom and dad had theirs, so me and my sister had to take turns. But then when mom and dad get tired of playing records, we go down there and play on the big speakers, you know what I'm sayin'. And we weren't, you know, no rich family. We were like lower middle class. Back then our house was worth maybe $70,000. I guess that was cool in the '70s. So we'd go down there and play it on the big speakers. And I used to just listen to records until I'd fall out on the floor. My sister would still be going through hers. So it's like the love for music, man, was just ALWAYS in the household. On a Sunday, when we cleaned up, we might let a Heat Wave album play all the way through, or Earth, Wind and Fire. Temptations. Christmas time, we'd play that famous Temptations album, just let it play.

Sa'id: That's one of the things that I wanted to get at. We've moved away from where music was a communal thing in the household.
DJ Toomp: YES SIR!

Sa'id: And now its become a like a "separate" thing—
DJ Toomp: YEAH, it's so private, I feel you!

Sa'id: Speak on that, how it affected you.
DJ Toomp: It definitely had an effect 'cuz believe it or not, I saw the beginning of it. The people started getting stuff like the Sony Walkman and whatnot. You know, with the radios on it. It was like people used to go a sneak and listen to music. Just when the Walkmans came out, that was the beginning. Before that, right before the Sony Walkmans came out, it was the boom boxes. You remember when Earth, Wind and Fire had that commercial back in the day, Panasonic Platinum. They came out with these radios and all of them was platinum color, that was like the flyest shit to have, the big boom box. You had some bigger than our whole upper body. So that's when LL Cool J says, "I play it even on the subway, I woulda got a summons but I ran away." That started given people summons for running around with these boom boxes playing loud, back in the day. I mean that's from New York and all over the country. And you started having noise ordinances. Even though it was just cassettes, when we made a mixtape or whatever, a cassette, we'd turn the record level up high. So on your boom box, it's going to play a lot louder than your average— And then they started getting better with the speakers on it. So you had boom boxes that were $500 back then. And when they started giving people ordinances and all that stuff, that's when they came out with the personal stuff, all the Sony Walkmans, and everybody else started coming, Toshiba. Where it sounded as good as a boom box, but it wasn't disturbing everybody. That was the beginning of it, right there.

Sa'id: Was music affecting you in class, what type of student were you?
DJ Toomp: Believe it or not, the way the music had an effect on me in the class room was, I wanted to get home, just get home and listen to music. I started DJ'ing in 8th grade, all the way up to '81. I mean I still touch the turntables, but when I was in high school and I was DJ'ing, I would just really try to finish all my work, just so I could go home and scratch! Just go home and listen to music and play. So my grades were good because I just couldn't wait to get home. I used to try to finish my homework quick, that way I'd have more turntable time at home — just scratchin', coming up with new routines and stuff like that.

Sa'id: Yeah, but at that time, who was doing it in Atlanta? Who got you into DJ'ing?
DJ Toomp: Believe it or not, man, I was so ahead of my time. Like my cousin, she's from Brooklyn, and she brought— She used to have mixtapes and stuff, and she just put me up on all the new rap stuff coming out of New York. It was like the early '80s. I been heard about the Crash Crew, Treacherous 3. A lot of people just knew about Sugar Hill Gang and Grandmaster Flash. I know all about the Cold Crush Brothers and all that. I saw the movie *Wild Style* at an early age, like when it first came out. A lot of people just catching on to *Wild Style* like right now. So I saw it. What made me interested [in DJ'ing] is when I heard the record, on Sugar Hill records, *The Adventures of Grandmaster Flash on the Wheels of Steel*. I heard that record, and this dude that stayed in my hood, his name's Jelly Dog, JD, JD Whitaker, he DJ'd but he was an old school DJ who just had two turntables and a mixer. But he didn't scratch or mix. So you know when he used to do all the parties in the neighborhood. When I heard this, it was like 1980/81 when I heard that record. And I kept hearing that [starts to emulate drum loop], and I'm like, Man, how is he starting the records over like that? How is he getting it to repeat? So I was trying to figure it out, but with my imagination, I was like, Man, I believe I know what he's doing. I think he's moving the needle back. And I was wrong. [Laughs] I went home and cried. That shit didn't work. [Laughs]. I messed up a few needles, you know what I mean, lying telling my parents I dropped the record and hit it. I didn't tell them I was trying to figure out how he got his sound.

And there was a DJ, I used to hear this DJ on the radio, his name was Reggie Reg, and it was an A.M. station, he used to mix, and I was like, *Damn, how he get them records on beat and just fade it out like that?* One day I heard him scratchin', but it was real slow like [starts to demonstrate the scractchin']. So I called him and was like, "Hey! [Laughs] How you do that?" 'Cuz they used to have like live remotes at a club, like 12 O'clock. He was like [starts to imitate his voice], "Well, you got to take the rubber off of the platter. And get either a cardboard from a record cover or some felt." I'm like, "What the hell is 'felt?' You know, I'm a kid." He's like, "You can go to a materials shop and cut out some felt." And I started doing it. So the guy JD, I use to sneak up to his house, 'cuz me and his son was cool. So when he'd go to work, we'd turn on the system. So I went in there and just started messing around, 'cuz I saw Grandmaster Flash doing it on *60 Minutes*. They was like introducing hip hop to the world, yeah they had him on *60 Minutes*. And they was talking about the movie *Wild Style*. Once I tried it and figured it out, like I said, I already knew I could do it, 'cuz when I heard it, I was like, I think I can do it.

Other people were just like, "I don't know how he's doing it." They thought it was just studio work. I knew! My cousin told me Flash used to be on turntables. She's from Brooklyn. but she knew all about the Bronx and hip hop. So the minute that I learned how to DJ, that's when I knew it was something going on! 'Cuz I begged my parents to buy me a turntable. My mom bought me a turntable, my dad bought me a mixer, you know what I'm sayin'. And this one dude in my neighborhood named Dee Dee — Dee Dee Tell — he gave me a turntable and I put my generator in it, 'cuz it didn't have a generator in it, it had burnt out. So I was always into electronics. Used to take VCRs loose, see how it worked. So the minute the heads went dirty, I knew how to clean the heads. So I knew how to work things. I just used to take stuff apart all the time and see if I could put it back together. But eventually, I learned it. So I started taking electro mechanics classes. And you know from all of that, being technical, and just being into equipment, I actually just started learning how to find the right type of stuff to really get my sound right on turntables. I found— I started digging into knowledge of the Technics 1200 turntable. Once I got into that and was able to do parties and sell tapes, I started hearing people talking about production. Even though I used to read on the back of album covers, like, What is producing? You know what I mean, like, "Produced by Quincy Jones," "Produced by Stevie Wonder." That was always in the back of my head. I already knew I had the ear for music. Next thing you know, I started going to studios. People gave me a chance and let me get in there and play around. You know they had to show me a few buttons. And it was like, I don't know, it was like I was always on some futuristic type stuff. People didn't really know what DJ'ing was [in Atlanta at that time], and people would say, "Toomp know how to DJ." First thing people would say, "Toomp be on the radio?" Like, "Nah, DJ'ing!" "What he do when he DJ'ing?" A lot of people just didn't know. Later on when they started seeing Jam Master Jay and Run-DMC, people were like, "Aw, that's that shit Toomp be doing."

Sa'id: At that time, a lot of people were looking at DJ'ing as an art and a craft, and some were trying to also make money from it. How much was money a role in it for you, at that time?
DJ Toomp: Well, 60 minute tapes for $5, 90 minute tapes for 8! And this was between '83 and '87. By about '87, my tapes got up to like $12, $15.

Sa'id: What kind of music were you mixing?
DJ Toomp: Hip hop stuff. One side might be fast, up-tempo Miami [Bass], you know, Pretty Tony, 2 Live Crew, Cybertron, Twilight 22, you know, "Electric Kingdom," all them fast records back then. "Planet Rock." And the other side might be slower: Grandmaster Flash, you know. Whoever you could think of that was out around those times.

Sa'id: How about parties, were you doing a lot of parties?
DJ Toomp: Yes! Man, I started off getting like $50 for a party. I used to have to use speakers from people houses. I brought mine, too. I used to have a home boy, you know, he had his license and he'd drive me around. Like whoever I'm doing a party for, like if I was doing a party at your house, I'd call and be like, "Ay, what kind of speakers you got over there? O.K., yeah, O.K., are they big? O.K., I'm going to plug 'em into my amp." So we'd have four speakers over there. Then somebody's next door neighbors might say, "Ay, we got some more!" So we'd run speakers in almost every room of the whole basement. You know, I dun blew a few amps and everything. Later on, once I get my own [big] speakers, my price went up to like $300, $400 a party.

Sa'id: So what did this give you? By you making money doing mixtapes, which is a private thing, and then doing parties, that's more of a communal thing. How does that manifest itself when you're making beats.
DJ Toomp: Want me to tell you how that played a part?

Sa'id: Indeed.
DJ Toomp: Aiight. Me— When other people [in Atlanta] started trying to get into the DJ'ing, which I had the craziest scratch patterns that nobody could really touch for a WHILE. So when more people started making mixtapes, I started getting competitive. I might talk at the beginning. So me, I used to do a trick, back in the day, with the pause button on the tape deck. So I might have a mixtape and record it into another tape deck and hit pause and just repeat a whole lotta stuff. And people were wondering how I did it. They were like, "Man, how you make it repeat like that?" And once again, that's game from New York! These guys called the Latin Rascals, they used to be on 98.7 Kiss [former New York radio station]. And I used to get those tapes, back in the days. And they used to actually edit in the studio. But I knew how to do all of their edit tricks with a pause button on an old school tape deck, you know what I mean. 'Cuz we let it off, the timing was so perfect. And when you do, you got to keep count like [demonstrates countdown], "1 – 2 – 3 – 4 – Boom!" And the counts, and the half-count, you could make it repeat. So after I started getting familiar with counts, first time I touched a drum machine and learned about bars and stuff, that's when I knew like, the first beat on something, the snare, where to let the pause off . So all the skills I had on the pause button play a part in me just being able — when I first got on the drum machine.

Sa'id: So you started understanding timing?
DJ Toomp: Aw, man, the timing was crazy! That's when I knew. I started listening to all the records I used to spin at parties, and was like, Oh, O.K., here go the intro, the breakdown right there, and there goes the end of the record. And I was like, I know I can do this shit. The same way I figured out DJ'ing. I KNOW I can make a record. And I made my first joint with this guy named Raheim Dream, that was in '85.

Sa'id: '85? What were you using to make that?
DJ Toomp: A DMX and a drumulator. The Drumulator was made by E-Mu, same people who make the Proteus and the Mophat.

Sa'id: What kind of track was your first joint? Was it up-tempo?
DJ Toomp: Honestly, it wasn't even up-tempo. See, in 1985, honestly, you gotta think, it was more like Rick Rubin stuff was jumping; '85, '86: you got the Rick Rubin sound. That was LL, Beastie Boys, and Run-DMC. So I was trying to make those type beats. Up-tempo Miami Bass wasn't even OUT, you know. That movement wasn't even out. So when I was doing that, me and Raheim, he was kind of rappin' like on an LL/Run-DMC style. And my beats were more

like, slower, like some Rick Rubin stuff — song called "Raheim The Dream."

Sa'id: So what did you start doing next? Did you say, "I'm bout to take this to another level in my life?"
DJ Toomp: Well, I was on some DJ Premier shit back then. I was actually scratchin' on the record. "Raheim The Dream" featuring DJ Toomp. I drew the artwork and everything on the label — had [the words] "DJ Toomp" coming out with some turntables. So I was scratchin' on the record, too, you know what I mean. It was a crazy record. It was in rotation. They played it like four times a day. I was able to start charging more for parties. So people was wanting to come see me spin.

Sa'id: So '85, who were the people, the producers that was taking your mind, that really influenced you as a producer?
DJ Toomp: The very first hip hop producer or producer, period?

Sa'id: Very first hip hop producer.
DJ Toomp: Kurtis Blow. That's where it starts, you know what I mean. He produced all his shit; "Christmas Rappin'." Anything you see Kurtis Blow, and what was that, Orange Crush, "I Want Action." Yeah, I think him and Russell Simmons produced that. Yeah, Kurtis Blow, he been a producer like that. He produced The Fat Boys. A lot of people don't give him his props. But yeah, I've been a fan of Kurtis Blow. Then later on, it was Rick Rubin, you know what I'm sayin'. And it was another cat, Larry Smith. He did a lot of stuff for Whoodini. I think Larry Smith must have had a deal on Jive back in the days, 'cuz everything that was on Jive/Zomba his name was on it. Steady B, everything. He produced a whole lot of stuff. Larry Smith, he was a hot producer, too. Who else...It's kind of hard when you get into it, too. 'Cuz when you listen to those Sugar Hill records, you don't really know who produced them! All you know is that it's Sylvia Robinson and its Sugar Hill Records. 'Cuz all their stuff was really a BAND! But like I said, later on after Rick Rubin and Larry Smith, believe it or not, I was fan of Thomas Dolby. He produced the first Whoodini record, "Magic Wand."

Sa'id: Thomas Dolby the pop artist?
DJ Toomp: Yeah [starts to sing like Thomas Dolby] "She blinded me with science." He was producing all Whoodini's shit when they first came out. And that's when I first got cable, and I used to be watching them dudes, and I was like, Aw, that's the dude, oh, O.K. Damn, he the one who did that record? A white guy? From England! 'Cuz see Whoodini used to record in England a lot. That's why their sound was so different from everybody's. When they started doing it here, it started blending in with everything else. But they had a real sound that couldn't be touched, you know what I mean, 'cuz that was just an England sound, from messing with Thomas Dolby. BUT, after that [after those producers, who really influenced me]? [enthusiastically] THE WORLD FAMOUS MARLEY MARL!

Sa'id: How did you react to Marley Marl and when sampling came in?
DJ Toomp: Man, I was TRIPPIN', because I was wondering how and the hell he did it! Where did he get those drum sounds! 'Cuz I knew the DMX didn't have it. I knew the Tom Sequencer didn't have it. I knew the drumulator didn't have it. I went through SEVERAL drum machines and was like, *Where is he getting these dirty ass kicks and snares?* And that's when I found out about the SP 12. And it only gave you 5 seconds of sampling time. So you was able to get some good drum sounds from some James Brown records and whatever. And that's when I noticed that his kicks and snares was coming from something old, 'cuz I heard the static. But I still didn't know how he got it. 'Cuz you know, I had the 808 drum machine, the 727. Back in the days, man, our studio used to be full of drum machines, 'cuz samplers weren't out. When they

came out with the SP 12 and the SP 1200, which were sampling machines, you were able to rob these machines for they sounds and just save 'em on a disk. Some people sold their 808; to this day they regret it. The original 808 drum machine, the black one with the buttons going out, man, like a lot of people. Like Andre 3000, he framed his. He paid top dollar for his 808; still look brand new. And that drum machine was used by everybody. Everything you heard was the 808 drum machine. But the thing about it, after the SP 12 and just— Sampling drum machines came out, people were able to just get sounds from all these drum machines, and they just faded out. But like I said, Marley Marl, when I first heard Marley Marl, I think it was "The Bridge." I was like, What the heck is that? [Starts to demonstrate drum beat from "The Bridge."] I'm like, Man, all these drum machines — I got the Roland R8, I got the Yamaha D5, I'm like, *Where are these drum sounds coming from?* I can't find this shit, you know what I mean. And that's when I found out it was a sampling machine. I was walking around Atlanta, 'cuz the way it's made, it looks like a big ol' EQ. Man, I was the first person to run around here with an SP! People didn't know what I was doing. And you had a lot of people who still really didn't even know what production was, straight up. Or really didn't know about drum machines too tough.

Sa'id: So basically, were you teaching yourself how to use it?
DJ Toomp: I had a homeboy, Mike Fresh. We figured it out. Mike Fresh, I've been knowing him, if you were to look at the old Shy D album covers, that's me and him. Yeah, we the ones who rekindled Sha D's career. We kept him going, 'cuz he had the first album, but we came and produced the second one. You know, we were responsible for his biggest song to this day, it was "Shake It." [Starts to demonstrate the hook from "Shake It."] That was the SP 1200 then. So me and Mike we figured it out, man, and just started taking over the city with it.

Sa'id: So did you go through an experimental process?
DJ Toomp: Yes. First we had the SP 12, like I said, that was 5 seconds of sampling time. It didn't have a disk drive. We used to save the data back-up on a cassette deck. A lot of people might not understand that, but you could actually put data on that digitally. Once we got to the SP 1200 — 10 seconds of sampling time — that's when we started buying records and just going through our record collections. We'd go over our aunties' and all parents' houses. We just started getting record collections. Brought them back to Mike Fresh house, and we'd just be down there sampling, going through some of everybody's stuff. It's stuff that we were looping back in '87 that folks just really finding now. So there were definitely influences. The first person I saw with an MPC was Jazzy Jeff. That's when they were on The Grammy's, him and Will Smith., when Jazzy Jeff and the Fresh Prince was on The Grammy's. He had an MPC. Everybody knew me from having an SP 12, and they was looking at mine like a new spaceship. But when they saw that, when that camera zoomed in on Jazzy Jeff's drum machine on The Grammy's, man, my phone just blew up! "Aw, Toomp, your boy got something else. You see that blue screen?" [Laughs] "Man, what kind of drum machine is that? It ain't got them slides, it's got 16 pads." I mean I had people who recorded The Grammy's on VHS and was like, "Man, Toomp, I'm gonna show you." And we would put it on pause. I'm like, Man, what kind of drum machine is that? I ain't have no internet or nothing like that back then. Man, I started going to this place called Rhythm City, it was a music store. They didn't know what I was talking about. I was like, "Man, I can just show you this video tape and let y'all see it." [Laughs] And later on somebody did their research and was like, "Nah, that's the new Roger Linn." We didn't even know it was an MPC, we just knew it as the new Roger Linn drum machine. It was the new MPC. And when we got it, it had maybe 15 seconds more, it was a cleaner sound than the SP, even though they both still 12 bit. But that Akai MPC, man, it just had something else. And that's when I started learning about sequencing and I started incorporating more keyboards into my music. 'Cuz at first, when we did the old Shy D stuff, it was mostly beat driven; just an SP, you know what I mean. It was mostly just beats, not too many melodies. But then later on, see, the SP

can MIDI-up with something. But a sequencer, it can control like four keyboards at one time.

Sa'id: A lot of people have gotten more into melody in the last 5 years, but by not having that solid drum beat background, their drums sound weak, the drum arrangements are weak—
DJ Toomp: Un huh.

Sa'id: Explain how you were able to get into the melody and still maintain the solid drumwork.
DJ Toomp: Well, melodies man, they stick in my head like for years. You know how some people will say they wanna replay The Ohio Players or they wanna replay this Michael Jackson record. Some people actually have to go and find that record. I remember all of the instruments and everything, when they go high and lower, I remember how the strings went. 'Cuz I used to sit down and just study music when I was a kid. Like I said, I didn't know that I would end up being a producer. But I just used to study it so much, and just melodies like that. That's how that song, "What You Know" [T.I.], that's a melody I always remembered when I was a kid. Whenever it got to the end of that Roberta Flack record, that [demonstrates melody part of song, "What You Know."] That part just feels so good. That melody's been in my head since the '70s. So I just decided to really just bring you know, right when it was finger-snappin', I just decided to bring— Like even before "What You Know," I noticed that's what really gave a song identity. The beats were one thing but the melody keeps it going. 'Cuz at one time, DJs used to scratch [demonstrates two hard scratches], like that'll be the music. You know what I mean.

Sa'id: Yeah, like a key stab.
DJ Toomp: Yeah, just a stab, there you go. After while, more people started getting familiar with, "Oh, shit, I can sync this keyboard up where it stays on beat with the drum machine." And if you add any kind of musical skills or your ear was just tuned in any way, you could become a melody player. And I just had so many melodies in my head. And I just kept my drums hitting hard. What I did was, I still incorporate the 808 sounds and a lot of stuff. Even when I sample old school records. Just like with Jay-Z, "Say Hello." I almost went with some harder, more East Coast drums, but I decided to keep the 808 claps and the kicks, just to still keep it that Southern bounce; that way it'll still have that Toomp identity, you know what I mean. No matter what I sample. I might sample something that sound like straight East Coast, but when that beat come in, you're going to know it's a Toomp beat.

Sa'id: One thing that I would say distinguish your beats, aside from the bounce, is the swing. I call it the "Toomp Swing."
DJ Toomp: Un huh.

Sa'id: It's a little different. Was that something that you intended to do?
DJ Toomp: Honestly, it was something that I naturally did. But once people started bringing it to my attention, like, "Hey, man, your songs don't sound alike, but you got this certain little…" I used to be like, "Word? Tell me what part of it is it." They'd be like, "I don't know." And what happened is, I just took time and really went through a lot of my songs, and it's the way that I do my hi-hats, you know what I mean. It's a certain way that I put em down. It's a certain count that I do that the average person don't do; where I be more *between* the beat. And it's just a certain way that it just bounce!

Sa'id: So you play all of your drum hats with two hands?
DJ Toomp: Yeah, yeah, it's a real natural feel, AND I do it in real time!

Sa'id: Please speak on that. When you're doing it in real time, do you keep it on 1/16th or Triplets?
DJ Toomp: Nah, well, see, REAL TIME is WITHOUT!

Sa'id: So you take timing correct completely off?
DJ Toomp: TAKE IT OFF! It's certain stuff that I might put in there, maybe a certain snare [demonstrates snare sound and unique placement of], but the hi-hats and everything— 'Cuz really what you do, once you find that one kick or either snare, at least one of those [may] need to be time correct, you know what I mean. It could be like 1/8th, 1/16th. But it depends. But I double time my stuff just to get a certain feel.

Sa'id: That's what I want you to open up about. People need to understand that you don't have to use timing correct, especially on a drum—
DJ Toomp: Man, exactly! But honestly, timing correct is a thing to where like, you can use it, but it's almost like training wheels! [Laughs] Timing correct is really training wheels. So sometimes you may hear some of my joints where you be like, "Oh, shit, it's locked in." Sometimes I might let certain beats slide by, but a song with a certain feel to it? If it's a sample that I've done chopped up [demonstrates incredibly solid drum pattern with his hands on baseboard of mixing console], it's got to be live. Who can duplicate my rhythm and the way that I decide to do it? But you let the machine do it, it's gonna go [demonstrates the same pattern, but now it sounds "stuck," less rhythmic and natural], and it's going to be *too* accurate. So I gotta do it the way you breathe [demonstrates the solid drum pattern first heard]. You don't breathe on no metronome — "click, click, click…" So I just [demonstrates solid drum pattern]. That's what keeps it LIVE! But if you just let that machine lock it in to where it's mechanical sounding— That's why, you know, you got cats— That's why you can hear people who can produce and some people who program. You can hear the programming of a machine to do something. That's just learning the technical side of it. O.K., I can program this. Uh, put this block right here and this block right here, and this gon make a beat. Like, you know all these new programs on the computer and whatnot. They cool, I use some of them, but I still incorporate my *live feel*. I don't just take squares and put em somewhere and make it be "bass, snare, and kick." Like, somewhere, some *rhythm* gotta be there! I gotta be tappin' or tappin' my feet or somethin', you know what I mean. So that's what plays a part in my sound.

Sa'id: Describe your work ethic.
DJ Toomp: Man, it's crazy. Sometimes I might do like 18 hours a day. Sometimes 14. Sometimes 10. I may get 3 good days out of the week and rest the other days, and chill with my daughter, or just kick it, READ, watch T.V.: UFC, IFL, cage boxing, cage fights, all that shit. I love that, that's my favorite sport right now.

Sa'id: You do one beat at a time or you work on several beats at a time?
DJ Toomp: I might make— When I come through here [his studio], I might have like, eight joints. I'll have eight different sequences, but—

Sa'id: Eight different sequences on the MPC?
DJ Toomp: On the MPC, Yeah. But, out of that eight, three of them may get finished that day. You know what I mean, from beginning to end: break down, hook, verse. But on the other ones, it might just be a crazy ass sequence, that's just like, Ooooh. Some people would rap over the whole thing and let their hook be the hook, you know what I mean, the beat just be the same all the way through.

Sa'id: A lot of producers lack quality control.
DJ Toomp: Yeah.

Sa'id: Meaning they'll do 30 beats and they'll try to get all of those 30 beats off to somebody.
DJ Toomp: Dumb move. I deal with quality more than quantity, you know what I mean. Like I even got old tracks from '94 that I could still load up, on disk, from when I had my first MPC. And some people will hear those beats and be like, "Man, I'll take that beat right now." And I'm like, "Man, that's kind of old." Like, that's what music was in '94. That's some Pete Rock shit right there. But some people be like, "Man, I'll take it now." But even if they wanna pay top dollar for it, I still got to take it and do something else to it. I just can't sell that track like that, man. I don't care how much they love it or whatever, like nah, my name is on it. I don't look at it as trash, I look at it like, these beats need to be updated somewhat, you know.

Sa'id: Let me give you this scenario, and for you it's a very realistic scenario. Let's say you get three or four different beat requests from four separate artists and you have a three-week window.
DJ Toomp: Un huh. [Laughs]. Gosh, somebody must've told you what's going on around here! [Laughs]

Sa'id: And in a case like this, you don't really have time to pussy-foot around. What do you reach for? Like when a hitman has to do work, there's a certain gun or weapon he reaches for. When you come in the studio, what are you reaching for first?
DJ Toomp: Aight, when it come to my East Coast artists, sometimes I go to my ASR-10, call up my Roland Fantom and my MPC. West Coast artists, most of em, that's Reason, you know, Reason software.

Sa'id: Are you controlling Reason with the Fantom?
DJ Toomp: I do it with the Fantom, or sometimes I just be home with a MIDI controller. And it's just a certain sound that I get out of Reason. Down South artists, that can be everything, you know, we sample down here, too. Certain sounds in Reason, the drums are there, but most of the stuff that people wanna hear from me down South, most of those drums are in my MPC, you know what I mean. Like 90% of T.I., Jeezy, Rick Ross, you know what I mean. Most of the Kanye was done on— Like, "Big Brother" was done on Reason. "Good Life" was done with the MPC, Fantom, and ASR. "Can't Tell Me Nothin'" that was MPC, Fantom, and my boy Mike Dean added the extra strings on it, and he used the Logic program, so that was a combination, you know what I mean. So like it varies, man, when it comes to weapons. When it came down to Jay-Z for his album, he was like, "We need something for *American* Gangster. Yo, we wanna get some of the old school feel." I was like, "Aiight!" I tried to shoot some original stuff first, you know what I mean, ain't nothin' like owning all your publishing. So he was like, "Nah, pull up some samples Toomp." I was like, *He* said samples, so O.K., ASR-10 and MPC. And I turned Reason off, "click!" And next thing you know, I just went all crazy with it and that's the way you got "Hello To The Bad Guy."

Sa'id: You said you used Reason for "Big Brother," but you can't tell—
DJ Toomp: Yeah, it's crazy. Well, you see, the drums are a little different. I'm-a tell you, one of the snares from my MPC, I dragged into Reason. Yeah, but "Big Brother" was done in Reason, and I had a live guitar player. And that was the only extra instrument I put in there. I started to get some real strings, but curtains was closing on the album and when I finished in time, I went on and let it go with the strings I had from Reason. It was crazy man, 'cuz what happened we was supposed to had used an artist's record man that didn't get cleared. So what I did was I had to come back home for 8 hours and build a whole new "Big Brother" and fly back to New

York. And when I brought it back, Jay [Jay-Z] and Kanye was like, "I bet you it ain't gonna be better than the original." And I was like, "Shiiid, I bet you it will!" And I pressed play and everybody just lost their mind.

Sa'id: So you used the Reason sounds or were you just sampling and putting sounds into Reason?
DJ Toomp: I mainly used the Reason sounds, I just drag one little drum library in there, you know, from the MPC. Just so I still kind of feel like I'm on the MPC. But it still don't add up to the feel from hittin' these square pads right here [starts to tap on the pads of the MPC 60 II that sits next to him], you know what I mean, just start, play and record. Knowing that this machine can run all this. Now, I incorporate Reason with the MPC just so I can still have that sound, you know what I mean.

Sa'id: You still have me scratchin' my head as to how you got Reason to sound the way it does on "Big Brother," tell me more about how you did it.
DJ Toomp: When I first got Reason, I knew how to program on it, but I didn't know how to produce on it, see what I'm sayin'. I was still tryin' to learn how to work it — how could I even be a producer on it? So after a while, I started learning about the EQ, EQ'ing my drums. Cuz if I play you a track from '03, when I first got Reason, you'd puke. So by the time of "Big Brother," I had learned how to EQ drums, knew how to pan my synths and make em move around. I knew how to make a track move. 'Cuz the program is really a mixing board and every sound effect that you need, outboard gear you know, compressors, limiters, vocoders, and all that. So what I did was just started learning how to get more technical with it. You know what I mean, 'cuz the quality still didn't match what I was getting from my MPC and the ASR. So once I started, people were telling me like, "Man, let me hear some of the beats you made with the MPC." And I was like to myself, Aw, man, that means these Reason beats are kind of weak. You know what I mean. Let me start trying to match these up to my MPC beats. So after while, I started learning how to actually EQ in Reason and get it to *sound* like the MPC. You know, to get it to sound like the analog stuff. But sometimes when I track, I go through the analog board. But that particular one I was in a rush to where, I couldn't even track it out. All I could do is just get my computer and go to New York. And boy, it was beautiful.

Sa'id: Another thing you've told me before is that you like to play through fluid, no loops. Break that down.
DJ Toomp: O.K, you mean like 8-bars, 4-bars, *step by step?*

Said: Yeah.
DJ Toomp: Yeah, 'cuz I never received no type of lessons, like piano lessons. So sometimes, to this day, I still don't know what key, what note is going to make what sound. I do melodies by ear. I whistle that music. You know T.I.'s "Motivation?" I whistled that flute melody for about an hour, just riding in my Denali; I had a little black Denali back then. I just kept whistling. I was like, I ain't gonna answer the phone, I'm not gonna turn the radio on, I'm not talking to no-body. I got this melody. And when I got to my keyboard, I just played it. Like anything I hear in my head, I can play it. But I don't know how to read music at all.

Sa'id: Wow, so what do you do, do you use like an anchor finger and find the tone on the keyboard?
DJ Toomp: I just find it, then go to work [demonstrates keyboard play of a made up melody]. I hit the bend and all of that. I can play, and I learned how to play my stuff all the way through, 'cuz I forced myself to learn how to play. You know if you keep doing it step by step, you'll never get good. You'll end up just being a sequence producer, a sequencing producer. But yeah,

I started forcing myself, even on 16-bar records, I'd play the bass line all the way through, in real time, just so it'll sound like a real bass player. If you do it step by step, I don't know, sometimes it's just you letting the machine take over like that.

Sa'id: So how often do you use the Fantom?
DJ Toomp: [starts smiling)] Man, that's the answer to a whole lot of stuff, man.

Sa'id: A lot of dudes don't understand.
DJ Toomp: Oh, you play with that?
Sa'id: Yeah, I fuck with the Fantom.
DJ Toomp: Yeah, man, hit a few chords and then take that one chord.

Sa'id: You can drop your elbow down on the keyboard and go back and sample that shit—
DJ Toomp: Swwwwiiiirr!!! And it's gonna be something when you use it, yeah, that's how you do it. I learned— What I did was I learned which chords are gonna sound good when I move them around. So you might hit one chord like this, and it might sound like [demonstrates sound]. But the minute you sample it and send it back and you go up here and it don't sound the same. So you have to find them ones that's gonna sound good, and where you can also look to another chord, and it'll be a whole 'nother sound. That's why really, from not having lessons and not really just being programmed to go by the laws of music theory and the rules, it's like I'm against the grain. Like what we do is really— Like you may hear some stuff that the average musician will be like, "Nah, that shouldn't go there!" But the world love it! Like if I'm just going by this guideline that YOU usually go by.

Sa'id: Even with the thing that you just said, you know, although a lot of people think that making beats is a simple process. You know the importance of the "arrangement" aspect of it. Get into that.
DJ Toomp: It's very important, 'cuz really, man, you got some people— I heard folks who try to duplicate my sound, right. And it's funny, 'cuz some people think that it requires a whole lot of instruments. NO! What you gotta do is find which instruments give you that full blend, you know what I'm sayin'. Like instead of having four or five strings, nah, you can have two strings. It's that right synthesizer that's got to sit up under there to make that string sound fuller. It's going to bring out certain things. Then you gotta think about frequency. It's almost like shockwaves in your body. You got this, this, and this. You gotta have something that's going to cover the top end, which is the highs, the mids and the lows. That's why the bass make people move — you got to feel it, 'cuz it's catching the lower part of your body. It's really science, but I didn't learn anything about that shit until I started reading books about shockwaves in the body and how things work. I was like, Aw, that's why when that bass hit you catch that lower end, and it makes you move. When you catch them highs, that be like Lil Jon. Remember how Lil Jon was using all them high pitch sounds in his records? That plays a part in that high end. So arrangement, you got to know where to put each instrument, what part. That's why some of the high parts don't even need to go while the rapper is rappin'. That's why when the hook come, that's when the high part come, you know what I mean. So once you learn that, and some people have to go to college, you know, music school to learn that. Honestly, it takes YEARS. It may take a certain amount of years in school. But long as you got hands-on experience and can walk in a studio on a regular basis, man, it'll take the average person [just] maybe two years to catch up on it.

Sa'id: Touch on this: If I give somebody Toomp's gear list, why are they not going be able to have the same sounds?
DJ Toomp: Man, you're GOOD, man. That's a good ass question! The reason why a person

couldn't just duplicate my sound, no matter if they came and sat in this studio and used the exact same thing, it's because, first of all, you gotta look at the ASR-10. You got some people who are so ignorant to the fact that this drum machine doesn't have ANY internal sounds. It forces you to be the most creative person in the world. It forces you to FIND sounds, almost like you're in the woods, like, How am I going to survive, this all I got? What can I do? If I was in a beat battle, I would be going up against niggas with this one keyboard. Like how many producers can sit in one box room, by THEMSELVES, and create a record? No drum machines, no sequencers, only this one keyboard. It's only a few of us out here. And so, what I have with the ASR, these are sounds that I just decided to MAKE. I might take a sound from one of these machines, but by the time I get it into the ASR the texture of that sound is not going to be the same. 'Cuz you got boost, you can normalize the gain, it's a lot of stuff you can do with the ASR. You got your own custom library, same thing with the MPC, and almost the same thing with any machine. Like, a person can get a Proteus 2000 and I may have the exact same sounds that they have, no expansions or nothin', just straight factory. But, you got some people who go through machines and be like, "Oh, that sound all right…" and go with that immediately. Me, I'm playing with the envelopes, I'm going to tweak it a certain way to where, yeah, you might have a Proteus, but you're not gonna go this far. You're not going to go through all these obstacles to get at these sounds.

Sa'id: Yeah, 'cuz a lot of people now settle on the preset.
DJ Toomp: Yeah! I like to have my sound, something that I created, you know what I mean, I designed the bass to sound like this. So it's almost like— And it's a certain way that I just touch, you know what I mean. I've seen people get on one of my keyboards, make my strings sound way better than I do. That be the real keyboard players. Certain way they know how to touch it. They may be looking at me like, "How did you get it to sound like that.?" That's what I learned. It's just your whole touch, your whole VIBE. And then you know, way beyond the equipment. I'm-a tell you: A person can go to school, man, you can get taught the science of music, the science of music frequencies, and you can get 50 million books, but if your ears are not tuned to hear certain shit? I don't care how much education, how much you get educated on music and the technical side — the engineering and just mixing — if your ears are not tuned, it is almost impossible for you to be able to be successful.

Sa'id: That's what I'm getting at, that road block for a new producer, it ain't the gear or programs, it's actually listening to music; learning the history of music.
DJ Toomp: Yeah! The history of it and just being able to tune in. Almost like you know if you go to a psychiatrist and they show you a weird picture and be like, "What do you see?" When a song come on the radio, I listen to it totally different from the average person. When it first come on, I'm like, I know what sample he used. O.K., he got some Autotone…ooh, sound like live strings, O.K., live drums, too, oh, that's hot…oh, I know where they got that sound from. So I'm sitting there just analyzing that whole track, while the other person's just dancing. I hear everything, and that's the first time. And when you play it again, that's when you get into the whole song. But a lot of time, I can get into all of that at one point. Like from the intro to the first verse that's when I'm listening to all of that, so after the hook come, then I listen to the record.

Sa'id: To you, what is music supposed to do? What is music's chief obligation?
DJ Toomp: Music. The obligation of music is to entertain your walks of life. I heard Quincy Jones say "The soundtrack of your life." It's that soundtrack. And that's another thing, when I listen to old school music on the radio, I'm listening to it like [remembering]. Man, being in the back yard, mom and dad, everybody's living, times was good, riding in the Lincoln Mark IV Continental. It's like when I hear music, I'm thinking of everything that I was doing. Certain

song may come on, and I be like, Aw, that's when I was dating such and such in the 10th grade. We used to listen to this record and be on the phone up to 12 midnight. So I hear it, and you can relate every song to so much. That's why I think that music is almost like a calendar, you know what I mean. It's a soundtrack of your whole life. And that's what it does.

Sa'id: Some people can't make music with other things going on.
DJ Toomp: I think I done mastered that.

Sa'id: Speak about it.
DJ Toomp: Well, it started really from DJ'ing. First of all, I'm left-handed, but I'm also right-handed, too — write with my left hand, punch and throw with my right. And so, with DJ'ing, that was excellent. Some people had their two turntables on one side. I always had my mixer in the middle, to where I use my left hand to scratch and my right. So when this right hand is doing one thing, I can scratch over here, I can be moving the cross fader over here. It comes from DJ'ing, being how to focus on more than one thing at once. When I'm DJ'ing a party, there's so much going on at one time. All of that applies to the music now, as far as being able to run the mixer, run the turntable all at once.

Sa'id: When somebody commissions you to do music for them, what is your responsibility to them? Like, does your responsibility to them overshadow your responsibility to the fans?
DJ Toomp: Honestly, it's both. I pay attention to what the fans want, just in case an artist hasn't been doing his homework, going to the club. You know, some of them don't wanna go out. Some of them get tired of folks, some of them can't deal with people running up on them. I can deal with it. I know how to handle when people say, "Hey, man, when you gonna do something for me?" "Man, hey, I got a manager…He's not going to drop the price for you, he's not your friend. I'm your friend, but I'm not the one you're doing business with. Me and you gon' be homeboys forever. I don't even wanna tell you my price…" I make sure that a person leaves with something hot. That's why I hang out,, I see what people like. It might be a song on the radio that I thought was just aiight. But if I go to the club and see the crowd go crazy over it, I'm-a take my time to find out what makes that record what it is. What part… I ask women, "You kow, y'all go crazy when that shit come on. What part is it that y'all like?" Believe it or not, a lot of people don't wanna admit it, but at one point we had gotten to cool to dance. That way you started coming up with the cool dances, like the "Bankhead bounce." Ain't too much foot moving, that's for the cool dudes. But at one point, it was cool to get down [dance], do the split. But I don't know what happened in our generation to where we was like, "That's lame!" But now, people are starting to dance again. Dancing is cool again, so now, just from paying attention to that, for certain types of artists, I got up-tempo tracks, too. So I'm ready to entertain anybody who's taking their time to see what the people want. But at the same time, ain't nothin' like doing what you do and bringing them into your world, too. I'm also on that.

Sa'id: But I also think your responsibility goes a little further than people randomly know. Nowadays, people are just basically "donating" beats, as Buckwild puts it. Speak on how that comes into play, how sending off a beat CD as opposed to you actually being there.
DJ Toomp: YEAH. I got to be there, 'cuz I got to feel that artist, you know what I mean. On the first— On *Kingdom Come*, the Jay-Z album, I sent tracks for that, but it's so easy to send the wrong track; especially if you don't know the feel or the theme of the album.

Sa'id: Or where they're at at that time—
DJ Toomp: Or where they're at, yeah. I'm like, I have to sit in the room with y'all, let me just hear what y'all talkin' about. Let me just feel it, play a few songs off the album. If I'm not there

to hear at least 5 joints that's gon make it on the album, it's like I'm shooting at an invisible target. And I stress that so hard. And people be like, "Aw, man, you're being stingy." I'm not being stingy, I wanna produce. If I just send you this beat [CD] and I'm not there and you're just picking through it, [saying] "Aw, they're cool, but they don't fit with what we're doing." In the back of your mind, Toomp falling off, 'cuz you couldn't find nothing that [I gave you on that beat CD]. I ain't falling off, I'm not falling off by a long shot! But, if y'all arrange it to where y'all fly me up to that city and I come sit with you, oh, you're gon get that shit. So if I just send you a beat CD, you're just buying a beat. You're not being produced by me! You're buying a beat. I sold you a beat…"Beat sold by DJ Toomp!" That should be the credits.

Sa'id: I've long maintained that there should be two separate credits: "Beat by…" and "Produced by…" 'cuz it's two separate things these days.
DJ Toomp: And I love producing. And that's the thing about it, and there are some people who I work with to where I already see their style and know where they're going; it's easy to send them beats. Because I already know their flow. See, sometimes it does work, you feel me. If I know your style already, just really how you do it, I can do it without being there, sometimes. But 90% of the time, if it's a new artist, I definitely got to be there. And if you're album has a certain theme that you're trying to stick to, I wanna make sure I give you something. I can give you 10 of the wrong tracks, any day, all of them will be bangers. They might not fit on your album, but, boom, one of your artists or one of your homeboys up under you might be like, "Oh, shit, that's fire!" That might be the hottest thing, and you'll be wondering, "Man, you didn't have that on my CD." "Yes I did, you just didn't hear that track the way this artist did." That's why nowadays, when it comes down to it, I always say, you know, you got A&Rs, and you got artists, artists are good at what they do, A&Rs are good at what they do. But really, for an artist who's looking for tracks for an album, nobody can really pick tracks better than another producer. If I'm executive producing an album, and it's up to me, and I'm really overseeing this album, I'm-a let the A&R do his job, but I'm-a do a great job at. Like, if we go to Pharell or whoever, I'm going to make sure we get a banger from him. We're not just gon be glad to have him on the album. If I go to Timbaland, or any of these big, big name producers, me being a producer and an Executive Producer, I'm critical. We're gonna make sure if we're paying his price, we're getting a single! And a lot of people are just getting so caught up in, "Aw, man, we got Timbaland on the album, we got this, and this, and this…" And then you hear the song, and you're like, Wow. Then you turn around and you give Jay-Z the biggest single, it's like, Jay-Z knows how to choose tracks better. And from working with Timbaland, he knows what really fits. But when you got an A&R, who may not even really be a hip hop head, straight up, who really don't even know no kind of history, he might be somebody's nephew, just got dropped in that position, you dealing with a monster then!

Sa'id: So how do you deal with the Business? Would you say you work inside of the industry or outside of it?
DJ Toomp: I'm kind of outside still. I love the industry and I respect everybody that's in it. I'm considered "in" the industry to a certain degree. But, the way I work, I'm not just locked into nobody's production deal and what not. I do song deals, which I'm still on the outside. And whenever I do business, it's just being tallied up. If it's a 10 song deal, O.K., Toomp just did 5 over here at Def Jam; O.K., 5 songs gone. Oh, you got 5 more left, your deal's gonna be up. O.K., cool…boom, boom, boom, boom, boom… "Oh, shit, you delivered!" Mariah Carey, three on Kanye, damn, you did good. I ran through that quick.

Sa'id: Was business something difficult for you to learn or was it something that you caught on to quick?
DJ Toomp: I learned. Honestly, yeah, at the beginning of my career I didn't see my first

royalty check until '97. Been producing records since '85, but didn't see, never, ever saw a royalty check — what a royalty check looked like — until '97. Well, Shy D showed me one, one time. But I didn't know that I was suppose to get one. [Laughs] I signed something, it was a "work-for-hire" [contract]. See, all I knew was [what they told me], "Once you sign this piece of paper, then we gon cut the check." I was like, Aw, shit, I'm just cravin' to get the check; all I know is I made a beat. "Can't get it till you sign this." And it's a work-for-hire, which means I don't own the publishing or nothing. So how can I get points if I don't own nothing on the record. So I really went to "college" at an early age, as far as the music business. I really didn't have— There weren't too many books out here like that. It wasn't too many seminars that you could go to and learn about, you know, mechanicals, your licensing, and your publishing and all that. And now there's stuff available, and it's sad that you still have cats in the basement, trying to be the best beatmaker or programmer, but the minute that somebody gets one of their tracks and it's the hottest song in the world, they don't even know what the next step is! Like, you really need to put more energy into learning this business. If you're doing it as a hobby, let it be a hobby. If you wanna get in the music business, you gotta learn about the business.

Sa'id: Some people tend to focus on your time with T.I., but what's lesser known is what went on when you were working with Luke. How did you first meet Luke [Luke Skywalker], and how did that turn into an opportunity to where you got in the position to meet T.I.?
DJ Toomp: Well, starting off in Atlanta, being born here and everything...the rap scene... when it came to the hip hop/rap scene, it wasn't too strong here, you know what I mean. We only had one label, that was Itchabon Records. It wasn't too many people on that label. But it was still a stronger vibe coming from Florida. You had Luke, you had Pretty Tony, with his label, Forsite Records; Sun Town Records, "Give It All You Got," remember that?

Sa'id: Yeah.
DJ Toomp: It was so many record labels and stuff that was coming through my record pool, when I was DJ'ing, mostly from Florida. And I'm like, Man, this where the scene is. When everybody heard that Shy D had signed with a label in Florida, which was Luke Skywalker Records, that's when I was like, *You know what, I'm-a get down to Miami and see what's happening.* So I got with Shy D. But Shy D, he scooped me up, 'cuz I was DJ'ing at a step show at the Civic Center back in the days. And he saw me on the turntables and was like, "Yo, man, you wanna go on tour?" But at this time he didn't know that I was producing either. When I graduated, I went on the road with him, moved down there with him.
Sa'id: When you graduated high school?
DJ Toomp: Yeah, I was fresh out of high school, like, never left Georgia ever in my life, never flown on an airplane. First show I did with Shy D was in Nassau, Bahamas. Crazy, 18 years old, looking down from the airplane, half-scared but excited, just gone. So from that, it was like an experience watching Luke running his label at the age of 25, 26, selling millions of records. That dude was a millionaire at an early age, shipping records out of his club. His club was his office and his radio station. So he had a club, office, and radio station in one building. So a UPS truck would pull up at Luke's club 'bout three times a day. This was real, true independent. Like, I actually witnessed real independent record companies being ran. And my boy Michael Sterling, who wrote "Lovers and Friends," he's the original writer of that record.

Sa'id: Usher's joint?
DJ Toomp: Yeah, Michael Sterling. He put that record out a long time ago. Lil Jon just remade it. But Michael Sterling used to ship records right out of his garage. For "Lovers and Friends," that song had blew up. Like he made hundreds of thousands [of dollars], like half a million, just off of distributing records out of his garage. So when it came down to it, I'm-a tell you it's the mentality of the people who are in cities around ports. More people [there] understand

distribution and really running a business. Like New York. More independent record labels are out of there because they're in a port area where there's so much business. And then in California you had Macola Records, that was a big record label. They distributed everybody from King Tee, Eazy E, Ice Cube, Dr. Dre…Macola Records.

Sa'id: Is Luke from California?
DJ Toomp: Well, 2 Live Crew was from California, but Luke is from Miami. And they came down there to perform for Luke at his club. See, Luke was a show promoter and a DJ at first. And when 2 Live Crew had this record, he used to book them. And then one day they told him they wasn't happy with their record label. And Luke was like, "I might start a label. I'll put y'all out." And man, next thing you know, you see dude on the album cover.

Sa'id: So you took all that back to Atlanta?
DJ Toomp: Oh, yeah, what I brought back to Atlanta…Well, my thing was, the scene down there, around '92, or around '90— 'Cuz I was in the group Poison Clan, I was the original DJ for that group. Around that time I started reading more, and I had my homeboy getting in my ear, you know, telling me a few things, a dude named Mike Hamilton. Everybody know him as DJ Magic Mike. Yeah, he started educating me on a lot of stuff, cuz he was running his own record label, too, selling millions of record, on his own label, no distribution, selling gold and platinum records. It was a lot of million dollar record labels down there — INDEPENDENT — in Florida; 69 Boyz, all them. Wasn't no major distribution. But what they did was shut down a lot of those distributors that was working. See, it wasn't just no Warner or Jive that you had to deal with. You had different distributors in each region: Big State, Schartz Brothers. And you had different distributors who could get your stuff around the country. So that way you didn't have to deal with the major labels. So cats was getting a lot of money back then. But what happened when they shut those distribution companies down, we were forced to be with a major label. It was a few people who still hung in there and did it without them. But they started closing the walls, shutting everybody down, making it even harder just to be independent. So now, we're almost forced to deal with the majors. But at first, in the late '80s, you didn't need none of that. Profile Records, who was Profile distributed by? Themselves! They was just dealing with independent distributors. They weren't distributed by no major. Sugar Hill, they weren't distributed by no major label. They were the actual "major" label.

Too many people were getting rich, so when it started kind of slowing down for the independents that's when I heard L.A. [L.A. Reid] moved to Atlanta and started LaFace Records. But I was still in Miami, and then I'm like, O.K., wow, I wonder who they could be dealing with? I start hearing that they're working with Jermaine [Dupree], Dallas [Austin]; and these the same producers who I saw come up when I was dealing with Luke and them, you know, we had our movement. But I remember Dallas and Jermaine and them and they grind. And when L.A. and Face [Babyface] came up there, they put them boys on. And I started hearing about it and I was like, O.K., you know what, and I had just did this New Jack City soundtrack with Luke. Aiight, I got paid for the upfront for the track. But this mother sold 3 million records, and I didn't handle my business. And I started learning more, that's when I decided to move back to Atlanta. And my goal was to get to Atlanta and get somebody signed, find me an artist and make it happen. So first people I really dealt with when I got back was Lil Jon. And I produced a song for him called "Shawty Freak A Lil' Somethin'." It was an up-tempo joint. But I still had another sound that I wanted to introduce the world to. And that was that "trap sound" when I was using them organs and just playing around with the beats. I had a whole new studio and everything when I moved back up here. In my mom's house, you know what I'm sayin'. Starting over, literally! So that's when my homeboy who I went to school with always told me about his lil' cousin who rap — it end up being Clifford Harris —"T.I." And that's when I found my artist who could display my style of music, and show the world this is how you rap over these new tracks that this man is bringing out. It's like, it took for Ginuwine and Aliyah and them to show you how you sing over a Timbaland beat. Noreaga showed you how you're supposed to ride a Neptunes beat, with "Super Thug." A few people tried to, you know, when Neptunes did that Mase [sings] "Why you over there lookin' at me." That was cool but people still didn't really. The Neptunes didn't really just *grab* at that point. But when that damn "Super Thug" came out, "What, What, What…" That's when people were like, "Ooh, who did that track?" Like it's certain ways you do it. That's when The Neptunes sound started getting popular. So it just takes certain artists to introduce a sound. Just like it took the Goodie Mob and Outkast and them to introduce that Organized Noize sound, you know what I mean. 'Cuz the average rapper down here wouldn't have known how to *approach* those tracks. So it's like, for that style they had you have to have somebody who can wear that. It's like you being a model, you design a certain type of t-shirt, the person gotta be built a certain way to get out and model your shirts or your shoes. So my tracks are like a design.

Sa'id: Keeping along those lines of design, for you, what is the essence of drums? A lot of people nowadays use the main left and right outs, I'm assuming you use all 8 outs?
DJ Toomp: Un-huh. I start off, when I'm just putting an idea together— Sometimes I mean my machine can already be hooked up to where, I have a template the way all my drums are separated. But a lot of times when I get straight to it, when I don't have time to really do the routing, what I'll do is get a left and right, and just turn it up at a real nice level. 'Cuz my drums are kind of pre-EQ'd already. But I might just hit em again with the Mackie board [analog mixing console], with EQs and whatnot. But sometimes when I'm making a track I do it in stereo. Or then once I get into it, that's when I start seeing, Yeah, O.K., that kick can be harder, let me send that on its own channel. All right, let me send this snare on its own channel. And that way, I get a chance to really hear it. So when it's time to track it out that's when I start separating everything. But when I'm making it, that's when I have it in stereo, that way I ain't using too many channels.

Sa'id: So you only use the left and right going into the Mackie board?
DJ Toomp: Everything is separated, I mean, the jacks are going in here [points to 32 channell Mackie mixing board and its routing], but when I'm working and I just wanna jump right into it, instead of saying, O.K., the bass right here, let me turn this. I just have everything come out of stereo first.

Sa'id: OH, so you still have it separated but you're only listening to it through the stereo?
DJ Toomp: YEAH…Exactly!

Sa'id: 'Cuz you already got it set!
DJ Toomp: Exactly, it's already set. And sometimes I program it having them separated, sometimes I don't, but when I'm really just rolling, I just keep it stereo.

Sa'id: As far as sampling, why is it an art form and not just a simple case of thievery?
DJ Toomp: Honestly, sampling. I wouldn't use the word "thievery." But sometimes if [all you do is] just let it roll, you're really just re-producing it. But what we do is recycle, when we sample. Any producer who takes time to chop it, to where you be like, Oooh, that song don't go like that, you know what I mean. And that comes from DJ'ing, too. Like when I used to beat juggle, change beats around. That's when I started getting into sampling, like, Aw, man, it's the same thing. Like the pause button, same thing, you're catching each part. 'Cuz you know, they weren't rolling off of a metronome back then, that was real time, so that the track might slow down a little bit and speed back up. So when I sample, for me, I chop it up and get creative with it, instead of just running a straight loop. That can be lazy, to a certain degree.

But, if you get that loop and you just got it in the pocket and you do something else and add more music to it, now THAT shows more creativity.

Sa'id: That's the thing where hip hop gets a bad eye. For instance, right now you can go to pretty much any major university and they have a jazz major program but there's no major program for hip hop. Why do you think that exists, when jazz today isn't as commercially viable as it once was — but you can still get a Masters Degree in jazz. Mind you, I like jazz, so it's not a knock against jazz. I think that there should indeed be a jazz major program at all major universities.

DJ Toomp: Honestly, man, it's like sending your kids to private school or a public school. Or you might just have home school. And that's what I got: home school, you know what I mean. A person wanna really learn and just get straight to the business, he come to home school. I'm teaching you stuff that's in the books but it's beyond the books. And I'm teaching you stuff that you're gonna actually use. And it's like, the only music program you have is jazz, so you're forcing me to do this. So it's like, I don't know, it's just a whole 'nother set of people who just got they hands covered on that. But if it's something that I got control of, or if I'm starting a music division at a black college or any other college that don't have it, oh, yeah I'm going to make sure that they have hip hop, I'm going to make sure they cover all genres of music. And hip hop is what's really keeping certain jazz musicians paid right now. Come on, man. You know when we started sampling and we had all them sampling, Pete Rock and all of them…diggin' into them…Ron Carter…Donald Byrd…man, it's a long list…Bob James, you know what I'm sayin'. *Nautilus*, how many people used *Nautilus*? Brought em back. Bob James is getting a nice ass check for that "Mardis Gras," you know what I mean. And they scratched it, so that was like sampling, but instead of putting in a sampler they kept scratchin' it and starting it over, that was dope…and put, you know, the 808 behind it. But yeah, they should include hip hop at [colleges], 'cuz hip hop is keeping it alive. Hip hop is what's making people wanna do their history. You see what I'm sayin'.

DJ PREMIER

Is there any beatmaker (producer) held in higher regard than DJ Premier? Not only is he one of the most important pioneers of beatmaking (hip hop/rap production), he's also one-half of Gang Starr, perhaps the most consistent hip hop/rap group of all time. He's also arguably the greatest beatmaker (producer) of all time.

Notable discography: Gang Starr, M.O.P., Nas, Jay-Z, Notorious B.I.G. (Biggie Smalls), AZ, Cormega, Fat Joe, Screwball, ***the list really goes on!!!***

DJ Premier's setup: Akai S950 & Akai MPC 60 II, E-Mu Planet Phat (sound module), Oxygen 48 (MIDI Controller), Pro Tools HD, Apple G4 (2016: Akai MPC Renaissance, Mac Pro)

Sa'id: You're actually one of the people who helped pioneer the terms we now use like, *chopping*.
DJ Premier: Yeah, Showbiz taught me that. Showbiz, from Showbiz and AG. I gotta give him credit. He's the one that taught me how to chop. I learned about filtering from Large Professor. Like I said, *these are things that I didn't even know how to do!!* But if I was shown how to do it, I knew I could master it, but still not do it like they did it. Me and Show don't chop the same way. Show has a room here [HeadQCourterz Studios, formerly D&D Studios]. He's down with us now, he's got his studio setup in the other room back there. And he's got mad records, and he's like, "Yo, take whatever you want." We can borrow each other's records. Like, when I did "Can't Stop the Prophet" for Jeru [Jeru The Damaja], he [Showbiz] gave me the "Shingaling" drums. He used them first on "Catchin' Wreck." I was like, "Damn, I loved to do a joint to them drums." He was like, "Here, you gonna do it different anyway. I wanna see what you're going to come up with." So I came up with "Can't Stop the Prophet." Show called and was like, "Yo, you melted it!" 'Cuz he knows that I'm going to use it wisely, where even the artist won't be like, "Awgh, you ruined my shit, you rap niggas." When, we chop, we do it in a way that even the artists who are really against how rappers use shit would appreciate how we put it into a different form, out of respect! All of that pours into the way that I make beats. That's what always keeps me fresh. Some people be like, "Aw, he used the same hi-hat, same this." I started using less hi-hat to show that I can still keep it funky. Take the snare away, I'll still keep it funky, it doesn't matter. It's still how I put it together.

Sa'id: Were you heavy into music when you were younger? Did you go to concerts?
DJ Premier: I used to beg my mother to let me go see Parliament. Like my moms keeps up, my moms really keeps up with music. And I learned a lot from her, you know. I went to Chakka Khan with her. And I was a young motherfucker, I was still in elementary. And I remember my moms took me to a Quincy Jones concert. My mother's a concert fanatic, so am I. I'm really big on concerts. I have a big ticket stub book of every concert that I go to. I went to Iron Maiden, I went to Ozzy Osbourne, I've been to Van Halen—before David Lee Roth left the group. Like I said I'm 40, so I've been around. I graduated high school in *1984*, for those that don't know. So I went to Genesis, went to Phil Collins. I went to Motley Crue. I went to U2, way back. I was into U2 from their first album, *1981*, I think it was, when they came out with "Boy," and then "October." I was a U2 fan from back then. And it was rebellious.

I'm really into lyrics, and I used to hear what they sang; they were always protesting war and stuff. I felt them. I went to The Police — before they broke up. I remember all this shit, and all that applies to what I do now!

Sa'id: Your drums are probably the most well-known in the production game, when you first began producing, is that something that you intentionally set out to focus on?
DJ Premier: Well, I play drums. One of my neighbors, his name was Jack Webster, him and his brother Travis had a band with their cousin. Their cousin played bass, Jack played drums. I used to go over there and just be fascinated. They were into Cameo, Slave, and they were really into The Brothers Johnson. I was just influenced by hip hop records that had the hard drums. Jack and them taught me how to play, and I'm not incredible, but I can get by. But the records I used to hear, like "South Bronx" and all the shit Ced G from Ultramagnetic used to do. Their drums were just smackin'. And I was like, "Yo, my drums gotta smack, too!"

Sa'id: Of all of the volumes of music that you've produced, what have you produced that surprised you the most?
DJ Premier: Hmm… Good question… Jadakiss, "None of Ya'll Better"…Um…" "Ten Crack Commandments," that was an accident. 'Cuz I was on the phone talking to somebody and I kept just scratchin' that little sample, so I could just hunt for something. I'm the type of person that can talk on the phone and work at the same time.

Sa'id: You had the track already laid out, with the bass and everything for that joint?
DJ Premier: Nah, just the drums. As I was scratchin', I was like, Damn, this sounds like how I need to do it'. So I just sampled myself scratchin' it and [I] looped my scratch — which I don't really do. But that was the only way that it was going to keep doing it *on time*. So I said, let me just sample myself. So I armed the machine, you know, the old S950. The Akai S950, you can arm it to do it exactly when you start. I let the drum machine keep going so I could keep the timing of it right. And I just did it, and I looped it. That's one of my favorites… "Mass Appeal" is one of my favorites. "Above The Clouds," with Inspectah Deck… "You Know My Steez" is definitely one of my all time, all time favorites. 'Cuz that was a rebirth of a another Gang Starr moment.

Sa'id: How do you see yourself as a producer?
DJ Premier: I'm always a consumer first. Then I'm a DJ. Then I'm a producer. And then I'm an artist! I've been a recording artist with Gang Starr since 1988. And I don't enjoy being a recording artist all the time, because of the politics, how the industry dealt with us on a major label. It's a headache. Furthermore, I'm just not a spotlight person. I always like to play the cut, and just get my money on the low. Because of that, I've always gone with that mentality. I was given a chance to do music as a consumer. The problem with the record companies now is the fact that they don't buy records anymore. You just saw what I bought. [He literally pull's each CD out of bag] I just bought Ray Cash, I just bought the new Dogg Pound, I just bought Shawna; I bought Field Mob; and I bought Mr. Lif! I knew about J Dilla, I know about Stones Throw; I know about the underground, and I still know all about the major people. And that's what keeps me fresher than most producers, because they don't go outside a certain realm of their craft. I was raised on the '70s and the '60s and all the good '80s music. I was into Punk Rock, New Wave — Duran Duran, Susie and the Banchies, The Smiths. You know, groups that you'd be like, "Damn, Premier listens to that shit?" Hell yeah! 'Cuz it was good music. Good music is good music! But when it comes to hip hop, I'm really, really adamant about keepin' it hard. That's the way I was raised on it. I saw it from the very beginning. And I lived in Texas at the time, and I still saw it from the very beginning, because my roots in Brooklyn were through my grandfather, my mother's father. I used to be in Brooklyn so much. He took me

everywhere, you know, in the early '70s and the early '80s, when niggas was just break dancin' for money and there were no records out yet. By the time I was 13, visiting my grandpa, I felt like I was a New Yorker, then. So when I moved here in '85, everything wasn't new. The same people I fucked with, still rollin' with me. And from there I just expanded into what I do now. But like I said, being a consumer and a DJ is the number one thing for me!

Sa'id: You recommend that producers have to listen to other music outside of hip hop?
DJ Premier: You don't *have* to. But it's good to listen to other forms of music, so that you understand what made hip hop great. Hip hop borrowed. This is why we sample. We're borrowing from music that was already here and just, like Rakim said, we converted into hip hop form. Hip hop can take anything and just make an ill beat. It's just about who's constructing it and understanding the science of it and understanding how to listen to it. A lot of people don't even know how to listen to records!

Sa'id: Is speed an issue with you, when you produce?
DJ Premier: The time part shouldn't even be a factor. It's about how does it feel when you listen to it! And without being programmed. Like a lot of people get programmed by radio. But if you're a true head, you're not going to accept what the radio plays if it sounds like bullshit. And if you're a hip hop head and you're street — and street doesn't mean that you have to be from the city, you can be from the country and all that — if you're a hip hop head, you know how to tell the difference between a good record and a bad record. These so-called mix DJs who are also ruining the game. 'Cuz they be like, "Yo, this the hottest shit out," and it be BULLSHIT! I'm like, YO, what do you hear that makes this record so great?

Sa'id: Really, they're no different than a radio DJ, 'cuz they are not blending or mixing or doing nothing like that. All they're doing is playing records.
DJ Premier: EXACTLY! And they call themselves mix show DJs or mixtape DJs. They're compilation DJs! There needs to be a new category. There should be compilation DJs and mixtape DJs. If there's no scratchin' or cuttin' or mixin' on it, it is NOT a mixtape and it's NOT a mix show!

Sa'id: Right now, do you look at radio as a reflection of quality music or is it a reflection of brand name producers?
DJ Premier: HELL NO!!! Radio is a reflection of murder to our culture!!! That's what it is. They're murderers. They're killing our culture off! They don't care, 'cuz they're still gettin' their checks. There are program directors that know what they're supposed to be doing, but they just keep sticking to it. As long as they're gettin' a check, they could care less.

Sa'id: If you were a program director, how would you implement change?
DJ Premier: For one, you can't only dedicate an hour a day to what made hip hop great. [hip hop] was born here, in this city [New York]. This city still suppose to dictate the way things drive, 'cuz hip hop was born and raised here. But there's no one from the culture that really, really gives a fuck that's involved in making sure that the culture still stands. And they're like, "No, the demographics are different and the kids are 18 or whatever." Nah, hip hop has grown to where now it's ages 6 to 56! There's a lot of 40 and 50 year old people that were around when it started. And they know how great it used to be. Hip hop ain't something that you outgrow. I ain't gonna be like at 50 years going, "I used to listen to that rap shit, when I was young." Nah, I'll love this shit forever.

Sa'id: You know Arif Marin, the legendary producer, just recently past, at age 74. And up until 74, he was producing. Do you see yourself like that?

DJ Premier: Yeah. Producing. It's just like with Christina [Aguilera]. I'm not going to cross a certain line to ruin my reputation as DJ Premier. We met in the middle, where my audience would be like, "Yo, that shit that you did with Christina is hot." And the people that fuck with her are gonna go, "Yo, that record you did with Premier is hot." I didn't soften up, I didn't water down what I do. I kept it raw. And she hired me based on what she loves about me anyway. So she's gonna get more of that. I still know how to attach my style to the artist. Guru always calls me a *beat tailor*. Just how a tailor hooks you up with a nice suit, once they look at your body and your frame. Or like a chef, I know how to cook up the proper plate. I know how to put the right meat in there. I know how to put the right sauce. It's all based on the artist. And I have to have some type of feeling about them to know how to make it match. And a lot of producers don't do that. A lot of producers just make beats and lay it down. They're not producers.

Sa'id: How do you distinguish between a beatmaker and a producer?
DJ Premier: A producer has to arrange the song! Know how to coach a vocal. Know when something needs to be fixed, based on your ear — your ear is everything that makes you great. My ears are definitely not fucked up. My ears are really on point because, for one, I respect hip hop *culture*, and I respect rap music. A lot of people don't respect— They listen to music, but they don't *respect* music. You have to respect it. If you respect it, you will always do hot shit! So even when I don't sell a lot of records, my shit is still respected, even though someone else might've sold platinum. I know why they are platinum and why I'm not! Because I don't conform.

Sa'id: You got all of your drums from vinyl or did you use sample CDs?
DJ Premier: Most of them are from vinyl, yeah…just find a little clip…and then I widen it, you know, or beef it up.

Sa'id: You was telling me that Large Professor showed you how to Filter?
DJ Premier: Un huh…I used to go over to the two deejays house, K-Cut and Sean [former members of Main Source], and Large Professor used to always be over there, and he used to show me how to filter on the SP 12.

Sa'id: How did you take what he showed you to the next level? Where did you go with it, in which direction?
DJ Premier: With records like "Ex Girl, To Next Girl." Pretty much, filtering was a hot thing at that time. Pete Rock started to layer 'em. I didn't understand how to layer 'em. He would have the filter and the sample going underneath each other, where he created his own bass out of filtering the original sample.

Sa'id: Like having the sample, copy that, have the original playing at the same time.
DJ Premier: Yeah, Yeah!!! Look at "Reminisce." You hear the sax, then all of sudden you hear the *boom, boom*. It's the same exact sample but he fuckin' put it underneath. That shit just happened to work. He murdered that shit, man. He murdered it!

Sa'id: What gear setup did you first start with?
DJ Premier: Professionally, or back when I was doing my demos?

Sa'id: Back when you were doing your demos.
DJ Premier: I used to borrow a buddy of mine's SP 12. His name is Carlos, he's the one who actually got me into the whole business; he's from Texas, too.

BeatTips: It was the SP 12, not the SP 1200?
DJ Premier: Yeah, it was the SP 12. The 1200 wasn't made yet. We would've been buggin' if we seen one of them.

Sa'id: You were doing your demos in Texas or were you in New York by this time?
DJ Premier: Nah, Texas. I was doing them in Texas. I was going to college. I had a crew down there. One of them was from Boston. The main dude, his name was Top Ski. I was doing parties and stuff, 'cuz my father worked at the college that I went to. It's an all-Black college called Prairie View A&M University. All Black. A bangin' ass school. We had one of the best bands. During the football season and all that, our band was ill. I got a lot of my experiences from being down there, too, that made me funky. But like I was sayin', I met Carlos at a record shop, in the hood. All the locals went there. He got me a job there. And that's how I got to hookin' up with Gang Starr. Prior to that, I have always collected records. My mother has an ill record collection.

Sa'id: What was the name of your group back then?
DJ Premier: We were called MCs In Control (M.I.C.). I was the DJ. But I was called Wax Master C, 'cuz my real name is Christopher. When I joined Gang Starr, the owner of the label, he didn't like my name, so he told me to see if I could come up with somethin' else, so I came up with DJ Premier. Me and mother. I showed my mother a list of names that I had, Premier was one of them. I just wanted something unique, that really represented who I am.

Sa'id: So how long was it between the time you sent your demo and when you and Guru made it happen?
DJ Premier: Probably like a year, 'cuz I was still with my group. But we had changed our name to ICP, we were called the Inner Circle Posse. We were shopping our demo. Wild Pitch Records, which Gang Starr was on, they didn't like my dudes, they liked me. And they wanted me to be in the group. And I said nah, not without my dudes, so I pulled out and said no deal. About a couple of months later, somewhere between 2 and 6 months, I really can't remember, but I remember the day and what happened. Sugar Pop couldn't afford to stay in New York and Styli was in the military, and the lead dude, Top, went to the military, and he had a four year thing before he would come back home. And I was stunned!!! I was like, "Yo, just put us in the studio and let us cut a demo in a real studio." They [Wild Pitch Records] even paid for that, and they still didn't like it, you know, when we updated our demo. They still didn't like it. But at least they gave us a shot. 'Pop got frustrated and left. So now I'm by myself. So I called and said, "If ya'll still want me, I'll get down." And that's how I got with Gang Starr.

Sa'id: You're known for a couple of very distinct sounds. But when do you think that you got past all the jazz association and everything? In my opinion, I think when you started working with M.O.P., it inspired you to go in a different direction, and you went somewhere else with it, and your sound expanded.
DJ Premier: Right…It was before M.O.P., really. I'm a person that's just such a fan of good artists, I'm like, Damn, if we ever got together we'd make somethin' hot. I know. Like I know with Nas, we make hot shit. I know it. I'm gonna make a good record regardless, but there's certain artists where it's like, YO!'… You know it's gonna come off. Like, say if I see Janet Jackson back in the studio with Jimmy Jam and Terry Lewis. I'm like, good, good. 'Cuz their formula works!

Sa'id: So the thing is certain artists challenge you to go somewhere else with your production.
DJ Premier: Oh, yeah! Anybody that come with a banger. I'm like, fuck that, I'm going to

the studio. When I hear a record that's dope, I'm goin' into the studio. Like, when I heard— I remember Rakim told me that Dre did the record that 50 did, it's on the "Get Rich, Or Die Tryin'" album, the song with the gun cockin', where it goes [he starts rhymin'] "I'll kill you, I ain't playin', you know what I'm sayin'." 50 murdered that. He murdered it. And I was like, *aiight*, I'm going in to make a joint. And NOT bite that. DON'T BITE. Bitin' used to get your ass kicked, when I was comin' up. We was seeing niggas get jumped for bitin'. Now, bitin's cool.

Sa'id: You got a couple sounds right now, how do you describe them?
DJ Premier: What it is, I'm still doing the same thing I've been doing. I'm just updating the formula. That's it. I'm just updating the same formula. So you do that gradually, you don't do it in big steps. If you do it in big steps— You don't want to lose the people that already get you — the ones that already understand you, you don't never want to lose them! I never want to lose my street niggas! I wanted to get the hard niggas to like me because of the fact I can relate to them. So being that I can relate to them, they'll understand my music. I'm just doing it in a music form, where they'll go, "Yeah, nigga, you understand us." They're just misunderstood and that's why there's so much crime and crazy shit going on. The ghetto's a really beautiful, balanced place, just like anywhere else, I gotta represent for that!

Sa'id: Who do you produce for? Do you produce for the fan first, do you produce for the artist, or do you produce for both at the same time?
DJ Premier: Both, but I gotta love it first. And I know when a record sounds good to me. Again, that's my DJ and consumer mentality. Every time I make a record, I literally act like I'm not the same person, that I'm not me, that I'm another person, whoever, and I listen to it like a regular person would, like, "Check out this new joint Premier did." Knowing when I hit good ones, vs. my aiight ones. Even my aiight ones I'm comfortable with putting them out. If they can leave the studio. And my *aiights* is better than a lot of niggas joints. And again, not a pat on my own back, it's out of the respect for music and knowing how to pick and choose. The record companies, I don't know how they hired these people they got.

Sa'id: What do you recommend for a producer, let's say who's been doing it for a couple of years, who hasn't been able to get on…How do you suggest he try to get on? Should he have a track price, etc., what's the best route?
DJ Premier: Nowadays, it's just so weird man, because it was so hard to try to break in when I was coming up. Now, it's really easy for everybody! You got the internet, you can start your own page, site and create your own business. You can even do that new thing, Burn Lounge, and actually become your own record company and do your own retail and collect your paper. Those are some recommendations, BurnLounge. I write my own blogs and everything. I haven't done one in a while, but I'm a start being more consistent 'cuz I'm home now. I've been on tour a lot. I was even doing them while I was on tour. We went to Hong Kong and all that shit. We want to understand the whole aspect of what we do as our career. This is our career. I want to master all of it and take it to other levels.

Sa'id: Do you think that new producers should try to get their music to well-known producers or A&Rs?
DJ Premier: Yeah, producers. Ya'll can always submit tracks to me. But make it on a level where I would really appreciate it. When I [first] submitted shit, my shit was on a level where I was like, *Yeah, I'm going to give this to Marley Marl*. And I went and saw Marley Marl. I always tease him about it, 'cuz he don't remember, but I remember that day. They were about to do "We Write The Songs" on the *In Control* album, with Heavy D. And he was waiting for Biz [Markie] to get there. I went to BLS [radio station 107.5 WBLS - NYC], he had a show with Mr. Magic, the Rap Attack…Wow.

Sa'id: Do you think that hip hop/rap producers need a union?
DJ Premier: I'VE ALWAYS SAID THAT, I always said that we need a union!!! But ain't enough niggas ready to take it there. You know the consequences of that, we ain't even gotta be discussing it, you know the consequences of that. I was down to ride.

Sa'id: Would you ever help a producer get placed?
DJ Premier: Yeah, but it's gotta blow my mind. That's why I got Show in here. Showbiz got a whole arsenal of bangin' beats, it's like next level. He's got a whole new sound, but it's still Show, and they bangin'. And he got a crew of producers he's bringing up. Some of them do the South stuff, one of them is from the South and the other one's from Jersey and they got totally opposite styles, but to the level where I'm like, yeah, we can work with that. So we're about to do a Works of Mart [Premier's production company] thing. But everybody'll get credit for what they do. I'm not going to start having them do shit, then I put my name on it! I can't never do that, even though some producers do that. I can't do that!

Sa'id: At this point, are you still mixing all the things that you do?
DJ Premier: Yeah, I've been mixing ever since we moved here [HeadQCourterz Studios, formerly, D&D Studios]. I talked to my old Engineer, Eddie Sancho, recently. I told him I'm going to bring him back and start working. Yeah, 'cuz he was a *BIG* part of my sound, from 1992 when I met 'em and I started doing the *Daily Operation* album with Gang Starr. And that's how I started to work with him. 'Cuz showbiz came to do a remix for Lord Finesse for "Return of the Funky Man." And they wanted me to do the scratches on it. So I came down here to do it with them. And Eddie engineered the session. And they gave me a cassette tape. I had a bangin' system in my MPV. I had one of the illest MPVs out, one of the banginist systems ever in New York! Master Ace will tell you, I was that nigga. It was clear and loud. And when I played that fuckin' mix — that Showbiz did with Eddie — in my car, it was so dope. I said, I'm going to start working here. I came in, started working with Eddie. He's the one that showed me how to use the MPC 60II! He was like, "Yo, you should use *this*." I was using the Alesis drum machine at that time. He was like, "Yo, you should use the MPC man, the way you're trying to divide your tracks, and they way that you're laying them down. You could do it all on there and do a straight print." I was like, "Word?!" So I bought his. And then boom! I started working with that. See, I got that motherfucker [MPC 60II] still there, and the 950.

Sa'id: Do you use two 950s at the same time?
DJ Premier: Nah, the other one, that one's broke, it needs to get fixed. I collect them.

Sa'id: So the only gear that you added was the Mo'phatt rack?
DJ Premier: Un huh, the Planet Phat. Bass. Yeah, I just switch it up and stuff.

Sa'id: You working with keyboards now, too?
DJ Premier: Yeah, I got my lil' Oxygen right there.

Sa'id: Oh, so you trigger the module with the Oxygen?
DJ Premier: Yeah. And Pro Tools has things, too, like the Indigos and stuff, you know, where you can do basses and keys, separate guitars, and have all the different variations of all the different guitars and stuff. Everything I do is experimentation anyway. It's like being a scientist in the lab. I experiment 'til it sounds like it's got my neck just *poppin'*. Once my neck pops, I'm rollin' with it!

Sa'id: Have you tried usin' production software, what do you think of that?
DJ Premier: Nah, that's just not my shit, my style. I love this style, and as long as this equipment

work, and I can keep getting them fixed by my people upstairs [DBM Audio Repair]. And I'm into new shit, just when I'm ready to roll there. Now, Jazzy Jeff, he's a gadget man. He puts me on to everything. I got people that still keep me in the loop.

Sa'id: For a new dude coming into production, what setup would you advise?
DJ Premier: I would say look, the shit I got is what I recommend the most. But that's so old, it's hard to find 'em. But there are newer versions of it, I don't know how to operate 'em. Even the MPC 3000, I don't know how to work.

Sa'id: You use the MPC 60 II just as a sequencer?
DJ Premier: Yeah, and I sample with the S950. Marley Marl was using that shit, Ced G and all of them. So I was like, O.K, I want one of those. Once I learned it. The King of Chill taught me how to work it, before I even locked it up to a drum machine to trigger it. He was teaching me how to loop it, chop it down and all that, and even do time stretching. And it's limited on the time. That's what I like about the S950, 'cuz I don't over sample. It's limited on the time, so I gotta take that little bit of time to make something. And that's what makes you strain and go, How can I flip this and make it dope.

Sa'id: You use the Timestretch on the 950?
DJ Premier: Yeah, a couple of times…on "Crush," Big Shug.

Sa'id: When you sample and sequence, are you looping the sample inside the 950 or are you choppin' it and lopping it in the sequencer?
DJ Premier: Nah, I'm doin' it in the 950. I loop it and then if I want to pitch it, I timestretch that and put it on a different pad. And then assign the same outputs to cut'em off, boom! Then it's all about where you land it.

Sa'id: The funny thing is when I got the MPC 60II. Rone [fellow friend and producer, Mike Rone] came to my crib and showed me everything you showed him.
DJ Premier: Yeah, Yeah [Laughs].

Sa'id: But I wouldn't even put everything on one track.
DJ Premier: Awgh, see, nah, nah, I can't do that. I gotta separate it. I separate it in the MPC, and then I do the individual outputs and lay it. I construct it first, then I separate everything.

Sa'id: What do you think your legacy has been on hip hop, thus far? And what do you think it's going to be?
DJ Premier: I feel like it's already in the history books. I got a Hall Of Fame DJ Award from Jam Master Jay and Grandmaster Flash. And I got the picture, too, of them presenting that to me. And that's ill! Things like that let me know I made it. All the people that I wanted to love my shit, love me. I wanted Run-DMC to love me, I wanted EPMD to love my shit. I wanted Rakim to love me…KRS ONE…Big Daddy Kane…Kool G Rap and Polo…Biz…Heavy D and The Boyz…Marley…Red Alert…Just Ice…MC Lyte…Audio Two… I wanted all of them to say "You *dope*!" And they all said that. So I done made it. If I stop today, I'm good.

Sa'id: Do you see yourself teaching hip hop/rap production in the future, similar to how Spike Lee teaches film over at NYU, or how Winton Marsalis teaches?
DJ Premier: I wouldn't be able to answer that now. Not that it couldn't never happen. I just have my own way of teaching people. It could come along. Right now, no, but you never know.

Sa'id: Knowing all that you know, do you recommend hip hop/rap production as a career choice?
DJ Premier: If you respect music, yes. If you don't respect music, no. Even if you make it big and have millions of dollars, you'll still be a sucker to real niggas. And why would you want to be a sucker to real niggas? When real people is who you want to be around. Be around real people, you'll enjoy life a LOT better.

Sa'id: How much should producers charge for tracks?
DJ Premier: If you're new, understand the business is funny. You gotta know the economy that you're living in. Shit is fucked up right now. Don't ever charge high, until you can really claim that you've done enough groundwork and paid dues to charge high numbers, you know what I'm sayin'. Don't rape the game when you haven't paid dues. *I paid dues…I did mad scrapin'*… Did things I wasn't even supposed to be doing, just for the sake of wanting to get this. But I did it in a way that I got through. Respect was on my mind the whole time!

Sa'id: Back then when you first started producing, how much were you charging for a track?
DJ Premier: Things were different. I mean, back then, $2,000 was a lot to me, you know. I did "Unbelievable" for 5 [$5,000.00] for Biggie and I was already making about 15, 20 grand a track at that time in '93, '94.

Sa'id: So you gave Biggie a break?
DJ Premier: Yeah, same thing with Jay [Jay-Z]. I liked Jay, I knew he was talented.

Sa'id: How much do you charge for a track now?
DJ Premier: I'm negotiable, that's all I can say, my prices vary.

Sa'id: Would you ever do a track for free for somebody?
DJ Premier: I've BEEN doing that!!! [Laughs]…Like, I'll do M.O.P shit for free…Yeah, M.O.P.'s for free.

Sa'id: The only reason I ask you that is 'cuz a lot of dudes need to understand you're going to have to do some favors…
DJ Premier: If you don't pay dues, what the fuck are you expecting? You know what I'm sayin'. Like the morals and development of artists and people involved in the music business have been taken away. I was *developed* into an artist and as an entertainer. I didn't know nothing about shows. I knew how to spin, and I stayed behind that table and kept quiet, I didn't talk on the mic. Now I understand how to put myself out there at the right times, I know when to speak and when to be quiet. You gotta know how to put yourself through this shit. This shit is *rough*, it's real rough! If you don't understand it, platinum or not, ya'll are all going to be right back in the poor house, soon. I've seen it a billion times. And it happened to me; I didn't hit the poor house, but I went flat…I had some flat tires, for real.

Sa'id: How did you get through those times?
DJ Premier: I utilized gettin' gigs that paid good money and still enjoyed the gigs that I was gettin'. I went overseas, I said, "Fuck it, I'm big over there." Went over there and worked and had a beautiful time. And it set up everything that I planned on doing to fix what was going on in the states, you know, to bring me back up. So that's from understanding the industry and how it works. I talk shit about how fucked up things are, but I do it in a way where I know it's not just me I'm speaking for, I'm speaking for a mass of people. Still, I just do it in a musical format.

Sa'id: What do you have coming up?
DJ Premier: I started a label called Year Round Records. I have three artists signed. The NYGz. They're straight raw, ghetto dudes, Panche and my man, Shiggy Sha. They're very knowledgeable and intelligent, but straight hood. I like what they kick. We had the struggles of the time it takes to get things done, but they understand what I'm goin' through to rebuild the house. Like, I'm sayin', now we on the rebuild and we're all doing it together. I said, "Hey, I'm a take a short, too…" I ain't gonna buy a new whip, no new jewelry, which I could do that, I use to do that all the time. But not before getting our work done… And I always get a new car every couple years. Always, two cars, minimum. And these last six years I have not bought a new vehicle. SIX YEARS!!! Because we've been on this mission, since then, to get our shit on another plane. And I'm still riding in the same 'ol beatup fuckin' Suburban. It's cool, I got music in it, and my shit is fast. I did soup it up, I did soup up my engine, and I did dual it out, so it will out run a lot of cats who got rims. I have no rims, my shit is dirty all the time and the window don't roll down, and the tints peelin'. People can't see me like that 'cuz I'm Premier. Fuck all that, I'm real, nigga, that's what's up. So fuck how I look. I got my niggas, and I got myself…

9th WONDER

From his beatwork with his former group, Little Brother, to an impressive list of credits that are as balanced and broad as Jay-Z and MURS, 9th Wonder has always been steadfastly shaping his position in the history of beatmaking (hip hop production).

Notable discography: Little Brother, Jay-Z, MURS, Buckshot, Skyzoo, Destiny's Child, Sean Price, Masta Ace.

9th Wonder's setup: FL Studio (2016: Native Instruments Maschine)

Sa'id: Give me a glimpse of your life as a child.
9th Wonder: I had a great childhood, man. I had an outstanding childhood as a matter of fact. I learned a lot; I got to see both sides. I went to a predominantly white elementary school. My mom was a teacher at this elementary school; she was a kindergarten assistant. So you know, I got a lot of leeway with that situation. But at the same time, I had an uncle that was a kingpin in Winston-Salem, North Carolina. And I got to see that side of the game. The crazy thing about it is, I never saw any drugs, I never saw any of the work. I did see, you know, lots of money, you know what I'm sayin'. My cousins used to get mopeds and stuff like that for Christmas. And I got to see from my cousins who were in the game, I got to see that first hand. So you know, I kind of got the best of both worlds. I got the whole academic side, with me being in different academic programs in elementary school, because I was quote on quote, "academically gifted." And then at the same time, the flipside, I would be running through the projects with my cousins. It was real. eclectic.

Sa'id: Were your parents together at the time when you were coming up?
9th Wonder: Yeah. My parents are separated now — although they don't act like it. My parents separated when I was in Jr. High School. I grew up with my parents. My dad worked a lot, you know what I'm sayin'. My mom was a school teacher, so I was with her most of the time. My dad built his house with his bare hands. My dad is (was) a professional landscaper. He did that for many years before he got to RJ Reynolds Tobacco Company, that's the company that makes Winstons and Salems and Camels (cigarettes). That's my mom and dad. And I have one older brother. I had an older sister, but she died in a car accident in '77. I don't remember her.

Sa'id: How old were you when she passed?
9th Wonder: I was 2 years old. I don't remember her at all, but my brother does. My brother was a year older than her. So that kind of took my family through some things. That's my childhood as a whole.

Sa'id: So how did music— Was it the typical black thing, did music play a big part in your family life?
9th Wonder: My mom and dad were in a choir called the MPT Celestial Choir. It was a choir started by a man named Marion Pete Thomas. That's what "MPT" stands for. They would tour with the choir and whatnot, so you know, throughout all the gospel music that was played in

the house. And at the same time, I'm 33, my brother will be 45 this year, so all the music he would play was The Commodores; Earth, Wind, & Fire; The Gap Band; all of the late '70s, early '80s; Parliament Funkadelic; Jermaine Jackson "Let's Get Serious," all that stuff. I would hear all of that. He used to play "Easy Like Sunday Morning" all the time (by The Commodores). Everything in that era.

Sa'id: So your brother, he DJ'd or he just loved music like that?
9th Wonder: He just loved music like that. And you know, from going to different clubs in the Winston-Salem area, at the time when he was in high school. I just listened to the music that he would play, when I was about 5 or 6 years old. That was the situation. But it wasn't until I started kickin' it with my cousins. There was a projects, a housing development in Winston-Salem called Cleveland Avenue Homes. And Cleveland Projects was where I heard a lot of my first hip hop records. Actually, it's where I heard my first hip hop record. And my first hip hop record I ever heard was "Planet Rock" (by Afrika Bambaataa). And that was it.

Sa'id: As far as your name goes, all of the seven wonders of the world are solid structures—
9th Wonder: Right!

Sa'id: When you think of your name, are you putting it out there that you're a solid structure or that you come from a solid structure, that a solid family structure is important to you, is that part of the meaning?

9th Wonder: Un huh. I'm a big history buff, man. I know my seven my wonders—

Sa'id: So that didn't have anything to do with it?
9th Wonder: Nah, man. [Laughs]. You know what, I tried to think of a name that sounded like a beatmaker's name! Without having "producer" in the name or "beats" in the name. A name that you could shorten up. Pete Rock is "Petey," "PR." DJ Premier is "Preme," "Premo," you know. Something that just sounded like— You know, I wrote down a bunch of names, but I wrote 'em down "Produced by blah, blah, blah." And I just stuck with one that sounded the best. "Produced by 9th Wonder" sounded the best to me. And I wrote the whole thing out. That had a ring to me. "Produced by DJ Premier for Works of Mart;" "produced by Pete Rock for Mecca and the Soul Brother," or now it's "Soul Brother #1;" like, "Produced by Kanye West for Roc the World." That has a certain ring to it, a certain cinematic value to it or theatrical value to it, so I had to think of something: "Produced by 9th Wonder for It's a Wonderful World."

Sa'id: One thing I'm gonna throw at you. I pitched this to Buckwild, I said, the type of music that he makes and the type of music that Preme makes that they're both "beatmakers" at heart who are also producers. Would that be an accurate assessment of you?
9th Wonder: Yeah! Because when you work, in becoming a "producer," it has to be an experience, you know what I'm sayin'. It has to be a pilgrimage. It's a whole experience. Like the Buckshot records that I did, it's a whole experience: "I went to see 9th, and I stayed for two weeks" [quoting Buckshot]. That's how music is made, I think sometimes.

Sa'id: Expand on that, where your music is actually an extension of you.
9th Wonder: Right! It's definitely going down to be with a person, that you're going to make something together. It's just— North Carolina is an extension of me. So in order to understand the whole 9th Wonder experience, you have to come here. You got to understand the food that I eat, the spots that I go. Where do I get my inspiration from, where do I pull my inspiration out of? I talked to Sistah Souljah about a year ago, and she was like, "How do you get your beats to sound like this, but you look outside and see trees and pastures?" And I explained to

her that it's like, you know, I didn't grow up in New York City. I didn't see New York [until] 1987. I was in New York in 1987. My aunt lived there, she lives here now. I was in New York for three weeks. In my three-week period in New York in 1987, Scott La Rock was killed. I was in the Bronx at the time. I didn't go back to New York until 2001. And so all of the music that I heard, I didn't get a chance to experience that music. Every time I go to New York, I play rap records, 'cuz I'm trying to— When "Shook Ones" [Mobb Deep] came out, you could see Queensbridge! I had no way of feelin' it. Everything for me was in here [points to heart] or up here [points to head] or my imagination. So that's where I had to pull, you know, a lot of stuff from. But when you come here, you get all of that. You still get the New York-type sound. But then, once we're done with studio, it's country-boy time pretty much.

Sa'id: I've likened what you've been able to do with what Dr. Dre's reaction was when he first began. The fact that he couldn't do New York, but if you listen to early N.W.A., it has New York—
9th Wonder: Feelin' in it…

Sa'id: Feelin', right. But it has the West Coast, or what became the West Coast sound, it has that color. And what you're doing is, instead of trying to simply mimic New York, you took the part of New York that inspired you and sort of put it into a pot of where you were from. That being said, express— O.K., let's say if someone says, "If I get FL Studio or if I get Reason and Recycle…" Typically, the music that comes out — although they're sampling soul sounds — it sounds sort of synthetic, the feelin' is somehow sort of lost.
9th Wonder: Right!

Sa'id: What are some of the things that you do to maintain that feelin', whether it be your arrangement or your sampling technique?
9th Wonder: It comes with the history. I understand the authenticity of the type of music that I want to make. I understand we control— Man made machines, you know what I'm sayin'.

Sa'id: Exactly.
9th Wonder: You shouldn't put so much into a machine that we made, you should— What I mean is, you can tell a machine to do what you want it to do, you can tell it to do exactly what you want it to do. I get a lot of people sayin', you know, "I can't get Fruity Loops to…" What you mean, "You can't get Fruity Loops to do that?" "How do you get it to sound like…?" Man, you got to mess with it, and mess with it. That's what cats did with the MP [Akai MPC] that's what cats did with the SP [E-Mu SP 1200] to make it do things it's not *supposed* to do — that's hip hop, man! It used to be cats just take a record and let it run all the way to the end, then take the record off, put another record on, let it run all the way to the end. Some bright guy came and put two turntables and records together, two record players together, and was like, "I gotta figure out the way to keep the party going without stopping." That's what hip hop is: taking something that is not *suppose to be*, and turning it from what we're *used* to what we *want*. Timberland is a construction boot [Laughs], but we turned it into a style, a way of life. And so, that's like me and my beats. That's what cats don't understand, they put so much faith, and they put so much on a machine, but it's really not about the machine. It's about the man behind the machine.

Sa'id: But the point with you is that how you were using software was so ahead of everybody. There are some well-known beatmakers that I've interviewed who are just now getting into software like Reason and such, but although they may do *some* of their music with software, the things that they use Reason and the like are for the more cleaner, crispier type of beats.
9th Wonder: Uh huh.

Sa'id: But as far as when they do a dusty or sample joint, they go back to their old trusty [hardware gear].
9th Wonder: I can do both on the same machine.

Sa'id: That's my point—
9th Wonder: I think the thing about me using Fruity Loops, man, is I didn't have a choice. I didn't have 2, 3 grand to buy no beat machine. And I don't live in an area where you can grind to get a beat machine, through a hip hop type of way, like carrying crates [music crates]. Not here. In New York, yes, not here. It's not a big, big scene here. I didn't know what to do, you know what I'm sayin'. So a friend introduced me to a beatmaking program called Hammer and Cool Edit. You know, 'cuz at first, I was doing pause tapes. And so, he introduced me to that and I messed around, messed around with it. Then another cat after that introduced me to Fruity Loops.

Sa'id: When you got Fruity Loops, did you already have a MIDI controller that you were using?
9th Wonder: No. Still to this day I don't. My first time I ever used MIDI, man, was when I tracked out. I don't know what it was, but that was the first time, I used MIDI like a year ago. I don't use MIDI now, I don't use MIDI. For me, I just wanted to make beats, and that's what was working for me.

Sa'id: What I'm talking about for a song, like the three efforts that you did for Destiny's Child. There's a lot going on in those songs. So you're saying, there's no keyboard controller that's playing the sounds? You're just using the computer keyboard?
9th Wonder: Un uh. I had a Toshiba laptop and a wireless mouse.

Sa'id: So how did the long parts get played out?
9th Wonder: What long part?
Sa'id: The melody parts.
9th Wonder: You're talking about for "Girl?"

Sa'id: Right?
9th Wonder: Aw, that's sampled!

Sa'id: All of those are samples that you arranged around?
9th Wonder: Un huh.

Sa'id: So you don't even rock with a MIDI controller?
9th Wonder: Un uh. And I believe in— One thing I learned from Dr. Dre is, the best way for you to understand the importance of musicianship is if you let other musicians get involved. He let Scott Storch—

Sa'id: Do what he does—
9th Wonder: Right! My man is James Porser from The Roots. If I need— The keys that you hear on that Erykah Badu track is James Porser. He was on *The Minstrel Show*, too. And he's gonna be all over *The Wonder Years*. That's what I prefer doing. It just brings the unity in musicianship. So that's what connects me to a producer in the '80s, to a producer in the '70s, to a producer in the '60s. It's ragtime, jazz, soul, funk, hip hop; it's all connected, as long as you don't lose musicianship in the process.

Sa'id: Hip hop is a continuum. However, there are a lot of producers who love their position right now, but they really don't see it as something that they have to pass on. You seem more concerned with not fighting *against* whack music but fighting *for* good music.
9th Wonder: [Laughs] That's heavy!

Sa'id: You understand what I'm sayin'?
9th Wonder: That's my biggest thing! I don't. Cats can do what they wanna do. Cats can make the music they wanna make. But what I'm fighting for is a standard. We as black people, we don't have a standard, man. We need more. We're afraid to say, you know, "That just ain't right." We're afraid to say that. And we get called "haters" for saying something ain't right! We get called, "Aw, you just hatin'." We think that when a person makes money, yeah you need money to survive and to be comfortable and all of that, you know what I'm sayin'. But you can't take it with you. There is such a thing as legacy. That's my thing. I gotta fight for good music, man, because it's like, there is such a thing. And I just don't want 40 years from now, I don't want 40 years from now — our black people 40 years from now — to be completely lost, you know what I'm sayin'. I really don't. Because we take so much time putting people at the front of our culture because they have a boat load of money or because they're very visible. We don't necessarily look at their achievements, and put them in front. And another thing that we don't do…

Not only do I fight for good music, I fight for my elders, man. Because it's a lot of musicians out, a lot of black musicians out right now that don't care nothing about their elders! You know what I'm sayin'. They don't really talk about their influences, they have no respect. They're not even educated, they don't even know. A lot of these people that paved the way, a lot of these people that signed these bogus contracts, a lot of these people went through that so [you wouldn't have to]. You learn from their mistakes. And they don't say "Thank you" to those cats. Maybe in my music, the music that I make and the music I play, that's my way of saying "Thank you" to the cats who came before me. And I understand from a religious standpoint, everybody ain't put on earth to do the same thing. But my thing is, and maybe it's because I got this from my mom and dad, *"respect your elders!"* That's what you really gotta do, and that's what I fight for. It's not only good music, I FIGHT FOR THE PEOPLE WHO MADE GOOD MUSIC! I'll say Pete Rock or Premier before I say any producer. I still say Quincy, I still say Jim Jam, Terry Lewis. But I'm talking about the ones who *directly* affected me to do what I do. These are the cats that affected me, you know what I'm sayin'. You'll never hear Tiger Woods — as much money as he makes — get up there and say — as much as they try to say he's the greatest ever — he'll say, "There's still Ben Hogan, there's still Sam Snead, there's still Jack Nicklaus, there's still Arnold Palmer." He knows his history of the game, and he knows where he sits in that. Some new jacks come up and they don't know where they sit in the realm of the game. And you know how the excuse is, "Aw, they too young, they ain't suppose to know…" Yeah, they suppose to know! And they suppose to care. So I just fight for good music. I ain't got time to sit and try to fight against whack music.

Sa'id: You brought up Preme and Pete Rock, those two (two beatmakers whose drums stand out)… With your drums, do you sample your drums raw — dry — from records or do you use sample CDs, or do you download waves [.wav files]?
9th Wonder: It depends. I got 'em so many ways. I got 'em off CDs, I got 'em off records. Madlib said to me one time that I leave drums open for beatmakers [Laughs].

Sa'id: When you pull them, do you sample them dry or do you throw anything on 'em?
9th Wonder: Sometimes. Sometimes I sample them dry. Sometimes I throw something on 'em. It just depends on the record for me.

Sa'id: Your progression that has happened from the first Little Brother offering all the way to your *Dream Merchant* album, two things: your sound, overall, got bigger, more polished, but then your drums, specifically your snares, started getting this old school reverb sound—
9th Wonder: Right!

Sa'id: It started having much more presence, not louder but much more present. Was that something that you focused on?

9th Wonder: No. You know, I didn't really understand the magnitude of having certain sounds sounding a certain way until about a year, maybe two years ago. And the mixing of my records haven't been very consistent, which means… I mixed *The Listening*, Young Guru mixed the *The Minstrel Show*. I quick-mixed *Dream Merchant*. But then all my other records, like my man Mike Shaft mixed the "Honey Joint." I don't know who mixed the Destiny Child joints; Young Guru mixed "Threat." I don't know who mixed the Lloyd Banks joint. Young Guru mixed the Memphis Bleek joints. I don't know who mixed the Mary J. Blidge joint. But *The Formula* and T*he Wonder Years* are mixed by one guy, his name is Ian Shrier, he's from Raleigh. He's making my sound sound bigger. And I understand that, I understand what that means. I didn't understand that at first, but now I do.

Sa'id: With software, do you use drum pads for your drums or the mouse?
9th Wonder: Mouse.

Sa'id: So you're just placing it in like somebody drawing?
9th Wonder: Ungh huh.

Sa'id: That's incredible timing. Where does that come from, does that come from your musical understanding?
9th Wonder: It's just me understanding 4/4 time, me understanding measures and, you know, a half, an eight, a sixteenth. Me being classically trained from middle school, from me playing instruments in middle school, me playing in a concert band, marching band.

Sa'id: What instruments did you play?
9th Wonder: I played clarinet, I played the saxophone. My band teacher was just throwing instruments at me, "Try this. Try this," because I was playing stuff by ear. And by the time I got into marching band, I was playing drums. So you know, doing that in the daytime — I started middle school in 1986. From 1986 to 1993 was my middle and high school years. You know the albums that came out during that time.

Sa'id: Yeah, yeah.
9th Wonder: So I'm playing — and my mom bought me a keyboard for every Christmas — I'm playing stuff, overtures at school, but I'm coming home [at night] listening to rap records, not really understanding that the music the cats was using in the background were samples, you know what I'm sayin'. I'm thinking everybody's playing it [Laughs]. But they're sampling people that played instruments. So who said it can't be replayed over? So I was trying to replay it on my keyboard.

Sa'id: Keeping with that, for you, what makes sampling an art form, and not something that people outrageously call an "act of thievery?"
9th Wonder: I say it's like when you go to the Louvre in Paris, and you walk down the hall and you see this big mural of somebody who took a whole bunch of *Time Life Book* magazines and made a big mural of *Time Life* Magazines of the years and call it a collage. What's the difference?

They didn't contact every person from every book that they snatched a page out of and get permission. What's the difference? You know what I mean, I just don't understand that. And collages happen all of the time in art.

Sa'id: It's often been said — by writers and movie directors especially — that there's really no such thing as an "original" idea, only innovation. So I think what really is the gut of hip hop is sampling anyway, the ability to utilize something, then put something to it. That being said, what is your perception of sample clearance? Do you think it's a fair situation?
9th Wonder: They don't look at it like it's a trade off. You're dealing with a lot of people that we sample that's bitter. But you also deal with a lot of people that understand the *bridge* that we're trying to connect. If cats that we sample understood — I wouldn't say the newest producers, you know, cats just taking records and not really understanding the purpose — if cats really understood how much we worshipped them— A kid hit me on Myspace and said, "My dad said 'Thanks' for what you did to his record." And I hit him back and was like, "Who is your dad?" He said, "My dad is Dexter Wansell." I used [that sample for] "Smoke the Pain Away." I used a sample from Billy Paul, "I Think I'll Stay Home Today." And Dexter Wansell wrote it, but he was a part of the Gamble & Huff camp. And he appreciated what I had done to the record. I met Hamilton Bohannon's son. They understand the bridge. They understand that an 18 year old is not going to pick up their record and listen to the whole record and appreciate. But they'll appreciate it when we take and do something that they can get. And that's what Pete Rock did for me, when he sampled Tom Scott for "The Reminisce Over You." If I see Tom Scott in the street, I may go up and hug this man. 'Cuz if he didn't make "Honey Suckle Breeze" in 1966, Pete wouldn't have made "T.R.O.Y." in 1992, which would not have turned me on to what I'm doing now. So we owe you (Tom Scott). But you have to be able to embrace the love that we're giving you. When we sample, it's really paying homage.

Sa'id: Do you favor some sort of regulation when it comes to this? I mean for what you and other beatmakers do, every sample is not identifiable. But I'm sure that you know that, in fact, it's so-called "illegal" to sample anything — even a drum snare — without permission. That's ridiculous. But it seems to be no beatmakers who are arguing for this. And the newer beatmakers don't really even care; they'd rather get things rushed, and most of them don't even sample at all. When a sample is undistinguishable and nothing major, it should fall under "fair use."
9th Wonder: Right!

Sa'id: How do you speak to that whole situation? If you were called, what would be the parameters that you would throw out there, 'cuz I think this will eventually go before Congress.
9th Wonder: My thing is. What we need to do is to get the jazz musicians, the R&B musicians from the '60s and '70s to understand what we do. If I ever go to Congress, I'm not going by myself. It's not going to be just me and Russell Simmons. It's gonna be me and Roy Ayers; it's gonna be me and Gamble & Huff; it's going to be me and cats from that era who understand what it is that we do, who understand what we're trying to do for the next generation. We're just really trying to create a bridge. It's not about trying to "take" your record and just make a profit off of it. There is really an art form to this. All that we do — from chopping a record, taking a song that's 3/4 time and turning it into 4/4 time. All of that is art. And I wouldn't go [to Congress] by myself. I would take elders with me, and be like, "Look, you say that we're 'stealing,' these are the cats that I sample, these are the musicians that we use from time and time again." Bob James—"Nautilus" has been sampled so many times. And when I sampled "Nautilus" for the MURS record, he cleared it. Because the thing about him is he understood. When The RZA sampled "Nautilus" for "Daytona 500," he cleared it because he liked what

The RZA did to it. He said he took a song that was clean and pristine and dirtied it up, and gave it a whole new texture to the song. It's a tribute. What people outside of hip hop don't really understand is "Nautilus" is one of the holy grail songs of hip hop.

Sa'id: It's like gateway music.
9th Wonder: Right! It's gateway music, that's exactly what it is. There needs to be some type of council, like the Jedi council. Bob James, Roy Ayers, Gamble & Huff, man, Curtis Mayfield, you could go on.

Sa'id: You do a lot of projects, how did you get to a level where your workflow was organized enough for you to separate?
9th Wonder: You know what helped me do that? School. College helped me do that. College helps you to time manage. I treat my music like papers [essays]. I got a deadline on this paper. And I was a history major. So I treat it like papers. I was doing 25 page thesis [papers] in the 10th grade. So I treat it like school, it just helps me time manage. History majors can juggle many different things in their mind at one time. I think within the last three years, I've worked on 10 projects at the same time, simultaneously, it seems like.

Sa'id: When you get to that level, how do you protect from burning your ears out?
9th Wonder: Man, good music could never burn your ears out. I'm not at a point where I listen to it on high volume all the time. But I don't think I ever burn my ears out.

Sa'id: When you have an idea and you're carving it out in your head, do you have a set term of time or do you go where the beat takes you?
9th Wonder: I just go where the beat takes me. If I feel like I'm done, I feel like I'm done, for that particular moment, until I wanna flesh it out, as Young Guru says, "Add stuff to it."

Sa'id: So when the project came to you from Destiny's Child, what did you do, how did you shape your mind. As a history a major, you're looking at a paper, what did you give that paper, did it have a title? What did you say?
9th Wonder: The name of that title for Destiny's Child paper was "Be Yourself." That's what Beyoncé told me to be, "Do *you*! We hired you for *you*. We didn't hire you to do anything else." The biggest thing that Beyoncé said to me was, "You know, this particular album, all of the formats of the songs, it's like, we're looking at it from the situation like we're The Emotions." It was easy after that. They were like "Do *you*."

Sa'id: You can still get a masters in jazz at a major university, whereas with hip hop, you can't even get one instructional course at most major universities. Why do you think, when it comes to hip hop production, it's not being taken by those in higher education as a serious, legitimate music trade?
9th Wonder: Because of the same reason why people flip out when I say what Beyoncé said. TV dictates what people think about things; TV has painted such a terrible, terrible picture of hip hop, I don't think there's ever a way of turning back. According to TV, hip hop is a violent, misogynistic art form that calls women "bitches" and "hoes" in every song. And TV not only has told this to white Americans, black America believes that to. And not only does black America believe that, it's [also] used as a parting of the Red Sea between the older generation and the young generation. It's getting [to where] two generations not even wanting to learn each other. So trying to explain that to a professor, sometimes is the roughest thing. Trying to explain that to a black professor, in the *South*? Oh, wow. It's like, they don't understand the connection. They don't understand what it is that we do. They let TV tell them what we do. They let TV tell them, "This is what hip hoppers do." Like what we're really trying to do is

to get students to understand the importance of the history of black music. That's what we're really trying to do. I talk to a professor at UNC, he teaches a masters class, and his masters class is about making beats. Incredible, his class is like eight people in a class. And I went to speak to this class one time, and I was talking to the class, and the girl had a book open in the class, and he's going through the book, word for word, chapter by chapter; this is stuff that we know!

Sa'id: What book was it?
9th Wonder: It was a book called *Making Beats*. And it's just about that thick [demonstrates the smallness of the book]. And I know the cat who wrote the book.

Sa'id: Paul Schloss—
9th Wonder: Yes! He wrote the book on the *premise* of what me, Preme, Pete, Just, Kanye, all of us eat and sleep. We eat and sleep this stuff. We know it *verbatim*. It's like a rite of passage… So why don't we have this in [all] our schools, teaching our children….We're revitalizing the word "musician."

Sa'id: Exactly. That being said, do you think one of the things that kind of takes new beatmakers for a detour is that they don't go through DJ'ing? All of the beatmakers that you've mentioned have a DJ background. And I don't think that's a coincidence.
9th Wonder: I think it's a rite of passage. I learned to DJ first. Cats always told me, stuff that I hear in music, they don't hear. And a cat always told me, "All this stuff is going to manifest one day; it's gonna manifest into something. You have a gift…" So I decided that I wanted to learn how to DJ. And just learning that made me really understand the importance of BPMs and how stuff speeds up and how some beats are faster and some beats are slower. You know stuff like that, and drum tracks. All that type of stuff. Knowing what songs go with what. Not only what *feelin'*, but what genre.

Sa'id: How did it help you with arrangements?
9th Wonder: It helped me know how to arrange an album. When you DJ parties, it's like a movie. There's build up, and there's a climax in every movie. There's rising action climax, then there's falling action climax. Every party is like that.

Sa'id: Speak about your approach to adding "changes" in your music.
9th Wonder: Everything with me is off feeling, everything that I do comes from *feeling*, which turns into the next generation. What I mean is, something that James Brown would do on *accident, off of a feeling*, is what the next generation practices as being part of the formula. So with hip hop, everything that— Something that Marley Marl did, or something that Preme turned into "the formula." Something that I started to do on accident (off of a feeling), it's now got some kids using it as "This is the way I chop samples," as the formula. They're not really doing it off feeling; I started doing it off *feeling*. They started doing it because it's "the formula."

Sa'id: Give me an example of something you did by accident.
9th Wonder: Sampling voices, when they really didn't make any sense. A lot of cats ask me, "What is the sample saying?" *"Man, I don't know."* 'Cuz I'm actually trying to chop around the sample. It's just the fact that there's no instrumental version to the song. So I go to… you know what I'm sayin'. And I like the background, and whatever is being sang in it; if it's saying words, fine, if it not, that's fine, too. I really don't care. That's the thing for me. When I did "Loving It," what I like about it, I'm not listening to the [begins to sing] "Told me a lie, I wonder why." I'm listening to the [mimics the rhythm and groove] *"dunh, dunh, doon, dh, dh, dh, dh, denh…"* I'm listening to that. He just happened to be, "…do me, I can see…" And so, a kid may hear that and be like, "Oh, he chose the words." And I was going for the *feeling*, and he thinks that's the formula! Every generation does that, every generation of black music

does that. Somebody'll make up something, and the next generation they'll create something, and the next generation uses that as the formula. And it goes on and on and on.

Sa'id: You've spoken indirectly on how important it is to study making beats. There's this misperception that you can get the latest software or just, you know, get an MPC, and then boom: you're making beats!
9th Wonder: Right!

Sa'id: Speak about the fact that this is a serious field that you do have to study.
9th Wonder: You got to know this stuff! You have to know it. Like, to successfully— And it shows, it shows, the cat's who do music, but really don't have an understanding of the history of it, or understand [how to do it]. You either had to grow up around it or you had to be there, one of the two. To be "authentic," you just can't wake up in the morning, man, and be like, "I wanna sample," without understanding the art of sampling. You just can't do it. You gotta— If you wanna sample, you gotta study; go study the greats who sampled records. It's like, if you want to be a great trumpet player, you gotta know all of the great jazz trumpet players who came before. I KNOW SO MANY PRODUCERS WHO MAKE BEATS THAT KNOW NOTHING ABOUT THE HISTORY! They know nothing about the producers that came before them. No matter what I do, no matter what mainstream record I do, no matter who I make a record for — I've made a beat for Jay [Jay-Z]. My mainstream sales is Jay, Destiny's Child, the biggest Mary J. Blige record. And I've been blessed to have that run, but the thing about it is, I would never say I'm better than Buckwild! And that's what cats just don't get, man.

Sa'id: Real talk, one thing that I want to point out is that when students don't wanna learn anymore, we've got a problem. But when teachers don't wanna teach, culture is over! It's just that simple, you know what I'm sayin'.
9th Wonder: Right.

Sa'id: So I feel good that you have a history class.
9th Wonder: That's what I gotta do. I know what hip hop has done for me. I'm trying to get to a point where all universities— When it's time for hip hop to be studied as a curriculum and a concentration, I don't want them to go get just some, any ol' professor, man. It better be somebody that comes from the cloth!

Sa'id: Finally speak on the simplicity of hip hop. You know music theory, and you know that hip hop — unlike other forms of music — isn't based on progression.
9th Wonder: Un uh! Hip hop is not based on progression, or chord progressions or movements. That's not it! Like blues, there's a format to blues, it's been the same format, and it's a very, very simple format. I think new cats try to conform to what— Instead of really building on what we created, and leaving it "as is," they try to do things to conform hip hop to other types of music. That's cool, if that's what you wanna do, that's fine. But I think that does something to the music, though. I think that loses— I think that pulls in other people from other forms of music, who are like, "Well, you know, I think hip hop should be like this. It kind of bothers me that hip hop is a little monotonous." Well, get out! You know what I'm sayin'. This is something that Kool Herc [and them] started in the '70s in the Bronx. Something in the '70s that cats had going on — something a lot of people didn't want to have *nothing* to do with. Now that they see it's a profitable thing, they wanna come in and say, "Everything is kind of monotonous." No! Understand the beauty of hip hop for what we made it to be! Don't try to come in and *change* what we have, especially when you have so many other art forms that have been the same way for years. You can not go down to Augusta National in Augusta, GA for the Masters, and change the format. You just can't do it. You can bring in ESPN, you can

bring in ABC, you can bring in different commentators. The point of the matter is this: Every year, whoever wore the green jacket last year puts the green jacket on the person who won it this year; and every year the person who won the green jacket last year gets to choose the menu. That's what is called "tradition," man! It's *tradition*. They're jackin' up the tradition, man. There's a *tradition* in hip hop, there really is. And we let money ruin the tradition. They don't understand that long tradition makes lots of money. They have it confused, because they wanna make it "now!" It's gotta be right now…

Sa'id: It's the "me, now" culture—
9th Wonder: Me, now! They don't understand that tradition creates money for centuries. The point of the matter is— Like there are cats in baseball that are gonna uphold the tradition of baseball, no matter what. Who's doing that for hip hop? There's not enough of us doing it, 'cuz we're letting *anything* go. We're letting anything slide down the tube.

Sa'id: For the high school cats, the ones who are just getting interested in hip hop and making beats, give a couple of first steps that you think that they should approach.
9th Wonder: If they wanna make beats, the best thing for them to do is to go back and buy old records and old rap records. You know, understand little nuances like how Preme takes something and doubles it up at the end of the fourth measure. Or understand how Pete Rock can take five records and put 'em on top of each other. Understand how The Beatminerz take a bass sample and filter it out at the beginning of "Buck 'em Down.," and then understand how they bring in the highs. You have to study that type of stuff. Not only do you have to study that, then you have to go back and see who they sampled. You gotta understand all of that aesthetic first. Either you decide that this is something that you really wanna do— The more you sample, the more cats sample, the window of originality gets smaller and smaller. And I had to learn what all of the samplers before me were doing before me, before I decided what sound that I wanted to go for. 'Cuz, I mean, in the beginning, I sounded like Pete [Pete Rock], then I sounded like Preme one day, then I sounded like The RZA. Where can I get to the point where it's a 9th Wonder sound? That took some time. Once I got it, I built out of that. And that's what young producers gotta do.

AFTERWORD

The Beatmaking Tradition's Contribution to Modern Music

Beatmaking, a tradition that grew out of the broader hip hop culture and hip hop/rap music tradition, has changed modern music forever. In 40 years, it has substantially reconfigured the approach to modern music-making, and within the last quarter of the twentieth century in particular, the hip hop/rap music and beatmaking traditions brought forth a number of pivotal developments that have both transcended and built upon previous musical approaches.

As the beatmaking tradition has resulted in an entirely new musical process, and it has also given birth to a new kind of musician and composer. Beatmaking has also reexamined the relationship between creativity and technology more profoundly than any other music tradition in the world. The beatmaking tradition has even reestablished the didactic, do-it-yourself ethic and approach to making music. And, of course, the beatmaking tradition has made the music-making process more accessible to the common person more than any other music tradition in recent history. Today, beatmaking (hip hop/rap production) stands as the most easily accessible means for people to express their individual musical creativity. This has given more people than ever before the chance to go from consumer to producer in the world of music.

And what of the wave of cuts of music and arts education (programs) at elementary, jr. high, and high schools all across America?[196] Those cuts took away many of the traditional outlets that kids, teenagers, and young adults had used in the past to express their natural interest in music and their own musical creativity. Those music-program cuts have also reduced the broad worth of music to American society; moreover, they have shunned the intrinsic value in music and the arts in general. Music, perhaps the most socially important of all art forms, not only enhances academic achievement among students, it also encourages personality and character growth. More often than not, people well-oriented in music excel in mathematics and do well in the political sciences. Music also helps people to bolster the creative side of their character. This fact is even more crucial to the development of elementary, jr. high, and high school students, because at that time in their lives the nourishment of the creative (and intuitive) side of their character is critical to the cultivation of the logical, analytical side of their character. But egregious as the widespread music- and arts-program cuts were (are), they could (can) not wipe out the naturally creative

---

[196] What widespread efforts are still seriously being made to teach young adults about the musical process? For example, where are the associations like the Afro-American Music Opportunities Association (AAMOA) of 1969, or schools like Dorothy Maynor's School of the Arts at New York, and the Elma Lewis School at Boston?

curiosity that people have for music. Moreover, those cuts could (can) not curb the desire that many people have to become career music professionals. Beatmaking directly addresses the systematic music and arts program cuts in America, and it fills the gaping void left by the cuts, as it offers an alternative means to music education, instruction, and appreciation.

The beatmaking tradition has also resulted in an entirely new music-making profession; and this profession's influence over the psyche of modern popular music — especially in the United States, France, the UK, Brazil, Germany, and Japan — has been so vast that the beatmaking tradition has truly spawned the first great music compositional phenomenon of the twenty-first century. Actually, the beatmaking tradition has created a unique class of electronic music-makers who now represent what I call *common composers*.

These common composers have distinct ideas about music culture, and they are not intimidated by other music traditions of presumably greater prestige. The common composer does not blindly defer to music theory (the abstract knowledge of the Western classical tradition), nor does the he cower to the pretentious presuppositions and predispositions of other popular forms of music like rock 'n' roll. Instead, the common composer embraces (directly or indirectly) the core ideologies and sensibilities of the hip hop/rap music tradition. Furthermore, because the common composer is much more sensitive to the idea of relevance in popular culture, he is uniquely mindful of the most unifying priority of all music traditions: To make music (art) function in a way that improves the quality of life of people in any given society.

Growth of the Hip Hop/Rap Music and Beatmaking Traditions – Not Without Controversy

The extent of which the hip hop/rap music and beatmaking traditions have grown has not come about without controversy. There have been numerous compositional and ideological differences that have occurred throughout the 40-year history of the hip hop/rap music and beatmaking traditions. In the following section, it is useful to outline the highlights and possible resolutions of these differences.

The Notion of Evolution in Hip Hop/Rap Music, Why Hip Hop/Rap Can't Be Redefined, and the Need for Non-Hip Hop/Rap Music Categories

Although hip hop/rap music may have outgrown itself, commercially speaking, and may have attracted an explosive amount of new interest, the fragile socio-economic conditions from which hip hop/rap music and beatmaking stem have not improved at the same pace. Hence, the blanket claim of "evolution" is made more off base. Further, the fundamental story of beatmaking in the last ten years is not that of *evolution* by particular beatmakers. It's the story of inclusion of new beatmaking talent, the dominance of trap-based styles, the discovery of the art of sampling by younger beatmakers, and the co-option of the beatmaking and hip hop/rap music tradition by members of musical cultures and traditions that are outside of hip hop/rap. To be certain, any music form can be converted into some variation of hip hop/rap. But attempts to convert hip-hop/rap into another music form usually results in something awkward, contrived, or superficial at best. And while hip-hop/rap music is itself a hybrid musical composite, one must be careful to respect the actual elements that comprise this hybrid.

Thus, it does not suffice to offer merely a passing acknowledgement of where the preferred aesthetics of hip hop/rap come from; and it is certainly not plausible to ignore hip hop/rap's common links to its broader parent tradition — the African-American (Black) music tradition. This is not my attempt to lay some sort of racial or ethnic claim to hip-hop/rap music. This is an accurate recognition of what hip hop/rap fundamentally *is* — not what it *isn't* — based on the architecture of its fundamental design. This recognition is no different than the recognition that is immediately earned (rightfully so) by the blues, jazz, rhythm and blues, soul, and/or funk. Each one of those traditions also developed through the cross-utilization and use of one base tradition: the blues. However, none of those aforementioned traditions have had to suffer the degradation in the name of some misperceived notion of evolution.

The product of evolution (i.e. innovation) within any art form goes without saying. It is expected that for every new innovation, there will be new innovations to follow. But I suspect that the outcry of *evolution* that has invaded the hip hop/rap music and beatmaking traditions throughout the past seven years is more than a simple recognition of innovation, but rather a not-so subtle attempt by late-comers and profiteers to overshadow, circumvent, and totally reconceptualize the true fundamentals of the hip hop/rap music and beatmaking traditions.

To know whether my assessment is accurate or not, one need only to closely examine the chief propagators of the evolutionist theme. Specifically, one must ask, Why are they really stressing this theme? Moreover, What do they actually stand to gain? I would argue that the leaders of the *evolution* banter are actually three groups. First, there are those who, either willfully or perhaps through no fault of their own, are ignorant of the history and fundamental aesthetics and priorities of the hip hop/rap music and beatmaking traditions. Since they do not know the history, the culture, or its tradition, this group simply moves along as if there's no rich heritage to draw from. Subsequently, they raise the *evolution* banner — a response to anything that they do as being purportedly new — as a form of cover.

Second, there are those who have been unable to master the fundamental and most preferred aesthetics of the hip hop/rap music and beatmaking traditions. Essentially whatever this group can't make, they dislike and look down upon. Most of this group is comprised of late-comers who usually have backgrounds in other musical forms. And as is often the case, this group has recently taken up hip hop/rap because of its popular appeal and, more importantly, its fiscal potential. This group believes, in effect, that by propagating the *evolution* claim, they are exempting themselves from being held accountable for not being able to make the sort of beats that subscribe to the crux of the hip hop/rap music tradition. Furthermore, because this group can make nothing more than a superficial version of hip hop/rap, they inevitably rely on and attach (forcefully) processes, priorities, and ideologies of other music forms to hip hop/rap. Then they brand their so-called developments as hip hop's/rap's *evolution*. Finally, there are those veteran beatmakers (producers) who have made it — commercially and/or critically — and are now bent on distinguishing themselves from the pack. For many of these beatmakers (usually those who have reached some Billboard success or other status marker), even the term "hip hop producer" evokes some sort of disdain or shame. For the most part, these beatmakers believe that their so-called spot at the top is secured, provided many hip hop/rap music-makers continue to conform and/or water-down their musical efforts.

I believe that the call to describe the hip hop/rap production themes of the 2000s as *evolution* is really a thinly veiled attempt to downplay, disregard, and otherwise undermine the very tenets that make hip hop/rap music what it is and has always been: A music form that prioritizes rhythm and groove over harmony and melody; a music form that is rooted in the black vernacular music tradition; a music form that is non-conformist and anti-establishment; and a music form that is all-inclusive on its own terms.

The "Universal" Concept of Hip Hop/Rap Music, the Fusion of Musical Forms, and Hip Hop as a Giant Music Tradition

Being mindful of the "universal" concept of hip hop/rap music, my argument may trouble some who want to view it as a stance of racial or ethnic exclusion. But that couldn't be further from the truth. Just as Bonnie Rait — a white woman — can proudly lay claim to being able to sing the blues and soul, so can Eminem lay claim to rapping. More importantly, to neglect, or even worse, negate the actual role that race and ethnicity has played — and still does play — in hip hop/rap music is to dilute and undermine the hip hop/rap music and beatmaking traditions. Though such a dilution might make some comfortable, it must be remembered that hip hop/rap was never intended to be a comfortable cultural space for everybody. It was (is) built by and for those who appreciated and respected it as is, regardless of race or ethnic background. Furthermore, as I dsicussed earlier in this study, beatmaking is the most racially and ethnically inclusive and accessible creative element in the broader hip hop/rap music tradition. Thus, my point here is to demonstrate an inconsistency in the perceptions of twentieth-century (and early twenty-first century) popular American music.

No one disputes that the blues, jazz, rhythm and blues, and/or soul are all black vernacular musics. These musics are indeed respected and appreciated *as is*, even celebrated for as much. However, hip-hop/rap music analysis of the last decade of the twentieth century and the first decade of the twenty-first century often includes a very noticeable push to broadly identify hip hop/rap by the "universal" — non-racial or post-racial — moniker. At the same time, there's often a reluctance to recognize it in the same black vernacular musical orbit from which it came and still continues (steadfastly) to reside.

I concede the fact that when two or more music traditions are fused together, each tradition is change or diluted to some degree. More importantly perhaps, I recognize the fact that within this "fusion mix," one tradition serves as the basis (i.e. prism) through which the other tradition(s) is (are) interpreted. But when the result of this fusion is both distinctly recognizable and commercially sustainable, then a new musical genre or categorization becomes necessary, not only to protect the integrity of each tradition within the fusion mix, but also to provide clarity for audiences and consumers. For example, jazz has bebop, swing, fusion; soul has funk; reggae has ska, rock steady, and dance hall.

Within giant music traditions, for example, the blues, jazz, rhythm and blues, rock, soul, and reggae, each genre inevitably develops and accounts for its own sub-genres. Each of these pocket genres or off-shoots — variations upon the tradition-proper, the tradition's base foundation — gain their own distinct reputation. However, the growth of pocket genres should never be confused with being the evolution of the tradition-proper, the main tradition itself. When the *evolution* tag is allowed to fester and grow, critical links to the tradition-proper are broken.

This broken link to the tradition-proper has not occurred in any of the twentieth-century giant music traditions aforementioned. More specifically, none of the other giant music traditions of twentieth-century American popular music have been forced to shoulder the off-shoot musics that it spawned. That is to say, the blues is still fundamentally recognized for what it is. Jazz is still fundamentally recognized for what it is; and in those areas of jazz where hybridism is obviously in effect, it's always clearly noted, for example: free jazz, soul jazz, jazz fusion. Soul is still fundamentally recognized for what it is; and in those areas of soul where there is a "new" component to the music that seeks to combine elements of today with yesterday, it's clearly noted, for example: neo soul, retro soul. Reggae serves as another good example. Reggae, like the blues, jazz, and soul, is still fundamentally recognized for what it is, it can't be "redefined;" and in those areas where new music has parted company with tradition, there has been a new name left in the wake to legitimize the new music as its own specific genre. The best example of this would be the genre known as Jamaican dance hall.

Well, hip hop/rap music is now a giant music tradtion. As such, it should be recognized and looked upon with similar scrutiny to that of the other giant music traditions of the twentieth century. In other words, hip hop's/rap's pocket traditions must be recognized for their own merits if the tradition-*proper* — the overall, fundamental tradition and culture — is to survive. (When the lines between two music traditions become blurred, the result is inevitably a new tradition anyway.) Therefore, a new musical genre and/or category (or genres and categories) is (are) needed to preserve the core meaning of what hip hop/rap *is*. Without it, hip hop/rap music will be further commodified and trivialized, and it's core meaning and promise will be usurped by the interests of conformists and others who have no stake in preserving the rich heritage of the hip hop/rap music tradition.

This is why some new category or name is needed to distinguish hip hop/rap music from hip hop/rap off-shoots. The fundamental aesthetics, principles, and priorities of the hip hop/rap music tradition-proper should no longer be forced to burden the definitions of the off-shoot musics that hip hop/rap has spawned. Therefore, it is my recommendation that the term "urban hop" be used to generally describe all other hip hop/rap-spawned traditions that do not ascribe to the core compositional aesthetic and concept of the original, never duplicated, often imitated hip hop/rap music tradition. I have chosen the term urban hop because it more than adequately describes the amalgamation of all of the current off-shoots or pocket traditions of hip hop/rap music. Moreover, ther term "urban hop" gives some indication of its connection to hip hop/rap without misrepresenting and/or undermining the essence of the term "hip hop." For example, techno and drum and bass (both musics that owe a debt of pedigree to beatmaking in hip hop/rap music), clearly make up their own distinct genres, and therefore, they are never miscategorized as being "hip hop/rap music." Yet there are an increasing number of electronic music producers who consistently classify their music as "hip hop/rap." Here, let me be more clear: I'm not calling for some dogmatic board of authority that determines what is or isn't hip hop/rap music. People have the right to describe their music in the manner that they want. But just because you call country music modern disco doesn't mean it's so.

Here, I shoud point out that I'm not against the forms of music that I would ascribe to the genre of urban hop. But I would also never say that every musical effort that *purports* to use the core compositional aesthetic and concept of hip hop/rap music captures my favor. The core compositional aesthetic and concept of hip hop/rap music is composed of two components: (1) the creation of music through the use of pre-recorded music and other recorded (or electronic-generated) sounds; and (2) the creation of this music through the use of rhythm and groove — rather than harmony and melody — as the chief compositional guide. This compositional aesthetic and concept was critically important to the original architects and pioneers of hip hop/rap music and beatmaking traditions; and it was of extreme importance to a new wave of pioneers 10 years later, and 10 years later after that. In fact, the first core aesthetic — the creation of music through the use of pre-recorded music and other recorded sounds — has been the go-to essence since the cradle of hip hop. Therefore, there is absolutely no reason that hip hop/rap music should or ever could be *redefined*. Just as there is no reason that the blues, jazz, rhythm and blues, rock 'n' roll, soul, or funk — the other giant music traditions of twentieth-century American popular music — should or ever could be redefined.

Purists and Snobs

My counter argument to the *evolution* claim as well as the urban hop solution is not a typical old school vs. new school debate. Moreover, this is not the mere musings of a musical elitist. Actually, when it comes to music, I am and have always been as much as a populist as anything else. My concern here is with preserving an art form as opposed to undermining it, or forcing it to burden music genres and traditions that stand in stark contrast to its essence. If this unfair burden continues to be levied against the hip hop/rap music tradition, the origins and essence of hip hop/rap music will be damaged beyond repair.

My position aside, it must be recognized that the so-called hip hop/rap pursists and music snobs both negatively impact this discussion. The hip hop/rap purists — i.e. those who fervently cry what "real" hip hop/rap is or isn't — and the music snobs — i.e. those who tend to view hip hop/rap as a primitive form of music in need of music theory-based "guidance" — both spew out much dogma. But each group is often less informed or less honest about the truth of hip hop culture's actual origins or how the hip hop/rap music tradition grew from it.

Either purists don't know or they simply overlook the fact that hip hop/rap music has always had a party music (club function) and dance function to it. In fact, the "have fun" and "party" components of hip hop/rap music were very critical to the development and spread of hip hop/rap music. When some purists frown at the current club trends of hip hop/rap music, they are, in effect, frowning at part of the roots of hip hop/rap music. Furthermore, hip hop/rap has also always had a money-cars-new-clothes-jewelry-women component to it. Sure, in its innaugral years, most of its practitioners participated in hip hop, in large part, for the love of it. But no one should be confused here: When presented with the opportunity, *all* of the architects and pioneers also took the money, the women, the new clothes, jewelry, and cars! Kool Herc, Grandmaster Flash, and Afrika Bambaataa, the three most visible architects and pioneers of hip hop/rap music, all eventually moved on to regular paying DJ gigs. This does not mean that they didn't "love" what they were doing. But it also doesn't mean that they didn't care about getting paid for it either. I suspect that they loved making hip hop/rap music; and they loved getting paid for it; and they loved the new clothes they could buy; and, of course, most of them loved the ladies that came with their celebrity status.

Similarly, music snobs either do not know about, or simply refuse to acknowledge, the fact that hip hop/rap music has its own rich tradition. The history of the hip hop/rap music and beatmaking traditions is deep. It contains a distinct music ideology; moreover, its compositional elements, principles, and priorities are well-established and well-understood by its architects and most authentic practitioners.

Although not all so-called classically trained musicians in hip hop/rap are music snobs, there are however some who approach hip hop/rap from their classical background and who, subsequently, exemplify an air of musical authority and superiority. These snobs typically try to discredit sampling especially, echoing the woefully misguided view of sampling as stealing and not creative or original. In doing so, these snobs nullify one of the earliest and most important foundations of the hip hop/rap music tradition. Furthermore, most of these music snobs tend not to embrace or even recognize the role DJ'ing/pre-recorded music played in the development of hip hop/rap music. Also, many music snobs do not even embrace or recognize the non-sample-based compositional styles of the hip hop/rap music tradition. Finally, trained music snobs who *slum* with hip hop/rap music are analogous to trained fashion designers who *visit* the streets. In both cases, each draws inspiration and direction from a phenomenon they typically know very little about. The interest of such borrowers is not so much in borrowing the pulse or essence of the phenomenon, or what informs and drives the phenomenon. Instead, their aim is to capture the *result,* and hopefully the popular reaction, of the aesthetic, not the aesthetic itself. But where some trained musicians further separate themselves in this analogy is in their tendency to look down upon the aesthetic from which they drew (admittedly) from.

Both the purists and snobs can be very condescending. Furthermore, both seem to want hip hop/rap music to be one way: *their way*. Also, both seemingly ignore the fact that, despite its humble beginnings, hip hop/rap music contains a hodgepodge of all sorts of styles, sounds, and approaches. But what both hip hop/rap purists and trained music snobs need to realize most is this: You can not redefine the fundamental tradition of a particular art form, it's existence is permanent, and it co-exists despite any new artistic genre or medium that it fosters.

Revisionist History and Instant Gratifiers

> Young kids today don't have the patience anymore. They go to cooking school for two years, then they get out and want to be a top chef. Just like with any other art, if you want to be successful you have to learn your craft. –Wolfgang Puck

As I alluded to earlier in this Afterword, there is a small but growing block of beatmakers (both "outsiders" and "insiders") who are disconnecting from, and downplaying, the actual roots of the hip hop/rap music and beatmaking traditions. In my view, this trend is actually part of a broader campaign by two groups in particular, instant gratifiers and music elitists, to negate the origins and roots of hip hop/rap music and beatmaking for their own selfish gain. This widespread negation of the early historical context of the hip hop/rap music and beatmaking traditions, specifically their valued aesthetics, well-established practices, principles, and priorities, is contributing to the declining integrity of hip hop/rap music and its chief compositional process: beatmaking. This rather disheartening phenomenon is serving as the primary catalyst to revise and rewrite the history hip hop/rap music in its entirety.

I have already discussed, to some degree, music elitists. Therefore here, it is useful to outline what I mean by the "instant gratifiers" within hip hop/rap music. I use the term "instant gratifiers" to describe those beatmakers and other musicians that simply want and, dare I say, expect great beatmaking skills (and the presumed money and fame) *instantly*. But the art and history of beatmaking in the hip hop/rap music tradition is not a form of goods or an item that can be subject to conspicuous consumption; it is not something that one can buy into and instantly obtain a skill and talent for. However, the saturation of gear and equipment marketed directly to hip hop/rap consumers seems to suggest otherwise. Likewise, the ever increasing number of new beatmakers perhaps justifies such a marketing/manufacturing blitz. But unlike other contemporary components of hip hop/rap mass culture, beatmaking can not be "pop"-marketed, neatly packaged, and/or sold like other random pop items. Still, many of these instant gratifiers are increasingly being enabled by the advent of a new wave of recording technology, specifically new beatmaking tools that have been designed more with speed, portability, and mobile capability in mind than quality beatmaking.

Fortunately, not all new beatmakers want the quick-fix. I believe that the majority of new beatmakers want to learn how to create quality beats. I also believe that they enter into beatmaking with the sort of drive, determination, and patience that it takes to amass serious beatmaking knowledge, a prerequisite for developing true skills. Unfortunately, however, there is a sizeable number of new beatmakers who willfully ignore this approach. Thus, the larger the number of new beatmakers who share this *instant* sentiment, the lower the bar for quality beats (music) goes.

There are also those who use hip hop/rap music, but at the same time, they try to swap out and replace the already well-established aesthetic values of the hip hop/rap music and beatmaking traditions with the aesthetic values and priorities of other music forms. This condescending ethos is akin to when many label owners — throughout the 1950s and early 1960s — recorded African American artists, then marketed the music with album cover images that included white artists, not the original black artists.

I am disheartened that some people (even now some veteran beatmakers) treat hip hop/rap music as it is an inferior music, devoid of any creativity and any set aesthetic values. And I am particularly disturbed by those musicians who use terms like "evolve" and "evolution" as code words for *better*. If these trends go unchecked, they will turn out to be the biggest contributing factors to the total revision and rewrite of the history of the hip hop/rap music and beatmaking traditions. A rewrite of this nature and magnitude will reduce hip hop's/rap's most prominent originators to mere footnotes; it will swap out or repurpose pivotal hip hop/rap and beatmaking architects and pioneers as well as critical moments throughout the first seven beatmaking periods. If this happens, hip hop/rap music will be so disproportionately co-opted by the mainstream at large that all significant aesthetic links to the origins and roots of hip hop/rap will be irreversibly neutralized, if not wiped out altogether. This will dramatically curb or undo the meaning, scope, importance, and impact of hip hop culture in general. And it will, in turn, chart a course for hip hop that will eventually end when "hip hop" is finally reduced to nothing more than a mere non-reflective, non-representative moniker of a general sector of the recording industry. Of course, should this happen, hip hop won't even be a shell of a representation of what it once stood for.

Hip Hop or Rap?

It is also worth briefly analyzing how the extensive use of the term "hip hop" rather than "rap" has had the effect of neutralizing the significance of the art of rapping. By removing "rap" as an identifier of hip hop music, hip hop has been presented as a music tradition that is equally agreeable to more familiar oral traditions, i.e. singing and the like. In turn, this sentiment has downplayed the fact that hip hop/rap music is and will always be most agreeable with its original oral tradition: rapping. Stripping hip hop of its native oral tradition makes it easier for people outside of the hip hop/rap music tradition to flirt with hip hop and to, therefore, capitalize on its widespread appeal to contemporary music audiences. The lingering effects of this is that the importance of lyrics wane, which leads to a drop in the overall quality of lyricism: Lyrics get shorter and lyric styles become more of the sing-along variety. Should this continue, the art of rapping, as we once knew it, may also disappear altogether.

The Future of Beatmaking in Hip Hop/Rap

Future Growth

From its humble beginnings in the early 1970s, the art of beatmaking has grown in size, complexity, and stature. So I anticipate that the sheer number of beatmakers will dramatically increase in the future. And as a result, serious interest in the study of beatmaking and hip hop/rap music, specifically at high schools and institutions of higher learning, will also continue to grow. This is because possessing a beatmaking (hip hop/rap) skill-set is increasingly becoming important for all musicians, especially those who are uninterested in the traditional band setting as well as those who want to participate in the popular global music market.

Naturally, as the interest in beatmaking grows (necessarily), I anticipate that EMPI manufacturers will continue to increase their involvement within the beatmaking (hip hop/rap music production) field. The big three EMPI brands (manufacturers) — Akai, Roland, and Yamaha — have been a presence since the start of the modern beatmaking tradition. And over the past 10 years, each has further increased its participation in the hip hop/rap production trade. More recently, however, a number of upstart software EMPI makers — like Ableton, Propeller Head, and Native Instruments — have ramped up their product lines on the bet that popular interest in beatmaking will grow.

And what of institutions of higher learning? Truth is, there has been an insular approach to serious music studies in America. That is to say, Western classical or jazz studies and sometimes popular music seminars — typically on rock 'n' roll — are the exclusive areas of scholarship at most college and university music programs. However, I expect that the rising interest in the art of beatmaking, and its undeniable significance as a musical process, will dictate that colleges and universities include beatmaking (hip hop/rap music production) courses and programs. I anticipate the more aggressive and forward-thinking institutions will soon begin to offer full curriculums that are designed around the beatmaking tradition of hip hop/rap music.

The Advent of a Beatmakers Union

In the preface of this study, I point out that the fundamental purpose of the book (as well the BeatTips network of websites) is to preserve the beatmaking tradition. Moreover, I want to draw more attention to the fact that beatmaking, as a music compositional method, has increasingly become significant around the globe. Thus, in every way possible, I want *The BeatTips Manual* and BeatTips.com to take the rich heritage and traditions of beatmaking from out of the throws of obscurity, and to bring them front and center into the world of acclaimed musical processes.

In addition to this fundamental purpose, one of my main auxiliary goals for BeatTips is to have it serve as the catalyst for a beatmakers union. For more than 15 years, I've worked to help unify and expand the community of beatmakers. And while most beatmakers are steadfastly committed to their art and craft, many do not recognize that beatmaking (hip hop production) is also a powerful trade. Hence, I've been committed to raising attention to the artisanship of beatmaking, and I believe the advent of a beatmakers union is not only helpful in this regard, it's necessary as the craft moves forward.

United Beatmakers Guild (UBG): The BeatTips Proposal for a Beatmakers Union

Amid the beat market exchange, a growing number of talented beatmakers, and desperation beat prices, a beatmakers union holds the answer to a more powerful beatmaking community

IIn order to ensure the rights for a rapidly growing number of professional beatmakers, I strongly believe that beatmakers must unionize. The BeatTips proposal for a beatmakers union includes four main points or recommendations:

- I recommend that the name of the union be United Beatmakers Guild (UBG). In my view, beatmaker has always carried a much more significant tone.

Beatmakers are the artisans of one of the world's newest and fastest growing music traditions. As such, beatmaker is a term that's distinguished from "producer," which can and often does signifies something altogether different. Further, beatmaker represents a specific form and category of music producer; thus, I find it more befitting (and powerful) that a union bear the name beatmaker. Still, I recognize the ubiquitous nature of the term "producer," therefore, United Producers Guild (UPG) works as well.

- I recommend that UBG focus on three fundamental areas: (1) guaranteed labor contracts with the RIAA, comparable to those held with the American Federation of Musicians (incidentally, beatmakers should also be members of the AFM — beatmakers are indeed musicians, and the AFM should recognize this fact and expand their membership to include beatmakers); (2) a fair compensation system, which includes prompt delivery of payment, fair minimum beat prices, a tiered pricing scheme, and a formal system for assigning proper credits; and (3) standards and best practices — upholding beatmaking/production standards, quality control, and preserving the integrity of the beatmaking craft.

- I recommend that UBG be modeled, in as many ways as possible, on the Screen Actors Guild (SAG).

- I recommend that the majority — if not all — UBG executive leadership posts be held by actual beatmakers (producers). I further recommend that UBG not be lead by beat brokers or owners of similar cottage industry outlets. It is crucial that any beatmakers union not be co-opted by beat placement organizations, beat-broker types or outer-fringe producer managers. This group's argument will be that they have the connections and infrastructure already in place. But if their connections where so strong and infrastructure so undeniably solid, they'd have far more beatmakers (producers) using their services now; they'd also have a lot more influence in the music industry. In truth, they're middle men with minimal power in a world where essentially anyone can contact anyone. Also, this group has been vocal about encouraging non-sample-based beats over sample-based beats. Union leadership should represent beatmakers of both major production styles — sample-based and non-sample-based — and they should not favor one beatmaking style and sound over another regardless of the complexities that may arise from one production style.

- I recommend that membership be restricted to beatmakers/music producers of both major production styles — sample-based and non-sample based. Under no circumstances can anyone who is not, nor has never made beats (produced) be a member of UBG. Persons who are not beatmakers (producers) or have never made beats, for example so-called producer managers, beat brokers, etc. should only be affiliated as independent contractors (if need be), or they could perhaps serve as advisors for limited times (if need be). In some rare cases, proven producer managers could hold pivotal staff administration positions or executive positions if need be.

Understanding What UBG Would Look Like

To have a better understanding of what I envision for UBG, I thought that it would be helpful to share Uh-Oh Beats' question to me on this matter, along with my detailed response. Here is Uh-Oh's comments and questions to me in full:

I agree with the union idea. How does one go about entering the union though? Like when I think of a "union," I think of all them old white dudes my dad knows who get together and throw parties and do city work and etc., etc. And to get in the union you have to know someone in the union. Would it be similar to that? And what would be the driving points to get beatmakers to want to join? Because honestly, I would want to join if I was guaranteed $3000 a beat. But honestly, how many beats would I be selling? I'd be happy to get $1000 for a beat, hell to be honest, if someone gave me $500 I'd be amazed and jump all over it. So what's to say struggling beatmakers with no connections other then the internet, what would be stopping them from going around the union? I think that's the main point of interest we have to look at and address to really make this happen. Because just the other day I sold five beats for $1000, which is the most money I've ever made off my music at one time. (The previous was five beats for $250.

I just find it so hard to sell beats as is, when I'm letting them go for $150 for exclusive and $50 to lease. (Frown upon me all you want lol. I love making beats and it's that much better getting paid to do something I love. Gotta go cheap if you want to sell ANYTHING with the market so flooded). I can't imagine honestly asking someone to pay $3000 for one unless their seriously established and working on a serious project.

But the union would also have to have a cap for the amount of members wouldn't it? and serious artists would go to the union for beats. but if there's so many members how would one go about even looking for beats within it?

Before getting into my full response to the concerns and questions raised by Uh-Oh, I have to provide some important context about beat prices themselves. First, the $3,000 price point that Uh-Oh kept referring to in his question comes from an earlier discussion on TBC (The BeatTips Community forums) where I discussed the reality and evolution of beat prices. For years, the legend has been that beatmakers in the 1990s were getting extremely high prices for beats;

rumors of $25,000, $50,000, and even $100,000 beat prices were the norm and the sort of thing many budding beatmakers dreamed of obtaining one day. Legend aside, you can be sure that $100,000 for beats weren't the norm for most beatmakers (producers) in the '90s or the early 2000s. Some undoubtedly did receive upwards of $25,000 — but that was typically for multiple beats.

But the fact is — which labels and recording artists eventually came to realize — $25,000 has always been too much to pay for a beat in the first place. As mentioned earlier in the Business Part of this study, beatmaking is a new musical phenomenon, as such, the price parameters and ceiling was being set — in real time — in the 1990s. The price parameters and ceiling for beats was based on the model for previous music producers. But it soon became clear that not all beatmakers were actually in the studio with rappers "producing," helping out song ideas, vocal coaching, mixing, etc. Also, the number of able beatmakers grew exponentially over the pass 10 years, which lead to a dramatic drop in beat prices. In other words, the beat market prices corrected themselves, it was inevitable.

Second, some have blamed lower beat prices on poor record sales and illegal downloads, but poor music sales and illegal downloads are NOT the major culprit here; they're not the reason that beat prices have gone down. Poor record sales and illegal downloads merely helped people to see the obvious: beats (not production services) were long overpriced and automatically presumed to be production services in a more traditional sense. Beat prices of $25,000 and above were unreasonable in the first place; it just took a little time for the market to correct itself.

Beat prices actually began to go down more quickly than people realize. By 1994, prices were steadily going down for most acclaimed beatmakers; only a specific few were able to command exorbitant beat prices and fees. Sure, the likes of Dr. Dre, Darkchild, Timbaland, and The Neptunes saw their prices go up; but they didn't just supply beats, they supplied production services and a highly marketable brand name. But I'm sure they came down off of their prices as they saw their workloads being decreased. Why? It's simple: price point too high, and with no guaranteed hit, there were very few takers willing to absorb the risk or blow to their decreased recording budgets. Many recording artists wised up and started looking elsewhere for new talent, quality production (sometimes even knock-off sounds), and lower prices.

Thus, the true market price range for quality beats has, in reality, always been roughly $3,000-$7,000 per beat (lower obviously for less established names). A product always goes for what the market is willing to bear. While the market was unsure, beat prices were high; once there was more clarity in the market — about the product, about what one was actually getting for their money, about the growing number of qualified beatmakers — the market corrected itself. And consider this fact: In most cases, between 1989-1999, the bigger beat price tags for most acclaimed beatmakers typically covered multiple flat-rate beat deals, usually 3-8 beats (plus in-studio work) or the entire album depending on the beatmaker and the specific rapper or other artist involved. (In my interviews with Marley Marl, DJ Premier, and DJ Toomp, each made this clear about the nature and negotiations of beat prices.)

Here, I'll provide my full response to the concerns and questions raised by Uh-Oh.

(1) "When I think of a 'union,' I think of all them old white dudes my dad knows who get together and throw parties and do city work and etc."

There are a number of different unions, but essentially all "worker unions" share two primary goals for its members: fair wages and better labor conditions. The labor union that you're probably most familiar with is in the vein of an auto/trucking union, or city workers union, something along those lines. A musicians union — which is what a beatmakers union would be — is a creative arts-based union. Just like any other union, there are rotating wage concerns and labor situations. A beatmakers union would seek to secure better wages for ALL members as well as better labor conditions. A beatmakers union would guarantee a minimum sell price, the selling floor.

Also, a union would guarantee a top tier payment scale, both based on beatmaker status (name recognition and number of commercial releases) and the magnitude of the project; for instance, big-time major or indie commercial releases, free mixtapes, etc. In terms of UBG, there would be a standard fee, which is union scale. Then there would be a graduated scale fee, or better said, a "veteran's minimum." The veteran's minimum would be calculated on a beatmakers overall presence/time/significance in the field. Point is, it wouldn't matter simply "how long" some one's been around. There are many beatmakers who have been around for 15 years, that doesn't mean that they've had much of an impact on the hip hop/rap and/or beatmaking traditions.

Membership in a creative arts-based union is different than, let's say, the UAW (United Auto Workers). Union membership is NOT fundamentally based on "who you know." Instead, membership is based on your actual professional work. For instance, the Screen Actors Guild (SAG) is a union for professional actors. SAG has feature film, indie film, television commercial contracts, etc. What gets you into SAG is your first SAG sanctioned gig. So let's say you go to an open audition for an upcoming feature film. Whether you've acted before or not, if you get the role, you automatically have to become a member of SAG; if you do not join SAG before principle shooting begins, then the producers (the studio) are restricted from using you in the role if it's a SAG sanctioned feature. Once you're a member of SAG, you get a notice about the initial SAG entry fee and subsequent dues, which is based on a small percentage of your annual earnings.

Now, the very important thing to understand here about SAG is that they've already worked out the "starting point" for all of its members. That is to say, because of SAG, there is a minimum day rate (paid rate per each day) that ALL actors must get, based on the type and size — big budget feature, small budget feature, indie, etc. — of the film. This also includes labor conditions that must be met, for example: personal trailers for principle actors, guaranteed work breaks, guaranteed overtime pay, guaranteed lunch breaks and food, transportation, etc. Before there was an actors union, NONE OF THIS was guaranteed! Movie studios could, and routinely did, pay an actor whatever they wanted. In fact, before SAG, motion picture studios would sign actors to long-term, draconian contracts, loaning the actors out to other studios as they chose.

Further, because SAG has jurisdiction over so many areas, film/television production companies face hefty fines when they use a non-union member for a SAG-sanctioned project. Thus, film/television companies do not mess around with this, they ONLY use SAG members for SAG-sanctioned projects.

(2) "What would be the driving points to get beatmakers to join?"

That's easy: better wages, appropriate labor conditions, and the promise of more work.

(3) As for "getting around the union?"

As with SAG, if a beatmakers union secured the right agreements with major labels (RIAA) and indie labels, jurisdiction would make it impossible for non-union members to get work on those projects sanctioned by the union. Of course, there will be selfish people who think that they can (and will) go it alone. But the reality is this: the number of professionally qualified new beatmakers is steadily growing. A beatmakers union is the best way to harness that power and create an environment for more beatmakers to consistently get paid for their work. If done right, every talented beatmaker would join the union, as opportunities outside of UBG would be minimal.

Incidentally, I believe now is the right time to move forward with a beatmakers union, because ALL labels are weakened, particularly in terms of leverage; they know anyone can make and distribute their own music. If a beatmakers union can demonstrate how it can help turn around the larger sales picture, labels will likely make a number of important concessions to a beatmakers union. Bottom line: The labels want (need) to make money. If an exclusive deal with a powerful beatmakers union helps them achieve that goal, they'll be more than willing to work with UBG.

Keep in mind, in recent years, one of the major problems in hip hop/rap music has been quality control particularly in the area of beats. If a beatmakers union was powerful enough to show labels (big and small) that it was in their strategic advantage to do a deal with UBG, they would. Should the labels ignore such a powerful union, the alternative would mean that they'd have to compete with a united force of individuals who have much more influence over the internet and the streets than they do.

(4) "But the union would also have to have a cap for the amount of members wouldn't it?"

No! There's no cap on the amount of new projects someone can think of, create, and distribute for commercial purposes. So why would there be a cap on the number of members in a beatmakers union? Again, entry into UBG would be based on a beatmakers contribution to a commercially released project or professional mixtape. This project could be a beatmaker's own commercially released project, even a free mixtape if was distributed to a large enough audience (not a mixtape that was just handed to a handful of friends); such a mixtape would have to have had garnered some widespread level of critical acclaim. But in the union I envision, all of the parameters of entry could not be determined by just one person. The metrics would be simple and automatic, with a streamlined process for registering with UBG.

(5) "If there's so many members how would one go about even looking for beats within it?"

Each member would be registered with UBG, and labels and individuals could submit beat requests to what I would call the UBG's "Beat Request Registry." Each "BR" request would have a number and link to the actual request. ONLY members in good standing (meaning dues paid, no worker complaints, etc.) would have access to the BR filings.

It is my firm belief that a strong and united beatmakers union is the only way to assure decent beat prices and pay parity in the new beat market exchange, a phenomenon I detailed earlier in the Business Part of this study. I've been calling for the creation of a union for beatmakers for over ten years now. In that time, the bottom-lines of some of the most well-known beatmakers (producers) have been pinched, and there's been a tremendous rise in the number of talented beatmakers turning pro with different levels of production placements. Thus, right now is the time for serious strides towards a beatmakers union to be made. UBG can become a reality.

Outro

Hip hop/rap music is shaping up for another big revolution, something perhaps more edgier, more urgent, more unpolished and less accessible to mainstream culture. Contemporary hip hop/rap music has become perhaps too acceptable and easily digestible by mainstream culture. That is to say, hip hop/rap music has become "safe;" but that was never the initial aim or draw to hip hop/rap music. One of the most important things that made hip hop/rap music "hip" and unique was the fact that it was never about playing it safe for the masses. Hip hop/rap music began as a "bandit" music, something created, facilitated, and primarily executed by the forgotten, ignored, and despised fringe of American society: poor blacks and Latinos of the streets.

Although hip hop/rap music still fundamentally gets its cue from these same streets, the reality is, there's a sizeable and increasingly growing number of beatmakers who do not come from a street environment. Yet many of these aformentioned beatmakers, I would argue, are becoming increasingly more aware of, and sincerely concerned with, what hip hop/rap music was and what beatmaking commonly meant in its traditional sense. As this awareness and concern grows, I believe that there will be a major beatmaking renaissance, a widespread shift towards a beatmaking style and approach that defers to the more fundamental aesthetics and priorities of hip hop/rap music (rather than to pop, rock, or any other music form outside of hip hop/rap), while also relying upon developments in (or re-interpretations of) key hip hop/rap sub-styles like trap and grime.

Hip hop culture and hip hop/rap music was born in the South Bronx, and its earliest cultivation — including the development of a beatmaking tradition

— took place throughout the streets of New York City, and later the streets in cities all across America, and then all over the globe. Thus, there is no dispute that hip hop/rap comes from, first and foremost, the streets. And though there can be no debate that hip hop/rap music has certainly grown past the borders of its origins, it's important to recognize that, despite all attempts to compromise and dilute the culture and art form, hip hop begins and ends with the streets. No matter who embraces or celebrates it, hip hop is a street-based culture with mass appeal. Therefore, this is where its chief trends and innovations have taken and will always take place. Not coincidentally, this is why I believe that the culture and art form will ultimately survive in its fundamental form.

Finally, I'm compelled to point out that I consider this book to be an investment in the future of hip hop culture, specifically the hip hop/rap music and beatmaking traditions. My concern throughout this study has been, first and foremost, with beatmakers, especially the youngest ones among us. Also, I have been focused on those responsible, objective music professionals who have not had access to a thorough understanding of the beatmaking tradition of hip hop/rap music. My aim is, and has always been, to help elevate the beatmaking tradition of hip hop/rap to its proper place in contemporary music. To that end, I have strived to make *The BeatTips Manual* a formidable force that beatmakers everywhere can rally around. Moreover, I have designed this book to serve as a platform that beatmakers could use to help achieve their creative and professional production goals and aspirations. Also, I have created this book to serve as a means for beatmakers worldwide to connect with one another.

Appendix

Canon of Hip Hop/Rap Beatmakers: The BeatTips Top 125 Beatmakers of All Time

Every art form has its own canon of artists. Thus, in the following list, I will include 125 beatmakers that collectively comprise a solid canon of beatmakers. Each of which are worthy of some degree of study, but the first 30 on the BeatTips Top 125 list deserve extra attention.

Whenever lists of this sort appear, they're generally presented with little or no serious discussion about the nature of the list beforehand. Perhaps that's fine for pure entertainment purposes. But for readers to get the best learning experience from a list of this kind, I believe that there are a number of things that readers should know up front. So I'd like to offer an important disclaimer about the nature of the BeatTips Top 125 Beatmakers of All Time list and the criteria used to determine which beatmakers were included on it.

The Nature of this List

The BeatTips Top 125 Beatmakers of All Time list is one of the first sub-projects of the BeatTips Art of Beatmaking Education Project (ABEP). The fundamental purpose of the BeatTips ABEP is to help preserve, promote, and expand the beatmaking tradition of hip hop/rap music through a series of specialized projects. In this way, the BeatTips Top 125 Beatmakers of All Time list is meant to serve as a discussion, MusicStudy, and general research portal.

Next, the BeatTips Top 125 Beatmakers of All-Time purposely omits the word "producer," and here's why. In the hip hop/rap music and beatmaking traditions, the term "producer" is often synonymously used to describe a beatmaker. But as I've pointed out in this study, this is not always appropriate, particularly because the definition of "producer" can be murky. Again from earlier: *Hip hop production is the creation of hip hop music. And although this description broadly covers every dimension of hip hop/rap music, the term hip hop production is used most commonly to refer to the making of the hip hop/rap instrumental—the beat.* So technically speaking, a beatmaker, one who makes beats, is a hip hop producer; ergo, a beatmaker is a producer. But "producer" is a loose term that can be used to describe anyone within the process of the final sound of a recording. Simply put, a beatmaker is someone who actually makes beats. A beatmaker can indeed be a producer; in fact, most double as both. (Further, being a beatmaker is not in anyway less noble than being a producer!) However, and this is a critical point, a producer need not be a beatmaker. Hip hop/rap music is littered with people who have "producer" credits, even though they never actually made (or assisted in the making of) any beats. Thus, The BeatTips Top 125 Beatmakers of All Time List primarliy includes beatmakers. Of course, each beatmaker on this list has also rightfully earned the title of producer.

There are four other important things to know about the nature of The BeatTips Top 125 Beatmakers of All Time list. First, like *The BeatTips Manual* itself, the purpose of this list is to educate. Hopefully, new beatmakers will be introduced more appropriately to some prominent beatmakers that they've only heard about in passing; and veteran beatmakers will be reminded of just how far the beatmaking tradition has come. In either case, I'd like this list to prompt some serious exploration and reflection from readers. Preserving and expanding hip hop/rap's beatmaking tradition requires historical examination, present-day review, future speculation, and, at times, constructive debate.

Second, this isn't a list to appease anyone that I know personally. I can count a number of beatmakers as friends; and I've interviewed many well-known and lesser-known (but quite acclaimed) beatmakers. That aside, I've made no effort to show favoritism in the making of this list. My objectivity — and naturally subjectivity — in the making of this list was based on the catalog of work of each beatmaker that I seriously considered.

Third, this is not a list intended to be safe so as to not offend anyone. Top lists of any kind tend to offend one group or another, so I'm all right with that. I'm not interested in gathering up an easy list of names. Instead, I want readers to seriously think, perhaps even broaden their own thoughts about how, why, and where they rank their favorite beatmakers.

Fourth, The BeatTips Top 125 Beatmakers of All Time is not a "hottest in the game right now" type of list. I deeply respect longevity, particularly because it requires talent, drive, integrity, and hustle. I'm less interested on shining a light on just this moment in time. I believe all-time lists offer a better learning (and discovery) experience for readers. This is especially important for new beatmakers who are often less familiar with the names and critical works of earlier times.

The Criteria

When making the BeatTips Top 125 Beatmakers of All-Time list there were many different things that I considered, far too many to mention here. But there are eight main criteria that I used in making this list:

(1) Body of work. Without the work speaking for itself, there could be no serious consideration of any beatmaker who made this list. And while I did not deem it necessary that each beatmaker on the list had a massive catalog, the sheer number of beats (recognized and respected songs) of certain beatmakers could not be ignored. Therefore, a larger body of acclaimed work was appropriately given more preference. Also, special attention was paid to how many songs a beatmaker had within the cannon of hip hop/rap music, as well as whether or not a beatmaker contributed to the career of another pivotal hip hop/rap artist's career. I should further add that the body of work that I've considered here is hip hop/rap only. Whether a beatmaker could or did produce music outside of the hip hop/rap genre had no bearing on where I ranked them with respect to hip hop/rap music. If I were ranking all-time horror film directors, it would be silly to include the comedic works of those directors as consideration in where they should be ranked. Likewise, neo-soul, drum-n-bass, dub step, etc. has no influence on a hip hop/rap ranking.

(2) Critical acclaim for a clearly distinguishable and/or signature sound. Preference was given to those beatmakers who either established their own well-recognized signature sound or contributed considerably to one or more of the eight distinct periods of beatmaking.

(3) Minimum of at least three critically acclaimed (not just top sellers) songs, albums, collaborative works, etc. within the last 30 years. Part of being a standout in any art medium is recognition within the field. Sometimes this means big hits, other times it means well-respected songs that most skilled beatmakers know of or appreciate for what they are. And note, this particular criteria reflects the reality that some of the best in any given field are overlooked for various reasons. But this does not diminish their work. Moreover, history is loaded with artists who didn't get their proper appreciation until late in, or well after, their careers.

(4) The number of lyrically acclaimed rappers — in their prime — who rapped over their beats and/or the subsequent "classic" songs created over the last 30 years. This is of particular importance for two reasons. First, it serves as proof of a beatmaker's automatic place in the canon of hip hop/rap music.

Second, it demonstrates the popularity and respect of a beatmaker among the best rhymers of their time and beyond.

(5) Real, not misperceived, impact and influence on other top beatmakers of all time. Everybody has to be influenced by someone. But who influenced most of the beatmakers on the BeatTips Top 125 (especially the first 30) Beatmakers of All-Time list? Not surprisingly, many influenced each other.

(6) Real, not misperceived, overall impact (or likely impact) on the beatmaking tradition. In other words, what was their recognizable impact on the beatmaking tradition itself? For instance, what developments, styles, techniques, ideas, etc. did they contribute to the beatmaking tradition?

(7) Longevity. How long was a beatmaker able to maintain his career. For various reasons, some beatmaker's careers were cut short, while others have continued to blossom since they first began. Thus, longevity wasn't measured in a sheer number of years, but in terms of body of work within the frame of time a beatmaker made his name. Think of it this way: Jimi Hendrix's entire body of work is just four years.

(8) Projected influence and impact on future beatmakers. Of course, this is speculation at best. No one can predict the future. Still, we can recognize the lasting contributions made to the beatmaking tradition by certain beatmakers.

One final note about this list: It's not static. That is to say, the beatmaking tradition is constantly expanding. Therefore, this list will necessarily need to be adjusted to account for new production output by beatmakers, as well as new research by myself. In other words, this list will be updated, with each new edition or perhaps every new print run or e-version.

APPENDIX

Homage to DJ Kool Herc, Grandmaster Flash, and Afrika Bambaataa — the grandfathers of modern beatmaking.[197]

1. DJ Premier
2. Marley Marl — father of modern beatmaking[198]
3. The RZA
4. Pete Rock
5. Large Professor (Example of Paul C.'s biggest influence)
6. Dr. Dre
7. Kanye West
8. The Bomb Squad (Hank Shocklee, Eric "Vietnam" Sadler, Keith Shocklee, Chuck D)
9. J Dilla
10. Q-Tip and Ali Shaheed Muhammad (of A Tribe Called Quest)
11. DJ Toomp
12. The Neptunes
13. Just Blaze
14. Showbiz[199]
15. Nottz
16. 9th Wonder
17. DJ Paul and Juicy J
18. Prince Paul
19. Madlib
20. Buckwild
21. Alchemist
22. Havoc (of Mobb Deep)
23. DJ Khalil
24. Rick Rubin
25. The Beatnuts
26. Jake One
27. Bink
28. True Master
29. Dame Grease
30. Marco Polo
31. Kev Brown
32. The Hitmen (D-Dot, Nashiem Myrick, Chucky Thompson, Stevie J, Carlos "6 July" Broady, Sean C and LV)
33. Salaam Remi
34. Easy Mo Bee
35. Organized Noise
36. No I.D.[200]
37. Swizz Beatz
38. Erick Sermon
39. Larry Smith
40. Timbaland
41. Black Milk
42. Diamond D
43. Mannie Fresh
44. J.U.S.T.I.C.E. League (Rook, Colione, Kenny)
45. Metro Boomin
46. Noah "40" Shebib

---

[197] Though not entirely within this illustrious group, Arthur Baker does indeed deserve some level of honorable mention for his contributions to early sampling and his early work with Afrika Bambaataa.
[198] Since 1986, every beatmaker (producer) who's ever made a beat stands on the shoulders of Marley Marl.
[199] Who was chopping samples like Showbiz, before Showbiz? Without Showbiz, no DJ Premier, no Buckwild, and no Minnesota, as we know them.
[200] Without No I.D., no Kanye West!

47	DJ Quik
48	Hi-Tek
49	K-Def
50	Cardiak
51	Shawty Redd
52	Statik Selektah
53	DJ Mustard
54	Khrysis
55	El-P
56	!llmind
57	Apollo Brown
58	Mathematics
59	Da Beatminerz
60	M-Phazes
61	DJ Scratch
62	Scott Storch
63	Ski (AKA Ski Beatz)
64	Oddisee
65	Don Cannon
66	Bronze Nazareth
67	DJ Muggs
68	Boi 1-da
69	Mel-Man
70	RJD2
71	The Heatmakerz
72	Dan the Automator
73	Minnesota
74	EZ Elpee
75	DJ Jazzy Jeff
76	Lord Finesse
77	DJ Shadow
78	Focus
79	Scram Jones
80	Trackmasters
81	Megahertz
82	Steinski
83	Drumma Boy
84	Rockwilder
85	DJ Clark Kent (from Brooklyn)
86	Knxwledge
87	Paul C. (Had he not been murdered at the very start of his career, he most likely would have been in top 20)
88	Mike Will Made It
89	Flying Lotus
90	Harry Fraud
91	S1 (Symbolic One)
92	88-Keys
93	Domino
94	Ant Banks
95	MF Doom
96	Oh No
97	Lil Jon
98	Jermaine Dupri
99	J Zone
100	Apathy
101	Denaun Porter

102	Bangladesh
103	DJ Pooh
104	Exile
105	Lex Luger
106	Paul White
107	Emile
108	Ced Gee
109	Ron Browz
110	Diplo
111	Hit Boy
112	FredWreck
113	Jimi Kendrix
114	Gensu Dean
115	Frank Dukes
116	DJ Skizz
117	Big K.R.I.T.
118	Battlecat
119	Nick Speed
120	T-Minus
121	Sir Jinx
122	Ty Fyffe
123	Amadeus
124	Ayatollah
125	Jahlil Beats

Discography

Hip Hop/Rap

2 Live Crew. *As Nasty As They Wanna Be* (Luke, 1989); *Banned in the U.S.A.* (Luke, 1990).
3rd Bass. *The Cactus Album* (Def Jam, 1989).
9th Wonder [also see Little Brother]. *The Dream Merchant, Vol. 2* (6 Hole, 2007).
50 Cent. *Get Rich or Die Tryin'* (G-Unit, Aftermath, Shady, Interscope, 2003); *The Massacre* (G-Unit/Aftermath/Shady/Interscope, 2005); *Curtis* (G-Unit/Aftermath/Shady/Interscope, 2007).
A Tribe Called Quest. *People's Instinctive Travels and the Paths of Rhythm* (Jive, 1990); *The Low End Theory* (Jive, 1991); *Midnight Marauders* (Jive, 1993); *Beats, Rhymes and Life* (Jive, 1995).
A.Z. *Doe or Die* (EMI, 1995); *Pieces of A Man* (Virgin, 1998); *Aziatic* (Motown, 2002); *A.W.O.L.* (Quiet Money, 2005); *The Format* (Quiet Money/Fast Life, 2006).
Afrika Bambaataa. "Jazzy Sensation" (Tommy Boy, 1981); "Planet Rock" (Tommy Boy, 1982); "Looking for the Perfect Beat" (Tommy Boy, 1982); "Renegades of Funk" (Tommy Boy, 1983).
The Alkaholiks. *21 & Over* (Loud, 1993); *Coast II Coast* (Loud, 1995); *Likwidation* (Loud, 1997).
Akinyele. *Vagina Diner* (Interscope/Atlantic, 1993); *Put It In Your Mouth* (Stress/Zoo/BMG, 1996).
BDP (Boogie Down Productions). *Criminal Minded* (B-Boy, 1987); *By Any Means Necessary* (Jive/RCA, 1988); *Ghetto Music: The Blueprint of Hip Hop* (Jive/RCA, 1989); *Edutainment* (Jive/RCA, 1990).
Beanie Sigel. *The Truth* (Roc-A-Fella, 2000); *The Reason* (Roc-A-Fella, 2001); *The B. Coming*, (Dame Dash Music Group/Def Jam, 2005).
The Beastie Boys. *Licensed to Ill* (Def Jam, 1986); *Paul's Boutique* (Capitol, 1989).
The Beatnuts. *Intoxicated Demons: The EP* (Relativity/Violator, 1993); *Street Level* (Relativity/Violator, 1994).
Big Daddy Kane. *Long Live the Kane* (Cold Chillin', 1988); *It's A Big Daddy Thing* (Cold Chillin', 1989).
Biz Markie. *Goin' Off* (Cold Chillin'/Warner Bros., 1987); *The Biz Never Sleeps* (Cold Chillin'/Warner Bros., 1989); *I Need A Haircut* (Cold Chillin'/Warner Bros., 1993).
Black Moon. *Enta Da Stage* (Nervous, 1993).
Black Sheep. *A Wolf in Sheep's Clothing,* (Mercury/Polygram, 1991).
Black Star (Mos Def and Talib Kweli). *Mos Def & Talib Kweli Are Black Star* (Rawkus, 1998).
Bumpy Knuckles (aka Freddy Foxxx). *Industry Shakedown* (Landspeed, 2000).
Cam'Ron. *Confessions of Fire* (Untertainment/Epic, 1998); *Come Home With Me* (Diplomat/Roc-A-Fella/Def Jam, 2002).
Clipse. *Lord Willin'* (Star Trak/Arista, 2002).
The Cold Crush Brothers. "Fresh, Fly, Wild, and Bold" (1984); "Cold Crush Brothers Battle Tape," Pts. 1-5 (Ca. 1981). [CCB music only on cassette between 1978-1979]
Cormega. *The Realness* (Legal Hustle, 2001); *The True Meaning,* (Legal Hustle, 2002); *Legal Hustle* (Legal Hustle/Koch, 2004).
Common (previously known as Common Sense). *Can I Borrow a Dollar* (Relativity, 1992); *Resurrection* (Relativity, 1994); *One Day It'll All Make Sense* (Relativity, 1997); *Like Water for Chocolate* (MCA/Universal, 2000); *Be* (G.O.O.D./Geffen, 2005); Finding Forever (G.O.O.D./Geffen, 2007).
Cypress Hill. *Cypress Hill* (Ruffhouse/Columbia, 1991).
The D.O.C. *No One Can Do It Better* (Ruthless, 1989).
De La Soul. *3 Feet High and Rising* (Tommy Boy, 1989); *De La Soul Is Dead* (Tommy Boy, 1991); *Buhloone Mindstate* (Tommy Boy, 1993); *Stakes Is High* (Tommy Boy, 1996).
DMX. *It's Dark and Hell Is Hot* (Ruff Ryders/Def Jam, 1998); *Grand Champ* (Def Jam, 2003).
Dilated Peoples. "Worst Comes to Worst" (Capitol, 2001).
Diamond D. *Stunts, Blunts and Hip Hop* (Chemistry/Mercury, 1992).
Double X Posse. "Not Gonna Be Able to Do It" (Big Beat, 1992).
Doug E Fresh (with the Get Fresh Crew). "The Show" (Reality, 1985); "La Di Da Di" (Reality, 1985).
Dr. Dre. *The Chronic* (Death Row, 1992); *2001* (Aftermath, 1999).
Drake. *Thank Me Later* (Aspire/Young Money/Cash Money/Universal Motown, 2010); *Take Care* (Young Money/Cash Money/Republic, 2011); *Nothing Was the Same* (OVO Young Money Cash Money Republic, 2013); *If You're Reading This, It's Too Late* (Cash Money Young Money OVO Sound Republic, 2015).
EPMD. *Strictly Business* (Fresh/Sleeping Bag, 1988); *Unfinished Business* (Priority, 1989); *Business As Usual* (Priority, 1990); *Business Never Personal* (Def Jam, 1992).
Ed O. G and Da Bulldogs. *Life of a Kid in the Ghetto* (PWL/Mercury, 1991).
Eminem. *The Slim Shady LP* (Aftermath, 1999); *The Marshall Mathers LP* (Aftermath, 2000).
Eric B & Rakim. *Paid In Full* (4th & B'way, 1987); *Follow the Leader* (Uni/Mercury, 1988); *Let the Rhythm Hit 'Em* (MCA, 1990); *Don't Sweat the Technique* (MCA, 1992).
Fat Boys, The. *Fat Boys* (Sutra, 1984).
Fat Joe. *Represent* (Relativity, 1993); *Jealous One's Envy* (Terror Squad/Relativity, 1995).
Freeway. *Philadelphia Freeway* (Roc-A-Fella, 2003).
Future. *Pluto* (A1/Freebandz/Epic, 2012); *DS2* (A1 Freebandz Epic, 2015).

Funky Four (aka Funky Four Plus One). "That's the Joint" (1981); "Rappin' & Rockin' the House."
The Game. *The Documentary* (Aftermath/G-Unit, 2005); *Doctor's Advocate* (Geffen, 2006).
Gang Starr. *No More Mr. Nice Guy* (Wild Pitch, 1989); *Step in the Arena* (Chrysalis, 1991); *Daily Operation* (Chrysalis, 1992); *Hard to Earn* (Chrysalis, 1994); *Moment of Truth* (Noo Trybe/Virgin, 1998); *Full Clip: A Decade of Gang Starr* (Noo Trybe/Virgin, 1999); *The Ownerz* (Virgin, 2003).
The Geto Boys. *We Can't Be Stopped* (Rap-A-Lot, 1991).
Ghostface Killah [also see Wu-Tang Clan]. *Iron Man* (Razor Sharp/Epic, 1996); *Supreme Clientele* (Razor Sharp/Epic, 2000); *Bulletproof Wallets* (Epic, 2001); *The Pretty Toney Album* (Def Jam, 2004); *Fishscale* (Def Jam, 2006); *The Big Doe Rehab* (Def Jam, 2007).
Grandmaster Flash. *The Adventures of Grandmaster Flash on the Wheels of Steel* (Sugar Hill, 1981).
Grandmaster Flash and the Furious Five. *The Message* (Sugar Hill, 1982).
Grandmaster Melle Mel. "White Lines" (Sugar Hill, 1983).
The GZA [also see Wu-Tang Clan]. *Liquid Swords* (Geffen, 1995); *Beneath the Surface* (MCA, 1999).
House of Pain. *House of Pain* (Tommy Boy, 1992).
Ice Cube. *AmeriKKKa's Most Wanted* (Priority, 1991); *Death Certificate* (Priority, 1991); *The Predator* (Priority, 1992).
Ice T. *Rhyme Pays* (Sire/Warner, 1987); *Power* (Sire/Warner, 1987); *O.G. Original Gangster* (Sire/Warner, 1991).
Inspectah Deck [also see Wu-Tang Clan]. *Uncontrolled Substance* (Loud, 1999).
Jadakiss. *Kiss Tha Game Goodbye* (Ruff Ryders, 2001); *Kiss of Death* (Ruff Ryders, 2004).
Jay-Z. *Reasonable Doubt* (Roc-A-Fella, 1996); *In My Lifetime, Vol. 1* (Roc-A-Fella, 1997); *Vol. 2... Hard Knock Life* (Roc-A-Fella, 1998); *Vol. 3… Life and Times of S. Carter* (Roc-A-Fella, 1999); *The Dynasty: Roc La Familia* (Roc-A-Fella, 2000); *The Blueprint* (Roc-A-Fella, 2001); *The Blueprint²: The Gift & The Curse* (Roc-A-Fella, 2002); *The Black Album* (Roc-A-Fella, 2003); *Kingdom Come* (Roc-A-Fella, 2006); *American Gangster* (Roc-A-Fella, 2007).
Jeru the Damaja. *The Sun Rises in the East* (Pay Day/FFRR, 1994).
Jurrasic 5. "What's Golden" (Interscope, 2002).
Juvenile. *400 Degreez* (Cash Money, 1998).
Kanye West. *The College Dropout* (Roc-A-Fella, 2004); *Late Registration* (Roc-A-Fella, 2005); *Graduation* (Roc-A-Fella, 2007); *808s & Heartbreak* (Roc-A-Fella, 2008).
KMD. *Mr. Hood* (Elektra, 1991).
KRS-One [also see BDP]. *Return of the Boom Bap* (Jive, 1993).
King Tee. *Act a Fool* (Capitol, 1988); *At Your Own Risk* (Capitol, 1990).
Kool G Rap & DJ Polo. *Road to the Riches* (Cold Chillin', 1989); *Wanted: Dead or Alive* (Cold Chillin', 1990); *Live and Let Die* (Cold Chillin', 1992).
Kurtis Blow. *Kurtis Blow* (Mercury, 1980);
LL Cool J. *Radio* (Def Jam, 1985); *Bigger and Deffer* (Def Jam, 1987); *Walking with a Panther* (Def Jam, 1989); *Mama Said Knock You Out* (Def Jam, 1990); *14 Shots to the Dome* (Def Jam, 1993); *Mr. Smith* (Def Jam, 1995).
Large Professor [also see Main Source]. *1st Class* (Matador, 2002).
Leaders of the New School. *A Future without a Past* (Elektra, 1991).
Lil Jon & the East Side Boyz. *Get Crunk, Who U Wit: Da Album* (Mirror Image, 1997); *Kings of Crunk* (TVT, 2002); *Crunk Juice* (TVT, 2004).
Lil Wayne. *Tha Block is Hot* (Cash Money, 1999); *Tha Carter* (Cash Money, 2004); *Tha Carter III* (Cash Money/Young Money, 2008).
Little Brother. *The Listening* (ABB, 2003); *The Minstrel Show* (Atlantic/ABB, 2005).
The Lox. *Money, Power & Respect* (Bad Boy, 1997).
MC Hammer. *Let's Get It Started* (Capitol, 1988).
MC Lyte. *Lyte As a Rock* (First Priority, 1988); *Eyes On This* (First Priority, 1989).
M.O.P. *To the Death* (Select, 1994); *Firing Squad* (Relativity, 1996); *First Family 4 Life* (Relativity, 1998); *Warriorz* (Loud, 2000).
Madlib (as Quasimoto). *The Further Adventures of Lord Quas* (Stones Throw, 2005).
Madvillain [Madlib with MF Doom]. *Madvillainy* (Stones Throw, 2004).
Main Source. *Breaking Atoms* (Wild Pitch, 1991).
Marley Marl. *In Contol* (Cold Chillin', 1988).
Method Man [also see Wu-Tang Clan]. *Tical* (Def Jam, 1994); *Tical 2000: Judgement Day* (Def Jam, 2000).
Method Man and Redman. *Blackout* (Def Jam, 1999).
Mobb Deep. *Juvenile Hell* (4th & B'Way, 1993); *The Infamous* (Loud, 1995); *Hell On Earth* (Loud, 1996); *Murda Muzik* (Loud, 1999); *Infamy* (Loud, 2001); *Blood Money* (G-Unit, 2006).
Mos Def. *Black on Both Sides* (Rawkus, 1999).
NWA. *Straight Outta Compton* (Ruthless, 1988); *100 Miles and Runnin'* (Ruthless, 1990); *Niggaz4Life* (Ruthless, 1991).
Noreaga. *N.O.R.E.* (Penalty, 1998).
NYGz. *Welcome 2 G-Dom* (Year Round, 2007).
Nas. *Illmatic* (Columbia, 1994); *It Was Written* (Columbia, 1996); *I Am* (Columbia, 1999); *Nastradamus* (Columbia, 1999); *Stillmatic* (Ill Will/Columbia, 2001); *Nasir Jones: God's Son* [aka God's Son] (Ill Will/Columbia, 2002);

Street's Desciple (Ill Will/Columbia, 2004); *Hip Hop Is Dead* (Def Jam, 2006).
Nature. *For All Seasons* (Track Masters, 2000).
Naughty By Nature. *Naughty By Nature* (Tommy Boy, 1991); *19 Naughty III* (Tommy Boy, 1993).
Notorious B.I.G. [aka Biggie Smalls]. *Ready To Die* (Bad Boy, 1994); *Life After Death* (Bad Boy, 1997).
O.C. *Word…Life* (Wild Pitch, 1994); *Jewelz* (Payday, 1997).
Ol' Dirty Bastard [also see Wu-Tang Clan]. *Return to the 36 Chambers: The Dirty Version* (Elektra, 1995); *Nigga Please* (Elektra, 1999).
Onyx. *Bacdafucup* (Def Jam, 1993).
Pete Rock. *Soul Survivor* (Loud/RCA, 1998).
Outkast. *Southernplayalisticadillacmuzik* (LaFace, 1994); *ATLiens* (LaFace/Arista, 1996); *Aquemini* (LaFace/Arista, 1998); *Stankonia*, (LaFace/Arista, 2000); *Speakerboxxx/The Love Below* (LaFace/Arista, 2003).
The Pharcyde. *Bizarre Ride II the Pharcyde* (Delicious Vinyl, 1992); *Labcabincalifornia* (Delicious Vinyl, 1995).
Public Enemy. *Yo! Bum Rush the Show* (Def Jam, 1987); *It Takes a Nation of Millions to Hold Us Back* (Def Jam, 1988); *Fear of a Black Planet* (Def Jam, 1990).
Q-Tip [also see A Tribe Called Quest]. *Amplified* (Arista, 1999).
Raewkon [also see Wu-Tang Clan]. *Only Built 4 Cuban Linx* (Loud, 1995); *Immobilarity* (Loud, 1999); *Only Built 4 Cuban Linx… Pt. II* (Ice H2O, 2009). *Reflection Eternal* [Talib Kweli and Hi-Tek]. *Train of Thought* (Rawkus, 2000).
Redman. *Whut? Thee Album* (Def Jam, 1992); *Muddy Waters* (Def Jam, 1996).
Rich Boy. "Throw Some D's," 2006.
Royal Flush. *Ghetto Millionaire* (Blunt, 1997).
Royce Da 5'9. *Street Hop* (M.I.C./One, 2009).
Run-DMC. *Run-DMC* (Profile, 1984); *King of Rock* (Profile, 1985); *Raising Hell* (Profile, 1986); *Tougher Than Leather* (Profile, 1988).
The RZA [also see Wu-Tang Clan]. *Bobby Digital in Stereo* (Gee Street/V2, 1998).
Salt-N-Pepa. *Hot, Cool & Vicious* (Next Plateau, 1986); *A Salt with a Deadly Pepa* (Next Plateau/London, 1988).
Scarface [also see The Geto Boys]. *The Diary* (Rap-A-Lot, 1994); *The Fix* (Def Jam South, 2002).
Screwball, *Y2K The Album* (Tommy Boy, 2000); *Loyalty* (Landspeed, 2001).
Sean Price. *Monkey Barz* (Duck Down, 2005); *Jesus Price Supastar* (Duck Down, 2007).
Showbiz & AG. *Runaway Slave* (Payday, 1992).
Slum Village. *Fantastic, Vol. 2* (Good Vibe, 2000).
Slick Rick. *The Great Adventures of Slick Rick* (Def Jam, 1988).
Smif N' Wesson. *Dah Shinin'* (Wreck, 1995).
Smoothe Da Hustler. *Once Upon a Time in America* (Profile, 1996).
Snoop Doggy Dog. *Doggytyle* (Death Row, 1993); *Tha Doggfather* (Death Row, 1996).
Soulja Boy Tell 'Em. *souljaboytellem.com* (Collipark/Stacks on Deck/Interscope, 2007).
Souls of Mischief. *93 'til Infinity* (Jive, 1993).
Special Ed. *Youngest In Charge* (Profile, 1989).
Spoonie Gee. "Love Rap" (ca. 1979/80).
Styles P. *A Gangster and a Gentleman* (Ruff Ryders, 2002); *Super Gangster* (Extraordinary Gentleman) (Koch, 2007).
Sugar Hill Gang. "Rapper's Delight" (Sugar Hill Records, 1979).
T.I. *I'm Serious* (Ghett-O-Vision/LaFace, 2001); *Trap Muzik* (Grand Hustle/Atlantic, 2003); *Urban Legend* (Grand Hustle/Atlantic, 2004); *King* (Grand Hustle/Atlantic, 2006); *T.I. vs. T.I.P.* (Grand Hustle/Atlantic, 2007); *Paper Trail* (Grand Hustle/Atlantic, 2008).
Talib Kweli [also see Reflection Eternal]. *Quality* (Rawkus, 2002).
Three Six Mafia. *When the Smoke Clears: Sixty 6, Sixty 1* (Loud, 200); *Da Unbreakables* (Columbia, 2003); *Most Known Unknown* (Sony, 2005).
Too Short. *Born to Mack* (Dangerous/Jive, 1987); *Life Is… Too Short* (Jive, 1988).
Treacherous Three. "Feel The Heartbeat" (1981).
Tupac. *2Pacalypse Now* (Jive, 1991); *Strictly 4 My N.I.G.G.A.Z.* (Atlantic, 1993); *Me Against the World* (Atlantic, 1995); *All Eyez On Me* (Death Row, 1996).
Whoodini. *Escape* (Jive, 1984).
Wu-Tang Clan. *Enter the Wu-Tang* (36 Chambers) (Loud, 1993); *Wu-Tang Forever* (Loud, 1997); *The W* (Loud, 2000); *Iron Flag* (Loud, 2001); *8 Diagrams* (SRC, 2007).
Young Jeezy. *Let's Get It: Thug Motivation 101* (Corporate Thugz Entertainment/Def Jam, 2005); *The Inspiration* (Corporate Thugz/Def Jam, 2006); *The Recession* (Corporate Thugz Entertainment/Def Jam, 2008).
Yo Yo. *Make Way for the Motherlode* (East West America, 1991).
Young Black Teenagers. *Dead Enz Kidz Doin'* Lifetime Bidz (MCA, 1993).

Blues

Dixon, Willie. *Willie's Blues* (Bluesville, 1959).
Hooker, John Lee. "Hobo Blues" (Modern, 1948); "Boogie Chillen" (Modern, 1948).

Howlin' Wolf. *Moanin' in the Moonlight* (Chess, 1959); "Spoonful" (Chess, 1960); "Shake It For Me" (Chess, 1964).
James, Etta. *At Last* (Chess, 1961).
King, B.B. *Singin' The Blues* (Crown, 1956); *The Blues* (Crown, 1958); *My Kind of Blues* (EMI, 1961).
Little Walter. "Juke" (Chess, 1952); "My Babe" (Chess, 1955).
Muddy Waters. "Rollin' Stone" (Chess, 1950); "Hoochie Coochie Man" (Chess, 1954); "Got My Mojo Working" (Chess, 1956); *The Best of Muddy* (Chess, 1958); *Waters* (Chess, 1958).
Smith, Bessie. "Downhearted Blues" (ca. 1923); "Ain't Nobody's Business" (ca. 1925).
T-Bone Walker. "Mean Old World" (Capitol, 1942); "Call It Stormy Monday (But Tuesday Is Just as Bad)" (1947).
Turner, Big Joe. "Roll 'Em, Pete" (1938); "Shake, Rattle, and Roll" (1954); *The Boss of the Blues* (Atlantic, 1956).

Jazz

Armstrong, Louis. "St. Louis Blues" (1929, Okeh); "All of Me" (Columbia, 1932); *Louis Armstrong Plays W. C. Handy* (Columbia, 1954); Porgy and Bess (Verve, 1958); "Hello Dolly!" (Kaap, 1964); "What a Wonderful World" (ABC, 1968).
Blakey, Art (with the Jazz Messengers) *Art Blakey with the Original Jazz Messengers* (Columbia, 1956); *Moanin'* (Blue Note, 1958).
Count Basie. *Swinging the Blues 1930-1939* (Jazz Legends, 2004) [orignal recordings 1930-1939].
Count Basie [with Joe Williams]. *One O'Clock Jump* (Verve, 1957).
Coltrane, John [also see Miles Davis Quintet, I]. *Coltrane* (Prestige, 1957); *Blue Train* (Blue Note, 1957); *Soultrane* (Prestige, 1958); *Giant Steps* (Atlantic, 1960); *My Favorite Things* (Atlantic, 1961); *Coltrane Plays the Blues* (Atlantic, 1962).
Davis, Miles. *Birth of Cool* (Capitol, 1949); *Blue Haze* (Prestige, 1954); *Miles Davis and the Modern Jazz Giants* (Prestige, 1956); *Miles Ahead* (Columbia, 1957); *Milestones* (Columbia, 1958); *Porgry and Bess* (Columbia, 1958); *Kind of Blue* (Columbia, 1959); *Sketches of Spain* (Columbia, 1960);
Davis, Miles Quintet (I). *Miles: The New Miles Davis Quintet* (Prestige, 1956); *Cookin' with The Miles Davis Quintet* (Prestige, 1957); "So What" (Robert Herridge Theater [television show] "The Sound of Miles of Davis" CBS, 1959).
Davis, Miles Quintet (II). *E.S.P.* (Columbia, 1965); *Miles Smiles* (Columbia, 1966); *Miles in the Sky* (Columbia, 1968); *Filles de Kilimanjaro* (Columbia, 1969).
Ellington, Duke. "Mood Indigo" (Brunswick, 1930); *It Don't Mean a Thing* (If It Ain't Got That Swing) (Brunswick, 1932); Take the "A" Train (1939).
Fats Waller. "Honeysuckle Rose" (1929); "This Joint Is Jump'in'" (ca. 1934).
Hancock, Herbie [also see Miles Davis Quintet, II; also see The Headhunters]. *Inventions and Dimensions* (Blue Note, 1964); *The Prisoner* (Blue Note, 1969); *Fat Albert Rotunda* (Warner, 1969); *Sextant* (Columbia, 1973).
Holiday, Billie. "Strange Fruit" (Columbia, 1939); "God Bless the Child" (Okeh, 1942); "Mack the Knife" (Columbia, 1955); *Lady Sings the Blues* (Verve, 1956); "Ain't Nobody's Business" (Decca, ca. 1945).
Jamal, Ahmad. *The Awakening* (Impulse, 1970).
Jones, Quincy. *The Quintessence* (Impulse, 1961); *Walking in Space* (A&M, 1969); *Body Heat* (A&M, 1974).
Klemmer, John. *Blowin' Gold* (Cadet, 1969).
Monk, Thelonius. *Monk* (Prestige, 1954); *The Unique Thelonious Monk* (Riverside, 1956); *Thelonious Monk with John Coltrane* (Milsesone, 1957); *Thelonious Himself* (Riverside, 1959).
Parker, Charlie. "Ko-Ko" (Savoy, 1945); "Ornithology" (Dial, 1946).
Roach, Max (with Miles Davis). *Birth of Cool* (Capitol, 1949).
Rollins, Sonny. *The Bridge* (Bluebird, 1962).

Gospel

Caravan, The. "Swing Low, Sweet Chariot" (1958).
Clara Ward Singers, The. "How I Got Over" (1950); "Didn't Rain" (ca. 1952); "Swing Low, Sweet Chariot" (ca. 1952).
Dixie Hummingbirds, The. "When the Gates Swing Open" (ca. 1950s); "Holding On" (ca. 1950s).
Dorsey, Thomas A. "Take My Hand, Precious Lord" (aka "Precious Lord, Take My Hand") (ca. 1932).
Franklin, Aretha. *Aretha Franklin Amazing Grace (with James Cleveland and the Southern California Community Choir)* (Atlantic, 1972).
Golden Gate Quartet (aka The Golden Gate Jubilee Quartet). "The General Jumped at Dawn" (1944); "Golden Gate Gospel Train" (Ca. early 1940s); "Joshua Fit the Battle" (1949).
Jackson, Mahalia. Bless This House (Columbia, 1956).
Sister Rosetta Tharpe. "Down By The Riverside" (ca. 1944); "Didn't It Rain" (ca. 1964).
Soul Stirrers. "Wade in the Water" (ca. 1946); "I'm A Pilgrim" (ca. 1947).
Soul Stirrers with Sam Cooke. "Nearer to Thee" (ca. 1950); "Peace in the Valley" (Specialty, 1950).
Ward, Clara [also see The Clara Ward Singers]. "When the Gates Swing Open" (ca. 1949).

Country

Autry, Gene. "Back in the Saddle Again" (Columbia, 1939).
Cash, Johnny. "I Walk the Line" (Sun, 1956); *Now Here's Johnny Cash* (Sun, 1968).
Rodgers, Jimmie. "Blue Yodel No. 1" (T for Texas) (Victor, 1927).
Williams, Hank. *Moanin' the Blues* (MGM, 1952); *Ramblin' Man* (MGM, 1954).

Rhythm & Blues

Brown, Ruth. "Teardrops From My Eyes" (Atlantic, 1950); "(Mama) He Treats Your Daughter Mean" (Atlantic, 1952).
Charles, Ray. *Hallelujah I Love Her So* (Atlantic, 1957); *What'd I Say* (Atlantic, 1959); *Ain't Nobody Here But Us Chickens* (Atlantic, 1960). *The Genius Hits the Road* (ABC, 1960); *Dedicated to You* (ABC, 1971).
Cooke, Sam. *Ain't That Good News* (RCA, 1964).
Otis, Johnny. "Willie and the Hand Jive" (Capitol, 1958).
Jordan, Louis. "Ain't Nobody Here But Us Chickens" (1946); "Let the Good Times Roll" (1946); "Beans and Cornbread" (1949); "Saturday Night Fish Fry" (1949).
Thomas, Rufus. *Walking the Dog* (Stax, 1963).

1950s Rock 'N' Roll

Berry, Chuck. "Maybellene" (Chess, 1955); "Roll Over Beethoven" (Chess, 1956); "No Particular Place to Go" (Chess, 1964).
Bill Haley and His Comets. "Shake, Rattle and Roll" (Decca, 1954) [originally recorded by Big Joe Turner]; "Rock Around the Clock" (Decca, 1954).
Fats Domino. "The Fat Man" (Imperial, 1949); "Hide Away Blues" (Imperial, 1950); "Ain't That a Shame" (Imperial, 1956); "My Blue Heaven" (Imperial, 1956); "Blueberry Hill" (Imperial, 1956); "I'm Walkin'" (Imperial, 1957).

Soul

Brown, James. *Please, Please, Please* (King, 1956); *Prisoner of Love* (King, 1963); Out of Sight (Smash, 1964).
Cooke, Sam. *Sam Cooke* (Keen, 1957); *Night Beat* (RCA, 1963); *Ain't That Good News* (RCA, 1964).
Chaka Khan, *Chaka* (Warner, 1978); *Naughty* (Warner, 1980).
Charles, Ray. *Hallelujah I Love Her So* (Atlantic, 1957); *What'd I Say* (Atlantic, 1959); *Ain't Nobody Here But Us Chickens* (Atlantic, 1960); *The Genius Hits the Road* (ABC, 1960); *Ingredients in a Recipe for Soul* (ABC, 1963).
Connors, Norman. *You Are My Starship* (Buddah, 1976).
Delfonics, The. *La La Means I Love You* (Philly Groove, 1968); *Sound of Sexy Soul* (Philly Groove, 1969); *The Delfonics* (1970).
Dells, The. *Love Is Blue* (Cadet, 1969); *Like It Is, Like It Was* (Cadet, 1971); *Sweet As Funk Can Be* (Cadet, 1972); *Give Your Baby a Standing Ovation* (Cadet, 1973); *The Dells* (Cadet, 1973); *The Mighty Mighty Dells* (Cadet, 1974); *The Dells vs. The Dramatics* (Cadet, 1975).
Dramatics, The. *Whatcha See Is Whatcha Get* (Volt, 1972); *A Dramatic Experience* (Volt, 1973); *The Dells vs. The Dramatics* (Cadet, 1975).
Earth, Wind & Fire. *That's the Way of the World* (Columbia, 1975); *Gratitude* (Columbia, 1975); *Spirit* (Columbia, 1976).
Emotions, The. *So I Can Love You* (Stax, 1970); *Untouched* (Stax, 1972); *Flowers* (Columbia, 1976).
Franklin, Aretha. *I Never Loved a Man the Way I Love You* (Atlantic, 1967); *Lady Soul* (Atlantic, 1968); *Soul '69* (Atlantic, 1969); *Aretha's Gold* (Atlantic, 1969); *The Girl's In Love With You* (Atlantic, 1970); *Spirit in the Dark* (Atlantic, 1970); *Young, Gifted and Black* (Atlantic, 1972); *Hey Now Hey* (The Other Side of the Sky) (Atlantic, 1973); *Let Me in Your* Life (Atlantic, 1974); *You* (Atlantic, 1975); *Sparkle* (Atlantic, 1976).
Green, Al. *Let's Stay Together* (Hi, 1972); *I'm Still In Love With You* (Hi, 1972).
Harold Melvin and The Blue Notes featuring Theodore Pendergrass. *I Miss You* [aka If You Don't Know Me by Now] (Philadelphia International, 1972).
Hathaway, Donny. *Everything is Everything* (Atco, 1970); *Donny Hathaway* (Atco, 1970); *Come Back, Charleston Blue* (Atco, 1972); *Roberta Flack & Donny Hathaway* (Atlantic, 1972); *Extension of a Man* (Atco, 1973).
Hayes, Isaac. *Hot Buttered Soul* (Enterprise, 1969); *The Isaac Hayes Movement* (Enterprise, 1970); *…To Be Continued* (Enterprise, 1970); *Shaft* (Enterprise, 1971); *Black Moses* (Enterprise, 1971).
Hutch, Willie. *Soul Portrait* (RCA, 1969); *Fully Exposed* (Motown, 1973); *The Mack* (Motown, 1973); *Foxy Brown* (Motown, 1975).
Impressions, The. *The Impressions* (Paramount, 1963); *Keep on Pushing* (Paramount, 1964); *People Get Ready* (Paramount, 1965); *Ridin' High* (Paramount, 1966); *We're a Winner* (Universal/MCA, 1968); *This Is My Country* (Curtom, 1968); *The Young Mod's Forgotten Story* (Curtom, 1969).

Intruders, The. *The Intruders Are Together* (Gamble, 1966); *Cowboys to Girls* (Gamble, 1968); *When We Get Married* (Gamble, 1970); *Save the Children* (Gamble, 1973).
Jackson, Michael [also see The Jackson 5 and The Jacksons]. *Off The Wall* (Epic, 1979); *Thriller* (Epic, 1982).
Jackson 5, The. *ABC* (Motown, 1970); *Third Album* (Motown, 1970); *Maybe Tomorrow* (Motown, 1971); *Lookin' Through the Window* (Motown, 1972); *Dancing Machine* (Motown, 1974).
Jacksons, The. *The Jacksons* (CBS, 1976); *Goin' Places* (CBS, 1977); *Destiny* (CBS, 1978).
James, Etta. *At Last* (Chess, 1961).
Kendricks, Eddie. *Peoople...Hold On* (Motown, 1972); *Eddie Kendricks* (Motown, 1973).
Gladys Knight & The Pips. *If I Were Your Woman* (Motown, 1971); *Neither One of Us* (Motown, 1973); *Imagination* (Motown, 1973); *Claudine* (Buddah, 1974).
Marie, Teena. *Wild and Peaceful* (Motown, 1979); *Lady T* (Motown, 1980); *Irons in the Fire* (Motwon, 1980); *It Must Be Magic* (Motown, 1981); *Robbery* (Epic, 1983); *Starchild* (Epic, 1984).
Mayfield, Curtis [also see The Impressions]. *Curtis* (Curtom, 1970); *Roots* (Curtom, 1971); *Super Fly* (Curtom, 1972); *Back to the World* (Curtom, 1973); *Sweet Exorcist* (Curtom, 1974); *There's No Place Like America Today* (Curtom, 1975).
Moments, The. *A Moment with the Moments* (Stang, 1970); *Those Sexy Moments* (Stang, 1974).
O'Jays, The. *Back Stabbers* (Philadelphia International, 1972); *Ship Ahoy* (Philadelphia International, 1973); *Survival* (Philadelphia International, 1975); *Family Reunion* (Philadelphia International, 1975); *Message in the Music* (Philadelphia International, 1976).
Paul, Billy. *360 Degrees of Billy Paul* (Philadelphia International, 1972).
Redding, Otis. *Pain in My Heart* (Atco, 1964); *Otis Blue: Otis Sings Soul* (Stax, 1965).
Ripperton, Minnie. *Perfect Angel* (Epic, 1974); *Minnie* (Capitol, 1979).
Rufus (aka Rufus featuring Chaka Khan) *Rags to Rufus* (ABC, 1974); *Rufus Featuring Chaka Khan* (ABC, 1975).
Scott-Heron, Gil. *Winter in America* (Strata-East, 1974).
Sly and The Family Stone. *Dance to the Music* (Epic, 1968); *Stand!* (Epic, 1969); *There's a Riot Goin' On* (Epic, 1971).
Smokey Robinson. *A Quiet Storm* (Tamla, 1975).
Staples Singers, The. *Be Attitude: Respect Yourself* (Stax, 1972); *Let's Do It Again* (Curtom, 1975).
Stevie Wonder. *Innervisions* (Tamla, 1973); *Songs in the Key of Life* (Tamla, 1976); *Hotter than July* (Tamla, 1980).
Taylor, Johnnie. "Who's Making Love" (Stax, 1968); "Jody's Got Your Girl and Gone" (Stax, 1970); "Doin' My Own Thing" (Stax, 1972); "Cheaper to Keep Her" (Stax, 1973); "You're the Best Girl in the World" (Columbia, 1976).
Wilson, Jackie. "Lonely Teardrops" (Brunswick, 1958); "That's Why (I Love You So)" (Brunswick, 1959).

Pre-Hip Hop Rap/Spoken Word

Last Poets, The. *The Last Poets* (1970); *This Is Madness* (Douglas, 1971).
Lightnin' Rod. *Hustler's Convention* (United Artist, 1973).
Scott-Heron, Gil. *Small Talk at 125th and Lenox* (Flying Dutchman, 1970); *Pieces of a Man* (Flying Dutchman, 1971); *Winter in America* (Strata-East, 1974).

African Soul/Afrobeat

Fela Kuti. *Why Black Man Dey Suffer* (Wrasse, 1971); *Open & Close* (Wrasse, 1972); *Expensive Shit* (Wrasse, 1975).
Hugh Masekela. *The Promise of a Future* (Uni, 1968); *Masekela Uni* (Uni, 1968); *The African Connection* (Impulse, 1973).

Funk

Bar-Kays, The. *Soul Finger* (Votl, 1967); *Gotta Groove* (Volt, 1969); *Black Rock* (Volt, 1971).
Baby Huey. *The Baby Huey Story: The Living Legend* (Curtom, 1970).
Bataan, Joe. *Mr. New York & The East Side Kids* (Fania, 1971); *Sweet Soul* (Fania, 1972); *Saint Latin's Day Massacre* (Fania, 1972); *Salsoul* (Mericana, 1973).
Beginning of the End, The. *Funky Nassau* (Alston, 1971).
Blackbyrds, The. *The Blackbyrds* (Fantasy, 1973).
Black Heat. *Black Heat* (Atlantic, 1972); *No Time to Burn* (Atlantic, 1974).
Black Ivory. *Don't Turn Around.* (Today, 1972); *Baby, Won't You Change Your Mind* (Today, 1972).
Black Nasty. "Party on 4th Street" (1972).
Booker T. & the MGs. *Soul Limbo* (Stax, 1968); *The Booker T. Set* (Stax, 1969); *McLemore Avenue* (Stax, 1970); *Melting Pot* (Stax, 1971); *The MGs* (Stax, 1973).
Boris Gardiner Happening, The. *Is What's Happening* (Dynamic, 1973).
Brown, James. *Out of Sight* (Smash,1964); *Papa's Got a Brand New Bag* (King, 1965); *Cold Sweat* (1967); *Say It Loud—I'm Black and I'm Proud* (King, 1968); *It's a Mother* (King, 1969); *Sex Machine* (King, 1970); *On the Good*

Foot (Poyldor, 1971); *The Payback* (Polydor, 1973); *Hell* (Polydor, 1974).
Byrd, Bobby [also see James Brown]. "I Need Help" (1970); "I Know You Got Soul" (1971).
Carbo, Chuck. "Can I Be Your Squeeze" (1970).
Collins, Lynn. *Think* (About It) (People, 1972).
Counts, The (aka The Fabulous Counts). *What's Up Front That Counts* (ca. 1971).
Creative Funk. "Moving World." (ca. early 1970s).
Cymande. Cymande (Janus, 1972); *Second Time Around* (Janus, 1973); *Promised Heights* (Janus, 1974).
David Batiste & The Gladiators. "Funky Soul" (Soulin', ca. 1971).
Dayton Sidewinders. *Let's Go Down To Funksville* (1972).
Dells, The. *Sweet As Funk Can Be* (Cadet, 1972).
Dynamics, The. *What A Shame.* (Black Gold, 1973).
Earth, Wind & Fire. *That's the Way of the World* (Columbia, 1975); *Gratitude* (Columbia, 1975); *Spirit* (Columbia, 1976).
Eight Minutes, The. *An American Family.*
Eliminators, The. *Loving Explosion.* (1974).
Fabulous Originals, The. "It Ain't Fair But It's Fun" (1971).
Fabulous Three. "Answer Me Softly" (Psycho, ca. 1972).
Freddie and the Kinfolk. "Mashed potato popcorn" (ca. 1972).
Gaturs, The. "Gator Bait" (1970); *Wasted.* (1970).
Harvey & The Phenomenals. *Soul & Sunshine* (1971).
Headhunters, The. *The Head Hunters* (1973); *Thrust* (Columbia, 1974).
Hitson, Herman. "Ain't No Other Way" (Sweet Rose, 1972).
Honey Drippers, The. "Impeach the President" (1973).
Huck Daniels Co., The. "Foolish Man (Pt.2)" (Kent, 1971).
Identities, The. "Hey Brother" (1970).
Jackson 5, The. *Dancing Machine* (Motown, 1974).
Jimmy Castor Bunch, The. *It's Just Begun* (RCA, 1972).
Kool and The Gang. *Kool and The Gang* (De-Lite, 1969); *Music Is the Message* (De-Lite, 1972); *Good Times* (De-Lite, 1973); *Wild and Peaceful* (De-Lite, 1973).
Latin Breed, The. "I Turn You On" (ca. 1971).
Lucien, Jon. *I Am Now* (RCA, 1970); *Rashida* (RCA, 1973).
Majestics, The. "Funky Chick" (ca. 1969).
Meters, The. *The Meters* (Sundazed, 1969); *Look-Ka Py Py* (Josie, 1969); *Struttin'* (Josie, 1970).
Mobile Blue, The. "Puffin'" (1969).
Mohawks, The. "The Champ" (Contillion, ca. 1969).
New Birth. *The New Birth* (RCA, 1971); *Ain't No Big Thing, But It's Growing* (RCA, 1971); *Birth Day* (RCA, 1973); *It's Been a Long Time* (RCA, 1974); *Blind Baby* (Buddah, 1975).
Nite-Liters, The [also see New Birth]. *Nite-Liters* (RCA, 1970); *Morning, Noon & the Nite-Liters* (RCA, 1971); *Different Strokes* (RCA, 1972).
Ohio Players, The. *Observations in Time* (Capitol, 1969); *Pain* (Westbound, 1972); *Pleasure* (Westbound, 1972); *Ecstacy* (Westbound, 1973); *Skin Tight* (Mercury, 1974); *Fire* (Mercury, 1974); *Honey* (Mercury, 1975); *Contradiction* (Mercury, 1976)
Politicians, The. *Psycha-Soula-Funkadelic.* (ca. 1972).
Reid, Clarence. "Funky Party" (ca. 1971); "Winter Man" (ca. 1973).
Nina Simone. "Ain't Got No...I've Got Life;" (RCA, 1970); *Black Gold* (RCA, 1970).
Sexton, Ann. "You're Losing Me" (1973).
Skin Williams and the Soulfadelics. "Skins Funk" (ca. early 1970s).
Skull Snaps. *Skull Snaps* (GSF, 1974); "It's a New Day." (1973); "All of Sudden" (1974).
Sly and The Family Stone. *Dance to the Music* (Epic, 1968); *Stand!* (Epic, 1969); *There's a Riot Goin' On* (Epic, 1971).
Thomas, Rufus. "Do That Breakdown Chillin'" (Stax, ca. 1973); "The Funky Chicken" (Stax, ca. 1973).
Unemployed, The. "They Won't Let Me" (Contillion, 1971).
Yellow Sunshine. "Yellow Sunshine" (1973).

Dub

Big Youth. *Screaming Target* (Gussie/Jaguar, 1972).
Upsetters, The. *Musical Bones* (DIP, 1975).
U-Roy. "Earth's Rightful Ruler" (1969); "Wake the Town" (1970).

'60s and '70s Rock/Progressive Rock/Art Rock/Hard Rock/Southern Rock

Allman Brothers, The. *The Allman Brothers Band* (Capricorn/Atco, 1969); *Idlewild South* (Capricorn/Atco, 1970); *Eat*

GLOSSARY

a Peach (Capricorn, 1972); *Brothers and Sisters* (Capricorn, 1973).
Band, The. *Music from the Big Pink* (Capitol, 1968); *The Band* (Capitol, 1969).
Beatles, The. *Please, Please Me* (Parlophone, 1963); *Meet the Beatles* (Capitol, 1964); *The Beatles' Second Album* (Capitol, 1964); *A Hard Day's Night* (Parlophone, 1964); *Beatles '65* (Capitol, 1964); *Beatles VI* (Capitol, 1965); *Help* (Capitol, 1965); *Rubber Soul* (Capitol, 1965); Revolver (Capitol, 1966); *Sgt. Pepper's Lonely Heart Club Band* (Capitol/Parlophone, 1967); *Magical Mystery Tour* (Capitol/Parlophone, 1967); *The Beatles* (aka "The White Album") (Capitol/Apple/Parlophone, 1968); *Yellow Submarine* (Apple/Capitol, 1969); *Abbey Road* (Capitol/Parlophone, 1969); *Let It Be* (Apple/Capitol, 1970).
Bluesbreakers with Eric Clapton. *Bluesbreakers with Eric Clapton* (Decca, 1966).
Clapton, Eric. *Eric Clapton* (Atco, 1970); *461 Ocean Boulevard* (RSO, 1974).
Cream. *Fresh Cream* (Atco, 1966); *Disraeli Gears* (Atco, 1967).
Doobie Brothers, The. *The Doobie Brothers* (Warner, 1971); *Toulouse Street* (Warner, 1972); *The Captain and Me* (Warner, 1973); *What Were Once Vices Are Now Habits* (Warner, 1974); *Takin' It to the Streets* (Warner, 1976).
Hendrix, Jimi. *Are You Experienced* (Track, 1967); *Electric Ladyland* (Reprise, 1968).
Joel, Billy. *Piano Man* (Columbia/Family Productions, 1973); *Streetlife Serenade* (Columbia/Family Productions, 1974); *Turnstiles* (Columbia/Family Productions, 1976).
Jethro Tulle. *This Was* (Reprise, 1969); *War Child* (Chrysalis, 1974).
Joplin, Janis. *Pearl* (Columbia, 1971).
Led Zeppelin. *Led Zeppelin* (Atlantic, 1969); *Led Zeppelin II* (Atlantic, 1969); *Led Zeppelin III* (Atlantic, 1970); *Led Zeppelin IV* (Atlantic, 1971); *House of the Holy* (Atlantic, 1973); *Physical Graffiti* (Swan Song, 1975).
Morrison, Van. *Astral Weeks* (Warner, 1968); *Moondance* (Warner, 1970).
Rolling Stones, The. *The Rolling Stones* (Decca, 1964); *The Rolling Stones No. 2* (Decca, 1965); *Out of Our Heads* (London, 1965); *December's Children (And Everybody's)* (London, 1965); *Aftermath* (London, 1966); *Between the Buttons* (London, 1967); *Their Satanic Majesties Request* (London, 1967); *Beggars Banquet* (London, 1968); *Let It Bleed* (London, 1969); *Sticky Fingers* (London, 1971); *Exile on Main Street* (Rolling Stones/Atlantic, 1972); *Goats Head Soup* (Rolling Stones/Atlantic, 1973); *It's Only Rock 'n' Roll* (Rolling Stones/Atlantic, 1974).
Santana. *Santana* (Columbia, 1969); *Abraxas* (Columbia, 1970); *Santana [aka Santana III]* (Columbia, 1971); *Borboletta* (CBS, 1974).
Toussaint, Allen. *Toussaint* (Scepter/DJM, 1970).
The Yardbirds [also see Eric Clapton]. *For Your Love* (Epic, 1965); *Having a Rave Up* (Epic, 1965); *Roger the Engineer* (Epic, 1966); Little Games (Epic, 1967).

Punk/British Ska/New Wave/'80s Pop Rock

Beat, The (aka The English Beat). *I Just Can't Stop It* (Go Feet/Sire, 1980); *Wha'ppen* (Go Feet/Sire, 1981); *Special Beat Service* (Go Feet/IRS, 1982).
Clash, The. *The Clash* (CBS, 1977); *London Calling* (CBS, 1979); *Combat Rock* (Epic, 1982).
Duran Duran. *Duran Duran* (EMI/Capitol, 1981); *Rio* (EMI/Capitol, 1982); *Seven and the Ragged Tiger* (EMI/Capitol, 1983).
Police, The. *Outlandos d'Amour* (A&M, 1978); *Reggatta de Blanc* (A&M, 1979); *Zenyattà Mondatta* (A&M, 1980); *Ghost in the Machine* (A&M, 1980); *Synchronicity* (A&M, 1983).
Specials, The (aka The Specials AKA). *Specials* (2 Tone, 1979); *More Specials* (2 Tone, 1980).
Talking Heads. *Talking Heads: 77* (Sire, 1977); *More Songs About Buildings and Food* (Sire, 1978); *Fear of Music* (Sire, 1979); *Remain in Light* (Sire, 1980).
Van Halen. *Van Halen* (Warner, 1978); *1984* (Warner, 1984).

Western Classical

Beethoven, Ludwig van. *Beethoven Symphony No. 5 in c minor; Symphony No. 9 in d minor;* performed by The Philadelphia Orchestra (2005).
Mozart, Wolfgang Amadeus. *Piano Concerto No. 24*, performed by Philharmonia Orchestra of London (1997).
Copland, Aaron. *Symphony no. 3 (aka Third Symphony)*, performed by the New York Philharmonic (Deutsche Grammophon, 1990).
Bernstein, Leonard. *Serenade for Solo Violin, Strings, Harp and Percussion (after Plato's "Symposium")*, performed by New York Philharmonic. From the album Bernstein: *Symphony No. 2; Serenade after Plato's Symposium* (Sony, 1998).

Bibliography

Bailyn, Bernard. *The Ideological Origins of the American Revolution*, Enlarged Edition. Harvard University Press: Cambridge, 1990.

Berman, Marshall. *All That Is Solid Melts Into Air: The Experience of Modernity.* New York: Simon and Schuster, 1982.

Burnim, Mellonee V. and Portia K. Maultsby. *African American Music: An Introduction.* New York: Routledge, 2006.

Chang, Jeff. *Can't Stop Won't Stop.* New York: St. Martin's Press, 2005.

Chapple, Steve and Reebee Garofalo. *Rock 'N' Roll Is Here to Pay: The History and Politics of the Music Industry.* Chicago: Nelson/Hall, 1978.

Chernoff, John Miller. *African Rhythm and African Sensibility.* Chicago: University of Chicago Press, 1979.

Fitch, Robert. *The Assassination of New York.* New York: Verso, 1993.

Flash, Grandmaster with David Ritz. *The Adventures of Grandmaster Flash: My Life, My Beats.* New York: Broadway Books, 2008.

Floyd, Jr., Samuel A. *The Power of Black Music: Interpreting Its History From Africa to the United States.* New York: Oxford, 1995.

Gates, Jr., Henry Louis. *Black Literatue & Literary Theory.* New York: Methuen, 1984.

Hager, Steven. *Hip Hop: The Illustrated History of Break Dancing, Rap Music, and Graffiti.* New York: St. Martin's Press, 1984.

Hebdige, Dick. *Cut 'N' Mix: Culture, Identity and Caribbean Music.* New York and London: Metheun, 1987.

Holloway, Joseph E. *Africanisms in American Culture.* Bloomington: 1990.

Miller, Michael. *The Complete Idiot's Guide to Music Theory, Second Edition.* New York: Penguin, 2005.

Neal, Mark Anthony. *Soul Babies: Black Popular Culture and The Post-Soul Aesthetic.* New York: Routledge, 2002.

Norek, Josh. "'You Can't Sing Without the Bling': The Toll of Excessive Sample License Fees on Creativity in Hip-Hop Music and the Need For a Compulsory Sound Recording Sample License System," 11 *UCLA Ent. L. Rev.* 83, 90 (2004).

Perkins, William Eric. *Droppin' Science: Critical Essays on Rap Music and Hip Hop Culture.* Philadelphia: Temple University Press, 1996.

Poe, Randy. *Music Publishing:: A Songwriter's Guide, Revised Edition.* Cincinnati: Writer's Digest Books, 1997.

H. Raine. 'US Housing Program in South Bronx Called a Waste by Moynihan.' *New York Daily News* 20 Dec 1978, p. 3.

Rose, Tricia. *Black Noise: Rap Music and Black Culture in Contemporary America.* Hanover: Wesleyan University Press, 1994.

'Text of the Moynihan Memorandum on the Status of Negroes.' *New York Times*, 30 January 1970, p. 3.

'Taki 183 Spawns Pen Pals.' *New York Times,* 21 July 1971.

"Plunderphonics: An Interview with John Oswald, Norman Ingma, *Retrofuturism Magazine,* Jan. 1990, no. 12, 1533-38.

Ramsey, Jr., Guthrie P. *Race Music: Black Cultures From Bebop to Hip Hop.* Berkeley: University of California Press, 2003.

Schloss, Joseph. *Making Beats: The Art of Sample-Based Hip-Hop.* Middletown: Wesleyan University Press, 2004.

Small, Christopher. *Music—Society—Education: An Examination of the Function of Music in Western, Eastern and African Cultures With Its Impact On Society and Its Use In Education.* New York: Schirmer Books, 1977.

Snead, James A. "On Repetition in Black Culture." In *Black American Literature Forum*, vol. 15, no. 4, 1981.

Southern, Eileen. *The Music of Black Americans: A History.* New York: W.W. Norton & Company, 1971.

Toop, David. *The Rap Attack: African Jive to New York Hip Hop.* New York: Pluto Press, 1984.

Vaidhyanathan, Siva. *Copyrights and Copywrongs: The Rise of Intellectual Property and How It Threatens Creativity.* New York: New York University Press, 2001.

Wallace, Deborah and Rodrick Wallace. *A Plague On Your Houses: How New York Was Burned Down and National Public Health Crumbled.* New York: Verso, 1998.

Glossary (Key Words)

Aftertouch
In regards to keyboards. This is where the signal of the keyboard strike is controlled and determined by the pressure one applies to keys on a keyboard.

Ambiance
Refers to the "mood" of the sound. Ambiance is usually created by the addition and subsequent combination of various sounds, effects, processors and equalization.

Arrangement
The process of creatively organizing the components, pieces, and subsequent "music blocks" into a conscious thematic order. In simpler terms, arrangement in beatmaking refers to the approach that beatmakers take when *arranging the elements* of their beats. Also, there's two ways you can look at arrangement: (1) you can look at it as the order and measure (length) of sounds and sequences within a song (composition); or (2) you can look at it as the pattern in which sounds correspond sequentially within any song (composition).

Bandwidth
The specific range of frequencies passed by an electronic circuit, like a filter, etc. Bandwidth settings determine the clarity of replicated (sampled/bounced) sounds.

Channel (in regards to MIDI)
Refers to 1 of 16 possible data channels over which MIDI data may be sent.

Channel (in regards to Mixing)
This is a single control strip of equalization. A typical channel strip on a standard mixing console has three fundamental frequency controls: Hi, Mid, and Low, (think of it like Hi treble, Mid treble, and bass).

Chopping (Chop)
The most fundamental way in which beatmakers edit and manipulate their samples (and other sounds). It's the altering of a sample (or other sound) by dividing it into smaller desired segments. Moreover, it's the process of removing or trimming unwanted sections from a sample. Typically, it involves trimming sections from the start and end of a sample.

Chord
Three or more different musical notes played at the same time.

Chorus
Just like it sounds, think "doubling" or "tripling" of a sound. Chorus is typically achieved by doubling up a signal, then adding some delay and pitch.

Clipping
When the sound signal is "too hot" and moving past the maximum (peak) level that a piece of equipment (e.g. a mixing console) can handle, that sound is "clipping."

Compression
The reducing, or rather *evening out*, of the dynamic range of an audio signal. It's generally achieved by simply either reducing the high level and/or increasing the low level audio signals.

Compressor
A processor (device) used for "compression," that is, the reducing, or rather *evening out* the dynamic range of an audio signal. It's generally achieved by simply either reducing the high levels and/or increasing the low levels.

DAW (Digital Audio Workstation)
Refers to a general combination of audio multitrack software and audio hardware. It's any system—usually software-based—designed to record, edit and play back music tracks. A key feature of DAWs is the ability to freely manipulate recorded sounds, much like a word processor manipulates typed words.

Decay
This is the dropping of a signal level until it reaches your preset sustain level.

Default Workflow System
A Default Workflow System is any stored beatmaking (production) template, like a default drum sequence (pattern)

or a default method, style, and/or technique.

"Dope"
A slang term often used in hip hop culture to describe something that is of unique style and high quality. Something that is considered "dope" in hip hop means that it is highly respected.

Drum Shell
A very pivotal type of Default Workflow System, it's a default drum sequence (pattern). It's any pre-made/pre-used drum sequence extracted from beats one has *already* made, attempted to make, or are currently making. Once a beatmaker creates a beat, he (or she) can always scrap the non-drum music and keep the drums. This left over drum pattern is what I call a *Drum Shell*.

Dynamic Range
This is the audible (sound) range between the highest signal and the lowest signal, typically described as the range from bass to treble. Much of today's music lacks true dynamic range, because everything is mixed so loudly at pretty much the same level, with very little dynamic range.

Equalizer (EQ)
This is a device used for "coloring" a sound. An Equalizer has the ability to boost or cut the Hi, Mid, and Low frequencies of a sound. (See also Graphic Equalizer).

EMPI
Electronic Music Production Instrument.

Event (in terms of a sequence)
An ***event*** or ***step*** within a sequence is the point at which any action (programmed hit) takes place. An event can be anything. It can be as simple as a kick-stab; it can be a sample of any length. The event (hit) serves to represent when and where the action takes place within a sequence.

Event (in term of MIDI)
A single unit of MIDI data.

Event Strike
Every event that you actively program within a sequence is what I call an ***event strike***. For example, tapping a drum pad is an event strike. Playing a key on a keyboard is an event strike.

Filter
A filter is an electronic component—within a sampler, keyboard and the like—that is used for emphasizing, deemphasizing and/or accentuating a specific range of frequencies. Generally, in beatmaking, filters are used to beef up bass sounds and cut down high sounds, or to cut bass sounds and beef up high sounds.

"Flip" or Flippin'
Flippin' (or to "flip" something) is the process of manipulating or modifying a sound (usually a sample), technique, or device in a way that produces a new (creative) result that is respected in hip hop. "Flippin'" a sample usually means that the sample is manipulated so much that you can't even tell where it came from. Still, there are other cases where a sample can be *flipped*, even while it contains its original identity. Flippin' can also be used to as a term to describe any reinterpretation or reconceptualization of an established style, sound, practice, and/or theme.

Gain
Think signal volume. Gain can amplify or de-amplify a signal level.

Graphic Equalizer
This is the visual manifestation of an equalizer, whereby multiple segments of the audio spectrum are represented by individual faders or knobs.

Headroom
This is the safety range between the highest peak signal that's being passed and the maximum signal level a piece of equipment can handle.

High Pass Filter
This is a filter used for accentuating or emphasizing high frequencies. It works by cutting off or detaining low frequencies, while letting high frequencies *pass* through.

Interface

This is simply a device that acts as a intermediary, a "connector," if you will, between two or more pieces of equipment, e.g. a sound card that allows audio to be recorded into a computer.

Latency
The delay (generally in milliseconds) of a signal from any hardware device to another. For example, the signal delay from a hard drive to sound card, or drum machine and keyboard.

Layering
The process of combining two or more sounds into one. It is typically achieved by taking one sound and placing it on top of the other. Layering is an excellent example of the high level of musicianship and application of advanced audio/sonic concepts in beatmaking.

Limiter
A limiter controls the gain (volume loudness or lowness) of an audio signal. It prevents a signal from exceeding a preset level. A limiter is similar to a compressor, but without the danger of "squashing" the signal.

Loop
A sound or measure of music of any length that is programmed to play for a predetermined amount of time before it returns—*loops*—back to it's beginning and repeats. The loop is the cornerstone structure of beatmaking. It's the repetitive instruction for a sequence and/or series of sequences.

Loop Point
In regards to sequencing and structuring a loop, the "loop point" is the audibly dead point, right before the loop turns over to the next sequence.

Low Pass Filter
This is a filter used for accentuating or rather emphasizing low frequencies. It works by cutting off or detaining high frequencies, while letting only low frequencies pass through.

Memory
Regarding computers, both personal and within EMPIs, there are two types of memory: (1) the standard hard drive memory; and (2) RAM. Standard hard drive memory is the *permanent* memory used by a computer to store programs and data. Here, all data is saved when the computer is turned off, whereas RAM (Random Access Memory) is the type of memory used by the computer for the temporary storage of programs and data. Here, all data is lost when the computer is turned off!

MIDI
The abbreviation stands for Musical Instrument Digital Interface. MIDI is the standard language by which all MIDI devices communicate and send data (instructions) to each other. There is NO audio involved with MIDI. MIDI is simply the instructional data for audio.

Octave
This is the 8th tone above a given pitch, with twice as many vibrations, or below a given pitch, with half as many vibrations.

"Out Front"
Regarding sound and sound placement, "out front" refers to the pre-recorded (sampled) drums (kick, snare) being amplified and/or higher up in the mix. Hip hop/rap is often characterized as a music that has the drums out front.

Placement (aks "Music Placement")
A placement is a confirmed beat and/or song on a commercially released album. The term has been around for some time now. It actually comes from the phrases: "Placed tracks and placed songs." During the 1980s and the mid- 1990s, these terms were not prominently used. But as beatmakers (producers) were increasingly marginalized, often only getting just one beat on a commercial release (rather than multiple beats), the use of the term "placement" increased.

Polyphony
Refers to the ability of an instrument to play two or more notes at the same time (simultaneously).

Pre-Mixing
The process of modifying your beats by using basic mixing concepts, before your beats and music are tracked and recorded into multitrack recording systems.

Processor

This is a device such as a compressor, gate, equalizer and the like. It's used for manipulating the dynamics or frequency of an audio signal.

Progressive Sequencing
The practice of programming sections into a song that are based more on progression rather than repetition.

Quantize or Quantizing
"Quantizing" involves moving notes recorded in a MIDI sequencer so that they line up (match) with the desired time values of a bar and/or sequence. Basically, it smoothens out the bumps when mixing two or more sounds together. It's particularly associated with lining up drums with non-drums so that the combination is right on time and not off line.

Resonance (in regards to low/high pass filters)
Resonance works as a "warming" or "fattening" agent of the audio signal selected for filtering.

Reverb
Reverb is the result of the sound reflections that occur in any given room. A reverb processor is used to give distance and space to a sound. It makes a sound last longer than it is, similar to an echo, but it's not necessarily delaying it, where you can hear it twice. Adding reverb also affects the way in which a sound resonates.

Sample Placement
The process of mapping samples out across the drum pads of a Drum Machine/Sequencer and/or across the keys of a keyboard or keyboard controller.

Scale
A scale is seven notes all in a row.

Sequence
A sequence is a program of chronological musical events (steps) within a measure of at least 1 bar.

Sequencing
Sequencing actually carries two meanings in beatmaking (hip hop/rap production). The first meaning of sequencing deals with structure, that is to say, the actual process of **programming the structure** of a beat. So a sequence is the recorded, arranged program data within a measure. The second meaning of "sequencing" refers to the process of linking up multiple EMPIs together.

Production Setup or Setup
The collective gear, equipment, and other instruments that a beatmaker (producer) uses to create his or her beats and music.

Timbre
The distinctive properties — characteristic, quality, or substance — of a sound or sound produced (made) by a particular instrument or voice.

Timestretch
A function/feature on an EMPI that changes the length of a sample (sound) *without* changing its tempo. Hence, it permits you to mesh together multiple pieces of music that contain slightly off-setting beat patterns. It's really a form of BPM matching. More specifically, it's useful for matching drums with non-drum music.

Track (In regards to recording/sequencing)
A track is an individual section on a mixing console, a virtual mixing console, and/or a sequencer, whereby audio data is recorded on (in) to.

Track (In regards to a complete composition)
A track is also another name often used for an entire beat, instrumental, or even a completed song.

Tracking
The process of recording audio data onto individual tracks within multirecording *(multitracking)* system.

Triggering
The process of playing a pre-programmed sound from one EMPI, via another; for example, using a drum pad from a drum machine to trigger a sampler or sound module; or likewise, using a keyboard or keyboard controller keys, computer keyboard keys, and the like.

Index

A

A Tribe Called Quest, 84-86, 88, 224, 467, 470, 475, 480, 559, 562, 564
African American (Black) Music Tradition, 40, 69, 154, 161, 228-30, 241, 301, 309, 312, 313, 332-34, 337, 344, 345, 348, 534
Afrika Bambaataa, 3, 30, 36, 41-43, 50, 60, 66, 67, 69-71, 74-77, 220, 231, 241, 246, 447, 520, 539, 559, 562
Akai, xv, xxi, 82, 89, 91-96, 101, 104, 105, 108, 113-16, 121, 129, 130, 134, 137, 138, 140, 141, 146, 160, 178, 179, 181, 184, 185, 214, 230-33, 251, 253-57, 260, 279, 455, 456, 464, 468, 473, 474, 477, 482, 490, 496, 509, 510, 521, 543
Anchor Technique, 172, 194, 293
Arrangement, 10, 82-87, 91, 93, 94, 97, 131, 137, 138, 147, 148, 152, 154, 157, 164-83, 186-88, 191, 193, 195, 197, 199, 201-05, 207, 209-11, 213, 217, 219, 226, 234, 235, 248, 249, 254, 258, 259 (see Chapter 6)
Arrangement Schemes, 202, 203, 205, 267
Assigning Sounds, 154, 159
Atonality, 212
Audio Bandwidth, 230, 260

B

B-Boy/B-Boying, xix, 1, 35, 37, 39, 40-45, 50, 54, 62, 66, 67, 70, 74, 77, 78, 221, 355, 356, 359
BPM matching, 183, 574
Bass Fill-Ins, 263, 264
Bass Filtering, 84, 88, 107, 108, 132, 141, 211, 251, 285, 256, 257, 411, 509, 512, 574
Bass Music, 67, 80, 81, 461, 471, 494
Beastie Boys, The, 78, 494, 562
Beat Broker, 373, 377-82, 386-89, 419-21, 545, 546
Beat CD, 317-20, 323, 324, 356, 406, 414, 434
Beat Prices, 374-77, 385, 389, 398, 400, 405, 407, 409, 421-27, 429, 439, 441, 451, 481, 494, 503, 504, 514, 517, 544-48, 551
Beat Structure, 181, 184, 186, 192, 219
Beatnuts, The, 69, 89, 559, 562
Benign Neglect, 23-28, 30-32, 62
Big Daddy Kane, 51, 53, 83, 456, 462, 469, 516, 562
Biz Markie, 83, 458, 514, 562
Blues, The, 1, 5, 9, 33, 47, 65, 69, 161, 229, 242, 259, 291, 292, 295-99, 309, 316, 318, 321, 333, 337, 342, 361, 528, 534, 536-38
Bomb Squad, The, 69, 81, 82, 232, 462, 469, 478, 559
Boogie Down Productions (BDP), 52, 478, 480, 562
Break-Beat, 62, 63, 69-72, 79, 83, 87, 148, 238, 239, 247, 248, 269, 340, 449, 450, 453, 485
Break-Beat Period, 69-72, 79
Break Dancing, (see B-Boy/B-Boying)
Brown, James, xviii, 41, 48, 54, 60, 63, 65, 69, 133, 193, 294, 321, 450, 454, 455, 466, 471, 482, 485, 495, 527, 566
Buckwild, 69, 82, 89, 237, 238, 464-81, 503, 520, 528, 559
Bumpin'-the-Sample, 210, 211

C

Chopping, 10, 52, 71, 80, 84, 107, 108, 127, 136, 153, 155, 170, 174, 197, 228, 233, 234, 249-55, 258, 261, 267, 271, 272, 274, 275, 281, 368, 449, 453, 471, 509, 525, 559, 571
Chopping, Basic, 252
Chopping, Complex, 252, 253, 258
Chopping, Mental-Intuitive, 249
Chopping, Phrase, 252
Chopping, Stab-, 252
Click-Fix Approach, 103
Clock Theory, 43, 71
Cold Crush Brothers, 48, 49, 51, 71, 492, 562
Complete Phrase, 191, 196, 209, 235, 248-50, 258, 260, 261, 274, 293
Compositional Ethic, 91, 309, 327-29, 349-52, 357, 358
Compositional Styles of Beatmaking, 169-78, 192, 195, 196m 200, 201, 209, 211, 225, 227-29, 235, 288-90, 293, 337, 540
Compositional Process, xvii, 1, 5, 8, 70, 95, 101, 166-68, 212, 229, 232, 306, 358, 359, 541
Consonance, 318, 336
Contracts, (see Chapter 13)
Core Drum Sounds, 82, 134, 140, 141, 218
Core Track, 205, 250, 258, 259
Counter-Melody, 211, 319
Crazy Legs, 44, 78
Cross Bronx Expressway, 18, 19
Culture of Sampling, 35, 54, 225, 226, 350
Cut/Cutting, 42, 43, 71-75, 79, 83, 85, 86, 116, 156, 167, 175, 182, 203, 215, 225, 234, 252, 253, 257, 261, 262, 279, 280, 333-35, 345, 347, 350, 449, 450, 452, 465, 466, 474, 484, 511, 516

D

DJ Premier, 69, 82, 84, 85, 87, 88, 89, 91, 93, 120, 121, 127, 129, 131, 139, 148, 193, 203, 220, 225, 232, 237, 238, 250, 254, 256, 261, 287, 300, 305, 341, 347, 419, 425, 450, 461, 481, 495, 509-18, 520, 523, 548, 559 (see interview with)
DJ Toomp, 64, 69, 80, 81, 89, 91, 92, 93, 95, 104, 120, 127, 129, 131, 148, 239, 287, 341, 418, 490-508, 548, 559 (see interview with)
DJ'ing, xix, 1, 10, 36, 37, 40, 41, 43, 48, 50, 59-61, 67, 70, 71, 74, 79, 81, 82, 90, 127, 169, 177, 225, 230, 231, 314, 447, 451, 456, 464-67, 491-94, 503, 505, 507, 527, 540
D.R. Period, ix, 89, 482-89 (see interview with)
Default Drum Programs, 162
Diamond D, 467, 468, 559, 562
Diggin' In The Crates, 82, 85, 86, 229, 234, 236, 237, 239-46, 450
Disco, 9, 41, 47, 63, 65, 69, 70, 72, 127, 169, 230, 231, 299, 300, 450, 538
Dissonance, 318, 336, 337
Downbeat, 259, 274, 320, 321, 432
Dr. Dre, 69, 77, 85-89, 91, 93, 120, 148, 177, 199, 203, 220, 232, 341, 426, 470, 471, 475, 477, 479, 506, 514, 521, 522, 547, 559, 562
Drum Framework(s), 82, 89, 91, 95, 97, 141, 154, 156, 157, 162, 168, 198, 218, 258, 274, 275, 338, 350

575

Drum Pattern(s), 81, 91, 97, 142, 147, 149-53, 157, 162, 168, 185, 258, 259, 269, 273, 281, 335, 482
Drum Programming, xvii, 84, 86, 87, 131, 133, 135, 137, 222, 223, 248, 264, 272, 273, 350, 414, 454, 478 (see chapter 5)
Drum Programming
  Break-Beat Blend, 148; Hit-Stab, 148
Drum Sound Library, 134-36, 164, 485
Drumwork, 84, 199-201, 203, 218, 223, 299, 497
Duke Bootee, 50, 75, 76

E

E-diggin', 128, 237, 240-45
East Coast Sound, 88, 287
Electronic Drum Machine Period, 69, 77, 80, 81, 94, 233

F

Fletcher, Ed, 50, 69, 75
Frequency Response Level, 260
Funk, 9, 41, 42, 44, 49, 60, 62, 63, 69, 70, 74-77, 81, 82, 85, 86, 89, 97, 107, 120, 127, 161, 169, 174, 230, 231, 242, 263, 291, 292, 297, 299, 300, 321, 342, 344, 361, 522, 534, 536, 538, 567

G

Gang Starr, 84, 85, 261, 509, 510, 513, 515, 563
Gangs, Street, 28, 29, 30, 35, 37
Graffiti, xix, 1, 37-40, 42, 43, 45, 50, 54, 55, 66, 67, 78, 94, 407
Grandmaster Caz, 48-51, 53, 78
Grandmaster Flash, 3, 30, 36, 41, 42, 43, 49, 50, 66-71, 74-77, 148, 220, 231, 240, 241, 304, 305, 363, 447, 449, 465, 466, 492, 493, 516, 539, 559, 563
Grandmaster Flash and the Furious Five, 49, 50, 71, 74, 75, 563
Grand Wizard Theodore, 69, 71
Group Map Assignment (GMA), 144, 178, 179

H

Harmonic Analysis, 317
Harmonic Rhythm, 318, 319
Harmony, 3, 6, 98, 114, 127, 172, 211, 267, 304, 315-318, 323, 324, 327, 328, 333-38, 343, 347, 349, 352, 357, 358, 360, 427, 491, 535, 538
Hathaway, Donny, 292, 566
Hip Hop Attitude, 54, 56, 57, 351, 352
Hip Hop DJ Style, 41, 59
Hip Hop Sensibility, 54-56, 67, 75, 77, 225, 226, 237, 310, 350, 352
Hip Hop/Rap Theory, 310, 332, 333
Housing Act of 1949, 20
Hustler's Convention, 48, 50, 52, 60, 63, 65, 567
Hybrid Beatmaking, 169
Hybrid Compositional style, 177

I

Image Line, 92-96

J

J Dilla, 69, 84, 86, 90, 91, 93, 120, 139, 148, 220, 283, 300, 388, 389, 510, 559, 564

Jazz, 5, 9, 33, 46, 49, 65, 69, 87, 107, 120, 127, 186, 229, 241, 259, 270, 284, 291, 292, 295, 304, 316, 320, 342, 361, 383, 478, 480, 508, 513, 516, 522, 525, 526, 528, 534, 536-38, 543, 565
Jones, Quincy, 33, 366, 367, 471, 493, 502, 509, 565

K

King Tim, 57, 72
Kool Herc, 3, 30, 36, 37, 41-43, 48, 49, 55, 59-66, 69-71, 231, 241, 447, 528, 539, 559
Kool G Rap, 51-53, 83, 389, 450, 456, 469, 516, 563
KRS ONE, 51, 52, 563
Kurtis Blow, 50, 51, 69, 74, 76, 78, 563

L

Large Professor, 69, 83-85, 87, 121, 148, 193, 220, 224, 232, 283, 449, 481, 509, 512, 526, 527, 559, 563
Layering, 80, 137, 138, 141, 213, 251, 261, 262, 267, 272, 322, 573
LL Cool J, 51, 78, 373, 458, 459, 492, 563
Lightnin' Rod, 48, 50, 567
Linear Progression, 3, 93-95, 186, 189, 312, 327-29, 333, 337, 344, 347, 349, 352

M

MIDI, 102, 108, 109, 111, 113, 134, 161, 173, 178, 179, 181, 193, 194, 214, 230, 234, 497, 499, 509, 522, 574, 572, 573
Main Source, 83, 85, 196, 512, 563
Marley, Bob (and The Wailers), 282, 295
Marley Marl, 1, 52, 58, 69, 74, 77, 79-83, 88, 89, 131, 148, 232, 282, 283, 285, 294, 305, 341, 373, 388, 389, 447-463, 469, 478, 495, 496, 514, 516, 527, 548, 559, 563 (see interview with)
Marketing Plan, 409-12, 416
Material Growth, 94, 95, 186, 327, 329, 347, 349, 350, 352
Mayfield, Curtis, 292, 490, 526, 567
Melendez, Benjy, 15, 22, 27, 30, 64
Melody, 3, 6, 41, 51, 70, 76, 85, 93, 98, 114, 127, 152, 170, 172, 173, 186, 187, 194, 195, 205, 208, 211, 216, 258, 267, 274, 288, 291, 292, 315-320, 323, 326-28, 333-36, 339, 340, 344, 347, 352, 357, 358, 427, 453, 475, 497, 500, 522, 535, 538
Meter, 50-52, 55, 320-22, 329
"Merry-Go-Round" Technique, 41, 71
Miami Bass, 69, 80, 81, 98, 494
Moses, Robert, 17-23, 26, 31
Moynihan, Daniel Patrick, 23-27, 31, 570
Music Theory, (see Part 3, Chapter 10),
xvii, 10, 170-73, 194-96, 204, 212, 219, 265, 266, 305, 307-313-17, 327-29, 332, 333, 341-44, 351, 352, 354-56, 359, 361, 363, 501, 528, 539, 570

N

Nas, 52, 87, 203, 346, 347, 464, 469, 482, 490, 509, 513, 563
Native Instruments, 94, 96, 519, 543
Needle Dropping, 42
Neptunes, The, 60, 90-93, 120, 139, 148, 220, 287, 426, 479, 484, 507, 547, 559
Nigger Twins, The, 41, 43

Nuriddin, Jalal, 48

O
Off-Beat/Off Beat, 86, 87, 146, 153, 223, 320

P
Paul C., 69, 83, 449, 559
Pete Rock, 69, 82, 84, 87, 139, 148, 193, 232, 250, 300, 388, 389, 463, 468, 475, 499, 508, 512, 520, 523, 525, 529, 559, 564
Pioneers/Avant-Garde Period, 69, 81, 82, 86, 88, 89, 94, 96, 107, 148, 181, 232, 233, 239
Post-Pioneers Period, 69, 89, 90, 93, 148, 357
Publishing, 373-78, 395, 427-437, 449, 505
Punch Phase, 43, 71

Q
Quik Mix Theory, 38, 63

R
Rand Corporation Fire Project, 22-24
Rapping, the Art of, xix, xx, 1, 37, 43-53, 67, 72, 73, 82, 334, 345, 346, 354, 355, 401, 477, 491, 536, 542, 543
Retro-Eclectic Period, 69, 93, 94, 97
Robinson, Sylvia, 58, 74, 75, 77, 175, 495
Rock 'n' Roll, 1, 161, 186, 231, 259, 295-98, 305, 308, 309, 321, 333, 361, 459, 533, 538, 543, 566
Rock Steady Crew, 43, 44, 78
Roland, xi, 81, 91-93, 104, 109, 114, 115, 119, 131, 147, 179, 214, 231-33, 484, 490, 496, 499, 543
Run-DMC, 50, 51, 458, 480, 493, 494, 516, 564
RZA, The, 69, 85-88, 139, 148, 193, 224, 232, 300, 341, 457, 525, 526, 529, 559

S
Sample-Based Beatmaking, 169, 227, 236, 237
Sample-Based Compositional Style, 170, 171, 176, 196, 209, 228, 229, 235, 540
Sample, Bumpin'-the-Sample, 210, 211
Sample Blending, 261
Sample Editing, 262
Sample Mapping, 114
Sample Placement, 574
Samples, Primary Samples, 180, 209, 210
Sampling, Forms of, 239, 247, 248
Sampling, Full Listen, 247
Sampling, Multi-Sampling, 261
Sampling, Paper-Clipping, Major/Minor, 258
Sampling, "Piggy-Back" Form, 247, 248, 284, 399
Sampling, The Sampling Equation, 234, 269
Sampling, Section Pieces, 248-50
Sampling, Spot-Listening, 247
Sampling, Spot-Note, 261, 262
Sequence Templates, 162
Sequencing, xvii, 10, 107, 108, 127, 163, 181, 193, 197, 234, 235, 368, 440, 472, 496, 500, 573
Setups, (see Chapter 4)
Shading Samples, 261, 262,
Shopping Beats, 373, 374, 419
Showbiz, 69, 82, 84, 232, 466-68, 509, 515, 559
Signal Chain, 234, 251, 266
Signature Sound, 84, 114, 139, 221-23, 409, 557

Slick Rick, 51, 53, 478, 480, 564
Smith, Larry, 69, 74, 76, 78, 81, 469, 495, 559
Sonic Quality, 64, 211, 214-16, 262, 263
Sonic Wall, 223
Soul (Music), 9, 16, 45, 48, 62, 63, 69, 82-89, 120, 127, 161, 169-74, 213, 217, 218, 230-33, 242, 269, 287, 290-92, 295, 297-300, 333, 342, 359, 361, 388, 466, 475, 480, 520-22, 534-38, 557, 566
Sound Frequencies, 136, 222, 223
Sound Rendition, 343, 344
Sound Signature, 114-16, 133
Song Structure, 89, 155, 186, 190, 191, 296
Sound-Stab, 83, 88, 170-72, 196, 199, 218, 227, 235, 248-53, 261, 266, 268, 281, 335
Sound-Tone, 248-50, 261
Southern Bounce Period, 69, 91-95
Spare-Part Phrase(s), 209, 235, 248-50
Spin Back, 42, 43, 71
Starr, Roger, 22, 25, 26, 31
Studio-Band Period, 50, 69, 72-77
Sugar Hill Gang, 50, 57, 58, 73, 492, 564
Sugar Hill Records, 57, 58, 73, 74, 77, 175, 492, 495
Syncopation, 91, 147, 153, 154, 159, 160, 171, 218, 322, 334, 339
Synthetic-Sounds-Based Compositional Style, 90, 154, 169, 172-77, 192, 195, 198, 201-03, 211, 214, 216, 222, 274, 292, 293, 336, 339, 340, 371

T
T La Rock, 51, 52, 78
"Tempo-ing Your Loop", 197
Timbre, 100, 104, 160, 173, 213, 215, 230, 263, 315, 322-26, 336, 343-46, 574
Time Signature, 148, 184, 191, 291, 321, 322
Time Stretch, 153, 516
Tonality, 212, 328, 352
Trap Based/Performance-Experimental Period, 69, 95-97
Triggering, 107, 108, 129, 161, 178, 179, 185, 234, 454, 574,
Tucking, 224

U
UDD (User Degree of Difficulty), 110

V
Velocity, 133, 136, 149, 155, 156, 160, 162, 263, 340, 341
Versioning, 46, 55, 228, 229, 238

W
West, Kanye, 69, 87, 90-93, 148, 220, 287, 470, 490, 499, 500, 504, 520, 527, 559, 563
West Coast Sound, 86-88, 98, 521
Westerm Classical Music, xxii, (see Chapter 10)
White Flight, 19
Williams, Alonzo, 69, 77, 81
Wonder, 9th 69, 94, 139, 237, 250 (see interview with)
Wu-Tang Clan, 82, 86, 87, 428, 563

Y
Yamaha, 113-115, 119, 231, 464, 490, 496, 543

Acknowledgements

Amir and Qamar, *Salaam Aikum wa Rahmatullah, wa-Baraktahu.* Thank you for talking with me about hip hop culture and hip hop/rap music, as well as science, philosophy, culture, mathematics, politics, and history. The discussions we shared helped give me new levels of clarity. The support, patience, advice, and, most importantly, the love and respect of both of you, was/is critical to me. I thank Allah for you both.

Amir Ali Said, my son, best friend, and Superchamp co-founder — Thank you for your friendship, knowledge, courage, and curiosity. And thank you for copy editing this manuscript. Remember, all the answers are in three places: Q, S, and YT. Samir Arts next.

Qamar, my son's mother — Your love, belief, and support through the years has meant, and will always mean, something incredibly special to me. Thank you.

I thank Allah for making you my son and best friend; and I'm grateful to Allah for having blessed you with such deep understanding and accurate insight.

Insight and information has been contributed to this study by many individuals. Therefore, I have not attempted to cite in the text all the authorities and sources consulted in the preparation of this study. To do so would require more space than is available. The list would include various beatmakers (producers), recording artists, recording engineers, A&Rs, lawyers, librarians, music retailers (owners, managers, associates), music writers, and other well-known "music people".

However, I would like to single out the following individuals, in particular, for their continued help, thoughts, encouragement, and overall support:

Mariella Gross, thank you for your unwavering commitment.

To EVERYONE I've ever interviewed, you have my deepest gratitude. Among those that I've interviewed, I would especially like to thank: **DJ Premier**, good-lookin' out, Preme. Your word is gold with me; **Buckwild**; **Bangout** (Salaam Alaikum wa-Rahmutallah); **Minnesota**; **True Master**; **D.R. Period**; **John King** (founder of Chung King Studios); **Rsonist** (of The Heatmakerz); **Dame Grease, Marco Polo, Rich Keller**; **EZ Elpee**; **DJ Clark Kent**; **Steve Sola**; **9th Wonder**; **DJ Toomp**; and **Marley Marl**.

Finally, I would also like to extend my respect and gratitude to Eileen Southern and to every unknown architect and pioneer who played a role in hip hop's foundation. Thank you.

About The Author

Amir Said is a writer, publisher, musician, and father from Brooklyn, NY. In addition to writing and managing the BeatTips Network of music education websites, Said also runs Superchamp Books, an independent publishing company. He is the founder of BeatTips, the leading resource for beatmaking/hip hop production education; and he has written a number of books, including *The Truth About New York*, *The Art of Sampling*, *Ghetto Brother*, and *The Truth About Paris* (co-written with John McNulty). His new novels, *Going Down to the Bungalow Bar* and *Feed the Meter*, are forthcoming in 2016 and 2017 respectively.

Sa'id, Dec. 1993

www.ingramcontent.com/pod-product-compliance
Lightning Source LLC
Chambersburg PA
CBHW080116020526
44112CB00037B/2754